D1274655

THE

CENTENARY EDITION

OF THE WORKS OF

NATHANIEL HAWTHORNE

Volume IV

THE MARBLE FAUN

EDITORS

NATHANIEL HAWTHORNE

THE MARBLE FAUN: OR, THE ROMANCE OF MONTE BENI

Ohio State University Press

CENTER FOR EDITIONS OF
AMERICAN AUTHORS

AN APPROVED TEXT

MODERN LANGUAGE
ASSOCIATION OF AMERICA

WILLIAM CHARVAT

FOR THE EDITORS of the Centenary Edition, William Charvat was *primus inter pares*. His superb understanding of the situation of the nineteenth-century American author, his capacity to discover and define the sorts of problems the editors would face, his fierce generosity, and his determination to get the job done—these made him by common consent the untitled chairman of the editorial board. The Centenary Edition itself was for him yet another stage in the development of his own major project—a study of the profession of authorship in the United States. Through insights gained from the work of the textual editors in particular, he was beginning to resolve some problems in stylistics and its relationship to economic and sociological factors affecting the American writer's image of himself and of the world for and in which he wrote. It was altogether characteristic of William Charvat that he was forever bound to learn, to insist on taking everything relevant into account, even if it meant agonizing revisions of his own work and a radical change in his own opinions. He bore well the burden of the scholar-critic's continuing incertitude and made it into an aspect of his deepest self. As in everything he undertook, it was that very self he committed to the Centenary Edition. The Edition, along with the fragments of his work-in-progress, constitutes a monument to a life which was, if not long enough, both full and fully lived.

R. H. P.

ACKNOWLEDGMENTS

THE EDITORS of the Centenary Hawthorne are grateful for the generous assistance given by librarians, scholars, and bibliophiles. We are indebted to C. Waller Barrett, Charlottesville, Virginia; William H. Bond and Roger E. Stoddard, Houghton Library, Harvard University; Herbert Cahoon, Pierpont Morgan Library; Kermit Cudd and Hyman W. Kritzer, Ohio State University Libraries; Donald Gallup and Miss Barbara D. Simison, Yale University Library; John D. Gordan, Berg Collection, Robert W. Hill, Manuscript Division, and Gilbert A. Cam, Reference Department, New York Public Library; James D. Hart, University of California at Berkeley; Parkman D. Howe, Boston, Massachusetts; Charles Mann, Pennsylvania State University Library; Norman Holmes Pearson, Yale University; Seven Gables Bookshop, New York City; Arnold Whitridge, New York City; and John Cook Wyllie, William H. Runge, and Miss Anne Freudenberg, Alderman Library, the University of Virginia.

Special acknowledgment is made for the work of Mrs. F. Russell Hart, Charlottesville; Mrs. Katharine Newland, Mrs. Sally Bulford, B. R. Brubaker, John Manning, and Robert Miller, Columbus, Ohio; Nolan E. Smith, New Haven, Connecticut; and T. A. J. Burnett, London, England.

We are particularly indebted to C. E. Frazer Clark, Jr., Detroit, Michigan.

ACKNOWLEDGMENTS

We thank the trustees of the British Museum for permission to edit from the manuscript of *The Marble Faun.*

We gratefully acknowledge the support of the National Endowment for the Humanities of the National Foundation on the Arts and Humanities.

The support of the following departments of the Ohio State University has made this project possible: The Department of English, the Graduate School, the University Libraries, the Office of Research, and the Research Foundation.

THE EDITORS

CONTENTS

Introduction to *The Marble Faun*		xix
Textual Introduction: *The Marble Faun*		xlv
Preface		1
I	Miriam, Hilda, Kenyon, Donatello	5
II	The Faun	12
III	Subterranean Reminiscences	20
IV	The Spectre of the Catacomb	28
V	Miriam's Studio	37
VI	The Virgin's Shrine	51
VII	Beatrice	62
VIII	The Suburban Villa	70
IX	The Faun and Nymph	77
X	The Sylvan Dance	85
XI	Fragmentary Sentences	92
XII	A Stroll on the Pincian	99
XIII	A Sculptor's Studio	113
XIV	Cleopatra	123
XV	An Æsthetic Company	131
XVI	A Moonlight Ramble	142

CONTENTS

XVII	Miriam's Trouble	153
XVIII	On the Edge of a Precipice	161
XIX	The Faun's Transformation	172
XX	The Burial Chaunt	178
XXI	The Dead Capuchin	187
XXII	The Medici Gardens	196
XXIII	Miriam and Hilda	202
XXIV	The Tower among the Apennines	213
XXV	Sunshine	221
XXVI	The Pedigree of Monte Beni	231
XXVII	Myths	242
XXVIII	The Owl-Tower	252
XXIX	On the Battlements	260
XXX	Donatello's Bust	270
XXXI	The Marble Saloon	277
XXXII	Scenes by the Way	288
XXXIII	Pictured Windows	300
XXXIV	Market-Day in Perugia	309
XXXV	The Bronze Pontiff's Benediction	316
XXXVI	Hilda's Tower	325
XXXVII	The Emptiness of Picture-Galleries	333
XXXVIII	Altars and Incense	344
XXXIX	The World's Cathedral	354
XL	Hilda and a Friend	363
XLI	Snow-Drops and Maidenly Delights	373
XLII	Reminiscences of Miriam	382
XLIII	The Extinction of a Lamp	390
XLIV	The Deserted Shrine	399

CONTENTS

XLV	The Flight of Hilda's Doves	409
XLVI	A Walk on the Campagna	418
XLVII	The Peasant and Contadina	426
XLVIII	A Scene in the Corso	436
XLIX	A Frolic of the Carnival	444
L	Miriam, Hilda, Kenyon, Donatello	455

Postscript 463

Textual Notes 471

Editorial Emendations in the Copy-Text 479

Rejected First-Edition Substantive Variants 501

Word-Division 507

Historical Collation 513

Alterations in the Manuscript 529

Compositorial Stints in *Transformation*, the First English Edition of 1860 577

The Centenary Texts: Editorial Principles 591

ILLUSTRATIONS

Folio 204 of the printer's-copy holograph manuscript of *The Marble Faun* in the British Museum (Add. 44889).

Folio 473 of the printer's-copy holograph manuscript of *The Marble Faun* in the British Museum (Add. 44890).

(between pages lxiv and lxv)

THE MARBLE FAUN

INTRODUCTION TO

THE MARBLE FAUN

WITHIN a year after the publication of *The Blithedale Romance* Hawthorne was appointed American consul at Liverpool, and during his term of office, 1853–57, he had no time for imaginative writing. His pen was not idle, to be sure: almost a hundred official dispatches to the State Department came from his office, and his journal-keeping amounted to some three hundred thousand words, later parceled out between *Our Old Home* and his wife's edition of *Passages from the English Note-Books*. But neither Hawthorne nor his Boston publishers Ticknor and Fields had forgotten the importance of keeping the author before the public.[1] Perhaps in answer to a direct query, Hawthorne wrote Ticknor early in 1855 that "there is the germ of a new Romance in my mind, which will be all the better for ripening slowly."[2] This was probably the idea of an American's pilgrimage to his ancestral English home, set down in his journal three months later in language suggesting that the idea was not new. At about the same time he heard the

[1] After *Blithedale* Hawthorne had been on the point of beginning another romance which he hoped would be "more genial" (October 13, 1852, to Horatio Bridge, MS, Bowdoin College Library). Randall Stewart, *Nathaniel Hawthorne: A Biography* (New Haven, 1948), p. 134, suggests that the "Agatha" story given him by Melville may have been in Hawthorne's mind, but nothing came of it.

[2] January 19, 1855, MS, Berg Collection, New York Public Library.

legend of the "bloody footstep,"[3] which he would later incorporate with the more general theme in both *Doctor Grimshawe's Secret* and *The Ancestral Footstep*. Toward the end of 1857, the consulship now behind him and a tidy $30,000 accumulated during his years in England,[4] he was not yet ready to resume serious writing, and advised Ticknor that no book could be soon expected. He would be seeing so much in his European travels that he would restrict himself to journal-keeping. He went on to express the conviction that "something would result" if he could be "perfectly quiet for a few months," evidently thinking of the projected English romance as his next work.[5]

In the spring of 1858 the Hawthornes arrived in Rome and began to engage in an intensive round of sightseeing. Hawthorne filled his Italian journals with accounts of visits to studios and meetings with artists, chiefly such American expatriates as William Wetmore Story, E. S. Bartholomew, Thomas Crawford, Cephas G. Thompson, Harriet Hosmer, and Maria Louisa Lander. Even more conspicuous in the notebooks is a voluminous record of museum-going, with close descriptions of painting and statuary, a great deal of which he afterward would transfer to the pages of *The Marble Faun*. On April 18 he recorded a family visit to the Villa Borghese, where he saw statues of two Fauns, one of them copied from Praxiteles:

> I like these strange, sweet, playful, rustic creatures, almost entirely human as they are, yet linked so prettily, without monstrosity, to the lower tribes by the long, furry ears, or by a modest tail; indicating a strain of honest wildness in them. Their character has never, that I know of, been wrought out in literature; and something very good, funny,

[3] Entries of April 12 and April 7, 1855, printed in Randall Stewart (ed.), *The English Notebooks by Nathaniel Hawthorne* (New York, 1941), pp. 107, 106.

[4] Stewart, *Nathaniel Hawthorne*, p. 181.

[5] November 5, 1857, MS, Berg Collection, New York Public Library.

and philosophical, as well as poetic, might very likely be educed from them.[6]

A few days later, in the sculpture gallery of the Capitol he looked at the Praxiteles original,[7] again conscious of the paradox of its being "friendly and wild at once."

> Its lengthened, but not preposterous ears, and the little tail which we infer, behind, have an exquisite effect, and make the spectator smile in his very heart. This race of fauns was the most delightful of all that antiquity imagined. It seems to me that a story, with all sorts of fun and pathos in it, might be contrived on the idea of their species having become intermingled with the human race; a family, with the faun-blo[o]d in them, having prolonged itself from the classic era till our own days. The tail might have disappeared by dint of constant intermarriages with ordinary mortals; but the pretty, hairy ears should occasionally reappear in members of the family; and the moral instincts and intellectual characteristics of the faun might be most picturesquely brought out, without detriment to the human interest of the story. Fancy this combination in the person of a young lady![8]

Hawthorne did not pursue the feminine possibilities his fancy had evoked, but his interest was quickened to the extent that he revisited the Capitol and on April 30 recorded a more minute account of the Praxiteles statue, "because the idea keeps recurring to me of writing a little Romance about it."[9]

On July 14, he noted in his 1858 pocket diary that he was "sketching plot" of a romance, and on July 17 he "began

---

[6] April 18, 1858, MS, Berg Collection, New York Public Library.

[7] It too may have been only a copy. Cf. H. W. Janson, *History of Art* (New York, 1962), p. 117: " . . . we do not have a single undisputed original by any of the famous sculptors of Greece."

[8] April 22, 1858, MS, Berg Collection, New York Public Library.

[9] MS, Pierpont Morgan Library. Sophia Hawthorne omitted the description from her edition of *Passages from the French and Italian Note-Books* (Boston, 1871), presumably because it was incorporated into the opening chapter of *The Marble Faun* with relatively minor reworking.

rough draft" of what there is every reason to believe was *The Marble Faun* in its first stages.[10] He and his family had moved to Florence for the summer months, settling first in the Casa del Bello across the street from the studio of the American sculptor Hiram Powers. For August and September they engaged the Villa Montauto, which Hawthorne described as "big enough to quarter a regiment." Writing to Fields, he continued: " . . . at one end of the house there is a moss-grown tower, haunted by owls and by the ghost of a monk, who was confined there in the thirteenth century, previous to being burnt at the stake in the principal square of Florence. I hire this villa, tower and all, at twenty-eight dollars a month; but I mean to take it away bodily and clap it into a Romance, which I have in my head ready to be written out." He had, he informed Fields, planned two romances, "one or both of which I could have ready for the press in a few months if I were either in England or America." The Italian atmosphere he did not consider conducive to steady work. "It is a pity; for I have really a plethora of ideas, and should feel relieved by discharging some of them upon the public." [11]

[10] MS, University of California Library, Berkeley. Hawthorne's pocket diaries—annuals with calendared divisions for the days of one week on facing pages—are to be distinguished from his journals (herein called also Italian notebooks). Hawthorne's diaries exist for 1856 (Morgan), 1858 (University of California, Berkeley), and 1859 (Berg); he very likely kept them during all his years abroad. Entries concern weather, correspondence, visits and visitors, family health, and the like. Only during the composition of *The Marble Faun* does he allude to his work as a writer, and then chiefly to note the amount or quality of his progress.

[11] September 3, 1858, MS, Huntington Library. Between August 4 and September 1 Hawthorne made only two entries in his notebook. On the latter date he explained that "few things journalizable" had occurred, "and, furthermore, I usually spend the whole day at home, having been engaged in planning and sketching out a Romance. I have now done with this for the present . . . " (MS, Pierpont Morgan Library).
The second romance he had planned was based on the "bloody footstep" legend he had heard in 1855. He filled eighty-eight pages of a copybook with daily entries between April 1 and May 19, 1858, but left it unfinished. As *The Ancestral Footstep* the manuscript was first printed in the Riverside Edition of *The Complete Works* (1883), Vol. XI.

In October the family returned to Rome and, despite distractions and the severe illness of his daughter Una, Hawthorne managed to work on his Italian story. The evidence is contained in scattered entries in his pocket diary. On October 25, "Began to write a Romance." On the three following days, "I scribbled romance"; "scribbled romance poorly"; "Scribbled Romance ineffectually." In mid-November three more entries, that of the twentieth being characteristic: "Forenoon, scribbled Romance a little, as usual." On the last day of the year he wrote: "So ends 1858. Since Nov. 25th I have scribbled more or less of Romance every day; &, with interruptions, from Oct. 26th."[12] In his new 1859 pocket diary he continued brief daily entries, noting on January 23, 1859, "Could not scribble Romance to-day, for the first time since Novr 25th." On January 30: "I finished, to-day, the rough draft of my Romance; intending to write it over after getting back to the Wayside."[13]

A few days later he announced to Fields that "Amid so much domestic trouble" he had been steadily at work, "trying to tear" a romance out of his mind. As usual, he was uncertain of his success. "I only know that I have produced what seems to me a larger amount of scribble than either of my former Romances, and that portions of it interested me a good deal while I was writing them . . ." He could have it ready by the time they were to leave Rome in April, "but my brain is tired of it just now," and revision must await the return to his Concord home in August.[14]

Soon afterward he wrote Ticknor to the same effect: "a month or two" would be required to make the necessary

[12] MS, University of California Library, Berkeley. This entry appears on the last leaf of the diary, with the notations: "Cut out from preceding page" and "(G P L[athrop] copied, Mar 22, '74)." Part of a leaf containing entries for August 5 and 9 has likewise been excised from the diary, but with no explanation or transcript of content.

[13] MS, Berg Collection, New York Public Library.

[14] February 3, 1859, MS, Huntington Library.

revisions, "trimming off of exuberances, and filling up of vacant spaces; . . . I shall do my best upon it, you may be sure; for I feel that I shall come before the public, after so long an interval, with all the uncertainties of a new author."[15] By the end of June the Hawthornes were in England, but their original plan of returning to America was suddenly changed. Fields had come to Europe on a combination business-pleasure trip and happened to be in London when the Hawthornes arrived. Within a few days he arranged for British publication of the new romance, and whereas he had secured £200 for the English rights to *The Blithedale Romance*, he now made an agreement whereby Smith, Elder & Co. would pay Hawthorne £600 for the English copyright in the new work.[16] Ticknor and Fields were to receive advance sheets so that there could be simultaneous publication on both sides of the Atlantic. Hawthorne determined therefore to finish the book without delay and remain in England until its publication in order to protect the copyright.

In search of seclusion he went to Whitby, but could find no suitable lodgings; several visits to St. Hilda's Abbey made their contribution by giving Hawthorne a name for the lady of the doves. On July 22, 1859, the family moved to Redcar, another seacoast spot in Yorkshire, and on the twenty-fourth Hawthorne recorded in his pocket diary the first of two days of preparation for rewriting his book. Then on July 26, "At about 10 °clock, began the Romance in great earnest, and wrote till 3." Thereafter his routine was almost unvarying—writing until two or three o'clock, dining, walking alone or with his son Julian, occasionally returning to his manuscript for an hour or two after the midday meal. Sometimes, as on July 29, he "scribbled fitfully . . . with many

[15] March 4, 1859, MS, Berg Collection, New York Public Library.

[16] Entry of July 5, 1859, in Hawthorne's pocket diary, MS, Berg Collection, New York Public Library.

idle pauses, & no good result." But the revision proceeded
at the rate of thirty-five or forty pages a week, and although
he complained to Fields that the going was slow because he
viewed his manuscript critically and made "many amendments," he felt the book would contain "some good chapters."[17] On September 10 he gave the completed portion
of the book to his wife Sophia to read—"rather more than
half," he estimated.[18] Early in October the family moved
from Redcar to Leamington for the winter, but by the ninth
Hawthorne had resumed work, and on the seventeenth dispatched the manuscript "as far as page 429" (through
Chapter XLII) to Smith, Elder & Co. Three weeks later,
on November 8, came the climactic entry in his pocket
diary: "Wrote till 5 minutes of 12, & finished the last page
of my Romance. 508 manuscript pages."

As had happened more than once before, Hawthorne
found it troublesome to decide on a title for his book. None
of his diary, journal, or epistolary references to the work in
progress identify it by theme, locale, character names, or any
other descriptive language; it is simply "the Romance." In
August he wrote Fields that he had no ideas for a title.[19]
Two months later he sent Fields a sheaf of possibilities, none
of which suited him exactly: " 'Monte Beni; or the Faun.

---

[17] August 6, 1859, MS, Collection of Arnold Whitridge.

[18] Hawthorne's pocket diary, MS, Berg Collection, New York Public
Library. Judging by later references to his progress, Hawthorne must have
finished about three hundred manuscript pages. It is tantalizing to think
that Sophia's reading may have been partly responsible for the change
in name of a major character. In the first three-fifths of the manuscript the
sculptor's name was originally Graydon, but commencing with fol. 304
(Centenary 275.32) the name Kenyon appears as an integral part of the
inscription; the substitution of Kenyon for Graydon in the earlier pages
is in Sophia's hand.

The manuscript reveals one other vagary in the process of settling on
character names. Until Hawthorne wrote the last page of Chapter II
(MS fol. 23), he had evidently not decided what he would call his dark
heroine, for he left space—often more than enough—for the name. The
first integrally inscribed appearance of Miriam's name is at Centenary 18.26.

[19] See note 17.

A Romance.' 'The Romance of a Faun.' 'The Faun of Monte Beni[.]' 'Monte Beni; a Romance.' 'Miriam; a Romance.' 'Hilda; a Romance.' 'Donatello; a Romance.' 'The Faun; a Romance.' 'Marble and Life; a Romance.'" He could see objections "to an Italian name, though perhaps Monte Beni might do. Neither do I wish, if I can help it, to make the fantastic aspect of the book too prominent by putting the Faun into the title page"—this despite the presence of that word in four of his proposed titles.[20]

At Fields's suggestion, Hawthorne settled on "The Romance of Monte Beni," but Smith, Elder & Co. demurred and he gave them a list of possible alternatives.[21] Reporting these developments to Ticknor on December 1, but with no knowledge of Smith, Elder's decision, Hawthorne added: " . . . their choice need not govern yours, and, if you wish to announce the book, I should like to have you call it 'Saint Hilda's Shrine.' We can change the title afterwards, should it appear advisable."[22] When he returned the first proof-sheets on December 6, his accompanying letter observed that despite Smith, Elder's disapproval of his original suggestion, the printers were using it (i.e., he could observe that "Romance of Monte Beni" was the running-title on all versos).[23] On December 12 he noted in his pocket diary that he had proposed "The Marble Faun" as the British title, and on the twenty-second he instructed Ticknor to

[20] October 10, 1859, MS, Huntington Library. In the last of his titles Hawthorne inserted and underlined "Man" above "Life", apparently as a further alternative.

[21] Hawthorne to Ticknor, December 1, 1859, MS, Berg Collection, New York Public Library. Hawthorne recorded his exchange with the English publishers in his pocket diary, November 11 and 13, 1859, but without listing the titles he proposed. Neither letter seems to have survived.

[22] MS, Berg Collection, New York Public Library. A New York trade periodical, *The Bookseller's Medium and Publisher's Advertiser*, II (February 1, 1860), 223, announced the forthcoming book under this title.

[23] MS, transcript courtesy of Professor Norman Holmes Pearson from the letter in the collection of Mrs. Reginald Smith. This and all other Hawthorne letters that were in the Smith collection are thought to be now in the archives of John Murray Ltd. and are not available at this time.

use it also for the American edition, saying that he had
rejected Smith, Elder's proposal, "The Transformation, or
the Romance of Monte Beni."[24] As late as January 26, 1860,
no decision on the British title had been reached,[25] but the
matter was settled soon thereafter when the publishers pointed
out that "Transformation" was in fact one of Hawthorne's
own suggestions.[26] He continued to rail against it, saying
to Fields that "Smith & Elder (who seem to be pig-headed
individuals) persist in calling the book 'Transformation,'
which gives me the idea of Harlequin in pantomine"; to
Ticknor he wrote that the British publishers "are determined
to take a title out of their own heads, though they affirm
that it was originally suggested by me . . . I beseech you
not to be influenced by their bad example."[27] A letter of
February 10 to Ticknor declared, "I am fully determined
not to retain their absurd title."[28] But on February 3 he had
capitulated to Smith, Elder "so far as the English edition is
concerned. In America I shall call the book 'The Marble
Faun.'"[29] And so it turned out. In both countries the subtitle
became *The Romance of Monte Beni*.[30]

[24] MSS, Berg Collection, New York Public Library.

[25] Hawthorne to Ticknor, MS, Berg Collection, New York Public
Library.

[26] Hawthorne's answer to Smith, Elder, February 3, 1860, acknowledged
that he had forgotten the title was his; he was glad that "in condemning
it, I shall criticize nobody but myself." It seemed to him "very flat and
inexpressive," but presumably his publishers could gauge British taste
better than he (MS, Collection of Mrs. Reginald Smith; quoted from
Norman Holmes Pearson's transcript). According to Hawthorne's son-in-
law George P. Lathrop (Introductory Note to *The Marble Faun*, Riverside
Edition, 1883, VI, 11), the title was shortened from "The Transformation
of the Faun." Cf. the heading of Chapter XIX: "The Faun's Transformation."

[27] February 11, 1860, MS, Huntington Library; February 3, 1860, MS,
Berg Collection, New York Public Library.

[28] MS, Berg Collection, New York Public Library.

[29] See note 26.

[30] An American reviewer made a case for the British title, saying that
Transformation was "more prosaic" than *The Marble Faun*, "but more
honest also, and more apocalyptic of the true nature of the book" (*New
York Times*, March 24, 1860, 3: 3).

At first it looked as though the book would be rushed into print for the Christmas trade, but when Hawthorne announced that he intended to remain some months longer in England, publication was deferred to the end of the following February.[31] Without this delay, it would have been impossible for Ticknor to prepare the American edition from British advance sheets in time for simultaneous publication. With Fields traveling on the Continent, it was Hawthorne who acted as intermediary between the London and Boston publishers. He attempted, as his letters show, to win further postponement from Smith, Elder and to expedite the dispatch of proof-sheets to Boston. But despite all he could do, the first sheets did not reach Ticknor until near the end of January and the final shipment did not leave London until early February.[32] *Transformation* came out as scheduled on February 28, priced at 31/6 for the three volumes, and Hawthorne, who duly presented himself in London on publication day to sign over the copyright to Smith, Elder, received his £600 promptly.[33]

Ticknor was unable to issue *The Marble Faun* on the same date as its English counterpart, but the American copyright was safe so long as he published the work before any English copies could be imported. On March 1 the *Boston Transcript* reviewed the book flatteringly from proof-sheets

[31] Hawthorne's 1859 pocket diary shows that he was reading proof steadily between December 6 and December 17. Initially the typesetting was going forward at the rate of fifty pages a day (Hawthorne to Ticknor, December 1, December 22, 1859, MSS, Berg Collection, New York Public Library; Hawthorne to Fields, December 30, 1859, MS, Huntington Library).

[32] Hawthorne to Ticknor, December 1, 1859, January 26, February 3, February 10, 1860, MSS, Berg Collection, New York Public Library; Hawthorne to Fields, February 11, 1860, MS, Huntington Library.

[33] Hawthorne to Ticknor, March 9, 1860, MS, Berg Collection, New York Public Library.

and announced the publication date as Wednesday, March 7. Advance promotion in the *Transcript* included the printing of five extracts from the romance, and another notice.[34]

The Marble Faun was issued in two volumes at a price of $1.50, less than one-fifth the cost of the English edition; Hawthorne's royalty was 15 per cent, or 22½ cents per copy. Initial advertisements by Ticknor and Fields announced that advance orders had almost exhausted the first printing; in point of fact, Ticknor had been optimistic enough to order three printings before publication, amounting to eight thousand sets.[35] And before the year was out, four more impressions were required, bringing the total to 14,500 sets— a figure exceeding the total American sales of any of his other romances during his lifetime. The size of the English printings is not known, but three impressions had been issued before the end of April.[36] During 1860 Tauchnitz issued a popular edition of *Transformation* on the Conti-

[34] The second review appeared on publication day. The extracts, with their assigned captions, were "Rome" (the famous sentence-paragraph of almost four hundred words opening Chapter XXXVI) and "Legend of the Fountain" (from Chapter XXVII), March 2, p. 1; "W. W. Story's Statue of Cleopatra" (from Chapter XIV), March 3, p. 4; "The Emptiness of Picture Galleries" (from Chapter XXXVII), March 5, p. 1; and "Guido's Beatrice Cenci" (from Chapter VII), March 8, p. 4.

[35] *New York Times*, March 7, 8, 9, 1860; *New York Tribune*, March 7, 1860. In the Ticknor and Fields Cost Books, the three printings are lumped together under dates of February 20, 23, and 27, 1860 (MS, Houghton Library, Harvard University). Advertisements of March 22 in both the *Times* and the *Tribune* announced the eighth thousand "now ready."

[36] These were: the original printing issued on February 28; a revised second printing containing the Postscript, advertised as the "Second Edition" in the *Athenæum*, April 7; and a true second edition (the first two volumes of which were reset, the third volume printed from standing type of the revised second printing), advertised as the "Third Edition . . . published next week" in the April 14 *Athenæum*, and as for sale in the issue of April 21. If the printings averaged a thousand sets each, Hawthorne would have more than earned the £600 copyright fee paid in lieu of royalty (15 per cent of 31/6 on slightly more than 2,500 sets would amount to £600).

nent,[37] but Hawthorne's return from this source cannot be estimated.[38]

Despite these evidences of popular acceptance, Hawthorne very quickly discovered that his readers were discontented with the resolution of his story. His friend Henry F. Chorley, in what was perhaps the earliest London notice, tempered generous praise with an invidious comparison between the "clear and forcible" ending of *The Scarlet Letter* and the "inconclusive and hazy" close of *Transformation*.[39] Chorley's disapproval was echoed in other reviews,[40] but before they were in print Hawthorne became aware that he had left his audience baffled. Within a week after publication he had begun to think of "adding a few explanatory pages, in the shape of a conversation between the author and Hilda or Kenyon, by means of which some further details may be elicited."[41] On March 7 he expressed his intention to Smith, Elder, and two days later he wrote Ticknor to the same effect, saying that "everybody" was complaining of the hazy

[37] Extra-illustrated copies of the Tauchnitz *Transformation* are often encountered, but these, not being identically interleaved, were evidently prepared for the purpose by booksellers and not by the publisher. In 1889 Houghton, Mifflin, acknowledging that visitors to Rome and Florence still collected photographs (or bought packets assembled by dealers) to embellish the romance, issued a handsome two-volume edition of *The Marble Faun* with fifty photogravures.

[38] That the Leipzig firm dealt honorably with authors in the days before international copyright is suggested by its treatment of Hawthorne. A letter from Baron Tauchnitz to Hawthorne, January 9, 1864 (MS, Houghton Library, Harvard University), announced the payment of $120 on sales of *The Scarlet Letter* and indicated that *Transformation* "was considered as an English book and I made an agreement about it signed by you and Messrs Smith Elder & Co." No further information concerning this contract has come to light.

[39] *Athenæum*, No. 1688 (March 3, 1860), 296–97.

[40] See, for example, *Saturday Review*, IX (March 17, 1860), 341–42, and Henry Bright's notice in the *Examiner*, No. 2722 (March 31, 1860), 197.

[41] Hawthorne to Francis Bennoch, March 4, 1860, MS, University of Virginia Library.

conclusion.[42] By March 16 the Postscript had been written, set in type, and proofread, and was duly incorporated in the second printing of the English edition and presumably in the fourth American printing.[43]

Despite his alacrity, Hawthorne protested that he would rather have left the story as it was. His reluctance to say more is evident in the opening paragraphs of the Postscript, which echo the beginning of the final chapter. As a romancer, he had warned the reader in his Preface that he intended to write "a fanciful story"; Italy afforded him "a sort of poetic or fairy precinct, where actualities would not be so terribly insisted upon, as they are . . . in America." But "actualities" come to occupy a strong place in the foreground as his quartet of characters move through museums and parks and other standard sights of the tourists' Rome. His scenic effects are so often dependent on the close rendering of circumstantial detail that the "fairy precinct" seems often subordinated to Roman tangibilities, into which a dash of religious and political intrigue has been melodramatically infused.

Hawthorne himself had observed what "disagreeable vibration of the nerves" could accompany a "perception of ambiguousness in familiar persons or affairs" (page 397). But in the original closing chapter he defended himself from the tediousness of tying up loose ends and "clearing up the romantic mysteries," on the ground that he disliked to destroy "fragile" effects, and—shifting to a totally opposite premise—that "The actual experience of even the most ordinary life

[42] Hawthorne to Smith, Elder & Co., MS, Collection of Mrs. Reginald Smith; transcript courtesy of Professor Norman Holmes Pearson; Hawthorne to Ticknor, MS, Berg Collection, New York Public Library.

[43] Hawthorne's note to Smith, Elder accompanying the return of proof is dated March 16 (MS, Collection of Mrs. Reginald Smith; transcript courtesy of Professor Norman Holmes Pearson). See footnote 5 of the Textual Introduction for discussion of a possible remainder issue of *The Marble Faun.*

is full of events that never explain themselves" (page 455).
In the Postscript he seems to grant that there is a valid distinction between curiosity about Donatello's ears and genuine
bafflement over the shadowiness of Miriam's identity, though
he gives the reader only a generalized formula for understanding Miriam's actions and attitudes. He summed up his
feelings in a candid outburst to the historian John Lothrop
Motley, who had written an appreciative letter declaring
that the outlines of the story were clear enough to an imaginative reader and that "It is exactly the romantic atmosphere
of the book in which I revel." [44] Hawthorne replied: " . . .
you take the book precisely as I meant it," whereas "These
beer-sodden English beefeaters do not know how to read a
Romance; neither can they praise it rightly, if ever so well
disposed." [45] In truth, the fault may have lain not with an
overly literal-minded public so much as with the mixture of
genres characteristic of Hawthorne's last three romances,
which created an attendant mixture of reader expectation.[46]

In general, critical response to the book was respectful.[47]

[44] March 29, 1860, MS, Berg Collection, New York Public Library.

[45] April 1, 1860, MS, Berg Collection, New York Public Library. G. P.
Lathrop omitted the "beefeaters" sentence when he quoted the letter in
his *A Study of Hawthorne* (Boston, 1876), p. 263.

[46] Ticknor and Fields themselves helped to foster the impression that
The Marble Faun was a piece of circumstantial reporting. Advertisements
in the *Boston Transcript*, beginning with the issue of April 28, 1860, and
running twice weekly through May, listed *The Marble Faun*, Charles
Eliot Norton's *Notes of Travel and Study in Italy*, and George S. Hillard's
Six Months in Italy as "The Best Guide Books to Italy."
The stir created by unresolved elements of Hawthorne's story provoked
at least one humorous exploitation. "*The Marble Faun*: Completed,"
published anonymously in *Knickerbocker*, LVI (July, 1860), 65–73, is a
heavy-handed spoof, more interesting as caricature than as wit or satire.

[47] In addition to Chorley's *Athenæum* review (*loc. cit.*), this discussion
draws upon the following notices: *Atlantic Monthly*, V (April, 1860),
509–10; *Literary Gazette*, n.s. IV (March 10, 1860), 306–7; *New York
Tribune*, March 8, 1860, 6: 1–6; *North American Review*, XC (April,
1860), 557–58; *Boston Daily Advertiser*, March 7, 1860, 2: 2; *New York
Times*, March 24, 1860, 3: 2–3; *Harper's New Monthly Magazine*, XXI
(June, 1860), 128; *Dublin University Magazine*, LV (June, 1860), 679–88;
Westminster Review, LXXIII (April, 1860), 624–27; *Universal Review*,
III (June, 1860), 742–71; *Albion*, XXXVIII (March 17, 1860), 129;
Times (London), April 7, 1860, 5: 1–4; *National Review*, XI (October,
1860), 453–81.

But aside from Lowell's unalloyed praise in the *Atlantic,* almost every notice expressed some reservation. Hawthorne's style received highest acclaim, and most reviewers accepted the author's theory of the romance. Wide divergence of opinion appeared, however, in comment on plot, tone, theme, characters, and setting.

The *Literary Gazette* called the plot "simply romance run mad," and denounced the book as "a vapid extravagance." The *New York Tribune* remarked on the "saturnine spirit and grim features of the narrative," declaring that the reader "will shrink from the stifling air of the charnel-house with which he is oppressed." But to the *North American Review* and the *Boston Advertiser* the book was healthier in tone than Hawthorne's other romances. The *New York Times* called *The Marble Faun* "a mere fermentation of impressions. Plot it has none, nor does any single dominant idea grow through it to the close"; the story was "desolately incoherent." The friendly imaginative understanding of Motley was not, however, without support. To George W. Curtis of *Harper's* the incompleteness of the plot was justifiable in a romance. He echoed Lowell, who said that he preferred conjecture to "any prosaic solution" of bafflements presented by the story. The *Dublin University Magazine* likewise defended Hawthorne against the literal-minded, arguing that Hawthorne had carefully prepared the reader for a shading off from reality to the fanciful.

Perhaps half the reviewers commented on the centrality of the Faun's transformation. Lowell, for instance, saw the book as concerned with "the most august truths of psychology" and offering "a profound parable of the development of the Christian Idea." Chorley, who described the crime as leading Donatello "to think, to feel,—lastly, to aspire," is representative of those who discerned the importance of the *felix culpa* argument, with which Miriam disturbed Kenyon and he in turn shocked Hilda. The Dublin commentator, however, insisted that Donatello, not being wholly human, could not illustrate the doctrine; the savage Faun on the fateful evening was reminiscent of an American Indian steeped in joy of the kill and unlikely to "gain an education by remorse for sin."

Chorley set the tone for discussing Hawthorne's characters. Miriam was derived from Zenobia, Hilda was "own cousin" to Phoebe. Kenyon was "a stone image, with little that appeals to our experience of men." The *Westminster Review* merely declared that the Americans were reintroduced from *The Blithedale Romance.* The *Literary Gazette,* taking a different tack, saw Miriam as "a damsel *errante,*" and found the independence of Hilda startling in her "disregard of the proprieties of female life"; Kenyon was the "only natural and rational member of the party." To George W. Curtis, however, Kenyon, "the only strictly human being in the book, is the least real of all." The *New York Tribune* considered Hilda "the loveliest type of American womanhood," whereas to the *Universal Review* she had "apparently little more relation than moonshine to any form of human passion." Donatello struck many critics as a happy fusion of Hawthorne's originality and fancy, but the *Albion* termed him "a monster . . . revolting to our instincts."

Hawthorne's descriptions of Italian scenery and life, Roman monuments and art objects, likewise received a mixed response. For Chorley the carefully sketched backgrounds "poetically and richly frame" some of the powerful scenes, and he especially commended Hawthorne's "sympathy with . . . St. Peter's." Most other British reviewers were unfriendly. The *Westminster Review,* for instance, felt that the guidebook material suggested "a strange flavour of the news letter, and not only so, but of news addressed to an American public." Typically irritated was the critic of the *Literary Gazette,* who observed that Hawthorne had become "thoroughly enthralled" by Rome and that "the body of the book is æsthetic . . . to a degree which is positively weari-some." But the London *Times* called *Transformation* "worth all the guide-books we ever met with, as regards the gems of Italian art, the characteristic features of Roman edifices, and the atmosphere of Roman life," and valued the "clear discernment" of his æsthetic eye. Lowell was glad to see references to American artists and their work, while Richard H. Hutton, writing in the *National Review*, scorned such commentary as "puffs, not in very good taste." Hutton con-sidered the "often powerful, and always subtle" art criticism to be "padding"; moreover, he deplored Hawthorne's "silly attacks upon nude figures." The *Westminster Review* also disliked the "provincial narrowness" of passages on nudity in statuary and on Gibson's tinted Venuses. The *Literary Gazette* expressed a not uncommon attitude in saying that the descriptive set pieces would be "acceptable" to readers not overly "familiar with the subjects"; Curtis, on the con-trary, doubted that such passages would interest persons unfamiliar with Italy. Many reviewers invoked the term "art-novel" to characterize unflatteringly at least part of Haw-thorne's intention, and the disparagement was likely to be particularized by some equivalent of the *Albion* phrase which described the work as an "exercise in psychological pathology."

Most of the factual detail in *The Marble Faun,* and even some of its tone, can be attributed to Hawthorne's preliminary "journalizing" in his Italian notebooks. His indebtedness has long been apparent, but it is even more pervasive than the published portions reveal, inasmuch as Sophia Hawthorne systematically omitted from *Passages* those sections in which the relationship is strongest. Hawthorne's characteristic method of using his journal savings bank may be observed in the makeup of three chapters (XVI–XVIII), describing a moonlight walk through central Rome which immediately precedes the fatal moments at the Tarpeian Rock. The itinerary from the Fountain of Trevi to the statue of Marcus Aurelius follows closely the walk of Hawthorne and his wife recorded in the notebook entry of April 25, 1858, only a small fraction of which has been published. At the fountain husband and wife leaned over the water to test a detail in Mme. de Staël's novel *Corinne*: they could not see the reflection of a face in the water, for three reasons which Hawthorne transferred to the *Marble Faun* scene. In the notebook entry he was not sure whether it was Corinne or Lord Nelvil who recognized the other's face—a point he cleared up in the *Faun*. Hawthorne's lukewarm appreciation of Bernini's rococo fountain statuary draws additionally from earlier reactions set down on February 7, 1858.

The Coliseum scene, freshly dramatized for Hawthorne's immediate purpose, is likewise animated with background detail from the notebook: the French sentinel, the young persons running races, a group of people sitting on the steps of the iron cross, the English and American sightseers who are probably trying to recapture Byron's moonlight experience. The walk through the Forum inspires rather tedious guidebook commentary which Hawthorne cannot much enliven, save for putting some of his own reactions into the mouths of his fictional spokesmen. He is more successful with Marcus Aurelius, whose "grand beneficence" reflected in the equestrian statue sets the tone for a discussion of worldly authority in which Kenyon, Miriam, and Hilda are neatly characterized by their individual attitudes. From the Campidoglio the Hawthornes had proceeded to the Corso and so homeward. In *The Marble Faun* the moonlight walk moves to its climax at the Tarpeian Rock, and here Hawthorne drew upon a journal passage for May 22, 1858, written after visiting the parapet with the Swedish author Fredrika Bremer. His reaction then had been that "it was a good idea of the stern old Romans, to fling political criminals down from the very height of that Capitoline hill on which stood the temples and public edifices, symbols of the institutions which they sought to violate." This sentiment he assigns to Kenyon, making it more explicit by naming Jove's temple and the Senate-House as the "emblems" of religious and political institutions.

Thus throughout this increasingly taut episode Hawthorne has drawn upon his journal for the pictorial background and the general evocative power of Rome's historical iconography. The specific gothic atmosphere of Miriam's growing crisis is a product of symbolically freighted conversation plus authorial comment, set against a background pictured as sinister and shadowy, time-stained in both pagan and Christian wickedness.

Critics justly noted an affinity between Hilda and Hawthorne's other virtuous blonde heroines, Phoebe and Priscilla. He drew upon his acquaintance with the expatriate Salem sculptress Maria Lander for his view of innocent independence which an unchaperoned female could paradoxically enjoy in corrupt Rome. Hilda's moral rigor, the priggishness of which Hawthorne surely underestimated, is a refraction of Sophia, despite her disclaimers.[48] Kenyon embodies many of Hawthorne's ideas and attitudes, often closely paraphrased from journal entries; the Preface to the novel acknowledges that he had attributed to Kenyon two figures by Paul Akers and had appropriated W. W. Story's figure of Cleopatra as Kenyon's work in progress, but otherwise Hawthorne does not seem to have levied significantly on specific artists in shaping Kenyon. Donatello, as the critics often remarked, was the most original of Hawthorne's cre-

[48] See, for example, her letter, probably of late October, 1859, printed in Rose Hawthorne Lathrop, *Memories of Hawthorne* (Boston, 1897), p. 348.

ations, a natural consequence of the Faun's role embodying an idea and little more. The Villa Montauto became the Count of Monte Beni's ancestral home, and the walking tour of Kenyon and Donatello recapitulates much of the Hawthorne family's sightseeing between Florence and Rome.

The most interesting and puzzling character here is Miriam Schaefer. Although her uncertain relationship to the tragic Cenci legend connects her most intimately with Italy, her imaginative origins lie outside Hawthorne's Italian experience. At a dinner given by the Lord Mayor of London in April, 1856, Hawthorne sat opposite a young woman who so impressed him that he devoted several hundred words to her in his journal.[49] His description there became the basis for a *Marble Faun* paragraph in which he uses Miriam's self-portrait as a device to reveal the essence of her appearance and personality. Salient in both accounts are her youth, her fine complexion neither sallow nor roseate, her haunting beauty, her black hair, abundant, not glossy, "Jewish hair." And both word-portraits link the striking figure with Old Testament women—with Rachel, worthy of Jacob's years of wooing; and with Judith, who was capable of slaying Holofernes. Whereas the notebook entry further enriches the image with the wry paradoxes of a Bathsheba without sin and an Eve too self-possessed to eat the apple, *The Marble Faun* suggests Miriam's temperamental affinity with her sketches of Jael and Judith and Salome, all of them "acting the part of a revengeful mischief towards man." But Hawthorne goes further with Miriam than to surround her with the aura of a strong woman, capable of violence in the primitive biblical exactions of the Mosaic law. He gives her an indistinct past, which he fills in with details that tantalize our curiosity rather than still it: she has a secret which

[49] Entry of April 13, 1856, *English Notebooks*, p. 321.

tortures her; she wishes she could forget one day in her life; the Model declares of her, "men have said, that this white hand had once a crimson stain"; and in another context he forbears to use her true name, "at which these leaves would shiver above our heads" (pages 97, 94).[50]

Hilda, in discussing her copy of the Guido Reni portrait of Beatrice Cenci, sees the sad figure as "a fallen angel, fallen, and yet sinless" (page 66), echoing one of Hawthorne's own impressions set down in his journal (February 20, 1858). This paradoxical characterization may apply also to Miriam, if we judge from a passage in which Hawthorne says, speaking omnisciently: "Yet, let us trust, there may have been no crime in Miriam, but only one of those fatalities . . . by which every crime is made to be the agony of many innocent persons, as well as of the single guilty one" (page 93). Miriam's background, then, is complex and equivocal; her past has left its shadow upon her. She belongs to a world in which violence may beget violence, in which she cannot imagine an Archangel triumphing over Satan without becoming disheveled and bloody himself. Hawthorne makes us understand the nature of her intense preoccupations, but without ever revealing their cause. When he finally allows her, near the denouement of the action, to settle some of the floating conjectures, he leaves the reader with other unexplained mysteries.

Surely one of these is the Cenci associations and what we are to make of them. The least subtle detail is the address

[50] Randall Stewart, in the Introduction to his edition of *The American Notebooks by Nathaniel Hawthorne* (New Haven, 1932), n. 381, suggested that "the name to be supplied would seem to be 'daughter' or, perhaps, 'sister'." But nothing in the novel gives warrant for thinking that the "iron chain" binding the two is kinship of this order; the Model's hold over her is menacing because he could, by disclosing her name, expose her to public shame for her part, no matter how innocent, in an unspecified evil episode.

to which Hilda takes Miriam's packet; the Palazzo Cenci must, if it stands for anything, connote an awkwardly literal connection between that family and the dark-haired artist of mysterious identity. Even a symbolic parallel between her secret and the incestuous cause of Beatrice's plight would require a harmony of details that Hawthorne does not bother to achieve. It is more confusing than deliciously suggestive to allow the reader to conjecture that Miriam may be a latter-day Cenci. But is this really his intention? Almost certainly he had read Melville's *Pierre,* in which a central motif is actual or possible incest, and in which the implicated young woman is said to resemble a copy of the same Beatrice portrait.[51] Hawthorne's extraordinary preoccupation with the Guido painting is attested in his Italian notebook; both he and Sophia set down extended descriptions of the painting. Moreover, Hawthorne became acquainted with other treatments of the subject, including a copy by Cephas Thompson and a sculptural version by Harriet Hosmer. In the important journal entry of February 20, 1858, he wishes that people could judge the Guido portrait without knowing Beatrice's history, thereby making it clear that his own response has been influenced by the legendary account of Beatrice as incestuous victim whose complicity in parricide seemed justifiable. For in both journal and romance he noted that the girl's expression of unutterable sadness is, as he finally put it, "the intimate consciousness of her father's sin that threw its shadow over her," a sinless person (page 205). This interpretation of the painting may explain Hawthorne's symbolic intentions in those moments when Miriam or Hilda resembles Beatrice. It is reinforced by the title "Innocence, dying of a Blood-stain," given a portrait of Hilda painted

51 Melville inscribed a copy of his book to the Hawthornes, August 13, 1852. See the catalogue of Sale No. 3911, American Art Association–Anderson Galleries, Inc., New York, April 29, 1931, item 28.

by Signor Panini after she had witnessed the midnight murder; Hawthorne pointedly suggests its resemblance to Guido's Beatrice. But if the symbolic correspondences are to work, almost all the Cenci legend must be ignored, leaving only a pure maiden whose grief comes from her consciousness of guilt in others. The resonance of the incest-parricide story is much too powerful to be thus dismissed, and in this respect Hawthorne has not effectively controlled the motifs he has introduced into the book.[52]

Offsetting the Cenci motif but perhaps not in conflict with it is Miriam's relationship to the Model and to a notorious event in recent history. She had refused to marry the marchese to whom her family had betrothed her at an early age—a much older man belonging to "another branch of her paternal house" (page 430). His streak of insanity evidently serves Hawthorne as a means of identifying him with the Model, a madman out of her past who is as anxious as she "to break the tie between us" (page 94), but who believes that fate has intertwined their lives. His hold over Miriam is not clearly explained, but a word from him would presumably have cast unjust suspicion on her innocence "in connection with a mysterious and terrible event" which had made her true name "familiar to the world." Hawthorne continues, in a sentence unusually explicit with reference to the world outside the novel: "The reader—if he think it

[52] The Cenci legend, which has repeatedly attracted painters, poets, and novelists, is imaginatively more satisfying, though no more lurid, than the actuality. A modern study of the evidence by Corrado Ricci, *Beatrice Cenci*, trans. Morris Bishop and Henry Longan Stuart (New York, 1925), shows that Beatrice was far from innocent, having had sexual relations with the man who became her father's assassin. Moreover, though her father was unspeakably brutal, the charge of incest was so belatedly introduced as to cast serious doubt upon it. Critics are disagreed about the portrait in the Barberini Gallery, some holding that it is by Guido Reni but does not represent Beatrice, others accepting Beatrice as the subject but denying the attribution to Guido. The state of knowledge in Hawthorne's day justifies his exploitation of legend and painting, if justification be needed.

worth while to recall some of the strange incidents which have been talked of, and forgotten, within no long time past—will remember Miriam's name" (page 430).

This is a commonplace fictional gambit, for which one need not expect to find a counterpart in actuality. But Hawthorne may not have wholly invented the sketchy outline of Miriam's fated life. His young English friend Henry Bright recalled that when Hawthorne visited London during the spring of 1860,

> we spent several hours wandering about and chatting. I told him I had heard that his Miriam (it was Arthur Penrhyn Stanley's idea) was Mdlle. de Luzzy, the governess of the Duc de Praslyn. He was much amused. "Well, I dare say she was," he said. "I knew I had some dim recollection of some crime, but I didn't know what." [53]

Dean Stanley's hint concerns a Paris scandal of 1847 widely publicized in America as well as Europe. Shortly after Henriette Deluzy-Desportes was discharged as governess, her employer, Charles Laure Hugues Théobald, Duc de Choiseul-Praslin, murdered his wife and a week later died of arsenic poisoning. The story has been reconstructed in detail by Nathalia Wright, who notes that "Mlle. Deluzy was held in custody for three months, during which time she was repeatedly interrogated. Although she established her innocence in court, the scandal about her name never entirely subsided." [54] She came to America in 1849 as Henriette Desportes, taught in a New York private school, and in 1851 married Henry Field, a Congregational minister of West Springfield, Massachusetts. Miss Wright thinks it possible that Haw-

[53] Undated letter, Bright to Julian Hawthorne, quoted in the latter's *Nathaniel Hawthorne and His Wife* (Boston, 1884), II, 236.

[54] "Hawthorne and the Praslin Murder," *New England Quarterly*, XV (March, 1942), 7.

thorne could have met her in Stockbridge in the summer of that year.

As Miss Wright points out, the principal link with *The Marble Faun* lies in the prosecution's hypothesis that Mlle. Deluzy "incited the Duke to murder his wife"[55] and thereby became implicated, just as Miriam's glance which prompts Donatello also implicates her; the parallel continues in Beatrice Cenci's complicity in the murder of her father, though it was carried out by others. The French governess was presumably innocent, despite popular suspicions to the contrary; we are allowed to believe the same of Miriam in the now-forgotten episode. Both escape to foreign lands, change their names, enter a new way of life, and try to escape from haunting accusations. But where Mrs. Field achieved respectability, Miriam was pursued by her nemesis: " . . . the shadow fell upon me, innocent," she says, "but I went astray in it, and wandered . . . into crime" (page 430). Miss Wright does not insist that the Praslin affair stimulated Hawthorne directly, preferring to say simply that it contributed to the background of the book.

The Marble Faun was the last of Hawthorne's important fictions. Soon after his return to America the Civil War broke out and its strong personal impact on him distracted his energies. The only full-length publication of his last years was *Our Old Home,* a bittersweet memoir and travel book which almost composed itself from the pages of his English journals. Several romances were on his desk in various states of disarray, but whether the mood of the war years inhibited concentration, or physical debility sapped his creative energy, the result was depressing for him. In his Italian romance, as in his earlier books, he was preoccupied with the psychology of guilt and problems of human

[55] *Ibid.,* p. 12.

responsibility, but his theater of action had broadened noticeably from the constricted milieu of *The Scarlet Letter*. In saying this, one points to sources of weakness as well as strength, for the domain of the romancer is constantly jeopardized by the strong claims of a real world, superficial though its picturesqueness may appear. Pages of *The Marble Faun* show Hawthorne's skill in rendering minute particulars with the fidelity he admired in Dutch painters. Nevertheless, the centers of deepest interest lie in a moral not a physical locale, and "The World's Cathedral," a phrase he originally applied to St. Peter's, comes to symbolize the inescapable arena in which man must wrestle with his problems of belief and conduct.

C. M. S.

TEXTUAL INTRODUCTION:

THE MARBLE FAUN

UNDER its English title of *Transformation, The Marble Faun* was published in three volumes, on February 28, 1860, in London, by Smith, Elder & Co., who were also the printers. The first printing collates: Vol. I, π^8 1–17^8 18^2, 146 leaves, pp. [i–v] vi–xiv [xv–xvi], [1] 2–273 [274–276]; p. i, half-title; p. ii, blank; p. iii, title; p. iv, translation notice; pp. v–xiv, preface; p. xv, contents; p. xvi, blank; pp. 1–273, text; p. 274, blank; p. 275, colophon; p. 276, blank. Vol. II, π^2 19–36^8 37^4, 150 leaves, pp. [i–iv], [1] 2–294 [295–296]; p. i, title; p. ii, translation notice; p. iii, contents; p. iv, blank; pp. 1–294, text; p. 295, colophon; p. 296, blank. Vol. III, π^2 38–55^8, 146 leaves, pp. [i–iv], [1] 2–285 [286–288]; p. i, title; p. ii, translation notice; p. iii, contents; p. iv, blank; pp. 1–285, text; p. 286, colophon; pp. 287–288, advertisements.

This printing, here referred to as E1^a, was made from type-metal, and not from plates.

Shortly after March 16, 1860 (the date that Hawthorne returned proof of the Postscript to Smith, Elder),[1] a second printing from this type (E1^b)—called the second edition on the title—was published, containing the added Postscript.

---

[1] Here and elsewhere in this Textual Introduction the evidence for dates already provided in Professor Simpson's Introduction will not be footnoted again.

The Postscript starts on p. 286 of signature 55, and ends on p. 294 subscribed *"Leamington, March 14th, 1860."*, followed by the finis and a one-line colophon. Book advertisements are printed on the final leaf, pp. 295–96. The collation of this third volume in its second printing is: π^2 38–55^8 56^4, 150 leaves, pp. [i–iv], [1] 2–294 [295–296]. Trifling corrections were made in this printing in the standing type in Vol. I, 197.7, and in Vol. III in the running-title of 223. These are without authority; moreover, changes requested by Hawthorne on March 7 were not included.[2]

Later in the year, between April 14 and 21, a second edition (E2)—calling itself the third edition—was published. This was a line-for-line resetting of E1^b for the first two volumes, but the third volume was printed from the standing type of E1^b. In the reset type the usual reprint variation occurs, but the two requested corrections in Hawthorne's letter of March 7 are finally made.[3] For E2 the error at III,

[2] On March 7, 1860, Hawthorne wrote to Smith, Elder that on reading the printed book he had noticed two or three unimportant errors of the press, but remembered only the following two: II,9.6 (Centenary 157.15) in which "with foot" should read "with her foot" and II,30.19 (Centenary 169.2) in which "literary" should read "literally". MS, transcript courtesy of Professor Norman Holmes Pearson, from the letter in the collection of Mrs. Reginald Smith. This and all other Hawthorne letters that were in the Smith collection are thought to be now in the archives of John Murray Ltd. and are not available at this time.

[3] The circumstances surrounding the first of these corrections, that in sheet 19 at II,9.6, are in some part obscure. That is, in the copies of E2 at Pennsylvania State University and the Berg Collection of the New York Public Library the sheet is reset, like the rest of Vol. II, and the reading is corrected as Hawthorne wished to "with her foot". In addition, three unauthoritative but useful punctuation changes are made (particularly the provision of a comma after "praying" at II,5.4 [Centenary 155.9] which returns to the reading of the manuscript). Only three copies of E2 have been located by the editors; but in one of these—the Ohio State University copy—this sheet is present in its original E1^b setting. The most viable hypothesis for this anomalous copy is that surplus E1^b sheets were used to piece out the E2 edition's second volume, just possibly after some copies of reset sheet 19 manufactured for the E2 edition had been inserted in a late binding-up of E1^b not now identified. The hypothesis also may accord with the evidence for the sheet 19 copy-text of E3, for which see note 4 below. (This hypothesis runs into the difficulty that

256.4 (Centenary 446.31) was corrected in the E1^b standing type, as was a misprint at III,289.4 (Centenary 464.28). A small punctuation change for consistency in a series was made at III,230.2 (Centenary 433.1), and an error occurred when the pronoun "I" beginning a line at III,112.7 (Centenary 369.31) dropped out. No change in E2, whether in reset or in standing type, can be identified as authoritative except for the two specifically requested corrections.

In 1861 Smith, Elder produced what they called "A New Edition" (E3) in one volume, plated. No authoritative alterations occur, and this edition merely exemplifies the continued degeneration of the text. Despite its agreement with the E2 Hawthorne corrections at Centenary 157.15 and 169.2 (II,9.6 and 30.19), and a few other shared readings with E2, the copy-text for E3 was clearly E1^b, corrected.[4]

no copies of E1^b with the interchanged E2 reset corrected sheet have come to light except for a hypothetical reconstructed copy, for which see footnote 4 below. Last, no attempt seemingly was made in a similar manner [if correction were the motive] to furnish E1^b with a reset E2 sheet 20 containing the corrected reading at II,30.19.)

The following Ohio State University Libraries copies of *Transformation* were completely machined: E1^a–PS 1862.A1. 1860.v.1–3, PS 1862.A1. 1860g.v.1 and 3; E1^b–PS 1862.A1.1860c.v.1–3, PS 1862.A1. 1860c.copy 2.v.1–3, PS 1862.A1. 1860c.copy 3.v.2–3; E2–PS 1862.A1. 1860g.v.2. Also completely machined were E1^a ViU Barrett PS 1862.A1. 1860d.566230–2.v.1–3, and E2 PSt T813.H31m.1860b2.v.1–3. The following copies of E3 were sight-collated: OU uncat. and ViU PS 1862.A1.1861. The printings of *The Marble Faun* completely machined were: A v.1–OU PS 1862.A1.1860, PS 1862.A1.1860.copy 4; A v.2–PS 1862.A1.1860.copy 2, PS 1862.A1.1860.copy 4; B v.1–PS 1862.A1.1860.copy 5, PS 1862.A1.-1860.copy 11; B v.2–PS 1862.A1.1860.copy 8, PS 1862.A1.1860.copy 10; C v.1–PS 1862.A1.1860.copy 3, PS 1862.A1.1860b.copy 3; C v.2–PS 1862.A1.1860.copy 3, PS 1862.A1.1860.copy 12; D v.2–PS 1862.A1.1860b, PS 1862.A1.1860b.copy 8; E v.1–PS 1862.A1.1860b.copy 4; and the following loan copies: E v.1–OHi 813.H318m, CtY Iw.H318.86obb, and E v.2–CtY Iw.H318.86obb. Copies of *The Marble Faun* spot-checked were: v.1–PS 1862.A1.1860.copies 2,6,7,8,9,10,12 and PS 1862.A1.1860b.copies 2,5,6,7,8,9,10,12,13; v.2–PS 1862.A1.1860.copies 5,6,7,9,11, and PS 1862.-A1.1860b.copies 2,3,5,6,7,9,10.

4 However, the reset sheet 19 of Vol. II as found in the Pennsylvania State University and Berg Collection copies of E2, containing the first of Hawthorne's requested corrections on II,9.6 and the punctuation changes mentioned above in footnote 3, served as the copy for the printer

The first American edition, set, stereotyped, and printed by H. O. Houghton & Co. at the Riverside Press, Cambridge, was published by Ticknor and Fields, presumably on March 7, 1860.[5] In the first pre-publication printing (I^a) the collation is: Vol. I, $[1-18]^8$ (signed in 12's as $1-12^{12}$, with 1_5 signed 1^*), 144 leaves, pp. [i–v] vi–xi [xii–xiv] [15] 16–283 [284–288]; p. i, half-title; p. ii, blank; p. iii, title; p. iv, copyright notice and imprint; pp. v–xi, preface; p. xii, blank; p. xiii, contents; p. xiv, blank; pp. 15–283, text; pp. 284–288, blank. Vol. II, $[1-18]^8$ (signed in 12's as $1-12^{12}$, with 1_5 signed 1^*), 144 leaves, pp. [i–vi] [7] 8–284 [285–288]; p. i, half-title; p. ii, blank; p. iii, title; p. iv, copyright notice and imprint; p. v, contents; p. vi, blank; pp. 7–284, text; pp. 285–288, blank.

In the second printing (I^b), also pre-publication, both volumes are gathered in 12's according to their signing,[6] but

---

of E3. The E2 reading from sheet 20 at II,30.19 was corrected according to Hawthorne's instructions but the rest of the sheet was set from $E1^b$, as was the whole of the volume, sheet 19 excepted. Later English printings or editions can have no authority and have not been consulted in the preparation of the present text.

5 The Ticknor and Fields Cost Books have the date of publication as February 28, but this was either wishful thinking or else window-dressing in case of trouble about the copyright. Seemingly more trustworthy is the *Boston Transcript* news item on March 1 that the book would be published on March 7.

That there was a remainder issue of this first printing of *The Marble Faun* is suggested by a set in the C. Waller Barrett Library of the University of Virginia Library (Barrett PS 1862.A1.1860e.573970–1). Bound in BD cloth without a publisher's imprint stamped on the spine, both volumes are in the A form of the Ticknor and Fields sheets and both have the original title page; Volume II does not have the Conclusion. At the back of Volume II is an inserted four-page catalogue of books for sale by T. O. H. P. Burnham of Boston. On the basis of these ads BAL #7621 speculates that "this secondary binding was prepared either late in 1860 or early in 1861." Accordingly, it seems very probable that Ticknor and Fields disposed of a small number of unbound sheets to Burnham after the Conclusion had been added to the romance. A second set in the remainder binding, which we have not examined, has been located in the private collection of Parkman D. Howe.

6 One can only guess why the sheets were originally printed and gathered in 8's though signed for 12's, and, moreover, manufactured in

owing to an error in imposition the contents leaf in Vol. I precedes the Preface so that the fifth leaf signed 1* is now p. vii, not p. ix as in the first printing. The pagination formula for Vol. I, therefore, may be given as pp. [i–iv] [xiii–xiv] [v] vi–xi [xii] [15] 16–283 [284–288].

Finally, in the third pre-publication printing (I^c) the contents leaf in Vol. I is reimposed to follow the Preface as in the first printing, but in the process the signing notation 1* was removed, and the collational formula for this and subsequent printings therefore becomes [1]^{12} 2–12^{12}. In this third printing another signing anomaly was straightened out by removing a wrongly placed signature. In I^a at II,197, the third leaf of the gathering signed 9, the signature 4* appears. This notation is doubly wrong in that the gathering is 9, not 4, and also in that the signature should have appeared on the fifth leaf (since the gathering is in 12's); and in fact 9* is present on p. 201, the fifth leaf, correctly. In I^b the signing error was detected and 4* changed to 9*; and in I^c the superfluous and wrongly placed signature was excised. Other than this removal of the signature on p. 197, in this third printing two textual plate changes were made in the first volume and twelve in the second. All but one of these alter the I^c readings to conform to those in E1^a (the same as MS), and that one is an attempted correction that was misunderstood and resulted, instead, in an error at Centenary 180.10.[7] (One of the changes, at 391.22, restores the MS and E1^a capital but maintains the E1^a and I^{a-b} spelling "Error" instead of MS "Errour".)

12's in all later impressions. Just possibly the size of the paper that was immediately available dictated the change in imposition for the first printing.

[7] These plate alterations, and the details of the early printings in Boston, were recorded by Matthew J. Bruccoli in "Concealed Printings in Hawthorne," *Papers of the Bibliographical Society of America*, LVII (First Quarter, 1963), 45–49. For an analysis of these variants and their authority, see below, pp. xcv–cii.

These three printings would seem to be covered by the three bills listed in unpublished sections of the Ticknor and Fields Cost Books in the Houghton Library, Harvard University, under February 20, 23, and 27. The fourth printing (I^d), listed in the Cost Books under "Fourth Edition" for which bills are dated March 22 and April 3, is possibly the one that first contained the postscript "Conclusion" added on pp. 284–88 of the second volume.[8] However, the Cost Books do not record charges for its typesetting and plating, nor, oddly, was the addition advertised. (Possibly the lack of publicity for the new Conclusion reflects the publisher's concern to dispose of all stock from earlier printings, but one must note that the association of the Conclusion with the fourth printing is not entirely confirmed as a fact.) In this, or in one of the two unidentified printings (probably intervening between I^d and I^e in May and July) from the seven in 1860 noted in the Cost Books, five textual changes were made in resetting and replating p. 98 of the second volume (presumably to repair an accident to the plate), all

[8] On March 7, 1860, Hawthorne proposed to Smith, Elder that he add a new ending; on March 9 he wrote to Ticknor, " . . . I intend to add a few pages to the concluding chapter. . . . The additional matter, when written, shall be sent you in manuscript." The March 10 letter to Henry Bright quoted below shows that the structure of the Postscript, the three-part conversation, was already established, but the language could suggest that the addition was not yet on paper. Since he wrote to Smith, Elder on March 16 returning proof, it might be queried whether the date March 14 subscribed to the Postscript represents the date of composition or the date he passed it in proof. However, on the analogy of his MS subscription of the Preface, we should expect the date to represent the completion of the writing; and indeed the same date, March 14, appended to the Conclusion in the Boston edition, sent to Ticknor in manuscript, confirms this hypothesis. If so, it would need to be received in London on March 15, set that day, and put in the mails immediately in order to be received in Leamington by March 16. The duplicate manuscript sent to Boston, under these conditions, saved only two days if it was mailed on March 14, as is probable. But Ticknor may have been holding up the fourth printing in order to include it, and time was precious.

of them extremely careless misprints.[9] Probably in the seventh printing (I^e) in September of 1860 the slug "Seventeenth Thousand" was added to the copyright page, and some plate alterations were performed, ten in Vol. I, spread individually (with two on only one page) between pp. 17 and 269; and twelve in Vol. II, between pp. 9 and 230, with somewhat more concentration.[10] Since various of these only make more consistent the American spelling or punctuation style and in this respect go contrary to $E1^a$ and also, frequently, to MS, they are without authority and were very likely ordered by a copyreader.

According to the Cost Books two printings of 280 sets each were made in 1864, and one printing of 500 in 1865; these impressions still retain the "Seventeenth Thousand" notation.

The Little Classics Edition of 1876, published by James R. Osgood and Company, introduced a new typesetting (II) derived from the first-edition plates in their I^e form, with no infusion of fresh authority but with some corruption as is to be expected in a reprint. Various "editions" (i.e., impressions) were manufactured from these plates, including the Popular Edition (1891), the Salem (1894), and the Concord (1899).

The famed Riverside Edition of 1883 (III), edited by Hawthorne's son-in-law, George Parsons Lathrop, and published by Houghton, Mifflin and Company, was set from the Little Classics text and was issued originally both in

[9] A further variant, the absence of a comma after "ever" in I^d Vol. II,118.4 appears to have resulted from plate batter and not from deliberate alteration.

[10] Professor Bruccoli had not personally checked the copy with these changes in Vol. II at the time of his *PBSA* article cited in note 7 above, but see the table below on pp. cxxxvi–cxxxviii. They occur in I^e Vol. II at 9.27, 9.29, 17.2, 17.3, 84.24, 92.28, 92.28, 93.27, 93.28, 99.10, 230.5, and 230.7.

trade and in large-paper form.[11] The text of this edition is notoriously corrupt. The last of the collected editions collated for the Centenary text is the Autograph Edition of 1900 (IV) set from the Riverside text (III) and published by Houghton, Mifflin in a white binding with tipped-in signed illustrations, and in a blue binding with unsigned illustrations. Both appear to be bound from sheets of the same impression.[12] The further history of these Autograph plates has not been investigated for the purpose of the Centenary text, although one may note an Old Manse impression printed from them in 1904.

Abroad, the Tauchnitz edition of 1860, set from E1^b (including the E1^b setting of sheet 19), has been collated for the information of the editors, but since no authoritative variants were found in it, and since it is out of the main line of textual transmission, the results are not presented in the Historical Collation.

The manuscript of *The Marble Faun* (wanting the Postscript, however) is preserved in the British Museum, its two volumes catalogued as Add. MSS. 44889, 44890. The manuscript carries the note in both volumes, "Presented by Mrs. E. P. Merivale in memory of her father, the late H. A. Bright, 10 Oct. 1936.", and on the front cover of Vol. I is pasted a slip stating, "This Manuscript of the MARBLE FAUN is presented to the BRITISH MUSEUM by ELIZABETH PHEBE MERIVALE in memory of her father HENRY ARTHUR BRIGHT to whom it was given by his friend NATHANIEL HAWTHORNE."

[11] Evidence from *The Scarlet Letter* (Centenary Edition, 1962), pp. lix–lx, suggests that the plates for the trade edition were made from the typesetting before printing and were thereupon corrected in a few details before reimpression in a second trade printing, followed by printing of the large-paper copies from type-metal. These details have not been investigated in *The Marble Faun*.

[12] The Historical Collation has been prepared from a copy with the blue binding in the Ohio State University Libraries.

Bound in is a letter from Hawthorne to Bright, a prosperous Liverpool littérateur and manuscript collector with whom Hawthorne had been especially friendly. The letter is dated March 10, 1860, from 21 Bath Street, Leamington, and reads in part:

Dear Mr. Bright,

I thank you very much for your letter, and am glad you like the Romance so far, and so well. I shall really be gratified if you will review it. Very likely you are right about Donatello; for though the idea in my mind was an agreeable and beautiful one, it was not easy so to present it to the reader.

Smith & Elder certainly do take strange liberties with the titles of books. I wanted to call it "The Marble Faun"; but they insisted upon "Transformation," which will lead the reader to anticipate a sort of pantomime. They wrote me, some days ago, that the edition was nearly all sold, and that they are going to print another; to which I mean to append a few pages, in the shape of a conversation between Kenyon, Hilda, and the author, throwing some further light on matters which seem to have been left too much in the dark. For my own part, however, I should prefer the book as it now stands.

It so happened, that, at the very time you were writing, Una was making up a parcel of the manuscript, to send to you. There is a further, portion now in the hands of Smith & Elder, which I will procure when I go to London; that is, if you do not consider this immense mass more than enough. . . . I remain

Most sincerely your friend
Nath¹ Hawthorne.

The plan to pick up the remaining manuscript was not carried out, as attested by another bound-in letter, this from Hawthorne to Smith, Elder, dated March 24, 1860, from 13 Charles Street, Bath:

Gentlemen,

I have quitted Leamington, and any communications for me may be directed as above.

A portion of the MS. of "Transformation" remains in your hands; and you would much oblige me by forwarding it to Henry A. Bright, Esq. Sandheys, West Derby, near Liverpool. . . . [13]

Also bound in is a note from 13 Charles Street, Bath, dated April 23, 1860:

Dear Mr. Bright,

Here is this preface, which I somehow neglected to send with the former package of rubbish. . . . Sincerely yours, Nath[l] Hawthorne

Pasted on the verso of the presentation leaf of the first volume is the engraving of Hawthorne after his portrait by Cephas G. Thompson that had been distributed by Ticknor, Reed, and Fields. Before the Preface is a watercolor title-page in the Greek style, to which reference is made in a bound-in letter to Henry Bright from the artist John Eliot Hodgkin dated September 19, 1860. Another version of this title-page also precedes the second volume. Finally, pasted on the verso of a leaf placed before Chapter I is a representation of the Faun by Praxiteles.

The manuscript itself consists of 505 leaves of white laid paper, each sheet folded once across the short axis to form two leaves (measuring 8 15/16″ x 7 3/8″, trimmed and gilded edges), the later sheets bearing an oval blindstamped seal with an eagle figure and the legend "LONDON SUPERFINE". The black ink is now faded to a somewhat grayish brown. With three exceptions, folios 43, 370^r, and 508, the inscription is only on the rectos.

[13] Unfortunately, Smith, Elder appear not to have included in this mailing the manuscript for the Postscript, which is therefore not present in the British Museum volumes and is probably lost.

Several systems of numeration are present on the leaves. The British Museum authorities are responsible for having numbered the folios consecutively for each volume, starting with the watercolor title in the first volume as 1, the Preface as 2–6, the inserted leaf with the Praxiteles representation as 7–8, and the beginning of Chapter I as 9, proceeding through the slip that ends Vol. I of *Transformation* as 175,[14] continuing with the start of the printed Vol. II on the remaining portion of the original leaf as 176, and ending with 245. The pencil numbering begins afresh with 1 on the watercolor title prefixed to the second volume of the manuscript, and concludes with 265 on the recto of the final leaf of the volume. These details make it certain that the pencil numbering is a post-printing system. It is, also, a strict foliation system, since text on the verso of leaves (like the ending of Chapter IV of the first volume on Hawthorne's p. 43) is not enumerated.

Hawthorne started originally to number the leaves in ink as he wrote, with 1 at Chapter I, and so continued through 410, which is the second leaf of "The Extinction of a Lamp." These numbers are centrally placed at the head of every inscribed page (excluding the insert on 370ᵛ). The abandonment of this system coincides with the sending of the MS through the preceding chapter "as far as page 429" (his revised numbering) on October 17, 1859, to Smith, Elder.

It is clear that the Preface, subscribed Leamington, October 15, 1859, accompanied this initial batch of copy to the publisher.[15] This Preface starts with Hawthorne's number 2, in

14 Hawthorne had begun the first chapter of the second volume on the same fol. 174 (according to his own final enumeration) as the end of Chapter XVI of Vol. I. The printer cut the leaf into two parts for assignment to different compositors, and the pencil numbering (though not Hawthorne's) counts each part separately.

15 The dates indicate that Hawthorne wrote the Preface at this point in order to include it in the first bundle of copy sent to the publisher. (From his pocket diary for October 14: "Wrote till 3— the Preface of my

an independent numbering (indicating the loss of his own inscribed title that he would have counted as 1) and concludes on 6. Thereupon Hawthorne renumbered the pages in the upper right-hand corner, starting with 7 for old page 1 on Chapter I. At the start he renumbered only every other leaf (that is, the first leaf of the fold), and so continued through 148, but beginning with 149 he numbered each page, concluding with 508. However, before copy was sent off (and thus between October 15 and 17, also) Sophia Hawthorne clarified for the printer the numbering of the pages by deleting the now-rejected centered numbering (a few are merely altered) and writing after it, in ink, the corrected figure according to Hawthorne's right-hand corner enumeration, though numbering every page. When at 148 Hawthorne starts his consecutive enumeration, Sophia merely deletes the original centered numbering and allows the right-hand corner figures to stand, and so continues through p. 431, the last of the centrally numbered pages.

All Centenary references to the manuscript by page or leaf are to Hawthorne's revised system of enumeration, that in the right-hand corner of the leaves.

Hawthorne's final numbering, followed by the second hand so far as it goes, is accurate. But the original centered enumeration has its irregularities. An interesting anomaly occurs at the start of Chapter V of the first volume, originally numbered 31 in the centered system but 44 according to the

---

book. It is not yet finished by 60 or 70 pages.") One may notice, also, that according to Hawthorne's letter of April 23, 1860, to Bright, he had had the Preface in his possession although it seems not to have been placed with the rest of the first section of the manuscript. No compositorial markings are present in the manuscript for the Preface, and it is likely that typesetting was done apart from the regular routine of the text. Preliminaries were almost invariably printed last; and in this case the first gathering, containing the Preface and title, could not be finally passed for the press until several months later, perhaps as late as early February, when the title *Transformation* was reluctantly accepted. On the other hand, the printed subscription December 15 (replacing manuscript October 15) suggests proof before the final decision about the title.

revised scheme, a difference that is thereupon maintained up to the next irregularity. What seems to have happened is this. Folio 42 (originally 36) contains on its verso the conclusion of Chapter IV, paged 43, this 43 being numbered centrally by Sophia (who, incidentally, when she continues with the next folio, deleting 31 at the head of Chapter V, initially writes 43 but alters to 44 before continuing with 45). Evidently, at some time after the start of Chapter V Hawthorne had revised some of the preceding manuscript material by rewriting to expand it by seven manuscript pages.

That this rewriting was not confined to Chapter IV, as it stands, but must have started earlier, is indicated by the fact that Chapter IV is 11 manuscript pages, as against 16 for Chapter V, 12 for Chapter VI, 9 for Chapter VII, 8 for Chapter VIII, and 9 for Chapter IX. Chapter I is 8, Chapter II is 9, and Chapter III is 9 also. If seven pages had been added within Chapter IV alone, the original chapter would have been only 4 pages, an improbably short unit.

Fortunately, complete precision in pinpointing the revision is afforded by physical evidence in the manuscript. Although the pen and ink of fols. 2–22 and then fol. 44 (beginning Chapter V) and following are alike, a different pen and ink inscribe fols. 23–43 which contain the last page of Chapter II followed by Chapters III and IV complete. This clearly delineated insertion, therefore, must cover the area of revision. Of considerable interest, corroborative evidence may exist in the question of Miriam's name. Professor Simpson first noticed that the spacing revealed the insertion of Miriam's name in blanks left for the purpose within the early pages, fols. 9–22, but normal inscription starting with fol. 23.[16] The fact that the name was inserted in blanks in

16 An observation made from his Xerox copy that was confirmed by some occasional differences in the ink between the name and surrounding text later observed in the manuscript by the textual editor. The important matter of the integral inscription of the name on fol. 23 has been independently checked and confirmed in MS by Messrs. L. N. Smith

Chapters I and II (save for the last page of Chapter II) but not in Chapters III and IV (or Chapter V) suggests that blanks may originally have been left later than fol. 22 and that the normal inscription of the name in fol. 23 and presumably in fols. 24–43 results from the revision of these pages. Because of the differences in the pen and ink in fols. 23–43, and the start of current inscription of Miriam's name with fol. 23, Chapters I and II must represent the original, unrevised material, with the revision starting with the last leaf of Chapter II and continuing through Chapters III and IV. Even so, since Chapters III and IV now total 20 pages, and before expansion would have totalled only 13, they are still suspiciously short.

The answer seems to be the obvious one. Not only the consistent differences in their ink but also the position of the chapter numbers throughout the manuscript indicate that they are later additions, just as the chapter titles (at least in the earlier part) were added at one time after the inscription of the text. (This practice conforms to that in *The House of the Seven Gables* manuscript.) Thus the chapter now numbered V on MS fol. 44 was not, according to the evidence, numbered at all at the time the preceding leaves were revised, since all of the first four chapters exhibit the same evidence as in the fifth chapter, and later, that the numbers and titles were subsequently inscribed in spaces left for the purpose.[17] Instead, then, of a nine-leaf original Chapter III and a four-

---

and T. A. J. Burnett. Fols. 23 and 24, which should be a fold, are disjunct. This fact does not seem to have any application to the problem of the revision but probably is to be explained by the cutting apart of the fold at the printing house consequent upon the assignment to Hobson of a take starting with fol. 24 and the new chapter. We may note that Hawthorne's system of renumbering only the first page of a fold provides a page number on 23 but not on 24, thus demonstrating that 23 and 24 were conjunct when sent to the printer.

[17] For this reason, Miriam's name in the title of Chapter I is normally inscribed.

leaf original Chapter IV, the evidence favors the hypothesis that what we now know as Chapters III and IV was only one chapter, probably dealing with the trip through the Catacomb of Saint Calixtus, and that at some time after the inscription of what is now Chapter V[18] this one chapter was expanded by seven manuscript pages and divided into two separate chapters.

It can be only guesswork, but one may notice that the account of Miriam that begins Chapter III takes up five manuscript pages (Centenary 20.1–24.4) to the start of the true narrative of the tour through the Catacomb bridged at 24.5 with "We now proceed with our narrative." Thus it is tempting to speculate that after he had written the account of Miriam's rooms, now found at the start of Chapter V, "Miriam's Studio," Hawthorne enlarged the discussion of her background at the beginning of "Subterranean Reminiscences" either by the invention of new material or (less likely, in view of the sixteen-page length of Chapter V) by transferring material from the "Miriam's Studio" section. That this interest in developing Miriam's background here was associated with the decision about her name seems reasonable to assume, and indeed it may be that it waited upon Hawthorne's invention of, or decision to emphasize, the rumor of her Jewish banking ancestry (22.32–23.4) which any reader would believe to accord better with her wealth and oriental appearance than the second rumor that she was a German princess.

Finally, since the rewriting actually started with the last manuscript page of Chapter II ("set of features. . . . ", 18.21), it is possible that the reason lay in the early intro-

18 The only *terminus ad quem* discernible for the expansion is fol. 304 of the manuscript (Centenary 275.32), written about September 10, 1859, at which point the inscription of the name Graydon ceased and that of Kenyon began. Throughout these first chapters Graydon is regularly altered to Kenyon, as usual.

duction of the Model at the end of Chapter II, which provides the occasion for the opening paragraph of Chapter III that quickly disposes of him and goes on to Miriam in a slightly awkward manner. (Centenary 21.28–31 is also a trifle oddly phrased coming after the first two chapters.)

The centered numeration and Hawthorne's final numbering continue with a difference of thirteen instead of six up to Chapter XII, "A Stroll on the Pincian." The last page of Chapter XI, "Fragmentary Sentences," had been numbered 100, altered to 113; but Chapter XII begins on a leaf centrally numbered 93 altered to 114. This anomaly can be explained by the fact that Chapter XI had also begun on centered page number 93, and thus can be exposed as a complete insertion. One may notice in this connection that in "A Stroll on the Pincian" the view Hilda and Kenyon have first of Donatello and then of Miriam and the Model does not require the information in "Fragmentary Sentences" but could readily follow on the end of Chapter X, "The Sylvan Dance," in which Donatello is ordered to leave Miriam after the appearance of the Model. The inserted Chapter XI, therefore, is very likely another indication of the development of the Model and his connection with Miriam's mysterious past in a more detailed manner than had been adumbrated in the earlier expansion of Chapter III to become Chapters III and IV, and certainly beyond that in the draft from which Hawthorne was making his fair copy. Whatever the date of this insertion of Chapter XI, it was accomplished, obviously, before the chapters were numbered, and also before the decision was made to alter *Graydon* to *Kenyon* (see below, pp. lxviii–lxix).

From this point the altered numbering continues, with original 93 now page 114, up to the last page of the centered numbering, 410 altered to 431. No irregularity thereafter exists following page 432 in what must have been Hawthorne's current numbering of the pages at the time of inscription up to the final 508.

The numerous examples of false starts and corrected eyeskips in the inscription of the manuscript (recorded in the appendix Alterations in the Manuscript, along with the evidence for revision of the draft as he wrote) suggest that, as he had done with *The House of the Seven Gables* and *The Blithedale Romance,* Hawthorne in this manuscript was making a fair copy of an earlier form. References to this lost antecedent manuscript may be found in the Introduction, ranging from the start of a rough draft on July 17, 1858, to the apparent beginning of the true antecedent copy on October 25, 1858, which was finished on January 30, 1859. The start of the present manuscript revised fair copy may be marked as July 26, 1859, with inscription proceeding at some thirty-five to forty pages a week. On October 17 the manuscript, through page 429, the end of his Chapter X of the third volume, "Reminiscences of Miriam" (Centenary, Chapter XLII), was sent off to Smith, Elder accompanied by the Preface. As shown by the numbering, at the time of this dispatch he was about to start p. 432 ("yon looked upon the group. . . . ", 391.30). Just before noon on November 8, 1859, he completed the last page, 508.

The first proof, in sheets paged and probably imposed and folded to make gatherings, reached him on or just before December 6, but he did not finish discussion of the title and reluctantly accept *Transformation* until early February 1860. Hence we must suppose that Smith, Elder, although refusing to accept the proffered "Romance of Monte Beni" title as final, in desperation chose it for the verso running-titles in order to start proofs while arguing about what final form the title was to take on the title-page. That the present verso running-titles are the originals, and not a reset series, may be shown by a remark in the December 6 letter accompanying the return of the first proof: "In reply to a letter of yours, disapproving of the title, I sent you a choice of several others; but I see that the printers adhere to the first one." On fol. 387^r of the manuscript appears the printer's pencil notation, "Romance of Monte Beni or Transformation [Sig. 42] page 65". This is the one time that "Transformation" is mentioned in these printer's notes, and it may indicate roughly the time, somewhere in early January, when Smith, Elder definitely decided on the title.

The manuscript ranges from about thirty to thirty-four lines per page. No page fails to show alteration of some variety made during the course of inscription or as part of a general review. Much of the alteration was made *currente calamo*, ordinarily by wiping out with a finger while the ink was still wet and writing over the same space. In the appendix Alterations in the Manuscript these changes are distinguished from the interlineations, which presumably were made at a later time, at least after the ink had dried.

The alterations over wiped-out letters and words offer the most serious difficulty to recovering the readings of the initial inscription, especially as no more than a letter or two, often, may have been written before the error was detected or a change decided on. Whenever anything of the original can be recovered, it is listed in the appendix, since sometimes even a single letter, in context, can suggest the probable word that was started, and the critic of Hawthorne's style can secure an insight into his self-criticism. (Frequently a wiped-out word, or start of a word, is not corrected but deferred in favor of expanded phrasing, a practice characteristic of Hawthorne's manuscripts.) Less commonly, substitute words were written over the discarded original when little or no obliteration had been attempted beforehand. The manuscript displays hundreds of cases of apparent alteration which, on examination, prove to be no more than the tracing-over of an identical original word, or some letters in a word, in order to increase legibility. Occasionally, the same word is interlined for clarity to this end. No attempt has been made in the appendix to record these tracings or interlined duplications, whether of words or of letters, when legibility alone was their purpose.

Although it is evident that the majority of Hawthorne's own alterations were made at the moment of inscription, some classes of alteration, like interlineations with or without deletion, cannot be pinpointed in time, nor can the various corrections made by mending. Alterations made over erasures or scraped paper are Hawthorne's own, as indicated by the handwriting at 128.34 where original "tell" has been erased and "say" interlined. On at least one occasion (though generalization from this may be difficult) the erasure and correction seem to have been made within a few pages of the original inscription. For example, on pp. 383–86 the "d" of "dome" is several times erased and then altered to "D" (Centenary 348.25, 349.2, 350.10, 351.7, 351.23), but in the second line of the next chapter, on p. 389 (354.2), and thereafter, the word is inscribed "Dome". However, some corrections must have been last-minute affairs, as suggested by the pocket-diary entries immediately preceding the dispatch of the first lot of copy to the printer on October 17, 1859: October 15, "Looked over manuscript of Romance till 3"; October 16, "Looked over manuscript &c."

As already remarked, Hawthorne left the spaces for the chapter numbers and titles vacant (as he had done in the manuscript of *The House of the Seven Gables*) and filled them in at a later time. The differences in ink indicate that the title and the chapter number were written at different times, the numbers ordinarily in a lighter ink. On the evidence that this lighter ink was often used to underline the titles to indicate capitalization, it would seem that the titles were first written and later the numbers; and corroboration in at least one instance comes on fol. 468 when the title of "The Peasant and Contadina" (Centenary Chapter XLVII) was first started too high beneath the end of the preceding chapter on the same page, and the "The" had to be wiped out and the title written farther down in order to leave sufficient space for the chapter number. Although it is clear that in the earlier part of the manuscript the chapter titles were added in a vacant space left in the text, and then, at a still later time, the chapter numbers, as the romance progresses, the similarity of ink between chapter title and text suggests that a number of the later titles were written currently with the text. However, the differences in inks and hence in time of inscription of the chapter numbers persist to the end even after the first package of copy through fol. 429 had been sent to the printer and Hawthorne was completing the romance.

The first sixteen chapter headings that comprise the first volume of the printed text all began on a fresh page. But Chapter I of the second volume (Centenary XVII) was placed on the same leaf (fol. 174) as the end of Chapter XVI, although subsequently cut apart by the printer. That this placement coincides with the end of a volume is fortuitous (especially since it is probable that at the time of inscription the chapter numbers, let alone the volume indications, had not been filled in) and is most likely due to the fact that Chapter XVI ended the page with only five lines of text, on fol. 174, whereas by chance all preceding chapter endings had occupied most of the leaf and thus had wasted little or no paper. However, the system of beginning a fresh chapter on a new page may have been deliberate at the start while Hawthorne was in some part working out major alterations during the course of revising and copying

The sculptor looked more attentively at the young man, and was surprised and alarmed to observe how entirely the fine, fresh glow of animal spirits had departed out of his face. Hitherto, moreover, even while he was standing perfectly still, there had been a kind of possible gambol indicated in his aspect. It was quite gone, now. All his youthful gaiety, and with it his simplicity of manner, was eclipsed, if not utterly extinct.

"You are surely ill, my dear fellow!" exclaimed Kenyon.

"Am I? Perhaps so," said Donatello indifferently. "I never have been ill, and know not what it may be."

"Do not make the poor lad fancy-sick," whispered Miriam, pulling the sculptor's sleeve. "He is of a nature to lie down and die, at once, if he finds himself drawing such melancholy breaths as we ordinary people are enforced to burthen our lungs withal. But we must get him away from this old, dreamy, and dreary Rome, where nobody but himself ever thought of being gay. Its influences are too heavy to sustain the life of such a creature."

The above conversation had passed chiefly on the steps of the Cappuccini; and, having said much, Miriam lifted the leathern curtain that hangs before all church-doors, in Italy.

"Hilda has forgotten her appointment," she observed, "or else her maiden slumbers are very sound, this morning. We will wait for her no longer."

They entered the nave. The interior of the church was of moderate compass, but of good architecture, with a vaulted roof over the nave, and a row of dusky chapels on either side of it, instead of the customary side-aisles. Each chapel had its saintly

Folio 204 of the printer's-copy holograph manuscript of
The Marble Faun in the British Museum (Add. 44889).

der of the fatality that seems to [haunt your footsteps, and throws a shadow of crime about your path,
you being guiltless."

225 - 52 - Vol iii
Hobson
231

"There was such a fatality," said Miriam. "Yes;
the shadow fell upon me, innocent, but I went astray in it,
and wandered — as Hilda would tell you — into crime."

She went on to say, that, while yet a child, she
had lost her English mother. From a very early period of her life, there had been a contract of betrothal
between herself and a certain marchese, the representative of another branch of her paternal house;
a family arrangement, between two persons of disproportioned ages, and in which feeling went for nothing. Most
Italian girls of noble rank would have yielded themselves to such a marriage, as an affair of course. But
there was something in Miriam's blood, in her mixed
race, in her recollections of her mother — some characteristic, finally, in her own nature — which had given
her freedom of thought, and force of will, and made this
pre-arranged connection odious to her. Moreover,
the character of her destined husband would have been
a sufficient and insuperable objection; for it betrayed
traits so evil, so treacherous, so wild, and yet so strangely subtle, as would only be accounted for by the insanity
which often developes itself in old, close-kept races
of men, when long unmixed with newer blood. Reaching the age when the marriage-contract should have
been fulfilled, Miriam had utterly repudiated it.

Sometime afterward had occurred that terrible event to which Miriam alluded, when she revealed
her name; an event, the frightful and mysterious cir-

Folio 473 of the printer's-copy holograph manuscript of
The Marble Faun in the British Museum (Add. 44890).

the draft manuscript, as in the rewritten Chapters III and IV, and the inserted Chapter XI. Thereafter, in the second volume Chapters X, XI, and XIV (Centenary XXVI, XXVII, XXX), with 12, 3, and 6 lines of text of chapter ending above them, respectively, begin part-way down a page; and in the third volume[19] Chapters III, IV, VIII, XII, XIII, XIV, XV, and XVI (Centenary XXXV, XXXVI, XL, XLIV, XLV, XLVI, XLVII, XLVIII), with 8, 6, 6, 6, 3, 21, 23, and 4 lines of chapter-ending above them, respectively. Obviously, some attempt had been made to save space and paper as the manuscript neared its close.

Hawthorne had designated "Miriam's Trouble" (Centenary XVII) as the first chapter of the English edition's second volume, and "Pictured Windows" (Centenary XXXIII) as the first chapter of the third volume. Probably in order to make all three volumes of approximately equal length, but surely for no literary design, the printers ignored his marking for the third volume and, adding "Pictured Windows" as Chapter XVII to Vol. II, they marked "Market-Day in Perugia" (Centenary XXXIV), the original second chapter, as Chapter I of Vol. III. Hawthorne's division is more meaningful. That, on another occasion, he concerned himself with the placement of his volume endings may be indicated by the direction, even though utilitarian, that he gave to Ticknor to begin the American edition's second volume with what is now Centenary XXVI.[20] When on September 10, 1859, he handed "rather more than half" of the manuscript to Sophia

[19] These third-volume numbers are the manuscript's. Because the printer renumbered them after beginning his Vol. III one chapter later than Hawthorne had directed, in *Transformation* they would be Chapters II, III, VII, XI, etc.

[20] "The exact middle of the work is at the 10th chapter (called "the Pedigree of Monte Beni") of the Second volume; and you must commence your Second volume with that chapter."—Hawthorne to Ticknor, December 22, 1859 (MS, Berg Collection, New York Public Library).

to read (estimated by Professor Simpson as about three hundred pages),[21] it is likely that she then, or shortly before the first batch of copy was bundled for the printer through fol. 429,[22] began to assist her husband chiefly by touching up a large number of words for legibility. Fortunately she used a noticeably finer pen and perhaps a different ink which has not faded but still differentiates itself from the now grayish color of Hawthorne's by its jet blackness. (This latter distinction could be more apparent than real, however, since it may possibly result from her having freshly dipped her pen before each alteration. The best test remains the fineness of the nib of the pen she used.) These ministrations also continue after fol. 430, the start of the second and final section of copy sent to the printer.

If Sophia had confined herself to improving the clarity of the manuscript for the benefit of the printer, no problems would have been presented. In fact, she was not content to be the simple handmaiden, but busied herself with the various corrections and suggestions.[23] On some occasions she would mark the word to be discussed with a pencil cross and when she had a specific suggestion, not just a query, she would pencil on a convenient verso the change she supported.

[21] If, as probable, he gave her the manuscript at the end of a chapter, he could have written the first page of Chapter XIV "Donatello's Bust" of the second volume (Centenary XXX) on fol. 298 beneath the ending of Chapter XIII, or else handed her manuscript to fol. 297, adding fol. 298 later. Chapter XIII begins on fol. 287. Chapter XV begins on fol. 306, but XIV contains the change in names from *Graydon* to *Kenyon*.

[22] The correctness of Professor Simpson's surmise that Sophia's reading of the manuscript was responsible for the change of *Graydon* to *Kenyon* would seem to be indicated by the evidence of the first such change as early as Centenary 7.12 (see below). This being so, her marking of the manuscript must have started immediately upon her first reading.

[23] The complete list of Sophia's corrections and suggestions will be found in the Alterations in the Manuscript, indicated by daggers. The numerous touchings-up for legibility have not been recorded.

The more important of her suggestions concern questions of fact. Thus on fol. 239 (215.33) Hawthorne had written "a coat of stucco and white-wash"; a pencil cross appears in the text over "white" and on the verso of the facing leaf Sophia writes in pencil "x yellow". When, in the text, her hand then deletes "white" and interlines "yellow" we must suppose that they discussed the color of Italian houses and, on Hawthorne's agreement, Sophia proceeded to alter the manuscript in accord with her suggestion.

Other questions of detail are represented by fol. 164 (144.19) in which Hawthorne had written "with many niches, out of which looked Agrippa's legendary virgin,". Sophia placed a cross interlined after "niches" and on fol. 165ᵛ (the second leaf of the fold of paper) she pencilled "x bas-releifs". In the text her hand then deletes "many" and interlines "and many bas-reliefs,"[24] with a caret drawn over the original comma after "niches". Similarly, on fol. 173 (152.8) a pencil cross is interlined after "entrance", and on the facing verso she wrote in pencil "x at one side". In the text she then deletes original "between two of the splendid Corinthian columns;" and interlines "on one side;" with a caret. The difference between the pencilled suggestion "at" and the text interlineation "on" may represent Hawthorne's preference.

Sophia's suggestions were usually followed, as in the stylistic change on fol. 220 (197.17–18) where the text originally read "a being whom sorrow could not cling to!" Sophia put an x before "to" but did not pencil a suggestion. Presumably after her husband's agreement, however, she deleted final "to!", placed the exclamation after "cling", and interlined "to" with a caret after "being". However, in a few places Hawthorne chose to modify her stylistic suggestions.

[24] She spells "reliefs" correctly in making the change in the text, but a hesitation is apparent in the inscription when she comes to the "i".

For example, one of them comes on fol. 204 (181.15) with a cross above and below "thus" and on fol. 205ᵛ (the second leaf of the fold) her pencilled "x thus spoken". Hawthorne apparently did not like this rather stilted phrase and contented himself with suggesting a simpler modification; hence she deleted "thus" and interlined "so" to make the phrase read "having said so much". Occasionally she would query an error, as in the three times, once on fol. 215 and twice on fol. 218 (192.5, 194.22, 195.1), in which Hawthorne had had Miriam addressed as "Signora" and a pencil cross and Sophia's ink correction to "Signorina" appear. Very likely a pencil arrow on fol. 303ᵛ is hers. The mark indicates a close repetition of "tempting" on fol. 302, and Hawthorne has agreed with the tacit criticism and has deleted the first and interlined "melting" (274.10).

Hawthorne ignored her crosses only three times. On fol. 356 (323.16) a pencil cross without accompanying change appears above "guest". On fol. 322 (292.6) an ink cross is placed before the phrase "vinous enjoyment", an indication of Sophia's temperance convictions already noticed in her censorship of the manuscript of *The Blithedale Romance*. In this case, however, her husband resisted the objection. Thirdly, another ink cross appears in the last paragraph indention on fol. 386 (351.16), where the matter to be queried is not certain.

One of the important results of Sophia's reading the manuscript was probably, as Professor Simpson has suggested, the change of the sculptor's name from *Graydon* [25] to *Kenyon*

[25] Julian Hawthorne quotes Bright as stating, "Kenyon's name was originally Grayson . . ." (*Nathaniel Hawthorne and His Wife* [1884], II, 243). Bright's error was a natural one, shared in fact for some time by the textual editor. The name is so ambiguously inscribed most of the time that *Grayson* is an easy misreading. Fortunately, enough cases appear of clear intent to write *Graydon* that there can be no doubt about the name.

even though the ink cross on fol. 9 (7.12) is oddly placed.[26] Thereafter, she alters the name in the text automatically. In the section between fols. 254 and 277 (Centenary 230.17 —251.5) including Chapters X and XI of Vol. II, Hawthorne himself performs the alterations, except for four occurrences he overlooked (Centenary 236.21, 237.7, 247.31, 248.23).

Not all of Sophia's alterations are marked by crosses. The simplest of these cases are, of course, the touching-up of letters for legibility, or, as with "thorough" on fol. 115 (100.30), her deletion of a word Hawthorne had corrected and her interlineation of the same word more clearly written. From such helpful and textually innocuous gestures where no changes occur, she proceeded, however, to occasional corrections of spellings, as her alteration on fol. 15 (12.13) of Hawthorne's "Appennines" to "Apennines", or on fol. 133 (115.33) of Hawthorne's characteristic "stopt" to "stopped". The inference follows that when Sophia made an alteration in the text without the pencil cross, she was acting on her own responsibility without having consulted her husband in advance and thus without his approval of the change. For instance, on fol. 97 (84.2) she silently altered "they" to

[26] This cross is a little odd in three respects: (1) it is in ink instead of the customary pencil; (2) it does not resemble the pencil crosses which are plain, with each stroke about the same length, but instead (like the ink cross on fol. 386) it has an ornamental dot above and below the much shorter stroke at upper left and lower right; (3) it is not placed over or before the word to be queried but instead in the space left by the short last line of the preceding paragraph, the name appearing in the first line of the next paragraph. This positioning, as well as the appearance of the ornamental cross in a paragraph indention on fol. 386, might suggest a printer's mark since compositors' names may be written in precisely the same spaces. However, the occurrence within the text on fol. 322 of an ink cross (though without the ornamental dots) with exactly the same differences between the strokes, one that is clearly associated with a phrase that could touch Sophia on a tender nerve, shows that these three anomalous ink crosses are hers and thus establishes a connection between her intervention and the change of the sculptor's name.

"that" owing to a misunderstanding of the text, apparently, and this change seems to have later triggered a proof-alteration by Hawthorne that further compounded her original error (see Textual Note). These unauthoritative and presumably unblessed changes may range from her assumption on fol. 178 (156.34) that Hawthorne's exclamation point was a mistake and a query would be better, to her tinkering with his idiom as on fol. 179 (157.19) when she changes his "the" to "their" in "relieve the nerves".

Venial as these alterations may be, they sometimes confuse the sense and have a cumulative effect of chipping away at Hawthorne's true style and intentions. They may also present textual problems when their authority is seriously in question, as in the examples above from fols. 178–179 (156.34, 157.19).

When a cross is missing, therefore, no evidence can exist to show that Hawthorne knew of the change. Indeed, it is probable that in one final class of Sophia's alterations she did not choose to call her interference to her husband's attention, since no cross ever appears when she is manifestly censoring his language. Sophia's sensibilities were highly refined (as demonstrated by her censorship of Hawthorne's notebooks before publication), and she disliked words that her taste would regard as low and vulgar. Thus it is unlikely that any authority inheres to her silent change on fol. 30 (25.16), for example, of "appetite" to "fancy" or on fol. 473 (431.1) of "breeds of men" to "races of men". Similarly, on fol. 225 (203.6) she seems to have been offended by Hawthorne's doves which "were squatted in a corner of the piazza" and, without a cross, she changed "squatted" to "huddled".

That the British Museum manuscript was the printer's copy is abundantly demonstrated by the regular markings of the printing shop on its pages. These notations are of two general kinds. The first are made on the versos of leaves and concern the making-up of the type-pages into the signed gatherings. These are almost always in ink (rarely some part of the notation appears in pencil or brown crayon) and appear regularly in a fixed position, the verso facing the leaf of text that begins a new sheet, and in the recto text at the point of change. Thus on fol. 17 where sheet 2 and page 17 begin, an ink bracket is drawn and near it is written in ink "17–2 vol. 1." (the 7 written over an original 8). On the facing verso is written in ink a large figure 1 and near it "Romance of Monte Beni [Sig 1]" followed in pencil by "Page 1". A pencil 1 also appears in the inner margin of this verso, placed on its side. By this means a permanent record was made of the sheet just finished and of that to follow. Similarly, when on fol. 28 we have the start of sheet 3, the first word of its text is bracketed in ink with the notation "33–3" and on fol. 27^v near the head is found a circled inverted ink 2 and, near the foot, in ink, "Romance of Monte Beni [Sig 2]" and then in pencil "Page 17". In a position that was thereafter to be adopted almost consistently, a pencil number for the signature of the preceding sheet (in this case 2) is found written in the inner or outer margin of the verso of the annotated text-page (in this case fol. 28) or whatever leaf was the second in the fold. Beginning with the marking on fol. 37 for the start of sheet 4, the ink annotation of the page-signature-volume also includes the name of the compositor who was setting type at the break between the sheets, as "49–4 vol. 1. Jenkins". Perhaps as many as four hands are found in these markings concerned with the makeup of the sheets.

On the versos of the leaves marked for the first two sheets (fols. 16^v, 27^v) are found in pencil, respectively, "R by S" and (inverted) "R by Scott" (this "Scott" may be a little doubtful as the reading). This kind of annotation does not appear again except on fol. 271ᵛ where is found, in pencil, "Read by N. V. C".

Seven, possibly eight, compositors sign the pages, listed here in their order of entrance: Hobson, Orr, Spech (?), Farley, Shand, Jenkins, Mintern, and Barnett. Spech, if that is an accurate transcript of his name (he may be Shand), set only 22 lines of text in one take of fols. 11–12 before permanently disappearing. Somewhat similarly, Orr set a total of 183 lines in two takes of seven leaves (fols. 9–11 and 31–34) before he left for good. For the rest, working in shifting groups for simultaneous composition, Farley set 4,792 lines of type in 39 stints, Hobson 3,657 lines in 32 stints, Shand 2,993 lines in 21 stints, Mintern 2,364 lines in 20 stints, Barnett 1,941 lines in 16 stints, and Jenkins 1,927 lines in 14 stints. Barnett enters late at I,246.9 and drops out early at III,86.16. Mintern leaves at III,54.7. Jenkins, who had dropped out after II,24.13, was not brought back until III,151.0. Farley, Hobson, and Shand, therefore, are the only compositors whose work is spread evenly throughout the book. The usual take (the number of manuscript folios distributed at one time to a compositor) was about four leaves, but when a number of compositors were working simultaneously it could be systematically reduced to two leaves.

The compositors signed the first leaf of each of their takes in pencil in the left margin in the space provided by the indention of the first paragraph on that leaf. The purpose of this signing was to establish the point at which the compositor of each take had started to set type. Since at this time a group of simultaneously setting workmen do not set manuscript directly into pages, and these must be made up later, the start of the initial paragraph provided the first place in each take where a compositor could begin to set into galleys with a full line. This was a necessity, since only when a compositor began his stint with a chapter heading could he know, at the time, that he was starting a fresh page. When he had completed the text on the last folio of his take, a compositor would normally continue the typesetting over onto the first leaf of the next one's take until he came to the end of the paragraph above where the compositor of the next take had begun his typesetting with the line indicated by his signature at the paragraph opening. The number of type-lines would be entered in the foreman's book so that credit could be given each compositor for the linage set, on a piecework basis.[27]

On a few occasions a compositor might take over from another before his fellow had finished the last leaf of his normal take, as Farley did from Spech(?) at I,8.22, Jenkins from Orr at I,43.7, Hobson from Shand at II,31.9, Barnett from Farley at II,120.15, Hobson from Farley at II,257.19, Mintern from Barnett at II,262.6, Hobson from Barnett at II,279.18, Farley from Hobson at II,282.13, or Shand from Farley at II,291.8. These instances may in part be explained, as with Spech(?) and Orr, as sudden detachment for re-assignment of duty; as a compositor especially assigned to help finish a stint that is delaying the making-up of the sheet; or as one speedy compositor going back in his setting to help a slower companion so that pages could be made up without delay. A bracket and the compositor's name in the text at the point of taking over mark each one of these anomalies. A few pencil brackets in the text without an attached name appear; their significance is obscure. In some cases, at least, it seems clear that they do not represent any shift in compositors at that point, although it may be that such a shift was proposed and then abandoned.

Although any stint would vary considerably according to

[27] For a more detailed description of this system of marking takes for simultaneous composition, see *The House of the Seven Gables* (Centenary Edition, 1965), pp. xxxix–xli.

the position of the initial paragraph on the first leaf of a take, a respectable equalizing took place over the course of composition. The markedly longer stints were always due to an unusually large assigned take. The longest was Shand's eighth take of 19 leaves and 704 type-lines, the next was Barnett's first take of 16 leaves and 584 type-lines, and the next Barnett's fifth take of 12 leaves and 465 type-lines, coming immediately before Shand's longest take. The shortest was Barnett's helping-out, of 11 lines at II,253.1–11. Shand averaged 142.5 lines per take, Jenkins 137.6 lines, Farley 122.9 lines, Barnett 121.3 lines, Mintern 118.2 lines, and Hobson 114.3 lines, whereas Orr had a 91.5 average for two takes, and Spech(?) set only 22 lines before he was interrupted.

The textual theory adopted for the Centenary Edition establishes the British Museum manuscript as the copy-text, that is, as the major and direct basis for the edited text. Since this manuscript is a fair-copy holograph, it is clear that its accidentals, or the forms of its spelling, punctuation, capitalization, and word-division, must be more authoritative than the printing-house style imposed on this same copy by the compositors. On the other hand, if Hawthorne can be conjectured to have corrected or revised any of the substantives (i.e., the words themselves) in the course of reading proof, such variant first-edition substantives would represent his final intentions and would become more authoritative than the corresponding manuscript readings. Similarly, if any evidence existed (which it does not) that Hawthorne had sent to Boston for inclusion in the first American edition readings that represented his afterthoughts following his approval of the English proof, these would also come in the class of his final intentions and would be adopted as more authoritative than the original readings either of manuscript or of first edition.

Since indisputable evidence exists for Hawthorne's revisions in proof, the present edition adheres to Sir Walter Greg's classic exposition of the theory of copy-text[28] and has utilized, with only a few specific exceptions, the manuscript accidentals in preference to those of the first edition.[29] In this general texture of authoritative accidentals from the manuscript, all such variant substantive readings of the first edition have been incorporated that may be thought to represent Hawthorne's proof-alterations in the original typesetting from the manuscript or are necessary corrections that might have been made as readily by the compositor as by the author.

All in all, several thousand differences exist in the accidentals between the manuscript and the print of *Transformation*. That any great part of these should be taken as stemming from Hawthorne's proofreading is fantastic.[30] Authors then as now were accustomed to accepting the printer's house style that they found in their proofs. As a practical example, the characteristics of the print, in contrast to the manuscript, are just about the same in *The Blithedale Romance* as in *The House of the Seven Gables*, set in the same shop the previous year. One would scarcely wish to argue that Hawthorne made hundreds and hundreds of proof-alterations in the *Seven Gables* sheets contrary to the style of his manuscript, and then ignored the new system

---

[28] "The Rationale of Copy-Text," *Studies in Bibliography*, III (1950–51), 19–36. See also Fredson Bowers, "Textual Criticism," *The Aims and Methods of Scholarship*, ed. James Thorpe (Modern Language Association of America, 1963), pp. 23–42.

[29] Evidence indicating that Hawthorne could not have been responsible for the majority, at least, of customary differences in the accidentals between manuscript and print is discussed in the Textual Introduction to *The Blithedale Romance* (Centenary Edition, 1964), pp. xxxvii–xxxix.

[30] If the plate changes made in the accidentals in the third printing of the Boston first edition at II,198, 199, 217, 218, 223 actually represent proof markings in Er* galleys (see below, pp. xcv–cii), each one was a correction returning to the manuscript form, not a revision of the manuscript practice. This is the only possible concrete evidence that we have in the matter.

he had embraced and returned to his former ways in the manuscript of *The Blithedale Romance*—only to alter them once more in proof.

The matter comes down to the point, then, that whereas a critic can on literary grounds (aided by whatever bibliographical evidence is available) make some attempt to judge whether substantive alterations are authorial or not, no one can thus adjudicate the authority of most of the accidentals altered from the manuscript in the print. With comparatively few exceptions, therefore, a definitive edition must follow the accidentals of the manuscript and not of the first edition. In doing so, the editor will perhaps lose a small number of Hawthorne alterations in the accidentals;[31] but in the unknown and undeterminable cases he will at least preserve an authorial reading, even if not the final one, and he will protect himself from reproducing many hundreds of the printer's own house-style variants as if they were the author's.

Hence the Centenary text transcribes Hawthorne's manuscript accidentals in all their flavor[32] and with all the literary intent that ordinarily governed his usage. An author's accidentals are an important part of his total style by which he conveys meaning; indeed, on the evidence of the manuscripts, Hawthorne took some care to adjust the weight of his punctuation to the desired nuance of the content,[33] and

[31] For an almost classic case from an earlier period, but one quite pertinent to the nineteenth century, see Fredson Bowers, "Current Theories of Copy-Text, with an Illustration from Dryden," *Modern Philology*, LXVIII (1950), 12–20.

[32] Amusingly, Hawthorne in this manuscript out-Englished the English in anglicizing some of his spellings, as in such a form as "liquour", and was sometimes "corrected" by the compositors. In the manuscripts of *Our Old Home*, written between 1860 and 1863 for an American printer, he reverts to his usual spelling patterns, forsaking the exaggerated anglicizing that may have been adopted for the fancied benefit of the English compositors.

[33] After surveying the difference between reading Hawthorne in the manuscript and in the first-edition versions, the late Professor William Charvat was moved to write to the textual editor: "It comes to me now, for the first time, that Hawthorne's style is essentially parenthetical, and

thus his desires have been scrupulously preserved save where mechanical correctness requires alteration.

The textual problem in dealing with the substantives is considerably more complex. Any alteration in the wording between MS and E1ᵃ must be (1) an authoritative proof-alteration by Hawthorne[34] or (2) a printer's alteration (conscious or unconscious) that Hawthorne did not recognize and correct in proof. Either because of the conditions in which proof was read[35] or because Hawthorne seems to have been

---

that this characteristic reflects the basically essayistic, generalizing, and speculative quality of his fiction. His parentheses give him the latitude and flexibility that this quality requires. He modulates the degree of isolation of a unit by selecting (usually) just the right pair of separators: parentheses, or dashes, or commas. I don't think he did this selecting consciously, and probably the restoration of his own punctuation, after the compositors mangled it, looked like too much drudgery. Certainly, the compositors show very little sensitivity about his modulations." To this perceptive statement one can add only that the various examples of change exhibited in the manuscript in which Hawthorne usually weights more heavily, but occasionally lightens, the parenthetical punctuation during his making the fair copy might lead one to suppose that sometimes, at least, he had a quite clear idea of what he was doing and was consciously altering his original sense of the modulations. The list of Alterations in the Manuscript records a number of examples.

[34] That Sophia may have continued assistance (meaning influence) into the stage of reading proofs is possible, although we have no external evidence to this effect. Hence speculation is idle whether her hand may be seen in such variants as 52.19 MS "shoving" and E1ᵃ "pushing"; any conjectured proof-alteration (as distinguished from compositorial sophistication) must be accepted without query as Hawthorne's final intention so long as it does not rest (as does 414.15) on his misconception of how the compositor had altered the MS.

[35] The facts are far from clear whether or not copy was returned to Hawthorne with proof so that he could check MS—if he cared to—when he was doubtful what he had written. In the letter of December 6 in which he returns the first proof to Smith, Elder, he writes, "A friend of mine has requested to have the manuscript of this work, after it has gone through the press, and I beg that it may be preserved for him." Long after the publication, he wrote Smith, Elder on March 24, 1860, to forward to Bright "A portion of the M.S. of "Transformation" [that] remains in your hands"; and on March 27 he wrote Bright informing him that he had requested Smith, Elder "to send you the remainder of the MS." This evidence suggests that he did not retain any part of the MS even if it had been sent him with proof. Thus the first part of the MS that he mailed to Bright must have been returned to him by the publisher on request. On the other hand, the evidence does not deny the possibility that copy was sent and that he returned it with the corrected proof. Yet such a

a careless proofreader, the incidence of undetected printer's error may run relatively high. Indeed, on the evidence of the two earlier romances whose manuscripts have been preserved, the substantive printing-house corruption that passed into the first edition unchallenged could range from about one-third of the variants between MS and print as in *The Blithedale Romance* to an extraordinary two-thirds in *The House of the Seven Gables*. The number of substantive variants in *The Marble Faun* is larger than in the other romances, in some part owing to the cavalier treatment the English compositors seem to have given the American usage and idiom not always familiar to them. Hence, the problem of differentiating the authentic proof-correction from the undetected sophistication and error is a peculiarly difficult one. Fortunately, bibliographical techniques for identifying and adjudicating the evidence are of remarkable assistance for almost a third of the text, and thus a norm can be established by which to test that larger portion where critical inquiry must be one's main reliance, guided by what bibliographical inferences can be drawn.

But before the bibliographical investigation, one question of the treatment of authority within the manuscript must be settled. Forty-two identified markings of the manuscript by Sophia Hawthorne exist that are not just simple touching-up

---

procedure is perhaps doubtful. Under the system of sending proof a sheet or two at a time, the end leaves of the takes would not always be readily available; and whether the printer would wish to part so quickly with the only tangible evidence about the compositors' stints in case of dispute is doubtful. The inference follows that the return of copy may not have been the normal procedure, and that Hawthorne in this case was expected to read proof without it. (Certainly, the extreme rapidity with which he read and returned proof on the same day of receipt militates against any theory of careful checking.) If copy were not returned, therefore, Hawthorne would have no precise way of checking what exact word he had written other than his memory, and often might fail to distinguish whether he or the printer was responsible for words that seemed satisfactory, or even that seemed unsatisfactory. The matter is obscure, as are so many details in printing history at specific dates and places.

of words or letters for the benefit of the printer.[36] Of these, eight are associated exclusively with improving the legibility of the manuscript and involve no change in the form or wording of the original inscription.[37] Of the remaining thirty-four alterations, thirteen are marked by a pencil cross[38] plus one by a special ink cross applying to the first of the changes at Centenary 7.12 from *Graydon* to *Kenyon*. The interlined changes in Sophia's hand accompanying these crosses must be assumed to have Hawthorne's approval and as much authority as if he had written them in himself.

Twenty changes now remain that carry no external evidence to suggest that they are authoritative. Of these, five are Sophia's simple and necessary correction of her husband's misspellings and can therefore be accepted as editorially approved.[39] An additional three represent her interlineation of a necessary and almost inevitable word omitted in error in the manuscript.[40] Again, these are editorially acceptable.

A residue of twelve alterations, then, requires individual editorial decision. Sophia's change at 115.33 of Hawthorne's characteristic "stopt" to "stopped" indicates that not every one of her alterations without crosses was authorized; and certainly the change of "they" to "that" at 84.2 seems to

[36] This count of forty-two includes the first change of the name *Graydon* to *Kenyon* at 7.12 but excludes the dozens of subsequent alterations of the name. The addition of a dieresis in "Jaël" at 43.17 (but omitted in the several following occurrences) is doubtfully Sophia's but is included.

[37] These eight are at 100.30, 101.32, 102.13, 147.27, 179.3, 219.18, 219.33, and 229.10. Six of these represent Sophia's alteration to make one undivided word of a word divided between two lines or pages of the copy, as her change of "i-|lex" to "ilex" at 102.13 or of "ter-|ror" to "terror" at 229.10. Two, at 100.30 and 101.32, involve no more than her deletion of a word rendered doubtful by Hawthorne's mending or alteration and the interlineation of the same word in a clearer script.

[38] These are the alterations at 144.19, 152.8, 154.14, 154.17, 154.26, 154.29, 156.25, 181.15, 192.5, 194.22, 195.1, 197.17–18, and 215.33.

[39] These are at 12.13, 28.5, 303.9, 303.24, and 385.26.

[40] These supply "it" at 322.7, "in" at 365.3, and "hand" at 438.8.

represent a misunderstanding of the text. The textual theory of the Centenary Edition, therefore, follows the assumption that the original manuscript version of all but one of these twelve readings should be accepted as the only demonstrably authoritative one, and Sophia's alterations are to be rejected since none is strictly necessary.[41] That Hawthorne "passed them in proof" is incontrovertible. That he thereby "approved" them would be a naïve textual assumption when no evidence exists to suggest that he was conscious of the fact that his own version had been changed any more than he was conscious of the numerous printer's sophistications that he passed unwittingly but did not thereby authorize.

One additional reading must be treated as a special case, however. At 134.34 (fol. 154) Hawthorne is deprecating the tinted statutes of an English sculptor as turning goddesses into mere naked women. The manuscript reads "bedaubed with buff-colour, they stood forth to the eyes of the profane" and so on; but "buff" in what appears to be Sophia's hand (although not certainly so) has been written over some other word, although the hyphen remains Hawthorne's. Two unusual features attach themselves to this alteration. First, in all other places (except 154.14) Sophia has crossed through the word to be rejected and interlined her own substitution, but here she writes "buff" immediately

41 Thus her substantive changes are rejected at 25.16, 84.2, 157.19, 203.6, and 431.1; her spelling change at 115.33; and her punctuation changes at 43.17, 156.34, 339.29, 349.8, 403.13, and 434.19. These are noted in the List of Emendations so that a permanent record is created for them in the textual apparatus. The five unauthorized substantive readings that she inserted are recorded in the Rejected First-Edition Substantive Readings for the sake of a complete record; but there they must of course be differentiated from the others, which represent compositorial error. The interlined "her" at 282.10 is doubtful, perhaps, whether Hawthorne's or Sophia's, although it is accepted as authorial. One change at 87.33 from "contadina" to "contadine" may be Sophia's: her Italian was better than her husband's.

over Hawthorne's adjective so that it is thoroughly obscured. Second, although the original Hawthorne word appears almost certainly to be "rose", some signs of his typical wiping-out of a letter with his finger when it was still wet are present about the first letter or two of the original, and a descender as if for some letter like a "p" (pink?) still remains. One might put this unusual method of alteration down to Sophia's delicate sensibilities were it not that in his journal Hawthorne records these statues as being colored "buff" (MS, Italian Notebook, April 3, 1858, Berg Collection, New York Public Library). Insofar as one can reconstruct the circumstances, then, this alteration appears to be one that was immediately discussed as a question of fact when Sophia came to it; and when it was settled, she forthwith made the change, albeit in an unusual manner. It may be of some interest that John Gibson himself wrote of his famous tinted Venus, "I tinted the flesh like warm ivory scarcely red" (see Rupert Gunnis, *Dictionary of British Sculptors* [London, 1953]).

Finally, at Centenary 126.28 Sophia has deleted "sensual negro" before "lips" with her characteristic spiral. It is Hawthorne, however, who interlines "Nubian".

Some fifty-three recognizably significant variants exist between the first English edition in three volumes (E1ᵃ) and the first printing of the Boston edition in two volumes (Iᵃ)—see table pp. cxxxiv–cxxxv. These are unequally distributed in a pattern that must reflect some difference in the nature of the copy provided the Boston printer. That is, if for the present we exclude as a special case the variant at Centenary 4.18 which occurs in the preliminary sheet containing the Preface, only five of these fifty-three remaining variants appear in the Vol. I copy of E1ᵃ from which Iᵃ was set. Moreover, these five are specialized in their nature in that each is an E1ᵃ misprint or error that seems to have been corrected by the Boston compositors or proofreaders.[42] In short, when the first volume of E1ᵃ was the copy, the Boston edition was so correctly printed that in no case did it depart from E1ᵃ to create a "significant" error, and its few variants thus were all required changes of E1ᵃ misprints.[43]

On the other hand, when Vol. II of E1ᵃ served as the copy, twenty-seven significant variants appear between the two editions; and when Vol. III is the copy, there are twenty such variants. In only a few cases, moreover, do these variants represent the correction of E1ᵃ, as in Vol. I.

When we examine the variants in the Vol. II copy, we see a further odd fact. The text of this second volume of E1ᵃ begins with sheet 19 and ends with sheet 37. However, though only six variants appear in the seven sheets 20–26, a total of twenty-one occur in the eight sheets 30–37. In the first six variants not much textual significance can attach to the obvious Iᵃ correction at 169.2 of the E1ᵃ (sheet 20) "literary" to "literally",[44] the correction at 216.15 of inconsistent E1ᵃ (sheet 26) "Thomaso" to "Tomaso", the modernization of archaic E1ᵃ (sheet 21) "trode" to "trod" at 176.16, or the Iᵃ misprint of "grives" for "grieves" in E1ᵃ (sheet

---

[42] These are 21.10, E1ᵃ "these" corrected to Iᵃ "those"; 21.15 "then" to "than"; 32.22, "Hoffman" to "Hoffmann"; 39.23, "form" to "from"; and 42.8, "Mariam" to "Miriam". Except for the spelling of "Hoffmann" each of the Iᵃ corrections conforms to the reading of MS, but this coincidence is not significant except as demonstrating the fact of error in E1ᵃ. The errors are too clear-cut not to have been caught by careful reading in Boston, except for 32.22 which shows some special knowledge.

[43] For the sake of the record, these Boston corrections are found in Iᵃ sheets 3 (twice), 4, and 5 (twice) of Vol. I, which is composed of eighteen gatherings.

[44] It will be observed that this is one of the two misprints about which Hawthorne wrote to Smith, Elder although the correction was not made until E2. But there can be no connection with the Iᵃ variant since he did not spot the error until several days after the publication of E1ᵃ and thus after the printing of Iᵃ. It is interesting that this misprint was so obvious as to be corrected independently both in Iᵃ and in the Tauchnitz edition.

20) at 162.18. More interesting, because it seems to resemble a misreading of handwriting, is the I^a error "there" for correct "them" in E1^a (sheet 24) at 204.22;[45] and also the I^a memorial error or sophistication causing the omission of "as much" from E1^a (sheet 26) "as much as if" at 220.4–5.

No significant variants appear in E1^a sheets 27–29, but beginning with sheet 30 not only do the number and concentration increase through to the end of the volume,[46] but also the nature of the variants in some cases changes from misprints or memorial errors to what appear to be clear-cut substantive alteration of a distinctive kind. The same anomaly is found in the copy provided by E1^a Vol. III. In the first nine sheets 38–46 there are only two significant variants, one a correction of an E1^a (sheet 41) error at 337.30, and the other an addition of a necessary word omitted from E1^a (sheet 45) at 370.10. But beginning with sheet 47 and continuing for the next eight sheets through final sheet 55, the number, the concentration, and also occasionally the nature alter almost as markedly as in Vol. II. That is, in the first nine sheets of Vol. III two variants occur, but eighteen appear in the next nine sheets.[47]

The only hypothesis that will interpret these statistics in a reasonable manner is that Vol. I was sent to Boston in sheets that had been revised after Hawthorne's proof-corrections. Thus no differences appear that cannot be imputed to Boston correction of obvious errors. Similarly, it would appear that sheets 19–29 of Vol. II were mailed to Boston in a revised state, but sheets 30–37 from an early state without Hawthorne's proof-corrections. In Vol. III,

---

45 This variant is reconsidered below on p. xcvii where the error is, in fact, explained as having originated in the E1^a copy.

46 The figures are four in sheet 30, four in sheet 32, four in sheet 33, two in sheet 34, four in sheet 35, two in sheet 36, and one in sheet 37.

47 The figures are five in sheet 47, one in sheet 48, one in sheet 49, three in sheet 50, one in sheet 51, one in sheet 52, three in sheet 53, two in sheet 54, and one in sheet 55.

sheets 38–46 appear to have been sent in revised form, but sheets 47–55 in the early state.[48]

The Vol. I preliminary sheet is more difficult to judge. Since it contains a short expansion of the MS in both its English and American form, we must believe that I^a was set from a revised proof. Moreover, since the first page of text in the Boston edition begins on the eighth, and last, leaf of the first gathering of I^a, it is clear that the Boston printer had the Preface, and knew its length, at the time he set and imposed his first sheet. This being so, the variant at 4.18 between EI^a "noble" and the repetitive "admirable" of I^a seems to be an authoritative Hawthorne alteration made either by note to Smith, Elder after the return of the proofs or else in a special revise sheet for the preliminaries sent him for his final approval.[49] The latter is almost certainly the answer. The proof for the Preface must have been mailed to Hawthorne and sent back (as attested by its December 15 date altered from MS October 15) before about December 16, 1859, when all of Vol. I had been read and returned, and hence the expanded form must have been included in the package of Vol. I sheets sent to Boston by Smith, Elder

[48] Since a clear sequence begins with the accumulation of variants in sheet 47, the single variants in sheets 48, 49, 51, 52, and 55 appear to reflect merely a lack of very much proof-correction of a "significant" kind by Hawthorne and not anomalous revised sheets. Indeed, the variants in sheets 48, 49, and 52 seem to represent misreadings of MS perpetuated in I^a. That the sequential sheets in Vols. II and III provided uncorrected English proof-sheets for the Boston typesetting is more probable than that the manifest proof-corrections indicated by some of the EI^a readings as against the I^a variants came from revises further corrected by Hawthorne. We have no evidence that revises of the text sheets were submitted to Hawthorne or to any author of the period who had not specifically requested them. (But see below for the special case of the Preface in the preliminary sheet of Vol. I.) Finally, in view of Hawthorne's correspondence with Smith, Elder about their dispatch of sheets to Boston, it is clear that the variants could not have arisen from Hawthorne's having made a duplicate set of marked proofs to be sent to Boston as printer's copy. The case of the Postscript is another matter, one that will be considered later.

[49] The alternatives are (a) an unauthorized English change made after the return of Hawthorne's proofs; (b) a memorial error in I^a. These are less attractive.

on January 6, 1860. But since it was at least January, and perhaps even early February, before Hawthorne's objections to the title *Transformation* had been finally worn down, it seems probable that the π sheet of preliminaries sent to Boston was not the final revise but an intermediate proof, perhaps with only a tentative title-page. Thus the I[a] reading "admirable" would seem to represent an authoritative original within the first proof addition but one that was then changed to "noble" by Hawthorne in a later stage of the proof-sheet than was sent to Boston.

At this point we may survey what extant evidence we have about the proofreading of the E1[a] sheets and the mailing of copy to Boston. The first manuscript copy was sent off by Hawthorne, we know, on October 17, 1859, and the remainder on November 9. On November 17 he wrote to Fields that Smith, Elder had told him the book was in their printer's hands but no proof-sheets had been received,[50] and on December 1 he wrote to Ticknor to the same effect. On December 6, however, he returned to Smith, Elder "some proof-sheets of the Romance; being the first which I have received."[51] The only entries about proofreading in his pocket diary are as follows:

December 6,	"The first proof-sheets of my Romance arrived. Sent back the proof-sheets to Smith & Elder; likewise, a note to them."
December 7,	"Rec[d] & sent back a package of proof-sheets."
December 8,	"Rec[d] letter &c from Smith Elder & Co. Rec[d] & returned some proofs."
December 10,	"Rec[d] & returned a proof-sheet."
December 17,	"Proof-sheet from Smith & Elder; sent it back."

[50] MS, Huntington Library.
[51] MS, transcript courtesy of Professor Norman Holmes Pearson.

On December 22 he wrote to Ticknor: "I have received proof-sheets of the Romance as far as the commencement of the second volume. They were going on at the rate of 50 pages a day; and I was afraid that they would get the book out, on this side of the water, before Christmas, without waiting for you to get it through the press and publish simultaneously." On the same date he wrote to Francis Bennoch: "The printers have advanced into the second volume of my Romance, and would probably have finished it, by this time, if I had not interposed to retard their progress. At the rate they were going on, they would have had it out, on this side of the water, long before Ticknor could have been ready for publication in the States; and so I should have hazarded my American copyright." [52] Finally, on December 30 he wrote to Fields: "The printing of the book has advanced into the second volume; and they were going on at the rate of 50 pages a day, when I suggested to Smith & Elder that there was no occasion for such haste. . . . it appeared to be their intention to bring out the work at Christmas; but in that case, the American edition must have been left altogether in the lurch. They have sent me no proof for about a fortnight past; and I suppose they mean to publish in the Spring."

The statement on December 30 that he has received no proof for about the past fortnight combines with the December 15 dating of the Preface in proof and the various statements that printing had entered the second volume to suggest that by December 17 (the last entry in his diary) he received proof for the final sheets of Vol. I, including the Preface, and perhaps a sheet or two of Vol. II.[53] The evidence by

[52] MS, Clifton Waller Barrett Library of the University of Virginia Library.

[53] His repeated statements that at the rate the printers were going it seemed that Smith, Elder proposed to publish the book by Christmas might suggest that more of the second-volume proof had been received by December 17, but this alarm is patently absurd since under no normal

no means indicates, however, that at the time proof stopped in mid-December Vol. II had progressed as far as sheet 29 (page 177 marks the start of sheet 30), which is presumably the last of the revised sheets of the second volume to be sent to Boston.

Unfortunately, no other mention of the proof of the second volume has been discovered. On January 27, 1860, he wrote to Bennoch: " . . . this morning's proof-sheet brings it to the 192 page of the third volume";[54] i.e., through sheet 49 of a total of 55. The preceding day he had written Ticknor, "The printers are now nearly at the end of the third volume of the Romance." Finally, on February 3 he informed Ticknor, "Smith & Elder tell me that they shall send you the sheets of the 3ᵈ volume by this steamer and shall bring the book out on the 28th inst."[55] Between January 27 and about February 1, then, Hawthorne completed reading proof for the last six sheets of the third volume.

Some mix-up in arrangements about sending copy to Ticknor must have occurred at the start of the whole process. In the December 30, 1859, letter to Fields (when proofs were advanced into the second volume) Hawthorne wrote: "I shall certainly tell them to forward the sheets to Ticknor, and I have already written to him to inform him of the probable length of the book. I had the idea that you had made some arrangements about forwarding the sheets. Was not this so?" On January 8, 1860, he addressed Smith, Elder, "I presume Mr. Fields made arrangements with you in respect to sending the proof sheets of the Romance to his

conditions could the three volumes have been typeset, manufactured, and bound by Christmas according to the most liberal estimates of the proof sent him at this date. According to what can be determined from the diary entries (which cannot be complete), the first batches of proof were large accumulations but thereafter a sheet per day is recorded.

54 MS, Clifton Waller Barrett Library of the University of Virginia Library.

55 MSS, Berg Collection, New York Public Library.

house in Boston, as they come from the press. . . ." Again, on February 3 he wrote to the firm that as of January 10 Ticknor had not received "any portion of the advance sheets."[56] However, in a letter of February 10 to Ticknor Hawthorne states that Smith, Elder had sent the first volume as early as January 6; thus some arrangements must have been made before the January 8 letter. The next mention of the dispatch of proof is in the letter of February 3 to Ticknor mentioned above.

From the American side the evidence is equally scanty. In the February 10 letter to Ticknor we learn that the first-volume sheets sent January 6 reached Ticknor on or just before January 26. On February 23 Hawthorne wrote Smith, Elder that a letter of February 7 from Ticknor informed him that no sheets subsequent to the first volume had been received.[57] Unfortunately, no mention is made, independently, of the dispatch of Vol. II copy. All that we know is that Vol. I was mailed on January 6, and Vol. III on February 3.

The evidence that the printer's copy of the Boston edition represented different states of the $E1^a$ typesetting needs interpretation in the light of these few facts about the proof and the dispatch of copy to America. In writing of his own receipt of copy from Smith, Elder, Hawthorne invariably refers to the "proof-sheets", but he is inconsistent in his references to the copy to be sent to Boston. In the December 30 letter to Fields, it is, "I shall certainly tell them to forward the sheets to Ticknor. . . . I had the idea that you had made some arrangements about forwarding the sheets." In the January 8 letter to Smith, Elder he is precise in calling the copy to be sent to Ticknor the "proof sheets", and again

[56] Hawthorne to Smith, Elder, transcripts courtesy of Professor Norman Holmes Pearson.

[57] Hawthorne to Smith, Elder, transcript courtesy of Professor Norman Holmes Pearson.

on January 26 to Ticknor he writes that Smith, Elder "replied that they had already sent you the proof-sheets of the first volume. . . . " On February 3 to Ticknor the announcement that Smith, Elder will send the copy of the third volume calls it "the sheets". On the other hand, the February 3 letter to Smith, Elder informs them that as of January 10 Ticknor had not received "any portion of the advance sheets. Unless he shall have acknowledge to you the receipt of them, you would oblige me by sending him another copy of the two first volumes." On February 10 to Ticknor he is surprised that "the first volume of the Romance" has not sooner reached him. On February 23 to Smith, Elder it is that Ticknor informs him that as of February 7 "no sheets subsequent to those of the first volume" have been received in Boston.

Whether or not the original arrangement specified proof-sheets, or the advance sheets (or whether these were roughly synonymous terms),[58] it is evident that when Smith, Elder on January 6 sent off copy for the first volume it was in final form; and the difference between the return about December 15 of the last proof of this volume from Hawthorne and the date of dispatch strongly suggests that the copy Ticknor received for the first volume was (except for the preliminaries) either special proofs of the typesetting in its final revised form or else the actual English book-sheets. This hypothesis may help to clarify the anomaly of the

[58] Hawthorne's mention of "proof sheets . . . as they come from the press" on January 8 to Smith, Elder may suggest some confusion, especially in the light of his February 3 use of the term "advance sheets" to the firm. The evidence indicates that he probably had no very precise idea what form the Boston copy would take and in at least some instances was perhaps only repeating the various terms his correspondents had employed. True advance sheets, i.e., actually printed final sheets not yet bound (or specially pulled proofs from type-metal in final form, or plates), were the customary printer's copy to send abroad to another publisher, but obviously intermediate or early working proof-sheets could be utilized when a special need for haste existed.

mixed Boston copy for Vol. II, and especially for Vol. III which seems to consist of the final revised text for sheets 38–46 but of a largely unrevised form for sheets 47–55. That is, if Hawthorne received "this morning's sheet" 49 on January 27, and on February 3 Smith, Elder were prepared to dispatch Vol. III copy "by this steamer", the six final sheets 50–55 (especially if sent to Hawthorne at the rate of about one a day as implied in the diary entries for December 10 and 17 and especially in the reference to sheet 49)[59] at best could only just have been returned in corrected form by the date of dispatch. The evidence suggests that when Smith, Elder made up the package of copy for mailing Vol. III complete at the first possible moment, they sent the final revised proofs or, perhaps, the actual book-sheets (or a mixture of the two) for 38–46; but since sheets had not been printed at the time beyond 46 (or specially revised before printing), they added the available proofs for sheets 47–55, and these proofs were in an uncorrected state.[60] The evidence of Vol. II copy also indicates that the same procedure had obtained earlier when at some unknown date in January a mixed package of book-sheets and proof-sheets was sent to

[59] No striking evidence exists in the statistics for the typesetting of the final sheets to suggest that they were turned out much if any faster than their predecessors. It is true that beginning with sheet 49 at page 177 the stints of the three regular compositors were raised from an average of three to an average of four leaves, and that Shand later joined the three and set two takes. But Hobson's eight-leaf take beginning with page 241 would slow down operations. On the whole, not much change in the rate of sending proof-sheets to Hawthorne seems to have taken place after he wrote his letter on January 27.

[60] That is, uncorrected by Hawthorne. We have no information whether Smith, Elder read proof and corrected it for typographical and other errors before sending it in the original or in the form of revises to Hawthorne as the first proofs that he would receive. (The printing-house compositors were supposed to read their own proofs and correct the sheets before dispatch to the publisher or author.) If Smith, Elder did in fact go over the proofs first, however much this proof-correction might contribute to the styling of Hawthorne's text, it would not catch the plausible compositorial departures from copy that made sense since proofreaders of fiction are not expected to collate the proofs back against the original copy.

Boston.[61] The date for the dispatch of Vol. III copy in relation to Hawthorne's receipt of sheet 49 turns out to be of significance in the reconstruction of events.

Following this hypothesis, then, we must take it that those variants in the portion of I^a set from E1^a book-sheets and final proofs 19–29 of Vol. II and 38–46 of Vol. III represent the changes of the Boston compositors.[62] The evidence equates very well with that for the sheets 1–18 of Vol. I complete which also provided copy in finally revised form. In Vol. II, for example, at Centenary 169.2 (sheet 20) Boston corrects to "literally" the obvious E1^a misprint "literary", and it makes consistent at 216.15 (sheet 26) the aberrant E1^a spelling "Thomaso". For the rest, I^a omits by error or sophistication "as much" at 220.4–5 (sheet 26). (In sheet 24 the I^a error "there" for E1^a "them" at 204.22 represents a special case that will be considered later.) The modernization of E1^a "trode" to "trod" is found at 176.16 (sheet 21) and the misprint "grives" for E1^a "grieves" at 162.18 (sheet 20). In Vol. III the Boston compositor at 337.30 (sheet 41) corrected the E1^a and MS error "Baberini" to "Barberini" and inserted at 370.10 (sheet 45) the required "as" omitted in MS and E1^a. These two are the only differences in the first nine sheets of Vol. III.

Correspondingly, in the early proof-copy for sheets 30–37 of Vol. II and 47–55 of Vol. III all substantive differences between I^a and E1^a that do not seem explicable in the light of the evidence for Boston variation within the area of the book-sheets or revised proofs, as detailed above, must repre-

[61] In Vol. II there would have been eleven book-sheets (or final revises) and eight early proof-sheets; in Vol. III there would have been nine book-sheets (or early revises) and nine early proof-sheets. Actually, if the hypothesis on pp. ci–cii below for the copy of Vol. II be accepted, the Vol. II packet sent to Boston would have consisted of four or five book-sheets, six or seven final proof-sheets, and eight early proof-sheets.

[62] Again assuming, as the evidence indicates, that in no case do they represent Hawthorne's independently communicated requests for alterations in the Boston edition.

sent I^a agreement with the readings in the proof of E_1^a which had not been corrected by Hawthorne. These variants are of three kinds: (1) obvious misprints which in the nature of the case cannot be assigned either to E_1^a or to I^a, though on the record I^a is more likely to correct E_1^a errors than to make mistakes; (2) clear-cut authorial revisions; (3) relatively indifferent readings that might represent compositorial error or sophistication or else, just possibly, authorial revision.[63]

The textual logic for dealing with these variants in a preliminary stage of inquiry is obvious. Whenever in the conjectured early proof-sheets MS and E_1^a agree and I^a differs, the I^a reading must represent either an E_1^a type-setting error corrected in proof but retained in its original early form in Boston, or else a I^a error made from correct E_1^a copy save for the rare case when I^a could correct a joint MS–E_1^a error. Whenever MS and I^a agree against E_1^a, the E_1^a reading must, of course, be authenticated as a subsequent Hawthorne proof-correction save in the rare case when E_1^a is a misprint which I^a could independently correct and thus return to the MS reading. Finally, whenever E_1^a and I^a agree against MS, the E_1^a–I^a reading must be either an original error in E_1^a repeated in I^a or else a natural E_1^a correction of a faulty MS reading. Thus, whenever MS and E_1^a agree against I^a the odds favor the hypothesis that the E_1^a reading is a Hawthorne proof-correction returning faulty proof to the MS form and should be accepted; whenever MS and I^a agree against E_1^a the odds favor the hypothesis that E_1^a should be accepted as a Hawthorne proof-revision; whenever E_1^a and I^a agree against MS the odds

---

[63] Again, on the record the Boston changes that are not simple misprints or simple corrections should be very few indeed.

favor the acceptance of the MS as the authentic reading.[64]

By using the first of these principles we can immediately discard, as errors that Hawthorne corrected in proof, the majority of the twenty-seven Boston variants in sheets 30–37 and 47–55 in which MS and E1[a] agree.[65] Several of these must, of course, represent the mistakes of the Boston compositors, but—on the evidence—not many. Some few are instantly to be identified as errors in the English proof, such as the easy confusion of Hawthorne's "could" as "would" at 248.34 (Hobson), 251.6 (Barnett), and 443.16 (Hobson) which Hawthorne in these cases detected. These may be compared with the identical confusion at 17.32 (Jenkins), 77.12 (Jenkins), 95.6 (Shand), 95.29 (Farley), 97.19 (Farley), 108.23 (Mintern), 269.22 (Farley), and 276.11 (Shand) that Hawthorne failed to notice in the proof, thereby establishing the errors as an integral part of both

[64] The only flaw in this reasoning would result from the possibility that completely uncorrected proof-sheets were sent to Boston, that subsequently Smith, Elder proofread them and had them revised before being sent to Hawthorne, and that Hawthorne did not detect the publisher's sophisticated readings inserted at this stage of the proof. However, the possibility is too remote (or at the least the number of readings that would be affected by such a contingency is too small) to be entertained seriously, given the sequence of dates as we have them. Moreover, even if the publisher proofread the sheets immediately on receipt and returned them to the print shop for revises before sending them to the author, we may suppose that the normal proof-sheet sent to Boston as copy would be in this revised condition, thus preventing I[a] variants from representing the differences between raw proof and its revises. The possibility always exists, of course, that the publisher's proofreader could survey and mark a copy of the proof while the other copy was with the author (or would resurvey and correct the author's proof on return) and then conflate the two, thus creating post-authorial alteration. But a possibility is not a probability; moreover, even if such a procedure had been adopted, it would not be reflected in the proof-sheets sent to Boston since these would seem to have been untouched by Hawthorne.

[65] These twenty-seven are 248.34, 251.6, 255.8, 264.14, 265.17, 269.8, 270.16, 276.15, 290.14, 290.20, 294.12, 296.19, 301.20, 302.11, 307.11, 391.10, 401.17, 404.27, 412.17, 421.10, 429.26, 434.33, 443.16, 445.25, 448.32, 455.11–12, and 460.25.

the English and American texts, along with other errors of a similar nature.

Remaining are ten variants (including 4.17–19 first, and then 4.18, in the Preface) which by the agreement of MS and I^a reveal in the E1^a reading Hawthorne's proof-revisions that must be accepted.[66]

Three additional variants represent special cases, in that MS, E1^a, and I^a all differ. In the first, at 285.9, Hawthorne had written in MS "heart-sustenance" which Shand seems to have misprinted as "heart, sustenance" the reading of I^a (unless the I^a reading is an independent error, as is possible). Since E1^a reads "heart sustenance", it would appear that Hawthorne (if the error actually stood in his proofs) removed the offending comma without substituting the MS hyphen. In the second, at 446.31 Hawthorne had written in MS "to let him blood" which Farley had misprinted as "to him let him blood" but Hawthorne had not corrected the error in proof. The Boston compositor, faced with the E1^a reading in his copy of the proof for sheet 53, did what he could to make sense by sophisticating to "to him to let him take blood". The third is more subtle. Hawthorne had written, at 414.15, in parallel structure in a series, "or to alight on the shrine, on the church-angels, and on the roofs"; but since his inscription of "on" and of "or" are usually indistinguishable, Jenkins had misread the word and must have set originally the phrase "or the church-angels", which is the reading perpetuated in I^a. When in E1^a we find "shrine, or on the church-angels" it seems evident that Hawthorne recognized an error, but not recalling the exact form of MS (which may not have been available) he patched the proof on the

---

[66] These ten are 4.17–19 (π), 4.18 (π), 247.30 (30), 274.19 (33), 274.26 (33), 275.2 (33), 281.23 (34), 387.26 (47), 391.14 (47), and 392.23 (47), and represent Hawthorne's correction or revision of readings in which the proof had coincided with MS.

assumption that a word had been omitted and thus created a reading that differed from his original.[67]

At this point we have specific information about forty variants, most of which can be established as authorial markings in the proof.[68] From these some extrapolation is possible to reveal the care (or lack of care) with which Hawthorne read proof, and also the incidence of error in the work of the various compositors, both of which will be of service when the main problem is tackled of the authority of the larger group of variants for which little or no direct bibliographical evidence is present to aid a decision. But, first, one other piece of evidence must be surveyed since it appears to bear on this central problem.

In what can be established as the third pre-publication Boston printing (I[c]) in late February appears a series of fourteen textual plate-changes. Two come in the part of Boston Vol. I that represents setting from E1[a] Vol. II sheets 22 and 24 (Centenary 180.10, 204.22). The remaining are in Boston Vol. II. The first two of these correct obvious misprints at 301.20 and 307.11 (E1[a] Vol. II sheets 36, 37); but then three at 390.16, 391.10, 391.22, clustered in E1[a] Vol. III sheet 47, are followed by three at 406.8, 406.33, 410.33, clustered in E1[a] sheet 49; then by the correction of two misprints at 412.17 and 421.10 from E1[a] sheet 50, a minor change at 423.19 from sheet 51, and another at 443.18 from sheet 53. (The first two plate-changes in Vol. II are in Boston sheets 4 and 5; the three from E1[a] sheet 47 are

---

[67] Editorial theory is clear that at 446.31 the MS is the only authoritative reading. However, at 414.15 two authoritative versions exist. Under the circumstances, however, Hawthorne was not attempting to revise but merely to correct; hence since his correction was made without knowledge of his original reading, MS is still to be preferred as better representing his purest intention.

[68] These forty are the total of footnotes 65 and 66, plus the three readings discussed in the text (285.9, 414.15, and 446.31).

in Boston sheet 9, and the remaining—except for the final one—in Boston sheet 10.) The I^c Vol. II plate-changes have these special points of interest: the clusters start with sheet 47 of E1^a, which was the first of the unrevised proof-sheets of Vol. III sent to Boston; also, in each of these cases the change in I^c returns the I^a variant to the exact reading of MS and E1^a, except for the special case at 391.22 where MS and E1^a differ.

Two explanations are possible for this oddity: (1) a Boston proofreader happened to devote his attention to these sheets; (2) in some manner corrections made in English copy subsequent to the dispatch of the original sheets were sent to Boston.

The first could (and perhaps does) hold for the alteration of the manifest misprints at 301.20 and 307.11. It could also hold, if the sheet being in sequence after 49 has no significance, for the perhaps equally obvious errors in original sheet 50 at 412.17 and 421.10. A copyreader working over the adjacent Boston sheets of I^{a-b} could notice the errors in the punctuation at the end of a paragraph at 390.16 and 443.18. He could also see that the comma at 410.33 violated consistency in the marking of a parenthetical expression since it was matched with a dash, and possibly he would have known at 423.19 that an apostrophe was needed after "de". But that he would by chance be so scrupulous as to personify "Error" and "Evil" as Hawthorne had done at 391.22, or change to a capital the rather consistent Boston lower-case "h" in "Heaven" at 406.33, is doubtful, and a splendid guess that "heart" at 391.10, which makes excellent sense, was really an error for "art" might well seem beyond him. Fortunately, speculation of this sort is not needed, for we are bound to assume that all the plate changes in I^c had a common origin except for whatever few like those at 301.20 or 307.11 might be assigned to an independent source in

Boston who was resurveying the sheets as a consequence of some special circumstance.

In this respect the evidence of the isolated change in Vol. I at Boston 225.22 in sheet 10 (Centenary 180.9–10) becomes of vital import. The manuscript had read, "There is certainly a Providence on purpose for Hilda, if for no other human creature"; but the inscription of the "on" was so ambiguous that Mintern very naturally read it as "or", in which form it was printed in $E1^a$ and thence transferred to I^a. However, in the I^c plate-change an absolute error is created when in what must be an attempt to restore MS "on" the error is untouched and the "on" substituted for "for" so that the reading is the confused, "There is certainly a Providence or purpose for Hilda, if on no other human creature." The only reasonable explanation for this mistake is that the workman charged with correcting the plate either misread or misunderstood his instructions (whatever they were) and altered the wrong word.

What is of significance, of course, is that this proposed change of "on" for "or" should somehow have been transmitted to Boston although, apparently, it was never made in any English printing or edition.[69] This being so, the plate-change also made in isolation in Vol. I, 252.30 (sheet 11 of I^c) at Centenary 204.22, from $I^{a\text{-}b}$ "there" to the correct I^c "them" (the reading of MS, $E1^a$), gains in significance as almost certainly from the same source and hence not, as might have been supposed, the correction of an original Boston misprint but instead the correction of an English misreading of MS in the copy that Boston had followed ($E1^a$, sheet 24).

A comprehensive explanation for these phenomena must

[69] That is, unless it proves to be a very late press-correction in $E1^b$, printed from the standing-type of $E1^a$, with E3 set from the earlier state. So far the only three copies of $E1^b$ located have been checked without disclosing any reading other than "or".

necessarily be speculative in the absence of positive evidence. However, we may at least provisionally take it that the six changes in I^c Vol. II sheets 9 and 10, from E1^a sheets 47 and 49, are too precise in returning to the present E1^a and MS readings to be independent Boston copyreader's corrections. If so, since the sequence starts at the very sheet 47 where unrevised proof-sheets had been mailed as copy to Ticknor, we may then guess that when corrected proof-sheets were received from Hawthorne (or made available by the printer after the correction of the type-pages), Smith, Elder sent certain information from them to Boston in an attempt to correct errors in the Vol. III copy that had been previously dispatched. This information may have taken the form of mailing the author's own corrected sheets, now no longer needed, or a duplicate marked-up set. On the other hand, it is possible that a list of alterations was compiled and the information sent in that form, for economy of postage.

Some such hypothesis is necessary to explain these changes in sheets 47 and 49, at least; but it is not without its difficulties. For example, in sheet 47 at Centenary 387.26 what must be supposed to be an authorial proof-alteration from "trod" to "had trodden" is ignored, as is the alteration from "avails" to "proceeds" at 392.23 and even that from "Belvidere" at 391.14 to "Belvedere". In sheet 49 the Boston error "as" at 404.27 for MS, E1^a "at" is not affected. Just possibly the anomalies in these two particular sheets can be explained. None of the plate-changes accepted require expansion, which might cause trouble in fitting the reset type into the hole cut in the plate for the area of the change (except for the addition of "a" at 421.10), whereas most of what we may suppose to be the English proof-changes that do not appear in I^c involve possible trouble with respacing, notably as in

387.26 "had trodden" to replace simple "trod". This is at least a possible explanation for these sheets.[70]

The problem then remains, if sheets 47 and 49 were later mailed in corrected form (or the substantially complete information from them), what happened to sheet 48 and to the supposed Hawthorne proof-correction at 401.17 of "where" to "when", much more likely as an original misreading of Hawthorne's hand than as a Boston sophistication?[71] The question also arises whether the remaining sheets 51–55 were also sent in revised state; this last is more easily answered in the negative for sheets 53–55, at least, where the six substantive variants between E1^a and I^a are not touched, and the single I^c plate change (Centenary 443.18) in 53 does not require the hypothesis of corrected copy. However, the two misprints in sheet 50, at 412.17 and 421.10, would form an unusual concentration given the correctness of the Boston typesetting in the earlier pages where the E1^a final proofs or book-sheets served as copy,[72] and it is plausible to con-

[70] However, the retention of the error "as" for "at" at 404.27 would then need to be explained as an original Boston typesetting mistake (and later negligence in proofreading) and not as an English misreading of Hawthorne's hand transmitted to I^a. This is quite possible (though Hawthorne's final "s" in this word might be mistaken for a "t" in MS) since the sense is excellent either way. The I^a phrase is the more conventional, however, and error of this sort in the Boston typesetting is not otherwise seen. The failure to alter the misspelling "Belvidere" in sheet 47 at 391.14 may be either negligence or economy.

[71] See above and below for the parallel I^c plate change at 204.22 of "them" substituted for the I^{a-b} error "there".

[72] A possible oddity exists in sheet 50. At I^a II, 230.5,7 (Centenary 416.23,26) necessary question marks found in E1^a and MS are replaced by periods, an odd procedure in a reprint. These are not altered in I^c; but in the unauthoritative series of plate changes by a publisher's reader made in I^e they become queries. However, any hypothesis that these were proof-changes in E1^a neglected until I^e would be extremely far-fetched. One may also observe that at 416.34 where MS has an exclamation point, E1^a a query, and I^{a-e} a period, no change is ever made in the I plates although this is a more likely transmission of an original E1^a typesetting error than the other two.

jecture that this sheet can be associated with 47 and 49. Sheets 51 and 52 are neutral.[73] It would seem, then, that if corrected proofs or their equivalent in information were indeed sent to Ticknor after the first mailing, these may have been confined to no more than 47–50 and at the most to 47–52. Since these sheets seem to have composed a sequence, there is little choice except to guess that in sheet 48 the probable $E1^a$ proof misreading of "where" at 401.17 was overlooked. It is the only "significant" variant in the sheet that can be identified as a proof-correction. It may be part of a pattern that single variants in sheets 51 and 52 were also neglected in the I^c plate-changes.[74]

The status of the two isolated plate-changes in the first volume of I^c can now be conjectured on the hypothesis that at some point an attempt was made by Smith, Elder to transmit corrections for the American edition toward the end of the printing of the English third volume, that is, between February 3 when the original batch of Vol. III copy was mailed and whatever date would enable a supplementary notice to reach Boston in time to be incorporated in the third pre-publication printing that must have been completed, according to the Cost Books, about February 27.[75]

[73] If we wish to believe that sheet 51 is not neutral, we must treat the MS, $E1^a$ "we" and I^a "I" at 429.26 the same as the *at-as* variant at 404.27; that is, either as negligence in sending or negligence in making the change. Each is the only substantive variant in its sheet. In sheet 52 no plate changes were made, and the I^a misprint of "last" for MS-$E1^a$ "lost" at 434.33 (a possible English misreading since the vowel has been worked over in MS) is not touched.

[74] This ignoring of a single substantive variant in a sheet would hold for sheet 49 as well, and the variant of "as" and "at" (404.27) would then join this group, *if* we were to assess the punctuation and capitalization changes at 406.8, 406.33, and 410.33 as without relation to the corrections of $E1^a$ and as independent cleaning-up of errors by a Boston copyreader on the order of 301.20. This is a big *if*, however, though not impossible.

[75] Since no independent effort was made to correct the errors transmitted in the proof-sheets of $E1^a$ Vol. II that served as copy for I^a, we are bound to take it that the attempt to assist the Boston printer to

The attempted correction of "or purpose" to "on purpose" at 180.9 is not explicable in any manner save as a written-out instruction or an ambiguously marked printed page. It would seem that Hawthorne noticed the error after he had returned proof, and communicated it to Smith, Elder in the belief that it could be corrected; sheet 22 was already printed, however, and they forgot to make the change in the standing type that was to print $E1^b$. But it was passed on to Boston when the Vol. III corrections for sheets 47–50 were being prepared.

Economy of hypothesis for two similarly isolated variants in nearby sheets suggests that the variant at 204.22 (sheet 24) was similarly transmitted. Hence, for all we know, "them" may have been a correction for the typesetting error "there" passed in the original proof and sent to Smith, Elder—perhaps at the same time as the attempt to alter 180.9—but before sheet 24 was printed so that the correction "them" was successfully made in $E1^a$. In this case the person at Smith, Elder who sent the corrected material to Boston may have had the two requested alterations on one piece of paper. If this is so, and it seems the most reasonable conjecture, then it follows that these two corrections were probably not sent off to Boston in the form of marked printed pages (else the fact that 204.22 had been corrected in the book-sheet might have been confusing) but instead as written-out instructions.[76] (It also follows—if this hypothesis is accepted—that the copy sent to Boston for Vol. II sheets 19–22 [or

---

more correct copy was triggered by Hawthorne's return of Vol. III sheets and was hence confined to these sheets save for the two isolated changes from the printed sheets of Vol. II, which must have had some unusual circumstances attached to them that caused them to be remembered and attached to the Vol. III corrections (see below).

[76] The error by which "on" was substituted for "for'" instead of "or" at 180.10 could be neatly explained if the instructions took the form of the standard errata list: "*for* or *read* on" or "for 'or' read 'on'". But this may be too neat.

perhaps 19–23] consisted of book-sheets but that for sheets 23[or 24]–29 of late-stage proof-sheets.) We do not know, of course, whether a similar list of the errors to be corrected in sheets 47–50 continued these instructions or whether marked individual pages or marked sheets (whether or not the originals) were appended.[77]

The plate-changes made in I^d are inadvertent errors, not part of an attempt at correction of the text; those in I^e are corrections but unauthoritative since they are aimed at making the Boston style more consistent in opposition to that of MS and E1^a. After I^e, therefore, changes in the American plates for the first edition have no bearing on the relation of the I^a typesetting to its English copy-text.

From what has been determined about this relationship above, some picture of Hawthorne as a proofreader can be built up on a more factual basis than was possible in the bibliographical investigation of his earlier romances for the Centenary editions. Of the variants between E1^a and I^a in the seventeen sheets (30–37, 47–55) conjectured as set in Boston from largely uncorrected English proofs, we see him detecting a maximum of twenty-nine ascertainable departures from what he had written in MS, although a very few of these are no doubt independent errors in the I^a setting not present in the English copy.[78] In the same sheets, however, he failed to notice at least forty-five substantive or "significant" compositorial departures from MS that as a consequence were printed in the first edition and up to the

[77] To review the possibilities, we have (a) instructions throughout; (b) instructions, plus marked sheets for 47–50 or 47–52; (c) instructions plus marked individual pages from the 47-50-52 series, in order to save postage. If the latter, single variants on a page might be overlooked and not sent.

[78] For twenty-seven of these variants see footnote 65 above. To this list must be added the special cases of 285.9 and 414.15 to make twenty-nine in all.

Centenary Edition have not been challenged as unauthoritative readings.[79]

In the matter of "significant" English printer's departures from copy, therefore, roughly three-fifths of the unauthorized variation from MS remains uncorrected in $E1^a$ in those sheets where a control in I^a (sheets 30–37 and 47–55, in which I^a was set from unrevised $E1^a$ proofs) permits us to distinguish with almost absolute exactness the nature of the readings. Some of this corruption of the text would be difficult for an author to detect unless he were scrupulously collating his manuscript with the proofs, such as the insertion of "the" in "of mid-" of MS at 259.5, the omission of "a" in "a nobler" at 262.19 or of "himself" at 278.12. That the plural nouns "penances" (432.12) and "secrets" (438.34) had been altered to singulars might easily be overlooked. Whether the manuscript read "further" and the proof "farther" (250.32, 266.29), "upward" or "upwards" (400.18), "goat's" or "goats'" (418.20) might not be recalled even if the forms in proof had been noticed. Hawthorne might readily have accepted as printing-house styling the alteration of "granducal" to "Grand-ducal" (254.12) or of "gensd'armes" to "gendarmes" (441.11, 442.27, 450.32). What is shocking for its potentialities, however, is the revelation of the extreme carelessness in proofreading that passed "mystery" for "misery" (281.18), "deep, mild" for "deep-hued" (294.32), "possesses" for "pursues" (298.27), "sorrow" for "horrour"

[79] These forty-five are: 247.32 (30), 250.32 (30), 254.12 (30), 254.20 (30), 259.5 (31), 259.21 (31), 262.19 (31), 266.29 (32), 269.23 (32), 271.13 (32), 276.11 (33), 277.16 (33), 278.12 (33), 279.8 (33), 281.18 (34), 287.4 (34), 290.3-4 (35), 292.14 (35), 292.17 (35), 294.32 (35), 296.18 (35), 298.27 (36), 306.17 (37), 306.33 (37), 307.28 (37), 400.18 (48), 402.18 (48), 404.31 (49), 410.13 (49), 415.13 (50), 418.20 (50), 431.6 (52), 432.12 (52), 433.20 (52), 433.24 (52), 434.8 (52), 438.34 (53), 441.11 (53), 442.27 (53), 444.3 (53), 446.24 (53), 446.31 (53), 450.32 (54), 456.11 (55), and 461.1 (55). These do not include the misprints 301.20 (36), 307.11 (37), 434.33 (52) which might have originated in I^a.

(446.24), and did not notice the blunder "to him let him blood" (446.31).

If we may trust all of the I[c] plate-changes in sheets 47 and 49,[80] Hawthorne occupied himself with the accidentals enough to personify by capitalization (391.22, 406.33), although the text of *Transformation* as printed is far from consistent in this matter. Less certainly he may have attended to some anomalous punctuation, as at 406.8 or 410.33, and he may have changed a comma to a period at 290.16.

Given the fact that the control sheets comprise almost one-third of the book, one can state with some certainty that Hawthorne was little concerned to improve his text by revising it in proof and that he read proof chiefly in the hope of correcting printer's errors, most of which, in fact, he did not recognize.[81]

Of the ten variants that in any strict sense can be called revisions (see footnote 66), the small expansion in the Preface at 4.17–19 represents a special case not touching the text of the romance proper. The one spelling change is of some interest since in ordinary circumstances no editor would be inclined to recognize it as authorial.[82] One variant deals with an essential matter of substantive meaning furnished by punctuation (281.23). One merely alters the tense of a verb (387.26). Only six of the lot, then, substitute one word or

---

[80] Some of the plate-changes may well have been ordered by the Boston copyreader whose attention was called to these sheets by the arrival of the few corrections from England and who read over the I[b] sheets in the area to make sure that more need for correction did not exist.

[81] The evidence of these control sheets in *The Marble Faun* confirms Hawthorne's expressed distrust in 1850–51 of printers' struggles with his handwriting and his desire to go over their work with care to restore his own readings: see *The House of the Seven Gables* (Centenary Edition, 1965), p. xlviii.

[82] This correction of "Belvidere" to "Belvedere" (391.14) may be included as a revision only by courtesy in that the error was also present in MS so that Hawthorne in altering it[c] went beyond the simple act of restoring an MS reading to proof.

phrase for another as part of a critical revision,[83] a very small figure indeed even if we add the substantive punctuation alteration and the non-corrective spelling change. It is of particular interest that in these revisions in proof no word is added to or subtracted from the text of the control sheets independently of some form of substitution. (One simple addition at 421.10 corrects a misprint, but is not a revision.)

A critic may regret the choice of a more modern noun for the old-fashioned "avails" (392.23). The rest are negligible improvements although on the evidence Hawthorne felt the readings important enough to alter. What is of editorial value is that they have some tendency to cluster in sheets: three (274.19, 274.26, 275.2) are in sheet 33, and three (387.26, 391.14, 392.23) are in sheet 47.

When we come to examine the authority of the 166 significant or substantive variants between MS and E1ᵃ in the remaining two-thirds of the sheets for which there is no control (these 166 variants are listed in notes 84–85, 87–89, 91–92), some preliminary narrowing of the evidence is possible. Thus if we exclude from any consideration the various uncounted examples in MS of dittography and inadvertent spelling errors (recorded in the list of Editorial Emendations, however), we are left with sixteen obvious errors in MS that were probably corrected by the compositors in the typesetting and have no relation to proof-changes.[84] Correspond-

---

[83] These are: "noble" for "admirable" (4.18), "persuasibility" for "persuadability" (247.30), "chanced to find" for "happened upon" (274.19), "figures" for "shows" (274.26), "sadder" for "sorrier" (275.2), and "proceeds" for "avails" (392.23).

[84] These E1ᵃ readings are all accepted by the Centenary text: 19.8 (Jenkins), 32.3 (Jenkins), 60.18 (Mintern), 63.3 (Hobson), 146.12 (Barnett), 147.9 (Barnett), 147.20 (Barnett), 178.4 (Mintern), 219.30 (Barnett), 236.21 (Shand), 237.7 (Shand), 244.7 (Shand), 318.8 (Mintern), 353.10 (Farley), 359.13 (Shand), and 370.13 (Farley). Two of these substitute "Kenyon" for undeleted "Graydon"; four represent the repair of omitted necessary words; and one omits an unnecessary word that crept into MS by anticipation. To this group one may add for the

ingly, the six simple compositorial misprints or blunders in
E_1^a that were passed in proof[85] may be subtracted from the
variants in these sheets that are under scrutiny for authority.

Another class of variants almost as clear-cut as the above
in assessment as compositorial error, once one compares the
E_1^a reading with the MS, comprises forty cases of substantive difference in which the misreading is quite definitely
due to some ambiguity in the manuscript inscription or at
least in which it is evident that the misreading could have
originated in the inscription given some real carelessness on
the part of the compositors.[86] These differences were, of
course, overlooked by Hawthorne in the proofreading, and
most of them have been a part of the textual tradition
stemming from E_1^a. If the statistics from the control sheets
are to hold, we may suppose that there were perhaps twenty

---

record: 247.31 (Hobson), 248.23 (Hobson), 249.23 (Hobson), 292.7
(Mintern), 398.19 (Farley), and 453.9 (Shand), which are readings
from the control sheets and hence almost certainly supplied by the compositors (whether of E_1^a or I^a).

[85] These six E_1^a readings are rejected by the Centenary text: 21.15
(Hobson), 39.23 (Hobson), 42.8 (Mintern), 157.15 (Farley), 157.34
(Farley), and 169.2 (Mintern). To these may be added from the control
sheets 281.18 (Mintern) and 446.31 (Farley), and doubtfully 301.20
(Hobson), 307.11 (Shand), and 421.10 (Jenkins) since these last three
may represent not E_1^a misprints followed by I^a but, instead, independent
I^a misprints.

[86] That is, the hand itself may have caused difficulty, as in the confusion of MS "would" as E_1^a "could" (17.32) or of MS "could" as E_1^a
"would" (77.12) or of "on" as "in" (18.1); or the question in MS at
25.25 whether in fact "my" had been deleted; or the important misreading
of faulty MS at 198.4 by which MS "un-|tentionally" was misinterpreted
as "intentionally" instead of correct "unintentionally". Some of these
variants may well represent memorial error or carelessness that cannot be
altogether blamed on MS. The inscription of "those" at 21.10 is perfectly
clear, but Hobson carelessly set it as "these"; there can be little question
about MS "tower" at 69.12, but Mintern set it as "lower". Others may
verge on compositorial sophistication. Farley's setting of "unmitigable"
(96.32) for MS "immitigable" and of "unfrequent" for "infrequent"
(346.18) may well be conscious, not a simple misreading, in view of
Hobson's "undistinguishable" for MS "indistinguishable" (290.3-4) and
Shand's "unmitigable" for MS "immitigable" (433.20). Perhaps E_1^a
"-fleckered" for MS "-flickered" (77.19) comes in this category.

to twenty-five more such errors that he detected and hence that have left no trace. Many of these errors represent the same sort of slight variation already seen in the rejected readings from the control sheets, the variation between singular and plural for instance, as in MS "affection" *vs.* E1ᵃ "affections" (105.9); between doublet forms like MS "around" *vs.* E1ᵃ "round" (26.34); or simple substitutions like MS "this" *vs.* E1ᵃ "their" (145.3) or MS "rejoined" *vs.* E1ᵃ "replied" (109.12). However, some produce astonishing variants that one is fortunate to be able to identify from MS as errors and to find in the inscription a clue to their source, like MS "adducing" *vs.* E1ᵃ "admiring" (60.34) or MS "movement" *vs.* E1ᵃ "moment" (85.5). The list also contains some egregious misprints that Hawthorne overlooked such as E1ᵃ "lower" for MS "tower" (69.12) or E1ᵃ "silver" for MS "sylvan" (90.7).[87]

Closely associated with the above misreadings, and not always to be distinguished from them, is a series of fifty-

[87] These forty readings in the E1ᵃ book-sheets or final proofs that provided the Iᵃ copy-text are theoretically due to misreading and are rejected in the Centenary text: 16.33 (Shand), 17.32 (Jenkins), 18.1 (Jenkins), 21.10 (Hobson), 25.25 (Farley), 26.34 (Orr), 52.30 (Jenkins), 57.20 (Shand), 60.34 (Mintern), 69.12 (Mintern), 77.12 (Jenkins), 77.19 (Jenkins), 85.5 (Farley), 86.19 (Farley), 90.7 (Mintern), 95.6 (Shand), 95.29 (Farley), 96.32 (Farley), 97.19 (Farley), 105.9 (Hobson), 108.23 (Mintern), 109.12 (Mintern), 110.10 (Shand), 119.11 (Farley), 145.3 (Barnett), 145.20 (Barnett), 150.1 (Barnett), 153.22 (Mintern), 166.1 (Mintern), 169.14 (Shand), 180.9 (Mintern), 198.4 (Hobson), 199.23 (Hobson), 239.16 (Shand), 240.2 (Shand), 321.10 (Farley), 335.5 (Farley), 346.18 (Farley), 375.24 (Farley), 375.29 (Farley). To these, for the record one may add from the control sheets the seventeen additional compositorial misreadings not detected by Hawthorne in the proofreading, comprising 266.29 (Shand), 269.23 (Farley), 276.11 (Shand), 279.8 (Mintern), 287.4 (Barnett), 290.3-4 (Hobson), 292.17 (Mintern), 294.32 (Farley), 298.27 (Hobson), 306.17 (Farley), 415.13 (Farley), 432.12 (Shand), 433.20 (Shand), 434.8 (Shand), 438.34 (Jenkins), 446.24 (Farley), and 456.11 (Shand). Also for the record one may list here the following thirteen conjectural misreadings from these control sheets that were corrected by Hawthorne, comprising 248.34 (Hobson), 264.14 (Farley), 270.16 (Mintern), 285.9 (Shand), 290.14 (Hobson), 290.20 (Hobson), 294.12 (Farley), 401.17 (Jenkins), 404.27 (Farley), 412.17 (Jenkins), 414.15 (Jenkins), 434.33 (Shand), and 443.16 (Hobson).

seven compositorial sophistications or inadvertent departures from copy. Sometimes one suspects that a careless reading of Hawthorne's hand caused the error; sometimes memorial error is the best explanation; and sometimes there seems to be a deliberate attempt to "improve" the style or syntax. Although this list lacks the visible evidence from the MS generally available for the group called misreadings, any argument for the authority of these variants would receive little support from the nature of Hawthorne's alterations in the control sheets; with few exceptions, therefore, no dispute will be encountered in labeling these as compositorial errors. This list, which also has become a part of the textual tradition after E1^a, is chiefly confined to questions of singular or plural, like MS "claw" *vs.* E1^a "claws" (8.30) or MS "weed" *vs.* E1^a "weeds" (38.7); of doublets like MS "further" *vs.* E1^a "farther" (21.14) or MS "subtile" *vs.* E1^a "subtle" (18.5) or MS "influencies" *vs.* E1^a "influences" (36.12) or MS "elder" *vs.* E1^a "older" (37.12); of grammar or usage like MS "neither" *vs.* E1^a "either" (14.2) or MS "is" *vs.* E1^a "are" (49.13) or MS "exceedingly" *vs.* E1^a "exceeding" (163.27) or MS "established" *vs.* E1^a "establishing" (241.22). These are clearly paralleled by similar compositorial departures in the control sheets and little or nothing can be said for them as Hawthorne proof-alterations.[88]

[88] These fifty-seven E1^a readings from non-control sheets are rejected by the Centenary text: 8.30 (Spech), 9.24 (Farley), 14.2 (Farley), 14.30 (Shand), 18.5 (Jenkins), 20.13 (Hobson; i.e., *shown-showed*), 21.14 (Hobson), 22.14 (Hobson), 28.18 (Orr), 36.12 (Farley), 37.12 (Hobson), 38.7 (Hobson), 43.10 (Mintern), 44.2 (Mintern), 44.4 (Mintern), 45.13 (Hobson), 49.13 (Farley), 52.30 (Jenkins), 55.1 (Jenkins), 55.17 (Shand), 58.2 (Shand), 59.25 (Mintern), 62.15 (Hobson), 72.4 (Mintern), 72.34 (Shand), 106.9 (Mintern), 106.16 (Mintern), 106.34 (Mintern), 113.5 (Farley), 124.5 (Mintern), 127.17 (Mintern), 137.13 (Jenkins), 149.18 (Barnett), 149.29 (Barnett), 154.12 (Mintern; i.e., *lie-lay*), 154.15 (Mintern), 154.18 (Mintern), 160.9 (Farley), 163.27 (Jenkins), 171.2 (Shand), 172.1 (Hobson), 180.7 (Mintern), 188.23 (Barnett), 207.8 (Barnett), 212.19 (Farley), 216.15 (Farley), 219.23 (Barnett), 225.15 (Barnett), 233.28 (Shand), 241.22 (Shand), 243.33

Eight substantive common errors of MS and E1[a] that need editorial correction may also be discarded.[89] More common readings than these exist between the two authorities that need editorial correction, of course, but they are not substantive or else not to be classed as actual errors.

We are left, then, with thirty-nine substantive variants in the non-control sheets about which some difference of opinion might develop (these thirty-nine are listed in notes 91–92). Before an attempt is made to classify these, some inquiry into the habits of the compositors who set them will be in order.

In the E1[a] control sheets 30–37 and 47–55 Farley set 1,480 lines, Hobson 1,476, Jenkins 937, Shand 874, Mintern 395, and Barnett 270. If we consolidate the 72 errors (listed in notes 65 and 79) made by these compositors regardless of whether Hawthorne did or did not correct them in proof, we may estimate that in these sheets Farley had a total of 23 significant departures from copy that were not corrections (1 misprint, 8 misreadings, 14 sophistications), Hobson a total of 15 (1 doubtful misprint, 6 misreadings, 8 sophistica-

---

(Shand), 245.6 (Shand), 324.2 (Mintern), 336.15 (Farley), 336.20 (Farley), 337.23 (Mintern), and 350.18 (Hobson). For the sake of the record one can add the following twenty-six departures from copy in the control sheets not detected by Hawthorne in the proofreading: 247.32 (Hobson), 250.32 (Barnett), 254.12 (Shand), 254.20 (Shand), 259.5 (Farley), 259.21 (Farley), 262.19 (Farley), 271.13 (Mintern), 277.16 (Farley), 278.12 (Barnett), 292.14 (Mintern), 296.18 (Shand), 306.33 (Farley), 307.28 (Shand), 400.18 (Jenkins), 402.18 (Jenkins), 404.31 (Farley), 410.13 (Hobson), 418.20 (Farley), 431.6 (Farley), 433.24 (Shand), 441.11 (Hobson), 442.27 (Hobson), 444.3 (Hobson), 450.32 (Jenkins), and 461.1 (Farley). Also for the record one may list here the eleven conjectural false readings from these sheets that were corrected by Hawthorne: 265.17 (Shand), 269.8 (Farley), 276.15 (Shand), 296.19 (Shand), 302.11 (Hobson), 391.10 (Jenkins), 429.26 (Farley), 445.25 (Hobson), 448.32 (Farley), 455.11–12 (Shand), and 460.25 (Farley).

[89] These eight are: "Signorina" for MS-E1[a] "Signora" (48.27), "had" for "have" (80.11), "di" for "della" (109.24 and 114.6), "Nelvil" for "Neville" (146.17 and 146.27), "di" for "da" (334.23), and "was as if" for "was if" (370.10).

tions), Jenkins a total of 8 (1 doubtful misprint, 3 misreadings, 4 sophistications), Shand a total of 17 (1 doubtful misprint, 7 misreadings, 9 sophistications), Mintern a total of 6 (1 misprint, 3 misreadings, 2 sophistications), and Barnett a total of 3 (2 misreadings, 1 sophistication). In the order of their fidelity to copy, then, the compositors rank as follows in these control sheets: Jenkins with one error per 117.1 lines (or .85 per 100 lines), Hobson with one per 98.4 lines (or 1.02 per 100), Barnett with one per 90.0 lines (or 1.11 per 100), Mintern with one per 65.8 lines (or 1.52 per 100), Farley with one per 64.3 lines (or 1.56 per 100), and Shand with one per 51.4 lines (or 1.95 per 100).

In the remaining, or non-control, sheets, Farley set a total of 3,312 lines, Hobson 2,181, Shand 2,119, Mintern 1,969, Barnett 1,671, and Jenkins 990. The 103 conjectural compositorial errors in these sheets (see notes 85, 87–88), as estimated in the first stage of the present inquiry, are Farley 26 (2 misprints, 12 misreadings, 12 sophistications), Hobson 15 (2 misprints, 4 misreadings, 9 sophistications), Shand 17 (7 misreadings, 10 sophistications), Mintern 26 (2 misprints, 8 misreadings, 16 sophistications), Barnett 9 (3 misreadings, 6 sophistications), and Jenkins 10 (5 misreadings, 5 sophistications). In the order of their assumed fidelity to copy, then, the compositors rank in these sheets as follows: Barnett with one error per 185.7 lines (or .54 per 100 lines), Hobson with one per 145.4 lines (or .69 per 100), Farley with one per 127.4 lines (or .78 per 100), Shand with one per 124.6 lines (or .80 per 100), Jenkins with one per 99.0 lines (or 1.01 per 100), and Mintern with one per 75.7 lines (or 1.32 per 100). These figures ignore the two errors by Orr and one by Spech (?).

The comparison shows several dramatic changes, the most striking of which are Hobson's rise in fidelity from one error per 98.4 lines to one in 145.4, Farley's rise from one per

64.3 to one per 127.4, and Shand's rise from one per 51.4 to one per 124.6. These differences are seemingly due less to the conjectural rate of error in the non-control pages versus the almost exactly ascertainable rate in the control pages than to the statistical adjustment that almost invariably takes place when a larger sampling is available. Barnett's 270 lines and Mintern's 395 in the first group provide too small a basis to be reliable. When the stints are fairly evenly divided between the two categories of sheets, as with Jenkins at 937 and 990 lines respectively, the statistics are more even: one error per 117.1 lines or .85 per 100, versus one error per 99 lines or 1.01 per 100. Considering the relatively few lines set by Jenkins, the results of these tests are encouraging.

Finally, when we put the two sets of figures together, we find that for those variants that up to this point have been assigned as compositorial error we have Farley with 4,792 lines and 49 errors (3 misprints, 20 misreadings, 26 sophistications), Hobson with 3,657 lines and 30 errors (3 misprints, 10 misreadings, 17 sophistications), Shand with 2,993 lines and 34 errors (1 misprint, 14 misreadings, 19 sophistications), Mintern with 2,364 lines and 32 errors (3 misprints, 11 misreadings, 18 sophistications), Barnett with 1,941 lines and 12 errors (5 misreadings, 7 sophistications), and Jenkins with 1,927 lines and 18 errors (1 misprint, 8 misreadings, 9 sophistications).

In tabular form the compositors provisionally rank as follows:

Consolidated		Non-Control		Control	
Barnett	161.7 (0.62)	Barnett	185.7 (0.54)	Jenkins	117.1 (0.85)
Hobson	121.9 (.82)	Hobson	145.4 (.69)	Hobson	98.4 (1.02)
Jenkins	107.1 (.93)	Farley	127.4 (.78)	Barnett	90.0 (1.11)
Farley	97.8 (1.02)	Shand	124.6 (.80)	Mintern	65.8 (1.52)
Shand	88.0 (1.14)	Jenkins	99.0 (1.01)	Farley	64.3 (1.56)
Mintern	73.9 (1.35)	Mintern	75.7 (1.32)	Shand	51.4 (1.95)

Although the leverage exerted by the figures for two-thirds of the sheets against one-third is considerable, it is of some interest to see that the consolidated list differs from the non-control sheets in its ranking only by dropping Jenkins two notches.

The ten significant proof-revisions from MS in the control sheets 30–37 and 47–55—including two in π—have already been established (see note 66). It now remains to examine the last undifferentiated thirty-nine readings of the non-control sheets in which E1^a (with I^a agreeing) differs from its copy-text manuscript (see notes 91 and 92). Some nineteen of the twenty-three of these listed in note 92 offer no serious difficulty. (The four more doubtful ones in 3.19, 3.32, 64.19, 331.33 are discussed in connection with the sixteen accepted Hawthorne proof-corrections below listed in note 91.) The printing-house variants already identified and rejected in the control sheets indicate the common substitution by the English compositors of one part of speech for another, the interchange of neutral verbal forms of roughly the same meaning, and the omission of simple connectives or link-words, chiefly articles and prepositions. Most of such small changes Hawthorne overlooked in the proofs of these sheets. Thus when we find E1^a "shall" for MS "should" (15.31, Shand), "in" for "at" (44.7, Mintern), "which" for "what" (72.3, Mintern), "the" for "a" (72.22, Mintern), "to" for "on" (88.34, Mintern), "of" for "in" (108.9, Mintern), "from" for "for" (352.27, Farley), every reason exists to prefer the MS form, especially when we notice that Mintern, the least reliable of the compositors and an especial offender in this form of change, is responsible for five of the seven, and that Shand and Farley, who share the other two, have a particularly high proportion of such sophistication or carelessness. Similarly, the omission of "up" (20.13, Hobson) and of "the" (110.32, Shand), or the addition of "a" in "or a" (241.13, Shand) are so neutral as to suggest compositorial error, not authorial proof-alteration.

The one-for-one substitution of E1ᵃ "possibility" for MS "probability" (122.5, Mintern) might be defended if made within the work of a more reliable compositor and if some legitimate shade of meaning were involved (which it is not). More clearly, "arena" for "area" (154.12, Mintern), "exclamation" for "explanation" (189.9, Barnett), "kindness" for "kindliness" (224.27, Barnett), and "treading" for "threading" (326.19, Barnett) also appear to be errors.[90] Farley's addition of "times" at 47.32 rests on a misunderstanding of Hawthorne's meaning and thus exposes itself as a sophistication (see the Textual Note). Mintern's omission of "attentively" at 88.30 certainly detracts from the sense; Jenkins' omission of "long" at 100.24 is so neutral (like Hobson's of "up" at 20.13) as scarcely to demand authorial intervention to alter a quite satisfactory phrase. (However, the rearrangement of the sentence structure and phrasing at 83.34 in Farley's stint is more easily explained not as compositorial meddling but as Hawthorne's attempt in proof to work over a bad reading he did not know had been created by Sophia's unauthorized intervention. The MS reading is to be preferred, therefore, but for a special reason.)

Sixteen variants listed in note 91 remain that may indeed represent Hawthorne's proof-alterations, but some few of these may be suspect, chiefly those that are simple additions or omissions, always the most difficult of variants to adjudicate. The addition of "actual" at 349.24 (Hobson) makes a

---

[90] Mintern's "arena" for "area" seems to be a fairly straight case of misreading. It is somewhat dashing to find this cluster of three from Barnett, who in the provisional rankings has been the most faithful of the regular compositors, though he set too few lines to provide a really sound basis for statistical analysis. But his "exclamation" is obviously wrong, and his reduction of "threading" to "treading" takes away from the sense and can be nothing but a sophistication. Hence little can be said in favor of his change of "kindliness" to "kindness", and MS must be preferred for each reading.

delicately superior sense beyond the range of sophistication. Some such word as "compelled" at 202.15 (Farley) seems required by the idiom, even though "she is to" in the sense of *she is obliged to* is a common idiom in the present or preterite tenses.

The acceptance of these readings requires no particular effort; and another—the deleting of "of Egypt" as the location of the Wilderness (315.11, Mintern)—is clearly an obligatory change made in proof. One may accept also the E1[a] excision of "probably" at 231.17 (Shand) as a definite improvement in incisiveness and directness of statement where indecision had no advantage. Yet whether there had been a faun-like inhabitant of Monte Beni "from a period beyond memory or record" as in E1[a], or MS "beyond human memory or record" (234.27, Shand) is a problem that neatly balances simple compositorial omission against the possibility that Hawthorne was abstracting a redundancy. What inclines one to accept the excision of the word as a deliberate proof-change is the fact that for all his faults Shand has no record other than at 231.17 and here at 234.27 for omitting words, and these two cases occur clustered in sheet 28. It would seem that they must stand or fall together; and thus the odds favor their standing as authoritative revisions. Similarly, an acceptable reason appears to lie behind the E1[a] removal at 214.12 (Barnett) of the phrase "in that kind" since it has no preceding reference and thus is anomalous.

A more delicate question concerns the two variants in Barnett's stint in sheet 16: the E1[a] addition of "the" before "divinest" (139.24) and the omission of "whitening" (143.34). At first view the matter of the "the" would seem to be another of those indifferent additions and subtractions that are the small-change of compositorial activity. But evidence exists in favor of a proof-change. When a simple series exists with two parallel nouns or adjectives as "the young Count as a listener or spectator" (241.13), MS usually does not repeat the modifying pronoun or article although in E1[a] Shand took it upon himself to repeat the "a". That the MS form is Hawthorne's preferred usage may be suggested not only by the custom of the manuscript elsewhere but also by the evidence of 292.14, in control sheet 35, that the E1[a]–I[a] addition of the second "its" by Mintern was unauthorized in the printed phrase "its gate and its surrounding walls" and MS must be retained. However, when the structure is not strictly parallel, Hawthorne was careful to insure unambiguous grammatical modification. For example, since it occurs in the control sheet 31, we can be sure that Farley's omission of "a" is an error when he sets MS "a more definite and a nobler individuality" (262.19) as "a more definite and nobler". On this analogy the odds favor Hawthorne at 139.24 restoring in proof his accidental omission of "the" in MS "the most beautiful and divinest figure" to correct in E1[a] to his preferred form, "the most beautiful and the divinest figure".

That the omission of "whitening" also comes in Barnett's stint in the same sheet is a point in favor of considering this omission as authorial since Hawthorne's proof-revisions (as distinguished from corrections) have a tendency to cluster within isolated sheets. Barnett is also one of the two most careful workmen (although some evidence exists to suggest that his supposed reliability might diminish if we had evidence from more typesetting). In this case, moreover, some slight literary reasons may perhaps be found to justify the deletion of the word in E1[a] as an authorial proof-change (see the Textual Note). However, the MS reading is so interesting that one could wish the variant had occurred in a control sheet where further evidence could have been obtained since the case is very doubtful indeed.

The omission of repetitive "then" in Hobson's stint at 383.1 is a toss-up as to whether it is a compositorial sophistication or an authorial second thought. Acceptance here of the E1ᵃ version is perhaps the least justified of the various cases of omission or addition, although most critics will perhaps favor E1ᵃ as more effective in its economy than MS. Moreover, Hobson is a superior workman.

An almost indifferent omission that might also be laid to the avoidance of repetition that had initially been thought effective but then discarded comes at 83.32 where E1ᵃ excises "they" before "twined". A case might be made out for this as a deletion in proof, on grounds of smoothness, but the compositor Farley is careless about adding or subtracting words. Thus the Cententary retention of MS "they" at this point may seem to be advisable even though it occurs only two lines above a conjectural Hawthorne proof-alteration mentioned above (83.34; see the Textual Note). It is also in the same sheet 10 as two rejected Mintern variants at 88.30 and 88.34, and is an omission that Hawthorne was scarcely likely to notice in proof.

Mintern is so suspect as a compositor that the addition of "been" before "understood" at 331.33 in his stint may not automatically be accepted as the necessary repair of a Hawthorne omission in MS. Indeed, if a rhetorical pause is made after "friends," the syntax though harsh is effective. It may well seem that this is another of Mintern's sophistications. In the Preface, set by an unknown compositor, "find it in my heart" (3.32) is the normal idiom as in E1ᵃ, but Hawthorne's more archaic "find in my heart" is justified in its MS and Centenary form by reference to *1 Henry IV*, II.iv.56.

A very odd case is the E_1^a omission in the Preface of "like" (3.19) so that MS "Romance and poetry, like ivy, lichens, and wall-flowers, need Ruin to make them grow" becomes in E_1^a–I^a "Romance and poetry, ivy, lichens, and wall-flowers, need . . . " The original use of a simile seems so much more natural than the forcefully yoked parallel series that ordinarily one would feel little difficulty in rejecting the E_1^a omission as a compositorial eyeskip. On the other hand, authors have a tendency to pay especial attention to their prefaces in which they speak in their own persons (and do not like to be misquoted). More particularly, we know from the expansion from MS at 4.17–19 that Hawthorne had proofread the preliminary sheet with some care. We also know from the later change of "admirable" to "noble" within the expansion (4.18) that he had continued to review the text of the Preface even after initial proof had been returned to the printer. Given this series of checks, it is not altogether easy to believe that such an obvious error as the omission of the comparative "like" would have escaped him since the effect of the series is considerably bolder as found in E_1^a. Yet the series is so forced that, with some trepidation, an editor may retain MS here and assign the E_1^a reading to an overlooked printer's error.

The rearranged syntax at 17.28 in Jenkins' stint is very likely authoritative. So few cases of this sort of variant exist, only one of them (a simple transposition) almost certainly ascertainable from the control sheets as a compositor's (302.11) and the other conjecturally assigned to Hawthorne (83.34), that something of a major operation like this appears to be authorial. The substitution at 52.19 (Jenkins) of "pushing" for the inelegant MS "shoving" and, in the same sheet, of "sending" for MS "projecting" (56.19, Shand) seems to bear the mark of an author, as does the superior

E1ᵃ "quick" for MS "much" (319.11, Mintern) despite its suspect compositor.

Three Farley variants may cause some concern. At 23.4 the substitution of "hinted" for the old-fashioned idiom "bore" could be a sophistication, but it more likely corresponds to such modernizations as Hawthorne made in the proof at 56.19 and 392.23; partly in its favor, also, is its appearance in sheet 2 accompanying the conjectured authorial proof-change at 17.28. At 309.9 the change from MS "only Italy" to "Italy alone" may be a Farley improvement, a process to which he was somewhat addicted, but at least it occurs in the same sheet 38 as the undoubted authorial change at 315.11 and has no strong reason to be denied acceptance. The switch at 208.26–27 to the third person in E1ᵃ "her . . . her . . . she" from MS "me . . . me . . . I" in Hilda's anguished interview with Miriam may be a bold compositorial interference, but the reason for Farley to alter MS would be obscure since the continued first-person pronouns are distinctly more natural. Thus one is forced to conclude that Hawthorne in changing his referent to "girl" at 208.25 from the preceding "I" had some idea of generalizing the statement of experience and perhaps of softening what might seem too egoistic an application.

One final variant remains, that at 64.19 in Hobson's stint, of E1ᵃ "eyes" versus MS "eyelids". This is a technical matter about how the artist of Beatrice Cenci's portrait had indicated the suggestion of a redness that gave rise to the fancy that the girl had been weeping. In his manuscript Italian journal (April 3, 1858) Hawthorne in describing the portrait at first hand had noted this effect and had used the exact word "eyelids"; hence his repetition in MS was undoubtedly drawn from these notes, like so much of his description of Italian art. Whereas it is possible that a subsequent discussion with Sophia when proof arrived may have induced him to provide a vaguer specification, to hypothesize such an imaginary conversation about the location of a spot or two of pigment as a reason for accepting E_1^a would be folly. No evidence exists to suggest that Hawthorne could have changed his mind in the proof-stage; thus it is a trifle easier to reject the E_1^a reading as Hobson's memorial contamination from "eyes" at 64.17 than to controvert the evidence of the Italian journal and of MS.

Of the thirty-nine variants in the non-control sheets, then, that have been reserved for final analysis, sixteen may be found acceptable as proof-revisions or necessary corrections.[91] Twenty-three may be rejected as compositorial errors that passed undetected in the proofs.[92] To the sixteen accepted alterations may be added the uncontested expansion in the Preface at 4.17–19, and the second-stage Preface change at 4.18. To the twenty-three alterations in this group (note 92) now assumed to be printer's errors one should add the 103 other errors previously established[93] to make a total of 126 departures from the text in significant readings that Haw-

[91] These sixteen Hawthorne proof-corrections are accepted by the Centenary text. Four of these appear in Farley, three each in Barnett and Shand, and two each in Mintern, Jenkins, and Hobson: 17.28 (Jenkins), 23.4 (Farley), 52.19 (Jenkins), 56.19 (Shand), 139.24 (Barnett), 143.34 (Barnett), 202.15 (Farley), 208.26–27 (Farley), 214.12 (Barnett), 231.17 (Shand), 234.27 (Shand), 309.9 (Farley), 315.11 (Mintern), 319.11 (Mintern), 349.24 (Hobson), 383.1 (Hobson).

[92] These twenty-three are returned to MS reading in the Centenary text. Nine of these appear in the work of Mintern, three each in Farley, Shand, and Barnett, two in Hobson, and one in Jenkins: 3.19 (anon.), 3.32 (anon.), 15.31 (Shand), 20.13 (Hobson), 44.7 (Mintern), 47.32 (Farley), 64.19 (Hobson), 72.3 (Mintern), 72.22 (Mintern), 83.32 (Farley), 88.30 (Mintern), 88.34 (Mintern), 100.24 (Jenkins), 108.9 (Mintern), 110.32 (Shand), 122.5 (Mintern), 154.12 (Mintern), 189.9 (Barnett), 224.27 (Barnett), 241.13 (Shand), 326.19 (Barnett), 331.33 (Mintern), 352.27 (Farley).

[93] These 103 errors consist of the 40 compositorial misreadings listed in note 87, and 57 compositorial changes listed in note 88, plus 6 special cases listed in note 85.

thorne did not detect. The proportion of revisions (not corrections) to printer's errors in the variants from MS in the non-control sheets is, then, 16 to 126, or 1 to 8, as compared with the 8 substantive revisions (excluding the Preface) versus the established 45 uncorrected errors in the control sheets, a little less than 1 to 6. Finally, the proportions of 16 revisions in 39 non-control sheets are alike, as well. 126 against 45 undetected errors, is at the rate of 3.23 per non-control sheet versus 2.65 per control sheet.

When we come to combine the statistics for the two classes of sheets, we add the 16 conjectural proof-alterations in non-control sheets 1–29 and 38–46 to the established 8 in control sheets 30–37 and 47–55 for a total of 24 authorial changes in proof from the readings of MS. Two proof-revisions appear in sheet π. To these may be added the 27 errors in the control sheets that Hawthorne corrected, for a total of 51 ascertained proof-alterations—or 54 including π and the mistaken proof-alteration in non-control 83.34. (The number of corrections, or returns to MS, that Hawthorne marked in the non-control sheets cannot be determined, of course.) The compositorial error in significant readings that can be recognized totals 198 variants,[94] of which Hawthorne is known to have corrected 27 (see note 65), to leave a net of about 172 (including 83.34) significant errors printed in $E1^a$, most of which became a part of the textual tradition of this romance.

When the adjustments from the examination of the last lot of variants are made to the compositorial records previously sketched on a provisional basis, Barnett remains as the most reliable compositor (an estimate that seems confirmed by qualitative as well as quantitative analysis), and the rank-

[94] These 198 compositorial errors are listed in note 65 (27), note 79 (45), note 85 (6), note 87 (40), note 88 (57), and note 92 (23).

ings remain stable although the percentage of error has been somewhat altered, of course, throughout:

	Errors	Lines Set	Lines per Error	Error per 100 Lines
Barnett	12 + 3 = 15	1,941	129.4	.77
Hobson	30 + 2 = 32	3,657	114.3	.88
Jenkins	18 + 1 = 19	1,927	101.4	.99
Farley	49 + 3 = 52	4,792	92.2	1.08
Shand	34 + 3 = 37	2,993	80.9	1.23
Mintern	32 + 9 = 41	2,364	57.7	1.73

The final textual problem concerns the Postscript, as it was called in England, or the Conclusion, the title given in the fourth Boston printing I^d in which it presumably first appeared in America. Unfortunately, the manuscript of this document has not been preserved. As early as March 4, 1860, in a letter to Bennoch, Hawthorne remarked that, "If it ever comes to a second edition, I have an idea of adding a few explanatory pages, in the shape of a conversation between the author and Hilda or Kenyon, by means of which some further details may be elicited." By March 7 when he announced his purpose to Smith, Elder the choice of a conversation between the author and either Hilda or Kenyon had hardened into "between the author, Kenyon, and Hilda". On March 9 to Ticknor he wrote that " . . . Smith & Elder wrote me, some days ago, that their edition was nearly exhausted, and that they were about printing another. . . . I intend to add a few pages to the concluding chapter, in order to make things a little clearer. The additional matter, when written, shall be sent you in manuscript." Sometime, then, between March 9 and March 14, the date subscribed to the Postscript and the Conclusion, he wrote the addendum.

Since on March 16 he wrote to Smith, Elder, "I return the proof of the postscript", the original copy must have been sent to them in time to be set in type and returned to Leamington by March 16.

The proposal to send Ticknor the added material in manuscript instead of waiting, as normally, for proof-sheets to serve as copy, is a clear indication that Hawthorne was concerned to get the new material across the Atlantic with the utmost expedition for inclusion in the first possible extra printing, the date of which would be unknown to him. His experience with the speed with which Smith, Elder had furnished proof in the past may not have prepared him, though, for the quickness with which (preparing a second printing) they now responded; but he could scarcely have contemplated a delay of more than a few days between his mailing of copy to Smith, Elder and the receipt of proof-sheets that he could send to Ticknor. Thus a strong sense of urgency in mailing copy to Ticknor is indicated, a point that may have something to do with the difficult question of the order of inscription of the respective manuscripts.

That the English Postscript and the Boston Conclusion were set from different manuscripts is beyond question. Although there is a fairly general concurrence in their accidentals (particularly close in some of the punctuation, like the use of semicolons) that must go back to a common origin, or archetype, some differences are unlikely to have arisen from Boston workmen setting from English proofs, especially the capitalization of "Author" and of "the Real and the Fantastic" in the American edition (Centenary 463.16,19; 464.4) —typical of the manuscript of the Preface—versus the lower case used by the English compositors in the Preface and Postscript. Moreover, the Boston use of parentheses at 464.14–15 suggests setting from a Hawthorne manuscript, whereas the English commas suggest the reduction of Hawthorne's parentheses to commas that is relatively common in the E1[a] typesetting.[95]

An inquiry about priority would exhibit only idle curiosity were it not that certain substantive variants existing between the two versions call for editorial decision. Obviously, the choice must rest with the latest form of the manuscript as representing Hawthorne's final intentions, modified perhaps only in E1[b] proof.

Among the variations between the two forms of the text the differences in paragraphing are of no assistance in solving the problem: the English printers had been accustomed to break up Hawthorne's longer paragraphs for typographical reasons relating to page-length, and the American workmen no doubt reserved for themselves a similar freedom. The variant accidentals also are of no service, since fidelity to these has no bearing here on the priority of the manuscript transcription; and their descent, under the circumstances, can scarcely be traced in the two prints.

One substantive reading might be of singular importance if the E1[b] version could be established as the actual reproduction of Hawthorne's manuscript. The English text reads (465.14–24):

> "You must recollect," replied Kenyon, with a glance of friendly commiseration at my obtuseness, "that Miriam had utterly disappeared, leaving no trace by which her whereabout could be known. In the meantime, the municipal authorities had become aware of the murder of the Capuchin; and, from many preceding circumstances, such as his strange persecution of Miriam, they must have been led to see an obvious connection between herself and that tragical event. Furthermore, there is reason to believe that Miriam was suspected of implication with some plot or political intrigue, of which there may have been tokens in the packet. . . . "

[95] As for instance (taking the earliest occurrences in E1[a] Vol. III) by Mintern at Centenary 315.22, Farley at 321.16–17, and Barnett at 327.16.

In this passage a cluster of variants occurs between the two editions. In Boston "whereabout" is "whereabouts", "strange" does not appear before "persecution", "must have been led to see" reads "must have seen", and for "implication" the word in Boston is, "Miriam was suspected of connection with some plot . . . " This particular American variant is unexceptionable, but it repeats the word "connection" just above ("obvious connection between herself") and it would seem that the English text's "implication" is in the nature of a revision. However, if we discard the faint possibility that the repeated "connection" is a misprint in Boston by contamination from the first, we are left with two equally viable explanations: (1) the Boston "connection" was the original reading, and Hawthorne revised it when he came to copy out the second manuscript for Smith, Elder; or (2) the word "connection" appeared in both typesettings, but the change to "implication" was a proof-revision on the order of the alteration in proof in the Preface of repetitive "admirable" (as in I^a) to "noble" (as in E1^a) at 4.18. If the first were true, the priority of inscription would be established; if the second, the variant has no bearing on the original order of the manuscripts.[96]

The other substantive variants in this paragraph do not, individually at least, clearly show priority. E1^b "whereabout" versus Boston "whereabouts" (465.16) is indifferent. The Capuchin's "strange persecution" of Miriam is perhaps a little more pertinent to the context than his "persecution" (465.19–20); but at 465.20 that the authorities "must have been led to see" or "must have seen" the connection between Miriam and the Capuchin's death suggests no very demon-

---

[96] That the superior idiom may be "implication in" and that the "with" in E1^b may just possibly be a vestigial remainder of the change from "connection" to "implication" may be true; but—either way—the question of the order of inscription is not affected in any demonstrable manner.

strable direction of change, although in context the first seems superior. The "whereabout" variant may perhaps be compositorial (in either edition) but the three others in the same paragraph must be interconnected and must be part of the same process of alteration. Cumulatively, their direction can only be toward improvement in the English text. The question remains, however, whether these superior readings result from proof-revision or from revision in a final inscription.

A scattering of other substantive variants offers little help. At 464.12–15, in E1ᵇ, "We three had climbed to the top of St. Peter's, and were looking down upon the Rome which we were soon to leave, but which, having already sinned sufficiently in that way, it is not my purpose further to describe." The absence of "which" in Iᵈ after "Rome" may as readily be compositorial (an addition in E1ᵇ or an eyeskip or memorial failure in Iᵈ) as an improvement in the E1ᵇ manuscript, or in the proof. Later, at 466.31,33, repeated "these" in E1ᵇ appears as "those" in the American edition. The second—" 'Is it possible that you need an answer to these questions?' "—is almost certainly right in the English text, for the questions are the ones that have just been asked by the author. The first is perhaps more likely "these" than "those" since the "consequences" referred to are the ones that have just been detailed, about which the author is inquiring; but the case may be arguable.[97] The probability is, nevertheless, that in either case, but very likely in Boston, a double error was created from a misreading of Hawthorne's

[97] Nevertheless, an argument for the correctness of the initial "those" runs into difficulty. If the first is right and the second wrong in Boston, contamination is a ready explanation. If so, however, we must simultaneously suppose that there has also been contamination in E1ᵇ, but in the more difficult reverse direction. In short, whether contamination or misreading, the first reading is more likely to have influenced the second than vice versa. If the second reading is correct in E1ᵇ, as suggested, then the first is likely to be so too, and Iᵈ exhibits double error.

hand. If so, no evidence can be gathered to establish the order of the manuscripts.

The most extensive piece of evidence, but unfortunately the most difficult to interpret, occurs at 467.9, on the same page below the *these-those* variation. In answer to the author's question, "'Where, at this moment, is Donatello?'", E1^b reads simply, "'In prison,' said Kenyon, sadly." The Boston edition is more elaborate: "'The Castle of Saint Angelo,' said Kenyon sadly, turning his face towards that sepulchral fortress, 'is no longer a prison; but there are others which have dungeons as deep, and in one of them, I fear, lies our poor Faun.'" From a critical point of view the evidence seems conflicting. That is, when he is revising, Hawthorne almost invariably expands and seldom condenses. On the other hand, since Donatello's imprisonment ought to impress the reader as a purgation, and not a hopeless punishment without foreseeable end, Hawthorne may well have felt that the longer form, with its reference to "sepulchral" fortress, "dungeons as deep", and "our poor Faun" gave too gloomy and contrary an impression, and a laconic statement would be less harrowing and would permit a reader, who chose, to join Hilda in feeling at least some optimism about Donatello's distant future (462.19–21).[98] The order of this revision must wait upon other considerations.

Although any reconstruction of events can only be speculative in the extreme, certain possibilities may bear on the physical evidence of the readings. Two major alternatives exist. First, Hawthorne wrote out a manuscript for the addendum and made a copy of it, sending the original to one publisher and the copy to the other. Second, Haw-

[98] It may be idle to point out that in a small way the longer form of the passage violates Hawthorne's promise at 464.14–15 to make no further description of Rome. But the clash between the last sentence of the original ending and this long version is more important.

thorne wrote a draft version and from this he made two fair copies, each of which went to his publishers. Whatever he did must have occurred within a relatively short time, since he presumably received proof on March 16, two days after the date appended to his Postscript. The March 14 date, then, must be authentic as applying to the completion of the Postscript manuscript and its English version of the text (barring proof-changes).

Either hypothesis shortly involves us in a morass of speculation. At first glance the initial option—that the original inscription of the addendum was used as printer's copy for one publisher, with a fair copy from it sent to the other— might appear to be impossible: if the variants between the two versions came into being while one was being copied directly from the other, no bar could have existed to transferring the second thoughts back into the original in order to bring it into conformity with the revised copy. On the other hand, if the two versions were substantially the same, and if the English manuscript, say, had been put into the mail immediately while the Boston copy was kept for a short time for further contemplation, then the major variant of Kenyon's reply could be a revision, and perhaps the important change of title as well.[99] In this case, all of the earlier variants (except for the two possible compositorial ones) would need to represent E1^b proof-alterations made on

[99] On March 16 in returning the proof to Smith, Elder, Hawthorne referred to the "postscript", and this, again, is the word he employed on April 4 to Bright: "However, the second edition is published, I believe, and my Postscript along with it" (MS, collection of Norman Holmes Pearson, transcript courtesy of Professor Pearson). These references suggest no dissatisfaction with an earlier choice of title. The alternative, of course, is to conjecture that the title always was "Postscript" and for reasons of his own Ticknor changed it to "Conclusion". That in his March 9 letter to Ticknor about the addition, Hawthorne's phrase is "to add a few pages to the concluding chapter" very likely means nothing as evidence either in favor of "Conclusion" as his own first choice or as Ticknor's substitution (MS, Berg Collection, New York Public Library).

March 16, granting the direction of change that has been assumed.[100] Yet if this is so, the question arises why, no more than two days later, Hawthorne did not mark in the E1^b proof some equivalent of the most important literary revision between the two forms.[101] If, to escape this dilemma, we reverse the order and conjecture that the Boston manuscript was mailed posthaste, with the English (whether original or copy) retained for further revision, some of which at least we see in E1^b, we come up against the uncomfortably short time interval between the March 14 subscription (in the morning?) and the letter returning proofs dated March 16 (in the evening?) that could have been mailed no later than March 17. However, of the two this explanation has the fewer problems attached, provided we accept the shorter form of Kenyon's answer as the revision.

Somewhat the same impasse is reached if, as is perhaps more probable in view of Hawthorne's usual method of composition, he wrote a draft and then made two fair copies. If the Boston is the earlier copy, we should need to conjecture that he had it mailed forthwith when completed on March 14, and then that he proceeded to copy the version that was to be sent to Smith, Elder, which was mailed either late on March 14 or just possibly early on March 15. If we reverse this and conjecture the English as the earlier, and the first mailed, with the Boston the later copy of the draft original, once again we must assign the

[100] That proof-correction exists in E1^b may perhaps be inferred from the correct form "Trinita de' Monti" at 466.19 (given the acceptable, at this time, lack of a grave accent in "Trinita") as against the Boston error "Trinità de' Monte" which may reflect the manuscript form. One might guess that this change is due to Sophia, who on several occasions in the manuscript of the romance had corrected her husband's uncertain Italian. On the other hand, the correction could have been made by the English compositor or copyreader.

[101] If the brief E1^b version of Kenyon's answer is also thought to be a proof-revision, then the matter of priority of the two inscriptions becomes of no editorial import since all E1^b variant readings would represent Hawthorne's final intentions as formulated in the proof. Such activity in proof, however, was not a characteristic of the text of this romance.

majority of the early E_1^b variants to proof-revision and query why, in proof, the important Boston revision of Kenyon's words was not even attempted.

On the whole, the most balanced hypothesis that seems best to fit all the evidence places the Boston version of the E_1^b Postscript as the earlier inscribed, with the succinct reference to Donatello's whereabouts as a revision probably made in copying from a common original, or else in a review of the second manuscript, after the Boston form had been mailed and was no longer available.[102] The other English variants would then be, in the main, revision made in the course of copying, or in review, with some admixture of proof-correction as in the almost certain proof-change of "Monte" to "Monti" (provided the English compositor or copyreader was not responsible).

The E_1^b printing of the Postscript, thus, has been chosen as copy-text for the Centenary Edition and its substantive readings have been followed, although some few borrowings from the Boston printing of the Conclusion have been made in the accidentals when they seemed to represent a more faithful rendering of Hawthorne's lost manuscript than is found in the English print; and a few minor accidentals changes have been made editorially for conformity with spellings normalized in the preceding text.

With the exception of this Postscript, then, the Centenary text of *The Marble Faun* is essentially an exact transcript

[102] If Hawthorne were so concerned to get copy to Ticknor that he did not wait for English proof-sheets, it is reasonable to suppose that he would prepare the Boston copy first and get it in the mail at the first moment in order not to miss a steamer. (The "Arabia" sailed from Liverpool on March 17. Presumably any packet would have missed the "City of Washington," which sailed on March 14.) Smith, Elder though in process of preparing a second printing had been alerted to the writing of the Postscript and could well wait a few hours, or a day. No emergency would seem to exist to rush copy to London at all costs, whereas Hawthorne might well suppose that Ticknor was about to release the next, or post-publication, printing and would not be inclined to delay merely on the promise of copy.

of the British Museum manuscript in its finally revised state save for the exclusion of twelve alterations conjectured to have been made without authority by Sophia Hawthorne. Substituted for manuscript readings are twenty-six substantive or other variants taken from the first edition ($E1^a$) believed to be Hawthorne's revisory proof-alterations (notes 66 and 91), and twenty-seven additional readings from the first edition thought to be Hawthorne's correction of manuscript errors, in case these escaped the compositors' correction (note 65), and fifty obvious manuscript slips doubtless corrected by the compositors in the setting.[103] Excluded are 172 first-edition substantive variants thought to represent unauthoritative printer's errors not corrected in the proofreading (notes 79, 85, 87–88, 92), or mistaken Hawthorne proof-corrections. For these the manuscript readings have been preferred.

In preparing his manuscript for the English printer Hawthorne for some forms adopted uncharacteristic spellings that he presumed to be English and hence would cause less trouble to the English compositors than his ordinary American spellings. Not all of these attempts at anglicizing his spelling were by any means consistent, and some few were not accepted by the compositors. These special manuscript spellings have been preserved for their linguistic interest, and, in accord with the editorial theory for Centenary texts, have been extended for consistency to encompass the inconsistent spellings of the same words which he inadvertently failed to anglicize. Most of these spellings concern the -*our* versus -*or* endings, in which Hawthorne made a valiant attempt to be an -*our* speller for this manuscript. In general, although

[103] These fifty accepted compositorial corrections consist of the sixteen in non-control sheets listed in note 84; sixteen dittographic slips in non-control (52.7, 53.26, 61.1, 62.3, 134.2, 151.12, 156.15, 169.8, 188.17, 199.15, 206.4, 244.1, 319.8, 354.8, 385.23, 385.24); and eighteen writing slips in control (247.18, 247.31, 248.23, 249.21, 249.23, 268.20, 268.34, 277.12, 292.7, 294.2, 307.28, 308.12, 387.34, 393.22, 397.8, 398.19, 439.14, 453.9).

he was inconsistent, he succeeded more often than not in his anglicizing so that Centenary editorial alteration for uniformity (all of which is recorded in the List of Emendations) ordinarily is based on the majority practice of the manuscript. However, for whatever obscure linguistic reason, Hawthorne so seldom used the *-our* ending in the single word *neighbor* that to emend this spelling to *neighbour* like the rest would have done considerable violence to the manuscript custom. Hence the very few appearances of *neighbour* have been normalized as *neighbor* in the contrary direction to other *-our* forms.

Some few other normalizations of inconsistent spelling forms customary in Hawthorne manuscripts have been made editorially in order to secure consistency of texture according to Hawthorne's majority practice. The editors have had to use their discretion in the transcription of a few words with *-ise* or *-ize* endings, since Hawthorne's inscription of *s* and *z* does not always differentiate the two letters clearly. Moreover, his minuscule *a* is sometimes left open and cannot always be distinguished firmly from his *u*. Thus the forms to reproduce must sometimes be determined from other occurrences in the manuscript or in similar documents. The editors have carefully considered each case on its merits and transcribed the form that seemed to be intended in the inscription and that was consistent with Hawthorne's established custom.

Critical emendation of the word-division has been undertaken to normalize anomalies according to forms customarily favored by Hawthorne.

Some punctuation emendations have proved necessary (a) to normalize anomalies, as above; (b) less often, to substitute necessary or manifestly superior first-edition punctuation which in a very few cases may be (though not necessarily) the result of proof-alteration; and (c) to correct a few manuscript errors reproduced in the print. All the foregoing have been recorded, with the immediate source of the emendation indicated. However, it must be understood that no edition after the first English printing of *Transformation* has any actual authority except for three specific readings, two of which appear in Hawthorne's letter to Smith, Elder and are corrected in E2, and the third conjectured to have been attempted in I^c, though never altered in any English edition.

An editorial attempt has also been made to introduce uniformity into Hawthorne's inconsistent use of personifying capitals.

The usual silent alterations, in the categories listed in the general discussion of textual procedures appended to this volume, have been effected. Manuscript spacing like "I 'll" or "had n't", not always consistent in the original though often characteristic of the period, has been silently modernized. Dashes that Hawthorne inserted to fill out the manuscript line to the right margin have been ignored unless ambiguous.

In the apparatus, non-substantive points of variance are ignored when they have nothing to do with the main purpose of the entry; in these circumstances the form of the variant in the MS copy-text is the only one noted. For example, if one were recording the editorial emendation to a capital the entry might read:

167.30 Dome] CENTENARY; dome MS, E1–E3, I–IV

That the manuscript might follow the word with a comma, E1^a with a semicolon, and other editions possibly with variable punctuation, is not recorded, since the punctuation in the text is that of MS and thus it is not the variant that is being listed as an emendation.

Apart from the divergences noted above and in the appendix discussion of general editorial procedures, the text of *The Marble Faun* is established here for the first time in the relative purity of its manuscript form.

F. B.

SIGNIFICANT VARIANTS BETWEEN THE FIRST ENGLISH EDITION (E1ª)
AND THE FIRST BOSTON EDITION (1ª)

NOTE: For the sole purpose of this specific investigation "significant" is used in the special sense of variants that are (a) truly substantive like 248.34, E1ª "could" vs. 1ª "would", or 275.2, "sadder" vs. 1ª "sorrier"; (b) substantive in the sense that a recognizable word is created even though by a misprint, like 290.14, E1ª "stern-" vs. 1ª "stain-", or 39.23, E1ª "form" vs. 1ª "from"; (c) changes in the number, tense, grammatical form, or doublet form of the same word, like 269.8, E1ª "sang" vs. 1ª "sung", or 296.19, E1ª "pincers" vs. 1ª "pinchers" (the subtile-subtile and farther-further doublets are excluded here as too much of a compositorial option to be "significant" bibliographically); (d) changes in the spelling of names, like 32.22 E1ª "Hoffman" vs. 1ª "Hoffmann"; or (e) simple misprints that might have been transmitted thoughtlessly, like 307.11, E1ª "dirty" vs. 1ª "dirty". The control sheets are 30-37 and 47-55.

Centenary	E1ª and Sheet	E1ª	1ª
4.18	I,xiii.16 (π)	noble	admirable
21.10	I,29.2 (2)	these	those (MS)
21.15	I,29.8 (2)	then	than (MS)
32.22	I,49.17 (4)	Hoffman (MS)	Hoffmann
39.23	I,63.19 (4)	form	from (MS)
42.8	I,68.18 (5)	Mariam	Miriam (MS)
162.18	II,18.13 (20)	grieves (MS)	grieves
169.2	II,30.19 (20)	literary	literally (MS)
176.16	II,45.1 (21)	trode (MS)	trod
204.22	II,95.14 (24)	them (MS)	there
216.15	II,118.11 (26)	Thomaso	Tomaso (MS)
220.4-5	II,125.17 (26)	as much as if (MS)	as if
247.30	II,177.22 (30)	persuasibility	persuadability (MS)
248.34	II,180.4 (30)	could (MS)	would
251.6	II,184.9 (30)	could (MS)	would
255.8	II,191.16 (30)	of the mid- (MS)	of mid-
264.14	II,209.11 (32)	life-line (MS)	lifetime
265.17	II,211.15 (32)	art (MS)	heart
269.8	II,219.1 (32)	sang (MS)	sung
270.16	II,222.3 (32)	kindly (MS)	kind
274.19	II,229.1 (33)	chanced to find	happened upon (MS)
274.26	II,229.10 (33)	figures	shows (MS)
275.2	II,230.1 (33)	sadder	sorrier (MS)
276.15	II,232.16 (33)	site (MS)	sight
281.23	II,242.13 (34)	moment, he	moment? He (MS)

SIGNIFICANT VARIANTS BETWEEN THE FIRST ENGLISH EDITION (E1ᵃ)
AND THE FIRST BOSTON EDITION (Iᵃ)—*Continued*

Centenary	E1ᵃ and Sheet	E1ᵃ	Iᵃ
285.9	II,249.13 (34)	heart sustenance	heart, sustenance*
290.14	II,259.7 (35)	stern- (MS)	stain-
290.20	II,259.14 (35)	sum (MS)	hum
294.12	II,266.21 (35)	caucus (MS)	canvass
296.19	II,271.8 (35)	pincers (MS)	pinchers
301.20	II,280.15 (36)	Etruscan (MS)	Etrucean
302.11	II,282.3 (36)	habitations such (MS)	such habitations
307.11	II,291.18 (37)	dirty (MS)	dirtly
337.30	III,52.21 (41)	Baberini (MS)	Barberini
370.10	III,113.2 (45)	*omit* (MS)	as
387.26	III,146.18 (47)	had trodden	trod (MS)
389.11	III,149.19 (47)	baioccho (MS)	baiocco
391.10	III,153.2 (47)	art (MS)	heart
391.14	III,153.7 (47)	Belvedere	Belvidere (MS)
392.23	III,155.17 (47)	proceeds	avails (MS)
401.17	III,172.10 (48)	when (MS)	where
404.27	III,178.18 (49)	at (MS)	as
412.17	III,193.10 (50)	dead (MS)	dread
414.15	III,197.8 (50)	shrine, or on the	shrine, or the†
421.10	III,208.21 (50)	a charge (MS)	charge
429.26	III,223.21 (51)	we (MS)	I
434.33	III,233.22 (52)	lost (MS)	last
443.16	III,249.22 (53)	could (MS)	would
445.25	III,253.20 (53)	aggregated (MS)	aggregate
446.31	III,256.4 (53)	to him let him blood	to him to let him take blood‡
448.32	III,260.4 (54)	Piazza (MS)	Palazzo
455.11–12	III,271.13–14 (54)	the web . . . its threads (MS)	its web . . . the threads
460.25	II,281.15 (55)	sentiment (MS)	sentiments

* MS reads "heart-sustenance".
† MS reads "shrine, on the".
‡ MS reads "to let him blood".

PLATE VARIANTS: "THE MARBLE FAUN"

VOLUME I

	A	B	C	D	E
Prelim	Pref-Cont	Cont-Pref	Pref-Cont		Pref-Cont
Gathered	8	12	12		12
Signed	12	12	12		12
Copyright page					SEVENTEENTH THOUSAND.

Centenary Page-Line	MS Reading	"Transformation" Sheet, Page-Line	"Transformation" Reading	"Marble Faun" Page-Line	A	B	C	D	E
				vii	∨	1*	∨		∨
				ix	1*	∨	∨		∨
7.6	gaily	1/I,14.19	gaily	17.17	gaily	⁓	⁓		gayly
40.31	Nature	5/I,66.5	nature	56.21	nature	⁓	⁓		Nature
58.33	face;—	7/I,99.21	face∧—	78.15	face∧—	⁓∧—	⁓∧—		⁓—
59.9	sensibility,	7/I,100.11	sensibility∧	78.24	sensibility,	⁓,	⁓,		⁓∧
68.27	bye	8/I,117.16	bye	90.4	bye	⁓	⁓		by
101.24	history∧—	12/I,177.19	history∧—	131.4	history∧—	⁓∧—	⁓∧—		⁓—
101.27	ink∧—	12/I,178.1	ink∧—	131.7	ink∧—	⁓∧—	⁓∧—		⁓—
152.14	slily	17/I,272.8	slily	192.12	slily	⁓	⁓		slyly
162.18	grieves	20/II,18.13	grieves	204.22	grives	⁓	⁓		grieves
180.10	for	22/II,52.1	for	225.22	for	⁓	on		⁓
204.22	them	24/II,95.14	them	252.30	there	⁓	them		⁓
218.19	nevertheless∧	26/II,122.13	nevertheless∧	269.22	nevertheless∧	⁓∧	⁓∧		⁓,

PLATE VARIANTS: "THE MARBLE FAUN"

VOLUME II

	A	B	C	D	E
Gathered	8	12	12	12	12
Signed	12	12	12	12	12
Copyright page					SEVENTEENTH THOUSAND.

Centenary Page-Line	MS Reading	"Transformation" Sheet, Page-Line	"Transformation" Reading	"Marble Faun" Page-Line	A	B	C	D	E
233.13	friend;	28/II,149.4	friend∧—	9.27	friend∧—	⌒⌇	⌒⌇	⌒⌇	⌒⌇	⌒⌇
233.15	woods;—	28/II,149.7	woods∧—	9.29	woods∧—	⌒∨	⌒∨	⌒∨	⌒∨	⌒⌇
239.4	era, (	28/II,160.19	era∧—	17.2	era∧—	⌒⌇	⌒⌇	⌒⌇	⌒⌇	⌒⌇
239.5	abundant,)	28/II,160.20	abundant∧—	17.3	abundant∧—	⌒∨	⌒∨	⌒∨	⌒∨	⌒⌇
294.22	intercourse,	35/II,267.12	intercourse,	84.24	intercourse,	⌒∨	⌒∨	⌒∨	⌒∨	⌒⌇
301.20	Etruscan	36/II,280.15	Etruscan	92.23	Etruscan		⌇	Etruscan	⌇	⌇
301.24	fall∧—	36/II,280.21	fall∧—	92.28	fall∧—	⌒⌇	⌒⌇	⌒⌇	⌒⌇	⌒⌇
301.24	away∧—	36/II,280.21	away∧—	92.28	away∧—	⌒∨	⌒∨	⌒∨	⌒∨	⌒⌇
302.18	country∧—	36/II,282.11	country∧—	93.27	country∧—	⌒∨	⌒∨	⌒∨	⌒∨	⌒⌇
302.18	here∧—	36/II,282.12	here∧—	93.28	here∧—	⌒⌇	⌒⌇	⌒⌇	⌒⌇	⌒⌇
306.3	strangely	37/II,289.9	strangely	98.3	strangely	⌇	⌇	⌇	strangelg	⌇
306.4	figure!	37/II,289.10	figure!	98.4	figure!	⌇	⌇	⌇	⌇	⌇
306.6	"it	37/II,289.12	"it	98.6	"it	⌇	"⌇	"	"it	"it
306.7	himself.	37/II,289.13	himself.	98.7	himself.	⌇	⌇	⌇	⌇	⌇
306.19	Belief	37/II,290.6	belief	98.20	belief	⌇	⌇	⌇	belife	⌇

VOLUME II—Continued

Centenary Page-Line	MS Reading	"Transformation" Sheet, Page-Line	"Transformation" Reading	"Marble Faun" Page-Line	A	B	C	D	E
307.3	boneless∧	37/II,291.9	boneless∧	99.10	boneless,	⌐'	⌐'	⌐'	⌐'
307.11	dirty	37/II,291.18	dirty	99.18	dirty	⌐	dirty	⌐	⌐
322.32	ever,	39/III,27.1	ever,	118.4	ever,	⌐'	⌐'	⌐'	⌐'
				197	4*	9*	<	<	<
390.16	medium.	47/III,152.4	medium.	198.16	medium,	⌐'	⌐'	⌐'	⌐'
391.10	art	47/III,153.2	ar	199.13	heart	⌐	art	⌐	⌐
391.22	Errour...Evil	47/III,153.17	Error...Evil	199.26	error...evil	}	Error...Evil	}	}
406.8	anxiety,	49/III,181.15	anxiety,	217.19	anxiety;	⌐;	⌐,	⌐'	⌐'
406.33	Heaven	49/III,182.22	Heaven	218.15	heaven	⌐	Heaven	⌐	⌐
410.33	before—	49/III,190.8-9	before—	223.8	before,	⌐'	⌐—	⌐|	⌐—
412.17	dead	50/III,193.10	dead	225.4	dread	⌐	dead	⌐	⌐
413.18	vain;	50/III,195.10	vain;	226.11	vain;	⌐<	⌐<	⌐<	⌐<
416.23	forever?	50/III,201.14	for ever?	230.5	forever.	⌐'	⌐'	⌐?	⌐?
416.26	aid?	50/III,201.17	aid?	230.7	aid.	⌐'	⌐'	⌐'	}
421.10	a charge	50/III,208.21	a charge	234.24	charge	⌐	a charge	}	}
423.19	de'	51/III,213.8	de'	237.14	de∧	⌐<	⌐'	⌐'	⌐'
443.18	bestrewn.	53/III,250.2	bestrewn.	260.30	bestrewn∧	⌐<	⌐'	⌐'	⌐'
			Conclusion..........No		No	No	No	Yes	Yes

THE MARBLE FAUN

PREFACE

I T IS NOW seven or eight years (so many, at all events,
that I cannot precisely remember the epoch) since the
Author of this Romance last appeared before the Public.
It had grown to be a custom with him, to introduce each of
his humble publications with a familiar kind of Preface,
addressed nominally to the Public at large, but really to a
character with whom he felt entitled to use far greater freedom. He meant it for that one congenial friend—more comprehensive of his purposes, more appreciative of his success,
more indulgent of his short-comings, and, in all respects,
closer and kinder than a brother—that all-sympathizing critic,
in short, whom an author never actually meets, but to whom
he implicitly makes his appeal, whenever he is conscious
of having done his best.

The antique fashion of Prefaces recognized this genial
personage as the 'Kind Reader,' the 'Gentle Reader,' the 'Beloved,' the 'Indulgent,' or, at coldest, the 'Honoured Reader,'
to whom the prim old author was wont to make his preliminary explanations and apologies, with the certainty that
they would be favourably received. I never personally encountered, nor corresponded through the Post, with this
Representative Essence of all delightful and desirable qualities
which a Reader can possess. But, fortunately for myself, I
never therefore concluded him to be merely a mythic character. I had always a sturdy faith in his actual existence, and

wrote for him, year after year, during which the great Eye of the Public (as well it might) almost utterly overlooked my small productions.

Unquestionably, this Gentle, Kind, Benevolent, Indulgent, and most Beloved and Honoured Reader, did once exist for me, and (in spite of the infinite chances against a letter's reaching its destination, without a definite address) duly received the scrolls which I flung upon whatever wind was blowing, in the faith that they would find him out. But, is he extant now? In these many years, since he last heard from me, may he not have deemed his earthly task accomplished, and have withdrawn to the Paradise of Gentle Readers, wherever it may be, to the enjoyments of which his kindly charity, on my behalf, must surely have entitled him? I have a sad foreboding that this may be the truth. The Gentle Reader, in the case of any individual author, is apt to be extremely short-lived; he seldom outlasts a literary fashion, and, except in very rare instances, closes his weary eyes before the writer has half done with him. If I find him at all, it will probably be under some mossy grave-stone, inscribed with a half-obliterated name, which I shall never recognize.

Therefore, I have little heart or confidence (especially, writing, as I do, in a foreign land, and after a long, long absence from my own) to presume upon the existence of that friend of friends, that unseen brother of the soul, whose apprehensive sympathy has so often encouraged me to be egotistical in my Prefaces, careless though unkindly eyes should skim over what was never meant for them. I stand upon ceremony, now, and, after stating a few particulars about the work which is here offered to the Public, must make my most reverential bow, and retire behind the curtain.

This Romance was sketched out during a residence of considerable length in Italy, and has been re-written and prepared for the press, in England. The author proposed to himself merely to write a fanciful story, evolving a thoughtful moral, and did not purpose attempting a portraiture of Italian manners and character. He has lived too long abroad, not to be aware that a foreigner seldom acquires that knowledge of a country, at once flexible and profound, which may justify him in endeavouring to idealize its traits.

Italy, as the site of his Romance, was chiefly valuable to him as affording a sort of poetic or fairy precinct, where actualities would not be so terribly insisted upon, as they are, and must needs be, in America. No author, without a trial, can conceive of the difficulty of writing a Romance about a country where there is no shadow, no antiquity, no mystery, no picturesque and gloomy wrong, nor anything but a common-place prosperity, in broad and simple daylight, as is happily the case with my dear native land. It will be very long, I trust, before romance-writers may find congenial and easily handled themes either in the annals of our stalwart Republic, or in any characteristic and probable events of our individual lives. Romance and poetry, like ivy, lichens, and wall-flowers, need Ruin to make them grow.

In re-writing these volumes, the Author was somewhat surprised to see the extent to which he had introduced descriptions of various Italian objects, antique, pictorial, and statuesque. Yet these things fill the mind, everywhere in Italy, and especially in Rome, and cannot easily be kept from flowing out upon the page, when one writes freely, and with self-enjoyment. And, again, while reproducing the book, on the broad and dreary sands of Redcar, with the gray German Ocean tumbling in upon me, and the northern blast always howling in my ears, the complete change of scene made these Italian reminiscences shine out so vividly, that I could not find in my heart to cancel them.

An act of justice remains to be performed towards two men of genius, with whose productions the Author has allowed himself to use a quite unwarrantable freedom. Having imagined a sculptor, in this Romance, it was necessary to provide him with such works in marble as should be in keeping with the artistic ability which he was supposed to possess. With this view, the Author laid felonious hands upon a certain bust of Milton and a statue of a Pearl-Diver, which he found in the studio of Mr. PAUL AKERS, and secretly conveyed them to the premises of his imaginary friend, in the Via Frezza. Not content even with these spoils, he committed a further robbery upon a magnificent statue of Cleopatra, the production of Mr. WILLIAM W. STORY, an artist whom his country and the world will not long fail to appreciate. He had thoughts of appropriating, likewise, a certain door of bronze, by Mr. RANDOLPH ROGERS, representing the history of Columbus in a series of admirable bas-reliefs, but was deterred by an unwillingness to meddle with public property. Were he capable of stealing from a lady, he would certainly have made free with Miss HOSMER's noble statue of Zenobia.

He now wishes to restore the above-mentioned beautiful pieces of sculpture to their proper owners, with many thanks, and the avowal of his sincere admiration. What he has said of them, in the Romance, does not partake of the fiction in which they are imbedded, but expresses his genuine opinion, which, he has little doubt, will be found in accordance with that of the Public. It is perhaps unnecessary to say, that, while stealing their designs, the Author has not taken a similar liberty with the personal characters of either of these gifted Sculptors; his own Man of Marble being entirely imaginary.

LEAMINGTON, October 15th, 1859

THE MARBLE FAUN: OR,
THE ROMANCE OF MONTE BENI

I

MIRIAM, HILDA, KENYON, DONATELLO

FOUR INDIVIDUALS, in whose fortunes we should be glad to interest the reader, happened to be standing in one of the saloons of the sculpture-gallery, in the Capitol, at Rome. It was that room (the first, after ascending the staircase) in the centre of which reclines the noble and most pathetic figure of the Dying Gladiator, just sinking into his death-swoon. Around the walls stand the Antinous, the Amazon, the Lycian Apollo, the Juno; all famous productions of antique sculpture, and still shining in the undiminished majesty and beauty of their ideal life, although the marble, that embodies them, is yellow with time, and perhaps corroded by the damp earth in which they lay buried for centuries. Here, likewise, is seen a symbol (as apt, at this moment, as it was two thousand years ago) of the Human Soul, with its choice of Innocence or Evil close at hand, in the pretty figure of a child, clasping a dove to her bosom, but assaulted by a snake.

From one of the windows of this saloon, we may see a flight of broad stone steps, descending alongside the antique and massive foundation of the Capitol, towards the battered triumphal arch of Septimius Severus, right below. Farther on, the eye skirts along the edge of the desolate Forum, (where Roman washerwomen hang out their linen to the sun,) passing over a shapeless confusion of modern edifices, piled rudely up with ancient brick and stone, and over the domes of Christian churches, built on the old pavements of heathen temples, and supported by the very pillars that once upheld them. At a distance beyond—yet but a little way, considering how much history is heaped into the intervening space—rises the great sweep of the Coliseum, with the blue sky brightening through its upper tier of arches. Far off, the view is shut in by the Alban mountains, looking just the same, amid all this decay and change, as when Romulus gazed thitherward over his half-finished wall.

We glance hastily at these things—at this bright sky, and those blue, distant mountains, and at the ruins, Etruscan, Roman, Christian, venerable with a threefold antiquity, and at the company of world-famous statues in the saloon—in the hope of putting the reader into that state of feeling which is experienced oftenest at Rome. It is a vague sense of ponderous remembrances; a perception of such weight and density in a by-gone life, of which this spot was the centre, that the present moment is pressed down or crowded out, and our individual affairs and interests are but half as real, here, as elsewhere. Viewed through this medium, our narrative— into which are woven some airy and unsubstantial threads, intermixed with others, twisted out of the commonest stuff of human existence—may seem not widely different from the texture of all our lives. Side by side with the massiveness of the Roman Past, all matters, that we handle or dream of, now-a-days, look evanescent and visionary alike.

It might be, that the four persons, whom we are seeking to introduce, were conscious of this dreamy character of the present, as compared with the square blocks of granite wherewith the Romans built their lives. Perhaps it even contributed to the fanciful merriment which was just now their mood. When we find ourselves fading into shadows and unrealities, it seems hardly worth while to be sad, but rather to laugh as gaily as we may, and ask little reason wherefore.

Of these four friends of ours, three were artists, or connected with Art; and, at this moment, they had been simultaneously struck by a resemblance between one of the antique statues, a well-known master-piece of Grecian sculpture, and a young Italian, the fourth member of their party.

"You must needs confess, Kenyon," said a dark-eyed young woman, whom her friends called Miriam, "that you never chiselled out of marble, nor wrought in clay, a more vivid likeness than this, cunning a bust-maker as you think yourself. The portraiture is perfect in character, sentiment, and feature. If it were a picture, the resemblance might be half-illusive and imaginary; but here, in this Pentelic marble, it is a substantial fact, and may be tested by absolute touch and measurement. Our friend Donatello is the very Faun of Praxiteles. Is it not true, Hilda?"

"Not quite—almost—yes, I really think so," replied Hilda, a slender, brown-haired, New England girl, whose perceptions of form and expression were wonderfully clear and delicate.— "If there is any difference between the two faces, the reason may be, I suppose, that the Faun dwelt in woods and fields, and consorted with his like; whereas, Donatello has known cities a little, and such people as ourselves. But the resemblance is very close, and very strange."

"Not so strange," whispered Miriam mischievously; "for no Faun in Arcadia was ever a greater simpleton than Donatello. He has hardly a man's share of wit, small as that may be. It is a pity there are no longer any of this congenial race of rustic creatures, for our friend to consort with!"

"Hush, naughty one!" returned Hilda. "You are very ungrateful, for you well know he has wit enough to worship you, at all events."

"Then the greater fool he!" said Miriam so bitterly that Hilda's quiet eyes were somewhat startled.

"Donatello, my dear friend," said Kenyon, in Italian, "pray gratify us all by taking the exact attitude of this statue."

The young man laughed, and threw himself into the position in which the statue has been standing for two or three thousand years. In truth, allowing for the difference of costume, and if a lion's skin could have been substituted for his modern Talma, and a rustic pipe for his stick, Donatello might have figured perfectly as the marble Faun, miraculously softened into flesh and blood.

"Yes; the resemblance is wonderful," observed Kenyon, after examining the marble and the man with the accuracy of a sculptor's eye.—"There is one point, however—or, rather, two points—in respect to which our friend Donatello's abundant curls will not permit us to say whether the likeness is carried into minute detail."

And the sculptor directed the attention of the party to the ears of the beautiful statue which they were contemplating.

But we must do more than merely refer to this exquisite work of art; it must be described, however inadequate may be the effort to express its magic peculiarity in words.

The Faun is the marble image of a young man, leaning his right arm on the trunk or stump of a tree; one hand hangs carelessly by his side; in the other, he holds the fragment of a pipe, or some such sylvan instrument of music. His only garment—a lion's skin, with the claw upon his shoulder—falls half-way down his back, leaving the limbs and entire front of the figure nude. The form, thus displayed, is marvellously graceful, but has a fuller and more rounded outline, more flesh, and less of heroic muscle, than the old sculptors were wont to assign to their types of masculine beauty. The character of the face corresponds with the figure; it is most agreeable in outline and feature, but rounded, and somewhat voluptuously developed, especially about the throat and chin; the nose is almost straight, but very slightly curves inward, thereby acquiring an indescribable charm of geniality and humour. The mouth, with its full, yet delicate lips, seems so nearly to smile outright, that it calls forth a responsive smile. The whole statue—unlike anything else that ever was wrought in that severe material of marble—conveys the idea of an amiable and sensual creature, easy, mirthful, apt for jollity, yet not incapable of being touched by pathos. It is impossible to gaze long at this stone image without conceiving a kindly sentiment towards it, as if its substance were warm to the touch, and imbued with actual life. It comes very close to some of our pleasantest sympathies.

Perhaps it is the very lack of moral severity, of any high and heroic ingredient in the character of the Faun, that makes it so delightful an object to the human eye and to the frailty of the human heart. The being, here represented, is endowed with no principle of virtue, and would be incapable of comprehending such. But he would be true and honest, by dint of his simplicity. We should expect from him no sacrifice nor effort for an abstract cause; there is not an atom of martyr's stuff in all that softened marble; but he has a capacity for strong and warm attachment, and might act devotedly through its impulse, and even die for it at need. It is possible, too, that the Faun might be educated through the medium of his emotions; so that the coarser, animal portion of his nature might eventually be thrown into the back-ground, though never utterly expelled.

The animal nature, indeed, is a most essential part of the Faun's composition; for the characteristics of the brute creation meet and combine with those of humanity, in this strange, yet true and natural conception of antique poetry and art. Praxiteles has subtly diffused, throughout his work, that mute mystery which so hopelessly perplexes us, whenever we attempt to gain an intellectual or sympathetic knowledge of the lower orders of creation. The riddle is indicated, however, only by two definite signs; these are the two ears of the Faun, which are leaf-shaped, terminating in little peaks, like those of some species of animals. Though not so seen in the marble, they are probably to be considered as clothed in fine, downy fur. In the coarser representations of this class of mythological creatures, there is another token of brute kindred—a certain caudal appendage—which, if the Faun of Praxiteles must be supposed to possess it at all, is hidden by the lion's skin that forms his garment. The pointed and furry ears, therefore, are the sole indications of his wild, forest nature.

Only a sculptor of the finest imagination, the most delicate taste, the sweetest feeling, and the rarest artistic skill—in a word, a sculptor and a poet too—could have first dreamed of a Faun in this guise, and then have succeeded in imprisoning the sportive and frisky thing, in marble. Neither man nor animal, and yet no monster, but a being in whom both races meet, on friendly ground! The idea grows coarse, as we handle it, and hardens in our grasp. But, if the spectator broods long over the statue, he will be conscious of its spell; all the pleasantness of sylvan life, all the genial and happy characteristics of creatures that dwell in woods and fields, will seem to be mingled and kneaded into one substance, along with the kindred qualities in the human soul. Trees, grass, flowers, woodland streamlets, cattle, deer, and unsophisticated man! The essence of all these was compressed long ago, and still exists, within that discoloured marble surface of the Faun of Praxiteles.

And, after all, the idea may have been no dream, but

rather a poet's reminiscence of a period when man's affinity with Nature was more strict, and his fellowship with every living thing more intimate and dear.

THE FAUN

D ONATELLO," playfully cried Miriam, "do not leave us in this perplexity! Shake aside those brown curls, my friend, and let us see whether this marvellous resemblance extends to the very tips of the ears. If so, we shall like you all the better!"

"No, no, dearest Signorina!" answered Donatello laughing, but with a certain earnestness.—"I entreat you to take the tips of my ears for granted."

As he spoke, the young Italian made a skip and jump, light enough for a veritable Faun; so as to place himself quite beyond the reach of the fair hand that was outstretched, as if to settle the matter by actual examination.

"I shall be like a wolf of the Apennines," he continued, taking his stand on the other side of the Dying Gladiator, "if you touch my ears ever so softly. None of my race could endure it. It has always been a tender point with my forefathers and me."

He spoke in Italian, with the Tuscan rusticity of accent, and an unshaped sort of utterance, betokening that he must heretofore have been chiefly conversant with rural people.

"Well, well," said Miriam, "your tender point—your two

tender points, if you have them—shall be safe, so far as I am concerned. But how strange this likeness is, after all!—and how delightful, if it really includes the pointed ears! Oh, it is impossible, of course," she continued, in English, "with a real and common-place young man, like Donatello; but you see how this peculiarity defines the position of the Faun, and, while putting him where he cannot exactly assert his brotherhood, still disposes us kindly towards the kindred creature. He is not supernatural, but just on the verge of Nature, and yet within it. What is the nameless charm of this idea, Hilda? You can feel it more delicately than I."

"It perplexes me," said Hilda, thoughtfully, and shrinking a little; "neither do I quite like to think about it."

"But, surely," said Kenyon, "you agree with Miriam and me, that there is something very touching and impressive in this statue of the Faun. In some long-past age, he must really have existed. Nature needed, and still needs, this beautiful creature, standing betwixt man and animal, sympathizing with each, comprehending the speech of either race, and interpreting the whole existence of one to the other. What a pity that he has forever vanished from the hard and dusty paths of life—unless," added the sculptor in a sportive whisper, "Donatello be actually he!"

"You cannot conceive how this fantasy takes hold of me," responded Miriam, between jest and earnest. "Imagine, now, a real being, similar to this mythic Faun; how happy, how genial, how satisfactory would be his life, enjoying the warm, sensuous, earthy side of Nature; revelling in the merriment of woods and streams; living as our four-footed kindred do—as mankind did in its innocent childhood, before sin, sorrow, or morality itself, had ever been thought of! Ah, Kenyon, if Hilda, and you, and I—if I, at least—had pointed ears! For I suppose the Faun had no conscience, no remorse, no burthen on the heart, no troublesome recollections of any sort; no dark future neither!"

"What a tragic tone was that last, Miriam!" said the sculptor; and looking into her face, he was startled to behold it pale and tear-stained. "How suddenly this mood has come over you!"

"Let it go as it came," said Miriam, "like a thunder-shower in this Roman sky. All is sunshine again, you see."

Donatello's refractoriness as regarded his ears had evidently cost him something; and he now came close to Miriam's side, gazing at her with an appealing air, as if to solicit forgiveness. His mute, helpless gesture of entreaty had something pathetic in it, and yet might well enough excite a laugh; so like it was to what you may see in the aspect of a hound, when he thinks himself in fault or disgrace. It was difficult to make out the character of this young man. So full of animal life as he was, so joyous in his deportment, so handsome, so physically well-developed, he made no impression of incompleteness, of maimed or stinted nature. And yet, in social intercourse, these familiar friends of his habitually and instinctively allowed for him, as for a child or some other lawless thing, exacting no strict obedience to conventional rules, and hardly noticing his eccentricities enough to pardon them. There was an indefinable characteristic about Donatello, that set him outside of rules.

He caught Miriam's hand, kissed it, and gazed into her eyes without saying a word. She smiled, and bestowed on him a little, careless caress, singularly like what one would give to a pet dog, when he puts himself in the way to receive it. Not that it was so decided a caress, neither, but only the merest touch, somewhere between a pat and a tap of the finger; it might be a mark of fondness, or perhaps a playful pretence of punishment. At all events, it appeared to afford Donatello exquisite pleasure; insomuch that he danced quite round the wooden railing that fences in the Dying Gladiator.

"It is the very step of the Dancing Faun," said Miriam apart to Hilda. "What a child, or what a simpleton, he is! I continually find myself treating Donatello as if he were the merest unfledged chicken; and yet he can claim no such privileges in the right of his tender age; for he is at least—how old should you think him, Hilda?"

"Twenty years, perhaps," replied Hilda, glancing at Donatello. "But, indeed, I cannot tell;—hardly so old, on second thoughts, or possibly older. He has nothing to do with time, but has a look of eternal youth in his face."

"All underwitted people have that look," said Miriam scornfully.

"Donatello has certainly the gift of eternal youth, as Hilda suggests," observed Kenyon laughing; "for, judging by the date of this statue, (which, I am more and more convinced, Praxiteles carved on purpose for him,) he must be at least twenty-five centuries old. And he still looks as young as ever."

"What age have you, Donatello?" asked Miriam.

"Signorina, I do not know," he answered. "No great age, however; for I have only lived since I met you."

"Now, what old man of society could have turned a silly compliment more smartly than that!" exclaimed Miriam. "Nature and art are just at one, sometimes. But what a happy ignorance is this of our friend Donatello! Not to know his own age! It is equivalent to being immortal on earth. If I could only forget mine!"

"It is too soon to wish that," observed the sculptor. "You are scarcely older than Donatello looks."

"I should be content, then," rejoined Miriam, "if I could only forget one day of all my life."—Then she seemed to repent of this allusion, and hastily added, "A woman's days are so tedious, that it is a boon to leave even one of them out of the account."

The foregoing conversation had been carried on in a mood in which all imaginative people, whether artists or poets, love to indulge. In this frame of mind, they sometimes find their profoundest truths side by side with the idlest jest, and utter one or the other, apparently without distinguishing which is the most valuable, or assigning any considerable value to either. The resemblance between the marble Faun and their living companion had made a deep, half-serious, half-mirthful impression on these three friends, and had taken them into a certain airy region, lifting up—as it is so pleasant to feel them lifted—their heavy, earthly feet from the actual soil of life. The world had been set afloat, as it were, for a moment, and relieved them, for just so long, of all customary responsibility for what they thought and said.

It might be under this influence, (or perhaps because sculptors always abuse one another's works,) that Kenyon threw in a criticism upon the Dying Gladiator.

"I used to admire this statue exceedingly," he remarked; "but, latterly, I find myself getting weary and annoyed that the man should be such a length of time leaning on his arm, in the very act of death. If he is so terribly hurt, why does he not sink down and die, without further ado? Flitting moments—imminent emergencies—imperceptible intervals between two breaths—ought not to be incrusted with the eternal repose of marble; in any sculptural subject, there should be a moral standstill, since there must of necessity be a physical one. Otherwise, it is like flinging a block of marble up into the air, and, by some trick or enchantment, causing it to stick there. You feel that it ought to come down, and are dissatisfied that it does not obey the natural law."

"I see," said Miriam, mischievously. "You think that sculpture should be a sort of fossilizing process. But, in truth, your frozen art has nothing like the scope and freedom of Hilda's and mine. In painting, there is no similar objection to the representation of brief snatches of time; perhaps because a story can be so much more fully told, in picture, and buttressed about with circumstances that give it an epoch. For instance, a painter never would have sent down yonder Faun out of his far antiquity, lonely and desolate, with no companion to keep his simple heart warm."

"Ah, the Faun!" cried Hilda, with a little gesture of impatience. "I have been looking at him too long; and now, instead of a beautiful statue, immortally young, I see only a corroded and discoloured stone. This change is very apt to occur in statues."

"And a similar one in pictures, surely!" retorted the sculptor. "It is the spectator's mood that transfigures the Transfiguration itself. I defy any painter to move and elevate me without my own consent and assistance."

"Then you are deficient of a sense," said Miriam.

The party now strayed onward from hall to hall of that rich gallery, pausing, here and there, to look at the multitude of noble and lovely shapes, which have been dug up out of the deep grave in which old Rome lies buried. And, still, the realization of the antique Faun, in the person of Donatello, gave a more vivid character to all these marble ghosts. Why should not each statue grow warm with life! Antinous might lift his brow, and tell us why he is forever sad. The Lycian Apollo might strike his lyre; and, at the first vibration, that other Faun in red marble, who keeps up a motionless dance, should frisk gaily forth, leading yonder Satyrs, with shaggy goat-shanks, to clatter their little hoofs upon the floor, and all join hands with Donatello! Bacchus, too, a rosy flush diffusing itself over his time-stained surface, would come down from his pedestal, and offer a cluster of purple grapes to Donatello's lips; because the god recognizes him as the woodland elf who so often shared his revels! And here, on this sarcophagus, the exquisitely carved figures might assume life, and chase one another round its verge with that wild merriment which is so strangely represented on those old burial coffers; though still with some subtile allusion to Death, carefully veiled, but forever peeping forth amid emblems of mirth and riot.

As the four friends descended the stairs, however, their play of fancy subsided into a much more sombre mood; a result apt to follow upon such exhilaration as that which had so recently taken possession of them.

"Do you know," said Miriam confidentially to Hilda, "I doubt the reality of this likeness of Donatello to the Faun, which we have been talking so much about? To say the truth, it never struck me so forcibly as it did Kenyon and yourself, though I gave in to whatever you were pleased to fancy, for the sake of a moment's mirth and wonder."

"I was certainly in earnest, and you seemed equally so," replied Hilda, glancing back at Donatello, as if to re-assure herself of the resemblance.—"But faces change so much, from hour to hour, that the same set of features has often no keeping with itself;—to an eye, at least, which looks at expression more than outline. How sad and sombre he has grown, all of a sudden!"

"Angry too, methinks!—nay, it is anger much more than sadness," said Miriam. "I have seen Donatello in this mood, once or twice before. If you consider him well, you will observe an odd mixture of the bull-dog, or some other equally fierce brute, in our friend's composition; a trait of savageness hardly to be expected in such a gentle creature as he usually is. Donatello is a very strange young man. I wish he would not haunt my footsteps so continually."

"You have bewitched the poor lad," said the sculptor laughing. "You have a faculty of bewitching people, and it is providing you with a singular train of followers. I see another of them behind yonder pillar; and it is his presence that has aroused Donatello's wrath."

They had now emerged from the gateway of the palace; and partly concealed by one of the pillars of the portico, stood a figure such as may often be encountered in the streets and piazzas of Rome, and nowhere else. He looked as if he might just have stept out of a picture, and, in truth, was likely enough to find his way into a dozen pictures; being no other than one of those living models, dark, bushy bearded, wild of aspect and attire, whom artists convert into Saints or assassins, according as their pictorial purposes demand.

"Miriam," whispered Hilda, a little startled, "it is your Model!"

III

SUBTERRANEAN REMINISCENCES

M IRIAM'S model has so important a connection with our story, that it is essential to describe the singular mode of his first appearance, and how he subsequently became a self-appointed follower of the young female artist. In the first place, however, we must devote a page or two to certain peculiarities in the position of Miriam herself.

There was an ambiguity about this young lady, which, though it did not necessarily imply anything wrong, would have operated unfavourably as regarded her reception in society, anywhere but in Rome. The truth was, that nobody knew anything about Miriam, either for good or evil. She had made her appearance without introduction, had taken a studio, put up her card upon the door, and shown very considerable talent as a painter in oils. Her fellow-professors of the brush, it is true, showered abundant criticisms upon her pictures, allowing them to be well enough for the idle half-efforts of an amateur, but lacking both the trained skill and the practice that distinguish the works of a true artist.

Nevertheless, be their faults what they might, Miriam's pictures met with good acceptance among the patrons of modern art. Whatever technical merit they lacked, its absence was more than supplied by a warmth and passionateness, which she had the faculty of putting into her productions, and which all the world could feel. Her nature had a great deal of colour, and, in accordance with it, so likewise had her pictures.

Miriam had great apparent freedom of intercourse; her manners were so far from evincing shyness, that it seemed easy to become acquainted with her, and not difficult to develope a casual acquaintance into intimacy. Such, at least, was the impression which she made, upon brief contact, but not such the ultimate conclusion of those who really sought to know her. So airy, free, and affable was Miriam's deportment towards all who came within her sphere, that possibly they might never be conscious of the fact; but so it was, that they did not get on, and were seldom any further advanced into her good graces to-day, than yesterday. By some subtile quality, she kept people at a distance, without so much as letting them know that they were excluded from her inner circle. She resembled one of those images of light, which conjurors evoke and cause to shine before us, in apparent tangibility, only an arm's length beyond our grasp; we make a step in advance, expecting to seize the illusion, but find it still precisely so far out of our reach. Finally, society began to recognize the impossibility of getting nearer to Miriam, and gruffly acquiesced.

There were two persons, however, whom she appeared to acknowledge as friends in the closer and truer sense of the word; and both of these more favoured individuals did credit to Miriam's selection. One was a young American sculptor, of high promise, and rapidly increasing celebrity; the other, a girl of the same country, a painter, like Miriam herself, but in a widely different sphere of art. Her heart flowed out towards these two; she requited herself by their society and friendship, (and especially by Hilda's,) for all the loneliness with which, as regarded the rest of the world, she chose to be surrounded. Her two friends were conscious of the strong, yearning grasp which Miriam laid upon them, and gave her their affection in full measure; Hilda, indeed, responding with the fervency of a girl's first friendship, and Kenyon with a manly regard, in which there was nothing akin to what is distinctively called Love.

A sort of intimacy subsequently grew up between these three friends and a fourth individual; it was a young Italian, who, casually visiting Rome, had been attracted by the beauty which Miriam possessed in a remarkable degree. He had sought her, followed her, and insisted, with simple persever-ance, upon being admitted at least to her acquaintance; a boon which had been granted, when a more artful character, seeking it by a more subtile mode of pursuit, would probably have failed to obtain it. This young man, though anything but intellectually brilliant, had many agreeable characteristics which won him the kindly and half-contemptuous regard of Miriam and her two friends. It was he whom they called Donatello, and whose wonderful resemblance to the Faun of Praxiteles forms the key-note of our narrative.

Such was the position in which we find Miriam, some few months after her establishment at Rome. It must be added, however, that the world did not permit her to hide her antecedents without making her the subject of a good deal of conjecture; as was natural enough, considering the abundance of her personal charms, and the degree of notice that she attracted as an artist. There were many stories about Miriam's origin and previous life, some of which had a very probable air, while others were evidently wild and romantic fables. We cite a few, leaving the reader to designate them either under the probable or the romantic head.

It was said, for example, that Miriam was the daughter and heiress of a great Jewish banker, (an idea perhaps sug-gested by a certain rich Oriental character in her face,) and had fled from her paternal home to escape a union with a cousin, the heir of another of that golden brotherhood; the object being, to retain their vast accumulation of wealth within the family. Another story hinted, that she was a German princess, whom, for reasons of state, it was proposed to give in marriage either to a decrepit sovereign or a prince still in his cradle. According to a third statement, she was the offspring of a Southern American planter, who had given her an elaborate education and endowed her with his wealth; but the one burning drop of African blood in her veins so affected her with a sense of ignominy, that she relinquished all, and fled her country. By still another account, she was the lady of an English nobleman, and, out of mere love and honour of art, had thrown aside the splendour of her rank, and come to seek a subsistence by her pencil in a Roman studio.

In all the above cases, the fable seemed to be instigated by the large and bounteous impression which Miriam invariably made, as if necessity and she could have nothing to do with one another. Whatever deprivations she underwent must needs be voluntary. But there were other surmises, taking such a common-place view, as that Miriam was the daughter of a merchant or financier, who had been ruined in a great commercial crisis; and, possessing a taste for art, she had attempted to support herself by the pencil, in preference to the alternative of going out as governess.

Be these things how they might, Miriam, fair as she looked, was plucked up out of a mystery, and had its roots still clinging to her. She was a beautiful and attractive woman, but based, as it were, upon a cloud, and all surrounded with misty substance, so that the result was to render her sprite-like in her most ordinary manifestations. This was the case even in respect to Kenyon and Hilda, her especial friends. But such was the effect of Miriam's natural language, her generosity, kindliness, and native truth of character, that these two received her as a dear friend into their hearts, taking her good qualities as evident and genuine, and never imagining that what was hidden must be therefore evil.

We now proceed with our narrative.

The same party of friends, whom we have seen at the Sculpture Gallery of the Capitol, chanced to have gone together, some months before, to the Catacomb of Saint Calixtus. They went joyously down into that vast tomb, and wandered by torch-light through a sort of dream, in which reminiscences of church-aisles and grimy cellars—and chiefly the latter—seemed to be broken into fragments and hopelessly intermingled. The intricate passages, along which they followed their guide, had been hewn, in some forgotten age, out of a dark-red, crumbly stone. On either side were horizontal niches, where, if they held their torches closely, the shape of a human body was discernible in white ashes, into which the entire mortality of a man or woman had resolved itself. Among all this extinct dust, there might perchance be a thigh-bone, which crumbled at a touch, or possibly a skull, grinning at its own wretched plight, as is the ugly and empty habit of the thing.

Sometimes their gloomy pathway tended upward, so that, through a crevice, a little daylight glimmered down upon them, or even a streak of sunshine peeped into a burial niche; then, again, they went downward by gradual descent, or by abrupt, rudely hewn steps, into deeper and deeper recesses of the earth. Here and there, the narrow and tortuous passages widened, somewhat, developing themselves into small chapels, which once, no doubt, had been adorned with marble-work and lighted with ever-burning lamps and tapers. All such illumination and ornament, however, had long since been extinguished and stript away; except, indeed, that the low roofs of a few of these ancient sites of worship were covered with dingy stucco, and frescoed with scriptural scenes and subjects, in the dreariest stage of ruin.

In one such chapel, the guide showed them a low arch, beneath which the body of Saint Cecilia had been buried after her martyrdom, and where it lay till a sculptor saw it, and rendered it forever beautiful in marble.

In a similar spot, they found two sarcophagi, one containing a skeleton, and the other a shrivelled body, which still wore the garments of its former lifetime.

"How dismal all this is!" said Hilda shuddering. "I do not know why we came here, nor why we should stay a moment longer."

"I hate it all!" cried Donatello, with peculiar energy. "Dear friends, let us hasten back into the blessed daylight!"

From the first, Donatello had shown little appetite for the expedition; for, like most Italians, and in especial accordance with the law of his own simple and physically happy nature, this young man had an infinite repugnance to graves and skulls, and to all that ghastliness which the Gothic mind loves to associate with the idea of death. He shuddered, and looked fearfully round, drawing nearer to Miriam, whose attractive influence alone had enticed him into that gloomy region.

"What a child you are, my poor Donatello!" she observed, with the freedom which she always used towards him. "You are afraid of ghosts?"

"Yes, Signorina; terribly afraid!" said the truthful Donatello.

"I also believe in ghosts," answered Miriam, "and could tremble at them, in a suitable place. But these sepulchres are so old, and these skulls and white ashes so very dry, that methinks they have ceased to be haunted. The most awful idea, connected with the catacombs, is their interminable extent, and the possibility of going astray into this labyrinth of darkness, which broods around the little glimmer of our tapers."

"Has any one ever been lost here?" asked Kenyon of the guide.

"Surely, Signor; one, no longer ago than my father's time," said the guide; and he added, with the air of a man who believed what he was telling:—"But the first that went astray here was a pagan of old Rome, who hid himself in order to spy out, and betray the blessed Saints, who then dwelt and worshipped in these dismal places. You have heard the story, Signor? A miracle was wrought upon the accursed one; and, ever since, (for fifteen centuries, at least,) he has been groping in the darkness, seeking his way out of the Catacomb!"

"Has he ever been seen?" asked Hilda, who had great and tremulous faith in marvels of this kind.

"These eyes of mine never beheld him, Signorina; the Saints forbid!" answered the guide. "But it is well known that he watches near parties that come into the Catacomb, especially if they be heretics, hoping to lead some straggler astray. What this lost wretch pines for, almost as much as for the blessed sunshine, is a companion to be miserable with him."

"Such an intense desire for sympathy indicates something amiable in the poor fellow, at all events," observed Kenyon.

They had now reached a larger chapel than those heretofore seen; it was of a circular shape, and, though hewn out of the solid mass of red sandstone, had pillars, and a carved roof, and other tokens of a regular architectural design. Nevertheless, considered as a church, it was exceedingly minute, being scarcely twice a man's stature in height, and only two or three paces from wall to wall; and while their collected torches illuminated this one, small, consecrated spot, the great darkness spread all around it, like that immenser mystery which envelopes our little life, and into which friends vanish from us, one by one.

"Why, where is Miriam?" cried Hilda.

The party gazed hurriedly from face to face, and became aware that one of their party had vanished into the great darkness, even while they were shuddering at the remote possibility of such a misfortune.

IV

THE SPECTRE OF THE CATACOMB

SURELY, she cannot be lost!" exclaimed Kenyon. "It is but a moment since she was speaking."

"No, no!" said Hilda, in great alarm. "She was behind us all; and it is a long while since we have heard her voice."

"Torches! Torches!" cried Donatello desperately. "I will seek her, be the darkness ever so dismal!"

But the guide held him back, and assured them all, that there was no possibility of assisting their lost companion, unless by shouting at the very top of their voices. As the sound would go very far along these close and narrow passages, there was a fair probability that Miriam might hear the call and be able to retrace her steps.

Accordingly, they all—Kenyon with his bass voice; Donatello with his tenor; the guide with that high and hard Italian cry, which makes the streets of Rome so resonant; and Hilda with her slender scream, piercing farther than the united uproar of the rest—began to shriek, halloo, and bellow, with the uttermost force of their lungs. And, not to prolong the reader's suspense, (for we do not particularly seek to interest him in this scene, telling it only on account of the trouble and strange entanglement which followed,) they soon heard a responsive call, in a female voice.

"It was the Signorina!" cried Donatello joyfully.

"Yes; it was certainly dear Miriam's voice," said Hilda. "And here she comes! Thank Heaven! Thank Heaven!"

The figure of their friend was now discernible by her own torch-light, approaching out of one of the cavernous passages. Miriam came forward, but not with the eagerness and tremulous joy of a fearful girl, just rescued from a labyrinth of gloomy mystery. She made no immediate response to their inquiries and tumultuous congratulations; and, as they afterwards remembered, there was something absorbed, thoughtful, and self-concentrated, in her deportment. She looked pale, as well she might, and held her torch with a nervous grasp, the tremour of which was seen in the irregular twinkling of the flame. This last was the chief perceptible sign of any recent agitation or alarm.

"Dearest, dearest Miriam," exclaimed Hilda, throwing her arms about her friend, "where have you been straying from us? Blessed be Providence, which has rescued you out of that miserable darkness!"

"Hush, dear Hilda!" whispered Miriam, with a strange little laugh. "Are you quite sure that it was Heaven's guidance which brought me back? If so, it was by an odd messenger, as you will confess. See; there he stands!"

Startled at Miriam's words and manner, Hilda gazed into the duskiness whither she pointed, and there beheld a figure standing just on the doubtful limit of obscurity, at the threshold of the small, illuminated chapel. Kenyon discerned him at the same instant, and drew nearer with his torch; although the guide attempted to dissuade him, averring that, once beyond the consecrated precincts of the chapel, the apparition would have power to tear him limb from limb. It struck the sculptor, however, when he afterwards recurred to these circumstances, that the guide manifested no such apprehension on his own account, as he professed on behalf of others; for he kept pace with Kenyon, as the latter approached the figure, though still endeavouring to restrain him.

In fine, they both drew near enough to get as good a view of the spectre, as the smoky light of their torches, struggling with the massive gloom, could supply.

The stranger was of exceedingly picturesque, and even melodramatic aspect. He was clad in a voluminous cloak, that seemed to be made of a buffalo's hide, and a pair of those goat-skin breeches, with the hair outward, which are still commonly worn by the peasants of the Roman Campagna. In this garb, they look like antique Satyrs; and, in truth, the Spectre of the Catacomb might have represented the last survivor of that vanished race, hiding himself in sepulchral gloom, and mourning over his lost life of woods and streams.

Furthermore, he had on a broad-brimmed, conical hat, beneath the shadow of which a wild visage was indistinctly seen, floating away, as it were, into a dusky wilderness of moustache and beard. His eyes winked, and turned uneasily from the torches, like a creature to whom midnight would be more congenial than noonday.

On the whole, the spectre might have made a considerable impression on the sculptor's nerves, only that he was in the habit of observing similar figures, almost every day, reclining on the Spanish Steps, and waiting for some artist to invite them within the magic realm of picture. Nor, even thus familiarized with the stranger's peculiarities of appearance, could Kenyon help wondering to see such a personage, shaping himself so suddenly out of the void darkness of the catacomb.

"What are you?" said the sculptor, advancing his torch nearer. "And how long have you been wandering here?"

"A thousand and five hundred years!" muttered the guide, loud enough to be heard by all the party. "It is the old pagan Phantom that I told you of, who sought to betray the blessed Saints!"

"Yes; it is a phantom!" cried Donatello with a shudder. "Ah, dearest Signorina, what fearful thing has beset you, in those dark corridors!"

"Nonsense, Donatello!" said the sculptor. "The man is no more a phantom than yourself. The only marvel is, how he comes to be hiding himself in the catacomb. Possibly, our guide might solve the riddle."

The spectre himself here settled the point of his tangibility, at all events, and physical substance, by approaching a step nearer, and laying his hand on Kenyon's arm.

"Inquire not what I am, nor wherefore I abide in the darkness," said he, in a hoarse, harsh voice, as if a great deal of damp were clustering in his throat. "Henceforth, I am nothing but a shadow behind her footsteps. She came to me when I sought her not. She has called me forth, and must abide the consequences of my re-appearance in the world."

"Holy Virgin! I wish the Signorina joy of her prize!" said the guide, half to himself. "And, in any case, the Catacomb is well rid of him!"

We need follow the scene no farther. So much is essential to the subsequent narrative, that, during the short period while astray in those tortuous passages, Miriam had encountered an unknown man, and led him forth with her, or was guided back by him, first into the torch-light, thence into the sunshine.

It was the further singularity of this affair, that the connection, thus briefly and casually formed, did not terminate with the incident that gave it birth. As if her service to him, or his service to her, whichever it might be, had given him an indefeasible claim on Miriam's regard and protection, the Spectre of the Catacomb never long allowed her to lose sight of him, from that day forward. He haunted her footsteps with more than the customary persistency of Italian mendicants, when once they have recognized a benefactor. For days together, it is true, he occasionally vanished, but always re-appeared, gliding after her through the narrow streets, or climbing the hundred steps of her staircase and sitting at her threshold.

Being often admitted to her studio, he left his features, or some shadow or reminiscence of them, in many of her sketches and pictures. The moral atmosphere of these productions was thereby so influenced, that rival painters pronounced it a case of hopeless mannerism, which would destroy all Miriam's prospects of true excellence in art.

The story of this adventure spread abroad, and made its way beyond the usual gossip of the Forestieri, even into Italian circles, where, enhanced by a still potent spirit of superstition, it grew far more wonderful than as above recounted. Thence, it came back among the Anglo-Saxons, and was communicated to the German artists, who so richly supplied it with romantic ornaments and excrescences, after their fashion, that it became a fantasy worthy of Tieck or Hoffmann. For, nobody has any conscience about adding to the improbabilities of a marvellous tale.

The most reasonable version of the incident, that could anywise be rendered acceptable to the auditors, was substantially the one suggested by the guide of the catacomb, in his allusion to the legend of Memmius. This man, or demon, or Man-Demon, was a spy during the persecutions of the early Christians, probably under the Emperour Diocletian, and penetrated into the Catacomb of Saint Calixtus, with the malignant purpose of tracing out the hiding-places of the refugees. But, while he stole craftily through those dark corridors, he chanced to come upon a little chapel, where tapers were burning before an Altar and a Crucifix, and a priest was in the performance of his sacred office. By Divine indulgence, there was a single moment's grace allowed to Memmius, during which, had he been capable of Christian faith and love, he might have knelt before the Cross, and received the holy light into his soul, and so have been blest forever. But he resisted the sacred impulse. As soon, therefore, as that one moment had glided by, the light of the consecrated tapers, which represent all truth, bewildered the wretched man with everlasting errour, and the blessed Cross itself was stamped as a seal upon his heart, so that it should never open to receive conviction.

Thenceforth, this heathen Memmius has haunted the wide and dreary precincts of the catacomb, seeking, as some say, to beguile new victims into his own misery, but, according to other statements, endeavouring to prevail on any unwary visitor to take him by the hand, and guide him out into the daylight. Should his wiles and entreaties take effect, however, the Man-Demon would remain only a little while above ground. He would gratify his fiendish malignity by perpetrating signal mischief on his benefactor, and perhaps bringing some old pestilence or other forgotten and long-buried evil on society—or, possibly, teaching the modern world some decayed and dusty kind of crime, which the antique Romans knew—and then would hasten back to the catacomb, which, after so long haunting it, has grown his most congenial home.

Miriam herself, with her chosen friends, the sculptor and the gentle Hilda, often laughed at the monstrous fictions that had gone abroad in reference to her adventure. Her two confidants (for such they were, on all ordinary subjects) had not failed to ask an explanation of the mystery; since, undeniably, a mystery there was, and one sufficiently perplexing itself, without any help from the imaginative faculty. And, sometimes, responding to their inquiries with a melancholy sort of playfulness, Miriam let her fancy run off into wilder

fables than any which German ingenuity or Italian superstition had contrived.

For example, with a strange air ot seriousness over all her
face, only belied by a laughing gleam in her dark eyes, she
would aver that the spectre (who had been an artist in his
mortal lifetime) had promised to teach her a long lost, but
invaluable secret of old Roman fresco-painting. The knowledge of this process would place Miriam at the head of modern
art; the sole condition being agreed upon, that she should
return with him into his sightless gloom, after enriching a
certain extent of stuccoed wall with the most brilliant and
lovely designs. And what true votary of Art would not
purchase unrivalled excellence, even at so vast a sacrifice!

Or, if her friends still solicited a soberer account, Miriam
replied, that, meeting the old infidel in one of the dismal
passages of the catacomb, she had entered into controversy
with him, hoping to achieve the glory and satisfaction of
converting him to the Christian faith. For the sake of so
excellent a result, she had even staked her own salvation
against his, binding herself to accompany him back into his
penal gloom, if, within a twelvemonth's space, she should not
have convinced him of the errours through which he had so
long groped and stumbled. But, alas! up to the present time,
the controversy had gone direfully in favour of the Man-
Demon; and Miriam (as she whispered in Hilda's ear) had
awful forebodings, that, in a few more months, she must
take an eternal farewell of the sun!

It was somewhat remarkable, that all her romantic fantasies
arrived at this self-same dreary termination; it appeared impossible for her even to imagine any other than a disastrous
result from her connection with her ill-omened attendant.

This singularity might have meant nothing, however, had
it not suggested a despondent state of mind, which was
likewise indicated by many other tokens. Miriam's friends

had no difficulty in perceiving, that, in one way or another, her happiness was very seriously compromised. Her spirits were often depressed into deep melancholy. If ever she was gay, it was seldom with a healthy cheerfulness. She grew moody, moreover, and subject to fits of passionate ill-temper, which usually wreaked itself on the heads of those who loved her best. Not that Miriam's indifferent acquaintances were safe from similar outbreaks of her displeasure, especially if they ventured upon any allusion to the Model. In such cases, they were left with little disposition to renew the subject, but inclined, on the other hand, to interpret the whole matter as much to her discredit as the least favourable colouring of the facts would allow.

It may occur to the reader, that there was really no demand for so much rumour and speculation in regard to an incident, which might well enough have been explained without going many steps beyond the limits of probability. The spectre might have been merely a Roman beggar, whose fraternity often harbour in stranger shelters than the catacombs; or one of those pilgrims, who still journey from remote countries to kneel and worship at the holy sites, among which these haunts of the early Christians are esteemed especially sacred. Or, as was perhaps a more plausible theory, he might be a thief of the city, a robber of the Campagna, a political offender, or an assassin with blood upon his hand, whom the negligence or connivance of the police allowed to take refuge in those subterranean fastnesses, where such outlaws have been accustomed to hide themselves, from a far antiquity downward.

Or, he might have been a lunatic, fleeing instinctively from man, and making it his dark pleasure to dwell among the tombs, like him whose awful cry echoes afar to us from Scripture times.

And, as for the stranger's attaching himself so devotedly to

Miriam, her personal magnetism might be allowed a certain weight in the explanation. For what remains, his pertinacity need not seem so very singular to those who consider how slight a link serves to connect these vagabonds of idle Italy with any person that may have the ill-hap to bestow charity, or be otherwise serviceable to them, or betray the slightest interest in their fortunes.

Thus, little would remain to be accounted for, except the deportment of Miriam herself; her reserve, her brooding melancholy, her petulance, and moody passion. If generously interpreted, even these morbid symptoms might have sufficient cause in the stimulating and exhausting influencies of an imaginative art, exercised by a delicate young woman, in the nervous and unwholesome atmosphere of Rome. Such, at least, was the view of the case which Hilda and Kenyon endeavoured to impress on their own minds, and impart to those whom their opinions might influence.

One of Miriam's friends took the matter sadly to heart. This was the young Italian. Donatello, as we have seen, had been an eye-witness of the stranger's first appearance, and had ever since nourished a singular prejudice against the mysterious, dusky, death-scented apparition. It resembled not so much a human dislike or hatred, as one of those instinctive, unreasoning antipathies which the lower animals sometimes display, and which generally prove more trustworthy than the acutest insight into character. The shadow of the Model, always flung into the light which Miriam diffused around her, caused no slight trouble to Donatello. Yet he was of a nature so remarkably genial and joyous, so simply happy, that he might well afford to have something subtracted from his comfort, and make tolerable shift to live upon what remained.

V

MIRIAM'S STUDIO

THE COURTYARD and staircase of a palace, built three hundred years ago, are a peculiar feature of modern Rome, and interest the stranger more than many things of which he has heard loftier descriptions. You pass through the grand breadth and height of a squalid entrance-way, and perhaps see a range of dusky pillars, forming a sort of cloister round the court; and in the intervals, from pillar to pillar, are strewn fragments of antique statues, headless and legless torsos, and busts that have invariably lost—what it might be well if living men could lay aside, in that unfragrant atmosphere—the nose. Bas-reliefs, the spoil of some far elder palace, are set in the surrounding walls, every stone of which has been ravished from the Coliseum, or any other imperial ruin which earlier barbarism had not already levelled with the earth. Between two of the pillars, moreover, stands an old sarcophagus without its lid, and with all its more prominently projecting sculptures broken off; perhaps it once held famous dust, and the bony frame-work of some historic man, although now only a receptacle for the rubbish of the courtyard and a half-worn broom.

In the centre of the court, under the blue Italian sky, and with the hundred windows of the vast palace gazing down upon it, from four sides, appears a fountain. It brims over from one stone basin to another, or gushes from a Naiad's urn, or spirts its many little jets from the mouths of nameless monsters, which were merely grotesque and artificial, when Bernini, or whoever was their unnatural father, first produced them; but now the patches of moss, the tufts of grass, the trailing maiden-hair, and all sorts of verdant weed that thrive in the cracks and crevices of moist marble, tell us that Nature takes the fountain back into her great heart, and cherishes it as kindly as if it were a woodland spring. And, hark, the pleasant murmur, the gurgle, the plash! You might hear just those tinkling sounds from any tiny waterfall in the forest, though here they gain a delicious pathos from the stately echoes that reverberate their natural language. So the fountain is not altogether glad, after all its three centuries of play!

In one of the angles of the courtyard, a pillared door-way gives access to the staircase, with its spacious breadth of low, marble steps, up which, in former times, have gone the princes and cardinals of the great Roman family who built this palace. Or they have come down, with still grander and loftier mien, on their way to the Vatican or the Quirinal, there to put off their scarlet hats in exchange for the triple crown. But, in fine, all these illustrious personages have gone down their hereditary staircase for the last time, leaving it to be the thoroughfare of ambassadours, English noblemen, American millionaires, artists, tradesmen, washerwomen, and people of every degree; all of whom find such gilded and marble-panelled saloons as their pomp and luxury demand, or such homely garrets as their necessity can pay for, within this one multifarious abode. Only, in not a single nook of the palace (built for splendour, and the accommodation of a vast retinue, but with no vision of a happy fireside or any mode of domestic enjoyment) does the humblest or the haughtiest occupant find comfort.

Up such a staircase, on the morning after the scene at the Sculpture Gallery, sprang the light foot of Donatello. He ascended from story to story, passing lofty door-ways, set within rich frames of sculptured marble, and climbing unweariedly upward, until the glories of the first piano and the elegance of the middle height were exchanged for a sort of Alpine region, cold and naked in its aspect. Steps of rough stone, rude wooden balustrades, a brick pavement in the passages, a dingy white-wash on the walls; these were here the palatial features. Finally, he paused before an oaken door, on which was pinned a card, bearing the name of Miriam Schaefer, artist in oils. Here Donatello knocked, and the door immediately fell somewhat ajar; its latch having been pulled up by means of a string on the inside. Passing through a little ante-room, he found himself in Miriam's presence.

"Come in, wild Faun," she said, "and tell me the latest news from Arcady!"

The artist was not just then at her easel, but was busied with the feminine task of mending a pair of gloves. There is something extremely pleasant, and even touching—at least, of very sweet, soft, and winning effect—in this peculiarity of needlework, distinguishing women from men. Our own sex is incapable of any such by-play, aside from the main business of life; but women—be they of what earthly rank they may, however gifted with intellect or genius, or endowed with awful beauty—have always some little handiwork ready to fill the tiny gap of every vacant moment. A needle is familiar to the fingers of them all. A queen, no doubt, plies it on occasion; the woman-poet can use it as adroitly as her pen; the woman's eye, that has discovered a new star, turns from its glory to send the polished little instrument gleaming along the hem of her kerchief, or to darn a casual fray in her dress. And they have greatly the advantage of us, in this respect. The slender thread of silk or cotton keeps them united with the small, familiar, gentle interests of life, the continually operating influences of which do so much for the health of the character, and carry off what would otherwise be a dangerous accumulation of morbid sensibility. A vast deal of human sympathy runs along this electric line, stretching from the throne to the wicker-chair of the humblest seamstress, and keeping high and low in a species of communion with their kindred beings. Methinks it is a token of healthy and gentle characteristics, when women of high thoughts and accomplishments love to sew; especially as they are never more at home with their own hearts than while so occupied.

And when the work falls in a woman's lap, of its own accord, and the needle involuntarily ceases to fly, it is a sign of trouble, quite as trustworthy as the throb of the heart itself. This was what happened to Miriam. Even while Donatello stood gazing at her, she seemed to have forgotten his presence, allowing him to drop out of her thoughts, and the torn glove to fall from her idle fingers. Simple as he was, the young man knew by his sympathies that something was amiss.

"Dear lady, you are sad!" said he, drawing close to her.

"It is nothing, Donatello," she replied, resuming her work. "Yes; a little sad, perhaps; but that is not strange for us people of the ordinary world, especially for women. You are of a cheerfuller race, my friend, and know nothing of this disease of sadness. But why do you come into this shadowy room of mine?"

"Why do you make it so shadowy?" asked he.

"We artists purposely exclude sunshine, and all but a partial light," said Miriam, "because we think it necessary to put ourselves at odds with Nature, before trying to imitate her. That strikes you very strangely, does it not? But we make very pretty pictures, sometimes, with our artfully arranged lights and shadows. Amuse yourself with some of mine, Donatello, and, by-and-by, I shall be in the mood to begin the portrait we were talking about."

The room had the customary aspect of a painter's studio; one of those delightful spots that hardly seem to belong to the actual world, but rather to be the outward type of a poet's haunted imagination, where there are glimpses, sketches, and half-developed hints of beings and objects, grander and more beautiful than we can anywhere find in reality. The windows were closed with shutters, or deeply curtained, except one, which was partly open to a sunless portion of the sky, admitting only, from high upward, that partial light which, with its strongly marked contrast of shadow, is the first requisite towards seeing objects pictorially. Pencil-drawings were pinned against the wall, or scattered on the tables. Unframed canvases turned their backs on the spectator, presenting only a blank to the eye, and churlishly concealing whatever riches of scenery, or human beauty, Miriam's skill had depicted on the other side.

In the obscurest part of the room, Donatello was half-startled at perceiving, duskily, a woman with long dark hair, who threw up her arms, with a wild gesture of tragic despair, and appeared to beckon him into the darkness along with her.

"Do not be afraid, Donatello," said Miriam, smiling to see him peering doubtfully into the mysterious dusk. "She means you no mischief, nor could perpetrate any, if she wished it ever so much. It is a lady of exceedingly pliable disposition; now a heroine of romance, and now a rustic maid; yet all for show, being created, indeed, on purpose to wear rich shawls and other garments in a becoming fashion. This is the true end of her being, although she pretends to assume the most varied duties and perform many parts in life, while really the poor puppet has nothing on earth to do. Upon my word, I am satirical unawares, and seem to be describing nine women out of ten in the person of my lay-figure! For most purposes, she has the advantage of the sisterhood. Would I were like her!"

"How it changes her aspect," exclaimed Donatello, "to know that she is but a jointed figure! When my eyes first fell upon her, I thought her arms moved, as if beckoning me to help her in some direful peril."

"Are you often troubled with such sinister freaks of fancy?" asked Miriam. "I should not have supposed it."

"To tell you the truth, dearest Signorina," answered the young Italian, "I am apt to be fearful in old, gloomy houses, and in the dark. I love no dark or dusky corners, except it be in a grotto, or among the thick green leaves of an arbour, or in some nook of the woods, such as I know many, in the neighborhood of my home. Even there, if a stray sunbeam steal in, the shadow is all the better for its cheerful glimmer."

"Yes; you are a Faun, you know," said the fair artist, laughing at the remembrance of the scene of the day before. "But the world is sadly changed, now-a-days; grievously changed, poor Donatello, since those happy times when your race used to dwell in the Arcadian woods, playing hide-and-seek with the nymphs in grottoes and nooks of shrubbery. You have re-appeared on earth some centuries too late."

"I do not understand you now," answered Donatello, looking perplexed. "Only, Signorina, I am glad to have my lifetime while you live; and where you are, be it in cities or fields, I would fain be there too."

"I wonder whether I ought to allow you to speak in this way," said Miriam, looking thoughtfully at him. "Many young women would think it behoved them to be offended. Hilda would never let you speak so, I dare say. But he is a mere boy," she added, aside, "a simple boy, putting his boyish heart to the proof on the first woman whom he chances to meet. If yonder lay-figure had had the luck to meet him first, she would have smitten him as deeply as I."

"Are you angry with me?" asked Donatello dolorously.

"Not in the least," answered Miriam, frankly giving him her hand. "Pray look over some of these sketches, till I have leisure to chat with you a little. I hardly think I am in spirits enough to begin your portrait to-day."

Donatello was as gentle and docile as a pet spaniel; as playful, too, in his general disposition, or saddening with his mistress's variable mood, like that, or any other kindly animal, which has the faculty of bestowing its sympathies more completely than man or woman can ever do. Accordingly, as Miriam bade him, he tried to turn his attention to a great pile and confusion of pen-and-ink sketches, and pencil-drawings, which lay tossed together on a table. As it chanced, however, they gave the poor youth little delight.

The first that he took up was a very impressive sketch, in which the artist had jotted down her rough ideas for a picture of Jael, driving the nail through the temples of Sisera. It was dashed off with remarkable power, and showed a touch or two that were actually lifelike and deathlike; as if Miriam had been standing by, when Jael gave the first stroke of her murderous hammer—or as if she herself were Jael, and felt irresistibly impelled to make her bloody confession, in this guise. Her first conception of the stern Jewess had evidently been that of perfect womanhood, a lovely form, and a high, heroic face of lofty beauty; but, dissatisfied either with her own work or the terrible story itself, Miriam had added a certain wayward quirk of her pencil, which at once converted the heroine into a vulgar murderess. It was evident that a Jael like this would be sure to search Sisera's pockets, as soon as the breath was out of his body.

In another sketch, she had attempted the story of Judith, which we see represented by the Old Masters so often, and in such various styles. Here, too, beginning with a passionate and fiery conception of the subject, in all earnestness, she had given the last touches in utter scorn, as it were, of the feeling which at first took such powerful possession of her hand. The head of Holofernes, (which, by-the-by, had a pair of twisted mustachios, like those of a certain potentate of the day,) being fairly cut off, was screwing its eyes upward and twirling its features into a diabolical grin of triumphant malice, which it flung right at Judith's face. On her part, she had the startled aspect that might be conceived of a cook, if a calf's head should sneer at her, when about to be popt into the dinner-pot.

Over and over again, there was the idea of woman, acting the part of a revengeful mischief towards man. It was, indeed, very singular to see how the artist's imagination seemed to run on these stories of bloodshed, in which woman's hand was crimsoned by the stain; and how, too—in one form or another, grotesque, or sternly sad—she failed not to bring out the moral, that woman must strike through her own heart to reach a human life, whatever were the motive that impelled her. One of the sketches represented the daughter of Herodias, receiving the head of John the Baptist in a charger. The general conception appeared to be taken from Bernardo Luini's picture, in the Uffizi gallery at Florence; but Miriam had imparted to the Saint's face a look of gentle and heavenly reproach, with sad and blessed eyes fixed upward at the maiden; by the force of which miraculous glance, her whole womanhood was at once awakened to love and endless remorse.

These sketches had a most disagreeable effect on Donatello's peculiar temperament. He gave a shudder; his face assumed a look of trouble, fear, and disgust; he snatched up one sketch after another, as if about to tear it in pieces. Finally, shoving away the pile of drawings, he shrank back from the table and clasped his hands over his eyes.

"What is the matter, Donatello?" asked Miriam, looking

up from a letter which she was now writing. "Ah! I did not mean you to see those drawings. They are ugly phantoms that stole out of my mind; not things that I created, but things that haunt me. See! Here are some trifles that perhaps will please you better."

She gave him a portfolio, the sketches in which indicated a happier mood of mind, and one, it is to be hoped, more truly characteristic of the artist. Supposing neither of these classes of subject to show anything of her own individuality, Miriam had evidently a great scope of fancy, and a singular faculty of putting what looked like heart into her productions. The latter sketches were domestic and common scenes, so finely and subtly idealized that they seemed such as we may see at any moment, and everywhere; while still there was the indefinable something added, or taken away, which makes all the difference between sordid life and an earthly paradise. The feeling and sympathy in all of them were deep and true. There was the scene, that comes once in every life, of the lover winning the soft and pure avowal of bashful affection from the maiden, whose slender form half leans towards his arm, half shrinks from it, we know not which. There was wedded affection, in its successive stages, represented in a series of delicately conceived designs, touched with a holy fire, that burned from youth to age in those two hearts, and gave one identical beauty to the faces, throughout all the changes of feature.

There was a drawing of an infant's shoe, half-worn out, with the airy print of the blessed foot within; a thing that would make a mother smile or weep out of the very depths of her heart; and yet an actual mother would not have been likely to appreciate the poetry of the little shoe, until Miriam revealed it to her. It was wonderful, the depth and force with which the above, and other kindred subjects, were depicted, and the profound significance which they often

acquired. The artist, still in her fresh youth, could not probably have drawn any of these dear and rich experiences from
her own life; unless, perchance, that first sketch of all, the
avowal of maiden affection, were a remembered incident, and
not a prophecy. But it is more delightful to believe, that,
from first to last, they were the productions of a beautiful
imagination, dealing with the warm and pure suggestions of
a woman's heart, and thus idealizing a truer and lovelier
picture of the life that belongs to woman, than an actual
acquaintance with some of its hard and dusty facts could
have inspired. So considered, the sketches intimated such a
force and variety of imaginative sympathies as would enable
Miriam to fill her life richly with the bliss and suffering of
womanhood, however barren it might individually be.

There was one observable point, indeed, betokening that
the artist relinquished, for her personal self, the happiness
which she could so profoundly appreciate for others. In all
those sketches of common life, and the affections that spir-
itualize it, a figure was pourtrayed apart; now, it peeped
between the branches of a shrubbery, amid which two lovers
sat; now, it was looking through a frosted window, from the
outside, while a young wedded pair sat at their new fireside,
within; and, once, it leaned from a chariot, which six horses
were whirling onward in pomp and pride, and gazed at a
scene of humble enjoyment by a cottage-door. Always, it was
the same figure, and always depicted with an expression of
deep sadness; and in every instance, slightly as they were
brought out, the face and form had the traits of Miriam's own.

"Do you like these sketches better, Donatello?" asked
Miriam.

"Yes," said Donatello, rather doubtfully.

"Not much, I fear," responded she, laughing. "And what
should a boy like you—a Faun, too—know about the joys and
sorrows, the intertwining light and shadow, of human life?

I forgot that you were a Faun. You cannot suffer deeply; therefore, you can but half enjoy. Here, now, is a subject which you can better appreciate."

The sketch represented merely a rustic dance, but with such extravagance of fun as was delightful to behold; and here there was no drawback, except that strange sigh and sadness which always come when we are merriest.

"I am going to paint the picture in oils," said the artist, "and I want you, Donatello, for the wildest dancer of them all. Will you sit for me, some day?—or, rather, dance for me?"

"Oh, most gladly, Signorina!" exclaimed Donatello. "See; it shall be like this."

And, forthwith, he began to dance, and flit about the studio, like an incarnate sprite of jollity, pausing at last on the extremity of one toe, as if that were the only portion of himself, whereby his frisky nature could come in contact with the earth. The effect in that shadowy chamber, whence the artist had so carefully excluded the sunshine, was as enlivening as if one bright ray had contrived to shimmer in, and frolic around the walls, and finally rest, just in the centre of the floor.

"That was admirable!" said Miriam, with an approving smile. "If I can catch you on my canvas, it will be a glorious picture; only I am afraid you will dance out of it, by the very truth of the representation, just when I shall have given it the last touch. We will try it, one of these days. And now, to reward you for that jolly exhibition, you shall see what has been shown to no one else."

She went to her easel, on which was placed a picture with its back turned towards the spectator. Reversing the position, there appeared the portrait of a beautiful woman, such as one sees only two or three, if even so many, in all a lifetime; so beautiful, that she seemed to get into your consciousness and memory, and could never afterwards be shut out, but haunted your dreams, for pleasure or for pain; holding your inner realm as a conquered territory, though without deigning to make herself at home there.

She was very youthful, and had what was usually thought to be a Jewish aspect; a complexion in which there was no roseate bloom, yet neither was it pale; dark eyes, into which you might look as deeply as your glance would go, and still be conscious of a depth that you had not sounded, though it lay open to the day. She had black, abundant hair, with none of the vulgar glossiness of other women's sable locks; if she were really of Jewish blood, then this was Jewish hair, and a dark glory such as crowns no Christian maiden's head. Gazing at this portrait, you saw what Rachael might have been, when Jacob deemed her worth the wooing seven years, and seven more; or perchance she might ripen to be what Judith was, when she vanquished Holofernes with her beauty, and slew him for too much adoring it.

Miriam watched Donatello's contemplation of the picture, and seeing his simple rapture, a smile of pleasure brightened on her face, mixed with a little scorn; at least, her lips curled and her eyes gleamed, as if she disdained either his admiration or her own enjoyment of it.

"Then you like the picture, Donatello?" she asked.

"Oh, beyond what I can tell!" he answered. "So beautiful!— so beautiful!"

"And do you recognize the likeness?"

"Signorina," exclaimed Donatello, turning from the picture to the artist, in astonishment that she should ask the question, "the resemblance is as little to be mistaken as if you had bent over the smooth surface of a fountain, and possessed the witchcraft to call forth the image that you made there! It is yourself!"

Donatello said the truth; and we forbore to speak descriptively of Miriam's beauty earlier in our narrative, because we foresaw this occasion to bring it perhaps more forcibly before the reader.

We know not whether the portrait were a flattered likeness; probably not, regarding it merely as the delineation of a lovely face; although Miriam, like all self-painters, may have endowed herself with certain graces which other eyes might not discern. Artists are fond of painting their own portraits; and, in Florence, there is a gallery of hundreds of them, including the most illustrious; in all of which there are autobiographical characteristics, so to speak; traits, expressions, loftinesses, and amenities, which would have been invisible, had they not been painted from within. Yet their reality and truth is none the less. Miriam, in like manner, had doubtless conveyed some of the intimate results of her heart-knowledge into her own portrait, and perhaps wished to try whether they would be perceptible to so simple and natural an observer as Donatello.

"Does the expression please you?" she asked.

"Yes," said Donatello, hesitatingly—"if it would only smile so like the sunshine as you sometimes do. No; it is sadder than I thought at first. Cannot you make yourself smile a little, Signorina?"

"A forced smile is uglier than a frown," said Miriam, a bright, natural smile breaking out over her face, even as she spoke.

"Oh, catch it now!" cried Donatello, clapping his hands. "Let it shine upon the picture! There; it has vanished already! And you are sad again, very sad; and the picture gazes sadly forth at me, as if some evil had befallen it in the little time since I looked last."

"How perplexed you seem, my friend!" answered Miriam. "I really half believe you are a Faun, there is such a mystery and terrour for you in these dark moods, which are just as natural as daylight to us people of ordinary mould. I advise you, at all events, to look at other faces, with those innocent and happy eyes, and never more to gaze at mine!"

"You speak in vain," replied the young man, with a deeper emphasis than she had ever before heard in his voice. "Shroud yourself in what gloom you will, I must needs follow you."

"Well, well, well!" said Miriam impatiently; "but leave me now, for, to speak plainly, my good friend, you grow a little wearisome. I walk, this afternoon, in the Borghese grounds. Meet me there, if it suits your pleasure."

VI

THE VIRGIN'S SHRINE

AFTER Donatello had left the studio, Miriam herself came forth, and taking her way through some of the intricacies of the city, entered what might be called either a widening of a street, or a small piazza. The neighborhood comprised a baker's oven, emitting the usual fragrance of sour bread; a shoe-shop; a linen-draper's shop; a pipe and cigar-shop; a lottery-office; a station for French soldiers, with a sentinel pacing in front; and a fruit-stand, at which a Roman matron was selling the dried kernels of chestnuts, wretched little figs, and some bouquets of yesterday. A church, of course, was near at hand, the façade of which ascended into lofty pinnacles, whereon were perched two or three winged figures of stone, either angelic or allegorical, blowing stone trumpets in close vicinity to the upper windows of an old and shabby palace. This palace was distinguished by a feature not very common in the architecture of Roman edifices; that is to say, a mediæval tower, square, massive, lofty, and battlemented and machicolated at the summit.

At one of the angles of the battlements stood a shrine of

the Virgin, such as we see everywhere at the street-corners of Rome, but seldom or never, except in this solitary instance, at a height above the ordinary level of men's views and aspirations. Connected with this old tower and its lofty shrine, there is a legend which we cannot here pause to tell; but, for centuries, a lamp has been burning before the Virgin's image, at noon, at midnight, and at all hours of the twenty-four, and must be kept burning forever, as long as the tower shall stand; or else the tower itself, the palace, and whatever estate belongs to it, shall pass from its hereditary possessor, in accordance with an ancient vow, and become the property of the Church.

As Miriam approached, she looked upward, and saw—not, indeed, the flame of the never-dying lamp, which was swallowed up in the broad sunlight that brightened the shrine—but a flock of white doves, skimming, fluttering, and wheeling about the topmost height of the tower, their silver wings flashing in the pure transparency of the air. Several of them sat on the ledge of the upper window, pushing one another off by their eager struggle for this favourite station, and all tapping their beaks and flapping their wings tumultuously against the panes; some had alighted in the street, far below, but flew hastily upward, at the sound of the window being thrust ajar, and opening in the middle, on rusty hinges, as Roman windows do.

A fair young girl, dressed in white, showed herself at the aperture, for a single instant, and threw forth as much as her two small hands could hold of some kind of food, for the flock of eleemosynary doves. It seemed greatly to the taste of the feathered people; for they tried to snatch beaksful of it from her grasp, caught it in the air, and rustled downward after it upon the pavement.

"What a pretty scene this is!" thought Miriam, with a kindly smile. "And how like a dove she is herself, the fair, pure creature! The other doves know her for a sister, I am sure."

Miriam passed beneath the deep portal of the palace, and turning to the left, began to mount flight after flight of a staircase, which, for the loftiness of its aspiration, was worthy to be Jacob's ladder, or, at all events, the staircase of the Tower of Babel. The city-bustle, which is heard even in Rome, the rumble of wheels over the uncomfortable paving-stones, the hard, harsh cries, re-echoing in the high and narrow streets, grew faint and died away; as the turmoil of the world will always die, if we set our faces to climb heavenward. Higher, and higher still; and now, glancing through the successive windows that threw in their narrow light upon the stairs, her view stretched across the roofs of the city, unimpeded even by the stateliest palaces. Only the domes of churches ascend into this airy region, and hold up their golden crosses on a level with her eye; except that, out of the very heart of Rome, the column of Antoninus thrusts itself upward, with Saint Paul upon its summit, the sole human form that seems to have kept her company.

Finally, the staircase came to an end; save that, on one side of the little entry where it terminated, a flight of a dozen steps gave access to the roof of the tower and the legendary shrine. On the other side was a door, at which Miriam knocked, but rather as a friendly announcement of her presence than with any doubt of hospitable welcome; for, awaiting no response, she lifted the latch and entered.

"What a hermitage you have found for yourself, dear Hilda!" she exclaimed. "You breathe sweet air, above all the evil scents of Rome; and even so, in your maiden elevation, you dwell above our vanities and passions, our moral dust and mud, with the doves and the angels for your near-est neighbors. I should not wonder if the Catholics were to make a Saint of you, like your namesake of old; especially as you have almost avowed yourself of their religion, by undertaking to keep the lamp a-light before the Virgin's shrine."

"No, no, Miriam!" said Hilda, who had come joyfully forward to greet her friend. "You must not call me a Catholic. A Christian girl—even a daughter of the Puritans—may surely pay honour to the idea of Divine Womanhood, without giving up the faith of her forefathers. But how kind you are to climb into my dove-cote!"

"It is no trifling proof of friendship, indeed," answered Miriam. "I should think there were three hundred stairs, at least."

"But it will do you good," continued Hilda. "A height of some fifty feet above the roofs of Rome gives me all the advantages that I could get from fifty miles of distance. The air so exhilarates my spirits, that sometimes I feel half-inclined to attempt a flight from the top of my tower, in the faith that I should float upward!"

"Oh, pray don't try it!" said Miriam laughing. "If it should turn out that you are less than an angel, you would find the stones of the Roman pavement very hard; and if an angel indeed, I am afraid you would never come down among us again."

This young American girl was an example of the freedom of life which it is possible for a female artist to enjoy at Rome. She dwelt in her tower, as free to descend into the corrupted atmosphere of the city beneath, as one of her companion-doves to fly downward into the street;—all alone, perfectly independent, under her own sole guardianship, unless watched over by the Virgin, whose shrine she tended;— doing what she liked, without a suspicion or a shadow upon the snowy whiteness of her fame. The customs of artist-life bestow such liberty upon the sex, which is elsewhere restricted within so much narrower limits; and it is perhaps an indication that, whenever we admit woman to a wider scope of pursuits and professions, we must also remove the shackles of our present conventional rules, which would then become an insufferable restraint on either maid or wife. The system seems to work unexceptionably in Rome; and in many other cases, as in Hilda's, purity of heart and life are allowed to assert themselves, and to be their own proof and security, to a degree unknown in the society of other cities.

Hilda, in her native land, had early shown what was pronounced by connoisseurs a decided genius for the pictorial art. Even in her school-days, (still not so very distant,) she had produced sketches that were seized upon by men of taste, and hoarded as among the choicest treasures of their portfolios; scenes delicately imagined, lacking, perhaps, the reality which comes only from a close acquaintance with life, but so softly touched with feeling and fancy, that you seemed to be looking at humanity with angel's eyes. With years and experience, she might be expected to attain a darker and more forcible touch, which would impart to her designs the relief they needed. Had Hilda remained in her own country, it is not improbable that she might have produced original works, worthy to hang in that gallery of native art, which, we hope, is destined to extend its rich length through many future centuries. An orphan, however, without near relatives, and possessed of a little property, she had found it within her possibilities to come to Italy; that central clime, whither the eyes and the heart of every artist turn, as if pictures could not be made to glow in any other atmosphere—as if statues could not assume grace and expression, save in that land of whitest marble.

Hilda's gentle courage had brought her safely over land and sea; her mild, unflagging perseverance had made a place for her in the famous city, even like a flower, that finds a chink for itself, and a little earth to grow in, on whatever ancient wall its slender roots may fasten. Here she dwelt, in her tower, possessing a friend or two in Rome, but no home-companion except the flock of doves, whose cote was in a ruinous chamber contiguous to her own. They soon became as familiar with the fair-haired Saxon girl as if she were a born sister of their brood; and her customary white robe bore such an analogy to their snowy plumage, that the confraternity of artists called Hilda The Dove, and recognized her aërial apartment as The Dove-cote. And while the other doves flew far and wide, in quest of what was good for them, Hilda likewise spread her wings, and sought such ethereal and imaginative sustenance as God ordains for creatures of her kind.

We know not whether the result of her Italian studies, so far as it could yet be seen, will be accepted as a good or desirable one. Certain it is, that, since her arrival in the pictorial land, Hilda seemed to have entirely lost the impulse of original design, which brought her thither. No doubt, the girl's early dreams had been, of sending forms and hues of beauty into the visible world out of her own mind; of compelling scenes of poetry and history to live before men's eyes, through conceptions and by methods individual to herself. But, more and more, as she grew familiar with the miracles of art that enrich so many galleries in Rome, Hilda had ceased to consider herself as an original artist. No wonder that this change should have befallen her. She was endowed with a deep and sensitive faculty of appreciation; she had the gift of discerning and worshipping excellence, in a most unusual measure. No other person, it is probable, recognized so adequately, and enjoyed with such deep delight, the pictorial wonders that were here displayed. She saw—no, not saw, but felt—through and through a picture; she bestowed upon it all the warmth and richness of a woman's sympathy; not by any intellectual effort, but by this strength of heart, and this guiding light of sympathy, she went straight to the central point, in which the Master had conceived his work. Thus, she viewed it, as it were, with his own eyes, and hence her comprehension of any picture that interested her was perfect.

This power and depth of appreciation depended partly upon Hilda's physical organization, which was at once healthful and exquisitely delicate; and, connected with this advantage, she had a command of hand, a nicety and force of touch, which is an endowment separate from pictorial genius, though indispensable to its exercise.

It has probably happened in many other instances, as it did in Hilda's case, that she ceased to aim at original achievement in consequence of the very gifts, which so exquisitely fitted her to profit by familiarity with the works of the mighty Old Masters. Reverencing these wonderful men so deeply, she was too grateful for all they bestowed upon her—too loyal—too humble, in their awful presence—to think of enrolling herself in their society. Beholding the miracles of beauty which they had achieved, the world seemed already rich enough in original designs, and nothing now was so desirable as to diffuse those self-same beauties more widely among mankind. All the youthful hopes and ambitions, the fanciful ideas which she had brought from home, of great pictures to be conceived in her feminine mind, were flung aside, and, so far as those most intimate with her could discern, relinquished without a sigh. All that she would henceforth attempt—and that, most reverently, not to say, religiously—was to catch and reflect some of the glory which had been shed upon canvas from the immortal pencils of old.

So Hilda became a copyist. In the Pinacotheca of the Vatican, in the galleries of the Pamfili-Doria palace, the Borghese, the Corsini, the Sciarra, her easel was set up before many a famous picture of Guido, Domenichino,

Raphael, and the devout painters of earlier schools than these. Other artists, and visitors from foreign lands, beheld her slender, girlish figure in front of some world-known work, absorbed, unconscious of everything around her, seeming to live only in what she sought to do. They smiled, no doubt, at the audacity which led her to dream of copying those mighty achievements. But, if they paused to look over her shoulder, and had sensibility enough to understand what was before their eyes, they soon felt inclined to believe that the spirits of the Old Masters were hovering over Hilda, and guiding her delicate white hand. In truth, from whatever realm of bliss and many-coloured beauty those spirits might descend, it would have been no unworthy errand, to help so gentle and pure a worshipper of their genius in giving the last divine touch to her repetitions of their works.

Her copies were indeed marvellous. Accuracy was not the phrase for them; a Chinese copy is accurate. Hilda's had that evanescent and ethereal life—that flitting fragrance, as it were, of the originals—which it is as difficult to catch and retain as it would be for a sculptor to get the very movement and varying colour of a living man into his marble bust. Only by watching the efforts of the most skilful copyists—men who spend a lifetime, as some of them do, in multiplying copies of a single picture—and observing how invariably they leave out just the indefinable charm that involves the last, inestimable value—can we understand the difficulties of the task which they undertake.

It was not Hilda's general practice to attempt reproducing the whole of a great picture, but to select some high, noble, and delicate portion of it, in which the spirit and essence of the picture culminated—the Virgin's celestial sorrow, for example, or a hovering Angel, imbued with immortal light, or a Saint, with the glow of Heaven in his dying face;— and these would be rendered with her whole soul. If a picture had darkened into an indistinct shadow, through time and neglect, or had been injured by cleaning, or retouched by some profane hand, she seemed to possess the faculty of seeing it in its pristine glory. The copy would come from her hands with what the beholder felt must be the light which the Old Master had left upon the original in bestowing his final and most ethereal touch. In some instances, even, (at least, so those believed, who best appreciated Hilda's power and sensibility,) she had been enabled to execute what the great Master had conceived in his imagination, but had not so perfectly succeeded in putting upon canvas;—a result surely not impossible when such depth of sympathy, as she possessed, was assisted by the delicate skill and accuracy of her slender hand. In such cases, the girl was but a finer instrument, a more exquisitely effective piece of mechanism, by the help of which the spirit of some great departed Painter now first achieved his ideal, centuries after his own earthly hand, that other tool, had turned to dust.

Not to describe her as too much a wonder, however, Hilda— or the Dove, as her well-wishers half-laughingly delighted to call her—had been pronounced by good judges incomparably the best copyist in Rome. After minute examination of her works, the most skilful artists declared that she had been led to her results by following precisely the same processes, step by step, through which the original painter had trodden to the development of his idea. Other copyists— if such they are worthy to be called—attempt only a superficial imitation. Copies of the Old Masters, in this sense, are produced by thousands; there are artists, as we have said, who spend their lives in painting the works, or perhaps one single work of one illustrious painter, over and over again; thus, they convert themselves into Guido machines, or Raphaelic machines. Their performances, it is true, are often wonderfully deceptive to a careless eye; but, working entirely from the outside, and seeking only to reproduce the surface, these men are sure to leave out that indefinable nothing, that inestimable something, that constitutes the life and soul through which the picture gets its immortality. Hilda was no such machine as this; she wrought religiously, and therefore wrought a miracle.

It strikes us that there is something far higher and nobler in all this—in her thus sacrificing herself to the devout recognition of the highest excellence in art—than there would have been in cultivating her not inconsiderable share of talent for the production of works from her own ideas. She might have set up for herself, and won no ignoble name; she might have helped to fill the already crowded and cumbered world with pictures, not destitute of merit, but falling short, if by ever so little, of the best that has been done; she might thus have gratified some tastes that were incapable of appreciating Raphael. But this could be done only by lowering the standard of art to the comprehension of the spectator. She chose the better, and loftier, and more unselfish part, laying her individual hopes, her fame, her prospects of enduring remembrance, at the feet of those great departed ones, whom she so loved and venerated. And therefore the world was the richer for this feeble girl. Since the beauty and glory of a great picture are confined within itself, she won out that glory by patient faith and self-devotion, and multiplied it for mankind. From the dark, chill corner of a gallery—from some curtained chapel in a church, where the light came seldom and aslant—from the prince's carefully guarded cabinet, where not one eye in thousands was permitted to behold it—she brought the wondrous picture into daylight, and gave all its magic splendour for the enjoyment of the world. Hilda's faculty of genuine admiration is one of the rarest to be found in human nature; and let us try to recompense her in kind by adducing her generous self-surrender, and **her** brave, humble magnanimity in choosing to be the handmaid of those old magicians, instead of a minor enchantress within a circle of her own.

The handmaid of Raphael, whom she loved with a virgin's love! Would it have been worth Hilda's while to relinquish this office, for the sake of giving the world a picture or two which it would call original; pretty fancies of snow and moonlight; the counterpart, in picture, of so many feminine achievements in literature!

VII

BEATRICE

M IRIAM was glad to find the Dove in her turret-home;
for being endowed with an infinite activity, and
taking exquisite delight in the sweet labour of which
her life was full, it was Hilda's practice to flee abroad betimes
and haunt the galleries till dusk. Happy were those (but they
were very few) whom she ever chose to be the companions
of her day; they saw the art-treasures of Rome, under her
guidance, as they had never seen them before. Not that Hilda
could dissertate, or talk learnedly about pictures; she would
probably have been puzzled by the technical terms of her
own art. Not that she had much to say about what she
most profoundly admired; but even her silent sympathy
was so powerful that it drew your own along with it, endowing you with a second-sight that enabled you to see
excellencies with almost the depth and delicacy of her
own perceptions.

All the Anglo-Saxon denizens of Rome, by this time, knew
Hilda by sight. Unconsciously, the poor child had become
one of the spectacles of the Eternal City, and was often
pointed out to strangers, sitting at her easel among the wild-
bearded young men, the white-haired old ones, and the

shabbily dressed, painfully plain women, who make up the throng of copyists. The old Custodes knew her well, and watched over her as their own child. Sometimes, a young artist, instead of going on with a copy of the picture before which he had placed his easel, would enrich his canvas with an original portrait of Hilda at her work. A lovelier subject could not have been selected, nor one which required nicer skill and insight in doing it anything like justice. She was pretty, at all times, in our native New England style, with her light brown ringlets, her delicately tinged, but healthful cheek, her sensitive, intelligent, yet most feminine and kindly face. But, every few moments, this pretty and girlish face grew beautiful and striking, as some inward thought and feeling brightened, rose to the surface, and then, as it were, passed out of sight again; so that, taking into view this constantly recurring change, it really seemed as if Hilda were only visible by the sunshine of her soul.

In other respects, she was a good subject for a portrait, being distinguished by a gentle picturesqueness, which was perhaps unconsciously bestowed by some minute peculiarity of dress, such as artists seldom fail to assume. The effect was to make her appear like an inhabitant of picture-land, a partly ideal creature, not to be handled, nor even approached too closely. In her feminine self, Hilda was natural, and of pleasant deportment, endowed with a mild cheerfulness of temper, not overflowing with animal spirits, but never long despondent. There was a certain simplicity that made every one her friend, but it was combined with a subtle attribute of reserve, that insensibly kept those at a distance who were not suited to her sphere.

Miriam was the dearest friend whom she had ever known. Being a year or two the elder, of longer acquaintance with Italy, and better fitted to deal with its crafty and selfish inhabitants, she had helped Hilda to arrange her way of life, and had encouraged her through those first weeks, when Rome is so dreary to every new-comer.

"But how lucky that you are at home to-day!" said Miriam, continuing the conversation which was begun, many pages back. "I hardly hoped to find you, though I had a favour to ask—a commission to put into your charge. But what picture is this?"

"See!" said Hilda, taking her friend's hand and leading her in front of the easel. "I wanted your opinion of it."

"If you have really succeeded," observed Miriam, recognizing the picture at the first glance, "it will be the greatest miracle you have yet achieved."

The picture represented simply a female head; a very youthful, girlish, perfectly beautiful face, enveloped in white drapery, from beneath which strayed a lock or two of what seemed a rich, though hidden luxuriance of auburn hair. The eyes were large and brown, and met those of the spectator, but evidently with a strange, ineffectual effort to escape. There was a little redness about the eyelids, very slightly indicated, so that you would question whether or no the girl had been weeping. The whole face was quiet; there was no distortion or disturbance of any single feature; nor was it easy to see why the expression was not cheerful, or why a single touch of the artist's pencil should not brighten it into joyousness. But, in fact, it was the very saddest picture ever painted or conceived; it involved an unfathomable depth of sorrow, the sense of which came to the observer by a sort of intuition. It was a sorrow that removed this beautiful girl out of the sphere of humanity, and set her in a far-off region, the remoteness of which—while yet her face is so close before us—makes us shiver as at a spectre.

"Yes, Hilda," said her friend, after closely examining the picture, "you have done nothing else so wonderful as this. But by what unheard-of solicitations or secret interest have you obtained leave to copy Guido's Beatrice Cenci? It is an unexampled favour; and the impossibility of getting a genuine copy has filled the Roman picture-shops with Beatrices, gay, grievous, or coquettish, but never a true one among them."

"There has been one exquisite copy, I have heard," said Hilda, "by an artist capable of appreciating the spirit of the picture. It was Thompson, who brought it away piece-meal, being forbidden (like the rest of us) to set up his easel before it. As for me, I knew the Prince Barberini would be deaf to all entreaties; so I had no resource but to sit down before the picture, day after day, and let it sink into my heart. I do believe it is now photographed there. It is a sad face to keep so close to one's heart; only, what is so very beautiful can never be quite a pain. Well; after studying it in this way, I know not how many times, I came home, and have done my best to transfer the image to canvas."

"Here it is then," said Miriam, contemplating Hilda's work with great interest and delight, mixed with the painful sympathy that the picture excited. "Everywhere we see oil-paintings, crayon-sketches, cameos, engravings, lithographs, pretending to be Beatrice, and representing the poor girl with blubbered eyes, a leer of coquetry, a merry look, as if she were dancing, a piteous look, as if she were beaten, and twenty other modes of fantastic mistake. But here is Guido's very Beatrice; she that slept in the dungeon, and awoke betimes, to ascend the scaffold. And now that you have done it, Hilda, can you interpret what the feeling is, that gives this picture such a mysterious force? For my part, though deeply sensible of its influence, I cannot seize it."

"Nor can I, in words," replied her friend. "But, while I was painting her, I felt all the time as if she were trying to escape from my gaze. She knows that her sorrow is so strange, and so immense, that she ought to be solitary forever, both for the world's sake and her own; and this is the reason we feel such a distance between Beatrice and ourselves, even when our eyes meet hers. It is infinitely heart-breaking to meet her glance, and to feel that nothing can be done to help or comfort her; neither does she ask help or comfort, knowing the hopelessness of her case better than we do. She is a fallen angel, fallen, and yet sinless; and it is only this depth of sorrow, with its weight and darkness, that keeps her down upon earth, and brings her within our view even while it sets her beyond our reach."

"You deem her sinless?" asked Miriam. "That is not so plain to me. If I can pretend to see at all into that dim region, whence she gazes so strangely and sadly at us, Beatrice's own conscience does not acquit her of something evil, and never to be forgiven."

"Sorrow so black as hers oppresses her very nearly as sin would," said Hilda.

"Then," inquired Miriam, "do you think that there was no sin in the deed for which she suffered?"

"Ah," replied Hilda shuddering, "I really had quite forgotten Beatrice's history, and was thinking of her only as the picture seems to reveal her character. Yes, yes; it was terrible guilt, an inexpiable crime, and she feels it to be so. Therefore it is that the forlorn creature so longs to elude our eyes, and forever vanish away into nothingness! Her doom is just."

"Oh, Hilda, your innocence is like a sharp steel sword," exclaimed her friend. "Your judgments are often terribly severe, though you seem all made up of gentleness and mercy. Beatrice's sin may not have been so great; perhaps it was no sin at all, but the best virtue possible in the circumstances. If she viewed it as a sin, it may have been because her nature was too feeble for the fate imposed upon her. Ah," continued Miriam passionately, "if I could only get within her consciousness! If I could but clasp Beatrice

Cenci's ghost, and draw it into myself! I would give my life to know whether she thought herself innocent, or the one great criminal since time began!"

As Miriam gave utterance to these words, Hilda looked from the picture into her face, and was startled to observe that her friend's expression had become almost exactly that of the portrait; as if her passionate wish and struggle to penetrate poor Beatrice's mystery had been successful.

"Oh, for Heaven's sake, Miriam, do not look so!" she cried. "What an actress you are! And I never guessed it before! Ah; now you are yourself again," she added, kissing her. "Leave Beatrice to me, in future."

"Cover up your magical picture then," replied her friend; "else I never can look away from it. It is strange, dear Hilda, how an innocent, delicate, white soul, like yours, has been able to seize the subtle mystery of this portrait; as you surely must, in order to reproduce it so perfectly. Well; we will not talk of it any more. Do you know, I have come to you, this morning, on a small matter of business? Will you undertake it for me?"

"Oh, certainly," said Hilda laughing; "if you choose to trust me with business."

"Nay, it is not a matter of any difficulty," answered Miriam. "Merely to take charge of this pacquet, and keep it for me awhile."

"But why not keep it yourself?" asked Hilda.

"Partly because it will be safer in your charge," said her friend. "I am a careless sort of person in ordinary things; while you, for all you dwell so high above the world, have certain good little housewifely ways of accuracy and order. The pacquet is of some slight importance; and yet, it may be, I shall not ask you for it again. In a week or two, you know, I am leaving Rome. You—setting at defiance the malaria-fever—mean to stay here, and haunt your beloved galleries through the summer. Now, four months hence, unless you hear more from me, I would have you deliver the pacquet according to its address."

Hilda read the direction; it was to Signor Luca Barboni, at the Palazzo Cenci, third piano.

"I will deliver it with my own hand," said she, "precisely four months from to-day, unless you bid me to the contrary. Perhaps I shall meet the ghost of Beatrice in that grim old palace of her forefathers."

"In that case," rejoined Miriam, "do not fail to speak to her, and try to win her confidence. Poor thing! She would be all the better for pouring her heart out freely, and would be glad to do it, if she were sure of sympathy. It irks my brain and heart to think of her, all shut up within herself."— She withdrew the cloth that Hilda had drawn over the picture, and took another long look at it.—"Poor sister Beatrice! For she was still a woman, Hilda, still a sister, be her sin or sorrow what they might. How well you have done it, Hilda! I know not whether Guido will thank you, or be jealous of your rivalship."

"Jealous, indeed!" exclaimed Hilda. "If Guido had not wrought through me, my pains would have been thrown away."

"After all," resumed Miriam, "if a woman had painted the original picture, there might have been something in it which we miss now. I have a great mind to undertake a copy myself, and try to give it what it lacks. Well; good bye! But, stay! I am going for a little airing to the grounds of the Villa Borghese, this afternoon. You will think it very foolish, but I always feel the safer in your company, Hilda, slender little maiden as you are! Will you come?"

"Ah, not to-day, dearest Miriam," she replied. "I have set my heart on giving another touch or two to this picture, and shall not stir abroad till nearly sunset."

"Farewell, then," said her visitor. "I leave you in your dove-cote. What a sweet, strange life you lead here; conversing with the souls of the Old Masters, feeding and fondling your sister-doves, and trimming the Virgin's lamp! Hilda, do you ever pray to the Virgin, while you tend her shrine?"

"Sometimes I have been moved to do so," replied the Dove, blushing and lowering her eyes.—"She was a woman once. Do you think it would be wrong?"

"Nay, that is for you to judge," said Miriam. "But, when you pray next, dear friend, remember me!"

She went down the long descent of the tower staircase; and, just as she reached the street, the flock of doves again took their hurried flight from the pavement to the topmost window. She threw her eyes upward, and beheld them hovering about Hilda's head; for, after her friend's departure, the girl had been more impressed than before by something very sad and troubled in her manner. She was therefore leaning forth from her airy abode, and flinging down a kind, maidenly kiss, and a gesture of farewell, in the hope that these might alight upon Miriam's heart, and comfort its unknown sorrow a little. Kenyon, the sculptor, who chanced to be passing the head of the street, took note of that ethereal kiss, and wished that he could have caught it in the air and got Hilda's leave to keep it!

VIII

THE SUBURBAN VILLA

D ONATELLO, while it was still a doubtful question betwixt afternoon and morning, set forth, to keep the appointment which Miriam had carelessly tendered him, in the grounds of the Villa Borghese.

The entrance to these grounds (as all my readers know, for everybody, now-a-days, has been in Rome) is just outside of the Porta del Popolo. Passing beneath that not very impressive specimen of Michel Angelo's architecture, a minute's walk will transport the visitor from the small, uneasy lava-stones of the Roman pavement into broad, gravelled carriage-drives; whence a little farther stroll brings him to the soft turf of a beautiful seclusion. A seclusion, but seldom a solitude; for priest, noble, and populace, stranger and native, all who breathe Roman air, find free admission, and come hither to taste the languid enjoyment of the day-dream that they call life.

But Donatello's enjoyment was of a livelier kind. He soon began to draw long and delightful breaths among those shadowy walks. Judging by the pleasure which the sylvan character of the scene excited in him, it might be no merely fanciful theory to set him down as the kinsman, not far remote, of that wild, sweet, playful, rustic creature, to whose marble image he bore so striking a resemblance. How mirthful a discovery would it be, (and yet with a touch of pathos in it,) if the breeze, which sported fondly with his clustering locks, were to waft them suddenly aside, and show a pair of leaf-shaped, furry ears! What an honest strain of wildness would it indicate! And into what regions of rich mystery would it extend Donatello's sympathies, to be thus linked (and by no monstrous chain) with what we call the inferiour tribes of being, whose simplicity, mingled with his human intelligence, might partly restore what man has lost of the divine!

The scenery, amid which the youth now strayed, was such as arrays itself in the imagination, when we read the beautiful old myths, and fancy a brighter sky, a softer turf, a more picturesque arrangement of venerable trees, than we find in the rude and untrained landscapes of the Western world. The ilex-trees, so ancient and time-honoured were they, seemed to have lived for ages undisturbed, and to feel no dread of profanation by the axe, any more than overthrow by the thunder-stroke. It had already passed out of their dreamy old memories, that, only a few years ago, they were grievously imperilled by the Gaul's last assault upon the walls of Rome. As if confident in the long peace of their lifetime, they assumed attitudes of indolent repose. They leaned over the green turf in ponderous grace, throwing abroad their great branches without danger of interfering with other trees; though other majestic trees grew near enough for dignified society, but too distant for constraint. Never was there a more venerable quietude than that which slept among their sheltering boughs; never a sweeter sunshine than that now gladdening the gentle gloom, which these leafy patriarchs strove to diffuse over the swelling and subsiding lawns.

In other portions of the grounds, the stone-pines lifted their dense clump of branches upon a slender length of stem, so high that they looked like green islands in the air; flinging down a shadow upon the turf, so far off that you hardly knew what tree had made it. Again, there were avenues of cypress, resembling dark flames of huge, funereal candles, which spread dusk and twilight roundabout them, instead of cheerful radiance. The more open spots were all a-bloom, even so early in the season, with anemones, of wondrous size, both white and rose-coloured, and violets, that betrayed themselves by their rich fragrance, even if their blue eyes failed to meet your own. Daisies, too, were abundant, but larger than the modest little English flower, and therefore of small account.

These wooded and flowery lawns are more beautiful than the finest of English park-scenery, more touching, more impressive, through the neglect that leaves Nature so much to her own ways and methods. Since man seldom interferes with her, she sets to work in her quiet way, and makes herself at home. There is enough of human care, it is true, bestowed long ago, and still bestowed, to prevent wildness from growing into deformity; and the result is an ideal landscape, a woodland scene, that seems to have been projected out of a poet's mind. If the ancient Faun were other than a mere creation of old poetry, and could have re-appeared anywhere, it must have been in such a scene as this.

In the openings of the wood, there are fountains plashing into marble basins, the depths of which are shaggy with water-weeds; or they tumble like natural cascades from rock to rock, sending their murmur afar, to make the quiet and silence more appreciable. Scattered here and there, with careless artifice, stand old altars, bearing Roman inscriptions. Statues, gray with the long corrosion of even that soft atmosphere, half hide and half reveal themselves, high on pedestals, or perhaps fallen and broken on the turf. Terminal figures, columns of marble or granite, porticoes, arches, are seen in the vistas of the wood-paths, either veritable relics of antiquity, or with so exquisite a touch of artful ruin on them, that they are better than if really antique. At all events, grass grows on the tops of the shattered pillars, and weeds and flowers root themselves in the chinks of the massive arches and fronts of temples, and clamber at large over their pediments, as if this were the thousandth summer since their winged seeds alighted there. What a strange idea—what a needless labour—to construct artificial ruins in Rome, the native soil of Ruin! But even these sportive imitations, wrought by man in emulation of what Time has done to temples and palaces, are perhaps centuries old, and, beginning as illusions, have grown to be venerable in sober earnest. The result of all is a scene, pensive, lovely, dreamlike, enjoyable, and sad, such as is to be found nowhere save in these princely villa-residences, in the neighborhood of Rome; a scene that must have required generations and ages, during which growth, decay, and man's intelligence, wrought kindly together, to render it so gently wild as we behold it now.

The final charm is bestowed by the Malaria. There is a piercing, thrilling, delicious kind of regret in the idea of so much beauty thrown away, or only enjoyable at its half-development, in winter and early spring, and never to be dwelt amongst, as the home-scenery of any human being. For if you come hither in summer, and stray through these glades in the golden sunset, Fever walks arm in arm with you, and Death awaits you at the end of the dim vista. Thus the scene is like Eden in its loveliness; like Eden, too, in the fatal spell that removes it beyond the scope of man's actual possessions.

But Donatello felt nothing of this dreamlike melancholy that haunts the spot. As he passed among the sunny shadows, his spirit seemed to acquire new elasticity. The flicker of the sunshine, the sparkle of the fountain's gush, the dance of the leaf upon the bough, the woodland fragrance, the green freshness, the old sylvan peace and freedom, were all intermingled in those long breaths which he drew. The ancient dust, the mouldiness of Rome, the dead atmosphere in which he had wasted so many months; the hard pavements, the smell of ruin, and decaying generations; the chill palaces, the convent-bells, the heavy incense of altars; the life that he had led in those dark, narrow streets, among priests, soldiers, nobles, artists, and women—all the sense of these things rose from the young man's consciousness like a cloud, which had darkened over him without his knowing how densely. He drank in the natural influences of the scene, and was intoxicated as by an exhilarating wine. He ran races with himself along the gleam and shadow of the wood-paths. He leapt up to catch the overhanging bough of an ilex, and swinging himself by it, alighted far onward, as if he had flown thither through the air. In a sudden rapture, he embraced the trunk of a sturdy tree, and seemed to imagine it a creature worthy of affection and capable of a tender response; he clasped it closely in his arms, as a Faun might have clasped the warm, feminine grace of the Nymph, whom antiquity supposed to dwell within that rough, encircling rind. Then, in order to bring himself closer to the genial earth, with which his kindred instincts linked him so strongly, he threw himself at full length on the turf, and pressed down his lips, kissing the violets and daisies, which kissed him back again, though shyly, in their maiden fashion.

While he lay there, it was pleasant to see how the green and blue lizards (who had been basking on some rock, or on a fallen pillar, that absorbed the warmth of the sun) scrupled not to scramble over him, with their small feet; and how the birds alighted on the nearest twigs and sang their little roundelays, unbroken by any chirrup of alarm. They recognized him, it may be, as something akin to themselves;

or else they fancied that he was rooted and grew there; for these wild pets of Nature dreaded him no more, in his buoyant life, than if a mound of soil, and grass, and flowers, had long since covered his dead body, converting it back to the sympathies from which human existence had estranged it.

All of us, after long abode in cities, have felt the blood gush more joyously through our veins with the first breath of rural air; few could feel it so much as Donatello, a creature of simple elements, bred in the sweet, sylvan life of Tuscany, and, for months back, dwelling amid the mouldy gloom and dim splendour of old Rome. Nature has been shut out for numberless centuries from those stony-hearted streets, to which he had latterly grown accustomed; there is no trace of her, except for what blades of grass spring out of the pavements of the less trodden piazzas, or what weeds cluster and tuft themselves on the cornices of ruins. Therefore his joy was like that of a child that had gone astray from home, and finds him suddenly in his mother's arms again.

At last, deeming it full time for Miriam to keep her tryst, he climbed to the tip-top of the tallest tree and thence looked about him, swaying to-and-fro in the gentle breeze, which was like the respiration of that great, leafy, living thing. Donatello saw beneath him the whole circuit of the enchanted ground; the statues and columns pointing upward from among the shrubbery; the fountains flashing in the sunlight; the paths winding hither and thither, and continually finding out some nook of new and ancient pleasantness. He saw the villa, too, with its marble front incrusted all over with bas-reliefs, and statues in its many niches; it was as beautiful as a fairy palace, and seemed an abode in which the lord and lady of this fair domain might fitly dwell, and come forth, each morning, to enjoy as sweet a life as their happiest dreams of the past night could have depicted. All this he saw; but his first glance had taken in too wide a sweep; and it was not till his eyes fell almost directly beneath him, that Donatello beheld Miriam just turning into the path that led across the roots of his very tree.

He descended among the foliage, waiting for her to come close to the trunk, and then suddenly dropt from an impending bough, and alighted at her side. It was as if the swaying of the branches had let a ray of sunlight through. The same ray likewise glimmered among the gloomy meditations that encompassed Miriam, and lit up the pale, dark beauty of her face, while it responded pleasantly to Donatello's glance.

"I hardly know," said she smiling, "whether you have sprouted out of the earth, or fallen from the clouds. In either case, you are welcome."

And they walked onward together.

IX

THE FAUN AND NYMPH

MIRIAM'S sadder mood, it might be, had at first an effect on Donatello's spirits. It checked the joyous ebullition into which they would otherwise have effervesced when he found himself in her society, not, as heretofore, in the old gloom of Rome, but under that bright, soft sky, and in those Arcadian woods. He was silent for awhile; it being, indeed, seldom Donatello's impulse to express himself copiously in words. His usual modes of demonstration were by the natural language of gesture, the instinctive movement of his agile frame, and the unconscious play of his features, which, within a limited range of thought and emotion, could speak volumes in a moment.

By-and-by, his own mood seemed to brighten Miriam's, and was reflected back upon himself. He began inevitably, as it were, to dance along the wood-path, flinging himself into attitudes of strange, comic grace. Often, too, he ran a little way in advance of his companion, and then stood to watch her as she approached along the shadowy and sun-flickered path. With every step she took, he expressed his joy at her nearer and nearer presence by what might be thought an extravagance of gesticulation, but which doubtless was the language of the natural man; though laid aside and forgotten by other men, now that words have been feebly substituted in the place of signs and symbols. He gave Miriam the idea of a being not precisely man, nor yet a child, but, in a high and beautiful sense, an animal; a creature in a state of development less than what mankind has attained, yet the more perfect within itself for that very deficiency. This idea filled her mobile imagination with agreeable fantasies, which, after smiling at them herself, she tried to convey to the young man.

"What are you, my friend?" she exclaimed, always keeping in mind his singular resemblance to the Faun of the Capitol.— "If you are, in good truth, that wild and pleasant creature whose face you wear, pray make me known to your kindred. They will be found hereabouts, if anywhere. Knock at the rough rind of this ilex-tree, and summon forth the Dryad! Ask the water-nymph to rise dripping from yonder fountain, and exchange a moist pressure of the hand with me! Do not fear that I shall shrink, even if one of your rough cousins, a hairy Satyr, should come capering on his goat-legs out of the haunts of far antiquity, and propose to dance with me among these lawns! And will not Bacchus—with whom you consorted so familiarly of old, and who loved you so well— will he not meet us here, and squeeze rich grapes into his cup for you and me?"

Donatello smiled; he laughed heartily, indeed, in sympathy with the mirth that gleamed out of Miriam's deep, dark eyes. But he did not seem quite to understand her mirthful talk, nor to be disposed to explain what kind of creature he was, or to inquire with what divine or poetic kindred his companion feigned to link him. He appeared only to know that Miriam was beautiful, and that she smiled graciously upon him; that the present moment was very sweet, and himself most happy with the sunshine, the sylvan scenery, and woman's kindly charm, which it inclosed within its small circumference. It was delightful to see the trust which he reposed in Miriam, and his pure joy in her propinquity; he asked nothing, sought nothing, save to be near the beloved object, and brimmed over with ecstasy at that simple boon. A creature of the happy tribes below us sometimes shows the capacity of this enjoyment; a man, seldom or never.

"Donatello," said Miriam, looking at him thoughtfully, but amused, yet not without a shade of sorrow, "you seem very happy! What makes you so?"

"Because I love you!" answered Donatello.

He made this momentous confession as if it were the most natural thing in the world; and, on her part—such was the contagion of his simplicity—Miriam heard it without anger or disturbance, though with no responding emotion. It was as if they had strayed across the limits of Arcadia, and come under a civil polity where young men might avow their passion with as little restraint as a bird pipes its notes, to a similar purpose.

"Why should you love me, foolish boy?" said she. "We have no points of sympathy at all. There are not two creatures more unlike, in this wide world, than you and I!"

"You are yourself, and I am Donatello," replied he. "Therefore I love you! There needs no other reason."

Certainly, there was no better or more explicable reason. It might have been imagined that Donatello's unsophisticated heart would be more readily attracted to a feminine nature of clear simplicity, like his own, than to one already turbid with grief or wrong, as Miriam's seemed to be. Perhaps, on the other hand, his character needed the dark element which it found in her. The force and energy of will, that sometimes flashed through her eyes, may have taken him captive; or, not improbably, the varying lights and shadows of her temper, now so mirthful, and anon so sad with mysterious gloom, had bewitched the youth. Analyze the matter as we may, the reason assigned by Donatello himself was as satisfactory as we are likely to attain.

Miriam could not think seriously of the avowal that had passed. He held out his love so freely, in his open palm, that she felt it could be nothing but a toy, which she might play with for an instant, and give back again. And yet Donatello's heart was so fresh a fountain, that, had Miriam been more world-worn than she was, she might have found it exquisite to slake her thirst with the feelings that welled up and brimmed over from it. She was far, very far, from the dusty mediæval epoch, when some women had a taste for such refreshment. Even for her, however, there was an inexpressible charm in the simplicity that prompted Donatello's words and deeds; though, unless she caught them in precisely the true light, they seemed but folly, the offspring of a maimed or imperfectly developed intellect. Alternately, she almost admired, or wholly scorned him, and knew not which estimate resulted from the deeper appreciation. But it could not, she decided for herself, be other than an innocent pastime, if they two—sure to be separated by their different paths in life, tomorrow—were to gather up some of the little pleasures that chanced to grow about their feet, like the violets and wood-anemones, to-day.

Yet an impulse of rectitude impelled Miriam to give him what she still held to be a needless warning against an imaginary peril.

"If you were wiser, Donatello, you would think me a dangerous person," said she. "If you follow my footsteps, they will lead you to no good. You ought to be afraid of me."

"I would as soon think of fearing the air we breathe!" he replied.

"And well you may, for it is full of malaria," said Miriam; she went on, hinting at an intangible confession, such as persons with overburthened hearts often make to children or dumb animals, or to holes in the earth, where they think their secrets may be at once revealed and buried.—"Those who come too near me are in danger of great mischiefs, I do assure you. Take warning therefore! It is a sad fatality that has brought you from your home among the Apennines—some rusty old castle, I suppose, with a village at its foot, and an Arcadian environment of vineyards, fig-trees, and olive-orchards—a sad mischance, I say, that has transported you to my side. You have had a happy life hitherto—have you not, Donatello?"

"Oh, yes," answered the young man; and, though not of a retrospective turn, he made the best effort he could to send his mind back into the past.—"I remember thinking it happiness to dance with the contadinas at a village-feast; to taste the new, sweet wine at vintage-time, and the old, ripened wine, which our Podere is famous for, in the cold winter evenings; and to devour great, luscious figs, and apricots, peaches, cherries, and melons. I was often happy in the woods, too, with hounds and horses, and very happy in watching all sorts of creatures and birds that haunt the leafy solitudes. But never half so happy as now!"

"In these delightful groves?" she asked.

"Here, and with you!" answered Donatello. "Just as we are now."

"What a fulness of content in him! How silly, and how delightful!" said Miriam to herself; then addressing him again—"But, Donatello, how long will this happiness last?"

"How long!" he exclaimed; for it perplexed him even more to think of the future than to remember the past.—"Why should it have any end? How long! Forever!—forever!—forever!"

"The child!—the simpleton!" said Miriam with sudden laughter, and checking it as suddenly.—"But, is he a simpleton indeed? Here, in those few, natural words, he has expressed that deep sense, that profound conviction of its own immortality, which genuine love never fails to bring. He perplexes me—yes, and bewitches me—wild, gentle, beautiful creature that he is! It is like playing with a young greyhound!"

Her eyes filled with tears, at the same time that a smile shone out of them. Then first she became sensible of a delight and grief, at once, in feeling this zephyr of a new affection, with its untainted freshness, blow over her weary, stifled heart, which had no right to be revived by it. The very exquisiteness of the enjoyment made her know that it ought to be a forbidden one.

"Donatello," she hastily exclaimed, "for your own sake, leave me! It is not such a happy thing as you imagine it, to wander in these woods with me, a girl from another land, burthened with a doom that she tells to none. I might make you dread me—perhaps hate me—if I chose; and I must choose, if I find you loving me too well!"

"I fear nothing!" said Donatello, looking into her unfathomable eyes, with perfect trust. "I love always!"

"I speak in vain," thought Miriam within herself. "Well, then, for this one hour, let me be such as he imagines me. Tomorrow will be time enough to come back to my reality. My reality! What is it? Is the past so indestructible?—the future so immitigable? Is the dark dream, in which I walk, of such solid, stony substance, that there can be no escape out of its dungeon? Be it so! There is, at least, that ethereal quality in my spirit, that it can make me as gay as Donatello himself—for this one hour!"

And immediately she brightened up, as if an inward flame, heretofore stifled, were now permitted to fill her with its happy lustre, glowing through her cheeks and dancing in her eye-beams. Donatello, brisk and cheerful as he seemed before, showed a sensibility to Miriam's gladdened mood by breaking into still wilder and ever-varying activity. He frisked around her, bubbling over with joy, which clothed itself in words that had little individual meaning, and in snatches of song that seemed as natural as bird-notes. Then they both laughed together, and heard their own laughter returning in the echoes, and laughed again at the response; so that the ancient and solemn grove became full of merriment for these two blithe spirits. A bird happening to sing cheerily, Donatello gave a peculiar call, and the little feathered creature came fluttering about his head, as if it had known him through many summers.

"How close he stands to Nature!" said Miriam, observing this pleasant familiarity between her companion and the bird. —"He shall make me as natural as himself—for this one hour!"

As they strayed through that sweet wilderness, she felt more and more the influence of his elastic temperament. Miriam was an impressible and impulsive creature, as unlike herself, in different moods, as if a melancholy maiden and a glad one were both bound within the girdle about her waist, and kept in magic thraldom by the brooch that clasped it. Naturally, it is true, she was the more inclined to melancholy, yet fully capable of that high frolic of the spirits which richly compensates for many gloomy hours; if her soul was apt to lurk in the darkness of a cavern, she could sport madly in the sunshine before the cavern's mouth. Except the freshest mirth of animal spirits, like Donatello's, there is no merriment, no wild exhilaration, comparable to that of melancholy people, escaping from the dark region in which it is their custom to keep themselves imprisoned.

So the shadowy Miriam almost outdid Donatello, on his own ground. They ran races with each other, side by side, with shouts and laughter; they pelted one another with early flowers, and gathering them up again, they twined them with green leaves into garlands for both their heads. They played together like children, or creatures of immortal youth;

for (so much had they flung aside the sombre habitudes of daily life) they seemed born to be sportive forever, and endowed with eternal mirthfulness instead of any deeper joy. It was a glimpse far backward into Arcadian life, or, farther still, into the Golden Age, before mankind was burthened with sin and sorrow, and before pleasure had been darkened with those shadows that bring it into high relief, and make it Happiness.

"Hark!" cried Donatello, stopping short, as he was about to bind Miriam's fair hands with flowers, and lead her along in triumph;—"there is music somewhere in the grove!"

"It is your kinsman Pan, most likely," said Miriam, "playing on his pipe. Let us go seek him, and make him puff out his rough cheeks and pipe his merriest air! Come; the strain of music will guide us onward like a gaily coloured thread of silk."

"Or like a chain of flowers!" responded Donatello, drawing her along by that which he had twined.—"This way!—come!"

X

THE SYLVAN DANCE

A S THE MUSIC CAME fresher on their ears, they danced to its cadence, extemporizing new steps and attitudes. Each varying movement had a grace which might have been worth putting into marble, for the long delight of days to come, but vanished with the moment that gave it birth, and was effaced from memory by another. In Miriam's motion, freely as she flung herself into the frolic of the hour, there was still an artful beauty; in Donatello's there was a charm of indescribable grotesqueness, hand in hand with grace; sweet, bewitching, most provocative of laughter, and yet akin to pathos, so deeply did it touch the heart. This was the ultimate peculiarity, the final touch, distinguishing between the sylvan creature and the beautiful companion at his side. Setting apart only this, Miriam resembled a Nymph, as much as Donatello did a Faun.

There were flitting moments, indeed, when she played the sylvan character as perfectly as he. Catching glimpses of her, then, you would have fancied that an oak had sundered its rough bark to let her dance freely forth, endowed with the same spirit in her human form as that which rustles in the leaves; or that she had emerged through the pebbly bottom of a fountain, a water-nymph, to play and sparkle in the sunshine, flinging a quivering light around her, and suddenly disappearing in a shower of rainbow drops.

As the fountain sometimes subsides into its basin, so in Miriam there were symptoms that the frolic of her spirits would at last tire itself out.

"Ah, Donatello," cried she laughing, as she stopt to take breath, "you have an unfair advantage over me! I am no true creature of the woods; while you are a real Faun, I do believe. When your curls shook, just now, methought I had a peep at the pointed ears!"

Donatello snapt his fingers above his head, as Fauns and Satyrs taught us first to do, and seemed to radiate jollity out of his whole nimble person. Nevertheless, there was a kind of dim apprehension in his face, as if he dreaded that a moment's pause might break the spell, and snatch away the sportive companion whom he had waited for through so many dreary months.

"Dance, dance!" cried he joyously. "If we take breath, we shall be as we were yesterday. Here, now, is the music, just beyond this clump of trees. Dance, Miriam, dance!"

They had now reached an open, grassy glade, (of which there are many, in that artfully constructed wilderness,) set round with stone-seats, on which the aged moss had kindly essayed to spread itself, instead of cushions. On one of the stone-benches sat the musicians, whose strains had enticed our wild couple thitherward. They proved to be a vagrant band, such as Rome, and all Italy, abounds with, comprising a harp, a flute, and a violin, which, though greatly the worse for wear, the performers had skill enough to provoke and modulate into tolerable harmony. It chanced to be a feast-day; and instead of playing in the sun-scorched piazzas of the city, or beneath the windows of some unresponsive palace, they had bethought themselves to try the echoes of these woods; for, on the festas of the Church, Rome scatters its merry-makers all abroad, ripe for the dance or any other pastime.

As Miriam and Donatello emerged from among the trees, the musicians scraped, tinkled, or blew, each according to his various kind of instrument, more inspiringly than ever. A dark-cheeked little girl, with bright black eyes, stood by, shaking a tambourine, set round with tinkling bells, and thumping it on its parchment-head. Without interrupting his brisk, though measured movement, Donatello snatched away this unmelodious contrivance, and flourishing it above his head, produced music of indescribable potency; still dancing with frisky step, and striking the tambourine, and ringing its little bells, all in one jovial act.

It might be that there was magic in the sound, or contagion, at least, in the spirit which had got possession of Miriam and himself; for, very soon, a number of festal people were drawn to the spot, and struck into the dance, singly, or in pairs, as if they were all gone mad with jollity. Among them were some of the plebeian damsels, whom we meet bareheaded in the Roman streets, with silver stilettos thrust through their glossy hair; the contadinas, too, from the Campagna and the villages, with their rich and picturesque costumes, of scarlet and all bright hues, such as fairer maidens might not venture to put on. Then came the modern Roman, from Trastevere, perchance, with his old cloak drawn about him like a toga, which, anon, as his active motion heated him, he flung aside. Three French soldiers capered freely into the throng, in wide scarlet trowsers, their short swords dangling at their sides; and three German artists, in gray flaccid hats, and flaunting beards; and one of the Pope's Swiss Guardsmen, in the strange motley garb which Michel Angelo contrived for them. Two young English tourists (one of them a lord) took contadine-partners, and dashed in; as did also a shaggy man in goat-skin breeches, who

looked like rustic Pan in person, and footed it as merrily
as he. Besides the above, there was a herdsman or two, from
the Campagna, and a few peasants in sky-blue jackets and
small-clothes, tied with ribbons at the knees;—haggard and
sallow were these last, poor serfs, having little to eat, and
nothing but the malaria to breathe; but still they plucked up
a momentary spirit, and joined hands in Donatello's dance.

Here, as it seemed, had the Golden Age come back again,
within the precincts of this sunny glade; thawing mankind
out of their cold formalities; releasing them from irksome
restraint; mingling them together in such childlike gaiety,
that new flowers (of which the old bosom of the Earth is
full) sprang up beneath their footsteps. The sole exception
to the geniality of the moment, as we have understood, was
seen in a countryman of our own, who sneered at the spectacle, and declined to compromise his dignity by making
part of it.

The harper thrummed with rapid fingers; the violin-player
flashed his bow back and forth across the strings; the flautist
poured his breath in quick puffs of jollity; while Donatello
shook the tambourine above his head, and led the merry
throng with unweariable steps. As they followed one another,
in a wild ring of mirth, it seemed the realization of one of
those bas-reliefs, where a dance of nymphs, satyrs, or bac-
chanals, is twined around the circle of an antique vase. Or
it was like the sculptured scene on the front and sides of
a sarcophagus, where, as often as any other device, a festive
procession mocks the ashes and white bones that are treasured
up, within. You might take it for a marriage-pageant; but,
after a while, if you look attentively at these merry-makers,
following them from end to end of the marble coffin, you
doubt whether their gay movement is leading them to a happy
close. A youth has suddenly fallen in the dance; a chariot is
overturned and broken, flinging the charioteer headlong on

the ground; a maiden seems to have grown faint or weary, and is drooping on the bosom of a friend. Always, some tragic incident is shadowed forth, or thrust sidelong into the spectacle; and when once it has caught your eye, you can look no more at the festal portions of the scene, except with reference to this one slightly suggested doom and sorrow.

As in its mirth, so in the darker characteristic here alluded to, there was an analogy between the sculptured scene on the sarcophagus and the wild dance which we have been describing. In the midst of its madness and riot, Miriam found herself suddenly confronted by a strange figure that shook its fantastic garments in the air, and pranced before her on its tiptoes, almost vying with the agility of Donatello himself. It was the Model.

A moment afterwards, Donatello was aware that she had retired from the dance. He hastened towards her and flung himself on the grass, beside the stone-bench on which Miriam was sitting. But a strange distance and unapproachableness had all at once enveloped her; and though he saw her within reach of his arm, yet the light of her eyes seemed as far off as that of a star; nor was there any warmth in the melancholy smile with which she regarded him.

"Come back!" cried he. "Why should this happy hour end so soon?"

"It must end here, Donatello," said she, in answer to his words and outstretched hand; "and such hours, I believe, do not often repeat themselves in a lifetime. Let me go, my friend! Let me vanish from you quietly, among the shadows of these trees. See; the companions of our pastime are vanishing already!"

Whether it was that the harp-strings were broken, the violin out of tune, or the flautist out of breath, so it chanced that the music had ceased, and the dancers come abruptly to a pause. All that motley throng of rioters was dissolved as suddenly as it had been drawn together. In Miriam's remembrance, the scene had a character of fantasy. It was as if a company of satyrs, fauns, and nymphs, with Pan in the midst of them, had been disporting themselves in these venerable woods, only a moment ago; and now, in another moment, because some profane eye had looked at them too closely, or some intruder had cast a shadow on their mirth, the sylvan pageant had utterly disappeared. If a few of the merry-makers lingered among the trees, they had hidden their racy peculiarities under the garb and aspect of ordinary people, and sheltered themselves in the weary common-place of daily life. Just an instant before, it was Arcadia, and the Golden Age. The spell being broken, it was now only that old tract of pleasure-ground, close by the people's gate of Rome; a tract where the crimes and calamities of ages, the many battles, blood recklessly poured out, and deaths of myriads, have corrupted all the soil, creating an influence that makes the air deadly to human lungs.

"You must leave me!" said Miriam to Donatello, more imperatively than before. "Have I not said it? Go; and look not behind you!"

"Miriam," whispered Donatello, grasping her hand forcibly, "who is it that stands in the shadow, yonder, beckoning you to follow him?"

"Hush; leave me!" repeated Miriam. "Your hour is past; his hour has come!"

Donatello still gazed in the direction which he had indicated; and the expression of his face was fearfully changed, being so disordered, perhaps with terrour—at all events, with anger and invincible repugnance—that Miriam hardly knew him. His lips were drawn apart, so as to disclose his set teeth, thus giving him a look of animal rage which we seldom see except in persons of the simplest and rudest

natures. A shudder seemed to pass through his very bones.
"I hate him!" muttered he.

"Be satisfied; I hate him too!" said Miriam.

She had no thought of making this avowal, but was irresistibly drawn to it by the sympathy of the dark emotion in her own breast with that so strongly expressed by Donatello. Two drops of water, or of blood, do not more naturally flow into each other, than did her hatred into his.

"Shall I clutch him by the throat?" whispered Donatello, with a savage scowl. "Bid me do so; and we are rid of him forever!"

"In Heaven's name, no violence!" exclaimed Miriam, affrighted out of the scornful controul which she had hitherto held over her companion, by the fierceness that he so suddenly developed.—"Oh, have pity on me, Donatello, if for nothing else, yet because, in the midst of my wretchedness, I let myself be your playmate for this one wild hour. Follow me no farther! Henceforth, leave me to my doom. Dear friend—kind, simple, loving friend—make me not more wretched by the remembrance of having thrown fierce hates or loves into the well-spring of your happy life!"

"Not follow you!" repeated Donatello, soothed from anger into sorrow, less by the purport of what she said than by the melancholy sweetness of her voice. "Not follow you! What other path have I?"

"We will talk of it once again," said Miriam, still soothingly. "Soon—tomorrow—when you will;—only, leave me now!"

XI

FRAGMENTARY SENTENCES

IN THE BORGHESE GROVE, so recently uproarious with merriment and music, there remained only Miriam and her strange follower.

A solitude had suddenly spread itself around them. It perhaps symbolized a peculiar character in the relation of these two, insulating them, and building up an insuperable barrier between their life-streams and other currents, which might seem to flow in close vicinity. For it is one of the chief earthly incommodities of some species of misfortune, or of a great crime, that it makes the actor in the one, or the sufferer of the other, an alien in the world, by interposing a wholly unsympathetic medium betwixt himself and those whom he yearns to meet.

Owing, it may be, to this moral estrangement—this chill remoteness of their position—there have come to us but a few vague whisperings of what passed in Miriam's interview, that afternoon, with the sinister personage who had dogged her footsteps ever since the visit to the catacomb. In weaving these mystic utterances into a continuous scene, we undertake a task resembling, in its perplexity, that of gathering up and piecing together the fragments of a letter, which has been torn and scattered to the winds. Many words of deep significance—many entire sentences, and those possibly the most important ones—have flown too far, on the winged breeze, to be recovered. If we insert our own conjectural amendments, we perhaps give a purport utterly at variance with the true one. Yet, unless we attempt something in this way, there must remain an unsightly gap, and a lack of continuousness and dependence in our narrative; so that it would arrive at certain inevitable catastrophes without due warning of their imminence.

Of so much we are sure, that there seemed to be a sadly mysterious fascination in the influence of this ill-omened person over Miriam; it was such as beasts and reptiles, of subtle and evil nature, sometimes exercise upon their victims. Marvellous it was, to see the hopelessness with which—being naturally of so courageous a spirit—she resigned herself to the thraldom in which he held her. That iron chain, of which some of the massive links were round her feminine waist, and the others in his ruthless hand—or which perhaps bound the pair together by a bond equally torturing to each—must have been forged in some such unhallowed furnace as is only kindled by evil passions and fed by evil deeds.

Yet, let us trust, there may have been no crime in Miriam, but only one of those fatalities which are among the most insoluble riddles propounded to mortal comprehension; the fatal decree, by which every crime is made to be the agony of many innocent persons, as well as of the single guilty one.

It was, at any rate, but a feeble and despairing kind of remonstrance which she had now the energy to oppose against his persecution.

"You follow me too closely," she said, in low, faultering accents. "You allow me too scanty room to draw my breath. Do you know what will be the end of this?"

"I know well what must be the end," he replied.

"Tell me, then," said Miriam, "that I may compare your foreboding with my own. Mine is a very dark one."

"There can be but one result, and that soon," answered the Model. "You must throw off your present mask, and assume another. You must vanish out of the scene, quit Rome with me, and leave no trace whereby to follow you. It is in my power, as you well know, to compel your acquiescence in my bidding. You are aware of the penalty of a refusal."

"Not that penalty with which you would terrify me," said Miriam. "Another there may be, but not so grievous."

"What is that other?" he inquired.

"Death! Simply, death!" she answered.

"Death," said her persecutor, "is not so simple and opportune a thing as you imagine. You are strong and warm with life. Sensitive and irritable as your spirit is, these many months of trouble—this latter thraldom in which I hold you— have scarcely made your cheek paler than I saw it in your girlhood. Miriam, (for I forbear to speak another name, at which these leaves would shiver above our heads,) Miriam, you cannot die!"

"Might not a dagger find my heart?" said she, for the first time meeting his eyes. "Would not poison make an end of me? Will not the Tiber drown me?"

"It might," he answered; "for I allow that you are mortal. But, Miriam, believe me, it is not your fate to die, while there remains so much to be sinned and suffered in the world. We have a destiny, which we must needs fulfil together. I, too, have struggled to escape it. I was as anxious as yourself to break the tie between us—to bury the past in a fathomless grave—to make it impossible that we should ever meet, until you confront me at the bar of Judgment! You little can imagine what steps I took to render all this secure. And what was the result? Our strange interview, in the bowels of the earth, convinced me of the futility of my design."

"Ah, fatal chance!" cried Miriam, covering her face with her hands.

"Yes; your heart trembled with horrour when you recognized me," rejoined he. "But, you did not guess, that there was an equal horrour in my own!"

"Why could not the weight of earth, above our heads, have crumbled down upon us both, forcing us apart, but burying us equally!" cried Miriam, in a burst of vehement passion. "Oh, that we could have wandered in those dismal passages till we both perished, taking opposite paths, in the darkness, so that, when we lay down to die, our last breaths might not mingle!"

"It were vain to wish it," said the Model. "In all that labyrinth of midnight paths, we should have found one another out, to live or die together. Our fates cross and are entangled. The threads are twisted into a strong cord, which is dragging us to an evil doom. Could the knots be severed, we might escape. But neither can your slender fingers untie those knots, nor my masculine force break them. We must submit!"

"Pray for rescue, as I have!" exclaimed Miriam. "Pray for deliverance from me, since I am your evil genius, as you mine! Dark as your life has been, I have known you to pray, in times past!"

At these words of Miriam, a tremour and horrour appeared to seize upon her persecutor, insomuch that he shook and grew ashy pale before her eyes. In this man's memory, there was something that made it awful for him to think of prayer; nor could any torture be more intolerable, than to be reminded of such Divine comfort and succour as await pious souls merely for the asking. This torment was perhaps the token of a native temperament deeply susceptible of religious impressions, but which had been wronged, violated, and debased, until, at length, it was capable only of terrour from the sources that were intended for our purest and loftiest consolation. He looked so fearfully at her, and with such intense pain struggling in his eyes, that Miriam felt pity.

And, now, all at once, it struck her that he might be mad. It was an idea that had never before seriously occurred to her mind, although, as soon as suggested, it fitted marvellously into many circumstances that lay within her knowledge. But, alas! such was her evil fortune, that, whether mad or no, his power over her remained the same, and was likely to be used only the more tyrannously if exercised by a lunatic.

"I would not give you pain," she said soothingly. "Your faith allows you the consolations of penance and absolution. Try what help there may be in these, and leave me to myself!"

"Do not think it, Miriam," said he. "We are bound together, and can never part again."

"Why should it seem so impossible?" she rejoined. "Think, how I had escaped from all the past! I had made for myself a new sphere, and found new friends, new occupations, new hopes and enjoyments. My heart, methinks, was almost as unburthened, as if there had been no miserable life behind me. The human spirit does not perish of a single wound, nor exhaust itself in a single trial of life. Let us but keep asunder, and all may go well for both."

"We fancied ourselves forever sundered," he replied. "Yet we met, once, in the bowels of the earth; and, were we to part now, our fates would fling us together again, in a desert, on a mountain-top, or in whatever spot seemed safest. You speak in vain, therefore."

"You mistake your own will for an iron necessity," said Miriam. "Otherwise, you might have suffered me to glide past you like a ghost, when we met among those ghosts of ancient days. Even now, you might bid me pass as freely."

"Never!" said he, with immitigable will. "Your re-appearance has destroyed the work of years. You know the power that I have over you. Obey my bidding; or, within short time, it shall be exercised—nor will I cease to haunt you, till the moment comes."

"Then," said Miriam, more calmly, "I foresee the end, and have already warned you of it. It will be death!"

"Your own death, Miriam—or mine?" he asked, looking fixedly at her.

"Do you imagine me a murderess?" said she, shuddering. "You, at least, have no right to think me so!"

"Yet," rejoined he, with a glance of dark meaning, "men have said, that this white hand had once a crimson stain."

He took her hand, as he spoke, and held it in his own, in spite of the repugnance, amounting to nothing short of agony, with which she struggled to regain it. Holding it up to the fading light, (for there was already dimness among the trees,) he appeared to examine it closely, as if to discover the imaginary blood-stain with which he taunted her. He smiled, as he let it go.

"It looks very white," said he; "but I have known hands as white, which all the water in the ocean could not have washed clean!"

"It had no stain," retorted Miriam bitterly, "until you grasped it in your own!"

The wind has blown away whatever else they may have spoken.

They went together towards the town, and, on their way, continued to make reference, no doubt, to some strange and dreadful history of their former life, belonging equally to this dark man and to the fair and youthful woman, whom he persecuted. In their words, or in the breath that uttered them, there seemed to be an odour of guilt, and a scent of blood. Yet, how can we imagine that a stain of ensanguined crime should attach to Miriam! Or, how, on the other hand, should spotless innocence be subjected to a thraldom like that which she endured from the spectre, whom she herself had evoked out of the darkness! Be this as it might, Miriam, we have reason to believe, still continued to beseech him, humbly, passionately, wildly, only to go his way, and leave her free to follow her own sad path.

Thus, they strayed onward through the green wilderness of the Borghese grounds, and soon came near the city-wall, where, had Miriam raised her eyes, she might have seen Hilda and the sculptor leaning on the parapet. But she walked in a mist of trouble, and could distinguish little beyond its limits. As they came within public observation, her persecutor fell behind, throwing off the imperious manner which he had assumed during their solitary interview. The Porta del Popolo swarmed with life. The merry-makers, who had spent the feast-day outside the walls, were now thronging in; a party of horsemen were entering beneath the arch; a travelling-carriage had been drawn up just within the verge, and was passing through the villainous ordeal of the Papal custom-house. In the broad piazza, too, there was a motley crowd.

But the stream of Miriam's trouble kept its way through this flood of human life, and neither mingled with it, nor was turned aside. With a sad kind of feminine ingenuity, she found a way to kneel before her tyrant, undetected, though in full sight of all the people, still beseeching him for freedom, and in vain.

XII

A STROLL ON THE PINCIAN

H ILDA, after giving the last touches to the picture of
Beatrice Cenci, had flown down from her dove-cote,
late in the afternoon, and gone to the Pincian Hill,
in the hope of hearing a strain or two of exhilarating music.
There, as it happened, she met the sculptor; for, to say the
truth, Kenyon had well noted the fair artist's ordinary way
of life, and was accustomed to shape his own movements so
as to bring him often within her sphere.

The Pincian Hill is the favourite promenade of the Roman
aristocracy. At the present day, however, like most other
Roman possessions, it belongs less to the native inhabitants
than to the barbarians from Gaul, Great Britain, and beyond
the sea, who have established a peaceful usurpation over
whatever is enjoyable or memorable in the Eternal City.
These foreign guests are indeed ungrateful, if they do not
breathe a prayer for Pope Clement, or whatever Holy Father
it may have been, who levelled the summit of the mount so
skilfully, and bounded it with the parapet of the city-wall;
who laid out those broad walks and drives, and overhung
them with the deepening shade of many kinds of tree; who
scattered the flowers of all seasons, and of every clime, abun-

dantly over those green, central lawns; who scooped out
hollows, in fit places, and, setting great basins of marble in
them, caused ever-gushing fountains to fill them to the brim;
who reared up the immemorial obelisk out of the soil that
had long hidden it; who placed pedestals along the borders
of the avenues, and crowned them with busts of that multitude of worthies—statesmen, heroes, artists, men of letters,
and of song—whom the whole world claims as its chief
ornaments, though Italy produced them all. In a word, the
Pincian Garden is one of the things that reconcile the
stranger (since he fully appreciates the enjoyment, and feels
nothing of the cost) to the rule of an irresponsible dynasty
of Holy Fathers, who seem to have aimed at making life
as agreeable an affair as it can well be.

In this pleasant spot, the red-trowsered French soldiers are
always to be seen; bearded and grizzled veterans, perhaps,
with medals of Algiers or the Crimea on their breasts. To
them is assigned the peaceful duty of seeing that children
do not trample on the flower-beds, nor any youthful lover
rifle them of their fragrant blossoms to stick in the beloved
one's hair. Here sits (drooping upon some marble bench, in
the treacherous sunshine) the consumptive girl, whose friends
have brought her, for cure, to a climate that instils poison
into its very purest breath. Here, all day long, come nursery-
maids, burthened with rosy English babies, or guiding the
footsteps of little travellers from the far Western world. Here,
in the sunny afternoons, roll and rumble all kinds of equipages, from the cardinal's old-fashioned and gorgeous purple
carriage, to the gay barouche of modern date. Here horsemen
gallop, on thorough-bred steeds. Here, in short, all the transitory population of Rome, the world's great watering-place,
rides, drives, or promenades; here are beautiful sunsets; and
here, whichever way you turn your eyes, are scenes as well-
worth gazing at, both in themselves and for their historic

interest, as any that the sun ever rose and set upon. Here, too, on certain afternoons of the week, a French military band flings out rich music over the poor old city, floating her with strains as loud as those of her own echoless triumphs.

Hilda and the sculptor (by the contrivance of the latter, who loved best to be alone with his young countrywoman) had wandered beyond the throng of promenaders, whom they left in a dense cluster around the music. They strayed, indeed, to the farthest point of the Pincian Hill, and leaned over the parapet, looking down upon the Muro Torto; a massive fragment of the oldest Roman wall, which juts over, as if ready to tumble down by its own weight, yet seems still the most indestructible piece of work that men's hands ever piled together. In the blue distance, rose Soracte, and other heights, which have gleamed afar, to our imaginations, but look scarcely real, to our bodily eyes; because, being dreamed about so much, they have taken the aërial tints which belong only to a dream. These, nevertheless, are the solid framework of hills that shut in Rome, and its wide surrounding Campagna; no land of dreams, but the broadest page of history, crowded so full with memorable events that one obliterates another; as if Time had crossed and re-crossed his own records till they grew illegible.

But, not to meddle with history—with which our narrative is no otherwise concerned, than that the very dust of Rome is historic, and inevitably settles on our page, and mingles with our ink—we will return to our two friends, who were still leaning over the wall. Beneath them lay the broad sweep of the Borghese grounds, covered with trees, amid which appeared the white gleam of pillars and statues, and the flash of an upspringing fountain; all to be overshadowed, at a later period of the year, by the thicker growth of foliage. The advance of vegetation, in this softer climate, is less abrupt than the inhabitant of the cold North is accustomed to observe. Beginning earlier—even in February—Spring is not compelled to burst into Summer with such headlong haste; there is time to dwell upon each opening beauty, and to enjoy the budding leaf, the tender green, the sweet youth and freshness of the year; it gives us its maiden charm, before settling into the married Summer, which, again, does not so soon sober itself into matronly Autumn. In our own country, the virgin Spring hastens to its bridal too abruptly. But, here, after a month or two of kindly growth, the leaves of the young trees, which cover that portion of the Borghese grounds nearest the city-wall, were still in their tender half-development.

In the remoter depths, among the old groves of ilex-trees, Hilda and Kenyon heard the faint sound of music, laughter, and mingling voices. It was probably the uproar—spreading even so far as the walls of Rome, and growing faded and melancholy, in its passage—of that wild sylvan merriment, which we have already attempted to describe. By-and-by, it ceased; although the two listeners still tried to distinguish it between the bursts of nearer music from the military band. But there was no renewal of that distant mirth. Soon afterwards, they saw a solitary figure, advancing along one of the paths that lead from the obscurer part of the grounds, towards the gateway.

"Look! Is it not Donatello?" said Hilda.

"He it is, beyond a doubt," replied the sculptor.—"But how gravely he walks, and with what long looks behind him! He seems either very weary, or very sad. I should not hesitate to call it sadness, if Donatello were a creature capable of the sin and folly of low-spirits. In all these hundred paces, while we have been watching him, he has not made one of those little caprioles in the air, which are a characteristic of his natural gait. I begin to doubt whether he is a veritable Faun!"

"Then," said Hilda, with perfect simplicity, "you have

thought him—and do think him—one of that strange, wild, happy race of creatures, that used to laugh and sport in the woods, in the old, old times? So do I, indeed! But I never quite believed, till now, that Fauns existed anywhere but in poetry."

The sculptor at first merely smiled. Then, as the idea took further possession of his mind, he laughed outright, and wished from the bottom of his heart (being in love with Hilda, though he had never told her so) that he could have rewarded or punished her for its pretty absurdity, with a kiss.

"Oh, Hilda, what a treasure of sweet faith and pure imagination you hide, under that little straw hat!" cried he, at length. "A Faun! A Faun! Great Pan is not dead, then, after all! The whole tribe of mythical creatures yet live in the moonlit seclusion of a young girl's fancy, and find it a lovelier abode and play-place, I doubt not, than their Arcadian haunts of yore. What bliss, if a man of marble, like myself, could stray thither too!"

"Why do you laugh so?" asked Hilda, reddening; for she was a little disturbed at Kenyon's ridicule, however kindly expressed.—"What can I have said, that you think so very foolish?"

"Well, not foolish, then," rejoined the sculptor, "but wiser, it may be, than I can fathom. Really, however, the idea does strike one as delightfully fresh, when we consider Donatello's position and external environment. Why, my dear Hilda, he is a Tuscan born, of an old, noble race in that part of Italy; and he has a moss-grown tower among the Apennines, where he and his forefathers have dwelt, under their own vines and fig-trees, from an unknown antiquity. His boyish passion for Miriam has introduced him familiarly to our little circle; and our republican and artistic simplicity of intercourse has included this young Italian, on the same terms as one of ourselves. But, if we paid due respect to rank and title, we should bend reverentially to Donatello, and salute him as his Excellency, the Count di Monte Beni."

"That is a droll idea—much droller than his being a Faun!" said Hilda, laughing in her turn. "This does not quite satisfy me, however;—especially as you yourself recognized and acknowledged his wonderful resemblance to the statue."

"Except as regards the pointed ears," said Kenyon; adding, aside—"and one other little peculiarity, generally observable in the statues of Fauns."

"As for his Excellency, the Count di Monte Beni's ears," replied Hilda, smiling again at the dignity with which this title invested their playful friend, "you know, we could never see their shape, on account of his clustering curls. Nay, I remember, he once started back, as shyly as a wild deer, when Miriam made a pretence of examining them. How do you explain that?"

"Oh, I certainly shall not contend against such a weight of evidence; the fact of his faunship being otherwise so probable," answered the sculptor, still hardly retaining his gravity.—"Faun or not, Donatello—or the Count di Monte Beni—is a singularly wild creature, and, as I have remarked on other occasions, though very gentle, does not love to be touched. Speaking in no harsh sense, there is a great deal of animal nature in him; as if he had been born in the woods, and had run wild, all his childhood, and were as yet but imperfectly domesticated. Life, even in our day, is very simple and unsophisticated, in some of the shaggy nooks of the Apennines."

"It annoys me very much," said Hilda, "this inclination, which most people have, to explain away the wonder and the mystery out of everything. Why could not you allow me—and yourself, too—the satisfaction of thinking him a Faun?"

"Pray keep your belief, dear Hilda, if it makes you any happier," said the sculptor; "and I shall do my best to become a convert. Donatello has asked me to spend the summer with him, in his ancestral tower, where I purpose investigating the pedigree of these sylvan counts, his forefathers; and if their shadows beckon me into Dream-land, I shall willingly follow. By-the-by, speaking of Donatello, there is a point on which I should like to be enlightened."

"Can I help you, then?" said Hilda, in answer to his look.

"Is there the slightest chance of his winning Miriam's affection?" suggested Kenyon.

"Miriam! She, so accomplished and gifted!" exclaimed Hilda.—"And he, a rude, uncultivated boy! No, no no!"

"It would seem impossible," said the sculptor. "But, on the other hand, a gifted woman flings away her affections so unaccountably, sometimes! Miriam, of late, has been very morbid and miserable, as we both know. Young as she is, the morning light seems already to have faded out of her life; and now comes Donatello, with natural sunshine enough for himself and her, and offers her the opportunity of making her heart and life all new and cheery again. People of high intellectual endowments do not require similar ones in those they love. They are just the persons to appreciate the wholesome gush of natural feeling, the honest affection, the simple joy, the fulness of contentment with what he loves, which Miriam sees in Donatello. True; she may call him a simpleton. It is a necessity of the case; for a man loses the capacity for this kind of affection, in proportion as he cultivates and refines himself."

"Dear me!" said Hilda, drawing imperceptibly away from her companion.—"Is this the penalty of refinement? Pardon me; I do not believe it. It is because you are a sculptor, that you think nothing can be finely wrought, except it be cold and hard, like the marble in which your ideas take shape. I am a painter, and know that the most delicate beauty may be softened and warmed throughout."

"I said a foolish thing, indeed," answered the sculptor.—
"It surprises me; for I might have drawn a wiser knowledge
out of my own experience. It is the surest test of genuine
love, that it brings back our early simplicity to the worldliest
of us."

Thus talking, they loitered slowly along beside the parapet,
which borders the level summit of the Pincian with its
irregular sweep. At intervals, they looked through the lattice-
work of their thoughts at the varied prospect that lay before
and beneath them.

From the terrace where they now stood, there is an abrupt
descent towards the Piazza del Popolo; and looking down into
its broad space, they beheld the tall, palatial edifices, the
church-domes, and the ornamented gateway, which grew and
were consolidated out of the thought of Michel Angelo. They
saw, too, the red granite obelisk—eldest of things, even in
Rome—which rises in the centre of the piazza, with a four-
fold fountain at its base. All Roman works and ruins (whether
of the Empire, the far-off Republic, or the still more distant
Kings) assume a transient, visionary, and impalpable character, when we think that this indestructible monument supplied one of the recollections, which Moses, and the Israelites,
bore from Egypt into the desert. Perchance, on beholding the
cloudy pillar and the fiery column, they whispered awe-
stricken to one another—"In its shape, it is like that old obelisk
which we and our fathers have so often seen, on the borders
of the Nile!"—And, now, that very obelisk, with hardly a
trace of decay upon it, is the first thing that the modern
traveller sees, after entering the Flaminian Gate!

Lifting their eyes, Hilda and her companion gazed westward, and saw, beyond the invisible Tiber, the Castle of
Sant' Angelo; that immense tomb of a pagan Emperour, with
the Archangel at its summit. Still farther off, appeared a
mighty pile of building, surmounted by the vast Dome, which

all of us have shaped, and swelled outward, like a huge
bubble, to the utmost scope of our imaginations, long before
we see it floating over the worship of the city. It may be
most worthily seen from precisely the point where our two
friends were now standing. At any nearer view, the grandeur
of Saint Peter's hides itself behind the immensity of its
separate parts; so that we see only the front, only the sides,
only the pillared length and loftiness of the portico, and not
the mighty whole. But, at this distance, the entire outline of
the world's Cathedral, as well as that of the palace of the
world's Chief-Priest, is taken in at once. In such remoteness,
moreover, the imagination is not debarred from lending its
assistance, even while we have the reality before our eyes,
and helping the weakness of human sense to do justice to so
grand an object. It requires both faith and fancy to enable
us to feel—what is, nevertheless, so true—that, yonder, in
front of the purple outline of hills, is the grandest edifice
ever built by man, painted against God's loveliest sky.

After contemplating, a little while, a scene which their
long residence in Rome had made familiar to them, Kenyon
and Hilda again let their glances fall into the piazza at their
feet. They there beheld Miriam, who had just entered the
Porta del Popolo, and was standing by the obelisk and
fountain. With a gesture that impressed Kenyon as at once
suppliant and imperious, she seemed to intimate to a figure
which had attended her thus far, that it was now her desire
to be left alone. The pertinacious Model, however, remained
immoveable.

And the sculptor here noted a circumstance, which, according to the interpretation he might put upon it, was either
too trivial to be mentioned, or else so mysteriously significant
that he found it difficult to believe his eyes. Miriam knelt
down on the steps of the fountain; so far, there could be no
question of the fact. To other observers, if any there were,

she probably appeared to take this attitude merely for the convenience of dipping her fingers into the gush of water from the mouth of one of the stone lions. But, as she clasped her hands together, after thus bathing them, and glanced upward at the Model, an idea took strong possession of Kenyon's mind, that Miriam was kneeling to this dark follower, there, in the world's face!

"Do you see it?" he said to Hilda.

"See what?" asked she, surprised at the emotion in his tone.—"I see Miriam, who has just bathed her hands in that delightfully cool water. I often dip my fingers into a Roman fountain, and think of the brook that used to be one of my playmates, in my New England village."

"I fancied I saw something else," said Kenyon; "but it was doubtless a mistake."

But—allowing that he had caught a true glimpse into the hidden significance of Miriam's gesture—what a terrible thraldom did it suggest! Free as she seemed to be—beggar as he looked—the nameless vagrant must then be dragging the beautiful Miriam through the streets of Rome, fettered and shackled more cruelly than any captive queen of yore, following in an Emperour's triumph. And was it conceivable that she could have been thus enthralled, unless some great errour—how great, Kenyon dared not think—or some fatal weakness, had given this dark adversary a vantage-ground?

"Hilda," said he abruptly, "who and what is Miriam? Pardon me; but, are you sure of her?"

"Sure of her!" repeated Hilda, with an angry blush for her friend's sake. "I am sure that she is kind, good, and generous—a true and faithful friend, whom I love dearly, and who loves me as well! What more than this need I be sure of?"

"And your delicate instincts say all this in her favour?— nothing against her?" continued the sculptor, without heeding the irritation of Hilda's tone.—"These are my own impressions too. But she is such a mystery! We do not even know whether she is a countrywoman of ours, or an Englishwoman, or a German. There is Anglo-Saxon blood in her veins, one would say, and a right English accent on her tongue, but much that is not English breeding, nor American. Nowhere else but in Rome, and as an artist, could she hold a place in society, without giving some clue to her past life."

"I love her dearly," said Hilda, still with displeasure in her tone, "and trust her most entirely."

"My heart trusts her, at least—whatever my head may do," rejoined Kenyon; "and Rome is not like one of our New England villages, where we need the permission of each individual neighbor for every act that we do, every word that we utter, and every friend that we make or keep. In these particulars, the Papal despotism allows us freer breath than our native air; and if we like to take generous views of our associates, we can do so, to a reasonable extent, without ruining ourselves."

"The music has ceased," said Hilda. "I am going now."

There are three streets that, beginning close beside each other, diverge from the Piazza del Popolo towards the heart of Rome; on the left, the Via del Babuino, on the right, the Via di Ripetta, and between these two, that world-famous avenue, the Corso. It appeared that Miriam and her strange companion were passing up the first-mentioned of these three, and were soon hidden from Hilda and the sculptor.

The two latter left the Pincian by the broad and stately walk that skirts along its brow. Beneath them, from the base of the abrupt descent, the city spread wide away, in a close contiguity of red-earthen roofs, above which rose eminent the domes of a hundred churches, besides here and there a tower, and the upper windows of some taller or higher situated palace, looking down on a multitude of palatial abodes. At a distance, ascending out of the central mass of edifices, they could see the top of the Antonine Column, and, near it, the circular roof of the Pantheon, looking heaven-ward with its ever-open eye. Except these two objects, almost everything that they beheld was mediæval, though built, indeed, of the massive old stones and indestructible bricks of imperial Rome; for the ruin of the Coliseum, the Golden House, and innumerable temples of Roman gods, and mansions of Caesars and senators, had supplied the material for all these gigantic hovels; and their walls were cemented with mortar of inestimable cost, being made of precious antique statues, burnt long ago for this petty purpose. Rome, as it now exists, has grown up under the Popes, and seems like nothing but a heap of broken rubbish, thrown into the great chasm between our own days and the Empire, merely to fill it up; and, for the better part of two thousand years, its annals of obscure policies, and wars, and continually recurring misfortunes, seem also but broken rubbish, as compared with its classic history.

If we consider the present city as at all connected with the famous one of old, it is only because we find it built over its grave. A depth of thirty feet of soil has covered up the Rome of ancient days; so that it lies like the dead corpse of a giant, decaying for centuries, with no survivor mighty enough even to bury it, until the dust of all those years has gathered slowly over its recumbent form and made a casual sepulchre. We know not how to characterize, in any accord-ant and compatible terms, the Rome that lies before us; its sunless alleys, and streets of palaces; its churches, lined with the gorgeous marbles that were originally polished for the adornment of pagan temples; its thousands of evil smells, mixed up with the fragrance of rich incense, diffused from as many censers; its little life, deriving feeble nutriment from what has long been dead. Everywhere, some fragment of ruin, suggesting the magnificence of a former epoch; everywhere, moreover, a Cross—and nastiness at the foot of it. As the sum of all, there are recollections that kindle the soul, and a gloom and languor that depress it beyond any depth of melancholic sentiment that can be elsewhere known.

Yet how is it possible to say an unkind or irreverential word of Rome?—the City of all time, and of all the world!—the spot for which Man's great life and deeds have done so much, and for which Decay has done whatever glory and dominion could not do!—At this moment, the evening sunshine is flinging its golden mantle over it, making all that we thought mean, magnificent; the bells of all the churches suddenly ring out, as if it were a peal of triumph, because Rome is still imperial.

"I sometimes fancy," said Hilda, on whose susceptibility the scene always made a strong impression, "that Rome—mere Rome—will crowd everything else out of my heart."

"Heaven forbid!" ejaculated the sculptor.

They had now reached the grand stairs that ascend from the Piazza di Spagna to the hither brow of the Pincian Hill. Old Beppo, the millionaire of his ragged fraternity, (it is a wonder that no artist paints him as the cripple whom Saint Peter heals, at the Beautiful Gate of the Temple,) was just mounting his donkey to depart, laden with the rich spoil of the day's beggary. Up the stairs, drawing his tattered cloak about his face, came the Model, at whom Beppo looked askance, jealous of an encroacher on his rightful domain. The figure passed away, however, up the Via Sistina. In the piazza below, near the foot of the magnificent steps, stood Miriam, with her eyes bent on the ground, as if she were counting those little, square, uncomfortable paving-stones, that make it a penitential pilgrimage to walk in Rome. She kept this attitude for several minutes, and when, at last, the importunities of a beggar disturbed her from it, she seemed bewildered, and pressed her hand upon her brow.

"She has been in some sad dream or other, poor thing!" said Kenyon sympathizingly; "and even now, she is imprisoned there in a kind of cage, the iron bars of which are made of her own thoughts."

"I fear she is not well," said Hilda.—"I am going down the stairs, and will join Miriam."

"Farewell then," said the sculptor.—"Dear Hilda, this is a perplexed and troubled world! It soothes me inexpressibly to think of you in your tower, with white doves and white thoughts for your companions, so high above us all, and with the Virgin for your household friend. You know not how far it throws its light—that lamp which you keep burning at her shrine! I passed beneath the tower, last night, and the ray cheered me—because you lighted it."

"It has for me a religious significance," replied Hilda quietly, "and yet I am no Catholic."

They parted, and Kenyon made haste along the Via Sistina, in the hope of overtaking the Model, whose haunts and character he was anxious to investigate, for Miriam's sake. He fancied that he saw him, a long way in advance, but before he reached the Fountain of the Triton, the dusky figure had vanished.

XIII

A SCULPTOR'S STUDIO

ABOUT this period, Miriam seems to have been goaded by a weary restlessness, that drove her abroad on any errand or none. She went, one morning, to visit Kenyon in his studio, whither he had invited her to see a new statue, on which he staked many hopes, and which was now almost completed in the clay. Next to Hilda, the person for whom Miriam felt most affection and confidence was Kenyon; and in all the difficulties that beset her life, it was her impulse to draw near Hilda for feminine sympathy, and the sculptor for brotherly counsel.

Yet it was to little purpose that she approached the edge of the voiceless gulf between herself and them. Standing on the utmost verge of that dark chasm, she might stretch out her hand, and never clasp a hand of theirs; she might strive to call out—'Help, friends, help!'—but, as with dreamers when they shout, her voice would perish inaudibly in the remoteness that seemed such a little way. This perception of an infinite, shivering solitude, amid which we cannot come close enough to human beings to be warmed by them, and where they turn to cold, chilly shapes of mist, is one of the most forlorn results of any accident, misfortune, crime, or peculiarity of character, that puts an individual ajar with the world.

Very often, as in Miriam's case, there is an insatiable instinct that demands friendship, love, and intimate communion, but is forced to pine in empty forms; a hunger of the heart, which finds only shadows to feed upon.

Kenyon's studio was in a cross-street, or, rather, an ugly and dirty little lane, between the Corso and the Via di Ripetta; and though chill, narrow, gloomy, and bordered with tall and shabby structures, the lane was not a whit more disagreeable than nine-tenths of the Roman streets. Over the door of one of the houses was a marble tablet, bearing an inscription, to the purport, that the sculpture-rooms within had formerly been occupied by the illustrious artist Canova. In these precincts (which Canova's genius was not quite of a character to render sacred, though it certainly made them interesting) the young American sculptor had now established himself.

The studio of a sculptor is generally but a rough and dreary-looking place, with a good deal the aspect, indeed, of a stone-mason's workshop. Bare floors of brick or plank, and plaistered walls; an old chair or two, or perhaps only a block of marble (containing, however, the possibility of ideal grace within it) to sit down upon; some hastily scrawled sketches of nude figures on the white-wash of the wall. These last are probably the sculptor's earliest glimpses of ideas that may hereafter be solidified into imperishable stone, or perhaps may remain as impalpable as a dream. Next, there are a few very roughly modelled little figures in clay or plaister, exhibiting the second stage of the Idea as it advances towards a marble immortality; and then is seen the exquisitely designed shape of clay, more interesting than even the final marble, as being the intimate production of the sculptor himself, moulded throughout with his loving hands, and nearest to his imagination and heart. In the plaister-cast, from this clay-model, the beauty of the statue strangely disappears, to shine forth again, with pure, white radiance, in the precious marble of Carrara. Works in all these stages of advancement, and some with the final touch upon them, might be found in Kenyon's studio.

Here might be witnessed the process of actually chiselling the marble, with which (as it is not quite satisfactory to think) a sculptor, in these days, has very little to do. In Italy, there is a class of men whose merely mechanical skill is perhaps more exquisite than was possessed by the ancient artificers, who wrought out the designs of Praxiteles, or, very possibly, by Praxiteles himself. Whatever of illusive representation can be effected in marble, they are capable of achieving, if the object be before their eyes. The sculptor has but to present these men with a plaister-cast of his design, and a sufficient block of marble, and tell them that the figure is imbedded in the stone, and must be freed from its encumbering super-fluities; and, in due time, without the necessity of his touch-ing the work with his own finger, he will see before him the statue that is to make him renowned. His creative power has wrought it with a word. In no other art, surely, does genius find such effective instruments, and so happily relieve itself of the drudgery of actual performance; doing wonder-fully nice things, by the hands of other people, when, it may be suspected, they could not always be done by the sculptor's own. And how much of the admiration which our artists get for their buttons and button-holes, their shoe-ties, their neckcloths—and these, at our present epoch of taste, make a large share of the renown—would be abated, if we were generally aware that the sculptor can claim no credit for such pretty performances, as immortalized in marble! They are not his work, but that of some nameless machine in human shape.

Miriam stopt, an instant, in an ante-chamber, to look at a half-finished bust, the features of which seemed to be struggling out of the stone, and, as it were, scattering and dissolving its hard substance by the glow of feeling and intelligence. As the skilful workman gave stroke after stroke of the chisel, with apparent carelessness, but sure effect, it was impossible not to think that the outer marble was merely an extraneous environment; the human countenance, within its embrace, must have existed there since the limestone ledges of Carrara were first made. Another bust was nearly completed, though still one of Kenyon's most trustworthy assistants was at work, giving delicate touches, shaving off an impalpable something, and leaving little heaps of marble-dust to attest it.

"As these busts in the block of marble," thought Miriam, "so does our individual fate exist in the limestone of Time. We fancy that we carve it out; but its ultimate shape is prior to all our action."

Kenyon was in the inner room, but, hearing a step in the ante-chamber, he threw a veil over what he was at work upon, and came out to receive his visitor. He was dressed in a gray blouse, with a little cap on the top of his head; a costume which became him better than the formal garments which he wore, whenever he passed out of his own domains. The sculptor had a face which, when time had done a little more for it, would offer a worthy subject for as good an artist as himself; features finely cut, as if already marble; an ideal forehead, deeply set eyes, and a mouth much hidden in a light brown beard, but apparently sensitive and delicate.

"I will not offer you my hand," said he;—"it is grimy with Cleopatra's clay."

"No; I will not touch clay; it is earthy and human," answered Miriam. "I have come to try whether there is any calm and coolness among your marbles. My own art is too nervous, too passionate, too full of agitation, for me to work at it whole days together, without intervals of repose. So, what have you to show me?"

"Pray look at everything here," said Kenyon. "I love to have painters see my work. Their judgment is unprejudiced, and more valuable than that of the world generally, from the light which their own art throws on mine. More valuable, too, than that of my brother-sculptors, who never judge me fairly—nor I them, perhaps."

To gratify him, Miriam looked round at the specimens in marble or plaister, of which there were several in the room, comprising originals or casts of most of the designs that Kenyon had thus far produced. He was still too young to have accumulated a large gallery of such things. What he had to show were chiefly the attempts and experiments, in various directions, of a beginner in art, acting as a stern tutor to himself, and profiting more by his failures than by any successes of which he was yet capable. Some of them, however, had great merit; and, in the pure, fine glow of the new marble, it may be, they dazzled the judgment into awarding them higher praise than they deserved. Miriam admired the statue of a beautiful youth, a pearl-fisher, who had got entangled in the weeds at the bottom of the sea, and lay dead among the pearl-oysters, the rich shells, and the sea-weeds, all of like value to him now.

"The poor young man has perished among the prizes that he sought," remarked she.—"But what a strange efficacy there is in Death! If we cannot all win pearls, it causes an empty shell to satisfy us just as well. I like this statue, though it is too cold and stern in its moral lesson; and, physically, the form has not settled itself into sufficient repose."

In another style, there was a grand, calm head of Milton, not copied from any one bust or picture, yet more authentic than any of them, because all known representations of the poet had been profoundly studied, and solved in the artist's mind. The bust over the tomb in Grey Friars Church, the original miniatures and pictures, wherever to be found, had mingled each its special truth in this one work; wherein, likewise, by long perusal and deep love of the *Paradise Lost,* the *Comus,* the *Lycidas,* and *L'Allegro,* the sculptor had succeeded, even better than he knew, in spiritualizing his marble with the poet's mighty genius. And this was a great thing to have achieved, such a length of time after the dry bones and dust of Milton were like those of any other dead man!

There were also several portrait-busts, comprising those of two or three of the illustrious men of our own country, whom Kenyon, before he left America, had asked permission to model. He had done so, because he sincerely believed that, whether he wrought the busts in marble or bronze, the one would corrode and the other crumble, in the long lapse of time, beneath these great men's immortality. Possibly, however, the young artist may have under-estimated the durability of his material. Other faces there were, too, of men who (if the brevity of their remembrance, after death, can be argued from their little value in life) should have been represented in snow rather than marble. Posterity will be puzzled what to do with busts like these, the concretions and petrifactions of a vain self-estimate, but will find, no doubt, that they serve to build into stone-walls, or burn into quick-lime, as well as if the marble had never been blocked into the guise of human heads.

But it is an awful thing, indeed, this endless endurance, this almost indestructibility, of a marble bust! Whether in our own case, or that of other men, it bids us sadly measure the little, little time, during which our lineaments are likely to be of interest to any human being. It is especially singular that Americans should care about perpetuating themselves in this mode. The brief duration of our families, as a hereditary household, renders it next to a certainty that the great-grandchildren will not know their father's grandfather, and that, half-a-century hence, at farthest, the hammer of the auctioneer will thump its knock-down blow against his block-head, sold at so much for the pound of stone! And it ought to make us shiver, the idea of leaving our features to be a dusty-white ghost among strangers of another generation, who will take our nose between their thumb and fingers, (as we have seen men do by Caesar's,) and infallibly break it off, if they can do so, without detection!

"Yes," observed Miriam, who had been revolving some such thoughts as the above, "it is a good state of mind for mortal man, when he is content to leave no more definite memorial than the grass, which will sprout kindly and speed-ily over his grave, if we do not make the spot barren with marble. Methinks, too, it will be a fresher and better world, when it flings off this great burthen of stony memories, which the ages have deemed it a piety to heap upon its back!"

"What you say," remarked Kenyon, "goes against my whole art. Sculpture, and the delight which men naturally take in it, appear to me a proof that it is good to work with all time before our view."

"Well, well," answered Miriam, "I must not quarrel with you for flinging your heavy stones at poor Posterity; and, to say the truth, I think you are as likely to hit the mark as anybody. These busts, now, much as I seem to scorn them, make me feel as if you were a magician. You turn feverish men into cool, quiet marble. What a blessed change for them! Would you could do as much for me!"

"Oh, gladly!" cried Kenyon, who had long wished to model that beautiful and most expressive face.—"When will you begin to sit?"

"Poh! That was not what I meant," said Miriam.—"Come; show me something else."

"Do you recognize this?" asked the sculptor.

He took out of his desk a little, old-fashioned, ivory coffer, yellow with age; it was richly carved with antique figures and foliage; and had Kenyon thought fit to say that Benvenuto Cellini wrought this precious box, the skill and elaborate fancy of the work would by no means have discredited his word, nor the old artist's fame. At least, it was evidently a production of Benvenuto's school and century, and might once have been the jewel-case of some grand lady at the court of the de' Medici.

Lifting the lid, however, no blaze of diamonds was disclosed, but only, lapt in fleecy cotton, a small, beautifully shaped hand, most delicately sculptured in marble. Such loving care and nicest art had been lavished here, that the palm really seemed to have a tenderness in its very substance. Touching those lovely fingers—had the jealous sculptor allowed you to touch—you could hardly believe that a virgin warmth would not steal from them into your heart.

"Ah, this is very beautiful!" exclaimed Miriam, with a genial smile. "It is as good, in its way, as Loulie's hand, with its baby-dimples, which Powers showed me at Florence, evidently valuing it as much as if he had wrought it out of a piece of his great heart! As good as Harriet Hosmer's clasped hands of Browning and his wife, symbolizing the individuality and heroic union of two high, poetic lives! Nay; I do not question that it is better than either of those, because you must have wrought it passionately, in spite of its maiden palm and dainty finger-tips."

"Then, you do recognize it?" asked Kenyon.

"There is but one right hand, on earth, that could have supplied the model," answered Miriam; "so small and slender, so perfectly symmetrical, and yet with a character of delicate energy! I have watched it, a hundred times, at its work. But

I did not dream that you had won Hilda so far! How have you persuaded that shy maiden to let you take her hand in marble?"

"Never! She never knew it!" hastily replied Kenyon, anxious to vindicate his mistress's maidenly reserve.—"I stole it from her. The hand is a reminiscence. After gazing at it so often—and even holding it once, for an instant, when Hilda was not thinking of me—I should be a bungler indeed, if I could not now reproduce it to something like the life."

"May you win the original, one day!" said Miriam, kindly.

"I have little ground to hope it," answered the sculptor despondingly.—"Hilda does not dwell in our mortal atmosphere; and, gentle and soft as she appears, it will be as difficult to win her heart, as to entice down a white bird from its sunny freedom in the sky. It is strange, with all her delicacy and fragility, the impression she makes of being utterly sufficient to herself! No; I shall never win her. She is abundantly capable of sympathy, and delights to receive it, but she has no need of love!"

"I partly agree with you," said Miriam.—"It is a mistaken idea which men generally entertain, that Nature has made women especially prone to throw their whole being into what is technically called Love. We have, to say the least, no more necessity for it than yourselves;—only, we have nothing else to do with our hearts. When women have other objects in life, they are not apt to fall in love. I can think of many women, distinguished in art, literature, and science—and multitudes whose hearts and minds find good employment, in less ostentatious ways—who lead high, lonely lives, and are conscious of no sacrifice, so far as your sex is concerned."

"And Hilda will be one of these!" said Kenyon sadly.—"The thought makes me shiver for myself—and—and for her too!"

"Well;" said Miriam smiling; "perhaps she may sprain the delicate wrist which you have sculptured to such perfection. In that case, you may hope! These Old Masters to whom she has vowed herself, and whom her slender hand and woman's heart serve so faithfully, are your only rivals."

The sculptor sighed, as he put away the treasure of Hilda's marble hand into the ivory coffer, and thought how slight was the probability that he should ever feel, responsive to his own, the tender clasp of the original. He dared not even kiss the image that he himself had made; it had assumed its share of Hilda's remote and shy divinity.

"And, now," said Miriam, "show me the new statue, which you asked me hither to see."

XIV

CLEOPATRA

M Y NEW STATUE!" said Kenyon, who had positively forgotten it, in the thought of Hilda.—"Here
it is, under this veil."

"Not a nude figure, I hope!" observed Miriam. "Every
young sculptor seems to think that he must give the world
some specimen of indecorous womanhood, and call it Eve,
Venus, a Nymph, or any name that may apologize for a lack
of decent clothing. I am weary, even more than I am ashamed,
of seeing such things. Now-a-days, people are as good as born
in their clothes, and there is practically not a nude human
being in existence. An artist, therefore,—as you must candidly
confess,—cannot sculpture nudity with a pure heart, if only
because he is compelled to steal guilty glimpses at hired
models. The marble inevitably loses its chastity under such
circumstances. An old Greek sculptor, no doubt, found his
models in the open sunshine, and among pure and princely
maidens, and thus the nude statues of antiquity are as modest
as violets, and sufficiently draped in their own beauty. But
as for Mr. Gibson's coloured Venuses, (stained, I believe,
with tobacco-juice,) and all other nudities of to-day, I really
do not understand what they have to say to this generation,

and would be glad to see as many heaps of quick-lime in their stead!"

"You are severe upon the professors of my art," said Kenyon, half-smiling, half-seriously.—"Not that you are wholly wrong, neither! We are bound to accept drapery of some kind, and make the best of it. But what are we to do? Must we adopt the costume of to-day, and carve, for example, a Venus in a hoop-petticoat?"

"That would be a boulder, indeed!" rejoined Miriam laughing.—"But the difficulty goes to confirm me in my belief, that, except for portrait-busts, sculpture has no longer a right to claim any place among living arts. It has wrought itself out, and come fairly to an end. There is never a new group now-a-days; never, even, so much as a new attitude. Greenough (I take my examples among men of merit) imagined nothing new; nor Crawford either, except in the tailoring-line. There are not—as you will own—more than half-a-dozen positively original statues or groups in the world, and these few are of immemorial antiquity. A person familiar with the Vatican, the Uffizi gallery, the Naples gallery, and the Louvre, will at once refer any modern production to its antique prototype—which, moreover, had begun to get out of fashion, even in old Roman days."

"Pray stop, Miriam," cried Kenyon, "or I shall fling away the chisel forever!"

"Fairly own to me, then, my friend," rejoined Miriam, whose disturbed mind found a certain relief in this declamation, "that you sculptors are, of necessity, the greatest plagiarists in the world."

"I do not own it," said Kenyon, "yet cannot utterly contradict you, as regards the actual state of the art. But as long as the Carrara quarries still yield pure blocks, and while my own country has marble mountains, probably as fine in quality, I shall steadfastly believe that future sculptors will revive this noblest of the beautiful arts, and people the world with new shapes of delicate grace and massive grandeur. Perhaps," he added smiling, "mankind will consent to wear a more manageable costume; or, at worst, we sculptors shall get the skill to make broadcloth transparent, and render a majestic human character visible through the coats and trowsers of the present day."

"Be it so!" said Miriam. "You are past my counsel. Show me the veiled figure, which, I am afraid, I have criticized beforehand. To make amends, I am in the mood to praise it now."

But, as Kenyon was about to take the cloth off the clay-model, she laid her hand on his arm.

"Tell me first what is the subject," said she; "for I have sometimes incurred great displeasure from members of your brotherhood, by being too obtuse to puzzle out the purport of their productions. It is so difficult, you know, to compress and define a character or story, and make it patent at a glance, within the narrow scope attainable by sculpture! Indeed, I fancy it is still the ordinary habit with sculptors, first to finish their group of statuary, (in such development as the particular block of marble will allow,) and then to choose the subject; as John of Bologna did, with his Rape of the Sabines. Have you followed that good example?"

"No; my statue is intended for Cleopatra," replied Kenyon, a little disturbed by Miriam's raillery. "The special epoch of her history, you must make out for yourself."

He drew away the cloth, that had served to keep the moisture of the clay-model from being exhaled. The sitting figure of a woman was seen. She was draped from head to foot in a costume, minutely and scrupulously studied from that of ancient Egypt, as revealed by the strange sculpture of that country, its coins, drawings, painted mummy-cases, and whatever other tokens have been dug out of its pyramids, graves, and catacombs. Even the stiff Egyptian head-dress was adhered to, but had been softened into a rich feminine adornment, without losing a particle of its truth. Difficulties, that might well have seemed insurmountable, had been courageously encountered, and made flexible to purposes of grace and dignity; so that Cleopatra sat attired in a garb proper to her historic and queenly state, as a daughter of the Ptolemies, and yet such as the beautiful woman would have put on, as best adapted to heighten the magnificence of her charms, and kindle a tropic fire in the cold eyes of Octavius.

A marvellous repose—that rare merit in statuary, except it be the lumpish repose native to the block of stone—was diffused throughout the figure. The spectator felt that Cleopatra had sunk down out of the fever and turmoil of her life, and, for one instant—as it were, between two pulse-throbs—had relinquished all activity, and was resting throughout every vein and muscle. It was the repose of despair, indeed; for Octavius had seen her, and remained insensible to her enchantments. But still there was a great, smouldering furnace, deep down in the woman's heart. The repose, no doubt, was as complete as if she were never to stir hand or foot again; and yet, such was the creature's latent energy and fierceness, she might spring upon you like a tigress, and stop the very breath that you were now drawing, midway in your throat.

The face was a miraculous success. The sculptor had not shunned to give the full Nubian lips, and other characteristics of the Egyptian physiognomy. His courage and integrity had been abundantly rewarded; for Cleopatra's beauty shone out richer, warmer, more triumphantly, beyond comparison, than if, shrinking timidly from the truth, he had chosen the tame Grecian type. The expression was of profound, gloomy, heavily revolving thought; a glance into her past life and present emergencies, while her spirit gathered itself up for some new struggle, or was getting sternly reconciled to impending doom. In one view, there was a certain softness and tenderness, how breathed into the statue, among so many strong and passionate elements, it is impossible to say. Catching another glimpse, you beheld her as implacable as a stone, and cruel as fire.

In a word, all Cleopatra—fierce, voluptuous, passionate, tender, wicked, terrible, and full of poisonous and rapturous enchantment—was kneaded into what, only a week or two before, had been a lump of wet clay from the Tiber. Soon, apotheosized in an indestructible material, she would be one of the images that men keep forever, finding a heat in them which does not cool down, throughout the centuries.

"What a woman is this!" exclaimed Miriam, after a long pause.—"Tell me, did she never try—even while you were creating her—to overcome you with her fury, or her love? Were you not afraid to touch her, as she grew more and more towards hot life, beneath your hand? My dear friend, it is a great work! How have you learned to do it?"

"It is the concretion of a good deal of thought, emotion, and toil of brain and hand," said Kenyon, not without a perception that his work was good.—"But I know not how it came about, at last. I kindled a great fire within my mind, and threw in the material—as Aaron threw the gold of the Israelites into the furnace—and, in the midmost heat, uprose Cleopatra, as you see her."

"What I most marvel at," said Miriam, "is the womanhood that you have so thoroughly mixed up with all those seemingly discordant elements. Where did you get that secret? You never found it in your gentle Hilda. Yet I recognize its truth."

"No, surely, it was not in Hilda," said Kenyon.—"Her womanhood is of the ethereal type, and incompatible with any shadow of darkness or evil."

"You are right," rejoined Miriam.—"There are women of that ethereal type, as you term it, and Hilda is one of them. She would die of her first wrong-doing;—supposing, for a moment, that she could be capable of doing wrong. Of sorrow, slender as she seems, Hilda might bear a great burthen;—of sin, not a feather's weight. Methinks, now, were it my doom, I could bear either, or both at once. But my conscience is still as white as Hilda's. Do you question it?"

"Heaven forbid, Miriam!" exclaimed the sculptor.

He was startled at the strange turn which she had so suddenly given to the conversation. Her voice too—so much emotion was stifled, rather than expressed in it—sounded unnatural.

"Oh, my friend," cried she, with sudden passion, "will you be my friend indeed? I am lonely, lonely, lonely! There is a secret in my heart that burns me!—that tortures me! Sometimes, I fear to go mad of it! Sometimes, I hope to die of it! But neither of the two happens. Ah, if I could but whisper it to only one human soul! And you—you see far into womanhood! You receive it widely into your large view! Perhaps—perhaps—but Heaven only knows—you might understand me! Oh, let me speak!"

"Miriam, dear friend," replied the sculptor, "if I can help you, speak freely, as to a brother."

"Help me? No!" said Miriam.

Kenyon's response had been perfectly frank and kind; and yet the subtlety of Miriam's emotion detected a certain reserve and alarm in his warmly expressed readiness to hear her story. In his secret soul, to say the truth, the sculptor doubted whether it were well for this poor, suffering girl to speak what she so yearned to say, or for him to listen. If there were any active duty of friendship to be performed, then, indeed, he would joyfully have come forward to do his best. But, if it were only a pent-up heart that sought an outlet? In that case, it was by no means so certain that a confession would do good. The more her secret struggled and fought to be told, the more certain would it be to change all former relations that had subsisted between herself and the friend to whom she might reveal it. Unless he could give her all the sympathy, and just the kind of sympathy, that the occasion required, Miriam would hate him, by-and-by, and herself still more, if he let her speak.

This was what Kenyon said to himself; but his reluctance, after all, and whether he were conscious of it or no, resulted from a suspicion that had crept into his heart, and lay there in a dark corner. Obscure as it was, when Miriam looked into his eyes, she detected it at once.

"Ah, I shall hate you!" cried she, echoing the thought which he had not spoken; she was half-choked with the gush of passion that was thus turned back upon her.—"You are as cold and pitiless as your own marble."

"No; but full of sympathy, God knows!" replied he.

In truth, his suspicions (however warranted by the mystery in which Miriam was enveloped) had vanished in the earnestness of his kindly and sorrowful emotion. He was now ready to receive her trust.

"Keep your sympathy, then, for sorrows that admit of such solace," said she, making a strong effort to compose herself.—"As for my griefs, I know how to manage them. It was all a mistake. You can do nothing for me, unless you petrify me into a marble companion for your Cleopatra there; and I am not of her sisterhood, I do assure you! Forget this foolish scene, my friend, and never let me see a reference to it in your eyes, when they meet mine hereafter."

"Since you desire it, all shall be forgotten," answered the

sculptor, pressing her hand as she departed; "or, if ever I can serve you, let my readiness to do so be remembered. Meanwhile, dear Miriam, let us meet in the same clear, friendly light as heretofore."

"You are less sincere than I thought you," said Miriam, "if you try to make me think that there will be no change."

As he attended her through the ante-chamber, she pointed to the statue of the pearl-diver.

"My secret is not a pearl," said she.—"Yet a man might drown himself in plunging after it!"

After Kenyon had closed the door, she went wearily down the staircase, but paused midway, as if debating with herself whether to return.

"The mischief was done," thought she; "and I might as well have had the solace that ought to come with it. I have lost—by staggering a little way beyond the mark, in the blindness of my distress—I have lost, as we shall hereafter find, the genuine friendship of this clear-minded, honourable, true-hearted young man; and all for nothing! What if I should go back, this moment, and compel him to listen?"

She ascended two or three of the stairs, but again paused, murmured to herself, and shook her head.

"No, no no," she thought; "and I wonder how I ever came to dream of it! Unless I had his heart for my own, (and that is Hilda's, nor would I steal it from her,) it should never be the treasure-place of my secret. It is no precious pearl, as I just now told him; but my dark-red carbuncle—red as blood—is too rich a gem to put into a stranger's casket!"

She went down the stairs, and found her Shadow waiting for her in the street.

XV

AN ÆSTHETIC COMPANY

O N THE EVENING after Miriam's visit to Kenyon's studio, there was an assemblage, composed almost entirely of Anglo-Saxons, and chiefly of American artists, with a sprinkling of their English brethren, and some few of the tourists who still lingered in Rome, now that Holy Week was past. Miriam, Hilda, and the sculptor, were all three present, and, with them, Donatello, whose life was so far turned from its natural bent, that, like a pet spaniel, he followed his beloved mistress wherever he could gain admittance.

The place of meeting was in the palatial, but somewhat faded and gloomy apartment of an eminent member of the æsthetic body. It was no more formal an occasion than one of those weekly receptions, common among the foreign residents of Rome, at which pleasant people—or disagreeable ones, as the case may be—encounter one another with little ceremony. If anywise interested in art, a man must be difficult to please, who cannot find fit companionship among a crowd of persons, whose ideas and pursuits all tend towards the general purpose of enlarging the world's stock of beautiful productions. One of the chief causes that make Rome the

favourite residence of artists—their ideal home, which they
sigh for, in advance, and are so loth to migrate from, after
once breathing its enchanted air—is, doubtless, that they there
find themselves in force, and are numerous enough to create
a congenial atmosphere. In every other clime, they are isolated
strangers; in this Land of Art, they are free citizens.

Not that, individually, or in the mass, there appears to be
any large stock of mutual affection among the brethren of the
chisel and the pencil. On the contrary, it will impress the
shrewd observer, that the jealousies and petty animosities,
which the poets of our day have flung aside, still irritate and
gnaw into the hearts of this kindred class of imaginative men.
It is not difficult to suggest reasons why this should be the
fact. The public, in whose good graces lie the sculptor's or
the painter's prospects of success, is infinitely smaller than
the public to which literary men make their appeal. It is
composed of a very limited body of wealthy patrons; and
these, as the artist well knows, are but blind judges, in matters
that require the utmost delicacy of perception. Thus, success
in art is apt to become partly an affair of intrigue; and it is
almost inevitable that even a gifted artist should look askance
at his gifted brother's fame, and be chary of the good word
that might help him to sell still another statue or picture.
You seldom hear a painter heap generous praise on anything
in his special line of art; a sculptor never has a favourable eye
for any marble but his own.

Nevertheless, in spite of all these professional grudges,
artists are conscious of a social warmth from each other's
presence and contiguity. They shiver at the remembrance
of their lonely studios in the unsympathizing cities of their
native land. For the sake of such brotherhood as they can
find, more than for any good that they get from galleries,
they linger year after year in Italy; while their originality
dies out of them, or is polished away as a barbarism.

The company, this evening, included several men and women whom the world has heard of, and many others, beyond all question, whom it ought to know. It would be a pleasure to introduce them upon our humble pages, name by name, and (had we confidence enough in our own taste) to crown each well-deserving brow according to its deserts. The opportunity is tempting, but not easily manageable, and far too perilous, both in respect to those individuals whom we might bring forward, and the far greater number that must needs be left in the shade. Ink, moreover, is apt to have a corrosive quality, and might chance to raise a blister, instead of any more agreeable titillation, on skins so sensitive as those of artists. We must therefore forego the delight of illuminating this chapter with personal allusions to men whose renown glows richly on canvas, or gleams in the white moonlight of marble.

Otherwise, we might point to an artist who has studied Nature with such tender love that she takes him to her intimacy, enabling him to reproduce her in landscapes that seem the reality of a better earth, and yet are but the truth of the very scenes around us, observed by the painter's insight and interpreted for us by his skill. By his magic, the moon throws her light far out of the picture, and the crimson of the summer-night absolutely glimmers on the beholder's face. Or we might indicate a poet-painter, whose song has the vividness of picture, and whose canvas is peopled with angels, fairies, and water-sprites, done to the ethereal life, because he saw them face to face in his poetic mood. Or we might bow before an artist, who has wrought too sincerely, too religiously, with too earnest a feeling, and too delicate a touch, for the world at once to recognize how much toil and thought are compressed into the stately brow of Prospero, and Miranda's maiden loveliness; or from what a depth within this painter's heart the Angel is leading forth Saint Peter.

Thus it would be easy to go on, perpetrating a score of little epigrammatical allusions, like the above, all kindly meant, but none of them quite hitting the mark, and often striking where they were not aimed. It may be allowable to say, however, that American art is much better represented at Rome in the pictorial than in the sculpturesque department. Yet the men of marble appear to have more weight with the public than the men of canvas; perhaps on account of the greater density and solid substance of the material in which they work, and the sort of physical advantage which their labours thus acquire over the illusive unreality of colour. To be a sculptor, seems a distinction in itself; whereas, a painter is nothing, unless individually eminent.

One sculptor there was, an Englishman, endowed with a beautiful fancy, and possessing at his fingers' ends the capability of doing beautiful things. He was a quiet, simple, elderly personage, with eyes brown and bright, under a slightly impending brow, and a Grecian profile, such as he might have cut with his own chisel. He had spent his life, for forty years, in making Venuses, Cupids, Bacchuses, and a vast deal of other marble progeny of dream-work, or, rather, frost-work; it was all a vapoury exhalation out of the Grecian mythology, crystallizing on the dull window-panes of to-day. Gifted with a more delicate power than any other man alive, he had foregone to be a Christian reality, and perverted himself into a pagan idealist, whose business or efficacy, in our present world, it would be exceedingly difficult to define. And, loving and reverencing the pure material in which he wrought, as surely this admirable sculptor did, he had nevertheless robbed the marble of its chastity by giving it an artificial warmth of hue. Thus, it became a sin and shame to look at his nude goddesses. They had revealed themselves to his imagination, no doubt, with all their deity about them; but, bedaubed with buff-colour, they stood forth to the eyes of the profane in the guise of naked women. But, whatever criticism may be ventured on his style, it was good to meet a man so modest, and yet imbued with such thorough and simple conviction of his own right principles and practice, and so quietly satisfied that his kind of antique achievement was all that sculpture could effect for modern life.

This eminent person's weight and authority among his artistic brethren were very evident; for, beginning unobtrusively to utter himself on a topic of art, he was soon the centre of a little crowd of younger sculptors. They drank in his wisdom, as if it would serve all the purposes of original inspiration; he, meanwhile, discoursing with gentle calmness, as if there could possibly be no other side, and often ratifying, as it were, his own conclusions by a mildly emphatic—'Yes!'

The veteran sculptor's unsought audience was composed mostly of our own countrymen. It is fair to say, that they were a body of very dextrous and capable artists, each of whom had probably given the delighted public a nude statue, or had won credit for even higher skill by the nice carving of button-holes, shoe-ties, coat-seams, shirt-bosoms, and other such graceful peculiarities of modern costume. Smart, practical men they doubtless were, and some of them far more than this, but, still, not precisely what an uninitiated person looks for in a sculptor. A sculptor, indeed, to meet the demands which our pre-conceptions make upon him, should be even more indispensably a poet than those who deal in measured verse and rhyme. His material, or instrument, which serves him in the stead of shifting and transitory language, is a pure, white, undecaying substance. It ensures immortality to whatever is wrought in it, and therefore makes it a religious obligation to commit no idea to its mighty guardianship, save such as may repay the marble for its faithful care, its incorruptible fidelity, by warming it with an ethereal life. Under this aspect, marble assumes a sacred character; and no man should dare to touch it unless he feels within himself a certain consecration and a priesthood, the only evidence of which, for the public eye, will be the high treatment of heroic subjects, or the delicate evolution of spiritual, through material beauty.

No ideas such as the foregoing—no misgivings suggested by them—probably troubled the self-complacency of most of these clever sculptors. Marble, in their view, had no such sanctity as we impute to it. It was merely a sort of white limestone from Carrara, cut into convenient blocks, and worth, in that state, about two or three dollars per pound; and it was susceptible of being wrought into certain shapes (by their own mechanical ingenuity, or that of artizans in their employment) which would enable them to sell it again at a much higher figure. Such men, on the strength of some small knack in handling clay, which might have been fitly employed in making waxwork, are bold to call themselves sculptors. How terrible should be the thought, that the nude woman whom the modern artist patches together, bit by bit, from a dozen heterogeneous models, meaning nothing by her, shall last as long as the Venus of the Capitol!—that his group of—no matter what, since it has no moral or intellectual existence—will not physically crumble any sooner than the immortal agony of the Laocoon!

Yet we love the artists, in every kind; even these, whose merits we are not quite able to appreciate. Sculptors, painters, crayon-sketchers, or whatever branch of æsthetics they adopted, were certainly pleasanter people, as we saw them that evening, than the average whom we meet in ordinary society. They were not wholly confined within the sordid compass of practical life; they had a pursuit which, if followed faithfully out, would lead them to the Beautiful, and always had a tendency thitherward, even if they lingered to gather up golden dross by the wayside. Their actual business (though they talked about it very much as other men talk of cotton, politics, flour-barrels, and sugar) necessarily illuminated their conversation with something akin to the Ideal. So, when the guests collected themselves in little groups, here and there, in the wide saloon, a cheerful and airy gossip began to be heard. The atmosphere ceased to be precisely that of common life; a faint, mellow tinge, such as we see in pictures, mingled itself with the lamplight.

This good effect was assisted by many curious little treasures of art, which the host had taken care to strew upon his tables. They were principally such bits of antiquity as the soil of Rome and its neighborhood is still rich in; seals, gems, small figures of bronze, mediæval carvings in ivory; things which had been obtained at little cost, yet might have borne no inconsiderable value in the museum of a virtuoso.

As interesting as any of these relics was a large portfolio of old drawings, some of which, in the opinion of their possessor, bore evidence on their faces of the touch of master-hands. Very ragged and ill-conditioned they mostly were, yellow with time, and tattered with rough usage; and, in their best estate, the designs had been scratched rudely with pen and ink, on coarse paper, or, if drawn with charcoal or a pencil, were now half-rubbed out. You would not anywhere see rougher and homelier things than these. But this hasty rudeness made the sketches only the more valuable; because the artist seemed to have bestirred himself at the pinch of the moment, snatching up whatever material was nearest, so as to seize the first glimpse of an idea that might vanish in the twinkling of an eye. Thus, by the spell of a creased, soiled, and discoloured scrap of paper, you were enabled to steal close to an Old Master, and watch him in the very effervescence of his genius.

According to the judgment of several connoisseurs, Raphael's own hand had communicated its magnetism to one of these sketches; and, if genuine, it was evidently his first conception of a favourite Madonna, now hanging in the private apartment of the Grand Duke, at Florence. Another drawing was attributed to Leonardo da Vinci, and appeared to be a somewhat varied design for his picture of Modesty and Vanity, in the Sciarra palace. There were at least half-a-dozen others, to which the owner assigned as high an origin. It was delightful to believe in their authenticity, at all events; for these things make the spectator more vividly sensible of a great painter's power, than the final glow and perfected art of the most consummate picture that may have been elaborated from them. There is an effluence of divinity in the first sketch; and there, if anywhere, you find the pure light of inspiration, which the subsequent toil of the artist serves to bring out in stronger lustre, indeed, but likewise adulterates it with what belongs to an inferiour mood. The aroma and fragrance of new thought were perceptible in these designs, after three centuries of wear and tear. The charm lay partly in their very imperfection; for this is suggestive, and sets the imagination at work; whereas, the finished picture, if a good one, leaves the spectator nothing to do, and, if bad, confuses, stupefies, disenchants, and disheartens him.

Hilda was greatly interested in this rich portfolio. She lingered so long over one particular sketch, that Miriam asked her what discovery she had made.

"Look at it carefully," replied Hilda, putting the sketch into her hands. "If you take pains to disentangle the design from those pencil-marks, that seem to have been scrawled over it, I think you will see something very curious."

"It is a hopeless affair, I am afraid," said Miriam. "I have

neither your faith, dear Hilda, nor your perceptive faculty.
Fie! What a blurred scrawl it is, indeed!"

The drawing had originally been very slight, and had
suffered more from time and hard usage than almost any
other in the collection; it appeared, too, that there had been
an attempt (perhaps by the very hand that drew it) to
obliterate the design. By Hilda's help, however, Miriam pretty
distinctly made out a winged figure with a drawn sword, and
a dragon, or a demon, prostrate at his feet.

"I am convinced," said Hilda, in a low, reverential tone,
"that Guido's own touches are on that ancient scrap of
paper! If so, it must be his original sketch for the picture
of the Archangel Michael, setting his foot upon the Demon,
in the Church of the Cappuccini. The composition and
general arrangement of the sketch are the same with those
of the picture; the only difference being, that the Demon
has a more upturned face, and scowls vindictively at the
Archangel, who turns away his eyes in painful disgust."

"No wonder!" responded Miriam.—"The expression suits
the daintiness of Michael's character, as Guido represents
him. He never could have looked the Demon in the face!"

"Miriam!" exclaimed her friend reproachfully. "You grieve
me, and you know it, by pretending to speak contemptuously
of the most beautiful and the divinest figure that mortal
painter ever drew."

"Forgive me, Hilda!" said Miriam. "You take these matters
more religiously than I can, for my life. Guido's Archangel
is a fine picture, of course, but it never impressed me as it
does you."

"Well; we will not talk of that," answered Hilda. "What
I wanted you to notice, in this sketch, is the face of the
Demon. It is entirely unlike the Demon of the finished
picture. Guido, you know, always affirmed that the resem-

blance to Cardinal Pamfili was either casual or imaginary. Now, here is the face as he first conceived it."

"And a more energetic Demon, altogether, than that of the finished picture!" said Kenyon, taking the sketch into his hand. "What a spirit is conveyed into the ugliness of this strong, writhing, squirming dragon, under the Archangel's foot! Neither is the face an impossible one. Upon my word, I have seen it somewhere, and on the shoulders of a living man!"

"And so have I," said Hilda. "It was what struck me from the first."

"Donatello, look at this face!" cried Kenyon.

The young Italian, as may be supposed, took little interest in matters of art, and seldom or never ventured an opinion respecting them. After holding the sketch a single instant in his hand, he flung it from him with a shudder of disgust and repugnance, and a frown that had all the bitterness of hatred.

"I know the face well!" whispered he. "It is Miriam's model!"

It was acknowledged both by Kenyon and Hilda that they had detected, or fancied, the resemblance which Donatello so strongly affirmed; and it added not a little to the grotesque and weird character which, half-playfully, half-seriously, they assigned to Miriam's attendant, to think of him as personating the Demon's part in a picture of more than two centuries ago. Had Guido, in his effort to imagine the utmost of sin and misery which his pencil could represent, hit ideally upon just this face? Or was it an actual portrait of somebody that haunted the Old Master, as Miriam was haunted now? Did the ominous shadow follow him through all the sunshine of his earlier career, and into the gloom that gathered about its close? And when Guido died, did the spectre betake himself to those ancient sepulchres, there awaiting a new victim, till it was Miriam's ill-hap to encounter him?

"I do not acknowledge the resemblance at all," said Miriam, looking narrowly at the sketch; "and, as I have drawn the face twenty times, I think you will own that I am the best judge."

A discussion here arose, in reference to Guido's Archangel, and it was agreed that these four friends should visit the Church of the Cappuccini, the next morning, and critically examine the picture in question; the similarity between it and the sketch being, at all events, a very curious circumstance.

It was now a little past ten o'clock, when some of the company, who had been standing in a balcony, declared the moonlight to be resplendent. They proposed a ramble through the streets, taking in their way some of those scenes of ruin, which produced their best effects under the splendour of the Italian moon.

XVI

A MOONLIGHT RAMBLE

THE PROPOSAL for a moonlight ramble was received with acclamation by all the younger portion of the company. They immediately set forth and descended from story to story, dimly lighting their way by waxen tapers, which are a necessary equipment to those whose thoroughfare, in the night-time, lies up and down a Roman staircase. Emerging from the courtyard of the edifice, they looked upward and saw the sky full of light, which seemed to have a delicate purple or crimson lustre, or, at least, some richer tinge than the cold, white moonshine of other skies. It gleamed over the front of the opposite palace, showing the architectural ornaments of its cornice and pillared portal, as well as the iron-barred basement-windows, that gave such a prison-like aspect to the structure, and the shabbiness and squalor that lay along its base. A cobler was just shutting up his little shop, in the basement of the palace; a cigar-vender's lantern flared in the blast that came through the archway; a French sentinel paced to-and-fro before the portal; a homeless dog, that haunted thereabouts, barked as obstreperously at the party as if he were the domestic guardian of the precincts.

The air was quietly full of the noise of falling water, the cause of which was nowhere visible, though apparently near at hand. This pleasant, natural sound, not unlike that of a distant cascade in the forest, may be heard in many of the Roman streets and piazzas, when the tumult at the city is hushed; for consuls, Emperours, and Popes, the great men of every age, have found no better way of immortalizing their memories than by the shifting, indestructible, ever new, yet unchanging, up-gush and downfall of water. They have written their names in that unstable element, and proved it a more durable record than brass or marble.

"Donatello, you had better take one of those gay, boyish artists for your companion," said Miriam, when she found the Italian youth at her side. "I am not now in a merry mood, as when we set all the world a-dancing, the other afternoon, in the Borghese grounds."

"I never wish to dance any more," answered Donatello.

"What a melancholy was in that tone!" exclaimed Miriam. "You are getting spoilt, in this dreary Rome, and will be as wise and as wretched as all the rest of mankind, unless you go back soon to your Tuscan vineyards. Well; give me your arm then! But take care that no friskiness comes over you. We must walk evenly and heavily, to-night!"

The party arranged itself according to its natural affinities or casual likings; a sculptor generally choosing a painter, and a painter a sculptor, for his companion, in preference to brethren of their own art. Kenyon would gladly have taken Hilda to himself, and have drawn her a little aside from the throng of merry wayfarers. But she kept near Miriam, and seemed, in her gentle and quiet way, to decline a separate alliance either with him or any other of her acquaintances.

So they set forth, and had gone but a little way, when the narrow street emerged into a piazza, on one side of which, glistening, and dimpling in the moonlight, was the most famous fountain in Rome. Its murmur—not to say, its uproar—had been in the ears of the company, ever since they came into the open air. It was the Fountain of Trevi, which draws its precious water from a source far beyond the walls, whence it flows hitherward through old subterranean aqueducts, and sparkles forth, as pure as the virgin who first led Agrippa to its well-spring, by her father's door.

"I shall sip as much of this water as the hollow of my hand will hold," said Miriam.—"I am leaving Rome in a few days; and the tradition goes, that a parting draught at the Fountain of Trevi ensures the traveller's return, whatever obstacles and improbabilities may seem to beset him. Will you drink, Donatello?"

"Signorina, what you drink, I drink," said the youth.

They, and the rest of the party, descended some steps to the water's brim, and, after a sip or two, stood gazing at the absurd design of the fountain, where some sculptor of Bernini's school had gone absolutely mad, in marble. It was a great palace-front, with niches and many bas-reliefs, out of which looked Agrippa's legendary virgin, and several of the allegoric sisterhood; while, at the base, appeared Neptune, with his floundering steeds, and Tritons blowing their horns about him, and twenty other artificial fantasies, which the calm moonlight soothed into better taste than was native to them.

And, after all, it was as magnificent a piece of work as ever human skill contrived. At the foot of the palatial façade, was strown, with careful art and ordered irregularity, a broad and broken heap of massive rock, looking as if it might have lain there since the deluge. Over a central precipice fell the water, in a semi-circular cascade; and from a hundred crevices, on all sides, snowy jets gushed up, and streams spouted out of the mouths and nostrils of stone-monsters, and fell in glistening drops; while other rivulets, that had run wild, came leaping from one rude step to another, over stones that were mossy, slimy, and green with sedge, because, in a century of this wild play, Nature had adopted the Fountain of Trevi, with all its elaborate devices, for her own. Finally, the water, tumbling, sparkling, and dashing, with joyous haste and never-ceasing murmur, poured itself into a great, marble-brimmed reservoir, and filled it with a quivering tide; on which was seen, continually, a snowy semi-circle of momentary foam from the principal cascade, as well as a multitude of snow-points from smaller jets. The basin occupied the whole breadth of the piazza, whence flights of steps descended to its border. A boat might float, and make voyages from one shore to another, in this mimic lake.

In the daytime, there is hardly a livelier scene in Rome than the neighborhood of the Fountain of Trevi; for the piazza is then filled with the stalls of vegetable and fruit-dealers, chestnut-roasters, cigar-venders, and other people, whose petty and wandering traffic is transacted in the open air. It is likewise thronged with idlers, lounging over the iron-railing, and with Forestieri, who come hither to see the famous fountain. Here, also, are seen men with buckets, urchins with cans, and maidens (a picture as old as the patriarchal times) bearing their pitchers upon their heads. For the water of Trevi is in request, far and wide, as the most refreshing draught for feverish lips, the pleasantest to mingle with wine, and the wholesomest to drink, in its native purity, that can anywhere be found. But, now, at nearly midnight, the piazza was a solitude; and it was a delight to behold this untameable water, sporting by itself in the moonshine, and compelling all the elaborate trivialities of art to assume a natural aspect, in accordance with its own powerful simplicity.

"What would be done with this water-power," suggested an artist, "if we had it in one of our American cities? Would they employ it to turn the machinery of a cotton-mill, I wonder!"

"The good people would pull down those rampant marble deities," said Kenyon; "and possibly they would give me a commission to carve the one-and-thirty (is that the number?) sister-States, each pouring a silver stream from a separate can into one vast basin, which should represent the grand reservoir of national prosperity."

"Or, if they wanted a bit of satire," remarked an English artist, "you could set those same one-and-thirty States to cleansing the national flag of any stains that it may have incurred. The Roman washerwomen at the lavatory yonder, plying their labour in the open air, would serve admirably as models."

"I have often intended to visit this fountain by moonlight," said Miriam, "because it was here that the interview took place between Corinne and Lord Nelvil, after their separation and temporary estrangement. Pray come behind me, one of you, and let me try whether the face can be recognized in the water."

Leaning over the stone-brim of the basin, she heard footsteps stealing behind her, and knew that somebody was looking over her shoulder. The moonshine fell directly behind Miriam, illuminating the palace-front and the whole scene of statues and rocks, and filling the basin, as it were, with tremulous and palpable light. Corinne, it will be remembered, knew Lord Nelvil by the reflection of his face in the water. In Miriam's case, however, (owing to the agitation of the water, its transparency, and the angle at which she was compelled to lean over,) no reflected image appeared; nor, from the same causes, would it have been possible for the recognition between Corinne and her lover to take place. The moon, indeed, flung Miriam's shadow at the bottom of the basin, as well as two more shadows of persons who had followed her, on either side.

"Three shadows!" exclaimed Miriam. "Three separate shadows, all so black and heavy that they sink in the water! There they lie on the bottom, as if all three were drowned together. This shadow on my right is Donatello; I know him by his curls, and the turn of his head. My left-hand companion puzzles me; a shapeless mass, as indistinct as the premonition of calamity! Which of you can it be? Ah!"

She had turned round, while speaking, and saw beside her the strange creature, whose attendance on her was already familiar, as a marvel and a jest, to the whole company of artists. A general burst of laughter followed the recognition; while the Model leaned towards Miriam, as she shrank from him, and muttered something that was inaudible to those who witnessed the scene. By his gestures, however, they concluded that he was inviting her to bathe her hands.

"He cannot be an Italian; at least, not a Roman," observed an artist. "I never knew one of them to care about ablution. See him, now! It is as if he were trying to wash off the time-stains and earthly soil of a thousand years!"

Dipping his hands into the capacious wash-bowl before him, the Model rubbed them together with the utmost vehemence. Ever and anon, too, he peeped into the water, as if expecting to see the whole Fountain of Trevi turbid with the results of his ablution. Miriam looked at him, some little time, with an aspect of real terrour, and even imitated him by leaning over to peep into the basin. Recovering herself, she took up some of the water in the hollow of her hand, and practised an old form of exorcism by flinging it in her persecutor's face.

"In the name of all the Saints," cried she, "vanish, Demon, and let me be free of you, now and forever!"

"It will not suffice," said some of the mirthful party, "unless the Fountain of Trevi gushes with holy-water."

In fact, the exorcism was quite ineffectual upon the pertinacious Demon, or whatever the apparition might be. Still he washed his brown, bony talons; still he peered into the vast basin, as if all the water of that great drinking-cup of Rome must needs be stained black or sanguine; and still he gesticulated to Miriam to follow his example. The spectators laughed loudly, but yet with a kind of constraint; for the creature's aspect was strangely repulsive and hideous.

Miriam felt her arm seized violently by Donatello. She looked at him, and beheld a tiger-like fury gleaming from his wild eyes.

"Bid me drown him!" whispered he, shuddering between rage and horrible disgust. "You shall hear his death-gurgle in another instant!"

"Peace, peace, Donatello!" said Miriam soothingly; for this naturally gentle and sportive being seemed all a-flame with animal rage.—"Do him no mischief! He is mad; and we are as mad as he, if we suffer ourselves to be disquieted by his antics. Let us leave him to bathe his hands till the fountain run dry, if he find solace and pastime in it. What is it to you or me, Donatello? There, there! Be quiet, foolish boy!"

Her tone and gesture were such as she might have used in taming down the wrath of a faithful hound, that had taken upon himself to avenge some supposed affront to his mistress. She smoothed the young man's curls, (for his fierce and sudden fury seemed to bristle among his hair,) and touched his cheek with her soft palm, till his angry mood was a little assuaged.

"Signorina, do I look as when you first knew me?" asked he, with a heavy, tremulous sigh, as they went onward, somewhat apart from their companions. "Methinks there has been a change upon me, these many months; and more and more, these last few days. The joy is gone out of my life; all gone!—all gone! Feel my hand! Is it not very hot? Ah; and my heart burns hotter still!"

"My poor Donatello, you are ill!" said Miriam, with deep sympathy and pity. "This melancholy and sickly Rome is stealing away the rich, joyous life that belongs to you. Go back, my dear friend, to your home among the hills, where (as I gather from what you have told me) your days were filled with simple and blameless delights! Have you found aught in the world that is worth what you there enjoyed? Tell me truly, Donatello!"

"Yes!" replied the young man.

"And what, in Heaven's name?" asked she.

"This burning pain in my heart," said Donatello; "for you are in the midst of it."

By this time, they had left the Fountain of Trevi considerably behind them. Little farther allusion was made to the scene at its margin; for the party regarded Miriam's persecutor as diseased in his wits, and were hardly to be surprised by any eccentricity in his deportment.

Threading several narrow streets, they passed through the Piazza of the Holy Apostles, and soon came to Trajan's forum. All over the surface of what once was Rome, it seems to be the effort of Time to bury up the ancient city, as if it were a corpse, and he the sexton; so that, in eighteen centuries, the soil over its grave has grown very deep, by the slow scattering of dust, and the accumulation of more modern decay upon elder ruin. This was the fate, also, of Trajan's forum, until some Papal antiquary, a few hundred years ago, began to hollow it out again, and disclosed the full height of the gigantic column, wreathed round with bas-reliefs of the old Emperour's warlike deeds. In the area before it, stands a **grove** of stone, consisting of the broken and unequal shafts of a vanished temple, still holding a majestic order, and apparently incapable of further demolition. The modern edifices of the piazza (wholly built, no doubt, out of the spoil of its old magnificence) look down into the hollow space whence these pillars rise.

One of the immense gray granite shafts lay in the piazza, on the verge of the area. It was a great, solid fact of the Past, making old Rome actually sensible to the touch and eye; and no study of history, nor force of thought, nor magic of song, could so vitally assure us that Rome once existed, as this sturdy specimen of what its rulers and people wrought.

"And, see!" said Kenyon, laying his hand upon it, "there is still a polish remaining on the hard substance of the pillar; and even now, late as it is, I can feel very sensibly the warmth of the noonday sun, which did its best to heat it through. This shaft will endure forever! The polish of eighteen centuries ago, as yet but half-rubbed off, and the heat of to-day's sunshine, lingering into the night, seem almost equally ephemeral in relation to it."

"There is comfort to be found in the pillar," remarked Miriam, "hard and heavy as it is. Lying here forever, as it will, it makes all human trouble appear but a momentary annoyance."

"And human happiness as evanescent too," observed Hilda sighing, "and beautiful art hardly less so! I do not love to think that this dull stone, merely by its massiveness, will last infinitely longer than any picture, in spite of the spiritual life that ought to give it immortality!"

"My poor little Hilda," said Miriam, kissing her compassionately, "would you sacrifice this greatest mortal consolation, which we derive from the transitoriness of all things—from the right of saying, in every conjuncture, 'This, too, will pass away'—would you give up this unspeakable boon, for the sake of making a picture eternal!"

Their moralizing strain was interrupted by a demonstration from the rest of the party, who, after talking and laughing together, suddenly joined their voices, and shouted at full pitch:—

"Trajan! Trajan!"

"Why do you deafen us with such an uproar?" inquired Miriam.

In truth, the whole piazza had been filled with their idle vociferation; the echoes from the surrounding houses reverberating the cry of 'Trajan,' on all sides; as if there was a great search for that imperial personage, and not so much as a handfull of his ashes to be found.

"Why, it was a good opportunity to air our voices in this resounding piazza," replied one of the artists.—"Besides, we had really some hopes of summoning Trajan to look at his column, which, you know, he never saw in his lifetime. Here is your Model (who, they say, lived and sinned before Trajan's death) still wandering about Rome; and why not the Emperour Trajan?"

"Dead Emperours have very little delight in their columns, I am afraid," observed Kenyon. "All that rich sculpture of Trajan's bloody warfare, twining from the base of the pillar to its capital, may be but an ugly spectacle for his ghostly eyes, if he considers that this huge, storied shaft must be laid before the judgment-seat, as a piece of the evidence of what he did in the flesh. If ever I am employed to sculpture a hero's monument, I shall think of this, as I put in the bas-reliefs of the pedestal!"

"There are sermons in stones," said Hilda, thoughtfully smiling at Kenyon's morality; "and especially in the stones of Rome."

The party moved on, but deviated a little from the straight way, in order to glance at the ponderous remains of the Temple of Mars Ultor, within which a convent of nuns is now established; a dove-cote, in the war-god's mansion. At only a little distance, they passed the portico of a Temple of Minerva, most rich and beautiful in architecture, but woefully gnawed by time and shattered by violence, besides being buried midway in the accumulation of soil, that rises over dead Rome like a flood-tide. Within this edifice of antique sanctity, a baker's shop was now established, with an entrance on one side; for, everywhere, the remnants of old grandeur and divinity have been made available for the meanest necessities of to-day.

"The baker is just drawing his loaves out of the oven," remarked Kenyon.—"Do you smell how sour they are? I should fancy that Minerva (in revenge for the desecration of her temple) had slily poured vinegar into the batch, if I did not know that the modern Romans prefer their bread in the acetous fermentation."

They turned into the Via Alessandria, and thus gained the rear of the Temple of Peace, and passing beneath its great arches, pursued their way along a hedge-bordered lane. In all probability, a stately Roman street lay buried beneath that rustic-looking pathway; for they had now emerged from the close and narrow avenues of the modern city, and were treading on a soil where the seeds of antique grandeur had not yet produced the squalid crop, that elsewhere sprouts from them. Grassy as the lane was, it skirted along heaps of shapeless ruin, and the bare site of the vast temple that Hadrian planned and built. It terminated on the edge of a somewhat abrupt descent, at the foot of which, with a muddy ditch between, rose, in the bright moonlight, the great curving wall and multitudinous arches of the Coliseum.

XVII

MIRIAM'S TROUBLE

A S USUAL, of a moonlight evening, several carriages
stood at the entrance of this famous ruin, and the
precincts and interiour were anything but a solitude.
The French sentinel, on duty beneath the principal archway,
eyed our party curiously, but offered no obstacle to their
admission. Within, the moonlight filled and flooded the
great empty space; it glowed upon tier above tier of ruined,
grass-grown arches, and made them even too distinctly visible.
The splendour of the revelation took away that inestimable
effect of dimness and mystery, by which the imagination
might be assisted to build a grander structure than the
Coliseum, and to shatter it with a more picturesque decay.
Byron's celebrated description is better than the reality. He
beheld the scene in his mind's eye, through the witchery
of many intervening years, and faintly illuminated it, as
if with starlight, instead of this broad glow of moonshine.

The party of our friends sat down, three or four of them
on a prostrate column; another, on a shapeless lump of marble,
once a Roman altar; others, on the steps of one of the
Christian shrines. Goths and barbarians though they were,
they chatted as gaily together as if they belonged to the
gentle and pleasant race of people who now inherit Italy.

There was much pastime and gaiety, just then, in the area of the Coliseum, where so many gladiators and wild beasts had fought and died, and where so much blood of Christian martyrs had been lapt up by that fiercest of wild beasts, the Roman populace of yore. Some youths and maidens were running merry races across the open space, and playing at hide-and-seek a little way within the duskiness of the ground-tier of arches; whence, now and then, you could hear the half-shriek, half-laugh, of a frolicksome girl, whom the shadow had betrayed into a young man's arms. Elder groups were seated on the fragments of pillars and blocks of marble, that lie round the verge of the area, talking in the quick, short ripple of the Italian tongue. On the steps of the great black cross, in the centre of the Coliseum, sat a party, singing scraps of song, with much laughter and merriment between the stanzas.

It was a strange place for song and mirth. That black cross marks one of the especial blood-spots of the earth, where, thousands of times over, the Dying Gladiator fell, and more of human agony has been endured, for the mere pastime of the multitude, than on the breadth of many battle-fields. From all this crime and suffering, however, the spot has derived a more than common sanctity. An inscription promises seven years' indulgence—seven years of remission from the pains of Purgatory, and earlier enjoyment of heavenly bliss—for each separate kiss imprinted on the black cross. What better use could be made of life (after middle-age, when the accumulated sins are many, and the remaining temptations few) than to spend it all in kissing the black cross of the Coliseum!

Besides its central consecration, the whole area has been made sacred by a range of shrines, which are erected round the circle, each commemorating some scene or circumstance of the Saviour's passion and suffering. In accordance with an ordinary custom, a pilgrim was making his progress from shrine to shrine, upon his knees, and saying a penitential prayer at each. Light-footed girls ran across the path along which he crept, or sported with their friends close by the shrines where he was kneeling. The pilgrim took no heed, and the girls meant no irreverence; for, in Italy, religion jostles along side by side with business and sport, after a fashion of its own; and people are accustomed to kneel down and pray, or see others praying, between two fits of merriment, or between two sins.

To make an end of our description, a red twinkle of light was visible amid the breadth of shadow, that fell across the upper part of the Coliseum. Now it glimmered through a line of arches, or threw a broader gleam, as it rose out of some profound abyss of ruin; now, it was muffled by a heap of shrubbery, which had adventurously clambered to that dizzy height; and so the red light kept ascending to loftier and loftier ranges of the structure, until it stood like a star, where the blue sky rested against the Coliseum's topmost wall. It indicated a party of English or Americans, paying the inevitable visit by moonlight, and exalting themselves with raptures that were Byron's, not their own.

Our company of artists sat on the fallen column, the pagan altar, and the steps of the Christian shrine, enjoying the moonlight and shadow, the present gaiety and the gloomy reminiscences of the scene, in almost equal share. Artists, indeed, are lifted by the ideality of their pursuits a little way off the earth, and are therefore able to catch the evanescent fragrance that floats in the atmosphere of life, above the heads of the ordinary crowd. Even if they seem endowed with little imagination, individually, yet there is a property, a gift, a talisman, common to their class, entitling them to partake, somewhat more bountifully than other people, in the thin delights of moonshine and romance.

"How delightful this is!" said Hilda; and she sighed, for very pleasure.

"Yes," said Kenyon, who sat on the column, at her side. "The Coliseum is far more delightful, as we enjoy it now, than when eighty thousand persons sat squeezed together, row above row, to see their fellow-creatures torn by lions and tigers limb from limb. What a strange thought, that the Coliseum was really built for us, and has not come to its best uses till almost two thousand years after it was finished!"

"The Emperour Vespasian scarcely had us in his mind," said Hilda smiling. "But I thank him none the less for building it."

"He gets small thanks, I fear, from the people whose bloody instincts he pampered," rejoined Kenyon. "Fancy a nightly assemblage of eighty thousand melancholy and re-morseful ghosts, looking down from those tiers of broken arches, striving to repent of the savage pleasures which they once enjoyed, but still longing to enjoy them over again!"

"You bring a Gothic horrour into this peaceful, moonlight scene," said Hilda.

"Nay, I have good authority for peopling the Coliseum with phantoms," replied the sculptor. "Do you remember that veritable scene in Benvenuto Cellini's autobiography, in which a necromancer of his acquaintance draws a magic circle, (just where the black cross stands now, I suppose,) and raises myriads of demons? Benvenuto saw them with his own eyes—giants, pygmies, and other creatures of frightful aspect—capering and dancing on yonder walls. Those spectres must have been Romans, in their lifetime, and frequenters of this bloody amphitheatre."

"I see a spectre, now!" said Hilda, with a little thrill of uneasiness. "Have you watched that pilgrim, who is going round the whole circle of shrines, on his knees, and praying with such fervency at every one! Now that he has revolved

so far in his orbit—and has the moonshine on his face, as
he turns towards us—methinks I recognize him!"

"And so do I," said Kenyon. "Poor Miriam! Do you think
she sees him?"

They looked round, and perceived that Miriam had risen
from the steps of the shrine, and disappeared. She had shrunk
back, in fact, into the deep obscurity of an arch that opened
just behind them.

Donatello (whose faithful watch was no more to be eluded
than that of a hound) had stolen after her, and became the
innocent witness of a spectacle that had its own kind of
horrour. Unaware of his presence, and fancying herself
wholly unseen, the beautiful Miriam began to gesticulate
extravagantly, gnashing her teeth, flinging her arms wildly
abroad, stamping with her foot. It was as if she had stept
aside, for an instant, solely to snatch the relief of a brief fit
of madness. Persons in acute trouble, or labouring under
strong excitement with a necessity for concealing it, are
prone to relieve the nerves in this wild way; although,
when practicable, they find a more effectual solace in
shrieking aloud.

Thus, as soon as she threw off her self-controul, under
the dusky arches of the Coliseum, we may consider Miriam
as a mad woman, concentrating the elements of a long insanity
into that instant.

"Signorina! Signorina! Have pity on me!" cried Donatello,
approaching her.—"This is too terrible!"

"How dare you look at me?" exclaimed Miriam, with a
start; then, whispering below her breath,—"Men have been
struck dead for a less offence!"

"If you desire it, or need it," said Donatello humbly,
"I shall not be loth to die."

"Donatello," said Miriam, coming close to the young man,
and speaking low, but still with the almost insanity of the

moment vibrating in her voice, "if you love yourself—if you desire those earthly blessings such as you, of all men, were made for—if you would come to a good old age among your olive-orchards and your Tuscan vines, as your forefathers did—if you would leave children to enjoy the same peaceful, happy, innocent life—then flee from me! Look not behind you! Get you gone without another word."

He gazed sadly at her, but did not stir.

"I tell you," Miriam went on, "there is a great evil hanging over me! I know it; I see it in the sky; I feel it in the air! It will overwhelm me as utterly as if this arch should crumble down upon our heads! It will crush you, too, if you stand at my side! Depart, then; and make the sign of the cross, as your faith bids you, when an evil spirit is nigh. Cast me off; or you are lost forever!"

A higher sentiment brightened upon Donatello's face, than had hitherto seemed to belong to its simple expression and sensuous beauty.

"I will never quit you," he said. "You cannot drive me from you!"

"Poor Donatello!" said Miriam in a changed tone, and rather to herself than him. "Is there no other that seeks me out, follows me, is obstinate to share my affliction and my doom—but only you! They call me beautiful; and I used to fancy that, at my need, I could bring the whole world to my feet. And, lo! here is my utmost need; and my beauty and my gifts have brought me only this poor, simple boy. Half-witted, they call him; and surely fit for nothing but to be happy! And I accept his aid! Tomorrow—tomorrow— I will tell him all. Ah, what a sin, to stain his joyous nature with the blackness of a woe like mine!"

She held out her hand to him, and smiled sadly as Donatello pressed it to his lips. They were now about to emerge from the depth of the arch; but, just then, the kneeling pilgrim, in his revolution round the orbit of the shrines, had reached the one on the steps of which Miriam had been sitting. There, as at the other shrines, he prayed, or seemed to pray. It struck Kenyon, however, (who sat close by, and saw his face distinctly,) that the suppliant was merely performing an enjoined penance, and without the penitence that ought to have given it effectual life. Even as he knelt, his eyes wandered, and Miriam soon felt that he had detected her, half-hidden as she was within the obscurity of the arch.

"He is evidently a good Catholic, however," whispered one of the party.—"After all, I fear, we cannot identify him with the ancient Pagan, who haunts the catacombs."

"The Doctors of the Propaganda may have converted him," said another. "They have had fifteen hundred years to perform the task."

The company now deemed it time to continue their ramble. Emerging from a side-entrance of the Coliseum, they had on their left the Arch of Constantine, and, above it, the shapeless ruins of the Palace of the Caesars; portions of which have taken shape anew, in mediæval convents and modern villas. They turned their faces cityward, and treading over the broad flag-stones of the old Roman pavement, passed through the Arch of Titus. The moon shone brightly enough, within it, to show the seven-branched Jewish candlestick, cut in the marble of the interiour. The original of that awful trophy lies buried, at this moment, in the yellow mud of the Tiber, and, could its gold of Ophir again be brought to light, it would be the most precious relic of past ages, in the estimation of both Jew and Gentile.

Standing amid so much ancient dust, it is difficult to spare the reader the common-places of enthusiasm, on which hundreds of tourists have already insisted. Over this half-worn pavement, and beneath this Arch of Titus, the Roman armies had trodden in their outward march, to fight battles, a world's width away. Returning, victorious, with royal captives and inestimable spoil, a Roman Triumph, that most gorgeous pageant of earthly pride, had streamed and flaunted, in hundredfold succession, over these same flag-stones, and through this yet stalwart archway. It is politic, however, to make few allusions to such a Past; nor, if we would create an interest in the characters of our story, is it wise to suggest how Cicero's foot may have stept on yonder stone, nor how Horace was wont to stroll near by, making his footsteps chime with the measure of the ode that was ringing in his mind. The very ghosts of that massive and stately epoch have so much density, that the actual people of to-day seem the thinner of the two, and stand more ghostlike by the arches and columns, letting the rich sculpture be discerned through their ill-compacted substance.

The party kept onward, often meeting pairs and groups of midnight strollers, like themselves. On such a moonlight night as this, Rome keeps itself awake and stirring, and is full of song and pastime, the noise of which mingles with your dreams, if you have gone betimes to bed. But it is better to be abroad, and take our own share of the enjoyable time; for the languor, that weighs so heavily in the Roman atmosphere, by day, is lightened beneath the moon and stars.

They had now reached the precincts of the Forum.

XVIII

ON THE EDGE OF A PRECIPICE

L ET US SETTLE IT," said Kenyon, stamping his foot firmly down, "that this is precisely the spot where the chasm opened, into which Curtius precipitated his good steed and himself. Imagine the great, dusky gap, impenetrably deep, and with half-shaped monsters and hideous faces looming upward out of it, to the vast affright of the good citizens who peeped over the brim! There, now, is a subject, hitherto unthought of, for a grim and ghastly story, and, methinks, with a moral as deep as the gulf itself. Within it, beyond a question, there were prophetic visions—intimations of all the future calamities of Rome—shades of Goths and Gauls, and even of the French soldiers of to-day. It was a pity to close it up so soon! I would give much for a peep into such a chasm."

"I fancy," remarked Miriam, "that every person takes a peep into it in moments of gloom and despondency; that is to say, in his moments of deepest insight."

"Where is it, then?" asked Hilda. "I never peeped into it."

"Wait, and it will open for you," replied her friend.—"The chasm was merely one of the orifices of that pit of blackness that lies beneath us, everywhere. The firmest substance of human happiness is but a thin crust spread over it, with just reality enough to bear up the illusive stage-scenery amid which we tread. It needs no earthquake to open the chasm. A footstep, a little heavier than ordinary, will serve; and we must step very daintily, not to break through the crust, at any moment. By-and-by, we inevitably sink! It was a foolish piece of heroism in Curtius to precipitate himself there, in advance; for all Rome, you see, has been swallowed up in that gulf, in spite of him. The Palace of the Caesars has gone down thither, with a hollow, rumbling sound of its fragments! All the temples have tumbled into it; and thousands of statues have been thrown after! All the armies and the triumphs have marched into the great chasm, with their martial music playing, as they stept over the brink. All the heroes, the statesmen, and the poets! All piled upon poor Curtius, who thought to have saved them all! I am loth to smile at the self-conceit of that gallant horseman, but cannot well avoid it."

"It grieves me to hear you speak thus, Miriam," said Hilda, whose natural and cheerful piety was shocked by her friend's gloomy view of human destinies. "It seems to me that there is no chasm, nor any hideous emptiness under our feet, except what the evil within us digs. If there be such a chasm, let us bridge it over with good thoughts and deeds, and we shall tread safely to the other side. It was the guilt of Rome, no doubt, that caused this gulf to open; and Curtius filled it up with his heroic self-sacrifice, and patriotism, which was the best virtue that the old Romans knew. Every wrong thing makes the gulf deeper; every right one helps to fill it up. As the evil of Rome was far more than its good, the whole commonwealth finally sank into it, indeed, but of no original necessity."

"Well, Hilda, it came to the same thing at last," answered Miriam despondingly.

"Doubtless, too," resumed the sculptor, (for his imagination was greatly excited by the idea of this wondrous chasm,) "all the blood that the Romans shed, whether on battle-fields, or in the Coliseum, or on the cross—in whatever public or private murder—ran into this fatal gulf, and formed a mighty subterranean lake of gore, right beneath our feet. The blood from the thirty wounds in Caesar's breast flowed hitherward, and that pure little rivulet from Virginia's bosom, too! Virginia, beyond all question, was stabbed by her father, precisely where we are standing."

"Then the spot is hallowed forever!" said Hilda.

"Is there such blessed potency in bloodshed?" asked Miriam. "Nay, Hilda, do not protest! I take your meaning rightly."

They again moved forward. And still, from the Forum and the Via Sacra, from beneath the arches of the Temple of Peace, on one side, and the acclivity of the Palace of the Caesars, on the other, there arose singing voices of parties that were strolling through the moonlight. Thus, the air was full of kindred melodies that encountered one another, and twined themselves into a broad, vague music, out of which no single strain could be disentangled. These good examples, as well as the harmonious influences of the hour, incited our artist-friends to make proof of their own vocal powers. With what skill and breath they had, they set up a choral strain—'Hail, Columbia!' we believe—which those old Roman echoes must have found it exceedingly difficult to repeat aright. Even Hilda poured the slender sweetness of her note into her country's song. Miriam was at first silent, being perhaps unfamiliar with the air and burthen. But, suddenly, she threw out such a swell and gush of sound, that it seemed to pervade the whole choir of other voices, and then to rise above them all, and become audible in what would else have been the silence of an upper region. That volume of melodious voice was one of the tokens of a great trouble. There had long been an impulse upon her—amounting, at last, to a necessity—to shriek aloud; but she had struggled against it, till the thunderous anthem gave her an opportunity to relieve her heart by a great cry.

They passed the solitary column of Phocas, and looked down into the excavated space, where a confusion of pillars, arches, pavements, and shattered blocks and shafts—the crumbs of various ruin, dropt from the devouring maw of Time—stand, or lie, at the base of the Capitoline Hill. That renowned hillock (for it is little more) now rose abruptly above them. The ponderous masonry, with which the hillside is built up, is as old as Rome itself, and looks likely to endure, while the world retains any substance or permanence. It once sustained the Capitol, and now bears up the great pile which the mediæval builders raised on the antique foundation, and that still loftier tower, which looks abroad upon a larger page, of deeper historic interest, than any other scene can show. On the same pedestal of Roman masonry, other structures will doubtless rise, and vanish like ephemeral things.

To a spectator on the spot, it is remarkable that the events of Roman history, and Roman life itself, appear not so distant as the Gothic ages which succeeded them. We stand in the Forum, or on the height of the Capitol, and seem to see the Roman epoch close at hand. We forget that a chasm extends between it and ourselves, in which lie all those dark, rude, unlettered centuries, around the birth-time of Christianity, as well as the age of chivalry and romance, the feudal system, and the infancy of a better civilization than that of Rome. Or, if we remember these mediæval times, they look farther off than the Augustan age. The reason may be, that the old Roman literature survives, and creates for us an intimacy

"Hush, hush! Do not let them hear you!" whispered Miriam. "I frighten you, you say. For Heaven's sake, how? Am I strange? Is there anything wild in my behaviour?"

"Only for that moment," replied Hilda, "because you seemed to doubt God's Providence."

"We will talk of that, another time," said her friend. "Just now, it is very dark to me."

On the left of the Piazza of the Campidoglio, as you face cityward, and at the head of the long and stately flight of steps, descending from the Capitoline Hill to the level of lower Rome, there is a narrow lane or passage. Into this, the party of our friends now turned. The path ascended a little, and ran along under the walls of a palace, but soon passed through a gateway, and terminated in a small, paved courtyard. It was bordered by a low parapet.

The spot, for some reason or other, impressed them as exceedingly lonely. On one side was the great height of the palace, with the moonshine falling over it, and showing all the windows barred and shuttered. Not a human eye could look down into the little courtyard, even if the seemingly deserted palace had a tenant. On all other sides of its narrow compass, there was nothing but the parapet, which, as it now appeared, was built right on the edge of a steep precipice. Gazing from its imminent brow, the party beheld a crowded confusion of roofs, spreading over the whole space between them and the line of hills that lay beyond the Tiber. A long, misty wreath, just dense enough to catch a little of the moonshine, floated above the houses, midway towards the hilly line, and showed the course of the unseen river. Far away, on the right, the moon gleamed on the Dome of Saint Peter's, as well as on many lesser and nearer domes.

"What a beautiful view of the city!" exclaimed Hilda. "And I never saw Rome from this point before!"

"It ought to afford a good prospect," said the sculptor; "for it was from this point—at least, we are at liberty to think so, if we choose—that many a famous Roman caught his last glimpse of his native city, and of all other earthly things. This is one of the sides of the Tarpeian Rock. Look over the parapet, and see what a sheer tumble there might still be for a traitor, in spite of the thirty feet of soil that have accumulated at the foot of the precipice!"

They all bent over, and saw that the cliff fell perpendicularly downward to about the depth, or rather more, at which the tall palace rose in height above their heads. Not that it was still the natural, shaggy front of the original precipice; for it appeared to be cased in ancient stone-work, through which the primeval rock showed its face, here and there, grimly and doubtfully. Mosses grew on the slight projections, and little shrubs sprouted out of the crevices, but could not much soften the stern aspect of the cliff. Brightly as the Italian moonlight fell a-down the height, it scarcely showed what portion of it was man's work, and what was Nature's, but left it all in very much the same kind of ambiguity and half-knowledge, in which antiquarians generally leave the identity of Roman remains.

The roofs of some poor-looking houses, which had been built against the base and sides of the cliff, rose nearly midway to the top; but, from an angle of the parapet, there was a precipitous plunge straight downward into a stone-paved court.

"I prefer this to any other site, as having been veritably the Traitor's Leap," said Kenyon, "because it was so convenient to the Capitol. It was an admirable idea of those stern old fellows, to fling their political criminals down from the very summit on which stood the Senate-House and Jove's temple; emblems of the institutions which they sought to violate. It symbolizes how sudden was the fall, in those days, from the utmost height of ambition to its profoundest ruin."

"Come, come; it is midnight," cried another artist; "too late to be moralizing here! We are literally dreaming on the edge of a precipice. Let us go home!"

"It is time, indeed," said Hilda.

The sculptor was not without hopes that he might be favoured with the sweet charge of escorting Hilda to the foot of her tower. Accordingly, when the party prepared to turn back, he offered her his arm. Hilda at first accepted it; but when they had partly threaded the passage between the little courtyard and the Piazza del Campidoglio, she discovered that Miriam had remained behind.

"I must go back," said she, withdrawing her arm from Kenyon's; "but pray do not come with me. Several times, this evening, I have had a fancy that Miriam has something on her mind—some sorrow or perplexity—which, perhaps, it would relieve her to tell me about. No, no; do not turn back! Donatello will be a sufficient guardian for Miriam and me."

The sculptor was a good deal mortified, and perhaps a little angry; but he knew Hilda's mood of gentle decision and independence too well not to obey her. He therefore suffered the fearless maiden to return alone.

Meanwhile, Miriam had not noticed the departure of the rest of the company; she remained on the edge of the precipice, and Donatello along with her.

"It would be a fatal fall, still!" she said to herself, looking over the parapet, and shuddering as her eye measured the depth. "Yes; surely, yes! Even without the weight of an over-burthened heart, a human body would fall heavily enough upon those stones to shake all its joints asunder. How soon it would be over!"

Donatello (of whose presence she was possibly not aware) now pressed closer to her side; and he, too, like Miriam, bent over the low parapet, and trembled violently. Yet he seemed to feel that perilous fascination which haunts the brow of precipices, tempting the unwary one to fling himself over, for the very horrour of the thing; for, after drawing hastily back, he again looked down, thrusting himself out farther than before. He then stood silent, a brief space, struggling, perhaps, to make himself conscious of the historic associations of the scene.

"What are you thinking of, Donatello?" asked Miriam.

"Who were they," said he, looking earnestly in her face, "who have been flung over here, in days gone by?"

"Men that cumbered the world," she replied. "Men whose lives were the bane of their fellow-creatures. Men who poisoned the air, which is the common breath of all, for their own selfish purposes. There was short work with such men, in old Roman times. Just in the moment of their triumph, a hand as of an avenging giant clutched them, and dashed the wretches down this precipice!"

"Was it well done?" asked the young man.

"It was well done," answered Miriam. "Innocent persons were saved by the destruction of a guilty one, who deserved his doom."

While this brief conversation passed, Donatello had once or twice glanced aside, with a watchful air, just as a hound may often be seen to take sidelong note of some suspicious object, while he gives his more direct attention to something nearer at hand. Miriam seemed now first to become aware of the silence that had followed upon the cheerful talk and laughter of a few moments before. Looking round, she perceived that all her company of merry friends had retired, and Hilda, too, in whose soft and quiet presence she had always an indescribable feeling of security. All gone; and only herself and Donatello left hanging over the brow of the ominous precipice!

Not so, however; not entirely alone! In the basement-wall of the palace, shaded from the moon, there was a deep, empty niche, that had probably once contained a statue; not empty, neither; for a figure now came forth from it, and approached Miriam. She must have had cause to dread some unspeakable evil from this strange persecutor, and to know that this was the very crisis of her calamity; for, as he drew near, such a cold, sick despair crept over her, that it impeded her breath, and benumbed her natural promptitude of thought. Miriam seemed dreamily to remember falling on her knees; but, in her whole recollection of that wild moment, she beheld herself as in a dim show, and could not well distinguish what was done and suffered; no, not even whether she were really an actor and sufferer in the scene.

Hilda, meanwhile, had separated herself from the sculptor, and turned back to rejoin her friend. At a distance, she still heard the mirth of her late companions, who were going down the cityward descent of the Capitoline Hill; they had set up a new stave of melody, in which her own soft voice, as well as the powerful sweetness of Miriam's, was sadly missed.

The door of the little courtyard had swung upon its hinges, and partly closed itself. Hilda (whose native gentleness pervaded all her movements) was quietly opening it, when she was startled, midway, by the noise of a struggle within, beginning and ending all in one breathless instant. Along with it, or closely succeeding it, was a loud, fearful cry, which quivered upward through the air, and sank quivering downward to the earth. Then, a silence! Poor Hilda had looked into the courtyard, and saw the whole quick passage of a deed, which took but that little time to grave itself in the eternal adamant.

XIX

THE FAUN'S TRANSFORMATION

THE DOOR of the courtyard swang slowly, and closed
itself of its own accord. Miriam and Donatello were
now alone there. She clasped her hands, and looked
wildly at the young man, whose form seemed to have dilated,
and whose eyes blazed with the fierce energy that had suddenly inspired him. It had kindled him into a man; it had
developed within him an intelligence which was no native
characteristic of the Donatello whom we have heretofore
known. But that simple and joyous creature was gone forever.

"What have you done!" said Miriam, in a horrour-stricken
whisper.

The glow of rage was still lurid on Donatello's face, and
now flashed out again from his eyes.

"I did what ought to be done to a traitor!" he replied. "I
did what your eyes bade me do, when I asked them with
mine, as I held the wretch over the precipice!"

These last words struck Miriam like a bullet. Could it be
so? Had her eyes provoked, or assented to this deed? She
had not known it. But, alas! Looking back into the frenzy
and turmoil of the scene just acted, she could not deny—she
was not sure whether it might be so, or no—that a wild joy
had flamed up in her heart, when she beheld her persecutor

in his mortal peril. Was it horrour?—or ecstasy?—or both in one? Be the emotion what it might, it had blazed up more madly, when Donatello flung his victim off the cliff, and more and more, while his shriek went quivering downward. With the dead thump upon the stones below, had come an unutterable horrour.

"And my eyes bade you do it!" repeated she.

They both leaned over the parapet, and gazed downward as earnestly as if some inestimable treasure had fallen over, and were yet recoverable. On the pavement, below, was a dark mass, lying in a heap, with little or nothing human in its appearance, except that the hands were stretched out, as if they might have clutched, for a moment, at the small, square stones. But there was no motion in them, now. Miriam watched the heap of mortality while she could count a hundred, which she took pains to do. No stir; not a finger moved.

"You have killed him, Donatello! He is quite dead," said she. "Stone dead! Would I were so, too!"

"Did you not mean that he should die?" sternly asked Donatello, still in the glow of that intelligence which passion had developed in him. "There was short time to weigh the matter; but he had his trial in that breath or two, while I held him over the cliff, and his sentence in that one glance, when your eyes responded to mine! Say that I have slain him against your will—say that he died without your whole consent—and, in another breath, you shall see me lying beside him!"

"Oh, never!" cried Miriam. "My one, own friend! Never, never, never!"

She turned to him—the guilty, blood-stained, lonely woman —she turned to her fellow-criminal, the youth, so lately innocent, whom she had drawn into her doom. She pressed him close, close to her bosom, with a clinging embrace that brought their two hearts together, till the horrour and agony of each was combined into one emotion, and that, a kind of rapture.

"Yes, Donatello, you speak the truth!" said she. "My heart consented to what you did. We two slew yonder wretch. The deed knots us together for time and eternity, like the coil of a serpent!"

They threw one other glance at the heap of death below, to assure themselves that it was there; so like a dream was the whole thing. Then they turned from that fatal precipice, and came out of the courtyard, arm in arm, heart in heart. Instinctively, they were heedful not to sever themselves so much as a pace or two from one another, for fear of the terrour and deadly chill that would thenceforth wait for them in solitude. Their deed—the crime which Donatello wrought, and Miriam accepted on the instant—had wreathed itself, as she said, like a serpent, in inextricable links about both their souls, and drew them into one, by its terrible contractile power. It was closer than a marriage-bond. So intimate, in those first moments, was the union, that it seemed as if their new sympathy annihilated all other ties, and that they were released from the chain of humanity; a new sphere, a special law, had been created for them alone. The world could not come near them; they were safe!

When they reached the flight of steps, leading downward from the Capitol, there was a far-off noise of singing and laughter. Swift, indeed, had been the rush of the crisis that was come and gone! This was still the merriment of the party that had so recently been their companions; they recognized the voices which, a little while ago, had accorded and sung in cadence with their own. But they were familiar voices no more; they sounded strangely, and, as it were, out of the depths of space; so remote was all that pertained to the past life of these guilty ones, in the moral seclusion that had suddenly extended itself around them. But how close, and ever closer, did the breadth of the immeasurable waste, that lay between them and all brotherhood or sisterhood, now press them one within the other!

"Oh, friend," cried Miriam, so putting her soul into that word that it took a heavy richness of meaning, and seemed never to have been spoken before.—"Oh, friend, are you conscious, as I am, of this companionship that knits our heart-strings together?"

"I feel it, Miriam," said Donatello. "We draw one breath; we live one life!"

"Only yesterday," continued Miriam; "nay, only a short half-hour ago, I shivered in an icy solitude. No friendship, no sisterhood, could come near enough to keep the warmth within my heart. In an instant, all is changed! There can be no more loneliness!"

"None, Miriam!" said Donatello.

"None, my beautiful one!" responded Miriam, gazing in his face, which had taken a higher, almost an heroic aspect from the strength of passion. "None, my innocent one! Surely, it is no crime that we have committed. One wretched and worthless life has been sacrificed, to cement two other lives forevermore."

"Forevermore, Miriam!" said Donatello. "Cemented with his blood!"

The young man started at the word which he had himself spoken; it may be that it brought home, to the simplicity of his imagination, what he had not before dreamed of—the ever-increasing loathsomeness of a union that consists in guilt. Cemented with blood, which would corrupt and grow more noisome, forever and forever, but bind them none the less strictly for that!

"Forget it! Cast it all behind you!" said Miriam, detecting, by her sympathy, the pang that was in his heart. "The deed has done its office, and has no existence any more."

They flung the past behind them, as she counselled, or else distilled from it a fiery intoxication, which sufficed to carry them triumphantly through those first moments of their doom. For, guilt has its moment of rapture, too. The foremost result of a broken law is ever an ecstatic sense of freedom. And thus there exhaled upward (out of their dark sympathy, at the base of which lay a human corpse) a bliss, or an insanity, which the unhappy pair imagined to be well-worth the sleepy innocence that was forever lost to them.

As their spirits rose to the solemn madness of the occasion, they went onward—not stealthily, not fearfully—but with a stately gait and aspect. Passion lent them (as it does to meaner shapes) its brief nobility of carriage. They trode through the streets of Rome, as if they, too, were among the majestic and guilty shadows, that, from ages long gone by, have haunted the blood-stained city. And, at Miriam's suggestion, they turned aside, for the sake of treading loftily past the old site of Pompey's forum.

"For there was a great deed done here!" she said—"a deed of blood, like ours! Who knows, but we may meet the high and ever-sad fraternity of Caesar's murderers, and exchange a salutation?"

"Are they our brethren, now?" asked Donatello.

"Yes; all of them," said Miriam; "and many another, whom the world little dreams of, has been made our brother or our sister, by what we have done within this hour!"

And, at the thought, she shivered. Where, then, was the seclusion, the remoteness, the strange, lonesome Paradise, into which she and her one companion had been transported by their crime? Was there, indeed, no such refuge, but only a crowded thoroughfare and jostling throng of criminals?

And was it true, that whatever hand had a blood-stain on it—or had poured out poison, or strangled a babe at its birth, or clutched a grandsire's throat, he sleeping, and robbed him of his few last breaths—had now the right to offer itself in fellowship with their two hands? Too certainly, that right existed. It is a terrible thought, that an individual wrong-doing melts into the great mass of human crime, and makes us—who dreamed only of our own little separate sin—makes us guilty of the whole. And thus Miriam and her lover were not an insulated pair, but members of an innumerable confraternity of guilty ones, all shuddering at each other.

"But not now; not yet!" she murmured to herself. "To-night, at least, there shall be no remorse!"

Wandering without a purpose, it so chanced that they turned into a street, at one extremity of which stood Hilda's tower. There was a light in her high chamber; a light, too, at the Virgin's shrine; and the glimmer of these two was the loftiest light beneath the stars. Miriam drew Donatello's arm, to make him stop; and while they stood at some distance, looking at Hilda's window, they beheld her approach and throw it open. She leaned far forth, and extended her clasped hands towards the sky.

"The good, pure child! She is praying, Donatello!"—said Miriam, with a kind of simple joy at witnessing the devoutness of her friend. Then her own sin rushed upon her, and she shouted, with the rich strength of her voice, "Pray for us, Hilda! We need it!"

Whether Hilda heard and recognized the voice, we cannot tell. The window was immediately closed, and her form disappeared from behind the snowy curtain. Miriam felt this to be a token that the cry of her condemned spirit was shut out of Heaven.

XX

THE BURIAL CHAUNT

THE CHURCH OF THE CAPUCHINS (where, as the reader may remember, some of our acquaintances had made an engagement to meet) stands a little aside from the Piazza Barberini. Thither, at the hour agreed upon, on the morning after the scenes last described, Miriam and Donatello directed their steps. At no time are people so sedulously careful to keep their trifling appointments, attend to their ordinary occupations, and thus put a common-place aspect on life, as when conscious of some secret that, if suspected, would make them look monstrous in the general eye.

Yet how tame and wearisome is the impression of all ordinary things, in the contrast with such a fact! How sick and tremulous, the next morning, is the spirit that has dared so much, only the night before! How icy cold is the heart, when the fervour, the wild ecstasy of passion, has faded away, and sunk down among the dead ashes of the fire that blazed so fiercely, and was fed by the very substance of its life! How faintly does the criminal stagger onward, lacking the impulse of that strong madness that hurried him into guilt, and treacherously deserts him in the midst of it!

When Miriam and Donatello drew near the church, they found only Kenyon awaiting them on the steps. Hilda had likewise promised to be of the party, but had not yet appeared. Meeting the sculptor, Miriam put a force upon herself, and succeeded in creating an artificial flow of spirits, which, to any but the nicest observation, was quite as effective as a natural one. She spoke sympathizingly to the sculptor on the subject of Hilda's absence, and somewhat annoyed him by alluding, in Donatello's hearing, to an attachment which had never been openly avowed, though perhaps plainly enough betrayed. He fancied that Miriam did not quite recognize the limits of the strictest delicacy; he even went so far as to generalize, and conclude within himself that this deficiency is a more general failing in woman than in man, the highest refinement being a masculine attribute.

But the idea was unjust to the sex at large, and especially so to this poor Miriam, who was hardly responsible for her frantic efforts to be gay. Possibly, moreover, the nice action of the mind is set ajar by any violent shock, as of great misfortune or great crime; so that the finer perceptions may be blurred thenceforth, and the effect be traceable in all the minutest conduct of life.

"Did you see anything of the dear child after you left us?" asked Miriam, still keeping Hilda as her topic of conversation. "I missed her sadly on my way homeward; for nothing ensures me such delightful and innocent dreams (I have experienced it twenty times) as a talk, late in the evening, with Hilda."

"So I should imagine," said the sculptor gravely; "but it is an advantage that I have little or no opportunity of enjoying. I know not what became of Hilda after my parting from you. She was not especially my companion in any part of our walk. The last I saw of her, she was hastening back to rejoin you in the courtyard of the Palazzo Caffarelli."

"Impossible!" cried Miriam starting.

"Then, did you not see her again?" inquired Kenyon in some alarm.

"Not there," answered Miriam quietly. "Indeed, I followed pretty closely on the heels of the rest of the party. But, do not be alarmed on Hilda's account. The Virgin is bound to watch over the good child, for the sake of the piety with which she keeps the lamp a-light at her shrine. And, besides, I have always felt that Hilda is just as safe, in these evil streets of Rome, as her white doves, when they fly downward from the tower-top, and run to-and-fro among the horses' feet. There is certainly a Providence on purpose for Hilda, if for no other human creature."

"I religiously believe it," rejoined the sculptor; "and yet my mind would be the easier, if I knew that she had returned safely to her tower."

"Then make yourself quite easy," answered Miriam. "I saw her (and it is the last sweet sight that I remember) leaning from her window, midway between earth and sky!"

Kenyon now looked at Donatello.

"You seem out of spirits, my dear friend," he observed. "This languid Roman atmosphere is not the airy wine that you were accustomed to breathe at home. I have not forgotten your hospitable invitation to meet you, this summer, at your castle among the Apennines. It is my fixed purpose to come, I assure you. We shall both be the better for some deep draughts of the mountain-breezes."

"It may be," said Donatello, with unwonted sombreness. "The old house seemed joyous, when I was a child. But, as I remember it now, it was a grim place too!"

The sculptor looked more attentively at the young man, and was surprised and alarmed to observe how entirely the fine, fresh glow of animal spirits had departed out of his face. Hitherto, moreover, even while he was standing perfectly still, there had been a kind of possible gambol indicated in his aspect. It was quite gone, now. All his youthful gaiety, and with it his simplicity of manner, was eclipsed, if not utterly extinct.

"You are surely ill, my dear fellow!" exclaimed Kenyon.

"Am I? Perhaps so," said Donatello indifferently. "I never have been ill, and know not what it may be."

"Do not make the poor lad fancy-sick," whispered Miriam, pulling the sculptor's sleeve. "He is of a nature to lie down and die, at once, if he finds himself drawing such melancholy breaths as we ordinary people are enforced to burthen our lungs withal. But we must get him away from this old, dreamy, and dreary Rome, where nobody but himself ever thought of being gay. Its influences are too heavy to sustain the life of such a creature."

The above conversation had passed chiefly on the steps of the Cappuccini; and, having said so much, Miriam lifted the leathern curtain that hangs before all church-doors, in Italy.

"Hilda has forgotten her appointment," she observed, "or else her maiden slumbers are very sound, this morning. We will wait for her no longer."

They entered the nave. The interiour of the church was of moderate compass, but of good architecture, with a vaulted roof over the nave, and a row of dusky chapels on either side of it, instead of the customary side-aisles. Each chapel had its saintly shrine, hung round with offerings; its picture above the altar, although closely veiled, if by any painter of renown; and its hallowed tapers, burning continually, to set a-light the devotion of the worshippers. The pavement of the nave was chiefly of marble, and looked old and broken, and was shabbily patched, here and there, with tiles of brick; it was inlaid, moreover, with tombstones of the mediæval taste, on which were quaintly sculptured borders, figures and portraits in bas-relief, and Latin epitaphs, now grown illegible by the tread of footsteps over them. The church appertains to a convent of Capuchin monks; and, as usually happens when a reverend brotherhood have such an edifice in charge, the floor seemed never to have been scrubbed or swept, and had as little the aspect of sanctity as a kennel; whereas, in all churches of nunneries, the maiden sisterhood invariably show the purity of their own hearts by the virgin cleanliness and visible consecration of the walls and pavement.

As our friends entered the church, their eyes rested at once on a remarkable object in the centre of the nave. It was either the actual body—or, as might rather have been supposed, at first glance, the cunningly wrought waxen face, and suitably draped figure—of a dead monk. This image of wax—or clay-cold reality, whichever it might be—lay on a slightly elevated bier, with three tall candles burning on each side, another tall candle at the head, and another at the foot. There was music, too, in harmony with so funereal a spectacle. From beneath the pavement of the church came the deep, lugubrious strain of a 'De Profundis,' which sounded like an utterance of the tomb itself; so dismally did it rumble through the burial-vaults, and ooze up among the flat grave-stones and sad epitaphs, filling the church as with a gloomy mist.

"I must look more closely at that dead monk, before we leave the church," remarked the sculptor. "In the study of my art, I have gained many a hint from the dead, which the living could never have given me."

"I can well imagine it," answered Miriam. "One clay image is readily copied from another. But let us first see Guido's picture. The light is favourable now."

Accordingly, they turned into the first chapel on the right hand, as you enter the nave; and there they beheld—not the picture, indeed—but a closely drawn curtain. The church-men of Italy make no scruple of sacrificing the very purpose for which a work of sacred art has been created—that of opening the way for religious sentiment through the quick medium of sight, by bringing angels, saints, and martyrs, down visibly upon earth—of sacrificing this high purpose, and, for aught they know, the welfare of many souls along with it, to the hope of a paltry fee. Every work, by an artist of celebrity, is hidden behind a veil, and seldom revealed except to Protestants, who scorn it as an object of devotion, and value it only for its artistic merit.

The sacristan was quickly found, however, and lost no time in disclosing the youthful Archangel, setting his divine foot on the head of his fallen adversary. It was an image of that greatest of future events, which we hope for so ardently, (at least, while we are young,) but find so very long in coming—the triumph of Goodness over the Evil Principle.

"Where can Hilda be?" exclaimed Kenyon. "It is not her custom ever to fail in an engagement; and the present one was made entirely on her account. Except herself, you know, we were all agreed in our recollection of the picture."

"But we were wrong, and Hilda right, as you perceive," said Miriam, directing his attention to the point on which their dispute, of the night before, had arisen. "It is not easy to detect her astray, as regards any picture on which those clear, soft eyes of hers have ever rested."

"And she has studied and admired few pictures so much as this," observed the sculptor. "No wonder; for there is hardly another so beautiful in the world. What an expression of heavenly severity in the Archangel's face! There is a degree of pain, trouble, and disgust at being brought in contact with sin, even for the purpose of quelling and punishing it; and yet a celestial tranquillity pervades his whole being."

"I have never been able," said Miriam, "to admire this picture nearly so much as Hilda does, in its moral and intellectual aspect. If it cost her more trouble to be good—if her soul were less white and pure—she would be a more competent critic of this picture, and would estimate it not half so high. I see its defects to-day more clearly than ever before."

"What are some of them?" asked Kenyon.

"That Archangel, now!" Miriam continued. "How fair he looks, with his unruffled wings, with his unhacked sword, and clad in his bright armour, and that exquisitely fitting sky-blue tunic, cut in the latest Paradisaical mode. What a dainty air of the first celestial society! With what half-scornful delicacy he sets his prettily sandalled foot on the head of his prostrate foe! But, is it thus that Virtue looks, the moment after its death-struggle with Evil? No, no! I could have told Guido better. A full third of the Archangel's feathers should have been torn from his wings; the rest all ruffled, till they looked like Satan's own! His sword should be streaming with blood, and perhaps broken half-way to the hilt; his armour crushed, his robes rent, his breast gory; a bleeding gash on his brow, cutting right across the stern scowl of battle! He should press his foot hard down upon the old Serpent, as if his very soul depended upon it, feeling him squirm mightily, and doubting whether the fight were half-over yet, and how the victory might turn! And, with all this fierceness, this grimness, this unutterable horrour, there should still be something high, tender, and holy, in Michael's eyes, and around his mouth. But the battle never was such child's play as Guido's dapper Archangel seems to have found it!"

"For Heaven's sake, Miriam," cried Kenyon, astonished at the wild energy of her talk, "paint the picture of man's struggle against sin, according to your own idea! I think it will be a master-piece."

"The picture would have its share of truth, I assure you," she answered; "but I am sadly afraid the victory would fall on the wrong side. Just fancy a smoke-blackened, fiery-eyed Demon, bestriding that nice young angel, clutching his white throat with one of his hinder claws, and giving a triumphant whisk of his scaly tail, with a poisonous dart at the end of it! That is what they risk, poor souls, who do battle with Michael's enemy."

It now perhaps struck Miriam, that her mental disquietude was impelling her to an undue vivacity; for she paused, and turned away from the picture, without saying a word more about it. All this while, moreover, Donatello had been very ill at ease, casting awe-stricken and inquiring glances at the dead monk; as if he could look nowhere but at that ghastly object, merely because it shocked him. Death has probably a peculiar horrour and ugliness, when forced upon the contemplation of a person so naturally joyous as Donatello, who lived with completeness in the present moment, and was able to form but vague images of the future.

"What is the matter, Donatello?" whispered Miriam soothingly. "You are quite in a tremble, my poor friend! What is it?"

"This awful chaunt from beneath the church!" answered Donatello. "It oppresses me; the air is so heavy with it that I can scarcely draw my breath. And yonder dead monk! I feel as if he were lying right across my heart!"

"Take courage!" whispered she again. "Come; we will approach close to the dead monk. The only way, in such cases, is to stare the ugly horrour right in the face; never a sidelong glance, nor a half-look, for those are what show a frightful thing in its frightfullest aspect. Lean on me, dearest friend! My heart is very strong for both of us. Be brave; and all is well!"

Donatello hung back, for a moment, but then pressed close to Miriam's side, and suffered her to lead him up to the bier. The sculptor followed. A number of persons, chiefly women, with several children among them, were standing about the corpse; and as our three friends drew nigh, a mother knelt down, and caused her little boy to kneel, both kissing the beads and crucifix that hung from the monk's girdle. Possibly, he had died in the odour of sanctity; or, at all events, Death, and his brown frock and cowl, made a sacred image of this reverend Father.

XXI

THE DEAD CAPUCHIN

THE DEAD MONK was clad, as when alive, in the brown woollen frock of the Capuchins, with the hood drawn over his head, but so as to leave the features and a portion of the beard uncovered. His rosary and cross hung at his side; his hands were folded over his breast; his feet (he was of a bare-footed order, in his lifetime, and continued so, in death) protruded from beneath his habit, stiff and stark, with a more waxen look than even his face. They were tied together at the ancles with a black ribbon.

The countenance, as we have already said, was fully displayed. It had a purplish hue upon it, unlike the paleness of an ordinary corpse, but as little resembling the flush of natural life. The eyelids were but partially drawn down, and showed the eyeballs beneath; as if the deceased friar were stealing a glimpse at the bystanders, to watch whether they were duly impressed with the solemnity of his obsequies. The shaggy eyebrows gave sternness to the look.

Miriam passed between two of the lighted candles, and stood close beside the bier.

"My God!" murmured she. "What is this?"

She grasped Donatello's hand, and, at the same instant, felt him give a convulsive shudder, which she knew to have been caused by a sudden and terrible throb of the heart. His hand, by an instantaneous change, became like ice within hers, which likewise grew so icy, that their insensible fingers might have rattled, one against the other. No wonder that their blood curdled; no wonder that their hearts leapt, and paused! The dead face of the monk, gazing at them beneath its half-closed eyelids, was the same visage that had glared upon their naked souls, the past midnight, as Donatello flung him over the precipice.

The sculptor was standing at the foot of the bier, and had not yet seen the monk's features.

"Those naked feet!" said he. "I know not why, but they affect me strangely. They have walked to-and-fro over the hard pavements of Rome, and through a hundred other rough ways of this life, where the monk went begging for his brotherhood; along the cloisters and dreary corridors of his convent, too, from his youth upward! It is a suggestive idea, to track those worn feet backward through all the paths they have trodden, ever since they were the tender and rosy little feet of a baby, and (cold as they now are) were kept warm in his mother's hand."

As his companions, whom the sculptor supposed to be close by him, made no response to his fanciful musings, he looked up, and saw them at the head of the bier. He advanced thither himself.

"Ha!" exclaimed he.

He cast a horrour-stricken and bewildered glance at Miriam, but withdrew it immediately. Not that he had any definite suspicion, or, it may be, even a remote idea, that she could be held responsible, in the least degree, for this man's sudden death. In truth, it seemed too wild a thought, to connect, in reality, Miriam's persecutor of many past months, and the vagabond of the preceding night, with the dead Capuchin of to-day. It resembled one of those unaccountable changes and interminglings of identity, which so often occur among the personages of a dream. But Kenyon, as befitted the professor of an imaginative art, was endowed with an exceedingly quick sensibility, which was apt to give him intimations of the true state of matters that lay beyond his actual vision. There was a whisper in his ear; it said, 'Hush!' Without asking himself wherefore, he resolved to be silent as regarded the mysterious discovery which he had made, and to leave any remark or explanation to be voluntarily offered by Miriam. If she never spoke, then let the riddle be unsolved.

And now occurred a circumstance that would seem too fantastic to be told, if it had not actually happened, precisely as we set it down. As the three friends stood by the bier, they saw that a little stream of blood had begun to ooze from the dead monk's nostrils; it crept slowly towards the thicket of his beard, where, in the course of a moment or two, it hid itself.

"How strange!" ejaculated Kenyon. "The monk died of apoplexy, I suppose, or by some sudden accident, and the blood has not yet congealed."

"Do you consider that a sufficient explanation?" asked Miriam, with a smile from which the sculptor involuntarily turned away his eyes. "Does it satisfy you?"

"And why not?" he inquired.

"Of course, you know the old superstition about this phenomenon of blood flowing from a dead body," she rejoined. "How can we tell but that the murderer of this monk (or, possibly, it may be only that privileged murderer, his physician) may have just entered the church?"

"I cannot jest about it," said Kenyon. "It is an ugly sight!"

"True, true; horrible to see, or dream of!" she replied, with one of those long, tremulous sighs, which so often betray a sick heart by escaping unexpectedly. "We will not look at it any more. Come away, Donatello. Let us escape from this dismal church. The sunshine will do you good."

When had ever a woman such a trial to sustain as this! By no possible supposition, could Miriam explain the identity of the dead Capuchin, quietly and decorously laid out in the nave of his convent-church, with that of her murdered persecutor, flung heedlessly at the foot of the precipice. The effect upon her imagination was as if a strange and unknown corpse had miraculously, while she was gazing at it, assumed the likeness of that face, so terrible henceforth in her remembrance. It was a symbol, perhaps, of the deadly iteration with which she was doomed to behold the image of her crime reflected back upon her, in a thousand ways, and converting the great, calm face of Nature, in the whole, and in its innumerable details, into a manifold reminiscence of that one dead visage.

No sooner had Miriam turned away from the bier, and gone a few steps, than she fancied the likeness altogether an illusion, which would vanish at a closer and colder view. She must look at it again, therefore, and at once; or else the grave would close over the face, and leave the awful fantasy that had connected itself therewith, fixed ineffaceably in her brain.

"Wait for me, one moment!" she said to her companions. "Only a moment!"

So she went back, and gazed once more at the corpse. Yes; these were the features that Miriam had known so well; this was the visage that she remembered from a far longer date than the most intimate of her friends suspected; this form of clay had held the evil spirit which blasted her sweet youth, and compelled her, as it were, to stain her womanhood with crime. But, whether it were the majesty of death, or something originally noble and lofty in the character of the dead, which the soul had stamped upon the features as it left them;

so it was that Miriam now quailed and shook, not for the vulgar horrour of the spectacle, but for the severe, reproachful glance that seemed to come from between those half-closed lids. True; there had been nothing, in his lifetime, viler than this man. She knew it; there was no other fact within her consciousness that she felt to be so certain; and yet, because her persecutor found himself safe and irrefutable in death, he frowned upon his victim, and threw back the blame on her!

"Is it thou, indeed?" she murmured, under her breath. "Then thou hast no right to scowl upon me so! But art thou real, or a vision?"

She bent down over the dead monk, till one of her rich curls brushed against his forehead. She touched one of his folded hands with her finger.

"It is he!" said Miriam. "There is the scar, that I know so well, on his brow. And it is no vision; he is palpable to my touch! I will question the fact no longer, but deal with it as I best can."

It was wonderful to see how the crisis developed in Miriam its own proper strength, and the faculty of sustaining the demands which it made upon her fortitude. She ceased to tremble; the beautiful woman gazed sternly at her dead enemy, endeavouring to meet and quell the look of accusation that he threw from between his half-closed eyelids.

"No; thou shalt not scowl me down!" said she. "Neither now, nor when we stand together at the Judgment Seat. I fear not to meet thee there. Farewell, till that next encounter!"

Haughtily waving her hand, Miriam rejoined her friends, who were awaiting her at the door of the church. As they went out, the sacristan stopped them and proposed to show the cemetery of the convent, where the deceased members of the fraternity are laid to rest in sacred earth, brought long ago from Jerusalem.

"And will yonder monk be buried there?" she asked.

"Brother Antonio?" exclaimed the sacristan. "Surely, our good brother will be put to bed there! His grave is already dug, and the last occupant has made room for him. Will you look at it, Signorina?"

"I will!" said Miriam.

"Then, excuse me," observed Kenyon; "for I shall leave you. One dead monk has more than sufficed me; and I am not bold enough to face the whole mortality of the convent."

It was easy to see, by Donatello's looks, that he, as well as the sculptor, would gladly have escaped a visit to the famous cemetery of the Cappuccini. But Miriam's nerves were strained to such a pitch, that she anticipated a certain solace and absolute relief in passing from one ghastly spectacle to another of long accumulated ugliness; and there was, besides, a singular sense of duty which impelled her to look at the final resting-place of the being whose fate had been so disastrously involved with her own. She therefore followed the sacristan's guidance, and drew her companion along with her, whispering encouragement as they went.

The cemetery is beneath the church, but entirely above ground, and lighted by a row of iron-grated windows without glass. A corridor runs along beside these windows, and gives access to three or four vaulted recesses, or chapels, of considerable breadth and height, the floor of which consists of the consecrated earth of Jerusalem. It is smoothed decorously over the deceased brethren of the convent, and is kept quite free from grass or weeds, such as would grow even in these gloomy recesses, if pains were not bestowed to root them up. But, as the cemetery is small, and it is a precious privilege to sleep in holy ground, the brotherhood are immemorially accustomed, when one of their number dies, to take the longest-buried skeleton out of the oldest grave, and lay the new slumberer there instead. Thus, each of the good friars, in his turn, enjoys the luxury of a consecrated bed, attended with the slight drawback of being forced to get up long before day-break, as it were, and make room for another lodger.

The arrangement of the unearthed skeletons is what makes the special interest of the cemetery. The arched and vaulted walls of the burial-recesses are supported by massive pillars and pilasters, made of thigh-bones and skulls; the whole material of the structure appears to be of a similar kind; and the knobs and embossed ornaments of this strange architecture are represented by the joints of the spine, and, the more delicate tracery, by the smaller bones of the human frame. The summits of the arches are adorned with entire skeletons, looking as if they were wrought most skilfully in bas-relief. There is no possibility of describing how ugly and grotesque is the effect, combined with a certain artistic merit; nor how much perverted ingenuity has been shown in this queer way; nor what a multitude of dead monks, through how many hundred years, must have contributed their bony frame-work to build up these great arches of mortality! On some of the skulls there are inscriptions, purporting that such a monk, who formerly made use of that particular head-piece, died on such a day and year; but vastly the greater number are piled up indistinguishably into the architectural design, like the many deaths that make up the one glory of a victory.

In the side-walls of the vaults are niches, where skeleton monks sit or stand, clad in the brown habits that they wore in life, and labelled with their names and the dates of their decease. Their skulls (some quite bare, and others still covered with yellow skin, and hair that has known the earth-damps) look out from beneath their hoods, grinning hideously repulsive. One reverend Father has his mouth wide open, as if he had died in the midst of a howl of terrour and remorse, which perhaps is even now screeching through eternity. As a general thing, however, these frocked and hooded skeletons seem to take a more cheerful view of their position, and try, with ghastly smiles, to turn it into a jest. But the cemetery of the Capuchins is no place to nourish celestial hopes; the soul sinks, forlorn and wretched, under all this burthen of dusty death; the holy earth from Jerusalem, so imbued is it with mortality, has grown as barren of the flowers of Paradise as it is of earthly weeds and grass. Thank Heaven for its blue sky; it needs a long, upward gaze, to give us back our faith! Not here can we feel ourselves immortal, where the very altars, in these chapels of horrible consecration, are heaps of human bones!

Yet, let us give the cemetery the praise that it deserves! There is no disagreeable scent, such as might have been expected from the decay of so many holy persons, in whatever odour of sanctity they may have taken their departure. The same number of living monks would not smell half so unexceptionably!

Miriam went gloomily along the corridor, from one vaulted Golgotha to another, until, in the farthest recess, she beheld an open grave.

"Is that for him who lies yonder in the nave?" she asked.

"Yes, Signorina, this is to be the resting-place of Brother Antonio, who came to his death, last night," answered the sacristan; "and in yonder niche, you see, sits a brother who was buried thirty years ago, and has risen to give him place."

"It is not a satisfactory idea," observed Miriam, "that you poor friars cannot call even your graves permanently your own. You must lie down in them, methinks, with a nervous anticipation of being disturbed, like weary men, who know that they shall be summoned out of bed at midnight. Is it not possible (if money were to be paid for the privilege) to leave Brother Antonio—if that be his name—in the occupancy of that narrow grave, till the last trumpet sounds?"

"By no means, Signorina, neither is it needful or desirable," answered the sacristan. "A quarter of a century's sleep, in the sweet earth of Jerusalem, is better than a thousand years in any other soil. Our brethren find good rest there. No ghost was ever known to steal out of this blessed cemetery."

"That is well," responded Miriam. "May he, whom you now lay to sleep, prove no exception to the rule!"

As they left the cemetery, she put money into the sacristan's hand, to an amount that made his eyes open wide and glisten, and requested that it might be expended in masses for the repose of Father Antonio's soul.

XXII

THE MEDICI GARDENS

D ONATELLO," said Miriam anxiously, as they came through the Piazza Barberini, "what can I do for you, my beloved friend? You are shaking as with the cold fit of the Roman fever!"

"Yes," said Donatello. "My heart shivers."

As soon as she could collect her thoughts, Miriam led the young man to the gardens of the Villa Medici, hoping that the quiet shade and sunshine of that delightful retreat would a little revive his spirits. The grounds are there laid out in the old fashion of straight paths, with borders of box, which form hedges of great height and density, and are shorn and trimmed to the evenness of a wall of stone, at the top and sides. There are green alleys, with long vistas, overshadowed by ilex-trees; and at each intersection of the paths, the visitor finds seats of lichen-covered stone to repose upon, and marble statues that look forlornly at him, regretful of their lost noses. In the more open portions of the garden, before the sculptured front of the villa, you see fountains and flower-beds, and, in their season, a profusion of roses, from which the genial sun of Italy distils a fragrance, to be scattered abroad by the no less genial breeze.

But Donatello drew no delight from these things. He walked onward in silent apathy, and looked at Miriam with strangely half-awakened and bewildered eyes, when she sought to bring his mind into sympathy with hers, and so relieve his heart of the burthen that lay lumpishly upon it.

She made him sit down on a stone-bench, where two embowered alleys crossed each other; so that they could discern the approach of any casual intruder, a long way down the path.

"My sweet friend," she said, taking one of his passive hands in both of hers, "what can I say to comfort you?"

"Nothing!" replied Donatello, with sombre reserve. "Nothing will ever comfort me."

"I accept my own misery," continued Miriam—"my own guilt, if guilt it be—and, whether guilt or misery, I shall know how to deal with it. But you, dearest friend, that were the rarest creature in all this world, and seemed a being to whom sorrow could not cling! You, whom I half fancied to belong to a race that had vanished forever, you only surviving, to show mankind how genial and how joyous life used to be, in some long-gone age! What had you to do with grief or crime?"

"They came to me as to other men," said Donatello broodingly. "Doubtless, I was born to them."

"No, no; they came with me!" replied Miriam. "Mine is the responsibility! Alas, wherefore was I born! Why did we ever meet! Why did I not drive you from me, knowing—for my heart foreboded it—that the cloud, in which I walked, would likewise envelope you!"

Donatello stirred uneasily, with the irritable impatience that is often combined with a mood of leaden despondency. A brown lizard with two tails—a monster often engendered by the Roman sunshine—ran across his foot, and made him start.

Then he sat silent awhile, and so did Miriam, trying to dissolve her whole heart into sympathy, and lavish it all upon him, were it only for a moment's cordial.

The young man lifted his hand to his breast, and, unintentionally, as Miriam's hand was within his, he lifted that along with it.

"I have a great weight here!" said he.

The fancy struck Miriam (but she drove it resolutely down) that Donatello almost imperceptibly shuddered, while, in pressing his own hand against his heart, he pressed hers there too.

"Rest your heart on me, dearest one!" she resumed. "Let me bear all its weight. I am well able to bear it; for I am a woman, and I love you! I love you, Donatello! Is there no comfort for you in this avowal? Look at me! Heretofore, you have found me pleasant to your sight. Gaze into my eyes! Gaze into my soul! Search as deeply as you may, you can never see half the tenderness and devotion that I henceforth cherish for you. All that I ask, is your acceptance of the utter self-sacrifice, (but it shall be no sacrifice, to my great love,) with which I seek to remedy the evil you have incurred for my sake!"

All this fervour on Miriam's part; on Donatello's, a heavy silence.

"Oh, speak to me!" she exclaimed. "Only promise me to be, by-and-by, a little happy!"

"Happy?" murmured Donatello. "Ah, never again! Never again!"

"Never? Ah, that is a terrible word to say to me!" answered Miriam. "A terrible word to let fall upon a woman's heart, when she loves you, and is conscious of having caused your misery! If you love me, Donatello, speak it not again. And surely you did love me?"

"I did," replied Donatello, gloomily and absently.

Miriam released the young man's hand, but suffered one of her own to lie close to his, and waited a moment to see whether he would make any effort to retain it. There was much depending upon that simple experiment.

With a deep sigh—as when, sometimes, a slumberer turns over, in a troubled dream—Donatello changed his position, and clasped both his hands over his forehead. The genial warmth of a Roman April, kindling into May, was in the atmosphere around them; but when Miriam saw that involuntary movement, and heard that sigh of relief, (for so she interpreted it,) a shiver ran through her frame, as if the iciest wind of the Apennines were blowing over her.

"He has done himself a greater wrong than I dreamed of," thought she, with unutterable compassion. "Alas, it was a sad mistake! He might have had a kind of bliss in the consequences of this deed, had he been impelled to it by a love vital enough to survive the frenzy of that terrible moment; mighty enough to make its own law, and justify itself against the natural remorse. But to have perpetrated a dreadful murder (and such was his crime, unless love, annihilating moral distinctions, made it otherwise) on no better warrant than a boy's idle fantasy! I pity him from the very depths of my soul! As for myself, I am past my own or others' pity."

She arose from the young man's side, and stood before him with a sad, commiserating aspect; it was the look of a ruined soul, bewailing, in him, a grief less than what her profounder sympathies imposed upon herself.

"Donatello, we must part," she said, with melancholy firmness. "Yes; leave me! Go back to your old tower, which overlooks the green valley you have told me of, among the Apennines. Then, all that has past will be recognized as but an ugly dream. For, in dreams, the conscience sleeps, and we often stain ourselves with guilt of which we should be incapable in our waking moments. The deed you seemed to do, last night, was no more than such a dream; there was as little substance in what you fancied yourself doing. Go; and forget it all!"

"Ah, that terrible face!" said Donatello, pressing his hands over his eyes. "Do you call that unreal?"

"Yes; for you beheld it with dreaming eyes," replied Miriam. "It was unreal; and, that you may feel it so, it is requisite that you see this face of mine no more. Once, you may have thought it beautiful; now, it has lost its charm. Yet it would still retain a miserable potency to bring back the past illusion, and, in its train, the remorse and anguish that would darken all your life. Leave me, therefore, and forget me!"

"Forget you, Miriam!" said Donatello, roused somewhat from his apathy of despair. "If I could remember you, and behold you, apart from that frightful visage which stares at me over your shoulder—that were a consolation, at least, if not a joy."

"But since that visage haunts you along with mine," rejoined Miriam, glancing behind her, "we needs must part. Farewell, then! But if ever—in distress, peril, shame, poverty, or whatever anguish is most poignant, whatever burthen heaviest—you should require a life to be given wholly, only to make your own a little easier, then summon me! As the case now stands between us, you have bought me dear, and find me of little worth. Fling me away, therefore! May you never need me more! But, if otherwise, a wish—almost an unuttered wish—will bring me to you!"

She stood a moment, expecting a reply. But Donatello's eyes had again fallen on the ground, and he had not, in his bewildered mind and overburthened heart, a word to respond.

"That hour I speak of may never come," said Miriam. "So farewell—farewell forever!"

"Farewell!" said Donatello.

His voice hardly made its way through the environment of unaccustomed thoughts and emotions, which had settled over him like a dense and dark cloud. Not improbably, he beheld Miriam through so dim a medium that she looked visionary; heard her speak only in a thin, faint echo.

She turned from the young man, and, much as her heart yearned towards him, she would not profane that heavy parting by an embrace, or even a pressure of the hand. So soon after the semblance of such mighty love, and after it had been the impulse to so terrible a deed, they parted, in all outward show, as coldly as people part, whose whole mutual intercourse has been encircled within a single hour.

And Donatello, when Miriam had departed, stretched himself at full length on the stone-bench, and drew his hat over his eyes, as the idle and light-hearted youths of dreamy Italy are accustomed to do, when they lie down in the first convenient shade, and snatch a noonday slumber. A stupour was upon him, which he mistook for such drowsiness as he had known in his innocent past life. But, by-and-by, he raised himself slowly, and left the garden. Sometimes, poor Donatello started, as if he heard a shriek; sometimes, he shrank back, as if a face, fearful to behold, were thrust close to his own. In this dismal mood, bewildered with the novelty of sin and grief, he had little left of that singular resemblance, on account of which, and for their sport, his three friends had fantastically recognized him as the veritable Faun of Praxiteles.

XXIII

MIRIAM AND HILDA

O N LEAVING the Medici Gardens, Miriam felt herself
astray in the world; and having no special reason to
seek one place more than another, she suffered chance
to direct her steps as it would. Thus it happened, that, involving herself in the crookedness of Rome, she saw Hilda's tower
rising before her, and was put in mind to climb up to the
young girl's aëry, and ask why she had broken her engagement at the Church of the Capuchins. People often do the
idlest acts of their lifetime, in their heaviest and most anxious
moments; so that it would have been no wonder, had Miriam
been impelled only by so slight a motive of curiosity as we
have indicated. But she remembered, too, and with a quaking
heart, what the sculptor had mentioned of Hilda's retracing
her steps towards the courtyard of the Palazzo Caffarelli, in
quest of Miriam herself. Had she been compelled to choose
between infamy in the eyes of the whole world, or in Hilda's
eyes alone, she would unhesitatingly have accepted the former,
on condition of remaining spotless in the estimation of her
white-souled friend. This possibility, therefore, that Hilda had
witnessed the scene of the past night, was unquestionably the

cause that drew Miriam to the tower, and made her linger and faulter as she approached it.

As she drew near, there were tokens to which her disturbed mind gave a sinister interpretation. Some of her friend's airy family, the doves, with their heads imbedded disconsolately in their bosoms, were squatted in a corner of the piazza; others had alighted on the heads, wings, shoulders, and trumpets, of the marble angels which adorned the façade of the neighboring church; two or three had betaken themselves to the Virgin's shrine; and as many as could find room were sitting on Hilda's window-sill. But all of them, so Miriam fancied, had a look of weary expectation and disappointment; no flights, no flutterings, no cooing murmur; something, that ought to have made their day glad and bright, was evidently left out of this day's history. And, furthermore, Hilda's white window-curtain was closely drawn, with only that one little aperture, at the side, which Miriam remembered noticing, the night before.

"Be quiet!" said Miriam to her own heart, pressing her hand hard upon it. "Why shouldst thou throb, now?—Hast thou not endured more terrible things than this?"

Whatever were her apprehensions, she would not turn back. It might be—and the solace would be worth a world— that Hilda, knowing nothing of the past night's calamity, would greet her friend with a sunny smile, and so restore a portion of the vital warmth, for lack of which her soul was frozen. But could Miriam, guilty as she was, permit Hilda to kiss her cheek, to clasp her hand, and thus be no longer so unspotted from the world as heretofore?

"I will never permit her sweet touch again," said Miriam, toiling up the staircase, "if I can find strength of heart to forbid it. But, Oh, it would be so soothing in this wintry fever-fit of my heart! There can be no harm to my white Hilda in one parting kiss. That shall be all!"

But, on reaching the upper landing-place, Miriam paused, and stirred not again till she had brought herself to an immoveable resolve.

"My lips—my hand—shall never meet Hilda's more!" said she.

Meanwhile, Hilda sat listlessly in her painting-room. Had you looked into the little adjoining chamber, you might have seen the slight imprint of her figure on the bed, but would also have detected, at once, that the white counterpane had not been turned down. The pillow was more disturbed; she had turned her face upon it, the poor child, and bedewed it with some of those tears, (among the most chill and forlorn that gush from human sorrow,) which the innocent heart pours forth, at its first actual discovery that sin is in the world. The young and pure are not apt to find out that miserable truth, until it is brought home to them by the guiltiness of some trusted friend. They may have heard much of the evil of the world, and seem to know it, but only as an impalpable theory. In due time, some mortal, whom they reverence too highly, is commissioned by Providence to teach them this direful lesson; he perpetrates a sin; and Adam falls anew, and Paradise, heretofore in unfaded bloom, is lost again, and closed forever, with the fiery swords gleaming at its gates.

The chair, in which Hilda sat, was near the portrait of Beatrice Cenci, which had not yet been taken from the easel. It is a peculiarity of this picture, that its profoundest expression eludes a straightforward glance, and can only be caught by side glimpses, or when the eye falls casually upon it; even as if the painted face had a life and consciousness of its own, and, resolving not to betray its secret of grief or guilt, permitted the true tokens to come forth only when it imagined itself unseen. No other such magical effect has ever been wrought by pencil.

Now, opposite the easel, hung a looking-glass, in which Beatrice's face and Hilda's were both reflected. In one of her weary, nerveless changes of position, Hilda happened to throw her eyes on the glass, and took in both these images at one unpremeditated glance. She fancied—nor was it without horrour—that Beatrice's expression, seen aside and vanishing in a moment, had been depicted in her own face, likewise, and flitted from it as timorously.

"Am I, too, stained with guilt?" thought the poor girl, hiding her face in her hands.

Not so, thank Heaven! But, as regards Beatrice's picture, the incident suggests a theory which may account for its unutterable grief and mysterious shadow of guilt, without detracting from the purity which we love to attribute to that ill-fated girl. Who, indeed, can look at that mouth—with its lips half-apart, as innocent as a baby's that has been crying— and not pronounce Beatrice sinless! It was the intimate consciousness of her father's sin that threw its shadow over her, and frightened her into a remote and inaccessible region, where no sympathy could come. It was the knowledge of Miriam's guilt that lent the same expression to Hilda's face.

But Hilda nervously moved her chair, so that the images in the glass should be no longer visible. She now watched a speck of sunshine that came through a shuttered window, and crept from object to object, indicating each with a touch of its bright finger, and then letting them all vanish successively. In like manner, her mind, so like sunlight in its natural cheerfulness, went from thought to thought, but found nothing that it could dwell upon for comfort. Never before had this young, energetic, active spirit, known what it is to be despondent. It was the unreality of the world that made her so. Her dearest friend, whose heart seemed the most solid and richest of Hilda's possessions, had no existence for her any more; and in that dreary void, out of which Miriam had disappeared, the substance, the truth, the integrity of life, the motives of effort, the joy of success, had departed along with her.

It was long past noon, when a step came up the staircase. It had passed beyond the limits where there was communication with the lower regions of the palace, and was mounting the successive flights which led only to Hilda's precincts. Faint as the tread was, she heard and recognized it. It startled her into sudden life. Her first impulse was to spring to the door of the studio, and fasten it with lock and bolt. But a second thought made her feel that this would be an unworthy cowardice, on her own part, and also that Miriam—only yesterday, her closest friend—had a right to be told, face to face, that thenceforth they must be forever strangers.

She heard Miriam pause, outside of the door. We have already seen what was the latter's resolve with respect to any kiss or pressure of the hand between Hilda and herself. We know not what became of the resolution. As Miriam was of a highly impulsive character, it may have vanished at the first sight of Hilda; but, at all events, she appeared to have dressed herself up in a garb of sunshine, and was disclosed, as the door swung open, in all the glow of her remarkable beauty. The truth was, her heart leaped convulsively towards the only refuge that it had, or hoped. She forgot, just one instant, all cause for holding herself aloof. Ordinarily there was a certain reserve in Miriam's demonstrations of affection, in consonance with the delicacy of her friend. To-day, she opened her arms to take Hilda in.

"Dearest, darling Hilda!" she exclaimed. "It gives me new life to see you!"

Hilda was standing in the middle of the room. When her friend made a step or two from the door, she put forth her hands with an involuntary repellent gesture, so expressive, that Miriam at once felt a great chasm opening itself between them two. They might gaze at one another from the opposite sides, but without the possibility of ever meeting more; or, at least, since the chasm could never be bridged over, they must tread the whole round of Eternity to meet on the other side. There was even a terrour in the thought of their meeting again. It was as if Hilda or Miriam were dead, and could no longer hold intercourse without violating a spiritual law.

Yet, in the wantonness of her despair, Miriam made one more step towards the friend whom she had lost.

"Do not come nearer, Miriam!" said Hilda.

Her look and tone were those of sorrowful entreaty, and yet they expressed a kind of confidence, as if the girl were conscious of a safeguard that could not be violated.

"What has happened between us, Hilda?" asked Miriam. "Are we not friends?"

"No, no!" said Hilda shuddering.

"At least, we have been friends," continued Miriam. "I loved you dearly! I love you still! You were to me as a younger sister; yes, dearer than sisters of the same blood; for you and I were so lonely, Hilda, that the whole world pressed us together by its solitude and strangeness. Then, will you not touch my hand? Am I not the same as yesterday?"

"Alas! No, Miriam!" said Hilda.

"Yes, the same—the same for you, Hilda," rejoined her lost friend. "Were you to touch my hand, you would find it as warm to your grasp as ever. If you were sick or suffering, I would watch night and day for you. It is in such simple offices that true affection shows itself; and so I speak of them. Yet now, Hilda, your very look seems to put me beyond the limits of humankind!"

"It is not I, Miriam," said Hilda; "not I, that have done this!"

"You, and you only, Hilda!" replied Miriam, stirred up to make her own cause good, by the repellent force which her friend opposed to her. "I am a woman, as I was yesterday;—endowed with the same truth of nature, the same warmth of heart, the same genuine and earnest love, which you have always known in me. In any regard that concerns yourself, I am not changed. And believe me, Hilda, when a human being has chosen a friend out of all the world, it is only some faithlessness between themselves, rendering true intercourse impossible, that can justify either friend in severing the bond. Have I deceived you? Then cast me off! Have I wronged you personally? Then forgive me, if you can! But, have I sinned against God and man, and deeply sinned? Then be more my friend than ever, for I need you more!"

"Do not bewilder me thus, Miriam!" exclaimed Hilda, who had not forborne to express, by look and gesture, the anguish which this interview inflicted on her. "If I were one of God's angels, with a nature incapable of stain, and garments that never could be spotted, I would keep ever at your side, and try to lead you upward. But I am a poor, lonely girl, whom God has set here in an evil world, and given her only a white robe, and bid her wear it back to Him, as white as when she put it on. Your powerful magnetism would be too much for me. The pure, white atmosphere, in which I try to discern what things are good and true, would be discoloured. And, therefore, Miriam, before it is too late, I mean to put faith in this awful heart-quake, which warns me henceforth to avoid you!"

"Ah, this is hard! Ah, this is terrible!" murmured Miriam, dropping her forehead in her hands. In a moment or two, she looked up again, as pale as death, but with a composed countenance.—"I always said, Hilda, that you were merciless; for I had a perception of it, even while you loved me best. You have no sin, nor any conception of what it is; and therefore you are so terribly severe! As an angel, you are not amiss; but, as a human creature, and a woman among earthly men and women, you need a sin to soften you!"

"God forgive me," said Hilda, "if I have said a needlessly cruel word!"

"Let it pass," answered Miriam. "I, whose heart it has smitten upon, forgive you. And tell me, before we part forever, what have you seen or known of me, since we last met?"

"A terrible thing, Miriam!" said Hilda, growing paler than before.

"Do you see it written in my face, or painted in my eyes?" inquired Miriam, her trouble seeking relief in a half-frenzied raillery. "I would fain know how it is that Providence, or Fate, brings eye-witnesses to watch us, when we fancy ourselves acting in the remotest privacy. Did all Rome see it, then? Or, at least, our merry company of artists? Or is it some blood-stain on me, or death-scent in my garments? They say that monstrous deformities sprout out of fiends, who once were lovely angels. Do you perceive such in me, already? Tell me, by our past friendship, Hilda, all you know!"

Thus adjured, and frightened by the wild emotion which Miriam could not suppress, Hilda strove to tell what she had witnessed.

"After the rest of the party had passed on, I went back to speak to you," she said; "for there seemed to be a trouble on your mind, and I wished to share it with you, if you could permit me. The door of the little courtyard was partly shut;

but I pushed it open, and saw you within, and Donatello, and a third person, whom I had before noticed in the shadow of a niche. He approached you, Miriam! You knelt to him! I saw Donatello spring upon him! I would have shrieked; but my throat was dry! I would have rushed forward; but my limbs seemed rooted to the earth! It was all like a flash of lightning. A look passed from your eyes to Donatello's— a look—"

"Yes, Hilda, yes!" exclaimed Miriam, with intense eagerness. "Do not pause now! That look?"

"It revealed all your heart, Miriam!" continued Hilda, covering her eyes as if to shut out the recollection. "A look of hatred, triumph, vengeance, and, as it were, joy at some unhoped for relief!"

"Ah, Donatello was right, then!" murmured Miriam, who shook throughout all her frame. "My eyes bade him do it! Go on, Hilda!"

"It all passed so quickly—all like a glare of lightning!" said Hilda. "And yet it seemed to me that Donatello had paused, while one might draw a breath. But that look!—Ah, Miriam, spare me! Need I tell more?"

"No more; there needs no more, Hilda," replied Miriam, bowing her head, as if listening to a sentence of condemnation from a supreme tribunal. "It is enough! You have satisfied my mind on a point where it was greatly disturbed. Henceforward, I shall be quiet. Thank you, Hilda!"

She was on the point of departing, but turned back again from the threshold.

"This is a terrible secret to be kept in a young girl's bosom," she observed. "What will you do with it, my poor child?"

"Heaven help and guide me," answered Hilda, bursting into tears; "for the burthen of it crushes me to the earth! It seems a crime to know of such a thing, and to keep it to myself. It knocks within my heart continually, threatening,

imploring, insisting to be let out! Oh, my mother! My mother!
Were she yet living, I would travel over land and sea to tell
her this dark secret, as I told all the little troubles of my
infancy. But I am alone—alone! Miriam, you were my dearest,
only friend! Advise me what to do!"

This was a singular appeal, no doubt, from the stainless
maiden to the guilty woman, whom she had just banished
from her heart forever. But it bore striking testimony to the
impression which Miriam's natural uprightness and impulsive
generosity had made on the friend who knew her best; and
it deeply comforted the poor criminal, by proving to her that
the bond between Hilda and herself was vital yet.

As far as she was able, Miriam at once responded to the
girl's cry for help.

"If I deemed it good for your peace of mind," she said, "to
bear testimony against me, for this deed, in the face of all
the world, no consideration of myself should weigh with me
an instant. But I believe that you would find no relief in
such a course. What men call justice lies chiefly in outward
formalities, and has never the close application and fitness
that would be satisfactory to a soul like yours. I cannot be
fairly tried and judged before an earthly tribunal; and of this,
Hilda, you would perhaps become fatally conscious, when it
was too late. Roman justice, above all things, is a by-word.
What have you to do with it? Leave all such thoughts aside!
Yet, Hilda, I would not have you keep my secret imprisoned
in your heart, if it tries to leap out, and stings you, like a
wild, venomous thing, when you thrust it back again. Have
you no other friend, now that you have been forced to give
me up?"

"No other!" answered Hilda sadly.

"Yes;—Kenyon!" rejoined Miriam.

"He cannot be my friend," said Hilda, "because—because—
I have fancied that he sought to be something more!"

"Fear nothing!" replied Miriam, shaking her head, with a strange smile. "This story will frighten his new-born love out of its little life, if that be what you wish. Tell him the secret, then, and take his wise and honourable counsel as to what should next be done. I know not what else to say."

"I never dreamed," said Hilda—"how could you think it?— of betraying you to justice. But I see how it is, Miriam. I must keep your secret, and die of it, unless God sends me some relief by methods which are now beyond my power to imagine. It is very dreadful. Ah, now I understand how the sins of generations past have created an atmosphere of sin for those that follow! While there is a single guilty person in the universe, each innocent one must feel his innocence tortured by that guilt. Your deed, Miriam, has darkened the whole sky!"

Poor Hilda turned from her unhappy friend, and, sinking on her knees in a corner of the chamber, could not be prevailed upon to utter another word. And Miriam, with a long regard from the threshold, bade farewell to this dove's nest, this one little nook of pure thoughts and innocent enthusiasms, into which she had brought such trouble. Every crime destroys more Edens than our own!

XXIV

THE TOWER AMONG THE APENNINES

I T WAS in June, that the sculptor, Kenyon, arrived on horseback at the gate of an ancient country-house (which, from some of its features, might almost be called a castle) situated in a part of Tuscany, somewhat remote from the ordinary track of tourists. Thither we must now accompany him, and endeavour to make our story flow onward, like a streamlet, past a gray tower that rises on the hill-side, over-looking a spacious valley, which is set in the grand frame-work of the Apennines.

The sculptor had left Rome with the retreating tide of foreign residents. For, as summer approaches, the Niobe of Nations is made to bewail anew, and doubtless with sincerity, the loss of that large part of her population which she derives from other lands, and on whom depends much of whatever remnant of prosperity she still enjoys. Rome, at this season, is pervaded and overhung with atmospheric terrours, and insulated within a charmed and deadly circle. The crowd of wandering tourists betake themselves to Switzerland, to the Rhine, or, from this central home of the world, to their native homes in England or America, which they are apt thence-forward to look upon as provincial, after once having yielded to the spell of the Eternal City. The artist, who contemplates an indefinite succession of winters in this home of art, (though his first thought was merely to improve himself by a brief visit,) goes forth, in the summer-time, to sketch scenery and costume among the Tuscan Hills, and pour, if he can, the purple air of Italy over his canvas. He studies the old schools of Art in the mountain-towns where they were born, and where they are still to be seen in the faded frescoes of Giotto and Cimabue, on the walls of many a church, or in the dark chapels, in which the sacristan draws aside the veil from a treasured picture of Perugino. Thence, the happy painter goes to walk the long, bright galleries of Florence, or to steal glowing colours from the miraculous works, which he finds in a score of Venetian palaces. Such summers as these, spent amid whatever is exquisite in art, or wild and picturesque in Nature, may not inadequately repay him for the chill neglect and disappointment through which he has probably languished, in his Roman winter. This sunny, shadowy, breezy, wandering life, in which he seeks for beauty as his treasure, and gathers for his winter's honey what is but a passing fragrance to all other men, is worth living for, come afterwards what may. Even if he die unrecognized, the artist has had his share of enjoyment and success.

Kenyon had seen, at a distance of many miles, the old villa or castle towards which his journey lay, looking from its height over a broad expanse of valley. As he drew nearer, however, it had been hidden among the inequalities of the hill-side, until the winding road brought him almost to the iron gateway. The sculptor found this substantial barrier fastened with lock and bolt. There was no bell, nor other instrument of sound; and after summoning the invisible garrison with his voice, instead of a trumpet, he had leisure to take a glance at the exterior of the fortress.

About thirty yards within the gateway rose a square tower, lofty enough to be a very prominent object in the landscape, and more than sufficiently massive in proportion to its height. Its antiquity was evidently such, that, in a climate of more abundant moisture, the ivy would have mantled it from head to foot in a garment that might, by this time, have been centuries old, though ever new. In the dry Italian air, however, Nature had only so far adopted this old pile of stone-work, as to cover almost every hand's breadth of it with close-clinging lichens and yellow moss; and the immemorial growth of these kindly productions rendered the general hue of the tower soft and venerable, and took away the aspect of nakedness, which would have made its age drearier than now.

Up and down the height of the tower were scattered three or four windows, the lower ones grated with iron bars, the upper ones vacant both of window-frames and glass. Besides these larger openings, there were several loop-holes and little, square apertures which might be supposed to light the stair-case, that doubtless climbed the interiour towards the battle-mented and machicolated summit. With this last-mentioned warlike garniture upon its stern old head and brow, the tower seemed evidently a stronghold of times long-past. Many a cross-bowman had shot his shafts from those windows and loop-holes, and from the vantage-height of those gray battle-ments; many a flight of arrows, too, had hit all roundabout the embrasures above, or the apertures below, where the helmet of a defender had momentarily glimmered. On festal nights, moreover, a hundred lamps had often gleamed afar over the valley, suspended from the iron hooks that were ranged for the purpose beneath the battlements and every window.

Connected with the tower, and extending behind it, there seemed to be a very spacious residence, chiefly of more modern date. It perhaps owed much of its fresher appearance, however, to a coat of stucco and yellow-wash, which is a sort of renovation very much in vogue with the Italians.

Kenyon noticed over a door-way, in the portion of the edifice immediately adjacent to the tower, a cross, which, with a bell suspended above the roof, indicated that this was a consecrated precinct, and the chapel of the mansion.

Meanwhile, the hot sun so incommoded the unsheltered traveller, that he shouted forth another impatient summons. Happening, at the same moment, to look upward, he saw a figure leaning from an embrasure of the battlements, and gazing down at him.

"Ho, Signor Count!" cried the sculptor, waving his straw hat; for he recognized the face, after a moment's doubt. "This is a warm reception, truly! Pray bid your porter let me in, before the sun shrivels me quite into a cinder!"

"I will come myself," responded Donatello, flinging down his voice out of the clouds, as it were. "Old Tomaso and old Stella are both asleep, no doubt, and the rest of the people are in the vineyard. But I have expected you, and you are welcome.'"

The young Count—as perhaps we had better designate him, in his ancestral tower—vanished from the battlements; and Kenyon saw his figure appear successively at each of the windows, as he descended. On every re-appearance, he turned his face towards the sculptor and gave a nod and smile; for a kindly impulse prompted him thus to assure his visitor of a welcome, after keeping him so long at an inhospitable threshold.

Kenyon, however, (naturally and professionally expert at reading the expression of the human countenance,) had a vague sense that this was not the young friend whom he had known so familiarly in Rome; not the sylvan and untutored youth, whom Miriam, Hilda, and himself, had liked, laughed at, and sported with; not the Donatello whose identity they had so playfully mixed up with that of the Faun of Praxiteles.

Finally, when his host had emerged from a side-portal of the mansion, and approached the gateway, the traveller still felt that there was something lost, or something gained, (he hardly knew which,) that set the Donatello of to-day irreconcileably at odds with him of yesterday. His very gait showed it, in a certain gravity, a weight and measure of step, that had nothing in common with the irregular buoyancy which used to distinguish him. His face was paler and thinner, and the lips less full, and less apart.

"I have looked for you a long while," said Donatello; and though his voice sounded differently, and cut out its words more sharply than had been its wont, still there was a smile shining on his face, that, for the moment, quite brought back the Faun. "I shall be more cheerful, perhaps, now that you have come. It is very solitary here."

"I have come slowly along, often lingering, often turning aside," replied Kenyon; "for I found a great deal to interest me in the mediæval sculpture, hidden away in the churches hereabouts. An artist, whether painter or sculptor, may be pardoned for loitering through such a region. But what a fine old tower! Its tall front is like a page of black-letter, taken from the history of the Italian republics."

"I know little or nothing of its history," said the Count, glancing upward at the battlements where he had just been standing. "But I thank my forefathers for building it so high. I like the windy summit better than the world below, and spend much of my time there, now-a-days."

"It is a pity you are not a star-gazer," observed Kenyon, also looking up. "It is higher than Galileo's tower, which I saw, a week or two ago, outside of the walls of Florence."

"A star-gazer? I am one," replied Donatello. "I sleep in the tower, and often watch very late on the battlements. There is a dismal old staircase to climb, however, before reaching the top, and a succession of dismal chambers, from story to story. Some of them were prison-chambers, in times past, as old Tomaso will tell you."

The repugnance, intimated in his tone, at the idea of this gloomy staircase and these ghostly, dimly lighted rooms, reminded Kenyon of the original Donatello, much more than his present custom of midnight vigils on the battlements.

"I shall be glad to share your watch," said the guest, "especially by moonlight. The prospect of this broad valley must be very fine. But I was not aware, my friend, that these were your country-habits. I have fancied you in a sort of Arcadian life, tasting rich figs, and squeezing the juice out of the sunniest grapes, and sleeping soundly, all night, after a day of simple pleasures."

"I may have known such a life, when I was younger," answered the Count gravely. "I am not a boy, now. Time flies over us, but leaves its shadow behind."

The sculptor could not but smile at the triteness of the remark, which, nevertheless had a kind of originality as coming from Donatello. He had thought it out from his own experience, and perhaps considered himself as communicating a new truth to mankind.

They were now advancing up the courtyard; and the long extent of the villa, with its iron-barred lower windows and balconied upper ones, became visible, stretching back towards a grove of trees.

"At some period of your family history," observed Kenyon, "the Counts of Monte Beni must have led a patriarchal life in this vast house. A great-grandsire and all his descendants might find ample verge here, and with space, too, for each separate brood of little ones to play within its own precincts. Is your present household a large one?"

"Only myself," answered Donatello, "and Tomaso, who has been butler since my grandfather's time, and old Stella, who goes sweeping and dusting about the chambers, and Girolamo, the cook, who has but an idle life of it. He shall send you up a chicken, forthwith. But, first of all, I must summon one of the contadini from the farm-house yonder, to take your horse to the stable."

Accordingly, the young Count shouted amain, and with such effect, that, after several repetitions of the outcry, an old gray woman protruded her head and a broom-handle from a chamber-window; the venerable butler emerged from a recess in the side of the house, where was a well, or reservoir, in which he had been cleansing a small wine-cask; and a sun-burnt contadino, in his shirt-sleeves, showed himself on the outskirts of the vineyard, with some kind of a farming-tool in his hand. Donatello found employment for all these retainers in providing accommodation for his guest and steed, and then ushered the sculptor into the vestibule of the house.

It was a square and lofty entrance-room, which, by the solidity of its construction, might have been an Etruscan tomb, being paved and walled with heavy blocks of stone, and vaulted almost as massively overhead. On two sides, there were doors, opening into long suites of ante-rooms and saloons; on the third side, a stone staircase, of spacious breadth, ascended, by dignified degrees and with wide resting-places, to another floor of similar extent. Through one of the doors, which was ajar, Kenyon beheld an almost interminable vista of apartments, opening one beyond the other, and reminding him of the hundred rooms in Blue Beard's castle, or the countless halls in some palace of the Arabian Nights.

It must have been a numerous family, indeed, that could ever have sufficed to people with human life so large an abode as this, and impart social warmth to such a wide world within doors. The sculptor confessed to himself, that Donatello could allege reason enough for growing melancholy, having only his own personality to vivify it all.

"How a woman's face would brighten it up!" he ejaculated, not intending to be overheard.

But, glancing at Donatello, he saw a stern and sorrowful look in his eyes, which altered his youthful face as much as if it had seen thirty years of trouble; and, at the same moment, old Stella showed herself through one of the door-ways, as the only representative of her sex at Monte Beni.

XXV

SUNSHINE

C OME," said the Count, "I see you already find the old house dismal. So do I, indeed! And yet it was a cheerful place in my boyhood. But, you see, in my father's days, (and the same was true of all my endless line of grandfathers, as I have heard,) there used to be uncles, aunts, and all manner of kindred, dwelling together as one family. They were a merry and kindly race of people, for the most part, and kept one another's hearts warm."

"Two hearts might be enough for warmth," observed the sculptor, "even in so large a house as this. One solitary heart, it is true, may be apt to shiver a little. But, I trust, my friend, that the genial blood of your race still flows in many veins besides your own?"

"I am the last," said Donatello gloomily. "They have all vanished from me, since my childhood. Old Tomaso will tell you that the air of Monte Beni is not so favourable to length of days, as it used to be. But that is not the secret of the quick extinction of my kindred."

"Then, you are aware of a more satisfactory reason?" suggested Kenyon.

"I thought of one, the other night, while I was gazing at the stars," answered Donatello; "but, pardon me, I do not mean to tell it. One cause, however, of the longer and healthier life of my forefathers was, that they had many pleasant customs, and means of making themselves glad, and their guests and friends along with them. Now-a-days, we have but one!"

"And what is that?" asked the sculptor.

"You shall see!" said his young host.

By this time, he had ushered the sculptor into one of the numberless saloons; and, calling for refreshment, old Stella placed a cold fowl upon the table, and quickly followed it with a savoury omelette, which Girolamo had lost no time in preparing. She also brought some cherries, plums, and apricots, and a plate-full of particularly delicate figs, of last year's growth. The butler showing his white head at the door, his master beckoned to him.

"Tomaso, bring some Sunshine!" said he.

The readiest method of obeying this order, one might suppose, would have been, to fling wide the green window-blinds, and let the glow of the summer-noon into the carefully shaded room. But, at Monte Beni, with provident caution against the wintry days, when there is little sunshine, and the rainy ones, when there is none, it was the hereditary custom to keep their Sunshine stored away in the cellar. Old Tomaso quickly produced some of it in a small, straw-covered flask, out of which he extracted the cork, and inserted a little cotton-wool, to absorb the olive oil that kept the precious liquid from the air.

"This is a wine," observed the Count, "the secret of making which has been kept in our family for centuries upon centuries; nor would it avail any man to steal the secret, unless he could also steal the vineyard, in which alone the Monte Beni grape can be produced. There is little else left me, save that patch of vines. Taste some of their juice, and tell me whether it is worthy to be called Sunshine! For that is its name."

"A glorious name, too!" cried the sculptor.

"Taste it," said Donatello, filling his friend's glass and pouring likewise a little into his own. "But first smell its fragrance; for the wine is very lavish of it, and will scatter it all abroad."

"Ah, how exquisite!" said Kenyon. "No other wine has a bouquet like this. The flavour must be rare indeed, if it fulfil the promise of this fragrance, which is like the airy sweetness of youthful hopes, that no realities will ever satisfy!"

This invaluable liquour was of a pale golden hue, like other of the rarest Italian wines, and, if carelessly and irreligiously quaffed, might have been mistaken for a very fine sort of Champagne. It was not, however, an effervescing wine, although its delicate piquancy produced a somewhat similar effect upon the palate. Sipping, the guest longed to sip again; but the wine demanded so deliberate a pause, in order to detect the hidden peculiarities and subtle exquisiteness of its flavour, that to drink it was really more a moral than a physical enjoyment. There was a deliciousness in it that eluded analysis, and—like whatever else is superlatively good— was perhaps better appreciated in the memory than by present consciousness. One of its most ethereal charms lay in the transitory life of the wine's richest qualities; for, while it required a certain leisure and delay, yet, if you lingered too long upon the draught, it became disenchanted both of its fragrance and its flavour.

The lustre should not be forgotten, among the other admirable endowments of the Monte Beni wine; for, as it stood in Kenyon's glass, a little circle of light glowed on the table roundabout it, as if it were really so much golden sunshine.

"I feel myself a better man for that ethereal potation," observed the sculptor. "The finest Orvieto, or that famous wine, the Est Est Est of Montefiascone, is vulgar in comparison. This is surely the wine of the Golden Age, such as Bacchus himself first taught mankind to press from the choicest of his grapes. My dear Count, why is it not illustrious? The pale, liquid gold, in every such flask as that, might be solidified into golden scudi, and would quickly make you a millionaire!"

Tomaso, the old butler, who was standing by the table, and enjoying the praises of the wine quite as much as if bestowed upon himself, made answer.

"We have a tradition, Signor," said he, "that this rare wine of our vineyard would lose all its wonderful qualities, if any of it were sent to market. The Counts of Monte Beni have never parted with a single flask of it for gold. At their banquets, in the olden time, they have entertained princes, cardinals, and once an Emperour, and once a Pope, with this delicious wine; and always, even to this day, it has been their custom to let it flow freely, when those whom they love and honour sit at the board. But the Grand Duke himself could not drink that wine, except it were under this very roof!"

"What you tell me, my good friend," replied Kenyon, "makes me venerate the Sunshine of Monte Beni even more abundantly than before. As I understand you, it is a sort of consecrated juice, and symbolizes the holy virtues of hospitality and social kindliness?"

"Why, partly so, Signor," said the old butler, with a shrewd twinkle in his eye; "but, to speak out all the truth, there is another excellent reason why neither a cask nor a flask of our precious vintage should ever be sent to market. The wine, Signor, is so fond of its native home, that a transportation of even a few miles turns it quite sour. And yet it is a wine that keeps well in the cellar, underneath this floor, and gathers fragrance, flavour, and brightness, in its dark dungeon. That very flask of Sunshine, now, has kept itself for you, Sir Guest, (as a maid reserves her sweetness till her lover comes for it,) ever since a merry vintage-time, when the Signor Count here was a boy!"

"You must not wait for Tomaso to end his discourse about the wine, before drinking off your glass," observed Donatello. "When once the flask is uncorked, its finest qualities lose little time in making their escape. I doubt whether your last sip will be quite so delicious as you found the first."

And, in truth, the sculptor fancied that the Sunshine became almost imperceptibly clouded, as he approached the bottom of the flask. The effect of the wine, however, was a gentle exhilaration, which did not so speedily pass away.

Being thus refreshed, Kenyon looked round him at the antique saloon in which they sat. It was constructed in a most ponderous style, with a stone floor, on which heavy pilasters were planted against the wall, supporting arches that crossed one another in the vaulted ceiling. The upright walls, as well as the compartments of the roof, were completely covered with frescoes, which doubtless had been brilliant when first executed, and perhaps for generations afterwards. The designs were of a festive and joyous character, representing Arcadian scenes, where Nymphs, Fauns, and Satyrs, disported themselves among mortal youths and maidens; and Pan, and the god of wine, and he of sunshine and music, disdained not to brighten some sylvan merry-making with the scarcely veiled glory of their presence. A wreath of dancing figures, in admirable variety of shape and motion, was festooned quite round the cornice of the room.

In its first splendour, the saloon must have presented an aspect both gorgeous and enlivening; for it invested some of the cheerfullest ideas and emotions, of which the human mind is susceptible, with the external reality of beautiful form and rich, harmonious glow and variety of colour. But the frescoes were now very ancient. They had been rubbed and scrubbed by old Stella and many a predecessor, and had been defaced in one spot, and retouched in another, and had peeled from the wall in patches, and had hidden some of their brightest portions under dreary dust; till the joyousness had quite vanished out of them all. It was often difficult to puzzle out the design; and even where it was more readily intelligible, the figures showed like the ghosts of dead and buried joys—the closer their resemblance to the happy past, the gloomier now. For it is thus, that, with only an inconsiderable change, the gladdest objects and existences become the saddest; Hope fading into Disappointment; Joy darkening into Grief, and festal splendour into funereal duskiness; and all evolving, as their moral, a grim identity between gay things and sorrowful ones. Only give them a little time, and they turn out to be just alike!

"There has been much festivity in this saloon, if I may judge by the character of its frescoes," remarked Kenyon, whose spirits were still upheld by the mild potency of the Monte Beni wine. "Your forefathers, my dear Count, must have been joyous fellows, keeping up the vintage merriment throughout the year. It does me good to think of them gladdening the hearts of men and women with their wine of Sunshine, even in the Iron age, as Pan and Bacchus, whom we see yonder, did in the Golden one!"

"Yes; there have been merry times in the banquet-hall of Monte Beni, even within my own remembrance," replied Donatello, looking gravely at the painted walls. "It was meant for mirth, as you see; and when I brought my own cheerfulness into the saloon, these frescoes looked cheerful too. But methinks they have all faded, since I saw them last."

"It would be a good idea," said the sculptor, falling into his companion's vein, and helping him out with an illustration which Donatello himself could not have put into shape, "to convert this saloon into a chapel; and when the priest tells his hearers of the instability of earthly joys, and would show how drearily they vanish, he may point to these pictures, that were so joyous, and are so dismal. He could not illustrate his theme so aptly in any other way."

"True, indeed," answered the Count, his former simplicity strangely mixing itself up with an experience that had changed him; "and yonder, where the minstrels used to stand, the altar shall be placed. A sinful man might do all the more effective penance in this old banquet-hall."

"But I should regret to have suggested so ungenial a transformation in your hospitable saloon," continued Kenyon, duly noting the change in Donatello's characteristics. "You startle me, my friend, by so ascetic a design! It would hardly have entered your head, when we first met. Pray do not—if I may take the freedom of a somewhat elder man to advise you," added he, smiling—"pray do not, under a notion of improvement, take upon yourself to be sombre, thoughtful, and penitential, like all the rest of us."

Donatello made no answer, but sat awhile, appearing to follow with his eyes one of the figures, which was repeated many times over in the groups upon the walls and ceiling. It formed the principal link of an allegory, by which (as is often the case, in such pictorial designs) the whole series of frescoes were bound together, but which it would be impossible, or, at least, very wearisome, to unravel. The sculptor's eyes took a similar direction, and soon began to trace through the vicissitudes—once gay, now sombre—in which the old artist had involved it, the same individual figure. He fancied a resemblance in it to Donatello himself; and it put him in mind of one of the purposes with which he had come to Monte Beni.

"My dear Count," said he, "I have a proposal to make. You must let me employ a little of my leisure in modelling your bust. You remember what a striking resemblance we all of us—Hilda, Miriam, and I—found between your features and those of the Faun of Praxiteles. Then, it seemed an identity; but, now that I know your face better, the likeness is far less apparent. Your head in marble would be a treasure to me. Shall I have it?"

"I have a weakness which I fear I cannot overcome," replied the Count, turning away his face. "It troubles me to be looked at steadfastly."

"I have observed it since we have been sitting here, though never before," rejoined the sculptor. "It is a kind of nervousness, I apprehend, which you caught in the Roman air, and which grows upon you, in your solitary life. It need be no hindrance to my taking your bust; for I will catch the likeness and expression by side-glimpses, which (if portrait-painters and bust-makers did but know it) always bring home richer results than a broad stare."

"You may take me if you have the power," said Donatello, but, even as he spoke, he turned away his face; "and if you can see what makes me shrink from you, you are welcome to put it in the bust. It is not my will, but my necessity, to avoid men's eyes. Only," he added with a smile, which made Kenyon doubt whether he might not as well copy the Faun, as model a new bust, "only, you know, you must not insist on my uncovering these ears of mine!"

"Nay; I never should dream of such a thing," answered the sculptor, laughing as the young Count shook his clustering curls. "I could not hope to persuade you, remembering how Miriam once failed!"

Nothing is more unaccountable than the spell that often lurks in a spoken word. A thought may be present to the mind, so distinctly that no utterance could make it more so; and two minds may be conscious of the same thought, in which one or both take the profoundest interest; but as long as it remains unspoken, their familiar talk flows quietly over the hidden idea, as a rivulet may sparkle and dimple over something sunken in its bed. But, speak the word; and it is like bringing up a drowned body out of the deepest pool of the rivulet, which has been aware of the horrible secret, all along, in spite of its smiling surface.

And even so, when Kenyon chanced to make a distinct reference to Donatello's relations with Miriam, (though the subject was already in both their minds,) a ghastly emotion rose up out of the depths of the young Count's heart. He trembled either with anger or terrour, and glared at the sculptor with wild eyes, like a wolf that meets you in the forest, and hesitates whether to flee or turn to bay. But, as Kenyon still looked calmly at him, his aspect gradually became less disturbed, though far from resuming its former quietude.

"You have spoken her name," said he, at last, in an altered and tremulous tone. "Tell me, now, all that you know of her!"

"I scarcely think that I have any later intelligence than yourself," answered Kenyon. "Miriam left Rome at about the time of your own departure. Within a day or two after our last meeting, at the Church of the Capuchins, I called at her studio and found it vacant. Whither she has gone, I cannot tell."

Donatello asked no further questions.

They rose from table, and strolled together about the premises, whiling away the afternoon with brief intervals of unsatisfactory conversation, and many shadowy silences. The sculptor had a perception of change in his companion, (possibly of growth and development, but certainly of change,) which saddened him, because it took away much of the simple grace that was the best of Donatello's peculiarities.

Kenyon betook himself to repose, that night, in a grim, old, vaulted apartment, which, in the lapse of five or six centuries, had probably been the birth, bridal, and death-chamber, of a great many generations of the Monte Beni family. He was aroused, soon after daylight, by the clamour of a tribe of beggars, who had taken their stand in a little rustic lane, that crept beside that portion of the villa, and were addressing their petitions to the open windows. By-and-by, they appeared to have received alms, and took their departure.

"Some charitable Christian has sent those vagabonds away," thought the sculptor, as he resumed his interrupted nap. "Who could it be? Donatello has his own rooms in the tower; Stella, Tomaso, and the cook are a world's width off; and I fancied myself the only inhabitant in this part of the house."

In the breadth and space, which so delightfully characterize an Italian Villa, a dozen guests might have had each his suite of apartments without infringing upon one another's ample precincts. But, so far as Kenyon knew, he was the only visitor beneath Donatello's widely extended roof.

XXVI

THE PEDIGREE OF MONTE BENI

FROM the old butler, whom he found to be a very gracious and affable personage, Kenyon soon learned many curious particulars about the family-history and hereditary peculiarities of the Counts of Monte Beni. There was a pedigree, the later portion of which (that is to say, for a little more than a thousand years) a genealogist would have found delight in tracing out, link by link, and authenticating by records and documentary evidences. It would have been as difficult, however, to follow up the stream of Donatello's ancestry to its dim source, as travellers have found it, to reach the mysterious fountains of the Nile. And, far beyond the region of definite and demonstrable fact, a romancer might have strayed into a region of old poetry, where the rich soil, so long uncultivated and untrodden, had lapsed into nearly its primeval state of wilderness. Among those antique paths, now overgrown with tangled and riotous vegetation, the wanderer must needs follow his own guidance, and arrive nowhither at last.

The race of Monte Beni, beyond a doubt, was one of the oldest in Italy, where families appear to survive, at least, if not to flourish on their half-decayed roots, oftener than in England or France. It came down in a broad track from the

Middle Ages; but, at epochs anteriour to those, it was distinctly visible in the gloom of the period before Chivalry put forth its flower; and farther still, (we are almost afraid to say,) it was seen, though with a fainter and wavering course, in the early morn of Christendom, when the Roman Empire had hardly begun to show symptoms of decline. At that venerable distance, the heralds gave up the lineage in despair.

But where written record left the genealogy of Monte Beni, Tradition took it up, and carried it, without dread or shame, beyond the Imperial ages into the times of the Roman Republic; beyond those, again, into the epoch of Kingly rule. Nor, even so remotely among the mossy centuries, did it pause, but strayed onward into that gray antiquity of which there is no token left, save its cavernous tombs, and a few bronzes, and some quaintly wrought ornaments of gold, and gems with mystic figures and inscriptions. There, or thereabouts, the line was supposed to have had its origin, in the sylvan life of Etruria, while Italy was yet guiltless of Rome.

Of course, as we regret to say, the earlier and very much the larger portion of this respectable descent (and the same is true of many briefer pedigrees) must be looked upon as altogether mythical. Still, it threw a romantic interest around the unquestionable antiquity of the Monte Beni family, and over that tract of their own vines and fig-trees, beneath the shade of which they had unquestionably dwelt for immemorial ages. And there they had laid the foundations of their tower, so long ago, that one half of its height was said to be sunken under the surface, and to hide subterranean chambers, which once were cheerful with the olden sunshine.

One story, or myth, that had mixed itself up with their mouldy genealogy, interested the sculptor by its wild, and perhaps grotesque, yet not unfascinating peculiarity. He caught at it the more eagerly, as it afforded a shadowy and whimsical semblance of explanation for the likeness, which he, with Miriam and Hilda, had seen, or fancied, between Donatello and the Faun of Praxiteles.

The Monte Beni family, as this legend averred, drew their origin from the Pelasgic race, who peopled Italy in times that may be called pre-historic. It was the same noble breed of men, of Asiatic birth, that settled in Greece; the same happy and poetic kindred who dwelt in Arcadia, and—whether they ever lived such life or not—enriched the world with dreams, at least, and fables, lovely, if unsubstantial, of a Golden Age. In those delicious times, when deities and demi-gods appeared familiarly on earth, mingling with its inhabitants as friend with friend; when nymphs, satyrs, and the whole train of classic faith or fable, hardly took pains to hide themselves in the primeval woods;—at that auspicious period, the lineage of Monte Beni had its rise. Its progenitor was a being not altogether human, yet partaking so largely of the gentlest human qualities, as to be neither awful nor shocking to the imagination. A sylvan creature, native among the woods, had loved a mortal maiden, and (perhaps by kindness, and the subtle courtesies which love might teach to his simplicity, or possibly by a ruder wooing) had won her to his haunts. In due time, he gained her womanly affection; and (making their bridal bower, for aught we know, in the hollow of a great tree) the pair spent a happy wedded life in that ancient neighborhood, where now stood Donatello's tower.

From this union sprung a vigorous progeny, that took its place unquestioned among human families. In that age, however, and long afterwards, it showed the ineffaceable lineaments of its wild paternity; it was a pleasant and kindly race of men, but capable of savage fierceness, and never quite restrainable within the trammels of social law. They were strong, active, genial, cheerful as the sunshine, passionate as the tornado. Their lives were rendered blissful by an unsought harmony with Nature.

But, as centuries passed away, the Faun's wild blood had necessarily been attempered with constant intermixtures from the more ordinary streams of human life. It lost many of its original qualities, and served, for the most part, only to bestow an unconquerable vigour, which kept the family from extinction, and enabled them to make their own part good, throughout the perils and rude emergencies of their interminable descent. In the constant wars with which Italy was plagued, by the dissensions of her petty states and republics, there was a demand for native hardihood. The successive members of the Monte Beni family showed valour and policy enough, at all events, to keep their hereditary possessions out of the clutch of grasping neighbors, and probably differed very little from the other feudal barons, with whom they fought and feasted. Such a degree of conformity with the manners of the generations, through which it survived, must have been essential to the prolonged continuance of the race.

It is well known, however, that any hereditary peculiarity— as a supernumerary finger, or an anomalous shape of feature, like the Austrian lip—is wont to show itself in a family after a very wayward fashion. It skips at its own pleasure along the line, and, latent for half-a-century or so, crops out again in a great-grandson. And thus, it was said, from a period beyond memory or record, there had ever and anon been a descendant of the Monte Benis, bearing nearly all the characteristics that were attributed to the original founder of the race. Some traditions even went so far as to enumerate the ears, covered with a delicate fur, and shaped like a pointed leaf, among the proofs of authentic descent which were seen in these favoured individuals. We appreciate the beauty of such tokens of a nearer kindred to the great family of Nature, than other mortals bear; but it would be idle to ask credit for a statement which might be deemed to partake so largely of the grotesque.

But it was indisputable, that, once in a century, or oftener, a son of Monte Beni gathered into himself the scattered qualities of his race, and reproduced the character that had been assigned to it from immemorial times. Beautiful, strong, brave, kindly, sincere, of honest impulses, and endowed with simple tastes, and the love of homely pleasures, he was believed to possess gifts by which he could associate himself with the wild things of the forests, and with the fowls of the air, and could feel a sympathy even with the trees, among which it was his joy to dwell. On the other hand, there were deficiencies both of intellect and heart, and especially, as it seemed, in the development of the higher portion of man's nature. These defects were less perceptible in early youth, but showed themselves more strongly with advancing age, when, as the animal spirits settled down upon a lower level, the representative of the Monte Benis was apt to become sensual, addicted to gross pleasures, heavy, unsympathizing, and insulated within the narrow limits of a surly selfishness.

A similar change, indeed, is no more than what we constantly observe to take place, in persons who are not careful to substitute other graces for those which they inevitably lose along with the quick sensibility and joyous vivacity of youth. At worst, the reigning Count of Monte Beni, as his hair grew white, was still a jolly old fellow over his flask of wine, the wine that Bacchus himself was fabled to have taught his sylvan ancestor how to express, and from what choicest grapes, which would ripen only in a certain divinely favoured portion of the Monte Beni vineyard.

The family, be it observed, were both proud and ashamed of these legends; but whatever part of them they might consent to incorporate into their ancestral history, they steadily repudiated all that referred to their one distinctive feature, the pointed and furry ears. In a great many years past, no sober credence had been yielded to the mythical portion of the pedigree. It might, however, be considered as typifying some such assemblage of qualities, (in this case, chiefly remarkable for their simplicity and naturalness,) as, when they re-appear in successive generations, constitute what we call family character. The sculptor found, moreover, on the evidence of some old portraits, that the physical features of the race had long been similar to what he now saw them in Donatello. With accumulating years, it is true, the Monte Beni face had a tendency to look grim and savage; and, in two or three instances, the family pictures glared at the spectator in the eyes, like some surly animal, that had lost its good humour when it outlived its playfulness.

The young Count accorded his guest full liberty to investigate the personal annals of these pictured worthies, as well as all the rest of his progenitors; and ample materials were at hand in many chests of worm-eaten papers and yellow parchments, that had been gathering into larger and dustier piles, ever since the Dark ages. But, to confess the truth, the information afforded by these musty documents was so much more prosaic than what Kenyon acquired from Tomaso's legends, that even the superiour authenticity of the former could not reconcile him to its dulness.

What especially delighted the sculptor was the analogy between Donatello's character, as he himself knew it, and those peculiar traits which the old butler's narrative assumed to have been long hereditary in the race. He was amused at finding, too, that not only Tomaso, but the peasantry of the estate and neighboring village recognized his friend as a genuine Monte Beni, of the original type. They seemed to cherish a great affection for the young Count, and were full of stories about his sportive childhood; how he had played among the little rustics, and been at once the wildest and the sweetest of them all; and how, in his very infancy, he had plunged into the deep pools of the streamlets, and never been drowned, and had clambered to the topmost branches of tall trees without ever breaking his neck. No such mischance could happen to the sylvan child, because, handling all the elements of Nature so fearlessly and freely, nothing had either the power or the will to do him harm. He grew up, said these humble friends, the playmate not only of all mortal kind, but of creatures of the woods; although, when Kenyon pressed them for some particulars of this latter mode of companionship, they could remember little more than a few anecdotes of a pet-fox, which used to growl and snap at everybody save Donatello himself.

But they enlarged (and never were weary of the theme) upon the blithesome effects of Donatello's presence in his rosy childhood and budding youth. Their hovels had always glowed like sunshine when he entered them; so that, as the peasants expressed it, their young Master had never darkened a door-way in his life. He was the soul of vintage-festivals. While he was a mere infant, scarcely able to run alone, it had been the custom to make him tread the wine-press with his tender little feet, if it were only to crush one cluster of the grapes. And the grape-juice, that gushed beneath his childish tread, be it ever so small in quantity, sufficed to impart a pleasant flavour to a whole cask of wine. The race of Monte Beni (so these rustic chroniclers assured the sculptor) had possessed the gift, from the oldest of old times, of expressing good wine from ordinary grapes, and a ravishing liquour from the choice growth of their vineyard.

In a word, as he listened to such tales as these, Kenyon could have imagined that the valleys and hill-sides about him were a veritable Arcadia, and that Donatello was not merely a sylvan Faun, but the genial wine-god in his very person. Making many allowances for the poetic fancies of Italian peasants, he set it down for fact, that his friend, in a simple way, and among rustic folks, had been an exceedingly delightful fellow in his younger days.

But the contadini sometimes added, shaking their heads and sighing, that the young Count was sadly changed, since he went to Rome. The village-girls now missed the merry smile with which he used to greet them.

The sculptor inquired of his good friend Tomaso, whether he, too, had noticed the shadow which was said to have recently fallen over Donatello's life.

"Ah, yes, Signor!" answered the old butler, "it is even so, since he came back from that wicked and miserable city. The world has grown either too evil, or else too wise and sad, for such men as the old Counts of Monte Beni used to be. His very first taste of it, as you see, has changed and spoilt my poor young lord. There had not been a single Count in the family, these hundred years and more, who was so true a Monte Beni, of the antique stamp, as this poor Signorino; and, now, it brings the tears into my eyes to hear him sighing over a cup of Sunshine! Ah; it is a sad world now!"

"Then, you think there was a merrier world once?" asked Kenyon.

"Surely, Signor," said Tomaso; "a merrier world, and merrier Counts of Monte Beni to live in it! Such tales of them as I have heard, when I was a child on my grandfather's knee! The good old man remembered a Lord of Monte Beni—at least, he had heard of such a one, though I will not make oath upon the holy crucifix that my grandsire lived in his time—who used to go into the woods and call pretty damsels out of the fountains, and out of the trunks of the old trees. That merry lord was known to dance with them, a whole, long summer-afternoon! When shall we see such frolics in our days?"

"Not soon, I am afraid," acquiesced the sculptor. "You are right, excellent Tomaso! The world is sadder now."

And, in truth, while our friend smiled at these wild fables, he sighed, in the same breath, to think how the once genial earth produces, in every successive generation, fewer flowers than used to gladden the preceding ones. Not that the modes and seeming possibilities of human enjoyment are rarer, in our refined and softened era, (on the contrary, they never before were nearly so abundant,) but that mankind are getting so far beyond the childhood of their race, that they scorn to be happy any longer. A simple and joyous character can find no place for itself among the sage and sombre figures that would put his unsophisticated cheerfulness to shame. The entire system of Man's affairs, as at present established, is built up purposely to exclude the careless and happy soul. The very children would upbraid the wretched individual who should endeavour to take life and the world as (what we might naturally suppose them meant for) a place and opportunity for enjoyment.

It is the iron rule in our days, to require an object and a purpose in life. It makes us all parts of a complicated scheme of progress, which can only result in our arrival at a colder and drearier region than we were born in. It insists upon everybody's adding somewhat (a mite, perhaps, but earned by incessant effort) to an accumulated pile of usefulness, of which the only use will be, to burthen our posterity with even heavier thoughts and more inordinate labour than our own. No life now wanders like an unfettered stream; there is a mill-wheel for the tiniest rivulet to turn. We go all wrong, by too strenuous a resolution to go all right.

Therefore it was (so, at least, the sculptor thought, although partly suspicious of Donatello's darker misfortune) that the young Count found it impossible, now-a-days, to be what his forefathers had been. He could not live their healthy life of animal spirits, in their sympathy with Nature, and brotherhood with all that breathed around them. Nature, in beast, fowl, and tree, and earth, flood, and sky, is what it was of old; but sin, care, and self-consciousness have set the human portion of the world askew; and thus the simplest character is ever the surest to go astray.

"At any rate, Tomaso," said Kenyon, doing his best to comfort the old man, "let us hope that your young lord will still enjoy himself at vintage-time. By the aspect of the vine-yard, I judge that this will be a famous year for the golden wine of Monte Beni. As long as your grapes produce that admirable liquour, sad as you think the world, neither the Count nor his guests will quite forget to smile!"

"Ah, Signor," rejoined the butler with a sigh, "but he scarcely wets his lips with the sunny juice!"

"There is yet another hope," observed Kenyon. "The young Count may fall in love, and bring home a fair and laughing wife to chase the gloom out of yonder old, frescoed saloon. Do you think he could do a better thing, my good Tomaso?"

"May be not, Signor," said the sage butler, looking earnestly at him; "and, may be, not a worse!"

The sculptor fancied that the good old man had it partly in his mind to make some remark, or communicate some fact, which, on second thoughts, he resolved to keep concealed in his own breast. He now took his departure cellar-ward, shaking his white head and muttering to himself, and did not re-appear till dinner-time, when he favoured Kenyon (whom he had taken far into his good graces) with a choicer flask of Sunshine than had yet blessed his palate.

To say the truth, this golden wine was no unnecessary ingredient towards making the life of Monte Beni palatable. It seemed a pity that Donatello did not drink a little more of it, and go jollily to bed, at least, even if he should awake with an accession of darker melancholy, the next morning.

Nevertheless, there was no lack of outward means for leading an agreeable life in the old villa. Wandering musicians haunted the precincts of Monte Beni, where they seemed to claim a prescriptive right; they made the lawn and shrubbery tuneful with the sound of fiddle, harp, and flute, and, now and then, with the tangled squeaking of a bag-pipe. Improvisatori likewise came, and told tales or recited verses to the contadini (among whom Kenyon often was an auditor) after their day's work in the vineyard. Jugglers, too, obtained permission to do feats of magic in the hall, where they set even the sage Tomaso, and Stella, Girolamo, and the peasant-girls from the farm-house, all of a broad grin, between merriment and wonder. These good people got food and lodging for their pleasant pains, and some of the small wine of Tuscany, and a reasonable handfull of the Grand Duke's copper coin, to keep up the hospitable renown of Monte Beni. But, very seldom had they the young Count as a listener or spectator. There were sometimes dances by moonlight on the lawn; but never, since he came from Rome, did Donatello's presence deepen the blushes of the pretty contadinas, or his footstep weary out the most agile partner or competitor, as once it was sure to do.

Paupers—for this kind of vermin infested the house of Monte Beni, worse than any other spot in beggar-haunted Italy—stood beneath all the windows, making loud supplication, or even established themselves on the marble steps of the grand entrance. They ate and drank, and filled their bags, and pocketed the little money that was given them, and went forth on their devious ways, showering blessings innumerable on the mansion and its lord, and on the souls of his deceased forefathers, who had always been just such simpletons as to be compassionate to beggary. But, in spite of their favourable prayers, (by which Italian philanthropists set great store,) a cloud seemed to hang over these once Arcadian precincts, and to be darkest around the summit of the tower, where Donatello was wont to sit and brood.

XXVII

MYTHS

A FTER the sculptor's arrival, however, the young Count sometimes came down from his forlorn elevation, and rambled with him among the neighboring woods and hills. He led his friend to many enchanting nooks, with which he himself had been familiar in his childhood. But, of late, as he remarked to Kenyon, a sort of strangeness had overgrown them, like clusters of dark shrubbery, so that he hardly recognized the places which he had known and loved so well.

To the sculptor's eye, nevertheless, they were still rich with beauty. They were picturesque in that sweetly impressive way, where wildness, in a long lapse of years, has crept over scenes that have been once adorned with the careful art and toil of man; and when man could do no more for them, Time and Nature came, and wrought hand in hand to bring them to a soft and venerable perfection. There grew the fig-tree that had run wild, and taken to wife the vine, which likewise had gone rampant out of all human controul; so that the two wild things had tangled and knotted themselves into a wild marriage-bond, and hung their various progeny—the luscious figs, the grapes, oozy with the southern juice, and both endowed with a wild flavour that added the final charm—on the same bough together.

In Kenyon's opinion, never was any other nook so lovely as a certain little dell which he and Donatello visited. It was hollowed in among the hills, and open to a glimpse of the broad, fertile valley. A fountain had its birth here, and fell into a marble basin, which was all covered with moss and shaggy with water-weeds. Over the gush of the small stream, with an urn in her arms, stood a marble nymph, whose nakedness the moss had kindly clothed as with a garment; and the long trails and tresses of the maiden-hair had done what they could in the poor thing's behalf, by hanging themselves about her waist. In former days, (it might be a remote antiquity,) this lady of the fountain had first received the infant tide into her urn, and poured it thence into the marble basin. But, now, the sculptured urn had a great crack, from top to bottom; and the discontented nymph was compelled to see the basin fill itself through a channel which she could not controul, although with water long ago consecrated to her.

For this reason, or some other, she looked terribly forlorn; and you might have fancied that the whole fountain was but the overflow of her lonely tears.

"This was a place that I used greatly to delight in," remarked Donatello sighing. "As a child, and as a boy, I have been very happy here."

"And, as a man, I should ask no fitter place to be happy in," answered Kenyon. "But you, my friend, are of such a social nature, that I should hardly have thought these lonely haunts would take your fancy. It is a place for a poet to dream in, and people it with the beings of his imagination."

"I am no poet, that I know of," said Donatello; "but, yet, as I tell you, I have been very happy here, in the company of this fountain and this nymph. It is said that a Faun, my eldest forefather, brought home hither, to this very spot, a human maiden, whom he loved and wedded. This spring of delicious water was their household-well."

"It is a most enchanting fable!" exclaimed Kenyon;—"that is, if it be not a fact!"

"And why not a fact?" said the simple Donatello. "There is likewise another sweet old story connected with this spot. But, now that I remember it, it seems to me more sad than sweet, though formerly the sorrow, in which it closes, did not so much impress me. If I had the gift of tale-telling, this one would be sure to interest you mightily."

"Pray tell it," said Kenyon, "no matter whether well or ill. These wild legends have often the most powerful charm when least artfully told."

So the young Count narrated a myth of one of his progenitors, (he might have lived a century ago, or a thousand years, or before the Christian epoch, for anything that Donatello knew to the contrary,) who had made acquaintance with a fair creature, belonging to this fountain. Whether woman or sprite, was a mystery, as was all else about her, except that her life and soul were somehow interfused throughout the gushing water. She was a fresh, cool, dewy thing, sunny and shadowy, full of pleasant little mischiefs, fitful and changeable with the whim of the moment, but yet as constant as her native stream, which kept the same gush and flow forever, while marble crumbled over and around it. The fountain-woman loved the youth, (a knight, as Donatello called him,) for, according to the legend, his race was akin to hers. At least, whether kin or no, there had been friendship and sympathy, of old, betwixt an ancestor of his, with furry ears, and the long-lived lady of the fountain. And, after all those ages, she was still as young as a May-morning, and as frolicsome as a bird upon a tree, or a breeze that makes merry with the leaves.

She taught him how to call her from her pebbly source, and they spent many a happy hour together, more especially in the fervour of the summer-days. For, often, as he sat waiting for her by the margin of the spring, she would suddenly fall down around him in a shower of sunny rain-drops, with a rainbow glowing through them, and forthwith gather herself up into the likeness of a beautiful girl, laughing —or was it the warble of the rill over the pebbles?—to see the youth's amazement. Thus, kind maiden that she was, the hot atmosphere became deliciously cool and fragrant for this favoured knight; and, furthermore, when he knelt down to drink out of the spring, nothing was more common than for a pair of rosy lips to come up out of its little depths, and touch his mouth with the thrill of a sweet, cool, dewy kiss!

"It is a delightful story for the hot noon of your Tuscan summer," observed the sculptor, at this point. "But the deport-ment of the watery lady must have had a most chilling influence in mid-winter. Her lover would find it, very literally, a cold reception!"

"I suppose," said Donatello rather sulkily, "you are making fun of the story. But I see nothing laughable in the thing itself, nor in what you say about it."

He went on to relate, that, for a long while, the knight found infinite pleasure and comfort in the friendship of the fountain-nymph. In his merriest hours, she gladdened him with her sportive humour. If ever he was annoyed with earthly trouble, she laid her moist hand upon his brow, and charmed the fret and fever quite away.

But, one day—one fatal noontide—the young knight came rushing with hasty and irregular steps to the accustomed fountain. He called the nymph; but—no doubt, because there was something unusual and frightful in his tone—she did not appear, nor answer him. He flung himself down, and washed his hands and bathed his feverish brow in the cool, pure water. And then, there was a sound of woe; it might have been a woman's voice; it might have been only the sighing of the brook over the pebbles. The water shrank away from the youth's hands, and left his brow as dry and feverish as before!

Donatello here came to a dead pause.

"Why did the water shrink from this unhappy knight?" inquired the sculptor.

"Because he had tried to wash off a blood-stain!" said the young Count, in a horrour-stricken whisper. "The guilty man had polluted the pure water. The nymph might have comforted him in sorrow, but could not cleanse his conscience of a crime."

"And did he never behold her more?" asked Kenyon.

"Never, but once," replied his friend. "He never beheld her blessed face, but once again; and then there was a blood-stain on the poor nymph's brow; it was the stain his guilt had left in the fountain where he tried to wash it off. He mourned for her, his whole life long, and employed the best sculptor of the time to carve this statue of the nymph from his description of her aspect. But, though my ancestor would fain have had the image wear her happiest look, the artist (unlike yourself) was so impressed with the mournfulness of the story, that, in spite of his best efforts, he made her forlorn, and forever weeping, as you see!"

Kenyon found a certain charm in this simple legend. Whether so intended, or not, he understood it as an apologue, typifying the soothing and genial effects of an habitual intercourse with Nature, in all ordinary cares and griefs; while, on the other hand, her mild influences fall short in their effect upon the ruder passions, and are altogether powerless in the dread fever-fit or deadly chill of guilt.

"Do you say," he asked, "that the nymph's face has never since been shown to any mortal? Methinks, you, by your native qualities, are as well entitled to her favour as ever your progenitor could have been. Why have you not summoned her?"

"I called her often, when I was a silly child," answered Donatello; and he added, in an inward voice,—"Thank Heaven, she did not come!"

"Then you never saw her?" said the sculptor.

"Never in my life!" rejoined the Count. "No, my dear friend, I have not seen the nymph; although here, by her fountain, I used to make many strange acquaintances; for, from my earliest childhood, I was familiar with whatever creatures haunt the woods. You would have laughed to see the friends I had among them; yes, among the wild, nimble things, that reckon man their deadliest enemy! How it was first taught me, I cannot tell; but there was a charm—a voice, a murmur, a kind of chaunt—by which I called the woodland inhabitants, the furry people and the feathered people, in a language that they seemed to understand."

"I have heard of such a gift," responded the sculptor gravely, "but never before met with a person endowed with it. Pray, try the charm; and lest I should frighten your friends away, I will withdraw into this thicket, and merely peep at them."

"I doubt," said Donatello, "whether they will remember my voice now. It changes, you know, as the boy grows towards manhood."

Nevertheless, (as the young Count's good nature and easy persuasibility were among his best characteristics,) he set about complying with Kenyon's request. The latter, in his concealment among the shrubbery, heard him send forth a sort of modulated breath, wild, rude, yet harmonious. It struck the auditor as at once the strangest and the most natural utterance that had ever reached his ears. Any idle boy, it should seem, singing to himself, and setting his wordless song to no other or more definite tune than the play of his own pulses, might produce a sound almost identical with this. And yet, it was as individual as a murmur of the breeze. Donatello tried it, over and over again, with many breaks, at first, and pauses of uncertainty; then with more confidence, and a fuller swell, like a wayfarer groping out of obscurity into the light, and moving with freer footsteps as it brightens around him.

Anon, his voice appeared to fill the air, yet not with an obtrusive clangour. The sound was of a murmurous character, soft, attractive, persuasive, friendly. The sculptor fancied that such might have been the original voice and utterance of the natural man, before the sophistication of the human intellect formed what we now call language. In this broad dialect— broad as the sympathies of Nature—the human brother might have spoken to his inarticulate brotherhood that prowl the woods, or soar upon the wing, and have been intelligible, to such extent as to win their confidence.

The sound had its pathos too. At some of its simple cadences, the tears came quietly into Kenyon's eyes. They welled up slowly from his heart, which was thrilling with an emotion more delightful than he had often felt before, but which he forbore to analyze, lest, if he seized it, it should at once perish in his grasp.

Donatello paused, two or three times, and seemed to listen; then, recommencing, he poured his spirit and life more earnestly into the strain. And, finally—or else the sculptor's hope and imagination deceived him—soft treads were audible upon the fallen leaves. There was a rustling among the shrubbery; a whir of wings, moreover, that hovered in the air. It may have been all an illusion; but Kenyon fancied that he could distinguish the stealthy, cat-like movement of some small forest-citizen, and that he could even see its doubtful shadow, if not really its substance. But, all at once, whatever might be the reason, there ensued a hurried rush and scamper of little feet; and then the sculptor heard a wild, sorrowful cry, and, through the crevices of the thicket, beheld Donatello fling himself on the ground.

Emerging from his hiding-place, he saw no living thing, save a brown lizard (it was of the tarantula species) rustling away through the sunshine. To all present appearance, this venomous reptile was the only creature that had responded to the young Count's efforts to renew his intercourse with the lower orders of Nature.

"What has happened to you?" exclaimed Kenyon, stooping down over his friend, and wondering at the anguish which he betrayed.

"Death, death!" sobbed Donatello. "They know it!"

He grovelled beside the fountain, in a fit of such passionate sobbing and weeping, that it seemed as if his heart had broken, and spilt its wild sorrows upon the ground. His unrestrained grief and childish tears made Kenyon sensible in how small a degree the customs and restraints of society had really acted upon this young man, in spite of the quietude of his ordinary deportment. In response to his friend's efforts to console him, he murmured words hardly more articulate than the strange chaunt, which he had so recently been breathing into the air.

"They know it!" was all that Kenyon could yet distinguish. "They know it!"

"Who know it?" asked the sculptor. "And what is it they know?"

"They know it!" repeated Donatello trembling. "They shun me! All Nature shrinks from me, and shudders at me! I live in the midst of a curse, that hems me round with a circle of fire! No innocent thing can come near me!"

"Be comforted, my dear friend," said Kenyon kneeling beside him. "You labour under some illusion, but no curse. As for this strange, natural spell, which you have been exercising, (and of which I have heard, before, though I never believed in, nor expected to witness it,) I am satisfied that you still possess it. It was my own half-concealed presence, no doubt, and some involuntary little movement of mine, that scared away your forest-friends."

"They are friends of mine, no longer," answered Donatello.

"We all of us, as we grow older," rejoined Kenyon, "lose somewhat of our proximity to Nature. It is the price we pay for experience."

"A heavy price, then!" said Donatello, rising from the ground. "But we will speak no more of it. Forget this scene, my dear friend. In your eyes, it must look very absurd. It is a grief, I presume, to all men, to find the pleasant privileges and properties of early life departing from them. That grief has now befallen me. Well; I shall waste no more tears for such a cause!"

Nothing else made Kenyon so sensible of a change in Donatello, as his newly acquired power of dealing with his own emotions, and, after a struggle more or less fierce, thrusting them down into the prison-cells where he usually kept them confined. The restraint which he now put upon himself, and the mask of dull composure which he succeeded in clasping over his still beautiful, and once faun-like face, affected the sensitive sculptor more sadly than even the unrestrained passion of the preceding scene. It is a very miserable epoch, when the evil necessities of life, in our tortuous world, first get the better of us so far, as to compel us to attempt throwing a cloud over our transparency. Simplicity increases in value, the longer we can keep it, and the further we carry it onward into life; the loss of a child's simplicity, in the inevitable lapse of years, causes but a natural sigh or two, because even his mother feared that he could not keep it always. But, after a young man has brought it through his childhood, and has still worn it in his bosom, not as an early dew-drop, but as a diamond of pure, white lustre,—it is a pity to lose it, then. And thus, when Kenyon saw how much his friend had now to hide, and how well he hid it, he could have wept, although his tears would have been even idler than those which Donatello had just shed.

They parted on the lawn before the house; the Count to climb his tower, and the sculptor to read an antique edition of Dante, which he had found among some old volumes of Catholic devotion, in a seldom-visited room. Tomaso met him in the entrance-hall, and showed a desire to speak.

"Our poor Signorino looks very sad to-day!" he said.

"Even so, good Tomaso," replied the sculptor. "Would that we could raise his spirits a little!"

"There might be means, Signor," answered the old butler, "if one might but be sure that they were the right ones. We men are but rough nurses for a sick body or a sick spirit."

"Women, you would say, my good friend, are better," said the sculptor, struck by an intelligence in the butler's face. "That is possible! But it depends."

"Ah; we will wait a little longer," said Tomaso, with the customary shake of his head.

XXVIII

THE OWL-TOWER

WILL YOU NOT SHOW ME YOUR TOWER?"
said the sculptor one day to his friend.

"It is plainly enough to be seen, methinks," answered the Count, with a kind of sulkiness that often appeared in him, as one of the little symptoms of inward trouble.

"Yes; its exteriour is visible, far and wide," said Kenyon. "But such a gray, moss-grown tower as this, however valuable as an object of scenery, will certainly be quite as interesting inside as out. It cannot be less than six hundred years old; the foundations and lower story are much older than that, I should judge; and traditions probably cling to the walls, within, quite as plentifully as the gray and yellow lichens cluster on its face, without."

"No doubt," replied Donatello. "But I know little of such things, and never could comprehend the interest which some of you Forestieri take in them. A year or two ago, an English Signor with a venerable white beard, (they say he was a magician, too,) came hither from as far off as Florence, just to see my tower."

"Ah; I have seen him at Florence," observed Kenyon. "He is a necromancer, as you say, and dwells in an old mansion of the Knights Templars, close by the Ponte Vecchio, with a great many ghostly books, pictures, and antiquities, to make the house gloomy, and one bright-eyed little girl to keep it cheerful!"

"I know him only by his white beard," said Donatello. "But he could have told you a great deal about the tower, and the sieges which it has stood, and the prisoners who have been confined in it. And he gathered up all the traditions of the Monte Beni family, and, among the rest, the sad one which I told you at the fountain, the other day. He had known mighty poets, he said, in his earlier life; and the most illustrious of them would have rejoiced to preserve such a legend in immortal rhyme—especially if he could have had some of our wine of Sunshine to help out his inspiration."

"Any man might be a poet, as well as Byron, with such wine and such a theme," rejoined the sculptor. "But, shall we climb your tower? The thunder-storm, gathering yonder among the hills, will be a spectacle worth witnessing."

"Come, then;" said the Count, adding with a sigh, "it has a weary staircase and dismal chambers, and it is very lonesome at the summit!"

"Like a man's life, when he has climbed to eminence," remarked the sculptor. "Or, let us rather say, with its difficult steps, and the dark prison-cells you speak of, your tower resembles the spiritual experience of many a sinful soul, which, nevertheless, may struggle upward into the pure air and light of Heaven, at last."

Donatello sighed again, and led the way up into the tower. Mounting the broad staircase that ascended from the entrance-hall, they traversed the great wilderness of a house, through some obscure passages, and came to a low, ancient door-way. It admitted them to a narrow turret-stair, which zig-zagged upward, lighted in its progress by loop-holes and iron-barred windows. Reaching the top of the first flight, the Count threw open a door of worm-eaten oak, and disclosed a chamber that occupied the whole area of the tower. It was most pitiably forlorn of aspect, with a brick-paved floor, bare holes through the massive walls, grated with iron, instead of windows, and, for furniture, an old stool, which increased the dreariness of the place tenfold, by suggesting an idea of its having once been tenanted.

"This was a prisoner's cell, in the old days," said Donatello. "The white-bearded necromancer, of whom I told you, found out that a certain famous monk was confined here, about five hundred years ago. He was a very holy man, and was afterwards burned at the stake in the Granducal square, at Firenze. There have always been stories, Tomaso says, of a hooded monk creeping up and down these stairs, or standing in the door-way of this chamber. It must needs be the ghost of the ancient prisoner. Do you believe in ghosts?"

"I can hardly tell," replied Kenyon. "On the whole, I think not."

"Neither do I," responded the Count; "for, if spirits ever came back, I should surely have met one, within these two months past. Ghosts never rise! So much I know, and am glad to know it."

Following the narrow staircase still higher, they came to another room of similar size and equally forlorn, but inhabited by two personages of a race which, from time immemorial, have held proprietorship and occupancy in ruined towers. These were a pair of owls, who, being doubtless acquainted with Donatello, showed little sign of alarm at the entrance of visitors. They gave a dismal croak or two, and hopped aside into the darkest corner; since it was not yet their hour to flap duskily abroad.

"They do not desert me, like my other feathered acquaintances," observed the young Count, with a sad smile, alluding to the scene which Kenyon had witnessed at the fountain-side. "When I was a wild, playful boy, the owls did not love me half so well!"

He made no further pause here, but led his friend up another flight of steps; while, at every stage, the windows and narrow loop-holes afforded Kenyon more extensive eye-shots over hill and valley, and allowed him to taste the cool purity of the mid-atmosphere. At length, they reached the topmost chamber, directly beneath the roof of the tower.

"This is my own abode," said Donatello; "my own owl's nest!"

In fact, the room was fitted up as a bed-chamber, though in a style of the utmost simplicity. It likewise served as an oratory; there being a crucifix in one corner, and a multitude of holy emblems, such as Catholics judge it necessary to help their devotion withal. Several ugly little prints, representing the sufferings of the Saviour and the martyrdoms of Saints, hung on the wall; and, behind the crucifix, there was a good copy of Titian's Magdalen of the Pitti Palace, clad only in the flow of her golden ringlets. She had a confident look, (but it was Titian's fault, not the penitent woman's,) as if expecting to win Heaven by the free display of her earthly charms. Inside of a glass case, appeared an image of the sacred Bambino, in the guise of a little waxen boy, very prettily made, reclining among flowers, like a Cupid, and holding up a heart that resembled a bit of red sealing wax. A small vase of precious marble was full of holy-water.

Beneath the crucifix, on a table, lay a human skull, which looked as if it might have been dug up out of some old grave. But, examining it more closely, Kenyon saw that it was carved in gray alabaster, most skilfully done to the death, with accurate imitation of the teeth, the sutures, the empty eye-caverns, and the fragile little bones of the nose. This hideous emblem rested on a cushion of white marble, so nicely wrought that you seemed to see the impression of the heavy skull in a silken and downy substance.

Donatello dipt his fingers into the holy-water vase, and crossed himself. After doing so, he trembled.

"I have no right to make the sacred symbol on a sinful breast!" he said.

"On what mortal breast can it be made, then?" asked the sculptor. "Is there one that hides no sin?"

"But, these blessed emblems make you smile, I fear," resumed the Count, looking askance at his friend.—"You heretics, I know, attempt to pray without even a crucifix to kneel at."

"I, at least, (whom you call a heretic,) reverence that holy symbol," answered Kenyon. "What I am most inclined to murmur at, is this death's head. I could laugh, moreover, in its ugly face! It is absurdly monstrous, my dear friend, thus to fling the dead weight of our mortality upon our immortal hopes. While we live on earth, 'tis true, we must needs carry our skeletons about with us; but, for Heaven's sake, do not let us burthen our spirits with them, in our feeble efforts to soar upward! Believe me, it will change the whole aspect of death, if you can once disconnect it, in your idea, with that corruption from which it disengages our higher part."

"I do not well understand you," said Donatello; and he took up the alabaster skull, shuddering, and evidently feeling it a kind of penance to touch it. "I only know that this skull has been in my family for centuries. Old Tomaso has a story, that it was copied by a famous sculptor from the skull of that same unhappy knight who loved the fountain-lady, and lost her by a blood-stain. He lived and died with a deep sense of sin upon him, and, on his death-bed, he ordained that this token of him should go down to his posterity. And my fore-

fathers, being a cheerful race of men, in their natural disposition, found it needful to have the skull often before their
eyes, because they dearly loved life and its enjoyments, and
hated the very thought of death."

"I am afraid," said Kenyon, "they liked it none the better,
for seeing its face under this abominable mask."

Without further discussion, the Count led the way up
one more flight of stairs, at the end of which they emerged
upon the summit of the tower. The sculptor felt as if his
being were suddenly magnified a hundred fold; so wide was
the Umbrian valley that suddenly opened before him, set in
its grand frame-work of nearer and more distant hills. It
seemed as if all Italy lay under his eyes, in that one picture.
For there was the broad, sunny smile of God, which we
fancy to be spread over that favoured land more abundantly
than on other regions, and, beneath it, glowed a most rich
and varied fertility. The trim vineyards were there, and the
fig-trees, and the mulberries, and the smoky-hued tracts of
the olive-orchards; there, too, were fields of every kind of
grain, among which waved the Indian corn, putting Kenyon
in mind of the fondly remembered acres of his father's homestead. White villas, gray convents, church-spires, villages,
towns, each with its battlemented walls and towered gateway,
were scattered upon this spacious map; a river gleamed across
it; and lakes opened their blue eyes in its face, reflecting
Heaven, lest mortals should forget that better land, when
they beheld the earth so beautiful.

What made the valley look still wider, was the two or
three varieties of weather that were visible on its surface, all
at the same instant of time. Here lay the quiet sunshine;
there, fell the great black patches of ominous shadow from
the clouds; and behind them, like a giant of league-long
strides, came hurrying the thunder-storm, which had already
swept midway across the plain. In the rear of the approach-

ing tempest, brightened forth again the sunny splendour, which its progress had darkened with so terrible a frown.

All round this majestic landscape, the bald-peaked or forest-crowned mountains descended boldly upon the plain. On many of their spurs and midway declivities, and even on their summits, stood cities, some of them famous of old; for these had been the seats and nurseries of early Art, where the flower of Beauty sprang out of a rocky soil, and in a high, keen atmosphere, when the richest and most sheltered gardens failed to nourish it.

"Thank God for letting me again behold this scene!" said the sculptor, a devout man in his way, reverently taking off his hat. "I have viewed it from many points, and never without as full a sensation of gratitude as my heart seems capable of feeling. How it strengthens the poor human spirit in its reliance on His Providence, to ascend but this little way above the common level, and so attain a somewhat wider glimpse of His dealings with mankind! He doeth all things right! His will be done!"

"You discern something that is hidden from me," observed Donatello gloomily, yet striving with unwonted grasp to catch the analogies which so cheered his friend. "I see sunshine on one spot, and cloud in another, and no reason for it in either case. The sun on you; the cloud on me! What comfort can I draw from this?"

"Nay; I cannot preach," said Kenyon, "with a page of heaven and a page of earth spread wide open before us! Only begin to read it, and you will find it interpreting itself without the aid of words. It is a great mistake to try to put our best thoughts into human language. When we ascend into the higher regions of emotion and spiritual enjoyment, they are only expressible by such grand hieroglyphics as these around us."

They stood, awhile, contemplating the scene; but, as inevitably happens after a spiritual flight, it was not long before the sculptor felt his wings flagging in the rarity of the upper atmosphere. He was glad to let himself quietly downward out of mid-sky, as it were, and alight on the solid platform of the battlemented tower. He looked about him, and beheld growing out of the stone pavement, which formed the roof, a little shrub, with green and glossy leaves. It was the only green thing there; and Heaven knows how its seeds had ever been planted, at that airy height, or how it had found nourishment for its small life, in the chinks of the stones; for it had no earth, and nothing more like soil than the crumbling mortar, which had been crammed into the crevices in a long-past age.

Yet the plant seemed fond of its native site; and Donatello said it had always grown there, from his earliest remembrance, and never, he believed, any smaller or any larger than they saw it now.

"I wonder if the shrub teaches you any good lesson," said he, observing the interest with which Kenyon examined it. "If the wide valley has a great meaning, this plant ought to have at least a little one; and it has been growing on our tower long enough to have learned how to speak it."

"Oh, certainly!" answered the sculptor. "The shrub has its moral, or it would have perished long ago. And, no doubt, it is for your use and edification, since you have had it before your eyes, all your lifetime, and now are moved to ask what may be its lesson."

"It teaches me nothing," said the simple Donatello, stooping over the plant, and perplexing himself with a minute scrutiny. "But here was a worm that would have killed it; an ugly creature, which I will fling over the battlements."

XXIX

ON THE BATTLEMENTS

THE SCULPTOR now looked through an embrasure, and threw down a bit of lime, watching its fall, till it struck upon a stone-bench at the rocky foundation of the tower, and flew into many fragments.

"Pray pardon me for helping Time to crumble away your ancestral walls," said he. "But I am one of those persons who have a natural tendency to climb heights, and to stand on the verge of them, measuring the depth below. If I were to do just as I like, at this moment, I should fling myself down after that bit of lime. It is a very singular temptation, and all but irresistible; partly, I believe, because it might be so easily done, and partly because such momentous consequences would ensue, without my being compelled to wait a moment for them. Have you never felt this strange impulse of an Evil Spirit at your back, shoving you towards a precipice?"

"Ah, no!" cried Donatello, shrinking from the battlemented wall with a face of horrour. "I cling to life in a way which you cannot conceive; it has been so rich, so warm, so sunny!—and beyond its verge, nothing but the chilly dark! And then a fall from a precipice is such an awful death!"

"Nay; if it be a great height," said Kenyon, "a man would leave his life in the air, and never feel the hard shock at the bottom."

"That is not the way with this kind of death!" exclaimed Donatello, in a low, horrour-stricken voice, which grew higher and more full of emotion, as he proceeded. "Imagine a fellow-creature—breathing, now, and looking you in the face—and now tumbling down, down, down, with a long shriek wavering after him, all the way! He does not leave his life in the air! No; but it keeps in him till he thumps against the stones, a horribly long while; then, he lies there frightfully quiet, a dead heap of bruised flesh and broken bones! A quiver runs through the crushed mass; and no more movement after that! No; not if you would give your soul to make him stir a finger! Ah, terrible! Yes, yes; I would fain fling myself down, for the very dread of it, that I might endure it once for all, and dream of it no more!"

"How forcibly—how frightfully—you conceive this!" said the sculptor, aghast at the passionate horrour which was betrayed in the Count's words, and still more in his wild gestures and ghastly look. "Nay; if the height of your tower affects your imagination thus, you do wrong to trust yourself here in solitude, and in the night-time, and at all unguarded hours. You are not safe in your chamber. It is but a step or two; and what if a vivid dream should lead you up hither, at midnight, and act itself out as a reality!"

Donatello had hidden his face in his hands, and was leaning against the parapet.

"No fear of that!" said he. "Whatever the dream may be, I am too genuine a coward to act out my own death in it."

The paroxysm passed away, and the two friends continued their desultory talk, very much as if no such interruption had occurred. Nevertheless, it affected the sculptor with infinite pity to see this young man, who had been born to gladness as an assured heritage, now involved in a misty bewilderment of grievous thoughts, amid which he seemed to go staggering blindfold. Kenyon (not without an unshaped suspicion of the definite fact) knew that his condition must have resulted from the weight and gloom of life, now first, through the agency of a secret trouble, making themselves felt on a character that had heretofore breathed only an atmosphere of joy. The effect of this hard lesson, upon Donatello's intellect and disposition, was very striking. It was perceptible that he had already had glimpses of strange and subtle matters in those dark caverns, into which all men must descend, if they would know anything beneath the surface and illusive pleasures of existence. And when they emerge, though dazzled and blinded by the first glare of daylight, they take truer and sadder views of life, forever afterwards.

From some mysterious source, as the sculptor felt assured, a soul had been inspired into the young Count's simplicity, since their intercourse in Rome. He now showed a far deeper sense, and an intelligence that began to deal with high subjects, though in a feeble and childish way. He evinced, too, a more definite and a nobler individuality, but developed out of grief and pain, and fearfully conscious of the pangs that had given it birth. Every human life, if it ascends to truth or delves down to reality, must undergo a similar change; but sometimes, perhaps, the instruction comes without the sorrow, and, oftener, the sorrow teaches no lesson that abides with us. In Donatello's case, it was pitiful, and almost ludicrous, to observe the confused struggle that he made; how completely he was taken by surprise; how ill-prepared he stood, on this old battle-field of the world, to fight with such an inevitable foe as mortal Calamity, and Sin for its stronger ally.

"And yet," thought Kenyon, "the poor fellow bears himself like a hero, too! If he would only tell me his trouble, or give me an opening to speak frankly about it, I might help him; but he finds it too horrible to be uttered, and fancies himself the only mortal that ever felt the anguish of remorse. Yes; he believes that nobody ever endured his agony before; so that—sharp enough in itself—it has all the additional zest of a torture just invented to plague him individually!"

The sculptor endeavoured to dismiss the painful subject from his mind; and, leaning against the battlements, he turned his face southward and westward, and gazed across the breadth of the valley. His thoughts flew far beyond even those wide boundaries, taking an air-line from Donatello's tower to another turret that ascended into the sky of the summer-afternoon, invisibly to him, above the roofs of distant Rome. Then rose tumultuously into his consciousness that strong love for Hilda, which it was his habit to confine in one of the heart's inner chambers, because he had found no encouragement to bring it forward. But, now, he felt a strange pull at his heart-strings. It could not have been more perceptible, if, all the way between these battlements and Hilda's dove-cote, had stretched an exquisitely sensitive cord, which, at the hither end, was knotted with his aforesaid heart-strings, and at the remoter one, was grasped by a gentle hand. His breath grew tremulous. He put his hand to his breast; so distinctly did he seem to feel that cord drawn once, and again, and again, as if—though still it was bashfully intimated—there were an importunate demand for his presence. Oh, for the white wings of Hilda's doves, that he might have flown thither, and alighted at the Virgin's shrine!

But lovers (and Kenyon knew it well) project so lifelike a copy of their mistresses out of their own imaginations, that it can pull at the heart-strings almost as perceptibly as the genuine original. No airy intimations are to be trusted; no evidences of responsive affection less positive than whispered and broken words, or tender pressures of the hand, allowed and half-returned, or glances, that distil many passionate avowals into one gleam of richly coloured light. Even these should be weighed rigorously, at the instant; for, in another instant, the imagination seizes on them as its property, and stamps them with its own arbitrary value. But Hilda's maidenly reserve had given her lover no such tokens, to be interpreted either by his hopes or fears.

"Yonder, over mountain and valley, lies Rome," said the sculptor. "Shall you return thither in the Autumn?"

"Never! I hate Rome," answered Donatello, "and have good cause."

"And yet it was a pleasant winter that we spent there," observed Kenyon, "and with pleasant friends about us. You would meet them again there, all of them."

"All?" asked Donatello.

"All, to the best of my belief," said the sculptor; "but you need not go to Rome to seek them. If there were one of those friends, whose life-line was twisted with your own, I am enough of a fatalist to feel assured that you will meet that one again, wander whither you may. Neither can we escape the companions whom Providence assigns for us, by climbing an old tower like this."

"Yet the stairs are steep and dark," rejoined the Count. "None but yourself would seek me here, or find me, if they sought."

As Donatello did not take advantage of this opening which his friend had kindly afforded him, to pour out his hidden troubles, the latter again threw aside the subject, and returned to the enjoyment of the scene before him. The thunder-storm, which he had beheld striding across the valley, had passed to the left of Monte Beni, and was continuing its march towards the hills that formed the boundary on the eastward. Above the whole valley, indeed, the sky was heavy with tumbling vapours, interspersed with which were tracts of blue, vividly brightened by the sun; but in the east, where the tempest was yet trailing its ragged skirts, lay a dusky region of cloud and sullen mist, in which some of the hills appeared of a dark purple hue. Others became so indistinct, that the spectator could not tell rocky height from impalpable cloud. Far into this misty cloud-region, however—within the domain of Chaos, as it were—hill-tops were seen brightening in the sunshine; they looked like fragments of the world, broken adrift and based on nothingness, or like portions of a sphere destined to exist, but not yet finally compacted.

The sculptor, habitually drawing many of the images and illustrations of his thoughts from the plastic art, fancied that the scene represented the process of the Creator, when He held the new, imperfect Earth in His hand, and modelled it.

"What a magic is in mist and vapour among the mountains!" he exclaimed. "With their help, one single scene becomes a thousand. The cloud-scenery gives such variety to a hilly landscape that it would be worth while to journalize its aspect, from hour to hour. A cloud, however, (as I have myself experienced,) is apt to grow solid, and as heavy as a stone, the instant that you take in hand to describe it. But, in my own art, I have found great use in clouds. Such silvery ones as those to the northward, for example, have often suggested sculpturesque groups, figures, and attitudes; they are especially rich in attitudes of living repose, which a sculptor only hits upon by the rarest good fortune. When I go back to my dear native land, the clouds along the horizon will be my only gallery of art!"

"I can see cloud-shapes, too," said Donatello. "Yonder is one that shifts strangely; it has been like people whom I knew. And now, if I watch it a little longer, it will take the figure of a monk reclining, with his cowl about his head and drawn partly over his face, and—Well! Did I not tell you so?"

"I think," remarked Kenyon, "we can hardly be gazing at the same cloud. What I behold is a reclining figure, to be sure, but feminine, and with a despondent air, wonderfully well expressed in the wavering outline from head to foot. It moves my very heart by something indefinable that it suggests."

"I see the figure, and almost the face," said the Count; adding, in a lower voice, "It is Miriam's!"

"No; not Miriam's," answered the sculptor.

While the two gazers thus found their own reminiscences and presentiments floating among the clouds, the day drew to its close, and now showed them the fair spectacle of an Italian sunset. The sky was soft and bright, but not so gorgeous as Kenyon had seen it, a thousand times, in America; for there the western sky is wont to be set a-flame with breadths and depths of colour, with which poets seek in vain to dye their verses, and which painters never dare to copy. As beheld from the tower of Monte Beni, the scene was tenderly magnificent, with mild gradations of hue, and a lavish outpouring of gold, but rather such gold as we see on the leaf of a bright flower than the burnished glow of metal from the mine. Or, if metallic, it looked airy and unsubstantial, like the glorified dreams of an alchemist. And speedily —more speedily than in our own clime—came the twilight, and, brightening through its gray transparency, the stars.

A swarm of minute insects, that had been hovering all day round the battlements, were now swept away by the freshness of a rising breeze. The two owls in the chamber beneath Donatello's, uttered their soft, melancholy cry, (which, with national avoidance of harsh sounds, Italian owls substitute for the hoot of their kindred in other countries,) and flew darkling forth among the shrubbery. A convent-bell rang out, near at hand, and was not only echoed among the hills, but answered by another bell, and still another, which doubtless had further and further responses, at various distances along the valley; for, like the English drum-beat around the globe, there is a chain of convent-bells from end to end, and crosswise, and in all possible directions, over priest-ridden Italy.

"Come," said the sculptor, "the evening air grows cool. It is time to descend."

"Time for you, my friend," replied the Count; and he

hesitated a little before adding, "I must keep a vigil here for some hours longer. It is my frequent custom to keep vigils; and sometimes the thought occurs to me whether it were not better to keep them in yonder Convent, the bell of which just now seemed to summon me. Would I do wisely, do you think, to exchange this old tower for a cell?"

"What! Turn monk?" exclaimed his friend. "A horrible idea!"

"True," said Donatello sighing. "Therefore, if at all, I purpose doing it."

"Then think of it no more, for Heaven's sake!" cried the sculptor. "There are a thousand better and more poignant methods of being miserable than that, if to be miserable is what you wish. Nay; I question whether a monk keeps himself up to the intellectual and spiritual height which misery implies. A monk—I judge from their sensual physiognomies, which meet me at every turn—is inevitably a beast! Their souls, if they have any to begin with, perish out of them, before their sluggish, swinish existence is half-done. Better, a million times, to stand star-gazing on these airy battlements, than to smother your new germ of a higher life in a monkish cell!"

"You make me tremble," said Donatello, "by your bold aspersion of men who have devoted themselves to God's service!"

"They serve neither God nor man, and themselves least of all, though their motives be utterly selfish," replied Kenyon. "Avoid the convent, my dear friend, as you would shun the death of the soul! But, for my own part, if I had an insupportable burthen—if, for any cause, I were bent upon sacrificing every earthly hope as a peace-offering towards Heaven—I would make the wide world my cell, and good deeds to mankind my prayer. Many penitent men have done this, and found peace in it."

"Ah; but you are a heretic!" said the Count.

Yet his face brightened beneath the stars; and, looking at it through the twilight, the sculptor's remembrance went back to that scene in the Capitol, where, both in features and expression, Donatello had seemed identical with the Faun. And still there was a resemblance; for now, when first the idea was suggested of living for the welfare of his fellow-creatures, the original beauty, which sorrow had partly effaced, came back elevated and spiritualized. In the black depths, the Faun had found a soul, and was struggling with it towards the light of Heaven.

The illumination, it is true, soon faded out of Donatello's face. The idea of life-long and unselfish effort was too high to be received by him with more than a momentary comprehension. An Italian, indeed, seldom dreams of being philanthropic, except in bestowing alms among the paupers who appeal to his beneficence at every step; nor does it occur to him that there are fitter modes of propitiating Heaven than by penances, pilgrimages, and offerings at shrines. Perhaps, too, their system has its share of moral advantages; they, at all events, cannot well pride themselves (as our own more energetic benevolence is apt to do) upon sharing in the counsels of Providence and kindly helping out its otherwise impracticable designs.

And now the broad valley twinkled with lights, that glimmered through its duskiness, like the fire-flies in the garden of a Florentine palace. A gleam of lightning from the rear of the tempest showed the circumference of hills, and the great space between, as the last cannon-flash of a retreating army reddens across the field where it has fought. The sculptor was on the point of descending the turret-stair, when, somewhere in the darkness that lay beneath them, a woman's voice was heard, singing a low, sad strain.

"Hark!" said he, laying his hand on Donatello's arm.

And Donatello had said 'Hark!' at the same instant.

The song (if song it could be called, that had only a wild rhythm, and flowed forth in the fitful measure of a wind-harp) did not clothe itself in the sharp brilliancy of the Italian tongue. The words, so far as they could be distinguished, were German, and therefore unintelligible to the Count, and hardly less so to the sculptor; being softened and molten, as it were, into the melancholy richness of the voice that sang them. It was as the murmur of a soul, bewildered amid the sinful gloom of earth, and retaining only enough memory of a better state to make sad music of the wail, which would else have been a despairing shriek. Never was there profounder pathos than breathed through that mysterious voice; it brought the tears into the sculptor's eyes, with remembrances and forebodings of whatever sorrow he had felt or apprehended; it made Donatello sob, as chiming in with the anguish that he found unutterable, and giving it the expression which he vaguely sought.

But, when the emotion was at its profoundest depth, the voice rose out of it, yet so gradually that a gloom seemed to pervade it, far upward from the abyss, and not entirely to fall away as it ascended into a higher and purer region. At last, the auditors could have fancied that the melody, with its rich sweetness all there, and much of its sorrow gone, was floating around the very summit of the tower.

"Donatello," said the sculptor, when there was silence again, "had that voice no message for your ear?"

"I dare not receive it," said Donatello. "The anguish, of which it spoke, abides with me; the hope dies away, with the breath that brought it hither. It is not good for me to hear that voice."

The sculptor sighed, and left the poor penitent, keeping his vigil on the tower.

XXX

DONATELLO'S BUST

K ENYON, it will be remembered, had asked Donatello's permission to model his bust. The work had now made considerable progress, and necessarily kept the sculptor's thoughts brooding much and often upon his host's personal characteristics. These it was his difficult office to bring out from their depths, and interpret them to all men, showing them what they could not discern for themselves, yet must be compelled to recognize at a glance, on the surface of a block of marble.

He had never undertaken a portrait-bust which gave him so much trouble as Donatello's; not that there was any special difficulty in hitting the likeness, though, even in this respect, the grace and harmony of the features seemed inconsistent with a prominent expression of individuality. But he was chiefly perplexed how to make this genial and kindly type of countenance the index of the mind within. His acuteness and his sympathies, indeed, were both somewhat at fault in their efforts to enlighten him as to the moral phase through which the Count was now passing. If, at one sitting, he caught a glimpse of what appeared to be a genuine and permanent trait, it would probably be less perceptible, on a second occasion, and perhaps have vanished entirely, at a third. So evanescent a show of character threw the sculptor into despair; not marble or clay, but cloud and vapour, was the material in which it ought to be represented. Even the ponderous depression, which constantly weighed upon Donatello's heart, could not compel him into the kind of repose which the plastic art requires.

Hopeless of a good result, Kenyon gave up all pre-conceptions about the character of his subject, and let his hands work, uncontrolled, with the clay, somewhat as a spiritual medium, while holding a pen, yields it to an unseen guidance other than that of her own will. Now and then, he fancied that this plan was destined to be the successful one. A skill and insight, beyond his consciousness, seemed occasionally to take up the task. The mystery, the miracle, of imbuing an inanimate substance with thought, feeling, and all the intangible attributes of the soul, appeared on the verge of being wrought. And now, as he flattered himself, the true image of his friend was about to emerge from the facile material, bringing with it more of Donatello's character than the keenest observer could detect, at any one moment, in the face of the original. Vain expectation! Some touch, whereby the artist thought to improve or hasten the result, interfered with the design of his unseen spiritual assistant, and spoilt the whole. There was still the moist, brown clay, indeed, and the features of Donatello, but without any semblance of intelligent and sympathetic life.

"The difficulty will drive me mad, I verily believe!" cried the sculptor nervously. "Look at the wretched piece of work yourself, my dear friend, and tell me whether you recognize any manner of likeness to your inner man!"

"None," replied Donatello, speaking the simple truth. "It is like looking a stranger in the face."

This frankly unfavourable testimony so wrought with the sensitive artist, that he fell into a passion with the stubborn image, and cared not what might happen to it thenceforward. Wielding that wonderful power which sculptors possess over moist clay, (however refractory it may show itself in certain respects,) he compressed, elongated, widened, and otherwise altered the features of the bust, in mere recklessness, and, at every change, inquired of the Count whether the expression became anywise more satisfactory.

"Stop!" cried Donatello, at last, catching the sculptor's hand. "Let it remain so!"

By some accidental handling of the clay, entirely independent of his own will, Kenyon had given the countenance a distorted and violent look, combining animal fierceness with intelligent hatred. Had Hilda, or had Miriam, seen the bust, with the expression which it had now assumed, they might have recognized Donatello's face as they beheld it at that terrible moment, when he held his victim over the edge of the precipice.

"What have I done?" said the sculptor, shocked at his own casual production. "It were a sin to let the clay, which bears your features, harden into a look like that. Cain never wore an uglier one!"

"For that very reason, let it remain!" answered the Count, who had grown pale as ashes at the aspect of his crime, thus strangely presented to him in another of the many guises, under which guilt stares the criminal in the face. "Do not alter it! Chisel it, rather, in eternal marble! I will set it up in my oratory and keep it continually before my eyes. Sadder and more horrible is a face like this, alive with my own crime, than the dead skull which my forefathers handed down to me!"

But, without in the least heeding Donatello's remonstrances, the sculptor again applied his artful fingers to the clay, and compelled the bust to dismiss the expression that had so startled them both.

"Believe me," said he, turning his eyes upon his friend, full of grave and tender sympathy, "you know not what is requisite for your spiritual growth, seeking, as you do, to keep your soul perpetually in the unwholesome region of remorse. It was needful for you to pass through that dark valley, but it is infinitely dangerous to linger there too long; there is poison in the atmosphere, when we sit down and brood in it, instead of girding up our loins to press onward. Not despondency, not slothful anguish, is what you now require—but effort! Has there been an unutterable evil in your young life? Then crowd it out with good, or it will lie corrupting there, forever, and cause your capacity for better things to partake its noisome corruption!"

"You stir up many thoughts," said Donatello, pressing his hand upon his brow, "but the multitude and the whirl of them make me dizzy!"

They now left the sculptor's temporary studio, without observing that his last accidental touches, with which he hurriedly effaced the look of deadly rage, had given the bust a higher and sweeter expression than it had hitherto worn. It is to be regretted that Kenyon had not seen it; for only an artist, perhaps, can conceive the irksomeness, the irritation of brain, the depression of spirits, that resulted from his failure to satisfy himself, after so much toil and thought as he had bestowed on Donatello's bust. In case of success, indeed, all this thoughtful toil would have been reckoned not only as well bestowed, but as among the happiest hours of his life; whereas, deeming himself to have failed, it was just so much of life that had better never have been lived; for thus does the good or ill result of his labour throw back sunshine or gloom upon the artist's mind. The sculptor, therefore, would have done well to glance again

at his work; for here were still the features of the antique
Faun, but now illuminated with a higher meaning, such as
the old marble never bore.

Donatello having quitted him, Kenyon spent the rest of
the day strolling about the pleasant precincts of Monte Beni,
where the summer was now so far advanced that it began,
indeed, to partake of the ripe wealth of autumn. Apricots
had long been abundant, and had past away, and plums and
cherries along with them. But now came great, juicy pears,
melting and delicious, and peaches, of goodly size and tempting aspect, though cold and watery to the palate, compared
with the sculptor's rich reminiscences of that fruit in America.
The purple figs had already enjoyed their day, and the white
ones were luscious now. The contadini (who, by this time,
knew Kenyon well) found many clusters of ripe grapes for
him, in every little globe of which was included a fragrant
draught of the sunny Monte Beni wine.

Unexpectedly, in a nook, close by the farm-house, he
chanced to find a spot where the vintage had actually com-
menced. A great heap of early ripened grapes had been
gathered, and thrown into a mighty tub. In the middle of it
stood a lusty and jolly contadino, nor stood, merely, but
stamped with all his might, and danced amain; while the
red juice bathed his feet, and threw its foam midway up his
brown and shaggy legs. Here, then, was the very process
that figures so picturesquely in Scripture and in poetry, of
treading out the wine-press and dyeing the feet and garments
with the crimson effusion, as with the blood of a battle-field.
The memory of the process does not make the Tuscan wine
taste more deliciously. The contadini hospitably offered
Kenyon a sample of the new liquour, that had already stood
fermenting for a day or two. He had tried a similar draught,
however, in years past, and was little inclined to make proof
of it again; for he knew that it would be a sour and bitter

juice, a wine of woe and tribulation, and that, the more a man drinks of such liquour, the sadder he is likely to be.

The scene reminded the sculptor of our New England vintages, where the big piles of golden and rosy apples lie under the orchard-trees, in the mild, autumnal sunshine; and the creaking cider-mill, set in motion by a circumgyratory horse, is all a-gush with the luscious juice. To speak frankly, the cider-making is the more picturesque sight of the two, and the new, sweet cider an infinitely better drink than the ordinary, unripe Tuscan wine. Such as it is, however, the latter fills thousands upon thousands of small, flat barrels, and, still growing thinner and sharper, loses the little life it had, as wine, and becomes apotheosized as a more praiseworthy vinegar.

Yet all these vineyard-scenes, and the processes connected with the culture of the grape, had a flavour of poetry about them. The toil, that produces those kindly gifts of Nature which are not the substance of life, but its luxury, is unlike other toil. We are inclined to fancy that it does not bend the sturdy frame, and stiffen the overwrought muscles, like the labour that is devoted in sad, hard earnest, to raise grain for sour bread. Certainly, the sun-burnt young men and dark-cheeked, laughing girls, who weeded the rich acres of Monte Beni, might well enough have passed for inhabitants of an unsophisticated Arcadia. Later in the season, when the true vintage-time should come, and the wine of Sunshine gush into the vats, it was hardly too wild a dream, that Bacchus himself might re-visit the haunts which he loved of old. But, alas, where now would he find the Faun, with whom we see him consorting in so many an antique group!

Donatello's remorseful anguish saddened this primitive and delightful life. Kenyon had a pain of his own, moreover, although not all a pain, in the never quiet, never satisfied yearning of his heart towards Hilda. He was authorized to use little freedom towards that shy maiden, even in his visions; so that he almost reproached himself, when, sometimes, his imagination pictured, in detail, the sweet years that they might spend together, in a retreat like this. It had just that rarest quality of remoteness from the actual and ordinary world, (a remoteness through which all delights might visit them freely, sifted from all troubles,) which lovers so reasonably insist upon, in their ideal arrangements for a happy union. It is possible, indeed, that even Donatello's grief, and Kenyon's pale, sunless affection, lent a charm to Monte Beni, which it could not have retained amid a more redundant joyousness. The sculptor strayed amid its vineyards and orchards, its dells and tangled shrubberies, with somewhat the sensations of an adventurer who should find his way to the site of ancient Eden, and behold its loveliness through the transparency of that gloom which has been brooding over those haunts of innocence, ever since the fall. Adam saw it in a brighter sunshine, but never knew the shade of pensive beauty which Eden won from his expulsion.

It was in the decline of the afternoon that Kenyon returned from his long, musing ramble. Old Tomaso (between whom and himself, for some time past, there had been a mysterious understanding) met him in the entrance-hall, and drew him a little aside.

"The Signorina would speak with you," he whispered.

"In the chapel?" asked the sculptor.

"No; in the saloon beyond it," answered the butler. "The entrance (you once saw the Signorina appear through it) is near the altar, hidden behind the tapestry."

Kenyon lost no time in obeying the summons.

XXXI

THE MARBLE SALOON

IN AN OLD TUSCAN VILLA, a chapel ordinarily makes one among the numerous apartments; though it often happens that the door is permanently closed, the key lost, and the place left to itself, in dusty sanctity, like that chamber in man's heart where he hides his religious awe. This was very much the case with the chapel of Monte Beni. One rainy day, however, in his wanderings through the great, intricate house, Kenyon had unexpectedly found his way into it, and been impressed by its solemn aspect. The arched windows, high upward in the wall, and darkened with dust and cobweb, threw down a dim light that showed the altar, with a picture of a martyrdom above, and some tall tapers ranged before it. They had apparently been lighted, and burned, an hour or two, and been extinguished, perhaps half-a-century before. The marble vase, at the entrance, held some hardened mud at the bottom, accruing from the dust that had settled into it during the gradual evaporation of the holy-water; and a spider (being an insect that delights in pointing the moral of desolation and neglect) had taken pains to weave a prodigiously thick tissue across the circular brim. An old family-banner, tattered by the moths, drooped from the vaulted roof. In niches, there were some mediæval busts of Donatello's forgotten ancestry, and among them, it might be, the forlorn visage of that hapless knight, between whom and the fountain-nymph had occurred such tender love-passages.

Throughout all the jovial prosperity of Monte Beni, this one spot within the domestic walls had kept itself silent, stern, and sad. When the individual or the family retired from song and mirth, they here sought those realities which men do not invite their festive associates to share. And here, on the occasion above referred to, the sculptor had discovered (accidentally, so far as he was concerned, though with a purpose on her part) that there was a guest under Donatello's roof, whose presence the Count himself did not suspect. An interview had since taken place, and he was now summoned to another.

He crossed the chapel, in compliance with Tomaso's instructions, and passing through the side-entrance, found himself in a saloon, of no great size, but more magnificent than he had supposed the villa to contain. As it was vacant, Kenyon had leisure to pace it, once or twice, and examine it with a careless sort of scrutiny, before any person appeared.

This beautiful hall was floored with rich marbles, in artistically arranged figures and compartments. The walls, likewise, were almost entirely cased in marble of various kinds, the prevalent variety being giallo antico, intermixed with verd antique, and others equally precious. The splendour of the giallo antico, however, was what gave character to the saloon; and the large and deep niches, apparently intended for full-length statues, along the walls, were lined with the same costly material. Without visiting Italy, one can have no idea of the beauty and magnificence that are produced by these fittings-up of polished marble. Without such experience, indeed, we do not even know what marble means, in any sense, save as the white limestone of which we carve our mantel-pieces. This rich hall of Monte Beni, moreover, was adorned, at its upper end, with two pillars that seemed to consist of Oriental alabaster; and wherever there was a space vacant of precious and variegated marble, it was frescoed with ornaments in arabesque. Above, there was a coved and vaulted ceiling, glowing with pictured scenes, which affected Kenyon with a vague sense of splendour, without his twisting his neck to gaze at them.

It is one of the special excellencies of such a saloon of polished and richly coloured marble, that decay can never tarnish it. Until the house crumbles down upon it, it shines indestructibly, and, with a little dusting, looks just as brilliant in its three hundredth year, as the day after the final slab of giallo antico was fitted into the wall. To the sculptor, at this first view of it, it seemed a hall where the sun was magically imprisoned, and must always shine. He anticipated Miriam's entrance, arrayed in queenly robes, and beaming with even more than the singular beauty that had heretofore distinguished her.

While this thought was passing through his mind, the pillared door, at the upper end of the saloon, was partly opened, and Miriam appeared. She was very pale, and dressed in deep mourning. As she advanced towards the sculptor, the feebleness of her step was so apparent that he made haste to meet her, apprehending that she might sink down on the marble floor, without the instant support of his arm.

But, with a gleam of her natural self-reliance, she declined his aid, and, after touching her cold hand to his, went and sat down on one of the cushioned divans, that were ranged against the wall.

"You are very ill, Miriam!" said Kenyon, much shocked at her appearance. "I had not thought of this."

"No; not so ill as I seem to you," she answered; adding despondently, "Yet I am ill enough, I believe, to die, unless some change speedily occurs."

"What, then, is your disorder?" asked the sculptor. "And what the remedy?"

"The disorder!" repeated Miriam. "There is none that I know of, save too much life and strength, without a purpose for one or the other. It is my too redundant energy that is slowly—or perhaps rapidly—wearing me away, because I can apply it to no use. The object, which I am bound to consider my only one on earth, fails me utterly. The sacrifice, which I yearn to make, of myself, my hopes, my everything, is coldly put aside. Nothing is left for me, but to brood, brood, brood, all day, all night, in unprofitable longings and repinings!"

"This is very sad, Miriam," said Kenyon.

"Aye, indeed; I fancy so!" she replied, with a short, unnatural laugh.

"With all your activity of mind," resumed he—"so fertile in plans as I have known you—can you imagine no method of bringing your resources into play?"

"My mind is not active any longer," answered Miriam, in a cold, indifferent tone. "It deals with one thought, and no more. One recollection paralyzes it. It is not remorse! Do not think it! I put myself out of the question, and feel neither regret nor penitence on my own behalf. But, what benumbs me—what robs me of all power—(it is no secret for a woman to tell a man, yet I care not though you know it)— is the certainty that I am, and must ever be, an object of horrour in Donatello's sight!"

The sculptor—a young man, and cherishing a love which insulated him from the wild experiences which some men gather—was startled to perceive how Miriam's rich, ill-regulated nature impelled her to fling herself, conscience and all, on one passion, the object of which, intellectually, seemed far beneath her.

"How have you obtained the certainty of which you speak?" asked he, after a pause.

"Oh, by a sure token!" said Miriam. "A gesture, merely; a shudder, a cold shiver that ran through him, one sunny morning, when his hand happened to touch mine! But, it was enough."

"I firmly believe, Miriam," said the sculptor, "that he loves you still."

She started, and a flush of colour came tremulously over the paleness of her cheek.

"Yes," repeated Kenyon, "if my interest in Donatello, (and in yourself, Miriam,) endows me with any true insight, he not only loves you still, but with a force and depth, proportioned to the stronger grasp of his faculties, in their new development."

"Do not deceive me!" said Miriam, growing pale again.

"Not for the world!" replied Kenyon. "Here is what I take to be the truth. There was an interval, no doubt, when the horrour of some calamity (which I need not shape out in my conjectures) threw Donatello into a stupour of misery. Connected with the first shock, there was an intolerable pain and shuddering repugnance, attaching themselves to all the circumstances and surroundings of the event that so terribly affected him. Was his dearest friend involved within the horrour of that moment, he would shrink from her, as he shrank, most of all, from himself. But, as his mind roused itself—as it rose to a higher life than he had hitherto experienced—whatever had been true and permanent within him revived by the self-same impulse! So has it been with his love."

"But, surely," said Miriam, "he knows that I am here! Why, then, (except that I am odious to him,) does he not bid me welcome?"

"He is, I believe, aware of your presence here," answered the sculptor. "Your song, a night or two ago, must have revealed it to him; and, in truth, I had fancied that there was already a consciousness of it in his mind. But, the more passionately he longs for your society, the more religiously he deems himself bound to avoid it. The idea of a life-long penance has taken strong possession of Donatello. He gropes blindly about him for some method of sharp self-torture, and finds, of course, no other so efficacious as this!"

"But, he loves me!" repeated Miriam, in a low voice, to herself.—"Yes; he loves me!"

It was strange to observe the womanly softness that came over her, as she admitted that comfort into her bosom. The cold, unnatural indifference of her manner, a kind of frozen passionateness, which had shocked and chilled the sculptor, disappeared. She blushed, and turned away her eyes, knowing that there was more surprise and joy in their dewy glances, than any man save one ought to detect there.

"In other respects," she inquired, at length, "is he much changed?"

"A wonderful process is going forward in Donatello's mind," answered the sculptor. "The germs of faculties, that have heretofore slept, are fast springing into activity. The world of thought is disclosing itself to his inward sight. He startles me, at times, with his perception of deep truths; and, quite as often, it must be owned, he compels me to smile by the intermixture of his former simplicity with a new intelligence. But, he is bewildered with the revelations that each day brings. Out of his bitter agony, a soul and intellect (I could almost say) have been inspired into him."

"Ah, I could help him here!" cried Miriam, clasping her hands. "And how sweet a toil to bend and adapt my whole nature to do him good! To instruct, to elevate, to enrich his mind, with the wealth that would flow in upon me, had I such a motive for acquiring it!—Who else can perform the task? Who else has the tender sympathy which he requires? Who else, save only me—a woman, a sharer in the same dread secret, a partaker in one identical guilt—could meet him on such terms of intimate equality as the case demands? With this object before me, I might feel a right to live! Without it, it is a shame for me to have lived so long!"

"I fully agree with you," said Kenyon, "that your true place is by his side."

"Surely it is," replied Miriam. "If Donatello is entitled to aught on earth, it is to my complete self-sacrifice for his sake. It does not weaken his claim, methinks, that my only prospect of happiness (a fearful word, however) lies in the good that may accrue to him from our intercourse. But he rejects me! He will not listen to the whisper of his heart, telling him that she, most wretched, who beguiled him into evil, might guide him to a higher innocence than that from which he fell. How is this first, great difficulty to be obviated?"

"It lies at your own option, Miriam, to do away the obstacle, at any moment," remarked the sculptor. "It is but to ascend Donatello's tower, and you will meet him there, under the Eye of God."

"I dare not!" answered Miriam. "No; I dare not!"

"Do you fear," asked the sculptor, "the dread Eye-Witness whom I have named?"

"No; for, as far as I can see into that cloudy and inscrutable thing, my heart, it has none but pure motives," replied Miriam. "But, my friend, you little know what a weak, or what a strong creature, a woman is! I fear not Heaven, (in this case, at least,) but—shall I confess it?—I am greatly in dread of Donatello. Once, he shuddered at my touch. If he shudder once again, or frown, I die!"

Kenyon could not but marvel at the subjection into which this proud and self-dependent woman had wilfully flung herself, hanging her life upon the chance of an angry or favourable regard from a person who, a little while before, had seemed the plaything of a moment. But, in Miriam's eyes, Donatello was always, thenceforth, invested with the tragic dignity of their hour of crime; and, furthermore, the keen and deep insight, with which her love endowed her, enabled her to know him far better than he could be known by ordinary observation. Beyond all question, since she loved him so, there was a force in Donatello worthy of her respect and love.

"You see my weakness," said Miriam, flinging out her hands, as a person does when a defect is acknowledged, and beyond remedy. "What I need, now, is an opportunity to show my strength."

"It has occurred to me," Kenyon remarked, "that the time is come, when it may be desirable to remove Donatello from the complete seclusion in which he buries himself. He has struggled long enough with one idea. He now needs a variety of thought, which cannot be otherwise so readily supplied to him as through the medium of a variety of scenes. His mind is awakened, now; his heart, though full of pain, is no longer benumbed. They should have food and solace. If he linger here much longer, I fear that he may sink back into a lethargy. The extreme excitability, which circumstances have imparted to his moral system, has its dangers, and its advantages; it being one of the dangers, that an obdurate scar may supervene upon its very tenderness. Solitude has done what it could for him; now, for a while, let him be enticed into the outer world."

"What is your plan, then?" asked Miriam.

"Simply," replied Kenyon, "to persuade Donatello to be my companion in a ramble among these hills and valleys. The little adventures and vicissitudes of travel will do him infinite good. After his recent profound experience, he will re-create the world by the new eyes with which he will regard it. He will escape, I hope, out of a morbid life, and find his way into a healthy one."

"And what is to be my part in this process?" inquired Miriam sadly, and not without jealousy. "You are taking him from me, and putting yourself, and all manner of living interests, into the place which I ought to fill!"

"It would rejoice me, Miriam, to yield the entire responsibility of this office to yourself," answered the sculptor. "I do not pretend to be the guide and counsellor whom Donatello needs; for, to mention no other obstacle, I am a man, and, between man and man, there is always an insuperable gulf. They can never quite grasp each other's hands; and therefore man never derives any intimate help, any heart-sustenance, from his brother man, but from woman—his mother, his sister, or his wife. Be Donatello's friend at need, therefore, and most gladly will I resign him!"

"It is not kind, to taunt me thus," said Miriam. "I have told you that I cannot do what you suggest, because I dare not."

"Well, then," rejoined the sculptor, "see if there is any possibility of adapting yourself to my scheme. The incidents of a journey often fling people together in the oddest, and therefore the most natural way. Supposing you were to find yourself on the same route, a re-union with Donatello might ensue, and Providence have a larger hand in it than either of us."

"It is not a hopeful plan," said Miriam, shaking her head, after a moment's thought. "Yet I will not reject it without a trial. Only, in case it fail, here is a resolution to which I bind myself, come what come may! You know the bronze statue of Pope Julius, in the great square of Perugia? I remember standing in the shadow of that statue, one sunny noontime, and being impressed by its paternal aspect, and fancying that a blessing fell upon me from its outstretched hand. Ever since, I have had a superstition, (you will call it foolish, but sad and ill-fated persons always dream such things,) that, if I waited long enough in that same spot, some good event would come to pass. Well, my friend, precisely a fortnight after you begin your tour, (unless we sooner meet,) bring Donatello, at noon, to the base of the statue. You will find me there!"

Kenyon assented to the proposed arrangement, and, after some conversation respecting his contemplated line of travel, prepared to take his leave. As he met Miriam's eyes, in bidding farewell, he was surprised at the new, tender gladness that beamed out of them, and at the appearance of health and bloom, which, in this little while, had overspread her face.

"May I tell you, Miriam," said he, smiling, "that you are still as beautiful as ever?"

"You have a right to notice it," she replied, "for, if it be so, my faded bloom has been revived by the hopes you give me. Do you, then, think me beautiful? I rejoice, most truly. Beauty—if I possess it—shall be one of the instruments by which I will try to educate and elevate him, to whose good I solely dedicate myself."

The sculptor had nearly reached the door, when, hearing her call him, he turned back, and beheld Miriam still standing where he had left her, in the magnificent hall, which seemed only a fit setting for her beauty. She beckoned him to return.

"You are a man of refined taste," said she. "More than that—a man of delicate sensibility. Now tell me frankly, and on your honour! Have I not shocked you, many times, during this interview, by my betrayal of woman's cause, my lack of feminine modesty, my reckless, passionate, most indecorous avowal, that I live only in the life of one who perhaps scorns and shudders at me?"

Thus adjured, however difficult the point to which she brought him, the sculptor was not a man to swerve aside from the simple truth.

"Miriam," replied he, "you exaggerate the impression made upon my mind; but it has been painful, and somewhat of the character which you suppose."

"I knew it," said Miriam, mournfully, but with no resentment. "What remains of my finer nature would have told me so, even if it had not been perceptible in all your manner. Well, my dear friend, when you go back to Rome, tell Hilda what her severity has done! She was all Womanhood to me; and when she cast me off, I had no longer any terms to keep with the reserves and decorums of my sex. Hilda has set me free! Pray tell her so, from Miriam, and thank her!"

"I shall tell Hilda nothing that will give her pain," answered Kenyon. "But, Miriam, (though I know not what passed between her and yourself,) I feel—and let the noble frankness of your disposition forgive me, if I say so—I feel that she was right. You have a thousand admirable qualities. Whatever mass of evil may have fallen into your life, (pardon me, but your own words suggest it,) you are still as capable as ever of many high and heroic virtues. But the white, shining purity of Hilda's nature is a thing apart; and she is bound, by the undefiled material of which God moulded her, to keep that severity which I, as well as you, have recognized."

"Oh, you are right!" said Miriam. "I never questioned it; though, as I told you, when she cast me off, it severed some few remaining bonds between me and decorous Womanhood. But, were there anything to forgive, I do forgive her. May you win her virgin heart; for, methinks, there can be few men, in this evil world, who are not more unworthy of her than yourself!"

XXXII

SCENES BY THE WAY

WHEN it came to the point of quitting the reposeful life of Monte Beni, the sculptor was not without regrets, and would willingly have dreamed, a little longer, of the sweet paradise on earth that Hilda's presence there might make. Nevertheless, amid all its repose, he had begun to be sensible of a restless melancholy, to which the cultivators of the ideal arts are more liable than sturdier men. On his own part, therefore, and leaving Donatello out of the case, he would have judged it well to go. He made parting visits to the legendary Dell, and to other delightful spots with which he had grown familiar; he climbed the tower again, and saw a sunset and a moonrise over the great valley; he drank, on the eve of his departure, one flask, and then another, of the Monte Beni Sunshine, and stored up its flavour in his memory, as the standard of what is exquisite in wine. These things accomplished, Kenyon was ready for the journey.

Donatello had not very easily been stirred out of the peculiar sluggishness, which enthrals and bewitches melancholy people. He had offered merely a passive resistance, however, not an active one, to his friend's schemes; and when the appointed hour came, he yielded to the impulse which

Kenyon failed not to apply, and was started upon the journey, before he had made up his mind to undertake it. They wandered forth at large, like two knights-errant, among the valleys, and the mountains, and the old mountain-towns, of that picturesque and lovely region. Save to keep the appointment with Miriam, a fortnight thereafter, in the great square of Perugia, there was nothing more definite in the sculptor's plan, than that they should let themselves be blown hither and thither, like winged seeds, that mount upon each wandering breeze. Yet there was an idea of fatality, implied in the simile of the winged seeds, which did not altogether suit Kenyon's fancy; for, if you look closely into the matter, it will be seen that whatever appears most vagrant, and utterly purposeless, turns out, in the end, to have been impelled the most surely on a pre-ordained and unswerving track. Chance and change love to deal with men's settled plans, not with their idle vagaries. If we desire unexpected and unimaginable events, we should contrive an iron frame-work, such as we fancy may compel the future to take one inevitable shape; then comes in the Unexpected, and shatters our design in fragments.

The travellers set forth on horseback, and purposed to perform much of their aimless journeyings, under the moon, and in the cool of the morning or evening twilight; the midday sun, while summer had hardly begun to trail its departing skirts over Tuscany, being still too fervid to allow of noontide exposure.

For a while, they wandered in that same broad valley which Kenyon had viewed with such delight from the Monte Beni tower. The sculptor soon began to enjoy the idle activity of their new life, which the lapse of a day or two sufficed to establish as a kind of system; it is so natural for mankind to be nomadic, that a very little taste of that primitive mode of existence subverts the settled habits of many preceding years.

Kenyon's cares, and whatever gloomy ideas before possessed him, seemed to be left at Monte Beni, and were scarcely remembered, by the time that its gray tower grew indistinguishable on the brown hill-side. His perceptive faculties (which had found little exercise of late, amid so thoughtful a way of life) became keen, and kept his eyes busy with a hundred agreeable scenes.

He delighted in the picturesque bits of rustic character and manners, so little of which ever comes upon the surface of our life at home. There, for example, were the old women, tending pigs or sheep by the wayside. As they followed the vagrant steps of their charge, these venerable ladies kept spinning yarn, with that elsewhere forgotten contrivance, the distaff; and so wrinkled and stern-looking were they, that you might have taken them for the Parcae, spinning the threads of human destiny. In contrast with their great-grandmothers were the children, leading goats of shaggy beard, tied by the horns, and letting them browze on branch and shrub. It is the fashion of Italy to add the petty industry of age and childhood to the sum of human toil. To the eyes of an observer from the Western world, it was a strange spectacle to see sturdy, sun-burnt creatures, in petticoats, but otherwise manlike, toiling side by side with male labourers, in the rudest work of the fields. These sturdy women (if as such we must recognize them) wore the high-crowned, broad-brimmed hat of Tuscan straw, the customary female head-apparel; and, as every breeze blew back its breadth of brim, the sunshine constantly added depth to the brown glow of their cheeks. The elder sisterhood, however, set off their witch-like ugliness to the worst advantage with black-felt hats, bequeathed them, one would fancy, by their long-buried husbands.

Another ordinary sight, as sylvan as the above, and more agreeable, was a girl, bearing on her back a huge bundle of green-twigs and shrubs, or grass, intermixed with scarlet poppies and blue flowers; the verdant burthen being sometimes of such size as to hide the bearer's figure, and seem a self-moving mass of fragrant bloom and verdure. Oftener, however, the bundle reached only half-way down the back of the rustic nymph, leaving in sight her well-developed lower limbs, and the crooked knife, hanging behind her, with which she had been reaping this strange harvest-sheaf. A pre-Raphaelite artist (he, for instance, who painted so marvellously a wind-swept heap of autumnal leaves) might find an admirable subject in one of these Tuscan girls, stepping with a free, erect, and graceful carriage. The miscellaneous herbage and tangled twigs and blossoms of her bundle, crowning her head, (while her ruddy, comely face looks out between the hanging side-festoons like a larger flower,) would give the painter boundless scope for the minute delineation which he loves.

Though mixed up with what was rude and earthlike, there was still a remote, dreamlike, Arcadian charm, which is scarcely to be found in the daily toil of other lands. Among the pleasant features of the wayside were always the vines, clambering on fig-trees, or other sturdy trunks; they wreathed themselves, in huge and rich festoons, from one tree to another, suspending clusters of ripening grapes in the interval between. Under such careless mode of culture, the luxuriant vine is a lovelier spectacle than where it produces a more precious liquour, and is therefore more artificially restrained and trimmed. Nothing can be more picturesque than an old grape-vine, with almost a trunk of its own, clinging fast around its supporting tree. Nor does the picture lack its moral. You might twist it to more than one grave purpose, as you saw how the knotted, serpentine growth imprisoned within its strong embrace the friend, that had supported its tender infancy; and how (as seemingly flexible natures are prone to do) it converted the sturdier tree entirely to its own selfish ends, extending its innumerable arms on every bough, and permitting hardly a leaf to sprout except its own. It occurred to Kenyon, that the enemies of the vine, in his native land, might here have seen an emblem of the remorseless gripe, which the habit of vinous enjoyment lays upon its victim, possessing him wholly, and letting him live no life but such as it bestows.

The scene was not less characteristic, when their path led the two wanderers through some small, ancient town. There, besides the peculiarities of present life, they saw tokens of the life that had long ago been lived and flung aside. The little town, such as we see in our mind's eye, would have its gate and surrounding walls, so ancient and massive that ages had not sufficed to crumble them away; but, in the lofty upper portion of the gateway (still standing over the empty arch, when there was no longer a gate to shut) there would be a dove-cote, and peaceful doves for the only warders. Pumpkins lay ripening in the open chambers of the structure. Then, as for the town-wall, on the outside, an orchard extends peacefully along its base, full, not of apple-trees, but of those old humourists with gnarled trunks and twisted boughs, the olives. Houses have been built upon the ramparts, or burrowed out of their ponderous foundation. Even the gray, martial towers, crowned with ruined turrets, have been converted into rustic habitations, from the windows of which hang ears of Indian corn. At a door (that has been broken through the massive stone-work, where it was meant to be strongest) some contadini are winnowing grain. Small windows, too, are pierced through the whole line of ancient wall, so that it seems a row of dwellings, with one continuous front, built in a strange style of needless strength; but remnants of the old battlements and machicolations are interspersed with the homely chambers and earthen-tiled house-

tops; and, all along its extent, both grape-vines and running
flower-shrubs are encouraged to clamber and sport over the
roughnesses of its decay.

Finally, the long grass, intermixed with weeds and wild-
flowers, waves on the uppermost height of the shattered
rampart; and it is exceedingly pleasant, in the golden sunshine of the afternoon, to behold the warlike precinct so
friendly, in its old days, and so overgrown with rural peace.
In its guard-rooms, its prison-chambers, and scooped out of
its ponderous breadth, there are dwellings, now-a-days, where
happy human lives are spent. Human parents and broods of
children nestle in them, even as the swallows nestle in the
little crevices along the broken summit of the wall.

Passing through the gateway of this same little town,
(challenged only by those watchful sentinels, the pigeons,)
we find ourselves in a long, narrow street, paved from side
to side with flag-stones, in the old Roman fashion. Nothing
can exceed the grim ugliness of the houses, most of which
are three or four stories high, stone-built, gray, dilapidated,
or half-covered with plaister in patches, and contiguous all
along from end to end of the town. Nature, in the shape of
tree, shrub, or grassy sidewalk, is as much shut out from the
one street of the rustic village, as from the heart of any
swarming city. The dark and half-ruinous habitations (with
their small windows, many of which are drearily closed with
wooden shutters) are but magnified hovels, piled story upon
story, and squalid with the grime that successive ages have
left behind them. It would be a hideous scene to contemplate
in a rainy day, or when no human life pervaded it. In the
summer-noon, however, it possesses vivacity enough to keep
itself cheerful; for all the within-doors of the village then
bubbles over upon the flag-stones, or looks out from the small
windows, and from here and there a balcony. Some of the
populace are at the butcher's shop; others are at the fountain,

which gushes into a marble basin that resembles an antique sarcophagus. A tailor is sewing before his door, with a young priest seated sociably beside him; a burly friar goes by, with an empty wine-barrel on his head; children are at play; women, at their own door-steps, mend clothes, embroider, weave hats of Tuscan straw, or twirl the distaff. Many idlers, meanwhile, strolling from one group to another, let the warm day slide by in the sweet, interminable task of doing nothing.

From all these people there comes a babblement that seems quite disproportioned to the number of tongues that make it. So many words are not uttered in a New England village throughout the year, (except it be at a political caucus or town-meeting,) as are spoken here, with no especial purpose, in a single day. Neither so many words, nor so much laughter; for people talk about nothing as if they were terribly in earnest, and make merry at nothing, as if it were the best of all possible jokes. In so long a time as they have existed, and within such narrow precincts, these little walled towns are brought into a closeness of society that makes them but a larger household. All the inhabitants are akin to each, and each to all; they assemble in the street as their common saloon, and thus live and die in a familiarity of intercourse, such as never can be known where a village is open at either end, and all roundabout, and has ample room within itself.

Stuck up beside the door of one house, in this village-street, is a withered bough; and, on a stone-seat, just under the shadow of the bough, sits a party of jolly drinkers, making proof of the new wine, or quaffing the old, as their often-tried and comfortable friend. Kenyon draws bridle here, (for the bough, or bush, is a symbol of the wine-shop, at this day, in Italy, as it was three hundred years ago, in England,) and calls for a goblet of the deep-hued purple juice, well diluted with water from the fountain. The Sunshine of Monte Beni would be welcome, now. Meanwhile, Donatello has

ridden onward, but alights where a shrine, with a burning
lamp before it, is built into the wall of an inn-stable. He
kneels, and crosses himself, and mutters a brief prayer, without attracting notice from the passers-by; many of whom are
parenthetically devout, in a similar fashion. By this time,
the sculptor has drunk off his wine-and-water, and our two
travellers resume their way, emerging from the opposite gate
of the village.

Before them, again, lies the broad valley, with a mist so
thinly scattered over it as to be perceptible only in the distance, and most so in the nooks of the hills. Now that we
have called it mist, it seems a mistake not rather to have
called it sunshine; the glory of so much light being mingled
with so little gloom, in the airy material of that vapour. Be
it mist or sunshine, it adds a touch of ideal beauty to the
scene, almost persuading the spectator that this valley and
those hills are visionary, because their visible atmosphere is
so like the substance of a dream.

Immediately about them, however, there were abundant
tokens that the country was not really the paradise it looked
to be, at a casual glance. Neither the wretched cottages nor
the dreary farm-houses seemed to partake of the prosperity,
with which so kindly a climate, and so fertile a portion of
Mother Earth's bosom, should have filled them, one and all.
But, possibly, the peasant-inhabitants do not exist in so grimy
a poverty, and in homes so comfortless, as a stranger, with his
native ideas of those matters, would be likely to imagine. The
Italians appear to possess none of that emulative pride which
we see in our New England villages, where every house-
holder, according to his taste and means, endeavours to make
his homestead an ornament to the grassy and elm-shadowed
wayside. In Italy, there are no neat door-steps and thresholds;
no pleasant, vine-sheltered porches; none of those grass-plots
or smoothly shorn lawns, which hospitably invite the imagina-

tion into the sweet domestic interiors of English life. Every-thing, however sunny and luxuriant may be the scene around, is especially disheartening in the immediate neighborhood of an Italian home.

An artist, it is true, might often thank his stars for those old houses, so picturesquely time-stained, and with the plais-ter falling in blotches from the ancient brick-work. The prison-like, iron-barred windows, and the wide-arched, dismal entrance, admitting on one hand to the stable, on the other to the kitchen, might impress him as far better worth his pencil than the newly painted pine-boxes, in which (if he be an American) his countrymen live and thrive. But there is reason to suspect that a people are waning to decay and ruin, the moment that their life becomes fascinating either in the poet's imagination or the painter's eye.

As usual, on Italian waysides, the wanderers passed great black Crosses, hung with all the instruments of the sacred agony and passion; there was the crown of thorns, the hammer and nails, the pincers, the spear, the sponge, and perched over the whole, the cock that crowed to Saint Peter's remorseful conscience. Thus, while the fertile scene showed the never-failing beneficence of the Creator towards man in his transitory state, these symbols reminded each wayfarer of the Saviour's infinitely greater love for him, as an immortal spirit. Beholding these consecrated stations, the idea seemed to strike Donatello of converting the otherwise aimless journey into a penitential pilgrimage. At each of them, he alighted, to kneel, and kiss the Cross, and humbly press his forehead against its foot; and this so invariably, that the sculptor soon learned to draw bridle of his own accord. It may be, too, heretic as he was, that Kenyon likewise put up a prayer, rendered more fervent by the symbols before his eyes, for the peace of his friend's conscience and the pardon of the sin that so oppressed him.

Not only at the Crosses did Donatello kneel, but at each of the many shrines, where the Blessed Virgin in fresco, (faded with sunshine and half-washed out with showers,) looked benignly at her worshipper; or where she was represented in a wooden image, or a bas-relief of plaister or marble, as accorded with the means of the devout person who built, or restored from a mediæval antiquity, these places of wayside worship. They were everywhere; under arched niches, or in little pent-houses with a brick-tiled roof, just large enough to shelter them; or perhaps in some bit of old Roman masonry, the founders of which had died before the Advent; or in the wall of a country-inn or farm-house; or at the midway point of a bridge; or in the shallow cavity of a natural rock, or high upward in the deep cuts of the road. It appeared to the sculptor, that Donatello prayed the more earnestly and the more hopefully at these shrines, because the mild face of the Madonna promised him to intercede, as a tender mother, betwixt the poor culprit and the awfulness of judgment.

It was beautiful to observe, indeed, how tender was the soul of man and woman towards the Virgin Mother, in recognition of the tenderness which, as their faith taught them, she immortally cherishes towards all human souls. In the wire-work screen, before each shrine, hung offerings of roses, or whatever flower was sweetest and most seasonable; some, already wilted and withered; some, fresh with that very morning's dew-drops. Flowers there were, too, that (being artificial) never bloomed on earth, nor would ever fade. The thought occurred to Kenyon, that flower-pots, with living plants, might be set within the niches, or even that rose-trees, and all kinds of flowering-shrubs, might be reared under the shrines and taught to twine and wreathe themselves around; so that the Virgin should dwell within a bower of verdure, bloom, and fragrant freshness, symbolizing a homage perpetually new. There are many things in the religious customs of these people that seem good; many things, at least, that might be both good and beautiful, if the soul of goodness and the sense of beauty were as much alive in the Italians, now, as they must have been, when those customs were first imagined and adopted. But, instead of blossoms on the shrub, or freshly gathered, with the dew-drops on their leaves, their worship, now-a-days, is best symbolized by the artificial flower.

The sculptor fancied, moreover, (but perhaps it was his heresy that suggested the idea,) that it would be of happy influence to place a comfortable and shady seat beneath every wayside shrine. Then, the weary and sun-scorched traveller, while resting himself under her protecting shadow, might thank the Virgin for her hospitality. Nor, perchance, were he to regale himself, even in such a consecrated spot, with the fragrance of a pipe, would it rise to Heaven more offensively than the smoke of priestly incense. We do ourselves wrong, and too meanly estimate the Holiness above us, when we deem that any act or enjoyment, good in itself, is not good to do religiously.

Whatever may be the iniquities of the Papal system, it was a wise and lovely sentiment, that set up the frequent shrine and Cross, along the roadside. No wayfarer, bent on whatever worldly errand, can fail to be reminded, at every mile or two, that this is not the business which most concerns him. The pleasure-seeker is silently admonished to look heavenward for a joy infinitely greater than he now pursues. The wretch in temptation beholds the Cross, and is warned, that, if he yield, the Saviour's agony for his sake will have been endured in vain. The stubborn criminal, whose heart has long been like a stone, feels it throb anew with dread and hope; and our poor Donatello, as he went kneeling from shrine to Cross, and from Cross to shrine, doubtless found an efficacy in these symbols that helped him towards a higher penitence.

Whether the young Count of Monte Beni noticed the fact, or no, there was more than one incident of their journey that led Kenyon to believe, that they were attended, or closely followed, or preceded, near at hand, by some one who took an interest in their motions. As it were, the step, the sweeping garment, the faintly heard breath, of an invisible companion, was beside them, as they went on their way. It was like a dream that had strayed out of their slumber and was haunting them in the daytime, when its shadowy substance could have neither density nor outline, in the too obtrusive light. After sunset, it grew a little more distinct.

"On the left of that last shrine," asked the sculptor, as they rode, under the moon, "did you observe the figure of a woman kneeling, with her face hidden in her hands?"

"I never looked that way," replied Donatello. "I was saying my own prayer. It was some penitent, perchance. May the Blessed Virgin be the more gracious to the poor soul, because she is a woman!"

XXXIII

PICTURED WINDOWS

A FTER wide wanderings through the valley, the two travellers directed their course towards its boundary of hills. Here, the natural scenery and men's modifications of it immediately took a different aspect from that of the fertile and smiling plain. Not unfrequently, there was a convent on the hill-side; or, on some insulated promontory, a ruined castle, once the den of a robber chieftain, who was accustomed to dash down from his commanding height upon the road that wound below. For ages back, the old fortress had been flinging down its crumbling ramparts, stone by stone, towards the grimy village at its foot.

Their road wound onward among the hills, which rose steep and lofty from the scanty level space that lay between them. They continually thrust their great bulks before the wayfarers, as if grimly resolute to forbid their passage, or closed abruptly behind them, when they still dared to proceed. A gigantic hill would set its foot right down before them, and only at the last moment, would grudgingly withdraw it, just far enough to let them creep towards another obstacle. Adown these rough heights were visible the dry tracks of many a mountain-torrent, that had lived a life too fierce and passionate to be a long one. Or, perhaps a stream was yet hurrying shyly along the edge of a far wider bed of pebbles and shelving rock than it seemed to need, though not too wide for the swollen rage of which this shy rivulet was capable. A stone bridge bestrode it, the ponderous arches of which were upheld and rendered indestructible by the weight of the very stones that threatened to crush them down. Old Roman toil was perceptible in the foundations of that massive bridge; the first weight that it ever bore was that of an army of the Republic.

Threading these defiles, they would arrive at some immemorial city, crowning the high summit of a hill with its cathedral, its many churches, and public edifices, all of Gothic architecture. With no more level ground than a single piazza, in the midst, the ancient town tumbled its crooked and narrow streets down the mountain-side, through arched passages and by steps of stone. The aspect of everything was awfully old; older, indeed, in its effect on the imagination, than Rome itself, because history does not lay its finger on these forgotten edifices and tell us all about their origin. Etruscan princes may have dwelt in them. A thousand years, at all events, would seem but a middle age for these structures. They are built of such huge, square stones, that their appearance of ponderous durability distresses the beholder with the idea that they can never fall—never crumble away—never be less fit than now for human habitation. Many of them may once have been palaces, and still retain a squalid grandeur. But, gazing at them, we recognize how undesirable it is to build the tabernacle of our brief lifetime out of permanent materials, and with a view to their being occupied by future generations.

All towns should be made capable of purification by fire, or of decay within each half-century. Otherwise, they become the hereditary haunts of vermin and noisomeness, besides standing apart from the possibility of such improvements as are constantly introduced into the rest of man's contrivances and accommodations. It is beautiful, no doubt, and exceedingly satisfactory to some of our natural instincts, to imagine our far posterity dwelling under the same roof-tree as ourselves. Still, when people insist on building indestructible houses, they incur, or their children do, a misfortune analogous to that of the Sibyl, when she obtained the grievous boon of immortality. So, we may build almost immortal habitations, it is true; but we cannot keep them from growing old, musty, unwholesome, dreary, full of death-scents, ghosts, and murder-stains; in short, habitations such as one sees everywhere in Italy, be they hovels or palaces.

"You should go with me to my native country," observed the sculptor to Donatello. "In that fortunate land, each generation has only its own sins and sorrows to bear. Here, it seems as if all the weary and dreary Past were piled upon the back of the Present. If I were to lose my spirits, in this country—if I were to suffer any heavy misfortune here—methinks it would be impossible to stand up against it, under such adverse influences!"

"The sky itself is an old roof, now," answered the Count; "and, no doubt, the sins of mankind have made it gloomier than it used to be."

"Oh, my poor Faun," thought Kenyon to himself, "how art thou changed!"

A city, like this of which we speak, seems a sort of stony growth out of the hill-side, or a fossilized town; so ancient and strange it looks, without enough of life and juiciness in it to be any longer susceptible of decay. An earthquake would afford it the only chance of being ruined, beyond its present ruin.

Yet, though dead to all the purposes for which we live to-day, the place has its glorious recollections, and not merely rude and warlike ones, but those of brighter and milder triumphs, the fruits of which we still enjoy. Italy can count several of these lifeless towns, which, four or five hundred years ago, were each the birth-place of its own school of art; nor have they yet forgotten to be proud of the dark, old pictures, and the faded frescoes, the pristine beauty of which was a light and gladness to the world. But, now, unless one happens to be a painter, these famous works make us miserably desperate. They are poor, dim ghosts of what, when Giotto or Cimabue first created them, threw a splendour along the stately aisles; so far gone towards nothingness, in our day, that scarcely a hint of design or expression can glimmer through the dusk. Those early artists did well to paint their frescoes. Glowing on the church-walls, they might be looked upon as symbols of the living spirit that made Catholicism a true religion, and that glorified it as long as it retained a genuine life; they filled the transepts with a radiant throng of Saints and Angels, and threw around the high altar a faint reflection (as much as mortals could see, or bear) of a Diviner Presence. But, now that the colours are so wretchedly bedimmed—now that blotches of plaistered wall dot the frescoes all over, like a mean reality thrusting itself through life's brightest illusions—the next best artist to Cimabue, or Giotto, or Ghirlandaio, or Pinturicchio, will be he that shall reverently cover their ruined master-pieces with white-wash!

Kenyon, however, being an earnest student and critic of Art, lingered long before these pathetic relics; and Donatello, in his present phase of penitence, thought no time spent amiss while he could be kneeling before an altar. Whenever they found a cathedral, therefore, or a Gothic church, the two travellers were of one mind to enter it. In some of these holy edifices, they saw pictures that time had not dimmed nor injured in the least, though they perhaps belonged to as old a school of Art as any that were perishing around them. These were the painted windows; and, as often as he gazed at them, the sculptor blessed the mediæval time, and its gorgeous contrivances of splendour; for surely the skill of man has never accomplished, nor his mind imagined, any other beauty or glory worthy to be compared with these.

It is the special excellence of pictured glass, that the light, which falls merely on the outside of other pictures, is here interfused throughout the work; it illuminates the design, and invests it with a living radiance; and, in requital, the unfading colours transmute the common daylight into a miracle of richness and glory, in its passage through the heavenly substance of the blessed and angelic shapes, which throng the high-arched window.

"It is a woeful thing," cried Kenyon, while one of these frail, yet enduring and fadeless pictures threw its hues on his face, and on the pavement of the church around him,—"a sad necessity, that any Christian soul should pass from earth, without once seeing an antique painted window, with the bright Italian sunshine glowing through it! There is no other such true symbol of the glories of the better world, where a celestial radiance will be inherent in all things and persons, and render each continually transparent to the sight of all."

"But what a horrour it would be," said Donatello sadly, "if there were a soul among them through which the light could not be transfused!"

"Yes; and perhaps this is to be the punishment of sin," replied the sculptor. "Not that it shall be made evident to the Universe, (which can profit nothing by such knowledge,) but that it shall insulate the sinner from all sweet society by rendering him impermeable to light, and therefore unrecognizable in the abode of heavenly simplicity and truth. Then, what remains for him, but the dreariness of infinite and eternal solitude!"

"That would be a horrible destiny, indeed!" said Donatello.

His voice, as he spoke the words, had a hollow and dreary cadence, as if he anticipated some such frozen solitude for himself. A figure in a dark robe was lurking in the obscurity of a side-chapel, close by, and made an impulsive movement forward, but hesitated, as Donatello spoke again.

"But there might be a more miserable torture than to be solitary forever," said he. "Think of having a single companion in eternity, and, instead of finding any consolation, or, at all events, variety of torture, to see your own weary, weary sin, repeated in that inseparable soul!"

"I think, my dear Count, you have never read Dante," observed Kenyon. "That idea is somewhat in his style, but I cannot help regretting that it came into your mind just then."

The dark-robed figure had shrunk back, and was quite lost to sight among the shadows of the chapel.

"There was an English poet," resumed Kenyon, turning again towards the window, "who speaks of the 'dim, religious light,' transmitted through painted glass. I always admired this richly descriptive phrase; but, though he was once in Italy, I question whether Milton ever saw any but the dingy pictures in the dusty windows of English cathedrals, imperfectly shown by the gray English daylight. He would else have illuminated that word, 'dim,' with some epithet that should not chase away the dimness, yet should make it glow like a million of rubies, sapphires, emeralds, and topazes. Is it not so with yonder window? The pictures are most brilliant in themselves, yet dim with tenderness and reverence, because God Himself is shining through them!"

"The pictures fill me with emotion, but not such as you seem to experience," said Donatello. "I tremble at those awful

Saints, and, most of all, at the figure above them. He glows with divine wrath!"

"My dear friend," exclaimed Kenyon, "how strangely your eyes have transmuted the expression of the figure! It is divine Love, not wrath!"

"To my eyes," said Donatello stubbornly, "it is wrath, not Love! Each must interpret for himself."

The friends left the church, and looking up, from the exteriour, at the window which they had just been contemplating within, nothing was visible but the merest outline of dusky shapes. Neither the individual likeness of Saint, Angel, nor Saviour, and far less the combined scheme and purport of the picture, could anywise be made out. That miracle of radiant art, thus viewed, was nothing better than an incomprehensible obscurity, without a gleam of beauty to induce the beholder to attempt unravelling it.

"And this," thought the sculptor, "is a most forcible emblem of the different aspect of religious truth and sacred story, as viewed from the warm interiour of Belief, or from its cold and dreary outside. Christian Faith is a grand Cathedral, with divinely pictured windows. Standing without, you see no glory, nor can possibly imagine any; standing within, every ray of light reveals a harmony of unspeakable splendours!"

After Kenyon and Donatello emerged from the church, however, they had better opportunity for acts of charity and mercy than for religious contemplation; being immediately surrounded by a swarm of beggars, who are the present possessors of Italy, and share the spoil of the stranger with the fleas and musquitoes, their formidable allies. These pests (the human ones) had hunted the two travellers at every stage of their journey. From village to village, ragged boys and girls kept almost under the horses' feet; hoary grandsires and grandams caught glimpses of their approach, and hobbled to intercept them at some point of vantage; blind men stared them out of countenance with their sightless orbs; women held up their unwashed babies; cripples displayed their wooden legs, their grievous scars, their dangling, boneless arms, their broken backs, their burthen of a hump, or whatever infirmity or deformity Providence had assigned them for an inheritance. On the highest mountain-summit—in the most shadowy ravine—there was a beggar waiting for them. In one small village, Kenyon had the curiosity to count merely how many children were crying, whining, and bellowing, all at once, for alms. They proved to be more than forty of as ragged and dirty little imps as any in the world; besides whom, all the wrinkled matrons, and most of the village-maids, and not a few stalwart men, held out their hands, grimly, piteously, or smilingly, in the forlorn hope of whatever trifle of coin might remain in pockets already so fearfully taxed. Had they been permitted, they would gladly have knelt down and worshipped the travellers, and have cursed them, without rising from their knees, if the expected boon failed to be awarded.

Yet they were not so miserably poor but that the grown people kept houses over their heads. In the way of food, they had, at least, vegetables in their little gardens, pigs and chickens to kill, eggs to fry into omelets with oil, wine to drink, and many other things to make life comfortable. As for the children, when no more small coin appeared to be forthcoming, they began to laugh, and play, and turn heels over head, showing themselves jolly and vivacious brats, and evidently as well fed as need be. The truth is, the Italian peasantry look upon strangers as the almoners of Providence, and therefore feel no more shame in asking and receiving alms, than in availing themselves of providential bounties in whatever other form.

In accordance with his nature, Donatello was always exceedingly charitable to these ragged battalions, and appeared to derive a certain consolation from the prayers which many of them put up in his behalf. In Italy, a copper coin of minute value will often make all the difference between a vindictive curse, (death by apoplexy being the favourite one,) mumbled in an old witch's toothless jaws, and a prayer from the same lips, so earnest that it would seem to reward the charitable soul with at least a puff of grateful breath, to help him heavenward. Good wishes being so cheap, though possibly not very efficacious, and anathemas so exceedingly bitter, (even if the greater portion of their poison remain in the mouth that utters them,) it may be wise to expend some reasonable amount in the purchase of the former. Donatello invariably did so; and as he distributed his alms under the pictured window, of which we have been speaking, no less than seven ancient women lifted their hands and besought blessings on his head.

"Come," said the sculptor, rejoicing at the happier expression which he saw in his friend's face, "I think your steed will not stumble with you to-day. Each of these old dames looks as much like Horace's Atra Cura as can well be conceived; but, though there are seven of them, they will make your burthen on horseback lighter, instead of heavier!"

"Are we to ride far?" asked the Count.

"A tolerable journey betwixt now and tomorrow noon," Kenyon replied; "for, at that hour, I purpose to be standing by the Pope's statue in the great square of Perugia."

XXXIV

MARKET-DAY IN PERUGIA

PERUGIA, on its lofty hill-top, was reached by the two
travellers before the sun had quite kissed away the
early freshness of the morning. Since midnight, there
had been a heavy rain, bringing infinite refreshment to the
scene of verdure and fertility amid which this ancient civilization stands; insomuch that Kenyon loitered, when they came
to the gray city-wall, and was loth to give up the prospect
of the sunny wilderness that lay below. It was as green as
England, and bright as Italy alone. There was the wide
valley, sweeping down and spreading away, on all sides, from
the weed-grown ramparts, and bounded afar by mountains,
which lay asleep in the sun, with thin mists and silvery
clouds floating about their heads by way of morning-dreams.

"It lacks still two hours of noon," said the sculptor to his
friend, as they stood under the arch of the gateway, waiting
for their passports to be examined. "Will you come with me
to see some admirable frescoes by Perugino? There is a hall
in the Exchange, of no great magnitude, but covered with
what must have been (at the time it was painted) such
magnificence and beauty as the world had not elsewhere
to show."

"It depresses me to look at old frescoes," responded the Count. "It is a pain, yet not enough of a pain to answer as a penance."

"Will you look at some pictures by Fra Angelico in the Church of San Domenico?" asked Kenyon. "They are full of religious sincerity. When one studies them faithfully, it is like holding a conversation about heavenly things with a tender and devout-minded man."

"You have shown me some of Fra Angelico's pictures, I remember," answered Donatello. "His angels look as if they had never taken a flight out of Heaven; and his Saints seem to have been born Saints, and always to have lived so. Young maidens, and all innocent persons, I doubt not, may find great delight and profit in looking at such holy pictures. But they are not for me."

"Your criticism, I fancy, has great moral depth," replied Kenyon; "and I see in it the reason why Hilda so highly appreciates Fra Angelico's pictures. Well; we will let all such matters pass, for to-day, and stroll about this fine old city till noon."

They wandered to-and-fro, accordingly, and lost themselves among the strange, precipitate passages which in Perugia are called streets. Some of them are like caverns, being arched all over, and plunging down abruptly towards an unknown darkness, which, when you have fathomed its depths, admits you to a daylight that you scarcely hoped to behold again. Here they met shabby men, and the care-worn wives and mothers of the people, some of whom guided children in leading-strings through those dim and antique thoroughfares, where a hundred generations had passed before the little feet of to-day began to tread them. Thence they climbed upward again, and came to the level plateau, on the summit of the hill, where are situated the grand piazza and the principal public edifices.

It happened to be market-day in Perugia. The great square therefore presented a far more vivacious spectacle than would have been witnessed in it, at any other time of the week, though not so lively as to overcome the gray solemnity of the architectural portion of the scene. In the shadow of the Cathedral and other old Gothic structures, (seeking shelter from the sunshine that fell across the rest of the piazza,) was a crowd of people, engaged as buyers or sellers in the petty traffic of a country-fair. Dealers had erected booths and stalls on the pavement, and overspread them with scanty awnings, beneath which they stood vociferously crying their merchandize; such as shoes, hats and caps, yarn stockings, cheap jewelry and cutlery, books, (chiefly little volumes of a religious character, and a few French novels,) toys, tin-ware, old iron, cloth, rosaries of beads, crucifixes, cakes, biscuits, sugar-plums, and innumerable little odds and ends, which we see no object in advertizing. Baskets of grapes, figs, and pears, stood on the ground. Donkeys, bearing panniers stuffed out with kitchen vegetables, and requiring an ample road-way, roughly shouldered aside the throng.

Crowded as the square was, a juggler found room to spread out a white cloth upon the pavement, and cover it with cups, plates, balls, cards—the whole material of his magic, in short— wherewith he proceeded to work miracles under the noonday sun. An organ-grinder, at one point, and a clarion and a flute, at another, accomplished what they could towards filling the wide space with tuneful noise. Their small uproar, however, was nearly drowned by the multitudinous voices of the people, bargaining, quarrelling, laughing, and babbling copiously at random; for the briskness of the mountain atmosphere, or some other cause, made everybody so loquacious that more words were wasted in Perugia on this one market-day, than the noisiest piazza of Rome would utter in a month.

Through all this petty tumult, which kept beguiling one's eyes and upper strata of thought, it was delightful to catch glimpses of the grand old architecture that stood around the square. The life of the flitting moment, existing in the antique shell of an age gone by, has a fascination which we do not find in either the past or present, taken by themselves. It might seem irreverent to make the gray Cathedral and the tall, time-worn palaces echo back the exuberant vociferation of the market; but they did so, and caused the sound to assume a kind of poetic rhythm, and themselves looked only the more majestic for their condescension.

On one side, there was an immense edifice devoted to public purposes, with an antique gallery, and a range of arched and stone-mullioned windows, running along its front; and, by way of entrance, it had a central Gothic arch, elaborately wreathed around with sculptured semi-circles, within which the spectator was aware of a stately and impressive gloom. Though merely the municipal Council-House and Exchange of a decayed country-town, this structure was worthy to have held, in one portion of it, the Parliament-hall of a nation, and in the other, the state-apartments of its ruler. On another side of the square, rose the mediæval front of the Cathedral, where the imagination of a Gothic architect had long ago flowered out indestructibly, achieving, in the first place, a grand design, and then covering it with such abundant detail of ornament, that the magnitude of the work seemed less a miracle than its minuteness. You would suppose that he must have softened the stone into wax, until his most delicate fancies were modelled in the pliant material, and then had hardened it to stone again. The whole was a vast, black-letter page of the richest and quaintest poetry. In fit keeping with all this old magnificence, was a great marble fountain, where, again, the Gothic imagination showed its overflow and gratuity of device in the manifold sculptures, which it lavished as freely as the water did its shifting shapes.

Besides the two venerable structures which we have described, there were lofty palaces, perhaps of as old a date, rising story above story, and adorned with balconies, whence, hundreds of years ago, the princely occupants had been accustomed to gaze down at the sports, business, and popular assemblages of the piazza. And, beyond all question, they thus witnessed the erection of a bronze statue, which, three centuries since, was placed on the pedestal that it still occupies.

"I never come to Perugia," said Kenyon, "without spending as much time as I can spare in studying yonder statue of Pope Julius the Third. Those sculptors of the Middle-Age have fitter lessons for the professors of my art than we can find in the Grecian master-pieces. They belong to our Christian civilization; and, being earnest works, they always express something which we do not get from the antique. Will you look at it?"

"Willingly," replied the Count; "for I see, even so far off, that the statue is bestowing a benediction, and there is a feeling in my heart that I may be permitted to share it."

Remembering the similar idea which Miriam, a short time before, had expressed, the sculptor smiled hopefully at the coincidence. They made their way through the throng of the market-place, and approached close to the iron-railing that protected the pedestal of the statue.

It was the figure of a Pope, arrayed in his pontifical robes, and crowned with the tiara. He sat in a bronze chair, elevated high above the pavement, and seemed to take kindly, yet authoritative cognizance of the busy scene which was, at that moment, passing before his eyes. His right hand was raised and spread abroad, as if in the act of shedding forth a benediction, which every man (so broad, so wise, and so serenely affectionate, was the bronze Pope's regard) might hope to feel quietly descending upon the need, or the distress, that he had closest at his heart. The statue had life and observation in it, as well as patriarchal majesty. An imaginative spectator could not but be impressed with the idea, that this benignly awful representative of Divine and human authority might rise from his brazen chair, should any great public exigency demand his interposition, and encourage or restrain the people by his gesture, or even by prophetic utterances worthy of so grand a presence.

And, in the long, calm intervals, amid the quiet lapse of ages, the Pontiff watched the daily turmoil around his seat, listening with majestic patience to the market-cries, and all the petty uproar that awoke the echoes of the stately old piazza. He was the enduring friend of these men, and of their forefathers, and children; the familiar face of generations.

"The Pope's blessing, methinks, has fallen upon you," observed the sculptor, looking at his friend.

In truth, Donatello's countenance indicated a healthier spirit than while he was brooding in his melancholy tower. The change of scene, the breaking up of custom, the fresh flow of incidents, the sense of being homeless, and therefore free, had done something for our poor Faun; these circumstances had at least promoted a re-action, which might else have been slower in its progress. Then, no doubt, the bright day, the gay spectacle of the market-place, and the sympathetic exhilaration of so many people's cheerfulness, had each their suitable effect on a temper naturally prone to be glad. Perhaps, too, he was magnetically conscious of a presence that formerly sufficed to make him happy. Be the cause what it might, Donatello's eyes shone with a serene and hopeful expression, while looking upward at the bronze Pope, to whose widely diffused blessing, it may be, he attributed all this good influence.

"Yes, my dear friend," said he, in reply to the sculptor's remark, "I feel the blessing upon my spirit."

"It is wonderful," said Kenyon, with a smile, "wonderful, and delightful, to think how long a good man's beneficence may be potent, even after his death! How great, then, must have been the efficacy of this excellent Pontiff's blessing, while he was alive!"

"I have heard," remarked the Count, "that there was a brazen image set up in the Wilderness, the sight of which healed the Israelites of their poisonous and rankling wounds. If it be the Blessed Virgin's pleasure, why should not this holy image before us do me equal good? A wound has long been rankling in my soul, and filling it with poison."

"I did wrong to smile," answered Kenyon. "It is not for me to limit Providence in its operations on man's spirit."

While they stood talking, the clock of the neighboring Cathedral told the hour, with twelve reverberating strokes, which it flung down upon the crowded market-place, as if warning one and all to take advantage of the bronze Pontiff's benediction, (or of Heaven's blessing, however proffered,) before the opportunity were lost.

"High noon!" said the sculptor. "It is Miriam's hour!"

XXXV

THE BRONZE PONTIFF'S BENEDICTION

WHEN the last of the twelve strokes had fallen from
the Cathedral clock, Kenyon threw his eyes over the
busy scene of the market-place, expecting to discern
Miriam somewhere in the crowd. He looked next towards
the Cathedral itself, where it was reasonable to imagine that
she might have taken shelter, while awaiting her appointed
time. Seeing no trace of her in either direction, his eyes
came back from their quest, somewhat disappointed, and
rested on a figure which was leaning, like Donatello and
himself, on the iron balustrade that surrounded the statue.
Only a moment before, they two had been alone.

It was the figure of a woman, with her head bowed on
her hands, as if she deeply felt (what we have been endeavouring to convey into our feeble description) the benign and
awe-inspiring influence which the Pontiff's statue exercises
upon a sensitive spectator. No matter though it were modelled
for a Catholic Chief-Priest; the desolate heart, whatever be
its religion, recognizes in that image the likeness of a Father!

"Miriam!" said the sculptor, with a tremour in his voice.
"Is it yourself?"

"It is I," she replied. "I am faithful to my engagement,
though with many fears."

She lifted her head, and revealed to Kenyon—revealed to Donatello, likewise—the well-remembered features of Miriam. They were pale and worn, but distinguished even now, though less gorgeously, by a beauty that might be imagined bright enough to glimmer with its own light in a dim cathedral aisle, and had no need to shrink from the severer test of the mid-day sun. But she seemed tremulous, and hardly able to go through with a scene which, at a distance, she had found courage to undertake.

"You are most welcome, Miriam!" said the sculptor, seeking to afford her the encouragement which, he saw, she so greatly required. "I have a hopeful trust that the result of this inter-view will be propitious. Come; let me lead you to Donatello!"

"No, Kenyon, no!" whispered Miriam, shrinking back. "Unless, of his own accord, he speaks my name—unless he bids me stay—no word shall ever pass between him and me. It is not that I take upon me to be proud, at this late hour. Among other feminine qualities, I threw away my pride, when Hilda cast me off."

"If not pride, what else restrains you?" Kenyon asked, a little angry at her unseasonable scruples, and also at this half-complaining reference to Hilda's just severity. "After daring so much, it is no time for fear! If we let him part from you, without a word, your opportunity of doing him inestimable good is lost forever."

"True; it will be lost forever!" repeated Miriam, sadly. "But, dear friend, will it be my fault? I willingly fling my woman's pride at his feet. But—do you not see?—his heart must be left freely to its own decision whether to recognize me, because on his voluntary choice, depends the whole question whether my devotion will do him good or harm. Except he feel an infinite need of me, I am a burthen and fatal obstruction to him!"

"Take your own course, then, Miriam," said Kenyon; "and doubtless, the crisis being what it is, your spirit is better instructed for its emergencies than mine."

While the foregoing words passed between them, they had withdrawn a little from the immediate vicinity of the statue, so as to be out of Donatello's hearing. Still, however, they were beneath the Pontiff's outstretched hand; and Miriam, with her beauty and her sorrow, looked up into his benignant face, as if she had come thither for his pardon and paternal affection, and despaired of so vast a boon.

Meanwhile, she had not stood thus long in the public square of Perugia, without attracting the observation of many eyes. With their quick sense of beauty, these Italians had recognized her loveliness, and spared not to take their fill of gazing at it; though their native gentleness and courtesy made their homage far less obtrusive than that of Germans, French, or Anglo-Saxons might have been. It is not improbable that Miriam had planned this momentous interview, on so public a spot and at high noon, with an eye to the sort of protection that would be thrown over it by a multitude of eye-witnesses. In circumstances of profound feeling and passion, there is often a sense that too great a seclusion cannot be endured; there is an indefinite dread of being quite alone with the object of our deepest interest. The species of solitude, that a crowd harbours within itself, is felt to be preferable, in certain conditions of the heart, to the remoteness of a desert or the depths of an untrodden wood. Hatred, love, or whatever kind of too intense emotion, or even indifference, where emotion has once been, instinctively seeks to interpose some barrier between itself and the corresponding passion in another breast. This, we suspect, was what Miriam had thought of, in coming to the thronged piazza; partly this, and partly, as she said, her superstition that the benign statue held good influences in store.

But Donatello remained leaning against the balustrade. She dared not glance towards him, to see whether he were pale and agitated, or calm as ice. Only, she knew that the moments were fleetly lapsing away, and that his heart must call her soon, or the voice would never reach her. She turned quite away from him, and spoke again to the sculptor.

"I have wished to meet you," said she, "for more than one reason. News have come to me respecting a dear friend of ours. Nay, not of mine! I dare not call her a friend of mine, though once the dearest."

"Do you speak of Hilda?" exclaimed Kenyon with quick alarm. "Has anything befallen her? When I last heard of her, she was still in Rome, and well."

"Hilda remains in Rome," replied Miriam, "nor is she ill, as regards physical health, though much depressed in spirits. She lives quite alone, in her dove-cote; not a friend near her, not one in Rome, which, you know, is deserted by all but its native inhabitants. I fear for her health, if she continue long in such solitude, with despondency preying on her mind. I tell you this, knowing the interest which the rare beauty of her character has awakened in you."

"I will go to Rome!" said the sculptor, in great emotion. "Hilda has never allowed me to manifest more than a friendly regard; but, at least, she cannot prevent my watching over her, at a humble distance. I will set out, this very hour!"

"Do not leave us now!" whispered Miriam imploringly, and laying her hand on his arm. "One moment more! Ah; he has no word for me!"

"Miriam!" said Donatello.

Though but a single word, and the first that he had spoken, its tone was a warrant of the sad and tender depth from which it came. It told Miriam things of infinite importance, and, first of all, that he still loved her. The sense of their mutual crime had stunned, but not destroyed the vitality of his affection; it was therefore indestructible. That tone, too, bespoke an altered and deepened character; it told of a vivified intellect, and of spiritual instruction that had come through sorrow and remorse; so that—instead of the wild boy, the thing of sportive, animal nature, the sylvan Faun—here was now the man of feeling and intelligence.

She turned towards him, while his voice still reverberated in the depths of her soul.

"You have called me!" said she.

"Because my deepest heart has need of you!" he replied. "Forgive, Miriam, the coldness, the hardness, with which I parted from you! I was bewildered with strange horrour and gloom."

"Alas! and it was I that brought it on you," said she. "What repentance, what self-sacrifice, can atone for that infinite wrong? There was something so sacred in the innocent and joyous life which you were leading! A happy person is such an unaccustomed and holy creature, in this sad world! And, encountering so rare a being, and gifted with the power of sympathy with his sunny life, it was my doom, mine, to bring him within the limits of sinful, sorrowful mortality! Bid me depart, Donatello! Fling me off! No good, through my agency, can follow upon such a mighty evil!"

"Miriam," said he, "our lot lies together. Is it not so? Tell me, in Heaven's name, if it be otherwise!"

Donatello's conscience was evidently perplexed with doubt, whether the communion of a crime, such as they two were jointly stained with, ought not to stifle all the instinctive motions of their hearts, impelling them one towards the other. Miriam, on the other hand, remorsefully questioned with herself, whether the misery, already accruing from her influence, should not warn her to withdraw from his path. In this momentous interview, therefore, two souls were groping for each other in the darkness of guilt and sorrow, and hardly were bold enough to grasp the cold hands that they found.

The sculptor stood watching the scene with earnest sympathy.

"It seems irreverent," said he, at length,—"intrusive, if not irreverent, for a third person to thrust himself between the two solely concerned in a crisis like the present. Yet, possibly, as a by-stander, though a deeply interested one, I may discern somewhat of truth that is hidden from you both—may, at least, interpret or suggest some ideas which you might not so readily convey to each other."

"Speak," said Miriam. "We confide in you."

"Speak," said Donatello. "You are true and upright."

"I well know," rejoined Kenyon, "that I shall not succeed in uttering the few, deep words which (in this matter, as in all others) include the absolute truth. But, here, Miriam, is one whom a terrible misfortune has begun to educate; it has taken him, and through your agency, out of a wild and happy state, which, within circumscribed limits, gave him joys that he cannot elsewhere find on earth. On his behalf, you have incurred a responsibility which you cannot fling aside. And, here, Donatello, is one whom Providence marks out as intimately connected with your destiny. The mysterious process, by which our earthly life instructs us for another state of being, was begun for you by her. She has rich gifts of heart and mind, a suggestive power, a magnetic influence, a sympathetic knowledge, which, wisely and religiously exercised, are what your condition needs. She possesses what you require, and, with utter self-devotion, will use it for your good. The bond betwixt you, therefore, is a true one, and never—except by Heaven's own act—should be rent asunder."

"Ah; he has spoken the truth!" cried Donatello, grasping Miriam's hand.

"The very truth, dear friend!" cried Miriam.

"But, take heed!" resumed the sculptor, anxious not to violate the integrity of his own conscience. "Take heed; for you love one another, and yet your bond is twined with such black threads, that you must never look upon it as identical with the ties that unite other loving souls. It is for mutual support; it is for one another's final good; it is for effort, for sacrifice, but not for earthly happiness! If such be your motive, believe me, friends, it were better to relinquish each other's hands, at this sad moment. There would be no holy sanction on your wedded life."

"None," said Donatello, shuddering. "We know it well."

"None," repeated Miriam, also shuddering. "United (miserably entangled with me, rather) by a bond of guilt, our union might be for eternity, indeed, and most intimate; but, through all that endless duration, I should be conscious of his horrour!"

"Not, for earthly bliss, therefore," said Kenyon, "but for mutual elevation and encouragement towards a severe and painful life, you take each other's hands. And if, out of toil, sacrifice, prayer, penitence, and earnest effort towards right things, there comes, at length, a sombre and thoughtful happiness, taste it, and thank Heaven! So that you live not for it—so that it be a wayside flower, springing along a path that leads to higher ends—it will be Heaven's gracious gift, and a token that it recognizes your union here below."

"Have you no more to say?" asked Miriam earnestly. "There is matter of sorrow and lofty consolation strangely mingled in your words."

"Only this, dear Miriam," said the sculptor. "If ever, in your lives, the highest duty should require from either of you the sacrifice of the other, meet the occasion without shrinking! This is all."

While Kenyon spoke, Donatello had evidently taken in the ideas which he propounded, and had enobled them by the sincerity of his reception. His aspect unconsciously assumed a dignity which, elevating his former beauty, accorded with the change that had long been taking place in his interiour self. He was a man, revolving grave and deep thoughts in his breast. He still held Miriam's hand; and there they stood, the beautiful man, the beautiful woman, united forever, as they felt, in the presence of these thousand eye-witnesses, who gazed so curiously at the unintelligible scene. Doubtless, the crowd recognized them as lovers, and fancied this a betrothal that was destined to result in life-long happiness. And, possibly, it might be so. Who can tell where happiness may come, or where, though an expected guest, it may never show its face? Perhaps—shy, subtle thing—it had crept into this sad marriage-bond, when the partners would have trembled at its presence, as a crime!

"Farewell!" said Kenyon. "I go to Rome."

"Farewell, true friend!" said Miriam.

"Farewell!" said Donatello too. "May you be happy! You have no guilt, to make you shrink from happiness."

At this moment, it so chanced that all the three friends, by one impulse, glanced upward at the statue of Pope Julius; and there was the majestic figure stretching out the hand of benediction over them, and bending down upon this guilty and repentant pair its visage of grand benignity. There is a singular effect, oftentimes, when out of the midst of engrossing thought and deep absorption, we suddenly look up, and catch a glimpse of external objects. We seem, at such moments, to look farther and deeper into them, than by any premeditated observation; it is as if they met our eyes alive, and with all their hidden meaning on the surface, but grew again inanimate and inscrutable, the instant that they become aware of our glances. So, now, at that unexpected glimpse, Miriam, Donatello, and the sculptor, all three imagined that they beheld the bronze Pontiff, endowed with spiritual life. A blessing was felt descending upon them from his outstretched hand; he approved, by look and gesture, the pledge of a deep union that had passed under his auspices.

XXXVI

HILDA'S TOWER

WHEN we have once known Rome, and left her where she lies, like a long decaying corpse, retaining a trace of the noble shape it was, but with accumulated dust and a fungous growth overspreading all its more admirable features;—left her in utter weariness, no doubt, of her narrow, crooked, intricate streets, so uncomfortably paved with little squares of lava that to tread over them is a penitential pilgrimage, so indescribably ugly, moreover, so cold, so alley-like, into which the sun never falls, and where a chill wind forces its deadly breath into our lungs;—left her, tired of the sight of those immense, seven-storied, yellow-washed hovels, or call them palaces, where all that is dreary in domestic life seems magnified and multiplied, and weary of climbing those staircases, which ascend from a ground-floor of cook-shops, coblers' stalls, stables, and regiments of cavalry, to a middle region of princes, cardinals, and ambassadours, and an upper tier of artists, just beneath the unattainable sky;—left her, worn out with shivering at the cheerless and smoky fireside, by day, and feasting with our own substance the ravenous little populace of a Roman bed, at night;—left her, sick at heart of Italian trickery, which has uprooted whatever faith in man's integrity had endured till now, and sick at stomach of sour bread, sour wine, rancid butter, and bad cookery, needlessly bestowed on evil meats;—left her, disgusted with the pretence of Holiness and the reality of Nastiness, each equally omnipresent;—left her, half-lifeless from the languid atmosphere, the vital principle of which has been used up, long ago, or corrupted by myriads of slaughters;—left her, crushed down in spirit with the desolation of her ruin, and the hopelessness of her future;—left her, in short, hating her with all our might, and adding our individual curse to the Infinite Anathema which her old crimes have unmistakeably brought down;—when we have left Rome in such mood as this, we are astonished by the discovery, by-and-by, that our heart-strings have mysteriously attached themselves to the Eternal City, and are drawing us thitherward again, as if it were more familiar, more intimately our home, than even the spot where we were born!

It is with a kindred sentiment, that we now follow the course of our story back through the Flaminian Gate, and threading our way to the Via Portoghese, climb the staircase to the upper chamber of the tower, where we last saw Hilda.

Hilda all along intended to pass the summer in Rome; for she had laid out many high and delightful tasks, which she could the better complete while her favourite haunts were deserted by the multitude that thronged them, throughout the winter and early spring. Nor did she dread the summer-atmosphere, although generally held to be so pestilential. She had already made trial of it, two years before, and found no worse effect than a kind of dreamy languor, which was dissipated by the first cool breezes that came with Autumn. The thickly populated centre of the city, indeed, is never affected by the feverish influence that lies in wait in the Campagna, like a besieging foe, and nightly haunts those beautiful lawns and woodlands, around the suburban villas, just at the season when they most resemble Paradise. What the flaming sword was to the first Eden, such is the malaria to these sweet gardens and groves. We may wander through them, of an afternoon, it is true; but they cannot be made a home and a reality, and to sleep among them is death. They are but illusions, therefore, like the show of gleaming waters and shadowy foliage, in a desert.

But Rome, within the walls, at this dreaded season, enjoys its festal days, and makes itself merry with characteristic and hereditary pastimes, for which its broad piazzas afford abundant room. It leads its own life with a freer spirit, now that the artists and foreign visitors are scattered abroad. No bloom, perhaps, would be visible in a cheek that should be unvisited, throughout the summer, by more invigorating winds than any within fifty miles of the city; no bloom, but yet (if the mind kept its healthy energy) a subdued and colourless well-being. There was consequently little risk in Hilda's purpose to pass the summer-days in the galleries of Roman palaces, and her nights in that aërial chamber, whither the heavy breath of the city and its suburbs could not aspire. It would probably harm her no more than it did the white doves, who sought the same high atmosphere, at sunset, and, when morning came, flew down into the narrow streets, about their daily business, as Hilda likewise did.

With the Virgin's aid and blessing, (which might be hoped for even by a heretic, who so religiously lit the lamp before her shrine,) the New England girl would sleep securely in her old Roman tower, and go forth on her pictorial pilgrimages without dread or peril. In view of such a summer, Hilda had anticipated many months of lonely, but unalloyed enjoyment. Not that she had a churlish disinclination to society, or needed to be told that we taste one intellectual pleasure twice, and with double the result, when we taste it with a friend. But, keeping a maiden heart within her bosom, she rejoiced in the freedom that enabled her still to choose her own sphere, and dwell in it, if she pleased, without another inmate.

Her expectation, however, of a delightful summer was woefully disappointed. Even had she formed no previous plan of remaining there, it is improbable that Hilda would have gathered energy to stir from Rome. A torpor, heretofore unknown to her vivacious, though quiet temperament, had possessed itself of the poor girl, like a half-dead serpent knotting its cold, inextricable wreaths about her limbs. It was that peculiar despair, that chill and heavy misery, which only the innocent can experience, although it possesses many of the gloomy characteristics that mark a sense of guilt. It was that heart-sickness, which, it is to be hoped, we may all of us have been pure enough to feel, once in our lives, but the capacity for which is usually exhausted early, and perhaps with a single agony. It was that dismal certainty of the existence of evil in the world, which (though we may fancy ourselves fully assured of the sad mystery, long before) never becomes a portion of our practical belief until it takes substance and reality from the sin of some guide, whom we have deeply trusted and revered, or some friend whom we have dearly loved.

When that knowledge comes, it is as if a cloud had suddenly gathered over the morning light; so dark a cloud, that there seems to be no longer any sunshine behind it or above it. The character of our individual beloved one having invested itself with all the attributes of right—that one friend being to us the symbol and representative of whatever is good and true—when he falls, the effect is almost as if the sky fell with him, bringing down in chaotic ruin the columns that upheld our faith. We struggle forth again, no doubt, bruised and bewildered. We stare wildly about us, and discover—or, it may be, we never make the discovery—that it was not actually the sky that has tumbled down, but merely a frail structure of our own rearing, which never rose higher than the house-tops, and has fallen because we founded it on nothing. But the crash, and the affright and trouble, are as overwhelming, for the time, as if the catastrophe involved the whole moral world. Remembering these things, let them suggest one generous motive for walking heedfully amid the defilement of earthly ways! Let us reflect, that the highest path is pointed out by the pure Ideal of those who look up to us, and who, if we tread less loftily, may never look so high again!

Hilda's situation was made infinitely more wretched by the necessity of confining all her trouble within her own consciousness. To this innocent girl, holding the knowledge of Miriam's crime within her tender and delicate soul, the effect was almost the same as if she herself had participated in the guilt. Indeed, partaking the human nature of those who could perpetrate such deeds, she felt her own spotlessness impugned.

Had there been but a single friend—or, not a friend, since friends were no longer to be confided in, after Miriam had betrayed her trust—but, had there been any calm, wise mind, any sympathizing intelligence, or, if not these, any dull, half-listening ear into which she might have flung the dreadful secret, as into an echoless cavern—what a relief would have ensued! But, this awful loneliness! It enveloped her whithersoever she went. It was a shadow in the sunshine of festal days; a mist between her eyes and the pictures at which she strove to look; a chill dungeon, which kept her in its gray twilight and fed her with its unwholesome air, fit only for a criminal to breathe and pine in! She could not escape from it. In the effort to do so, straying farther into the intricate passages of our nature, she stumbled, ever and again, over this deadly idea of mortal guilt.

Poor sufferer for another's sin! Poor well-spring of a virgin's heart, into which a murdered corpse had casually fallen, and whence it could not be drawn forth again, but lay there, day after day, night after night, tainting its sweet atmosphere with the scent of crime and ugly death!

The strange sorrow, that had befallen Hilda, did not fail to impress its mysterious seal upon her face, and to make itself perceptible to sensitive observers in her manner and carriage. A young Italian artist, who frequented the same galleries which Hilda haunted, grew deeply interested in her expression. One day, while she stood before Leonardo da Vinci's picture of Joanna of Aragon, but evidently without seeing it, (for, though it had attracted her eyes, a fancied resemblance to Miriam had immediately drawn away her thoughts,) this artist drew a hasty sketch, which he afterwards elaborated into a finished portrait. It represented Hilda as gazing, with sad and earnest horrour, at a blood-spot which she seemed just then to have discovered on her white robe. The picture attracted considerable notice. Copies of an engraving from it may still be found in the print-shops along the Corso. By many connoisseurs, the idea of the face was supposed to have been suggested by the portrait of Beatrice Cenci; and, in fact, there was a look somewhat similar to poor Beatrice's forlorn gaze out of the dreary isolation and remoteness, in which a terrible doom had involved a tender soul. But the modern artist strenuously upheld the originality of his own picture, as well as the stainless purity of its subject, and chose to call it, (and was laughed at for his pains,) 'Innocence, dying of a Blood-stain!'

"Your picture, Signor Panini, does you credit," remarked the picture-dealer, who had bought it of the young man for fifteen scudi, and afterwards sold it for ten times the sum;

"but it would be worth a better price if you had given it a more intelligible title. Looking at the face and expression of this fair Signorina, we seem to comprehend, readily enough, that she is undergoing one or another of those troubles of the heart, to which young ladies are but too liable. But what is this Blood-stain? And what has Innocence to do with it? Has she stabbed her perfidious lover with a bodkin?"

"She! She commit a crime!" cried the young artist. "Can you look at the innocent anguish in her face, and ask that question? No; but, as I read the mystery, a man has been slain in her presence, and the blood, spirting accidentally on her white robe, has made a stain which eats into her life."

"Then, in the name of her patron-saint," exclaimed the picture-dealer, "why don't she get the robe made white again, at the expense of a few baiocchi to her washerwoman? No, no, my dear Panini! The picture being now my property, I shall call it 'The Signorina's Vengeance.' She has stabbed her lover, over night, and is repenting it betimes, the next morning. So interpreted, the picture becomes an intelligible and very natural representation of a not uncommon fact."

Thus coarsely does the world translate all finer griefs that meet its eye! It is more a coarse world than an unkind one.

But Hilda sought nothing either from the world's delicacy or its pity, and never dreamed of its misinterpretations. Her doves often flew in through the windows of the tower, winged messengers, bringing her what sympathy they could, and uttering soft, tender, and complaining sounds, deep in their bosoms, which soothed the girl more than a distincter utterance might. And sometimes Hilda moaned quietly among the doves, teaching her voice to accord with theirs, and thus finding a temporary relief from the burthen of her incommunicable sorrow; as if a little portion of it, at least, had been told to these innocent friends, and understood, and pitied.

When she trimmed the lamp before the Virgin's shrine,

Hilda gazed at the sacred image, and, rude as was the workmanship, beheld, or fancied, (expressed with the quaint, powerful simplicity which sculptors sometimes had, five hundred years ago,) a woman's tenderness responding to her gaze. If she knelt—if she prayed—if her oppressed heart besought the sympathy of Divine Womanhood, afar in bliss, but not remote, because forever humanized by the memory of mortal griefs—was Hilda to be blamed? It was not a Catholic, kneeling at an idolatrous shrine, but a child, lifting its tear-stained face to seek comfort from a Mother!

XXXVII

THE EMPTINESS OF
PICTURE-GALLERIES

HILDA descended, day by day, from her dove-cote, and went to one or another of the great, old palaces—the Pamfili-Doria, the Corsini, the Sciarra, the Borghese, the Colonna—where the door-keepers knew her well, and offered her a kindly greeting. But they shook their heads and sighed, on observing the languid step with which the poor girl toiled up the grand marble staircases. There was no more of that cheery alacrity with which she used to flit upward, as if her doves had lent her their wings, nor of that glow of happy spirits which had been wont to set the tarnished gilding of the picture-frames, and the shabby splendour of the furniture, all a-glimmer, as she hastened to her congenial and delightful toil.

An old German artist, whom she often met in the galleries, once laid a paternal hand on Hilda's head, and bade her go back to her own country.

"Go back soon," he said, with kindly freedom and directness, "or you will go never more! And, if you go not, why, at least, do you spend the whole summer-time in Rome? The air has been breathed too often, in so many thousand years, and is not wholesome for a little foreign flower like you, my child, a delicate wood-anemone from the western forest-land!"

"I have no task nor duty anywhere but here," replied Hilda. "The Old Masters will not set me free!"

"Ah, those Old Masters!" cried the veteran artist, shaking his head. "They are a tyrannous race! You will find them of too mighty a spirit to be dealt with, for long together, by the slender hand, the fragile mind, and the delicate heart, of a young girl. Remember that Raphael's genius wore out that divinest painter before half his life was lived. Since you feel his influence powerfully enough to reproduce his miracles so well, it will assuredly consume you like a flame."

"That might have been my peril once," answered Hilda. "It is not so, now."

"Yes, fair maiden, you stand in that peril now!" insisted the kind old man; and he added, smiling, yet in a melancholy vein, and with a German grotesqueness of idea, "Some fine morning, I shall come to the Pinacotheca of the Vatican, with my palette and my brushes, and shall look for my little American artist that sees into the very heart of the grand pictures! And what shall I behold? A heap of white ashes on the marble floor, just in front of the divine Raphael's picture of the Madonna di Foligno! Nothing more, upon my word! The fire, which the poor child feels so fervently, will have gone into her innermost, and burnt her quite up!"

"It would be a happy martyrdom!" said Hilda, faintly smiling. "But I am far from being worthy of it. What troubles me much, among other troubles, is quite the reverse of what you think. The Old Masters hold me here, it is true, but they no longer warm me with their influence. It is not flame consuming, but torpor chilling me, that helps to make me wretched."

"Perchance, then," said the German, looking keenly at her, "Raphael has a rival in your heart? He was your first-love; but young maidens are not always constant, and one flame is sometimes extinguished by another!"

Hilda shook her head, and turned away.

She had spoken the truth, however, in alleging that torpor, rather than fire, was what she had now to dread. In these gloomy days that had befallen her, it was a great additional calamity that she felt conscious of the present dimness of an insight, which she once possessed in more than ordinary measure. She had lost—and she trembled lest it should have departed forever—the faculty of appreciating those great works of art, which heretofore had made so large a portion of her happiness. It was no wonder.

A picture, however admirable the painter's art, and wonderful his power, requires of the spectator a surrender of himself, in due proportion with the miracle which has been wrought. Let the canvas glow as it may, you must look with the eye of faith, or its highest excellence escapes you. There is always the necessity of helping out the painter's art with your own resources of sensibility and imagination. Not that these qualities shall really add anything to what the Master has effected; but they must be put so entirely under his controul, and work along with him to such an extent, that, in a different mood, (when you are cold and critical, instead of sympathetic,) you will be apt to fancy that the loftier merits of the picture were of your own dreaming, not of his creating.

Like all revelations of the better life, the adequate perception of a great work of art demands a gifted simplicity of vision. In this, and in her self-surrender, and the depth and tenderness of her sympathy, had lain Hilda's remarkable power as a copyist of the Old Masters. And now that her capacity of emotion was choked up with a horrible experience, it inevitably followed that she should seek in vain, among those Friends so venerated and beloved, for the marvels which they had heretofore shown her. In spite of a reverence that lingered longer than her recognition, their poor worshipper became almost an infidel, and sometimes doubted whether the pictorial art be not altogether a delusion.

For the first time in her life, Hilda now grew acquainted with that icy Demon of Weariness, who haunts great picture-galleries. He is a plausible Mephistophiles, and possesses the magic that is the destruction of all other magic. He annihilates colour, warmth, and, more especially, sentiment, and passion, at a touch. If he spare anything, it will be some such matter as an earthen pipkin or a bunch of herrings by Teniers; a brass kettle, in which you can see your face, by Gerard Douw; a furred robe, or the silken texture of a mantle, or a straw hat, by Van Mieris; or a long-stalked wine-glass, transparent and full of shifting reflections, or a bit of bread and cheese, or an over-ripe peach with a fly upon it, truer than reality itself, by the school of Dutch conjurors. These men, and a few Flemings, whispers the wicked Demon, were the only painters. The mighty Italian Masters, as you deem them, were not human, nor addressed their works to human sympathies, but to a false intellectual taste, which they themselves were the first to create. Well might they call their doings, 'Art,' for they substituted art instead of Nature. Their fashion is past, and ought, indeed, to have died and been buried along with them!

Then there is such a terrible lack of variety in their subjects! The churchmen, their great patrons, suggested most of their themes, and a dead mythology the rest. A quarter-part, probably, of any large collection of pictures, consists of Virgins and Infant Christs, repeated over and over again, in pretty much an identical spirit, and generally with no more mixture of the Divine than just enough to spoil them as representations of Maternity and Childhood, with which everybody's heart might have something to do. Half of the other pictures are Magdalens, Flights into Egypt, Crucifixions, Depositions from the Cross, Pietàs, Noli-me-tangeres, or the Sacrifice of Abraham, or Martyrdoms of Saints, originally painted as altar-pieces, or for the shrines of chapels, and woefully lacking the accompaniments which the artist had in view.

The remainder of the gallery comprises mythological subjects, such as nude Venuses, Ledas, Graces, and, in short, a general apotheosis of nudity, once fresh and rosy, perhaps, but yellow and dingy in our day, and retaining only a traditionary charm. These impure pictures are from the same illustrious and impious hands that adventured to call before us the august forms of Apostles and Saints, the Blessed Mother of the Redeemer, and her Son, at his death, and in his glory, and even the awfulness of Him, to whom the Martyrs, dead a thousand years ago, have not yet dared to raise their eyes. They seem to take up one task or the other— the disrobed woman whom they call Venus, or the type of highest and tenderest womanhood, in the mother of their Saviour—with equal readiness, but to achieve the former with far more satisfactory success. If an artist sometimes produced a picture of the Virgin, possessing warmth enough to excite devotional feeling, it was probably the object of his earthly love, to whom he thus paid the stupendous and fearful homage of setting up her portrait to be worshipped, not figuratively, as a mortal, but by religious souls in their earnest aspirations towards Divinity. And who can trust the religious sentiment of Raphael, or receive any of his Virgins as Heaven-descended likenesses, after seeing, for example, the Fornarina of the Barberini palace, and feeling how sensual the artist must have been, to paint such a brazen trollop of his own accord, and lovingly! Would the Blessed Mary reveal herself to his spiritual vision, and favour him with sittings, alternately with that type of glowing earthliness, the Fornarina!

But no sooner have we given expression to this irreverent criticism, than a throng of spiritual faces look reproachfully upon us. We see Cherubs, by Raphael, whose baby-innocence could only have been nursed in Paradise; Angels, by Raphael, as innocent as they, but whose serene intelligence embraces both earthly and celestial things; Madonnas, by Raphael, on whose lips he has impressed a holy and delicate reserve, implying sanctity on earth, and into whose soft eyes he has thrown a light which he never could have imagined, except by raising his own eyes with a pure aspiration heavenward. We remember, too, that Divinest countenance in the Transfiguration, and withdraw all that we have said.

Poor Hilda, however, in her gloomiest moments, was never guilty of the high-treason, suggested in the above remarks, against her beloved and honoured Raphael. She had a faculty (which, fortunately for themselves, pure women often have) of ignoring all moral blotches in a character that won her admiration. She purified the objects of her regard by the mere act of turning such spotless eyes upon them.

Hilda's despondency, nevertheless, while it dulled her perceptions in one respect, had deepened them in another; she saw beauty less vividly, but felt truth, or the lack of it, more profoundly. She began to suspect that some, at least, of her venerated painters, had left an inevitable hollowness in their works, because, in the most renowned of them, they essayed to express to the world what they had not in their own souls. They deified their light and wandering affections, and were continually playing off the tremendous jest, alluded to above, of offering the features of some venal beauty to be enshrined in the holiest places. A deficiency of earnestness and absolute truth is generally discoverable in Italian pictures, after the art had become consummate. When you demand what is deepest, these painters have not wherewithal to respond. They substituted a keen intellectual perception, and a marvellous knack of external arrangement, instead of the live sympathy and sentiment which should have been their inspiration. And hence it happens, that shallow and worldly men are among the best critics of their works; a taste for pictorial art is often no more than a polish upon the hard enamel of an artificial character. Hilda had lavished her whole heart upon it, and found (just as if she had lavished it upon a human idol) that the greater part was thrown away.

For some of the earlier painters, however, she still retained much of her former reverence. Fra Angelico, she felt, must have breathed a humble aspiration between every two touches of his brush, in order to have made the finished picture such a visible prayer as we behold it, in the guise of a prim Angel, or a Saint without the human nature. Through all these dusky centuries, his works may still help a struggling heart to pray. Perugino was evidently a devout man; and the Virgin, therefore, revealed herself to him in loftier and sweeter faces of celestial womanhood, (and yet with a kind of homeliness in their human mould,) than even the genius of Raphael could imagine. Sodoma, beyond a question, both prayed and wept, while painting his fresco, at Siena, of Christ bound to a pillar.

In her present need and hunger for a spiritual revelation, Hilda felt a vast and weary longing to see this last-mentioned picture once again. It is inexpressibly touching. So weary is the Saviour, and utterly worn out with agony, that his lips have fallen apart from mere exhaustion; his eyes seem to be set; he tries to lean his head against the pillar, but is kept from sinking down upon the ground only by the cords that bind him. One of the most striking effects produced, is the sense of loneliness. You behold Christ deserted both in Heaven and earth; that despair is in him, which wrung forth the saddest utterance man ever made—'Why hast Thou forsaken me?' Even in this extremity, however, he is still divine. The great and reverent painter has not suffered the Son of God to be merely an object of pity, though depicting him in a state so profoundly pitiful. He is rescued from it, we know not how—by nothing less than miracle—by a celestial majesty and beauty, and some quality of which these are the outward garniture. He is as much, and as visibly, our Redeemer, there bound, there fainting, and bleeding from the scourge, with the Cross in view, as if he sat on his throne of glory in the heavens! Sodoma, in this matchless picture, has done more towards reconciling the incongruity of Divine Omnipotence and outraged, suffering Humanity, combined in one person, than the theologians ever did.

This hallowed work of genius shows what pictorial art, devoutly exercised, might effect in behalf of religious truth; involving, as it does, deeper mysteries of Revelation, and bringing them closer to man's heart, and making him tenderer to be impressed by them, than the most eloquent words of preacher or prophet.

It is not of pictures like the above, that galleries, in Rome or elsewhere, are made up, but of productions immeasurably below them, and requiring to be appreciated by a very different frame of mind. Few amateurs are endowed with a tender susceptibility to the sentiment of a picture; they are not won from an evil life, nor anywise morally improved by it. The love of Art, therefore, differs widely in its influence from the love of Nature; whereas, if Art had not strayed away from its legitimate paths and aims, it ought to soften and sweeten the lives of its worshippers, in even a more exquisite degree than the contemplation of natural objects. But, of its own potency, it has no such effect; and it fails, likewise, in that other test of its moral value which poor Hilda was now involuntarily trying upon it. It cannot comfort the heart in affliction; it grows dim when the shadow is upon us.

So the melancholy girl wandered through those long galleries, and over the mosaic pavements of vast, solitary saloons, wondering what had become of the splendour that used to beam upon her from the walls. She grew sadly critical, and condemned almost everything that she was wont to admire. Heretofore, her sympathy went deeply into a picture, yet seemed to leave a depth which it was inadequate to sound; now, on the contrary, her perceptive faculty penetrated the canvas like a steel probe, and found but a crust of paint over an emptiness. Not that she gave up all Art as worthless; only, it had lost its consecration. One picture in ten thousand, perhaps, ought to live in the applause of mankind, from generation to generation, until the colours fade and blacken out of sight, or the canvas rot entirely away. For the rest, let them be piled in garrets, just as the tolerable poets are shelved, when their little day is over. Is a painter more sacred than a poet?

And as for these galleries of Roman palaces, they were to Hilda—though she still trode them with the forlorn hope of getting back her sympathies—they were drearier than the white-washed walls of a prison corridor. If a magnificent palace were founded, as was generally the case, on hardened guilt and a stony conscience—if the Prince or Cardinal, who stole the marble of his vast mansion from the Coliseum, or some Roman temple, had perpetrated still deadlier crimes, as probably he did—there could be no fitter punishment for his ghost than to wander perpetually through these long suites of rooms, over the cold marble or mosaic of the floors, growing chiller at every eternal footstep. Fancy the progenitor of the Dorias thus haunting those heavy halls where his posterity reside! Nor would it assuage his monotonous misery, but increase it manifold, to be compelled to scrutinize those master-pieces of art, which he collected with so much cost and care, and gazing at them unintelligently, still leave a further portion of his vital warmth at every one.

Such, or of a similar kind, is the torment of those who seek to enjoy pictures in an uncongenial mood. Every haunter of picture-galleries, we should imagine, must have experienced it, in greater or less degree; Hilda, never till now, but now most bitterly.

And now, for the first time in her lengthened absence, comprising so many years of her young life, she began to be acquainted with the exile's pain. Her pictorial imagination brought up vivid scenes of her native village, with its great, old elm-trees, and the neat, comfortable houses, scattered along the wide grassy margin of its street, and the white meeting-house, and her mother's very door, and the stream of gold-brown water, which her taste for colour had kept flowing, all this while, through her remembrance. Oh, dreary streets, palaces, churches, and imperial sepulchres of hot and dusty Rome, with the muddy Tiber eddying through the midst, instead of the gold-brown rivulet! How she pined under this crumbly magnificence, as if it were piled all upon her human heart! How she yearned for that native home-liness, those familiar sights, those faces which she had known always, those days that never brought any strange event, that life of sober week-days, and a solemn Sabbath at the close! The peculiar fragrance of a flower-bed, which Hilda used to cultivate, came freshly to her memory across the windy sea, and through the long years since the flowers had withered. Her heart grew faint at the hundred reminiscences that were awakened by that remembered smell of dead blossoms; it was like opening a drawer, where many things were laid away, and every one of them scented with lavender and dried rose-leaves!

We ought not to betray Hilda's secret; but it is the truth, that being so sad, and so utterly alone, and in such great need of sympathy, her thoughts sometimes recurred to the sculptor. Had she met him now, her heart, indeed, might not have been won, but her confidence would have flown to him like a bird to its nest. One summer-afternoon, especially, Hilda leaned upon the battlements of her tower, and looked over Rome, towards the distant mountains, whither Kenyon had told her that he was going.

"Oh, that he were here!" she sighed. "I perish under this terrible secret; and he might help me to endure it. Oh, that he were here!"

That very afternoon, as the reader may remember, Kenyon felt Hilda's hand pulling at the silken cord that was connected with his heart-strings, as he stood looking towards Rome from the battlements of Monte Beni.

XXXVIII

ALTARS AND INCENSE

R OME has a certain species of consolation readier at
hand, for all the necessitous, than any other spot under
the sky; and Hilda's despondent state made her peculiarly liable to the peril (if peril it can justly be termed) of
seeking, or consenting, to be thus consoled.

Had the Jesuits known the situation of this troubled heart,
her inheritance of New England puritanism would hardly
have protected the poor girl from the pious strategy of those
good Fathers. Knowing, as they do, how to work each proper
engine, it would have been ultimately impossible for Hilda
to resist the attractions of a faith, which so marvellously adapts
itself to every human need. Not, indeed, that it can satisfy
the soul's cravings, but, at least, it can sometimes help the
soul towards a higher satisfaction than the faith contains
within itself. It supplies a multitude of external forms, in
which the Spiritual may be clothed and manifested; it has
many painted windows, as it were, through which the celestial
sunshine, else disregarded, may make itself gloriously perceptible in visions of beauty and splendour. There is no one
want or weakness of human nature, for which Catholicism
will own itself without a remedy; cordials, certainly, it

possesses in abundance, and sedatives, in inexhaustible variety, and what may once have been genuine medicaments, though a little the worse for long keeping.

To do it justice, Catholicism is such a miracle of fitness for its own ends, (many of which might seem to be admirable ones,) that it is difficult to imagine it a contrivance of mere man. Its mighty machinery was forged and put together, not on middle earth, but either above or below. If there were but angels to work it, (instead of the very different class of engineers who now manage its cranks and safety-valves,) the system would soon vindicate the dignity and holiness of its origin.

Hilda had heretofore made many pilgrimages among the churches of Rome, for the sake of wondering at their gorgeousness. Without a glimpse at these palaces of worship, it is impossible to imagine the magnificence of the religion that reared them. Many of them shine with burnished gold. They glow with pictures. Their walls, columns, and arches, seem a quarry of precious stones, so beautiful and costly are the marbles with which they are inlaid. Their pavements are often a mosaic, of rare workmanship. Around their lofty cornices, hover flights of sculptured angels; and within the vault of the ceiling and the swelling interiour of the dome, there are frescoes of such brilliancy, and wrought with so artful a perspective, that the sky, peopled with sainted forms, appears to be opened, only a little way above the spectator. Then there are chapels, opening from the side-aisles and transepts, decorated by princes for their own burial-places, and as shrines for their especial Saints. In these, the splendour of the entire edifice is intensified and gathered to a focus. Unless words were gems, that would flame with many-coloured light upon the page, and throw thence a tremulous glimmer into the reader's eyes, it were vain to attempt a description of a princely chapel.

Restless with her trouble, Hilda now entered upon another pilgrimage among these altars and shrines. She climbed the hundred steps of the Ara Cœli; she trod the broad, silent nave of Saint John Lateran; she stood in the Pantheon, under the round opening in the Dome, through which the blue, sunny sky still gazes down, as it used to gaze when there were Roman deities in the antique niches. She went into every church that rose before her, but not now to wonder at its magnificence, which she hardly noticed, more than if it had been the pine-built interiour of a New England meeting-house.

She went (and it was a dangerous errand) to observe how closely and comfortingly the Popish faith applied itself to all human occasions. It was impossible to doubt that multitudes of people found their spiritual advantage in it, who would find none at all in our own formless mode of worship, which, besides, so far as the sympathy of prayerful souls is concerned, can be enjoyed only at stated and too infrequent periods. But, here, whenever the hunger for divine nutriment came upon the soul, it could on the instant be appeased. At one or another altar, the incense was forever ascending; the mass always being performed, and carrying upward with it the devotion of such as had not words for their own prayer. And yet, if the worshipper had his individual petition to offer, his own heart-secret to whisper below his breath, there were divine auditors ever ready to receive it from his lips; and what encouraged him still more, these auditors had not always been divine, but kept, within their heavenly memories, the tender humility of a human experience. Now, a Saint in Heaven, but, once, a man on earth!

Hilda saw peasants, citizens, soldiers, nobles, women with bare heads, ladies in their silks, entering the churches, individually, kneeling for moments, or for hours, and directing their inaudible devotions to the shrine of some Saint of their

own choice. In his hallowed person, they felt themselves
possessed of an own friend in Heaven. They were too humble
to approach the Deity directly. Conscious of their unworthiness, they asked the mediation of their sympathizing patron,
who, on the score of his ancient martyrdom, and after many
ages of celestial life, might venture to talk with the Divine
Presence almost as friend with friend. Though dumb before
its Judge, even Despair could speak, and pour out the misery
of its soul like water, to an advocate so wise to comprehend
the case, and eloquent to plead it, and powerful to win
pardon, whatever were the guilt. Hilda witnessed what she
deemed to be an example of this species of confidence
between a young man and his Saint. He stood before a shrine,
writhing, wringing his hands, contorting his whole frame, in
an agony of remorseful recollection, but finally knelt down to
weep and pray. If this youth had been a Protestant, he
would have kept all that torture pent up in his heart, and
let it burn there till it seared him into indifference.

Often, and long, Hilda lingered before the shrines and
chapels of the Virgin, and departed from them with reluctant
steps. Here, perhaps, strange as it may seem, her delicate
appreciation of Art stood her in good stead, and lost Catholicism a convert. If the painter had represented Mary with a
heavenly face, poor Hilda was now in the very mood to worship her, and adopt the faith in which she held so elevated a
position. But she saw that it was merely the flattered portrait
of an earthly beauty, the wife, at best, of the artist, or, it
might be, a peasant-girl of the Campagna, or some Roman
princess to whom he desired to pay his court. For love, or
some even less justifiable motive, the old painter had apotheosized these women; he thus gained for them, as far as his
skill would go, not only the meed of immortality, but the
privilege of presiding over Christian altars, and of being
worshipped with far holier fervours than while they dwelt

on earth. Hilda's fine sense of the fit and decorous could not be betrayed into kneeling at such a shrine.

She never found just the Virgin Mother whom she needed. Here, it was an earthly mother, worshipping the earthly baby in her lap, as any and every mother does from Eve's time downward. In another picture, there was a dim sense, shown in the mother's face, of some divine quality in the child. In a third, the artist seemed to have had a higher perception, and had striven hard to shadow out the Virgin's joy at bringing the Saviour into the world, and her awe and love, inextricably mingled, of the little form which she pressed against her bosom. So far was good. But still, Hilda looked for something more; a face of celestial beauty, but human as well as heavenly, and with the shadow of past grief upon it; bright with immortal youth, yet matronly and motherly, and endowed with a queenly dignity, but infinitely tender, as the highest and deepest attribute of her divinity.

"Ah," thought Hilda to herself, "why should not there be a Woman to listen to the prayers of women; a Mother in Heaven for all motherless girls like me! In all God's thought and care for us, can He have withheld this boon, which our weakness so much needs!"

Oftener than to the other churches, she wandered into Saint Peter's. Within its vast limits, she thought, and beneath the sweep of its great Dome, there should be space for all forms of Christian truth; room both for the faithful and the heretic to kneel; due help for every creature's spiritual want.

Hilda had not always been adequately impressed by the grandeur of this mighty Cathedral. When she first lifted the heavy-leathern curtain, at one of the doors, a shadowy edifice in her imagination had been dazzled out of sight by the reality. Her pre-conception of Saint Peter's was a structure of no definite outline, misty in its architecture, dim, and gray, and huge, stretching into an interminable perspective, and over-arched by a Dome like the cloudy firmament. Beneath that vast breadth and height, as she had fancied them, the personal man might feel his littleness, and the soul triumph in its immensity. So, in her earlier visits, when the compassed splendour of the actual interiour glowed before her eyes, she had profanely called it a great prettiness; a gay piece of cabinet-work on a Titanic scale; a jewel-casket, marvellously magnified.

This latter image best pleased her fancy; a casket, all inlaid, in the inside, with precious stones of various hue, so that there should not be a hair's breadth of the small interiour unadorned with its resplendent gem. Then, conceive this minute wonder of a mosaic-box, increased to the magnitude of a Cathedral, without losing the intense lustre of its littleness, but all its petty glory striving to be sublime. The magic transformation from the minute to the vast has not been so cunningly effected, but that the rich adornment still counteracts the impression of space and loftiness. The spectator is more sensible of its limits than of its extent.

Until after many visits, Hilda continued to mourn for that dim, illimitable interiour, which, with her eyes shut, she had seen from childhood, but which vanished at her first glimpse through the actual door. Her childish vision seemed preferable to the Cathedral which Michel Angelo, and all the great architects, had built; because, of the dream-edifice, she had said, 'How vast it is!'—while, of the real Saint Peter's, she could only say, 'After all, it is not so immense!' Besides, such as the church is, it can nowhere be made visible at one glance. It stands in its own way. You see an aisle or a transept; you see the nave, or the tribune; but, on account of its ponderous piers and other obstructions, it is only by this fragmentary process that you get an idea of the Cathedral.

There is no answering such objections. The great church smiles calmly upon its critics, and, for all response, says, 'Look at me!'—and if you still murmur for the loss of your shadowy perspective, there comes no reply, save, 'Look at me!'—in endless repetition, as the one thing to be said. And, after looking many times, with long intervals between, you discover that the Cathedral has gradually extended itself over the whole compass of your idea; it covers all the site of your visionary temple, and has room for its cloudy pinnacles beneath the Dome.

One afternoon, as Hilda entered Saint Peter's, in sombre mood, its interiour beamed upon her with all the effect of a new creation. It seemed an embodiment of whatever the imagination could conceive, or the heart desire, as a magnificent, comprehensive, majestic symbol of religious faith. All splendour was included within its verge, and there was space for all. She gazed with delight even at the multiplicity of ornament. She was glad of the cherubim that fluttered upon the pilasters, and of the marble doves, hovering, unexpectedly, with green olive-branches of precious stones. She could spare nothing, now, of the manifold magnificence that had been lavished, in a hundred places, richly enough to have made world-famous shrines, in any other church, but which here melted away into the vast, sunny breadth, and were of no separate account. Yet each contributed its little all towards the grandeur of the whole.

She would not have banished one of those grim Popes, who sit each over his own tomb, scattering cold benedictions out of their marble hands; nor a single frozen sister of the Allegoric family, to whom (as, like hired mourners at an English funeral, it costs them no wear and tear of heart) is assigned the office of weeping for the dead. If you choose to see these things, they present themselves; if you deem them unsuitable and out of place, they vanish, individually, but leave their life upon the walls.

The pavement! It stretched out illimitably, a plain of many-coloured marble, where thousands of worshippers might kneel together, and shadowless angels tread among them without brushing their heavenly garments against those earthly ones. The roof! The Dome! Rich, gorgeous, filled with sunshine, cheerfully sublime, and fadeless after centuries, those lofty depths seemed to translate the heavens to mortal comprehension, and help the spirit upward to a yet higher and wider sphere. Must not the Faith, that built this matchless edifice, and warmed, illuminated, and overflowed from it, include whatever can satisfy human aspirations, at the loftiest, or minister to human necessity at the sorest! If Religion had a material home, was it not here!

As the scene, which we but faintly suggest, shone calmly before the New England maiden, at her entrance, she moved, as if by very instinct, to one of the vases of holy-water, upborne against a column by two mighty cherubs. Hilda dipt her fingers, and had almost signed the cross upon her breast, but forbore, and trembled, while shaking the water from her finger-tips. She felt as if her mother's spirit, somewhere within the Dome, were looking down upon her child, the daughter of Puritan forefathers, and weeping to behold her ensnared by these gaudy superstitions. So, she strayed sadly onward, up the nave, and towards the hundred golden lights that swarm before the high altar. Seeing a woman, a priest, and a soldier, kneel to kiss the toe of the brazen Saint Peter, (who protrudes it beyond his pedestal, for the purpose, polished bright with former salutations,) while a child stood on tiptoe to do the same, the glory of the church was darkened before Hilda's eyes. But again she went onward into remoter regions. She turned into the right transept, and thence found her way to a shrine, in the extreme corner of the edifice, which is adorned with a mosaic copy of Guido's beautiful Archangel, treading on the prostrate fiend.

This was one of the few pictures, which, in these dreary days, had not faded nor deteriorated in Hilda's estimation; not that it was better than many in which she no longer took an interest; but the subtle delicacy of the painter's genius was peculiarly adapted to her character. She felt, while gazing at it, that the artist had done a great thing, not merely for the Church of Rome, but for the cause of Good. The moral of the picture (the immortal youth and loveliness of Virtue, and its irresistible might against ugly Evil) appealed as much to Puritans as Catholics.

Suddenly, and as if it were done in a dream, Hilda found herself kneeling before the shrine, under the ever-burning lamp that throws its ray upon the Archangel's face. She laid her forehead on the marble steps before the altar, and sobbed out a prayer; she hardly knew to whom, whether Michael, the Virgin, or the Father; she hardly knew for what, save only a vague longing, that thus the burthen of her spirit might be lightened a little.

In an instant, she snatched herself up, as it were, from her knees, all a-throb with the emotions which were struggling to force their way out of her heart by the avenue, that had so nearly been opened for them. Yet there was a strange sense of relief won by that momentary, passionate prayer; a strange joy, moreover, whether for what she had done, or for what she had escaped doing, Hilda could not tell. But she felt as one half-stifled, who has stolen a breath of air.

Next to the shrine where she had knelt, there is another, adorned with a picture by Guercino, representing a maiden's body in the jaws of the sepulchre, and her lover weeping over it; while her beatified spirit looks down upon the scene, in the society of the Saviour, and a throng of Saints. Hilda wondered if it were not possible, by some miracle of faith, so to rise above her present despondency that she might look down upon what she was, just as Petronilla in the picture looked at her own corpse. A hope, born of hysteric trouble, fluttered in her heart. A presentiment, or what she fancied such, whispered her, that, before she had finished the circuit of the Cathedral, relief would come.

The unhappy are continually tantalized by similar delusions of succour near at hand; at least, the despair is very dark that has no such Will-o'-the-Wisp to glimmer in it.

XXXIX

THE WORLD'S CATHEDRAL

STILL gliding onward, Hilda now looked up into the Dome, where the sunshine came through the western windows, and threw across long shafts of light. They rested upon the mosaic figures of two Evangelists, above the cornice. These great beams of radiance, traversing what seemed the empty space, were made visible, in misty glory, by the holy cloud of incense, else unseen, which had risen into the middle Dome. It was to Hilda as if she beheld the worship of the priest and people, ascending heavenward, purified from its alloy of earth, and acquiring celestial substance in the golden atmosphere to which it aspired. She wondered if Angels did not sometimes hover within the Dome, and show themselves (in brief glimpses, floating amid the sunshine and the glorified vapour) to those who devoutly worshipped on the pavement.

She had now come into the southern transept. Around this portion of the church are ranged a number of confessionals. They are small tabernacles of carved wood, with a closet for the priest in the centre, and, on either side, a space for a penitent to kneel, and breathe his confession through a perforated auricle into the good Father's ear. Observing this arrangement, though already familiar to her, our poor Hilda was anew impressed with the infinite convenience (if we may use so poor a phrase) of the Catholic religion to its devout believers.

Who, in truth, that considers the matter, can resist a similar impression! In the hottest fever-fit of life, they can always find, ready for their need, a cool, quiet, beautiful place of worship. They may enter its sacred precincts, at any hour, leaving the fret and trouble of the world behind them, and purifying themselves with a touch of holy-water at the threshold. In the calm interiour, fragrant of rich and soothing incense, they may hold converse with some Saint, their awful, kindly friend. And, most precious privilege of all, whatever perplexity, sorrow, guilt, may weigh upon their souls, they can fling down the dark burthen at the foot of the Cross, and go forth—to sin no more, nor be any longer disquieted—but to live again in the freshness and elasticity of innocence!

"Do not these inestimable advantages," thought Hilda, "or some of them, at least, belong to Christianity itself? Are they not a part of the blessings which the System was meant to bestow upon mankind? Can the faith, in which I was born and bred, be perfect, if it leave a weak girl like me to wander, desolate, with this great trouble crushing me down?"

A poignant anguish thrilled within her breast; it was like a thing that had life, and was struggling to get out.

"Oh, help! Oh, help!" cried Hilda. "I cannot, cannot bear it!"

Only by the reverberations that followed—arch echoing the sound to arch, and a Pope of bronze repeating it to a Pope of marble, as each sat enthroned over his tomb—did Hilda become aware that she had really spoken above her breath. But, in that great space, there is no need to hush up the heart within one's own bosom, so carefully as elsewhere; and, if the cry reached any distant auditor, it came broken into many fragments, and from various quarters of the church.

Approaching one of the confessionals, she saw a woman kneeling within. Just as Hilda drew near, the penitent rose, came forth, and kissed the hand of the priest, who regarded her with a look of paternal benignity, and appeared to be giving her some spiritual counsel, in a low voice. She then knelt to receive his blessing, which was fervently bestowed. Hilda was so struck with the peace and joy in the woman's face, that, as the latter retired, she could not help speaking to her.

"You look very happy!" said she. "Is it so sweet, then, to go to the Confessional?"

"Oh, very sweet, my dear Signorina!" answered the woman, with moistened eyes and an affectionate smile; for she was so thoroughly softened with what she had been doing, that she felt as if Hilda were her younger sister.— "My heart is at rest now. Thanks be to the Saviour, and the Blessed Virgin, and the Saints, and this good Father, there is no more trouble for poor Teresa!"

"I am glad for your sake," said Hilda, sighing for her own. "I am a poor heretic, but a human sister; and I rejoice for you!"

She went from one to another of the confessionals, and, looking at each, perceived that they were inscribed with gilt letters; on one, Pro Italica Lingua; on another, Pro Flandrica Lingua; on a third, Pro Polonica Lingua; on a fourth, Pro Illyrica Lingua; on a fifth, Pro Hispanica Lingua. In this vast and hospitable Cathedral, worthy to be the religious heart of the whole world, there was room for all nations; there was access to the Divine Grace for every Christian soul; there was an ear for what the overburthened heart might have to murmur, speak in what native tongue it would.

When Hilda had almost completed the circuit of the transept, she came to a confessional, (the central part was closed, but a mystic rod protruded from it, indicating the presence of a priest within,) on which was inscribed, PRO ANGLICA LINGUA.

It was the word in season! If she had heard her mother's voice from within the tabernacle, calling her, in her own mother-tongue, to come and lay her poor head in her lap, and sob out all her troubles, Hilda could not have responded with a more inevitable obedience. She did not think; she only felt. Within her heart, was a great need. Close at hand, within the veil of the confessional, was the relief. She flung herself down in the penitent's place; and, tremulously, passionately, with sobs, tears, and the turbulent overflow of emotion too long repressed, she poured out the dark story which had infused its poison into her innocent life.

Hilda had not seen, nor could she now see, the visage of the priest. But, at intervals, in the pauses of that strange confession, half-choked by the struggle of her feelings towards an outlet, she heard a mild, calm voice, somewhat mellowed by age. It spoke soothingly; it encouraged her; it led her on by apposite questions that seemed to be suggested by a great and tender interest, and acted like magnetism in attracting the girl's confidence to this unseen friend. The priest's share in the interview, indeed, resembled that of one who removes the stones, clustered branches, or whatever entanglements impede the current of a swollen stream. Hilda could have imagined—so much to the purpose were his inquiries—that he was already acquainted with some outline of what she strove to tell him.

Thus assisted, she revealed the whole of her terrible secret! The whole, except that no name escaped her lips!

And, ah, what a relief! When the hysteric gasp, the strife between words and sobs, had subsided, what a torture had passed away from her soul! It was all gone; her bosom was as pure now as in her childhood. She was a girl again; she was Hilda, of the dove-cote; not that doubtful creature whom her own doves had hardly recognized as their mistress and playmate, by reason of the death-scent that clung to her garments!

After she had ceased to speak, Hilda heard the priest bestir himself with an old man's reluctant movement. He stept out of the confessional; and as the girl was still kneeling in the penitential corner, he summoned her forth.

"Stand up, my daughter!" said the mild voice of the Confessor. "What we have further to say, must be spoken face to face."

Hilda did his bidding, and stood before him with a downcast visage, which flushed, and grew pale again. But it had the wonderful beauty which we may often observe in those who have recently gone through a great struggle, and won the peace that lies just on the other side. We see it in a new mother's face; we see it in the faces of the dead; and in Hilda's countenance, (which had always a rare natural charm for her friends,) this glory of peace made her as lovely as an angel.

On her part, Hilda beheld a venerable figure with hair as white as snow, and a face strikingly characterized by benevolence. It bore marks of thought, however, and penetrative insight; although the keen glances of the eyes were now somewhat bedimmed with tears, which the aged shed, or almost shed, on lighter stress of emotion than would elicit them from younger men.

"It has not escaped my observation, daughter," said the priest, "that this is your first acquaintance with the confessional. How is this?"

"Father," replied Hilda raising her eyes, and again letting them fall, "I am of New England birth, and was bred as what you call a heretic."

"From New England?" exclaimed the priest. "It was my own birth-place, likewise; nor have fifty years of absence made me cease to love it. But, a heretic! And are you reconciled to the Church?"

"Never, Father," said Hilda.

"And, that being the case," demanded the old man, "on what ground, my daughter, have you sought to avail yourself of these blessed privileges (confined exclusively to members of the one true Church) of Confession and Absolution?"

"Absolution, Father?" exclaimed Hilda, shrinking back. "Oh, no, no! I never dreamed of that! Only our Heavenly Father can forgive my sins; and it is only by sincere repentance of whatever wrong I may have done, and by my own best efforts towards a higher life, that I can hope for His forgiveness! God forbid that I should ask absolution from mortal man!"

"Then, wherefore," rejoined the priest, with somewhat less mildness in his tone—"wherefore, I ask again, have you taken possession, as I may term it, of this holy ordinance; being a heretic, and neither seeking to share, nor having faith in, the unspeakable advantages which the Church offers to its penitents?"

"Father," answered Hilda, trying to tell the old man the simple truth, "I am a motherless girl, and a stranger here in Italy. I had only God to take care of me, and be my closest friend; and the terrible, terrible crime, which I have revealed to you, thrust itself between Him and me; so that I groped for Him in the darkness, as it were, and found Him not—found nothing but a dreadful solitude, and this crime in the midst of it! I could not bear it. It seemed as if I made the awful guilt my own, by keeping it hidden in my heart. I grew a fearful thing to myself. I was going mad!"

"It was a grievous trial, my poor child!" observed the Confessor. "Your relief, I trust, will prove to be greater than you yet know."

"I feel already how immense it is!" said Hilda, looking gratefully in his face. "Surely, Father, it was the hand of Providence that led me hither, and made me feel that this vast temple of Christianity, this great home of Religion, must needs contain some cure, some ease, at least, for my un-utterable anguish. And it has proved so. I have told the hideous secret; told it under the sacred seal of the Con-fessional; and now it will burthen my poor heart no more!"

"But, daughter," answered the venerable priest, not unmoved by what Hilda said, "you forget!—you mistake!—you claim a privilege to which you have not entitled your-self! The seal of the Confessional, do you say? God forbid that it should ever be broken, where it has been fairly im-pressed; but it applies only to matters that have been confided to its keeping in a certain prescribed method, and by persons, moreover, who have faith in the sanctity of the ordinance. I hold myself (and any learned casuist of the Church would hold me) as free to disclose all the particulars of what you term your confession, as if they had come to my knowledge in a secular way."

"This is not right, Father!" said Hilda, fixing her eyes on the old man's.

"Do not you see, child," he rejoined, with some little heat—"with all your nicety of conscience, cannot you recognize it as my duty to make the story known to the proper authori-ties; a great crime against public justice being involved, and further evil consequencies likely to ensue?"

"No, Father, no!" answered Hilda, courageously, her cheeks flushing and her eyes brightening as she spoke. "Trust a girl's simple heart sooner than any casuist of your Church, however learned he may be. Trust your own heart, too! I came to your confessional, Father, as I devoutly believe, by the direct impulse of Heaven, which also brought you hither to-day, in its mercy and love, to relieve me of a torture that

I could no longer bear. I trusted in the pledge which your Church has always held sacred between the Priest and the human soul, which, through his medium, is struggling towards its Father above. What I have confided to you lies sacredly between God and yourself. Let it rest there, Father; for this is right, and if you do otherwise, you will perpetrate a great wrong, both as a priest and a man! And, believe me, no question, no torture, shall ever force my lips to utter what would be necessary, in order to make my confession available towards the punishment of the guilty ones. Leave Providence to deal with them!"

"My quiet little countrywoman," said the priest, with half a smile on his kindly old face, "you can pluck up a spirit, I perceive, when you fancy an occasion for one!"

"I have spirit only to do what I think right," replied Hilda simply. "In other respects, I am timorous."

"But you confuse yourself between right-feelings and very foolish inferences," continued the priest, "as is the wont of women, (so much I have learnt by long experience in the Confessional,) be they young or old. However, to set your heart at rest, there is no probable need for me to reveal the matter. What you have told, if I mistake not, and perhaps more, is already known in the quarter which it most concerns."

"Known!" exclaimed Hilda. "Known to the authorities of Rome! And what will be the consequence?"

"Hush!" answered the Confessor, laying his finger on his lips. "I tell you my supposition, (mind, it is no assertion of the fact,) in order that you may go the more cheerfully on your way, not deeming yourself burthened with any responsibility as concerns this dark deed. And, now, daughter, what have you to give in return for an old man's kindness and sympathy?"

"My grateful remembrance," said Hilda fervently, "as long as I live!"

"And nothing more?" the priest inquired with a persuasive smile. "Will you not reward him with a great joy; one of the last joys that he may know on earth, and a fit one to take with him into the better world? In a word, will you not allow him to bring you, as a stray lamb, into the true fold? You have experienced some little taste of the relief and comfort, which the Church keeps abundantly in store for all its faithful children. Come home, dear child—poor wanderer, who hast caught a glimpse of the heavenly light—come home, and be at rest!"

"Father," said Hilda, much moved by his kindly earnestness, (in which, however, genuine as it was, there might still be a leaven of professional craft,) "I dare not come a step farther than Providence shall guide me. Do not let it grieve you, therefore, if I never return to the Confessional; never dip my fingers in holy-water; never sign my bosom with the cross. I am a daughter of the Puritans. But, in spite of my heresy," she added, with a sweet, tearful smile, "you may one day see the poor girl, to whom you have done this great Christian kindness, coming to remind you of it, and thank you for it, in the better land!"

The old priest shook his head. But, as he stretched out his hands, at the same moment, in the act of benediction, Hilda knelt down and received the blessing with as devout a simplicity as any Catholic of them all.

XL

HILDA AND A FRIEND

WHEN Hilda knelt to receive the priest's benediction, the act was witnessed by a person who stood leaning against the marble balustrade that surrounds the hundred golden lights, before the high altar. He had stood there, indeed, from the moment of the girl's entrance into the confessional. His start of surprise, at first beholding her, and the anxious gloom that afterwards settled on his face, sufficiently betokened that he felt a deep and sad interest in what was going forward.

After Hilda had bidden the priest farewell, she came slowly towards the high altar. The individual, to whom we have alluded, seemed irresolute whether to advance or retire. His hesitation lasted so long, that the maiden, straying through a happy reverie, had crossed the wide extent of the pavement between the confessional and the altar, before he had decided whether to meet her. At last, when within a pace or two, she raised her eyes and recognized Kenyon.

"It is you!" she exclaimed with joyful surprise. "I am so happy!"

In truth, the sculptor had never before seen, nor hardly imagined, such a figure of peaceful beatitude as Hilda now presented. While coming towards him in the solemn radiance which, at that period of the day, is diffused through the transept and showered down beneath the Dome, she seemed of the same substance as the atmosphere that enveloped her. He could scarcely tell whether she was imbued with sunshine, or whether it was a glow of happiness that shone out of her.

At all events, it was a marvellous change from the sad girl, who had entered the confessional, bewildered with anguish, to this bright, yet softened image of religious consolation that emerged from it. It was as if one of the throng of angelic people, who might be hovering in the sunny depths of the Dome, had alighted on the pavement. Indeed, this capability of transfiguration (which we often see wrought by inward delight on persons far less capable of it than Hilda) suggests how angels come by their beauty. It grows out of their happiness, and lasts forever only because that is immortal.

She held out her hand; and Kenyon was glad to take it in his own, if only to assure himself that she was made of earthly material.

"Yes, Hilda, I see that you are very happy," he replied gloomily, and withdrawing his hand after a single pressure. "For me, I never was less so than at this moment."

"Has any misfortune befallen you?" asked Hilda with earnestness. "Pray tell me; and you shall have my sympathy, though I must still be very happy. Now, I know how it is, that the Saints above are touched by the sorrows of distressed people on earth, and yet are never made wretched by them. Not that I profess to be a Saint, you know," she added, smiling radiantly. "But the heart grows so large, and so rich, and so variously endowed, when it has a great sense of bliss, that it can give smiles to some and tears to others, with equal sincerity, and enjoy its own peace throughout all."

"Do not say you are no Saint!" answered Kenyon, with a smile, though he felt that the tears stood in his eyes. "You will still be Saint Hilda, whatever church may canonize you."

"Ah; you would not have said so, had you seen me but an hour ago!" murmured she. "I was so wretched, that there seemed a grievous sin in it."

"And what has made you so suddenly happy?" inquired the sculptor. "But, first, Hilda, will you not tell me why you were so wretched?"

"Had I met you, yesterday, I might have told you that," she replied. "To-day, there is no need."

"Your happiness, then?" said the sculptor, as sadly as before. "Whence comes it?"

"A great burthen has been lifted from my heart—from my conscience, I had almost said," answered Hilda, without shunning the glance that he fixed upon her. "I am a new creature, since this morning. Heaven be praised for it! It was a blessed hour—a blessed impulse—that brought me to this beautiful and glorious Cathedral. I shall hold it in loving remembrance, while I live, as the spot where I found infinite peace after infinite trouble!"

Her heart seemed so full, that it spilt its new gush of happiness, as it were, like rich and sunny wine out of an overbrimming goblet. Kenyon saw that she was in one of those moods of elevated feeling, when the soul is upheld by a strange tranquillity, which is really more passionate, and less controllable, than emotions far exceeding it in violence. He felt that there would be indelicacy (if he ought not rather to call it impiety) in his stealing upon Hilda, while she was thus beyond her own guardianship, and surprising her out of secrets which she might afterwards bitterly regret betraying to him. Therefore, though yearning to know what had happened, he resolved to forbear further question.

Simple and earnest people, however, being accustomed to speak from their genuine impulses, cannot easily, as craftier men do, avoid the subject which they have at heart. As often as the sculptor unclosed his lips, such words as these were ready to burst out:—

"Hilda, have you flung your angelic purity into that mass of unspeakable corruption, the Roman Church?"

"What were you saying?" she asked, as Kenyon forced back an almost uttered exclamation of this kind.

"I was thinking of what you have just remarked about the Cathedral," said he, looking up into the mighty hollow of the Dome. "It is indeed a magnificent structure, and an adequate expression of the Faith which built it. When I behold it in a proper mood—that is to say, when I bring my mind into a fair relation with the minds and purposes of its spiritual and material architects—I see but one or two criticisms to make. One is, that it needs painted windows."

"Oh, no!" said Hilda. "They would be quite inconsistent with so much richness of colour in the interiour of the church. Besides, it is a Gothic ornament, and only suited to that style of architecture, which requires a gorgeous dimness."

"Nevertheless," continued the sculptor, "yonder square apertures, filled with ordinary panes of glass, are quite out of keeping with the superabundant splendour of everything about them. They remind me of that portion of Aladdin's palace which he left unfinished, in order that his royal father-in-law might put the finishing touch. Daylight, in its natural state, ought not to be admitted here. It should stream through a brilliant illusion of Saints and Hierarchies, and old Scriptural images, and symbolized Dogmas, purple, blue, golden, and a broad flame of scarlet. Then, it would be just such an illumination as the Catholic faith allows to its believers. But, give me—to live and die in—the pure, white light of Heaven!"

"Why do you look so sorrowfully at me?" asked Hilda, quietly meeting his disturbed gaze. "What would you say to me? I love the white light, too!"

"I fancied so," answered Kenyon. "Forgive me, Hilda; but I must needs speak. You seemed to me a rare mixture of impressibility, sympathy, sensitiveness to many influences, with a certain quality of common sense;—no, not that, but a higher and finer attribute, for which I find no better word. However tremulously you might vibrate, this quality, I supposed, would always bring you back to the equipoise. You were a creature of imagination, and yet as truly a New England girl as any with whom you grew up in your native village. If there were one person in the world, whose native rectitude of thought, and something deeper, more reliable than thought, I would have trusted against all the arts of a priesthood—whose taste, alone, so exquisite and sincere that it rose to be a moral virtue, I would have rested upon as a sufficient safeguard—it was yourself!"

"I am conscious of no such high and delicate qualities as you allow me," answered Hilda. "But what have I done that a girl of New England birth and culture, with the right sense that her mother taught her, and the conscience that she developed in her, should not do?"

"Hilda, I saw you at the confessional!" said Kenyon.

"Ah, well, my dear friend," replied Hilda, casting down her eyes, and looking somewhat confused, yet not ashamed, "you must try to forgive me for that, (if you deem it wrong,) because it has saved my reason, and made me very happy. Had you been here, yesterday, I would have confessed to you."

"Would to Heaven I had!" ejaculated Kenyon.

"I think," Hilda resumed, "I shall never go to the Confessional again; for there can scarcely come such a sore trial twice in my life. If I had been a wiser girl, a stronger, and a more sensible, very likely I might not have gone to the Confessional at all. It was the sin of others that drove me thither; not my own, though it almost seemed so. Being what I am, I must either have done what you saw me doing, or have gone mad. Would that have been better?"

"Then, you are not a Catholic?" asked the sculptor earnestly.

"Really, I do not quite know what I am," replied Hilda, encountering his eyes with a frank and simple gaze. "I have a great deal of faith, and Catholicism seems to have a great deal of good. Why should not I be a Catholic, if I find there what I need, and what I cannot find elsewhere? The more I see of this worship, the more I wonder at the exuberance with which it adapts itself to all the demands of human infirmity. If its ministers were but a little more than human, above all errour, pure from all iniquity, what a religion would it be!"

"I need not fear your perversion to the Catholic faith," remarked Kenyon, "if you are at all aware of the bitter sarcasm implied in your last observation. It is very just. Only, the exceeding ingenuity of the system stamps it as the contrivance of man, or some worse author, not an emanation of the broad and simple wisdom from on high."

"It may be so," said Hilda; "but I meant no sarcasm."

Thus conversing, the two friends went together down the grand extent of the nave. Before leaving the church, they turned, to admire again its mighty breadth, the remoteness of the glory behind the altar, and the effect of visionary splendour and magnificence imparted by the long bars of smoky sunshine, which travelled so far before arriving at a place of rest.

"Thank Heaven for having brought me hither!" said Hilda fervently.

Kenyon's mind was deeply disturbed by his idea of her Catholic propensities; and, now, what he deemed her disproportionate and misapplied veneration for the sublime edifice, stung him into irreverence.

"The best thing I know of Saint Peter's," observed he, "is its equable temperature. We are now enjoying the coolness of last winter, which, a few months hence, will be the warmth of the present summer. It has no cure, I suspect, in all its length and breadth, for a sick soul, but it would make an admirable atmospheric hospital for sick bodies. What a delightful shelter would it be for the invalids who throng to Rome, where the Sirocco steals away their strength, and the Tramontana stabs them through and through, like cold steel with a poisoned point! But, within these walls, the thermometer never varies. Winter and Summer are married at the high altar, and dwell together in perfect harmony."

"Yes," said Hilda, "and I have always felt this soft, unchanging climate of Saint Peter's to be another manifestation of its sanctity."

"That is not precisely my idea," replied Kenyon. "But, what a delicious life it would be, if a colony of people with delicate lungs (or merely with delicate fancies) could take up their abode in this ever-mild and tranquil air! These architectural tombs of the Popes might serve for dwellings, and each brazen sepulchral door-way would become a domestic threshold. Then, the lover, if he dared, might say to his mistress, 'Will you share my tomb with me?'—and, winning her soft consent, he would lead her to the altar, and thence to yonder sepulchre of Pope Gregory, which should be their nuptial home. What a life would be theirs, Hilda, in their marble Eden!"

"It is not kind, nor like yourself," said Hilda gently, "to throw ridicule on emotions which are genuine. I revere this glorious church for itself and its purposes, and love it, moreover, because here I have found sweet peace, after a great anguish."

"Forgive me," answered the sculptor, "and I will do so no more. My heart is not so irreverent as my words."

They went through the Piazza of Saint Peter's, and the adjacent streets, silently, at first; but, before reaching the bridge of Sant' Angelo, Hilda's flow of spirits began to bubble forth, like the gush of a streamlet that has been shut up by frost, or by a heavy stone over its source. Kenyon had never found her so delightful as now; so softened out of the chillness of her virgin pride; so full of fresh thoughts, at which he was often moved to smile, although, on turning them over a little more, he sometimes discovered that they looked fanciful only because so absolutely true.

But, indeed, she was not quite in a normal state. Emerging from gloom into sudden cheerfulness, the effect upon Hilda was as if she were just now created. After long torpor, receiving back her intellectual activity, she derived an exquisite pleasure from the use of her faculties, which were set in motion by causes that seemed inadequate. She continually brought to Kenyon's mind the image of a child, making its plaything of every object, but sporting in good faith, and with a kind of seriousness. Looking up, for example, at the statue of Saint Michael, on the top of Hadrian's castellated tomb, Hilda fancied an interview between the Archangel and the old Emperour's ghost, who was naturally displeased at finding his mausoleum, which he had ordained for the stately and solemn repose of his ashes, converted to its present purposes.

"But Saint Michael, no doubt," she thoughtfully remarked, "would finally convince the Emperour Hadrian, that where a warlike despot is sown as the seed, a fortress and a prison are the only possible crop!"

They stopt on the bridge, to look into the swift, eddying flow of the yellow Tiber, a mud-puddle in strenuous motion; and Hilda wondered whether the seven-branched golden candlestick, the holy candlestick of the Jews, (which was lost at the Ponte Molle, in Constantine's time,) had yet been swept as far down the river as this.

"It probably stuck where it fell," said the sculptor, "and, by this time, is imbedded thirty feet deep in the mud of the Tiber. Nothing will ever bring it to light again."

"I fancy you are mistaken," replied Hilda smiling. "There was a meaning and purpose in each of its seven branches, and such a candlestick cannot be lost forever. When it is found again, and seven lights are kindled and burning in it, the whole world will gain the illumination which it needs. Would not this be an admirable idea for a mystic story, or parable, or seven-branched allegory, full of poetry, art, philosophy, and religion? It shall be called 'The Recovery of the Sacred Candlestick.' As each branch is lighted, it shall have a differently coloured lustre from the other six; and when all the seven are kindled, their radiance shall combine into the intense white light of Truth!"

"Positively, Hilda, this is a magnificent conception," cried Kenyon. "The more I look at it, the brighter it burns."

"I think so too," said Hilda, enjoying a childlike pleasure in her own idea. "The theme is better suited for verse than prose; and when I go home to America, I will suggest it to one of our poets. Or, seven poets might write the poem together, each lighting a separate branch of the Sacred Candlestick!"

"Then, you think of going home?" Kenyon asked.

"Only yesterday," she replied, "I longed to flee away. Now, all is changed, and, being happy again, I should feel deep regret at leaving the Pictorial Land. But, I cannot tell. In Rome, there is something dreary and awful, which we can never quite escape. At least, I thought so yesterday."

When they reached the Via Portoghese, and approached Hilda's tower, the doves, who were waiting aloft, flung themselves upon the air, and came floating down about her head. The girl caressed them, and responded to their cooings with similar sounds from her own lips, and with words of endearment; and their joyful flutterings and airy little flights, evidently impelled by pure exuberance of spirits, seemed to show that the doves had a real sympathy with their mistress's state of mind. For peace had descended upon her like a dove.

Bidding the sculptor farewell, Hilda climbed her tower, and came forth upon its summit to trim the Virgin's lamp. The doves, well knowing her custom, had flown up thither to meet her, and again hovered about her head; and very lovely was her aspect, in the evening sunlight, which had little further to do with the world, just then, save to fling a golden glory on Hilda's hair, and vanish.

Turning her eyes down into the dusky street, which she had just quitted, Hilda saw the sculptor still there, and waved her hand to him.

"How sad and dim he looks, down there in that dreary street!" she said to herself. "Something weighs upon his spirits. Would I could comfort him!"

"How like a spirit she looks, aloft there, with the evening glory round her head, and those winged creatures claiming her as akin to them!" thought Kenyon, on his part. "How far above me! How unattainable! Ah, if I could lift myself to her region! Or—if it be not a sin to wish it—would that I might draw her down to an earthly fireside!"

What a sweet reverence is that, when a young man deems his mistress a little more than mortal, and almost chides himself for longing to bring her close to his heart! A trifling circumstance, but such as lovers make much of, gave him hope. One of the doves, which had been resting on Hilda's shoulder, suddenly flew downward, (as if recognizing him as its mistress's dear friend, and perhaps commissioned with an errand of regard,) brushed his upturned face with its wings, and again soared aloft.

The sculptor watched the bird's return, and saw Hilda greet it with a smile.

XLI

SNOW-DROPS AND MAIDENLY
DELIGHTS

IT BEING still considerably earlier than the period at
which artists and tourists are accustomed to assemble in
Rome, the sculptor and Hilda found themselves comparatively alone there. The dense mass of native Roman
life, in the midst of which they were, served to press them
nearer to one another. It was as if they had been thrown
together on a desert island. Or, they seemed to have wandered,
by some strange chance, out of the common world, and encountered each other in a depopulated city, where there were
streets of lonely palaces, and unreckonable treasures of
beautiful and admirable things, of which they two became
the sole inheritors.

In such circumstances, Hilda's gentle reserve must have
been stronger than her kindly disposition permitted, if the
friendship between Kenyon and herself had not grown as
warm as a maiden's friendship can ever be, without absolutely and avowedly blooming into love. On the sculptor's
side, the amaranthine flower was already in full blow. But
it is very beautiful (though the lover's heart may grow chill
at the perception) to see how the snow will sometimes linger
in a virgin's breast, even after the Spring is well advanced.

In such alpine soils, the summer will not be anticipated; we seek vainly for passionate flowers, and blossoms of fervid hue and spicy fragrance, finding only snow-drops and sunless violets, when it is almost the full season for the crimson rose.

With so much tenderness as Hilda had in her nature, it was strange that she so reluctantly admitted the idea of love; especially as, in the sculptor, she found both congeniality and variety of taste, and likenesses and differences of character; these being as essential as those to any poignancy of mutual emotion.

So Hilda, as far as Kenyon could discern, still did not love him, though she admitted him within the quiet circle of her affections as a dear friend, and trusty counsellor. If we knew what is best for us, or could be content with what is reasonably good, the sculptor might well have been satisfied, for a season, with this calm intimacy, which so sweetly kept him a stranger in her heart, and a ceremonious guest, and yet allowed him the free enjoyment of all but its deeper recesses. The flowers, that grow outside of those inner sanctities, have a wild, hasty charm, which it is well to prove; there may be sweeter ones within the sacred precinct, but none that will die while you are handling them, and bequeathe you a delicious legacy, as these do, in the perception of their evanescence and unreality.

And this may be the reason, after all, why Hilda, like so many other maidens, lingered on the hither side of passion; her finer instinct and keener sensibility made her enjoy those pale delights in a degree of which men are incapable. She hesitated to grasp a richer happiness, as possessing already such measure of it as her heart could hold, and of a quality most agreeable to her virgin tastes.

Certainly, they both were very happy. Kenyon's genius, unconsciously wrought upon by Hilda's influence, took a more delicate character than heretofore. He modelled, among other things, a beautiful little statue of Maidenhood, gathering a Snow-drop. It was never put into marble, however; because the sculptor soon recognized it as one of those fragile creations which are true only to the moment that produces them, and are wronged, if we try to imprison their airy excellence in a permanent material.

On her part, Hilda returned to her customary occupations with a fresh love for them, and yet with a deeper look into the heart of things; such as those necessarily acquire, who have passed from picture-galleries into dungeon-gloom, and thence come back to the picture-gallery again. It is questionable whether she was ever so perfect a copyist, thenceforth. She could not yield herself up to the painter so unreservedly as in times past; her character had developed a sturdier quality, which made her less pliable to the influence of other minds. She saw into the picture as profoundly as ever, and perhaps more so, but not with the devout sympathy that had formerly given her entire possession of the Old Master's idea. She had known such a reality, that it taught her to distinguish inevitably the large portion that is unreal, in every work of art. Instructed by sorrow, she felt that there is something beyond almost all which pictorial genius has produced; and she never forgot those sad wanderings from gallery to gallery, and from church to church, when she had vainly sought a type of the Virgin Mother, or the Saviour, or Saint, or Martyr, which a soul in extreme need might recognize as the adequate one.

How, indeed, should she have found such! How could Holiness be revealed to the artists of an age when the greatest of them put genius and imagination in the place of spiritual insight, and when, from the Pope downward, all Christendom was corrupt!

Meanwhile, months wore away, and Rome received back that large portion of its life-blood which runs in the veins of

its foreign and temporary population. English visitors established themselves in the hotels, and in all the sunny suites
of apartments, in the streets convenient to the Piazza di
Spagna; the English tongue was heard familiarly along the
Corso, and English children sported in the Pincian Gardens.

The native Romans, on the other hand, like the butterflies
and grasshoppers, resigned themselves to the short, sharp
misery, which Winter brings to a people whose arrangements are made almost exclusively with a view to summer.
Keeping no fire within-doors, except possibly a spark or two
in the kitchen, they crept out of their cheerless houses into
the narrow, sunless, sepulchral streets, bringing their firesides
along with them in the shape of little earthen pots, vases,
or pipkins, full of lighted charcoal and warm ashes, over
which they held their tingling finger-ends. Even in this
half-torpid wretchedness, they still seemed to dread a pestilence in the sunshine, and kept on the shady side of the
piazzas, as scrupulously as in summer. Through the open
door-ways, (no need to shut them, when the weather within
was bleaker than without,) a glimpse into the interiour of
their dwellings showed the uncarpeted brick-floors, as dismal
as the pavement of a tomb.

They drew their old cloaks about them, nevertheless, and
threw the corners over their shoulders, with the dignity of
attitude and action that have come down to these modern
citizens, as their sole inheritance from the togaed nation.
Somehow or other, they managed to keep up their poor, frost-
bitten hearts against the pitiless atmosphere, with a quiet
and uncomplaining endurance that really seems the most
respectable point in the present Roman character. For, in
New England, or in Russia, or scarcely in a hut of the
Esquimaux, there is no such discomfort to be borne as by
Romans in wintry weather, when the orange-trees bear icy
fruit in the gardens; and when the rims of all the fountains

are shaggy with icicles, and the Fountain of Trevi skimmed almost across with a glassy surface; and when there is a slide in the Piazza of Saint Peter's, and a fringe of brown, frozen foam along the eastern shore of the Tiber, and sometimes a fall of great snow-flakes into the dreary lanes and alleys of the miserable city. Cold blasts, that bring death with them, now blow upon the shivering invalids, who came hither in the hope of breathing balmy airs.

Wherever we pass our summers, may all our inclement months, from November to April, henceforth be spent in some country that recognizes Winter as an integral portion of its year!

Now, too, there was especial discomfort in the stately picture-galleries, where nobody, indeed—not the princely or priestly founders, nor any who have inherited their cheerless magnificence—ever dreamed of such an impossibility as fire-side warmth, since those great palaces were built. Hilda, therefore, finding her fingers so much benumbed that the spiritual influence could not be transmitted to them, was persuaded to leave her easel before a picture, on one of these wintry days, and pay a visit to Kenyon's studio. But neither was the studio anything better than a dismal den, with its marble shapes shivering around the walls, cold as the snow-images which the sculptor used to model, in his boyhood, and sadly behold them weep themselves away, at the first thaw.

Kenyon's Roman artizans, all this while, had been at work on the Cleopatra. The fierce Egyptian queen had now struggled almost out of the imprisoning stone; or, rather, the workmen had found her within the mass of marble, imprisoned there by magic, but still fervid to the touch with fiery life, the fossil woman of an age that produced statelier, stronger, and more passionate creatures, than our own. You already felt her compressed heat, and were aware of a tiger-like character even in her repose. If Octavius should make his appearance, though the marble still held her within its embrace, it was evident that she would tear herself forth in a twinkling, either to spring enraged at his throat, or, sinking into his arms, to make one more proof of her rich blandishments, or falling lowly at his feet, to try the efficacy of a woman's tears.

"I am ashamed to tell you how much I admire this statue," said Hilda. "No other sculptor could have done it!"

"This is very sweet for me to hear," replied Kenyon; "and, since your reserve keeps you from saying more, I shall imagine you expressing everything that an artist would wish to hear said about his work."

"You will not easily go beyond my genuine opinion," answered Hilda, with a smile.

"Ah; your kind word makes me very happy," said the sculptor; "and I need it, just now, on behalf of my Cleopatra. That inevitable period has come, (for I have found it inevitable, in regard to all my works,) when I look at what I fancied to be a statue, lacking only breath to make it live, and find it a mere lump of senseless stone, into which I have not really succeeded in moulding the spiritual part of my idea. I should like, now—only it would be such shameful treatment for a discrowned queen, and my own offspring, too—I should like to hit poor Cleopatra a bitter blow on her Egyptian nose, with this mallet!"

"That is a blow which all statues seem doomed to receive, sooner or later, though seldom from the hand that sculptured them," said Hilda, laughing. "But you must not let yourself be too much disheartened by the decay of your faith in what you produce. I have heard a poet express similar distaste for his own most exquisite poems; and I am afraid that this final despair, and sense of short-coming, must always be the reward and punishment of those who try to grapple with a great or beautiful idea. It only proves that you have been able to imagine things too high for mortal faculties to execute. The Idea leaves you an imperfect image of itself, which you at first mistake for the ethereal reality, but soon find that the latter has escaped out of your closest embrace."

"And the only consolation is," remarked Kenyon, "that the blurred and imperfect image may still make a very respectable appearance in the eyes of those who have not seen the original."

"More than that," rejoined Hilda; "for there is a class of spectators whose sympathy will help them to see the Perfect, through a mist of imperfection. Nobody, I think, ought to read poetry, or look at pictures or statues, who cannot find a great deal more in them than the poet or artist has actually expressed. Their highest merit is suggestiveness."

"You, Hilda, are yourself the only critic in whom I have much faith," said Kenyon. "Had you condemned Cleopatra, nothing should have saved her."

"You invest me with such an awful responsibility," she replied, "that I shall not dare to say a single word about your other works."

"At least," said the sculptor, "tell me whether you recognize this bust."

He pointed to a bust of Donatello. It was not the one which Kenyon had begun to model at Monte Beni, but a reminiscence of the Count's face, wrought under the influence of all the sculptor's knowledge of his history, and of his personal and hereditary character. It stood on a wooden pedestal, not nearly finished, but with fine white dust and small chips of marble scattered about it, and itself incrusted all round with the white, shapeless substance of the block. In the midst, appeared the features, lacking sharpness, and very much resembling a fossil countenance, (but we have already used this simile, in reference to Cleopatra,) with the accumulations of long-past ages clinging to it.

And yet, strange to say, the face had an expression, and a more recognizable one than Kenyon had succeeded in putting into the clay-model, at Monte Beni. The reader is probably acquainted with Thorwaldsen's threefold analogy; —the Clay-model, the Life; the Plaister-cast, the Death; and the sculptured Marble, the Resurrection;—and it seemed to be made good by the spirit that was kindling up these imperfect features, like a lambent flame.

"I was not quite sure, at first glance, that I knew the face," observed Hilda. "The likeness surely is not a striking one. There is a good deal of external resemblance, still, to the features of the Faun of Praxiteles, between whom and Donatello, you know, we once insisted that there was a perfect twin-brotherhood. But the expression is now so very different!"

"What do you take it to be?" asked the sculptor.

"I hardly know how to define it," she answered. "But it has an effect as if I could see this countenance gradually brightening while I look at it. It gives the impression of a growing intellectual power and moral sense. Donatello's face used to evince little more than a genial, pleasurable sort of vivacity, and capability of enjoyment. But, here, a soul is being breathed into him; it is the Faun, but advancing towards a state of higher development."

"Hilda, do you see all this?" exclaimed Kenyon, in considerable surprise. "I may have had such an idea in my mind, but was quite unaware that I had succeeded in conveying it into the marble."

"Forgive me," said Hilda, "but I question whether this striking effect has been brought about by any skill or purpose on the sculptor's part. Is it not, perhaps, the chance-result of the bust being just so far shaped out, in the marble, as the process of moral growth had advanced, in the original? A few more strokes of the chisel might change the whole expression, and so spoil it for what it is now worth."

"I believe you are right," answered Kenyon, thoughtfully examining his work; "and, strangely enough, it was the very expression that I tried, unsuccessfully, to produce in the clay-model. Well; not another chip shall be struck from the marble."

And, accordingly, Donatello's bust (like that rude, rough mass of the head of Brutus, by Michel Angelo, at Florence) has ever since remained in an unfinished state. Most spectators mistake it for an unsuccessful attempt towards copying the features of the Faun of Praxiteles. One observer in a thousand is conscious of something more, and lingers long over this mysterious face, departing from it, reluctantly, and with many a glance thrown backward. What perplexes him is the riddle that he sees propounded there; the riddle of the Soul's growth, taking its first impulse amid remorse and pain, and struggling through the incrustations of the senses. It was the contemplation of this imperfect portrait of Donatello that originally interested us in his history, and impelled us to elicit from Kenyon what he knew of his friend's adventures.

REMINISCENCES OF MIRIAM

W HEN Hilda and himself turned away from the unfinished bust, the sculptor's mind still dwelt upon the reminiscences which it suggested.

"You have not seen Donatello recently," he remarked, "and therefore cannot be aware how sadly he is changed."

"No wonder!" exclaimed Hilda, growing pale.

The terrible scene which she had witnessed, when Donatello's face gleamed out in so fierce a light, came back upon her memory, almost for the first time since she knelt at the confessional. Hilda (as is sometimes the case with persons whose delicate organization requires a peculiar safeguard) had an elastic faculty of throwing off such recollections as would be too painful for endurance. The first shock of Donatello's and Miriam's crime had, indeed, broken through the frail defence of this voluntary forgetfulness; but, once enabled to relieve herself of the ponderous anguish over which she had so long brooded, she had practised a subtle watchfulness in preventing its return.

"No wonder, do you say?" repeated the sculptor, looking at her with interest, but not exactly with surprise; for he had long suspected that Hilda had a painful knowledge of events which he himself little more than surmised. "Then you know!—you have heard! But what can you possibly have heard, and through what channel?"

"Nothing!" replied Hilda, faintly. "Not one word has reached my ears from the lips of any human being. Let us never speak of it again! No, no! Never again!"

"And Miriam!" said Kenyon, with irrepressible interest. "Is it also forbidden to speak of her?"

"Hush! Do not even utter her name! Try not to think of it!" Hilda whispered. "It may bring terrible consequences!"

"My dear Hilda!" exclaimed Kenyon, regarding her with wonder and deep sympathy. "My sweet friend, have you had this secret hidden in your delicate, maidenly heart, through all these many months! No wonder that your life was withering out of you."

"It was so, indeed!" said Hilda, shuddering. "Even now, I sicken at the recollection."

"And how could it have come to your knowledge?" continued the sculptor. "But, no matter! Do not torture yourself with referring to the subject. Only, if at any time it should be a relief to you, remember that we can speak freely together, for Miriam has herself suggested a confidence between us."

"Miriam has suggested this!" exclaimed Hilda. "Yes, I remember, now, her advising that the secret should be shared with you. But I have survived the death-struggle that it cost me, and need make no further revelations. And Miriam has spoken to you! What manner of woman can she be, who, after sharing in such a deed, can make it a topic of conversation with her friends?"

"Ah, Hilda," replied Kenyon, "you do not know (for you could never learn it from your own heart, which is all purity and rectitude) what a mixture of good there may be in things evil; and how the greatest criminal, if you look at his conduct from his own point of view, or from any side-point, may seem not so unquestionably guilty, after all. So with Miriam;

so with Donatello. They are perhaps partners in what we must call awful guilt; and yet, I will own to you—when I think of the original cause, the motives, the feelings, the sudden concurrence of circumstances thrusting them onward, the urgency of the moment, and the sublime unselfishness on either part—I know not well how to distinguish it from much that the world calls heroism. Might we not render some such verdict as this?—'Worthy of Death, but not unworthy of Love!'"

"Never!" answered Hilda, looking at the matter through the clear, crystal medium of her own integrity. "This thing, as regards its causes, is all a mystery to me, and must remain so. But there is, I believe, only one right and one wrong; and I do not understand (and may God keep me from ever understanding) how two things so totally unlike can be mistaken for one another; nor how two mortal foes—as Right and Wrong surely are—can work together in the same deed. This is my faith; and I should be led astray, if you could persuade me to give it up."

"Alas, for poor human nature, then!" said Kenyon sadly, and yet half-smiling at Hilda's unworldly and impracticable theory. "I always felt you, my dear friend, a terribly severe judge, and have been perplexed to conceive how such tender sympathy could coexist with the remorselessness of a steel blade. You need no mercy, and therefore know not how to show any!"

"That sounds like a bitter gibe," said Hilda, with the tears springing into her eyes. "But I cannot help it. It does not alter my perception of the truth. If there be any such dreadful mixture of good and evil as you affirm, (and which appears to me almost more shocking than pure evil,) then the good is turned to poison, not the evil to wholesomeness."

The sculptor seemed disposed to say something more, but yielded to the gentle steadfastness with which Hilda declined to listen. She grew very sad; for a reference to this one dismal topic had set, as it were, a prison-door ajar, and allowed a throng of torturing recollections to escape from their dungeons into the pure air and white radiance of her soul. She bade Kenyon a briefer farewell than ordinary, and went homeward to her tower.

In spite of her efforts to withdraw them to other subjects, her thoughts dwelt upon Miriam; and, as had not heretofore happened, they brought with them a painful doubt whether a wrong had not been committed, on Hilda's part, towards the friend once so beloved. Something that Miriam had said, in their final conversation, recurred to her memory, and seemed now to deserve more weight than Hilda had assigned to it, in her horrour at the crime just perpetrated. It was not that the deed looked less wicked and terrible, in the retrospect; but she asked herself whether there were not other questions to be considered, aside from that single one of Miriam's guilt or innocence; as, for example, whether a close bond of friendship, in which we once voluntarily engage, ought to be severed on account of any unworthiness, which we subsequently detect in our friend. For, in these unions of hearts, (call them marriage, or whatever else,) we take each other for better, for worse. Availing ourselves of our friend's intimate affection, we pledge our own, as to be relied upon in every emergency. And what sadder, more desperate emergency could there be, than had befallen Miriam! Who more need the tender succour of the innocent, than wretches stained with guilt! And, must a selfish care for the spotlessness of our own garments keep us from pressing the guilty ones close to our hearts, wherein, for the very reason that we are innocent, lies their securest refuge from further ill!

It was a sad thing for Hilda to find this moral enigma propounded to her conscience, and to feel that, whichever way she might settle it, there would be a cry of wrong on the other side. Still, the idea stubbornly came back, that the tie between Miriam and herself had been real, the affection true, and that therefore the implied compact was not to be shaken off.

"Miriam loved me well," thought Hilda, remorsefully, "and I failed her at her sorest need!"

Miriam loved her well; and not less ardent had been the affection which Miriam's warm, tender, and generous characteristics had excited in Hilda's more reserved and quiet nature. It had never been extinguished; for, in part, the wretchedness, which Hilda had since endured, was but the struggle and writhing of her sensibility, still yearning towards her friend. And now, at the earliest encouragement, it awoke again, and cried out piteously, complaining of the violence that had been done it.

Recurring to the delinquencies of which she fancied—(we say 'fancied,' because we do not unhesitatingly adopt Hilda's present view, but rather suppose her misled by her feelings)— of which she fancied herself guilty towards her friend, she suddenly remembered a sealed pacquet that Miriam had confided to her. It had been put into her hands with earnest injunctions of secrecy and care, and if unclaimed after a certain period, was to be delivered according to its address. Hilda had forgotten it; or, rather, she had kept the thought of this commission in the back-ground of her consciousness, with all other thoughts referring to Miriam.

But, now, the recollection of this pacquet, and the evident stress which Miriam laid upon its delivery, at the specified time, impelled Hilda to hurry up the staircase of her tower, dreading lest the period should already have elapsed.

No; the hour had not gone by, but was on the very point of passing. Hilda read the brief note of instruction, on a corner of the envelope, and discovered, that, in case of

Miriam's absence from Rome, the pacquet was to be taken to its destination, that very day.

"How nearly I had violated my promise!" said Hilda. "And, since we are separated forever, it has the sacredness of an injunction from a dead friend. There is no time to be lost."

So Hilda set forth, in the decline of the afternoon, and pursued her way towards the quarter of the city, in which stands the Palazzo Cenci. Her habit of self-reliance was so simply strong, so natural, and now so well established by long use, that the idea of peril seldom or never occurred to Hilda, in her lonely life.

She differed, in this particular, from the generality of her sex; although the customs and character of her native land often produce women, who meet the world with gentle fearlessness, and discover that its terrours have been absurdly exaggerated by the tradition of mankind. In ninety-nine cases out of a hundred, the apprehensiveness of women is quite gratuitous. Even as matters now stand, they are really safer, in perilous situations and emergencies, than men, and might be still more so, if they trusted themselves more confidingly to the chivalry of manhood. In all her wanderings about Rome, Hilda had gone, and returned, as securely as she had been accustomed to tread the familiar street of her New England village, where every face wore a look of recognition. With respect to whatever was evil, foul, and ugly, in this populous and corrupt city, she had trodden as if invisible, and not only so, but blind. She was altogether unconscious of anything wicked that went along the same pathway, but without jostling or impeding her, any more than gross substance hinders the wanderings of a spirit. Thus it is, that, bad as the world is said to have grown, Innocence continues to make a Paradise around itself, and keep it still unfallen.

Hilda's present expedition led her into what was—physically, at least—the foulest and ugliest part of Rome. In that vicinity lies the Ghetto, where thousands of Jews are crowded within a narrow compass, and lead a close, unclean, and multitudinous life, resembling that of maggots when they overpopulate a decaying cheese.

Hilda passed on the borders of this region, but had no occasion to step within it. Its neighborhood, however, naturally partook of characteristics like its own. There was a confusion of black and hideous houses, piled massively out of the ruins of former ages, rude, and destitute of plan, as a pauper would build his hovel, and yet displaying here and there an arched gateway, a cornice, a pillar, or a broken arcade, that might have adorned a palace. Many of the houses, indeed, as they stood, might once have been palaces, and possessed still a squalid kind of grandeur. Dirt was everywhere, strewing the narrow streets, and incrusting the tall shabbiness of the edifices, from the foundations to the roofs; it lay upon the thresholds, and looked out of the windows, and assumed the guise of human life in the children, that seemed to be engendered out of it. Their father was the Sun, and their mother—a heap of Roman mud!

It is a question of speculative interest whether the ancient Romans were as unclean a people as we everywhere find those who have succeeded them. There appears to be a kind of malignant spell in the spots that have been inhabited by these masters of the world, or made famous in their history; an inherited and inalienable curse, impelling their successors to fling dirt and defilement upon whatever temple, column, ruined palace, or triumphal arch, may be nearest at hand, and on every monument that the old Romans built. It is most probably a classic trait, regularly transmitted downward, and perhaps a little modified by the better civilization of Christianity; so that Caesar may have trod narrower and filthier ways, in his path to the Capitol, than even those of modern Rome.

As the paternal abode of Beatrice, the gloomy old palace of the Cencis had an interest for Hilda; although not sufficiently strong, hitherto, to overcome the disheartening effect of the exteriour, and draw her over its threshold. The adjacent piazza, of poor aspect, contained only an old woman selling roasted chestnuts and baked squash-seeds; she looked sharply at Hilda, and inquired whether she had lost her way.

"No," said Hilda. "I seek the Palazzo Cenci."

"Yonder it is, fair Signorina," replied the Roman matron. "If you wish that pacquet delivered, which I see in your hand, my grandson Pietro shall run with it, for a baiòcco. The Cenci palace is a spot of ill-omen for young maidens."

Hilda thanked the old dame, but alleged the necessity of doing her errand in person. She approached the front of the palace, which, with all its immensity, had but a mean appearance, and seemed an abode which the lovely shade of Beatrice would not be apt to haunt, unless her doom made it inevitable. Some soldiers stood about the portal, and gazed at the brown-haired, fair-cheeked Anglo-Saxon girl, with approving glances, but not indecorously. Hilda began to ascend the staircase, three lofty flights of which were to be surmounted, before reaching the door whither she was bound.

XLIII

THE EXTINCTION OF A LAMP

B ETWEEN Hilda and the sculptor there had been a kind of half-expressed understanding, that both were to visit the galleries of the Vatican, the day subsequent to their meeting at the studio. Kenyon, accordingly, failed not to be there, and wandered through the vast ranges of apartments, but saw nothing of his expected friend. The marble faces, which stand innumerable along the walls, and have kept themselves so calm through the vicissitudes of twenty centuries, had no sympathy for his disappointment; and he, on the other hand, strode past these treasures and marvels of antique art, with the indifference which any pre-occupation of the feelings is apt to produce, in reference to objects of sculpture. Being of so cold and pure a substance, and mostly deriving their vitality more from thought than passion, they require to be seen through a perfectly trans-parent medium.

And, moreover, Kenyon had counted so much upon Hilda's delicate perceptions in enabling him to look at two or three of the statues, about which they had talked together, that the entire purpose of his visit was defeated by her absence. It is a delicious sort of mutual aid, when the united power of two sympathetic, yet dissimilar intelligences, is brought to bear upon a poem by reading it aloud, or upon a picture or statue, by viewing it in each other's company. Even if not a word of criticism be uttered, the insight of either party is wonderfully deepened, and the comprehension broadened; so that the inner mystery of a work of genius, hidden from one, will often reveal itself to two. Missing such help, Kenyon saw nothing at the Vatican which he had not seen a thousand times before, and more perfectly than now.

In the chill of his disappointment, he suspected that it was a very cold art to which he had devoted himself. He questioned, at that moment, whether Sculpture really ever softens and warms the material which it handles; whether carved marble is anything but limestone, after all; and whether the Apollo Belvedere itself possesses any merit above its physical beauty, or is beyond criticism even in that generally acknowledged excellence. In flitting glances, heretofore, he had seemed to behold this statue as something ethereal and godlike, but not now.

Nothing pleased him, unless it were the group of the Laocoon, which, in its immortal agony, impressed Kenyon as a type of the long, fierce struggle of Man, involved in the knotted entanglements of Errour and Evil, those two snakes, which (if no Divine help intervene) will be sure to strangle him and his children, in the end. What he most admired was the strange calmness, diffused through this bitter strife; so that it resembled the rage of the sea, made calm by its immensity, or the tumult of Niagara, which ceases to be tumult because it lasts forever. Thus, in the Laocoon, the horrour of a moment grew to be the Fate of interminable ages. Kenyon looked upon the group as the one triumph of Sculpture, creating the repose, which is essential to it, in the very acmé of turbulent effort; but, in truth, it was his mood of unwonted despondency that made him so sensitive to the terrible magnificence, as well as to the sad moral of this work. Hilda herself could not have helped him to see it with nearly such intelligence.

A good deal more depressed than the nature of the disappointment warranted, Kenyon went to his studio, and took in hand a great lump of clay. He soon found, however, that his plastic cunning had departed from him, for the time. So he wandered forth again into the uneasy streets of Rome, and walked up and down the Corso, where, at that period of the day, a throng of passers-by and loiterers choked up the narrow sidewalk. A penitent was thus brought in contact with the sculptor.

It was a figure in a white robe, with a kind of featureless mask over the face, through the apertures of which the eyes threw an unintelligible light. Such odd, questionable shapes are often seen gliding through the streets of Italian cities, and are understood to be usually persons of rank, who quit their palaces, their gaieties, their pomp and pride, and assume the penitential garb, for a season, with a view of thus expiating some crime, or atoning for the aggregate of petty sins that make up a worldly life. It is their custom to ask alms, and perhaps to measure the duration of their penance by the time requisite to accumulate a sum of money out of the little droppings of individual charity. The proceeds are devoted to some beneficent or religious purpose; so that the benefit accruing to their own souls is, in a manner, linked with a good done, or intended, to their fellow-men. These figures have a ghastly and startling effect, not so much from any very impressive peculiarity in the garb, as from the mystery which they bear about with them, and the sense that there is an acknowledged sinfulness as the nucleus of it.

In the present instance, however, the penitent asked no alms of Kenyon; although, for the space of a minute or two, they stood face to face, the hollow eyes of the mask encountering the sculptor's gaze. But, just as the crowd was about to separate them, the former spoke, in a voice not unfamiliar to Kenyon, though rendered remote and strange by the guilty veil through which it penetrated.

"Is all well with you, Signor?" inquired the penitent, out of the cloud in which he walked.

"All is well," answered Kenyon. "And with you?"

But the masked penitent returned no answer, being borne away by the pressure of the throng.

The sculptor stood watching the figure, and was almost of a mind to hurry after him and follow up the conversation that had been begun; but it occurred to him that there is a sanctity (or, as we might rather term it, an inviolable etiquette) which prohibits the recognition of persons who choose to walk under the veil of penitence.

"How strange!" thought Kenyon to himself. "It was surely Donatello! What can bring him to Rome, where his recollections must be so painful, and his presence not without peril? And Miriam! Can she have accompanied him?"

He walked on, thinking of the vast change in Donatello, since those days of gaiety and innocence, when the young Italian was new in Rome, and was just beginning to be sensible of a more poignant felicity than he had yet experienced, in the sunny warmth of Miriam's smile. The growth of a soul, which the sculptor half imagined that he had witnessed in his friend, seemed hardly worth the heavy price that it had cost, in the sacrifice of those simple enjoyments that were gone forever. A creature of antique healthfulness had vanished from the earth; and, in his stead, there was only one other morbid and remorseful man, among millions that were cast in the same indistinguishable mould.

The accident of thus meeting Donatello—the glad Faun of his imagination and memory, now transformed into a gloomy penitent—contributed to deepen the cloud that had fallen over Kenyon's spirits. It caused him to fancy (as we generally do, in the petty troubles which extend not a hand's breadth beyond our own sphere) that the whole world was saddening around him. It took the sinister aspect of an omen, although he could not distinctly see what trouble it might forebode.

If it had not been for a peculiar sort of pique, with which lovers are much conversant, (a preposterous kind of resentment which endeavours to wreak itself on the beloved object, and on one's own heart, in requital of mishaps for which neither are in fault,) Kenyon might at once have betaken himself to Hilda's studio, and asked why the appointment was not kept. But the interview of to-day was to have been so rich in present joy, and its results so important to his future life, that the bleak failure was too much for his equanimity. He was angry with poor Hilda, and censured her without a hearing; angry with himself, too, and therefore inflicted on this latter criminal the severest penalty in his power; angry with the day that was passing over him, and would not permit its latter hours to redeem the disappointment of the morning.

To confess the truth, it had been the sculptor's purpose to stake all his hopes on that interview in the galleries of the Vatican. Straying with Hilda through those long vistas of ideal beauty, he meant, at last, to utter himself upon that theme which lovers are fain to discuss in village-lanes, in wood-paths, on seaside sands, in crowded streets; it little matters where, indeed, since roses are sure to blush along the way, and daisies and violets to spring beneath the feet, if the spoken word be graciously received. He was resolved to make proof whether the kindness, that Hilda evinced for him, was the precious token of an individual preference, or merely the sweet fragrance of her disposition, which other friends might share as largely as himself. He would try if it were possible to take this shy, yet frank, and innocently fearless creature, captive, and imprison her in his heart, and make her sensible of a wider freedom, there, than in all the world besides.

It was hard, we must allow, to see the shadow of a wintry sunset falling upon a day that was to have been so bright, and to find himself just where yesterday had left him, only with a sense of being drearily baulked, and defeated without an opportunity for struggle. So much had been anticipated from these now vanished hours, that it seemed as if no other day could bring back the same golden hopes.

In a case like this, it is doubtful whether Kenyon could have done a much better thing than he actually did, by going to dine at the Café Nuovo, and drinking a flask of Montefiascone; longing, the while, for a beaker or two of Donatello's Sunshine. It would have been just the wine to cure a lover's melancholy by illuminating his heart with tender light and warmth, and suggestions of undefined hopes, too ethereal for his morbid humour to examine and reject them.

No decided improvement resulting from the draught of Montefiascone, he went to the Teatro Argentino, and sat gloomily to see an Italian comedy, which ought to have cheered him somewhat, being full of glancing merriment, and effective over everybody's risibilities except his own. The sculptor came out, however, before the close of the perform-ance, as disconsolate as he went in.

As he made his way through the complication of narrow streets, which perplex that portion of the city, a carriage passed him. It was driven rapidly, but not too fast for the light of a gas-lamp to flare upon a face within; especially as it was bent forward, appearing to recognize him, while a beckoning hand was protruded from the window. On his part, Kenyon at once knew the face, and hastened to the carriage, which had now stopped.

"Miriam! You in Rome?" he exclaimed. "And your friends know nothing of it?"

"Is all well with you?" she asked.

This inquiry, in the identical words which Donatello had so recently addressed to him, from beneath the penitent's mask, startled the sculptor. Either the previous disquietude of his mind, or some tone in Miriam's voice, or the unaccountableness of beholding her there, at all, made it seem ominous.

"All is well, I believe," answered he, doubtfully. "I am aware of no misfortune. Have you any to announce?"

He looked still more earnestly at Miriam, and felt a dreamy uncertainty whether it was really herself to whom he spoke. True; there were those beautiful features, the contour of which he had studied too often, and with a sculptor's accuracy of perception, to be in any doubt that it was Miriam's identical face. But he was conscious of a change, the nature of which he could not satisfactorily define; it might be merely her dress, which, imperfect as the light was, he saw to be richer than the simple garb that she had usually worn. The effect, he fancied, was partly owing to a gem which she had on her bosom; not a diamond, but something that glimmered with a clear, red lustre, like the stars in a southern sky. Somehow or other, this coloured light seemed an emanation of herself, as if all that was passionate and glowing, in her native disposition, had crystallized upon her breast, and were just now scintillating more brilliantly than ever, in sympathy with some emotion of her heart.

Of course, there could be no real doubt that it was Miriam, his artist-friend, with whom and Hilda he had spent so many pleasant and familiar hours, and whom he had last seen at Perugia, bending with Donatello beneath the bronze Pope's benediction. It must be that self-same Miriam; but the sensitive sculptor felt a difference of manner, which impressed him more than he conceived it possible to be affected, by so external a thing. He remembered the gossip so prevalent in Rome, on Miriam's first appearance; how that she was no real artist, but the daughter of an illustrious or golden lineage, who was merely playing at necessity; mingling with human struggle for her pastime; stepping out of her native sphere, only for an interlude, just as a princess might alight from her gilded equipage to go on foot through a rustic lane. And now, after a masque in which Love and Death had performed their several parts, she had resumed her proper character.

"Have you anything to tell me?" cried he, impatiently; for nothing causes a more disagreeable vibration of the nerves than this perception of ambiguousness in familiar persons or affairs. "Speak; for my spirits and patience have been much tried to-day."

Miriam put her finger on her lips, and seemed desirous that Kenyon should know of the presence of a third person. He now saw, indeed, that there was some one beside her in the carriage, hitherto concealed by her attitude; a man, it appeared, with a sallow Italian face, which the sculptor distinguished but imperfectly, and did not recognize.

"I can tell you nothing," she replied; and leaning towards him, she whispered, (appearing then more like the Miriam whom he knew, than in what had before passed,)—"Only, when the lamp goes out, do not despair!"

The carriage drove on, leaving Kenyon to muse over this unsatisfactory interview, which seemed to have served no better purpose than to fill his mind with more ominous forebodings than before. Why were Donatello and Miriam in Rome, where both, in all likelihood, might have much to dread? And why had one and the other addressed him with a question that seemed prompted by a knowledge of some calamity, either already fallen on his unconscious head, or impending closely over him?

"I am sluggish," muttered Kenyon to himself; "a weak, nerveless fool, devoid of energy and promptitude; or neither Donatello nor Miriam could have escaped me thus! They are aware of some misfortune that concerns me deeply. How soon am I to know it too?"

There seemed but a single calamity possible to happen, within so narrow a sphere as that with which the sculptor was connected; and even to that one mode of evil he could assign no definite shape, but only felt that it must have some reference to Hilda.

Flinging aside the morbid hesitation, and the dallyings with his own wishes, which he had permitted to influence his mind throughout the day, he now hastened to the Via Portoghese. Soon, the old palace stood before him, with its massive tower rising into the clouded night, obscured from view, at its midmost elevation, but revealed again, higher upward, by the Virgin's lamp that twinkled on the summit. Feeble as it was, in the broad, surrounding gloom, that little ray made no inconsiderable illumination among Kenyon's sombre thoughts; for, remembering Miriam's last words, a fantasy had seized him that he should find the sacred lamp extinguished.

And, even while he stood gazing, as a mariner at the star in which he puts his trust, the light quivered, sank, gleamed up again, and finally went out, leaving the battlements of Hilda's tower in utter darkness. For the first time in centuries, the consecrated and legendary flame, before the loftiest shrine in Rome, had ceased to burn.

XLIV

THE DESERTED SHRINE

K ENYON knew the sanctity which Hilda (faithful
Protestant, and daughter of the Puritans, as the girl
was) imputed to this shrine. He was aware of the
profound feeling of responsibility, as well earthly as religious,
with which her conscience had been impressed, when she
became the occupant of her aërial chamber, and undertook
the task of keeping the consecrated lamp a-light. There was
an accuracy and a certainty about Hilda's movements, as
regarded all matters that lay deep enough to have their roots
in right or wrong, which made it as possible and safe to rely
upon the timely and careful trimming of this lamp, (if she
were in life, and able to creep up the steps,) as upon the rising of tomorrow's sun, with lustre undiminished from to-day.

The sculptor could scarcely believe his eyes, therefore,
when he saw the flame flicker and expire. His sight had
surely deceived him. And now, since the light did not
re-appear, there must be some smoke-wreath or impenetrable
mist brooding about the tower's gray, old head, and obscuring
it from the lower world. But, no! For right over the dim
battlements, as the wind chased away a mass of clouds, he
beheld a star, and, moreover, by an earnest concentration of
his sight, was soon able to discern even the darkened shrine

itself. There was no obscurity around the tower; no infirmity of his own vision. The flame had exhausted its supply of oil, and become extinct. But where was Hilda!

A man in a cloak happened to be passing; and Kenyon (anxious to distrust the testimony of his senses, if he could get more acceptable evidence on the other side) appealed to him.

"Do me the favour, Signor," said he, "to look at the top of yonder tower, and tell me whether you see the lamp burning at the Virgin's shrine."

"The lamp, Signor!" answered the man, without at first troubling himself to look up. "The lamp that has burned, these four hundred years! How is it possible, Signor, that it should not be burning, now?"

"But, look!" said the sculptor impatiently.

With good-natured indulgence for what he seemed to consider as the whim of an eccentric Forestiero, the Italian carelessly threw his eyes upward; but, as soon as he perceived that there was really no light, he lifted his hands with a vivid expression of wonder and alarm.

"The lamp is extinguished!" cried he. "The lamp that has been burning, these four hundred years! This surely must portend some great misfortune; and, by my advice, Signor, you will hasten hence, lest the tower tumble on our heads. A priest once told me, that, if the Virgin withdrew her blessing, and the light went out, the old Palazzo del Torre would sink into the earth, with all that dwell in it. There will be a terrible crash before morning!"

The stranger made the best of his way from the doomed premises; while Kenyon (who would willingly have seen the tower crumble down before his eyes, on condition of Hilda's safety) determined, late as it was, to attempt ascertaining if she were in her dove-cote.

Passing through the arched entrance—which, as is often the case with Roman entrances, was as accessible at midnight as at noon—he groped his way to the broad staircase, and, lighting his wax-taper, went glimmering up the multitude of steps that led to Hilda's door. The hour being so unseasonable, he intended merely to knock, and, as soon as her voice from within should re-assure him, to retire, keeping his explanations and apologies for a fitter time. Accordingly, reaching the lofty height where the maiden, as he trusted, lay asleep, with angels watching over her, though the Virgin seemed to have suspended her care, he tapped lightly at the door-panels—then knocked more forcibly—then thundered an impatient summons. No answer came. Hilda evidently was not there.

After assuring himself that this must be the fact, Kenyon descended the stairs, but made a pause, at every successive stage, and knocked at the door of its apartment, regardless whose slumbers he might disturb, in his anxiety to learn when the girl had last been seen. But, at each closed entrance, there came those hollow echoes, which a chamber— or any dwelling, great or small—never sends out, in response to human knuckles or iron hammer, as long as there is life within to keep its heart from getting dreary.

Once, indeed, on the lower landing-place, the sculptor fancied that there was a momentary stir, inside the door, as if somebody were listening at the threshold. He hoped, at least, that the small, iron-barred aperture would be unclosed, through which Roman housekeepers are wont to take careful cognizance of applicants for admission, from a traditionary dread, perhaps, of letting in a robber or assassin. But it remained shut; neither was the sound repeated; and Kenyon concluded that his excited nerves had played a trick upon his senses, as they are apt to do when we most wish for the clear evidence of the latter.

There was nothing to be done, save to go heavily away, and await whatever good or ill tomorrow's daylight might disclose.

Betimes in the morning, therefore, Kenyon went back to the Via Portoghese, before the slant rays of the sun had descended half-way down the gray front of Hilda's tower. As he drew near its base, he saw the doves perched, in full session, on the sunny height of the battlements; and a pair of them (who were probably their mistress's especial pets, and the confidants of her bosom-secrets, if Hilda had any) came shooting down, and made a feint of alighting on his shoulder. But, though they evidently recognized him, their shyness would not yet allow so decided a demonstration. Kenyon's eyes followed them as they flew upward, hoping that they might have come as joyful messengers of the girl's safety, and that he should discern her slender form, half-hidden by the parapet, trimming the extinguished lamp at the Virgin's shrine, just as other maidens set about the little duties of a household. Or perhaps he might see her gentle and sweet face smiling down upon him, midway towards Heaven, as if she had flown thither for a day or two, just to visit her kindred, but had been drawn earthward again by the spell of unacknowledged love.

But his eyes were blessed by no such fair vision or reality; nor, in truth, were the eager, unquiet flutterings of the doves indicative of any joyful intelligence, which they longed to share with Hilda's friend, but of anxious inquiries that they knew not how to utter. They could not tell, any more than he, whither their lost companion had withdrawn herself, but were in the same void despondency with him, feeling their sunny and airy lives darkened and grown imperfect, now that her sweet society was taken out of it.

In the brisk morning air, Kenyon found it much easier to pursue his researches than at the preceding midnight, when, if any slumberers heard the clamour that he made, they had responded only with sullen and drowsy maledictions, and turned to sleep again. It must be a very dear and intimate reality for which people will be content to give up a dream. When the sun was fairly up, however, it was quite another thing. The heterogeneous population, inhabiting the lower floor of the old tower and the other extensive regions of the palace, were now willing to tell all they knew, and imagine a great deal more. The amiability of these Italians, assisted by their sharp and nimble wits, caused them to overflow with plausible suggestions, and to be very bounteous in their avowals of interest for the lost Hilda. In a less demonstrative people, such expressions would have implied an eagerness to search land and sea, and never rest till she were found. In the mouths that uttered them, they meant good wishes, and were so far better than indifference. There was little doubt that many of them felt a genuine kindness for the shy, brown-haired, delicate, young foreign maiden, who had flown from some distant land to alight upon their tower, where she consorted only with the doves. But their energy expended itself in exclamation; and they were content to leave all more active measures to Kenyon, and to the Virgin, whose affair it was, to see that the faithful votary of her lamp received no harm.

In a great Parisian domicile, multifarious as its inhabitants might be, the concierge under the archway would be cognizant of all their incomings and issuings-forth. But, except in rare cases, the general entrance and main staircase of a Roman house are left as free as the street, of which they form a sort of by-lane. The sculptor, therefore, could hope to find information about Hilda's movements only from casual observers.

On probing the knowledge of these people to the bottom, there was various testimony as to the period when the girl had last been seen. Some said, that it was four days since there had been a trace of her; but an English lady, in the second piano of the palace, was rather of opinion that she had met her, the morning before, with a drawing-book in her hand. Having no acquaintance with the young person, she had taken little notice, and might have been mistaken. A Count, on the piano next above, was very certain that he had lifted his hat to Hilda, under the archway, two afternoons ago. An old woman, who had formerly tended the shrine, threw some light upon the matter, by testifying that the lamp required to be replenished once, at least, in three days, though its reservoir of oil was exceedingly capacious.

On the whole, though there was other evidence enough to create some perplexity, Kenyon could not satisfy himself that she had been visible since the afternoon of the third preceding day, when a fruit-seller remembered her coming out of the arched passage, with a sealed pacquet in her hand. As nearly as he could ascertain, this was within an hour after Hilda had taken leave of the sculptor, at his own studio, with the understanding that they were to meet at the Vatican, the next day. Two nights, therefore, had intervened, during which the lost maiden was unaccounted for.

The door of Hilda's apartments was still locked, as on the preceding night; but Kenyon sought out the wife of the person who sub-let them, and prevailed on her to give him admittance by means of the duplicate-key, which the good woman had in her possession. On entering, the maidenly neatness and simple grace, recognizable in all the arrangements, made him visibly sensible that this was the daily haunt of a pure soul, in whom religion and the love of beauty were at one.

Thence, the sturdy Roman matron led the sculptor across a narrow passage, and threw open the door of a small chamber, on the threshold of which he reverently paused. Within, there was a bed, covered with white drapery, enclosed within snowy curtains, like a tent, and of barely width enough for a slender figure to repose upon it. The sight of this cool, airy, and secluded bower caused the lover's heart to stir, as if enough of Hilda's gentle dreams were lingering there to make him happy for a single instant. But then came the closer consciousness of her loss, bringing along with it a sharp sting of anguish.

"Behold, Signor!" said the matron. "Here is the little staircase, by which the Signorina used to ascend, and trim the Blessed Virgin's lamp. She was worthy to be a Catholic, such pains the good child bestowed to keep it burning; and doubtless the Blessed Mary will intercede for her, in consideration of her pious offices, heretic though she was. What will become of the old palazzo, now that the lamp is extinguished, the Saints above us only know! Will you mount, Signor, to the battlements, and see if she have left any trace of herself there?"

The sculptor stepped across the chamber, and ascended the little staircase, which gave him access to the breezy summit of the tower. It affected him inexpressibly to see a bouquet of beautiful flowers beneath the shrine, and to recognize in them an offering of his own to Hilda, who had put them in a vase of water and dedicated them to the Virgin, in a spirit partly fanciful, perhaps, but still partaking of the religious sentiment which so profoundly influenced her character. One rosebud, indeed, she had selected for herself from the rich mass of flowers; for Kenyon well remembered recognizing it in her bosom, when he last saw her, at his studio.

"That little part of my great love she took!" said he to himself. "The remainder she would have devoted to Heaven, but has left it withering in the sun and wind. Ah, Hilda, Hilda, had you given me a right to watch over you, this evil had not come!"

"Be not downcast, Signorino mio," said the Roman matron, in response to the deep sigh which struggled out of Kenyon's breast. "The dear little maiden, as we see, has decked yonder blessed shrine as devoutly as I myself, or any other good

Catholic woman, could have done. It is a religious act, and has more than the efficacy of a prayer. The Signorina will as surely come back as the sun will fall through the window, tomorrow no less than to-day. Her own doves have often been missing, for a day or two, but they were sure to come fluttering about her head again, when she least expected them. So will it be with this dove-like child!"

"It might be so," thought Kenyon, with yearning anxiety, "if a pure maiden were as safe as a dove, in this evil world of ours!"

As they returned through the studio, with the furniture and arrangements of which the sculptor was familiar, he missed a small, ebony writing-desk that he remembered as having always been placed on a table there. He knew that it was Hilda's custom to deposit her letters in this desk, as well as other little objects of which she wished to be specially careful.

"What has become of it?" he suddenly inquired, laying his hand on the table.

"Become of what, pray?" exclaimed the woman, a little disturbed. "Does the Signor suspect a robbery, then?"

"The Signorina's writing-desk is gone," replied Kenyon. "It always stood on this table, and I myself saw it there, only a few days ago."

"Ah, well!" said the woman, recovering her composure, which she seemed partly to have lost. "The Signorina has doubtless taken it away with her. The fact is of good omen; for it proves that she did not go unexpectedly, and is likely to return when it may best suit her convenience."

"This is very singular!" observed Kenyon. "Have the rooms been entered by yourself, or any other person, since the Signorina's disappearance?"

"Not by me, Signor—so help me Heaven and the Saints!" said the matron. "And I question whether there are more than two keys in Rome, that will suit this strange, old lock. Here is one; and as for the other, the Signorina carries it in her pocket."

The sculptor had no reason to doubt the word of this respectable dame. She appeared to be well-meaning and kind-hearted, as Roman matrons generally are; except when a fit of passion incites them to shower horrible curses on an obnoxious individual, or perhaps to stab him with the steel stiletto that serves them for a hair-pin. But Italian asseverations of any questionable fact, however true they may chance to be, have no witness of their truth in the faces of those who utter them. Their words are spoken with strange earnestness, and yet do not vouch for themselves as coming from any depth, like roots drawn out of the substance of the soul, with some of the soil clinging to them. There is always a something inscrutable, instead of frankness, in their eyes. In short, they lie so much like truth, and speak truth so much as if they were telling a lie, that their auditor suspects himself in the wrong, whether he believes or disbelieves them; it being the one thing certain, that falsehood is seldom an intolerable burthen to the tenderest of Italian consciences.

"It is very strange what can have become of the desk!" repeated Kenyon, looking the woman in the face.

"Very strange, indeed, Signor," she replied meekly, without turning away her eyes in the least, but checking his insight of them at about half-an-inch below the surface. "I think the Signorina must have taken it with her."

It seemed idle to linger here any longer. Kenyon therefore departed, after making an arrangement with the woman, by the terms of which she was to allow the apartments to remain in their present state, on his assuming the responsibility for the rent.

He spent the day in making such further search and investigation as he found practicable; and, though at first trammelled by an unwillingness to draw public attention to Hilda's affairs, the urgency of the circumstances soon compelled him to be thoroughly in earnest. In the course of a week, he tried all conceivable modes of fathoming the mystery, not merely by his personal efforts and those of his brother-artists and friends, but through the police, who readily undertook the task, and expressed strong confidence of success. But the Roman police has very little efficacy, except in the interest of the despotism of which it is a tool. With their cocked hats, shoulder-belts, and swords, they wear a sufficiently imposing aspect, and doubtless keep their eyes open wide enough to track a political offender, but are too often blind to private outrage, be it murder or any lesser crime. Kenyon counted little upon their assistance, and profited by it not at all.

Remembering the mystic words which Miriam had addressed to him, he was anxious to meet her, but knew not whither she had gone, nor how to obtain an interview either with herself or Donatello. The days wore away, and still there were no tidings of the lost one; no lamp rekindled before the Virgin's shrine; no light shining into the lover's heart; no star of Hope—he was ready to say, as he turned his eyes almost reproachfully upward—in Heaven itself!

XLV

THE FLIGHT OF HILDA'S DOVES

A LONG WITH the lamp on Hilda's tower, the sculptor now felt that a light had gone out, or, at least, was ominously obscured, to which he owed whatever cheerfulness had heretofore illuminated his cold, artistic life. The idea of this girl had been like a taper of virgin wax, burning with a pure and steady flame, and chasing away the evil spirits out of the magic circle of its beams. It had darted its rays afar, and modified the whole sphere in which Kenyon had his being. Beholding it no more, he at once found himself in darkness and astray.

This was the time, perhaps, when Kenyon first became sensible what a dreary city is Rome, and what a terrible weight is there imposed on human life, when any gloom within the heart corresponds to the spell of ruin, that has been thrown over the site of ancient empire. He wandered, as it were, and stumbled over the fallen columns, and among the tombs, and groped his way into the sepulchral darkness of the catacombs, and found no path emerging from them. The happy may well enough continue to be such, beneath the brilliant sky of Rome. But, if you go thither in melancholy mood—if you go with a ruin in your heart, or with a vacant site there, where once stood the airy fabric of happiness, now vanished—all the ponderous gloom of the Roman Past will pile itself upon that spot, and crush you down as with the heaped-up marble and granite, the earth-mounds, and multitudinous bricks, of its material decay.

It might be supposed that a melancholy man would here make acquaintance with a grim philosophy. He should learn to bear patiently his individual griefs, that endure only for one little lifetime, when here are the tokens of such infinite misfortune on an imperial scale, and when so many far land-marks of time, all around him, are bringing the remoteness of a thousand years ago into the sphere of yesterday. But it is in vain that you seek this shrub of bitter-sweetness among the plants that root themselves on the roughnesses of massive walls, or trail downward from the capitals of pillars, or spring out of the green turf in the Palace of the Caesars. It does not grow in Rome; not even among the five hundred various weeds which deck the grassy arches of the Coliseum. You look through a vista of century beyond century—through much shadow, and a little sunshine—through barbarism and civilization, alternating with one another, like actors that have pre-arranged their parts—through a broad pathway of progressive generations, bordered by palaces and temples, and bestridden by old, triumphal arches, until, in the distance, you behold the obelisks, with their unintelligible inscriptions, hinting at a Past infinitely more remote than history can define. Your own life is as nothing, when compared with that immeasurable distance; but still you demand, none the less earnestly, a gleam of sunshine, instead of a speck of shadow, on the step or two that will bring you to your quiet rest.

How exceedingly absurd! All men, from the date of the earliest obelisk—and of the whole world, moreover, since that far epoch, and before—have made a similar demand, and seldom had their wish. If they had it, what are they the better, now? But, even while you taunt yourself with this sad lesson, your heart cries out obstreperously for its small share of earthly happiness, and will not be appeased by the myriads of dead hopes that lie crushed into the soil of Rome. How wonderful, that this our narrow foothold of the Present should hold its own so constantly, and, while every moment changing, should still be like a rock betwixt the encountering tides of the long Past and the infinite To-come!

Man of marble though he was, the sculptor grieved for the Irrevocable. Looking back upon Hilda's way of life, he marvelled at his own blind stupidity, which had kept him from remonstrating—as a friend, if with no stronger right—against the risks that she continually encountered. Being so innocent, she had no means of estimating those risks, nor even a possibility of suspecting their existence. But he—who had spent years in Rome, with a man's far wider scope of observation and experience—knew things that made him shudder. It seemed to Kenyon, looking through the darkly coloured medium of his fears, that all modes of crime were crowded into the close intricacy of Roman streets, and that there was no redeeming element, such as exists in other dissolute and wicked cities.

For here was a priesthood, pampered, sensual, with red and bloated cheeks, and carnal eyes. With apparently a grosser development of animal life than most men, they were placed in an unnatural relation with woman, and thereby lost the healthy, human conscience that pertains to other human beings, who own the sweet household ties connecting them with wife and daughter. And here was an indolent nobility, with no high aims or opportunities, but cultivating a vicious way of life as if it were an art, and the only one which they cared to learn. Here was a population, high and low, that had no genuine belief in virtue; and if they recognized any act as criminal, they might throw off all care, remorse, and memory of it, by kneeling a little while at the confessional, and rising unburthened, active, elastic, and incited by fresh appetite for the next ensuing sin. Here was a soldiery, who felt Rome to be their conquered city, and doubtless considered themselves the legal inheritors of the foul license which Gaul, Goth, and Vandal have here exercised, in days gone by.

And what localities for new crime existed in those guilty sites, where the crime of departed ages used to be at home, and had its long, hereditary haunt! What street in Rome, what ancient ruin, what one place where man had standing-room, what fallen stone was there, unstained with one or another kind of guilt! In some of the vicissitudes of the city's pride, or its calamity, the dark tide of human evil had swelled over it, far higher than the Tiber ever rose against the acclivities of the seven hills. To Kenyon's morbid view, there appeared to be a contagious element, rising foglike from the ancient depravity of Rome, and brooding over the dead and half-rotten city, as nowhere else on earth. It prolonged the tendency to crime, and developed an instantaneous growth of it, whenever an opportunity was found. And where could it be found so readily as here! In those vast palaces, there were a hundred remote nooks where Innocence might shriek in vain. Beneath meaner houses, there were unsuspected dungeons that had once been princely chambers, and open to the daylight; but, on account of some wickedness there perpetrated, each passing age had thrown its handfull of dust upon the spot, and buried it from sight. Only ruffians knew of its existence, and kept it for murder, and worse crime.

Such was the city through which Hilda, for three years past, had been wandering without a protector or a guide. She had trodden lightly over the crumble of old crimes; she had taken her way amid the grime and corruption which Paganism had left there, and a perverted Christianity had made more noisome; walking saintlike through it all, with white, innocent feet; until, in some dark pitfall that lay right across her path, she had vanished out of sight. It was terrible to imagine what hideous outrage might have thrust her into that abyss!

Then the lover tried to comfort himself with the idea that Hilda's sanctity was a sufficient safeguard. Ah, yes; she was so pure! The angels, that were of the same sisterhood, would never let Hilda come to harm. A miracle would be wrought on her behalf, as naturally as a father would stretch out his hand to save a best-beloved child. Providence would keep a little area and atmosphere about her, as safe and wholesome as Heaven itself, although the flood of perilous iniquity might hem her round, and its black waves hang curling above her head! But these reflections were of slight avail. No doubt, they were the religious truth. Yet the ways of Providence are utterly inscrutable; and many a murder has been done, and many an innocent virgin has lifted her white arms, beseeching its aid in her extremity, and all in vain; so that, though Providence is infinitely good and wise, (and perhaps for that very reason,) it may be half an eternity before the great circle of its scheme shall bring us the superabundant recompense for all these sorrows! But what the lover asked, was such prompt consolation as might consist with the brief span of mortal life; the assurance of Hilda's present safety, and her restoration within that very hour.

An imaginative man, he suffered the penalty of his endowment in the hundred-fold variety of gloomily tinted scenes that it presented to him, in which Hilda was always a central figure. The sculptor forgot his marble. Rome ceased to be anything, for him, but a labyrinth of dismal streets, in one or another of which the lost girl had disappeared. He was haunted with the idea, that some circumstance, most important to be known, and perhaps easily discoverable, had hitherto been overlooked, and that, if he could lay hold of this one clue, it would guide him directly in the track of Hilda's footsteps. With this purpose in view, he went, every morning, to the Via Portoghese, and made it the starting-point of fresh investigations. After nightfall, too, he invariably returned thither, with a faint hope fluttering at his heart, that the lamp might again be shining on the summit of the tower, and would dispel this ugly mystery out of the circle consecrated by its rays. There being no point of which he could take firm hold, his mind was filled with unsubstantial hopes and fears. Once, Kenyon had seemed to cut his life in marble; now, he vaguely clutched at it, and found it vapour.

In his unstrung and despondent mood, one trifling circumstance affected him with an idle pang. The doves had at first been faithful to their lost mistress. They failed not to sit in a row upon her window-sill, or to alight on the shrine, on the church-angels, and on the roofs and portals of the neighboring houses, in evident expectation of her re-appearance. After the second week, however, they began to take flight, and dropping off, by pairs, betook themselves to other dove-cotes. Only a single dove remained, and brooded drearily beneath the shrine. The flock, that had departed, were like the many hopes that had vanished from Kenyon's heart; the one that still lingered, and looked so wretched—was it a Hope, or already a Despair?

In the street, one day, the sculptor met a priest of mild and venerable aspect; and as his mind dwelt continually upon Hilda, and was especially active in bringing up all incidents that had ever been connected with her, it immediately struck him that this was the very Father with whom he had seen her at the confessional. Such trust did Hilda inspire in him, that Kenyon had never asked what was the subject of the communication between herself and this old priest. He had no reason for imagining that it could have any relation with her disappearance, so long subsequently; but, being thus brought face to face with a personage, mysteriously associated, as he now remembered, with her whom he had lost, an impulse ran before his thoughts and led the sculptor to address him.

It might be, that the reverend kindliness of the old man's expression took Kenyon's heart by surprise; at all events, he spoke as if there were a recognized acquaintanceship, and an object of mutual interest between them.

"She has gone from me, Father!" said he.

"Of whom do you speak, my son?" inquired the priest.

"Of that sweet girl," answered Kenyon, "who knelt to you at the confessional. Surely, you must remember her, among all the mortals to whose confessions you have listened! For she, alone, could have had no sins to reveal."

"Yes; I remember," said the priest, with a gleam of recollection in his eyes. "She was made to bear a miraculous testimony to the efficacy of the Divine ordinances of the Church, by seizing forcibly upon one of them, and finding immediate relief from it, heretic though she was. It is my purpose to publish a brief narrative of this miracle for the edification of mankind, in Latin, Italian, and English, from the printing-press of the Propaganda. Poor child! Setting apart her heresy, she was spotless, as you say. And is she dead?"

"Heaven forbid, Father!" exclaimed Kenyon, shrinking back. "But, she has gone from me, I know not whither. It may be—yes, the idea seizes upon my mind—that what she revealed to you will suggest some clue to the mystery of her disappearance."

"None, my son, none!" answered the priest, shaking his head. "Nevertheless, I bid you be of good cheer. That young maiden is not doomed to die a heretic. Who knows what the Blessed Virgin may at this moment be doing for her soul! Perhaps, when you next behold her, she will be clad in the shining white robe of the true faith."

This latter suggestion did not convey all the comfort which the old priest possibly intended by it; but he imparted it to the sculptor, along with his blessing, as the two best things that he could bestow, and said nothing further, except to bid him farewell.

When they had parted, however, the idea of Hilda's conversion to Catholicism recurred to her lover's mind, bringing with it certain reflections that gave a new turn to his surmises about the mystery into which she had vanished. Not that he seriously apprehended (although the superabundance of her religious sentiment might mislead her, for a moment) that the New England girl would permanently succumb to the scarlet superstitions which surrounded her, in Italy. But the incident of the confessional—if known, as probably it was, to the eager propagandists who prowl about for souls, as cats to catch a mouse—would surely inspire the most confident expectations of bringing her over to the faith. With so pious an end in view, would Jesuitical morality be shocked at the thought of kidnapping the mortal body, for the sake of the immortal spirit that might otherwise be lost forever? Would not the kind old priest, himself, deem this to be infinitely the kindest service that he could perform for the stray lamb, who had so strangely sought his aid?

If these suppositions were well founded, Hilda was most likely a prisoner in one of the religious establishments that are so numerous in Rome. The idea, according to the aspect in which it was viewed, brought now a degree of comfort, and now an additional perplexity. On the one hand, Hilda was safe from any but spiritual assaults; on the other, where was the possibility of breaking through all those barred portals, and searching a thousand convent-cells, to set her free!

Kenyon, however, as it happened, was prevented from endeavouring to follow out this surmise, which only the state of hopeless uncertainty, that almost bewildered his reason, could have led him for a moment to entertain. A communication reached him by an unknown hand, in consequence of which, and within an hour after receiving it, he took his way through one of the gates of Rome.

XLVI

A WALK ON THE CAMPAGNA

I T WAS a bright forenoon of February; a month in which
the brief severity of a Roman winter is already past, and
when violets and daisies begin to show themselves in spots
favoured by the sun. The sculptor came out of the city by
the gate of San Sebastiano, and walked briskly along the
Appian Way.

For the space of a mile or two beyond the gate, this ancient
and famous road is as desolate and disagreeable as most of
the other Roman avenues. It extends over small, uncomfortable paving-stones, between brick and plaistered walls, which
are very solidly constructed, and so high as almost to exclude
a view of the surrounding country. The houses are of most
uninviting aspect, neither picturesque, nor homelike and
social; they have seldom or never a door opening on the wayside, but are accessible only from the rear, and frown in-
hospitably upon the traveller through iron-grated windows.
Here and there, appears a dreary inn, or a wine-shop,
designated by the withered bush beside the entrance; within
which you discern a stone-built and sepulchral interiour,
where guests refresh themselves with sour bread and goat's
milk cheese, washed down with wine of dolorous acerbity.

At frequent intervals along the roadside, uprises the ruin of an ancient tomb. As they stand now, these structures are immensely high and broken mounds of conglomerated brick, stone, pebbles, and earth, all molten by time into a mass as solid and indestructible as if each tomb were composed of a single boulder of granite. When first erected, they were cased externally, no doubt, with slabs of polished marble, artfully wrought bas-reliefs, and all such suitable adornments, and were rendered majestically beautiful by grand architectural designs. This antique splendour has long since been stolen from the dead, to decorate the palaces and churches of the living. Nothing remains to the dishonoured sepulchres, except their massiveness.

Even the pyramids form hardly a stranger spectacle, or are more alien from human sympathies, than the tombs of the Appian Way, with their gigantic height, breadth, and solidity, defying time and the elements, and far too mighty to be demolished by an ordinary earthquake. Here, you may see a modern dwelling, and a garden with its vines and olive-trees, perched on the lofty dilapidation of a tomb, which forms a precipice of fifty feet in depth on each of the four sides. There is a home on that funereal mound, where generations of children have been born, and successive lives been spent, undisturbed by the ghost of the stern Roman whose ashes were so preposterously burthened. Other sepulchres wear a crown of grass, shrubbery, and forest-trees, which throw out a broad sweep of branches, having had time, twice over, to be a thousand years of age. On one of them stands a tower, which, though immemorially more modern than the tomb, was itself built by immemorial hands, and is now rifted quite from top to bottom by a vast fissure of decay; the tomb-hillock, its foundation, being still as firm as ever, and likely to endure until the last trump shall rend it wide asunder, and summon forth its unknown dead.

Yes; its unknown dead! For, except in one or two doubtful instances, these mountainous sepulchral edifices have not availed to keep so much as the bare name of an individual or a family from oblivion. Ambitious of everlasting remembrance, as they were, the slumberers might just as well have gone quietly to rest, each in his pigeon-hole of a columbarium, or under his little green hillock, in a graveyard, without a headstone to mark the spot. It is rather satisfactory than otherwise, to think that all these idle pains have turned out so utterly abortive.

About two miles, or more, from the city-gate, and right upon the roadside, Kenyon passed an immense round pile, sepulchral in its original purposes, like those already mentioned. It was built of great blocks of hewn stone, on a vast, square foundation of rough, agglomerated material, such as composes the mass of all the other ruinous tombs. But, whatever might be the cause, it was in a far better state of preservation than they. On its broad summit rose the battlements of a mediæval fortress, out of the midst of which (so long since had time begun to crumble the supplemental structure, and cover it with soil, by means of wayside dust) grew trees, bushes, and thick festoons of ivy. This tomb of a woman had become the citadel and donjon-keep of a castle; and all the care that Caecilia Metella's husband could bestow, to secure endless peace for her beloved relics, had only sufficed to make that handfull of precious ashes the nucleus of battles, long ages after her death.

A little beyond this point, the sculptor turned aside from the Appian Way, and directed his course across the Campagna, guided by tokens that were obvious only to himself. On one side of him, but at a distance, the Claudian aqueduct was striding over fields and water-courses. Before him, many miles away, with a blue atmosphere between, rose the Alban Hills, brilliantly silvered with snow and sunshine.

He was not without a companion. A buffalo-calf, that seemed shy and sociable by the self-same impulse, had begun to make acquaintance with him, from the moment when he left the road. This frolicksome creature gambolled along, now before, now behind; standing a moment to gaze at him, with wild, curious eyes, he leaped aside and shook his shaggy head, as Kenyon advanced too nigh; then, after loitering in the rear, he came galloping up, like a charge of cavalry, but halted, all of a sudden, when the sculptor turned to look, and bolted across the Campagna, at the slightest signal of nearer approach. The young, sportive thing, Kenyon half fancied, was serving him as a guide, like the heifer that led Cadmus to the site of his destined city; for, in spite of a hundred vagaries, his general course was in the right direction, and along by several objects which the sculptor had noted, as landmarks of his way.

In this natural intercourse with a rude and healthy form of animal life, there was something that wonderfully revived Kenyon's spirits. The warm rays of the sun, too, were wholesome for him in body and soul; and so was a breeze that bestirred itself occasionally, as if for the sole purpose of breathing upon his cheek, and dying softly away, when he would fain have felt a little more decided kiss. This shy, but loving breeze reminded him strangely of what Hilda's deportment had sometimes been towards himself.

The weather had very much to do, no doubt, with these genial and delightful sensations, that made the sculptor so happy with mere life, in spite of a head and heart full of doleful thoughts, anxieties, and fears, which ought in all reason to have depressed him. It was like no weather that exists anywhere, save in Paradise and in Italy; certainly not in America, where it is always too strenuous on the side either of heat or cold. Young as the season was, and wintry as it would have been, under a more rigid sky, it resembled Summer rather than what we New Englanders recognize in our idea of Spring. But there was an indescribable something, sweet, fresh, and remotely affectionate, which the matronly Summer loses, and which thrilled, and, as it were, tickled Kenyon's heart, with a feeling partly of the senses, yet far more a spiritual delight. In a word, it was as if Hilda's delicate breath were on his cheek.

After walking at a brisk pace for about half-an-hour, he reached a spot where an excavation appeared to have been begun, at some not very distant period. There was a hollow space in the earth, looking exceedingly like a deserted cellar, being enclosed within old subterranean walls, constructed of thin Roman bricks, and made accessible by a narrow flight of stone steps. A suburban villa had probably stood over this site, in the imperial days of Rome, and these might have been the ruins of a bath-room, or some other apartment that was required to be wholly or partly under ground. A spade can scarcely be put into that soil, so rich in lost and forgotten things, without hitting upon some discovery which would attract all eyes, in any other land. If you dig but a little way, you gather bits of precious marble, coins, rings, and engraved gems; if you go deeper, you break into columbaria, or into sculptured and richly frescoed apartments that look like festive halls, but were only sepulchres.

The sculptor descended into the cellar-like cavity, and sat down on a block of stone. His eagerness had brought him thither sooner than the appointed hour. The sunshine fell slantwise into the hollow, and happened to be resting on what Kenyon at first took to be a shapeless fragment of stone —possibly, marble—which was partly concealed by the crumbling-down of earth.

But his practised eye was soon aware of something artistic in this rude object. To relieve the anxious tedium of his situation, he cleared away some of the soil (which seemed to have fallen very recently) and discovered a headless figure of marble. It was earth-stained, as well it might be, and had a slightly corroded surface, but at once impressed the sculptor as a Greek production, and wonderfully delicate and beautiful. The head was gone; both arms were broken off at the elbows. Protruding from the loose earth, however, Kenyon beheld the fingers of a marble hand; it was still appended to its arm, and a little further search enabled him to find the other. Placing these limbs in what the nice adjustment of the fractures proved to be their true position, the poor, fragmentary woman forthwith showed that she retained her modest instincts to the last. She had perished with them, and snatched them back at the moment of revival. For these long-buried hands immediately disposed themselves in the manner that nature prompts, as the antique artist knew, and as all the world has seen, in the Venus de' Medici.

"What a discovery is here!" thought Kenyon to himself. "I seek for Hilda, and find a marble woman! Is the omen good or ill?"

In a corner of the excavation, lay a small, round block of stone, much incrusted with earth that had dried and hardened upon it. So, at least, you would have described this object, until the sculptor lifted it, turned it hither and thither, in his hands, brushed off the clinging soil, and finally placed it on the slender neck of the newly discovered statue. The effect was magical. It immediately lighted up and vivified the whole figure, endowing it with personality, soul, and intelligence. The beautiful Idea at once asserted its immortality, and converted that heap of forlorn fragments into a whole, as perfect to the mind, if not to the eye, as when the new marble gleamed with snowy lustre; nor was the impression marred by the earth that still hung upon the exquisitely graceful limbs, and even filled the lovely crevice of the lips. Kenyon cleared it away from between them, and almost deemed himself rewarded with a living smile.

It was either the prototype or a better repetition of the Venus of the Tribune. But those, who have been dissatisfied with the small head, the narrow, soulless face, the button-hole eyelids, of that famous statue, and its mouth such as Nature never moulded, should see the genial breadth of this far nobler and sweeter countenance. It is one of the few works of antique sculpture in which we recognize Womanhood, and that, moreover, without prejudice to its divinity.

Here, then, was a treasure for the sculptor to have found! How happened it to be lying there, beside its grave of twenty centuries? Why were not the tidings of its discovery already noised abroad? The world was richer than yesterday, by something far more precious than gold. Forgotten beauty had come back, as beautiful as ever; a goddess had risen from her long slumber, and was a goddess still. Another cabinet in the Vatican was destined to shine as lustrously as that of the Apollo Belvedere; or, if the aged Pope should resign his claim, an Emperour would woo this tender marble, and win her as proudly as an imperial bride!

Such were the thoughts, with which Kenyon exaggerated to himself the importance of the newly discovered statue, and strove to feel at least a portion of the interest which this event would have inspired in him, a little while before. But, in reality, he found it difficult to fix his mind upon the subject. He could hardly, we fear, be reckoned a consummate artist, because there was something dearer to him than his art; and, by the greater strength of a human affection, the divine statue seemed to fall asunder again, and become only a heap of worthless fragments.

While the sculptor sat listlessly gazing at it, there was a sound of small hoofs, clumsily galloping on the Campagna; and, soon, his frisky acquaintance, the buffalo-calf, came and peeped over the edge of the excavation. Almost at the same moment, he heard voices, which approached nearer and nearer; a man's voice, and a feminine one, talking the musical tongue of Italy. Besides the hairy visage of his four-footed friend, Kenyon now saw the figures of a peasant and a contadina, making gestures of salutation to him, on the opposite verge of the hollow space.

XLVII

THE PEASANT AND CONTADINA

T HEY DESCENDED into the excavation; a young peasant, in the short blue jacket, the small-clothes buttoned at the knee, and buckled shoes, that compose one of the ugliest dresses ever worn by man, except the wearer's form have a grace which any garb, or the nudity of an antique statue, would equally set off; and, hand in hand with him, a village-girl, in one of those brilliant costumes, largely kindled up with scarlet, and decorated with gold embroidery, in which the contadinas array themselves on feast-days. But Kenyon was not deceived; he had recognized the voices of his friends, indeed, even before their disguised figures came between him and the sunlight. Donatello was the peasant; the contadina—with the airy smile, half-mirthful, though it shone out of melancholy eyes—was Miriam.

They both greeted the sculptor with a familiar kindness which reminded him of the days when Hilda, and they, and he, had lived so happily together, before the mysterious adventure of the catacomb. What a succession of sinister events had followed one spectral figure out of that gloomy labyrinth!

"It is Carnival-time, you know," said Miriam, as if in explanation of Donatello's and her own costume. "Do you remember how merrily we spent the Carnival, last year?"

"It seems many years ago," replied Kenyon. "We are all so changed!"

When individuals approach one another with deep purposes on both sides, they seldom come at once to the matter which they have most at heart. They dread the electric shock of a too sudden contact with it. A natural impulse leads them to steal gradually onward, hiding themselves, as it were, behind a closer, and still a closer topic, until they stand face to face with the true point of interest. Miriam was conscious of this impulse, and partially obeyed it.

"So, your instincts as a sculptor have brought you into the presence of our newly discovered statue," she observed. "Is it not beautiful? A far truer image of immortal Womanhood than the poor little damsel at Florence, world-famous though she be!"

"Most beautiful!" said Kenyon, casting an indifferent glance at the Venus. "The time has been, when the sight of this statue would have been enough to make the day memorable."

"And will it not do so, now?" Miriam asked. "I fancied so, indeed, when we discovered it, two days ago. It is Donatello's prize. We were sitting here together, planning an interview with you, when his keen eyes detected the fallen goddess, almost entirely buried under that heap of earth, which the clumsy excavators showered down upon her, I suppose. We congratulated ourselves, chiefly for your sake. The eyes of us three are the only ones to which she has yet revealed herself. Does it not frighten you a little, like the apparition of a lovely woman that lived of old, and has long lain in the grave?"

"Ah, Miriam, I cannot respond to you," said the sculptor, with irrepressible impatience. "Imagination and the love of art have both died out of me."

"Miriam," interposed Donatello, with gentle gravity, "why should we keep our friend in suspense? We know what anxiety he feels. Let us give him what intelligence we can."

"You are so direct and immediate, my beloved friend!" answered Miriam, with an unquiet smile. "There are several reasons why I should like to play round this matter, a little while, and cover it with fanciful thoughts, as we strew a grave with flowers."

"A grave!" exclaimed the sculptor.

"No grave in which your heart need be buried," she replied. "You have no such calamity to dread. But I linger, and hesitate, because every word I speak brings me nearer to a crisis from which I shrink. Ah, Donatello, let us live a little longer the life of these last few days! It is so bright, so airy, so childlike, so without either past or future! Here, on the wild Campagna, you seem to have found, both for yourself and me, the life that belonged to you in early youth; the sweet, irresponsible life which you inherited from your mythic ancestry, the Fauns of Monte Beni. Our stern and black reality will come upon us speedily enough. But, first, a brief time more of this strange happiness!"

"I dare not linger upon it," answered Donatello with an expression that reminded the sculptor of the gloomiest days of his remorse, at Monte Beni. "I dare to be so happy as you have seen me, only because I have felt the time to be so brief."

"One day, then!" pleaded Miriam. "One more day in the wild freedom of this sweet-scented air!"

"Well; one more day," said Donatello smiling; and his smile touched Kenyon with a pathos beyond words, there being gaiety and sadness both melted into it. "But, here is Hilda's friend, and our own. Comfort him, at least, and set his heart at rest, since you have it partly in your power."

"Ah, surely he might endure his pangs a little longer!" cried Miriam, turning to Kenyon with a tricksy, fitful kind of mirth, that served to hide some solemn necessity, too sad and serious to be looked at in its naked aspect. "You love us both, I think, and will be content to suffer for our sakes, one other day. Do I ask too much?"

"Tell me of Hilda!" replied the sculptor. "Tell me only that she is safe, and keep back what else you will."

"Hilda is safe," said Miriam. "There is a Providence purposely for Hilda, as I remember to have told you, long ago. But a great trouble—an evil deed, let us acknowledge it—has spread out its dark branches so widely, that the shadow falls on innocence as well as guilt. There was one slight link, that connected your sweet Hilda with a crime which it was her unhappy fortune to witness, but of which, I need not say, she was as guiltless as the angels that looked out of Heaven, and saw it too. No matter, now, what the consequence has been. You shall have your lost Hilda back, and—who knows?—perhaps tenderer than she was."

"But when will she return?" persisted the sculptor. "Tell me the when, and where, and how!"

"A little patience! Do not press me so!" said Miriam; and again Kenyon was struck by the spritelike, fitful characteristic of her manner, and a sort of hysteric gaiety, which seemed to be a Will-o'-the-Wisp from a sorrow stagnant at her heart. "You have more time to spare than we. First, listen to something that I have to tell. We will talk of Hilda by-and-by."

Then Miriam spoke of her own life, and told facts that threw a gleam of light over many things which had perplexed the sculptor, in all his previous knowledge of her. She described herself as springing from English parentage, on the mother's side, but with a vein, likewise, of Jewish blood, yet connected, through her father, with one of those few princely families of southern Italy, which still retain a great wealth and influence. And she revealed a name, at which her auditor started, and grew pale; for it was one, that, only a few years before, had been familiar to the world, in connection with a mysterious and terrible event. The reader— if he think it worth while to recall some of the strange incidents which have been talked of, and forgotten, within no long time past—will remember Miriam's name.

"You shudder at me, I perceive!" said Miriam, suddenly interrupting her narrative.

"No; you were innocent," replied the sculptor. "I shudder at the fatality that seems to haunt your footsteps, and throws a shadow of crime about your path, you being guiltless."

"There was such a fatality," said Miriam. "Yes; the shadow fell upon me, innocent, but I went astray in it, and wandered —as Hilda could tell you—into crime."

She went on to say, that, while yet a child, she had lost her English mother. From a very early period of her life, there had been a contract of betrothal between herself and a certain marchese, the representative of another branch of her paternal house; a family arrangement, between two persons of disproportioned ages, and in which feeling went for nothing. Most Italian girls of noble rank would have yielded themselves to such a marriage, as an affair of course. But there was something in Miriam's blood, in her mixed race, in her recollections of her mother—some characteristic, finally, in her own nature—which had given her freedom of thought, and force of will, and made this pre-arranged connection odious to her. Moreover, the character of her destined husband would have been a sufficient and insuperable objection; for it betrayed traits so evil, so treacherous, so wild, and yet so strangely subtle, as could only be accounted for by the insanity which often developes itself in old, close-kept breeds of men, when long unmixed with newer blood. Reaching the age when the marriage-contract should have been fulfilled, Miriam had utterly repudiated it.

Some time afterwards had occurred that terrible event to which Miriam alluded, when she revealed her name; an event, the frightful and mysterious circumstances of which will recur to many minds, but of which few or none can have found for themselves a satisfactory explanation. It only concerns the present narrative, inasmuch as the suspicion of being at least an accomplice in the crime fell darkly and directly upon Miriam herself.

"But, you know that I am innocent!" she cried, interrupting herself again, and looking Kenyon in the face.

"I know it by my deepest consciousness," he answered; "and I know it by Hilda's trust and entire affection, which you never could have won, had you been capable of guilt."

"That is sure ground, indeed, for pronouncing me innocent," said Miriam, with the tears gushing into her eyes. "Yet I have since become a horrour to your saintlike Hilda, by a crime which she herself saw me help to perpetrate!"

She proceeded with her story. The great influence of her family connections had shielded her from some of the consequences of her imputed guilt. But, in her despair, she had fled from home, and had surrounded her flight with such circumstances as rendered it the most probable conclusion that she had committed suicide. Miriam, however, was not of the feeble nature which takes advantage of that obvious and poor resource, in earthly difficulties. She flung herself upon the world, and speedily created a new sphere, in which Hilda's gentle purity, the sculptor's sensibility, clear thought, and genius, and Donatello's genial simplicity, had given her almost her first experience of happiness. Then came that ill-omened adventure of the catacomb. The spectral figure, which she encountered there, was the Evil Fate that had haunted her through life.

Looking back upon what had happened, Miriam observed, she now considered him a madman. Insanity must have been mixed up with his original composition, and developed by those very acts of depravity which it suggested, and still more intensified by the remorse that ultimately followed them. Nothing was stranger in his dark career, than the penitence which often seemed to go hand in hand with crime. Since his death, she had ascertained that it finally led him to a convent, where his severe and self-inflicted penances had even acquired him the reputation of unusual sanctity, and had been the cause of his enjoying greater freedom than is commonly allowed to monks.

"Need I tell you more?" asked Miriam, after proceeding thus far. "It is still a dim and dreary mystery, a gloomy twilight, into which I guide you; but, possibly, you may catch a glimpse of much that I myself can explain only by conjecture. At all events, you can comprehend what my situation must have been, after that fatal interview in the catacomb. My persecutor had gone thither for penance, but followed me forth with fresh impulses to crime. He had me in his power. Mad as he was—and wicked as he was—with one word, he could have blasted me, in the belief of all the world. In your belief, too, and Hilda's! Even Donatello would have shrunk from me with horrour!"

"Never," said Donatello. "My instinct would have known you innocent."

"Hilda, and Donatello, and myself—we three would have acquitted you," said Kenyon, "let the world say what it might. Ah, Miriam, you should have told us this sad story, sooner!"

"I thought often of revealing it to you," answered Miriam. "On one occasion, especially, (it was after you had shown me your Cleopatra,) it seemed to leap out of my heart, and got as far as my very lips. But, finding you cold to accept my confidence, I thrust it back again. Had I obeyed my first impulse, all would have turned out differently."

"And Hilda!" resumed the sculptor. "What can have been her connection with these dark incidents?"

"She will doubtless tell you with her own lips," replied Miriam. "Through sources of information which I possess, in Rome, I can assure you of her safety. In two days more— by the help of the special Providence that, as I love to tell you, watches over Hilda—she shall rejoin you."

"Still two days more!" murmured the sculptor.

"Ah, you are cruel, now! More cruel than you know!" exclaimed Miriam, with another gleam of that fantastic, fitful gaiety, which had more than once marked her manner, during this interview. "Spare your poor friends!"

"I know not what you mean, Miriam," said Kenyon.

"No matter," she replied. "You will understand, hereafter. But, could you think it? Here is Donatello haunted with strange remorse, and an immitigable resolve to obtain what he deems justice upon himself. He fancies (with a kind of direct simplicity, which I have vainly tried to combat) that, when a wrong has been done, the doer is bound to submit himself to whatever tribunal takes cognizance of such things, and abide its judgment. I have assured him that there is no such thing as earthly justice, and especially none here, under the Head of Christendom!"

"We will not argue the point again," said Donatello, smiling. "I have no head for argument, but only a sense, an impulse, an instinct, I believe, which sometimes leads me right. But why do we talk, now, of what may make us sorrowful? There are still two days more. Let us be happy!"

It appeared to Kenyon, that, since he last saw Donatello, some of the sweet and delightful characteristics of the antique

Faun had returned to him. There were slight, careless graces, pleasant and simple peculiarities, that had been obliterated by the heavy grief through which he was passing, at Monte Beni, and out of which he had hardly emerged, when the sculptor parted with Miriam and him, beneath the bronze Pontiff's outstretched hand. These happy blossoms had now re-appeared. A playfulness came out of his heart, and glimmered like firelight on his actions, alternating, or even closely intermingled, with profound sympathy and serious thought.

"Is he not beautiful?" said Miriam, watching the sculptor's eye as it dwelt admiringly on Donatello. "So changed, yet still, in a deeper sense, so much the same! He has travelled in a circle, as all things heavenly and earthly do, and now comes back to his original self, with an inestimable treasure of improvement won from an experience of pain. How wonderful is this! I tremble at my own thoughts, yet must needs probe them to their depths. Was the crime—in which he and I were wedded—was it a blessing in that strange disguise? Was it a means of education, bringing a simple and imperfect nature to a point of feeling and intelligence, which it could have reached under no other discipline?"

"You stir up deep and perilous matter, Miriam," replied Kenyon. "I dare not follow you into the unfathomable abysses, whither you are tending."

"Yet there is a pleasure in them! I delight to brood on the verge of this great mystery," returned she. "The story of the Fall of Man! Is it not repeated in our Romance of Monte Beni? And may we follow the analogy yet farther? Was that very sin—into which Adam precipitated himself and all his race—was it the destined means by which, over a long pathway of toil and sorrow, we are to attain a higher, brighter, and profounder happiness, than our lost birthright gave?

Will not this idea account for the permitted existence of sin, as no other theory can?"

"It is too dangerous, Miriam! I cannot follow you!" repeated the sculptor. "Mortal man has no right to tread on the ground where you now set your feet!"

"Ask Hilda what she thinks of it?" said Miriam, with a thoughtful smile. "At least, she might conclude that Sin—which Man chose instead of Good—has been so beneficently handled by Omniscience and Omnipotence, that, whereas our dark Enemy sought to destroy us by it, it has really become an instrument most effective in the education of intellect and soul."

Miriam paused a little longer among these meditations, which the sculptor rightly felt to be so perilous; she then pressed his hand, in token of farewell.

"The day after tomorrow," said she, "an hour before sunset, go to the Corso, and stand in front of the fifth house on your left, beyond the Antonine Column. You will learn tidings of a friend!"

Kenyon would have besought her for more definite intelligence, but she shook her head, put her finger on her lips, and turned away with an illusive smile. The fancy impressed him, that she, too, like Donatello, had reached a wayside Paradise, in their mysterious life-journey, where they both threw down the burthen of the Before and After, and, except for this interview with himself, were happy in the flitting moment. To-day, Donatello was the sylvan Faun; to-day, Miriam was his fit companion, a Nymph of grove or fountain; tomorrow—a remorseful Man and Woman, linked by a marriage-bond of crime—they would set forth towards an inevitable goal.

XLVIII

A SCENE IN THE CORSO

O N THE appointed afternoon, Kenyon failed not to make his appearance in the Corso, and at an hour much earlier than Miriam had named.

It was Carnival-time. The merriment of this famous festival was in full progress; and the stately avenue of the Corso was peopled with hundreds of fantastic shapes, some of which probably represented the mirth of ancient times, surviving, through all manner of calamity, ever since the days of the Roman Empire. For a few afternoons of early Spring, this mouldy gaiety strays into the sunshine; all the remainder of the year, it seems to be shut up in the catacombs, or some other sepulchral store-house of the past.

Besides these hereditary forms, at which a hundred generations have laughed, there were others of modern date, the humorous effluence of the day that was now passing. It is a day, however, and an age, that appears to be remarkably barren, when compared with the prolific originality of former times, in productions of a scenic and ceremonial character, whether grave or gay. To own the truth, the Carnival is alive, this present year, only because it has existed through centuries gone by. It is traditionary, not actual. If decrepit and melancholy Rome smiles, and laughs broadly, indeed, at Carnival-time, it is not in the old simplicity of real mirth, but with a half-conscious effort, like our self-deceptive pretence of jollity at a threadbare joke. Whatever it may once have been, it is now but a narrow stream of merriment, noisy of set purpose, running along the middle of the Corso, through the solemn heart of the decayed city, without extending its shallow influence on either side. Nor, even within its own limits, does it affect the mass of spectators, but only a comparatively few, in street and balcony, who carry on the warfare of nosegays and counterfeit sugar-plums. The populace look on with staid composure; the nobility and priesthood take little or no part in the matter; and but for the hordes of Anglo-Saxons, who annually take up the flagging mirth, the Carnival might long ago have been swept away, with the snow-drifts of confetti that whiten all the pavement.

No doubt, however, the worn-out festival is still new to the youthful and light-hearted, who make the worn-out world itself as fresh as Adam found it, on his first forenoon in Paradise. It may be only Age and Care that chill the life out of its grotesque and airy riot, with the impertinence of their cold criticism.

Kenyon, though young, had care enough within his breast to render the Carnival the emptiest of mockeries. Contrasting the stern anxiety of his present mood with the frolic spirit of the preceding year, he fancied that so much trouble had, at all events, brought wisdom in its train. But there is a Wisdom that looks grave, and sneers at merriment; and again a deeper Wisdom, that stoops to be gay as often as occasion serves, and oftenest avails itself of shallow and trifling grounds of mirth; because, if we wait for more substantial ones, we seldom can be gay at all. Therefore, had it been possible, Kenyon would have done well to mask himself in some wild, hairy visage, and plunge into the throng of other masquers, as at the Carnival before. Then, Donatello had danced along the Corso in all the equipment of a Faun, doing the part with wonderful felicity of execution, and revealing furry ears which looked absolutely real; and Miriam had been, alternately, a lady of the antique regime, in powder and brocade, and the prettiest peasant-girl of the Campagna, in the gayest of costumes; while Hilda, sitting demurely in a balcony, had hit the sculptor with a single rosebud—so sweet and fresh a bud that he knew at once whose hand had flung it.

These were all gone; all those dear friends whose sympathetic mirth had made him gay. Kenyon felt as if an interval of many years had passed since the last Carnival. He had grown old, the nimble jollity was tame, and the masquers dull and heavy; the Corso was but a narrow and shabby street of decaying palaces, and even the long, blue streamer of Italian sky, above it, not half so brightly blue as formerly.

Yet, if he could have beheld the scene with his clear, natural eye-sight, he might still have found both merriment and splendour in it. Everywhere, and all day long, there had been tokens of the festival, in the baskets brimming over with bouquets, for sale at the street-corners, or borne about on people's heads; while bushels upon bushels of variously coloured confetti were displayed, looking just like veritable sugar-plums; so that a stranger would have imagined that the whole commerce and business of stern old Rome lay in flowers and sweets. And, now, in the sunny afternoon, there could hardly be a spectacle more picturesque than the vista of that noble street, stretching into the interminable distance between two rows of lofty edifices, from every window of which, and many a balcony, flaunted gay and gorgeous carpets, bright silks, scarlet cloths with rich golden fringes, and Gobelin tapestry, still lustrous with varied hues, though the product of antique looms. Each separate palace had put on a gala-dress, and looked festive for the occasion, whatever sad or guilty secrets it might hide within. Every window, moreover, was alive with the faces of women, rosy girls, and children, all kindled into brisk and mirthful expression by the incidents in the street below. In the balconies, that projected along the palace-fronts, stood groups of ladies, some beautiful, all richly dressed, scattering forth their laughter, shrill, yet sweet, and the musical babble of their voices, to thicken into an airy tumult over the heads of common mortals.

All these innumerable eyes looked down into the street, the whole capacity of which was thronged with festal figures, in such fantastic variety that it had taken centuries to contrive them; and through the midst of the mad, merry stream of human life, rolled slowly onward a never-ending procession of all the vehicles in Rome, from the ducal carriage, with the powdered coachman high in front, and the three golden lacquies clinging in the rear, down to the rustic cart drawn by its single donkey. Among this various crowd, at windows and in balconies, in cart, cab, barouche, or gorgeous equipage, or bustling to-and-fro afoot, there was a sympathy of nonsense; a true and genial brotherhood and sisterhood, based on the honest purpose—and a wise one, too—of being foolish, all together. The sport of mankind, like its deepest earnest, is a battle; so these festive people fought one another with an ammunition of sugar-plums and flowers.

Not that they were veritable sugar-plums, however, but something that resembled them only as the apples of Sodom look like better fruit. They were concocted mostly of lime, with a grain of oat or some other worthless kernel in the midst. Besides the hail-storm of confetti, the combatants threw handfulls of flour or lime into the air, where it hung like smoke over a battle-field, or, descending, whitened a black coat or priestly robe, and made the curly locks of youth irreverently hoary.

At the same time with this acrid contest of quick-lime, (which caused much effusion of tears from suffering eyes,) a gentler warfare of flowers was carried on, principally between knights and ladies. Originally, no doubt, when this pretty custom was first instituted, it may have had a sincere and modest import. Each youth and damsel, gathering bouquets of field flowers—or the sweetest and fairest that grew in their own gardens, all fresh and virgin blossoms—flung them, with true aim, at the one, or few, whom they regarded with a sentiment of shy partiality, at least, if not with love. Often, the lover in the Corso may thus have received from his bright mistress, in her father's princely balcony, the first sweet intimation that his passionate glances had not struck against a heart of marble. What more appropriate mode of suggesting her tender secret could a maiden find, than by the soft hit of a rosebud against a young man's cheek!

This was the pastime and the earnest of a more innocent and homelier age. Now-a-days, the nosegays are gathered and tied up by sordid hands, chiefly of the most ordinary flowers, and are sold along the Corso at mean price, yet more than such venal things are worth. Buying a basket-full, you find them miserably wilted, as if they had flown hither and thither through two or three Carnival-days, already; muddy, too, having been fished up from the pavement, where a hundred feet have trampled on them. You may see throngs of men and boys who thrust themselves beneath the horses' hoofs to gather up bouquets that were aimed amiss from balcony and carriage; these they sell again, and yet once more, and ten times over, defiled as they all are with the wicked filth of Rome.

Such are the flowery favours—the fragrant bunches of sentiment—that fly between cavalier and dame, and back again, from one end of the Corso to the other. Perhaps they may symbolize, more aptly than was intended, the poor, battered, wilted hearts of those who fling them; hearts which —crumpled and crushed by former possessors, and stained with various mishap—have been passed from hand to hand, along the muddy street-way of life, instead of being treasured in one faithful bosom!

These venal and polluted flowers, therefore, and those deceptive bon-bons, are types of the small reality that still subsists in the observance of the Carnival. Yet the government seemed to imagine that there might be excitement enough, (wild mirth, perchance, following its antics beyond law, and frisking from frolic into earnest,) to render it expedient to guard the Corso with an imposing show of military power. Besides the ordinary force of gensd'armes, a strong patrol of Papal dragoons, in steel helmets and white cloaks, were stationed at all the street-corners. Detachments of French infantry stood by their stacked muskets in the Piazza del Popolo, at one extremity of the course, and before the palace of the Austrian embassy, at the other, and by the column of Antoninus, midway between. Had that chained tiger-cat, the Roman populace, shown only so much as the tips of his claws, the sabres would have been flashing and the bullets whistling, in right earnest, among the combatants who now pelted one another with mock sugar-plums and wilted flowers.

But, to do the Roman people justice, they were restrained by a better safeguard than the sabre or the bayonet; it was their own gentle courtesy, which imparted a sort of sacredness to the hereditary festival. At first sight of a spectacle so fantastic and extravagant, a cool observer might have imagined the whole town gone mad; but, in the end, he would see that all this apparently unbounded license is kept strictly within a limit of its own; he would admire a people who can so freely let loose their mirthful propensities, while muzzling those fiercer ones that tend to mischief. Everybody seemed lawless; nobody was rude. If any reveller overstept the mark, it was sure to be no Roman, but an Englishman or an American; and even the rougher play of this Gothic race was still softened by the insensible influence of a moral atmosphere more delicate, in some respects, than we breathe at home. Not that, after all, we like the fine Italian spirit better than our own; popular rudeness is sometimes the symptom of rude moral health. But, where a Carnival is in question, it would probably pass off, more decorously, as well as more airily and delightfully, in Rome, than in any Anglo-Saxon city.

When Kenyon emerged from a side-lane into the Corso, the mirth was at its height. Out of the seclusion of his own feelings, he looked forth at the tapestried and damask-curtained palaces, the slow-moving, double line of carriages, and the motley masquers that swarmed on foot, as if he were gazing through the iron lattice of a prison-window. So remote from the scene were his sympathies, that it affected him like a thin dream, through the dim, extravagant material of which he could discern more substantial objects, while too much under its controul to start forth broad awake. Just at that moment, too, there came another spectacle, making its way right through the masquerading throng.

It was, first and foremost, a full band of martial music, reverberating, in that narrow and confined, though stately avenue, between the walls of the lofty palaces, and roaring upward to the sky, with melody so powerful that it almost grew to discord. Next came a body of cavalry and mounted gensd'armes, with great display of military pomp. They were escorting a long train of equipages, each and all of which shone as gorgeously as Cinderella's coach, with paint and gilding. Like that, too, they were provided with coachmen, of mighty breadth, and enormously tall footmen, in immense, powdered wigs, and all the splendour of gold-laced, three-cornered hats, and embroidered silk coats and breeches. By the old-fashioned magnificence of this procession, it might worthily have included his Holiness in person, with a suite of attendant cardinals, if those sacred dignitaries would kindly have lent their aid to heighten the frolic of the Carnival. But, for all its show of a martial escort and its antique splendour of costume, it was but a train of the municipal authorities of Rome—illusive shadows, every one, and among them a phantom, styled the Roman Senator—proceeding to the Capitol.

The riotous interchange of nosegays and confetti was partially suspended, while the procession passed. One well-directed shot, however, (it was a double-handfull of powdered lime, flung by an impious New Englander,) hit the coachman of the Roman Senator full in the face, and hurt his dignity amazingly. It appeared to be his opinion, that the Republic was again crumbling into ruin, and that the dust of it now filled his nostrils; though, in fact, it could hardly be distinguished from the official powder with which he was already plentifully bestrewn.

While the sculptor, with his dreamy eyes, was taking idle note of this trifling circumstance, two figures passed before him, hand in hand. The countenance of each was covered with an impenetrable black mask; but one seemed a peasant of the Campagna—the other, a contadina in her holiday costume.

XLIX

A FROLIC OF THE CARNIVAL

THE CROWD and confusion, just at that moment, hindered the sculptor from pursuing these figures—the Peasant and the Contadina—who, indeed, were but two of a numerous tribe that thronged the Corso, in similar costume. As soon as he could squeeze a passage, Kenyon tried to follow in their footsteps, but quickly lost sight of them, and was thrown off the track by stopping to examine various groups of masqueraders, in which he fancied the objects of his search to be included. He found many a sallow peasant or herdsman of the Campagna, in such a dress as Donatello wore; many a contadina, too, brown, broad, and sturdy, in her finery of scarlet, and decked out with gold or coral beads, a pair of heavy ear-rings, a curiously wrought cameo or mosaic brooch, and a silver comb or long stiletto among her glossy hair. But those shapes of grace and beauty, which he sought, had vanished.

As soon as the procession of the Senator had passed, the merry-makers resumed their antics with fresh spirit, and the artillery of bouquets and sugar-plums, suspended for a moment, began anew. The sculptor himself being probably the most anxious and unquiet spectator there, was especially a mark for missiles from all quarters, and for the practical jokes which the license of the Carnival permits. In fact, his sad and contracted brow so ill accorded with the scene, that the revellers might be pardoned for thus using him as the butt of their idle mirth, since he evidently could not otherwise contribute to it.

Fantastic figures, with bulbous heads, the circumference of a bushel, grinned enormously in his face. Harlequins struck him with their wooden swords, and appeared to expect his immediate transformation into some jollier shape. A little, long-tailed, horned fiend sidled up to him, and suddenly blew at him through a tube, enveloping our poor friend in a whole harvest of winged seeds. A biped, with an ass's snout, brayed close to his ear, ending his discordant uproar with a peal of human laughter. Five strapping damsels (so, at least, their petticoats bespoke them, in spite of an awful freedom in the flourish of their legs) joined hands and danced around him, inviting him, by their gestures, to perform a horn-pipe in the midst. Released from these gay persecutors, a clown in motley rapped him on the back with a blown bladder, in which a handfull of dried peas rattled horribly.

Unquestionably, a care-stricken mortal has no business abroad, when the rest of mankind are at high carnival; they must either pelt him and absolutely martyr him with jests, and finally bury him beneath the aggregated heap; or else the potency of his darker mood (because the tissue of human life takes a sad dye more readily than a gay one) will quell their holiday humours, like the aspect of a death's head at a banquet. Only that we know Kenyon's errand, we could hardly forgive him for venturing into the Corso with that troubled face.

Even yet, his merry martyrdom was not half over. There came along a gigantic female figure, seven feet high, at least, and taking up a third of the street's breadth with the preposterously swelling sphere of her crinoline skirts. Singling out the sculptor, she began to make a ponderous assault upon his heart, throwing amorous glances at him out of her great, goggle-eyes, offering him a vast bouquet of sunflowers and nettles, and soliciting his pity by all sorts of pathetic and passionate dumb-show. Her suit meeting no favour, the rejected Titaness made a gesture of despair and rage; then suddenly drawing a huge pistol, she took aim right at the obdurate sculptor's breast, and pulled the trigger. The shot took effect, (for the abominable plaything went off by a spring, like a boy's pop-gun,) covering Kenyon with a cloud of lime-dust, under shelter of which the revengeful damsel strode away.

Hereupon, a whole host of absurd figures surrounded him, pretending to sympathize in his mishap. Clowns and parti-coloured harlequins; orang-outangs; bear-headed, bull-headed, and dog-headed individuals; faces that would have been human, but for their enormous noses; one terrific creature, with a visage right in the centre of his breast; and all other imaginable kinds of monstrosity and exaggeration. These apparitions appeared to be investigating the case, after the fashion of a coroner's jury, poking their pasteboard counte-nances close to the sculptor's, with an unchangeable grin that gave still more ludicrous effect to the comic alarm and horrour of their gestures. Just then, a figure came by, in a gray wig and rusty gown, with an ink-horn at his button-hole and a pen behind his ear; he announced himself as a notary, and offered to make the last will and testament of the assassinated man. This solemn duty, however, was interrupted by a surgeon, who brandished a lancet, three feet long, and proposed to let him blood.

The affair was so like a feverish dream, that Kenyon resigned himself to let it take its course. Fortunately, the humours of the Carnival pass from one absurdity to another, without lingering long enough on any, to wear out even the slightest of them. The passiveness of his demeanour afforded too little scope for such broad merriment as the masqueraders sought. In a few moments, they vanished from him, as dreams and spectres do, leaving him at liberty to pursue his quest, with no impediment except the crowd that blocked up the footway.

He had not gone far, when the Peasant and the Contadina met him. They were still hand in hand, and appeared to be straying through the grotesque and animated scene, taking as little part in it as himself. It might be because he recognized them, and knew their solemn secret, that the sculptor fancied a melancholy emotion to be expressed by the very movement and attitudes of these two figures; and even the grasp of their hands, uniting them so closely, seemed to set them in a sad remoteness from the world at which they gazed.

"I rejoice to meet you," said Kenyon.

But they looked at him through the eye-holes of their black masks, without answering a word.

"Pray give me a little light on the matter which I have so much at heart," said he. "If you know anything of Hilda, for Heaven's sake, speak!"

Still, they were silent; and the sculptor began to imagine that he must have mistaken the identity of these figures, there being such a multitude in similar costume. Yet there was no other Donatello; no other Miriam. He felt, too, that spiritual certainty which impresses us with the presence of our friends, apart from any testimony of the senses.

"You are unkind," resumed he—"knowing the anxiety which oppresses me—not to relieve it, if in your power."

The reproach evidently had its effect; for the Contadina now spoke, and it was Miriam's voice.

"We gave you all the light we could," said she. "You are yourself unkind, (though you little think how much so,) to come between us at this hour. There may be a sacred hour, even in Carnival-time!"

In another state of mind, Kenyon could have been amused by the impulsiveness of this response, and a sort of vivacity that he had often noted in Miriam's conversation. But he was conscious of a profound sadness in her tone, overpowering its momentary irritation, and assuring him that a pale, tear-stained face was hidden behind her mask.

"Forgive me!" said he.

Donatello here extended his hand, (not that which was clasping Miriam's,) and she, too, put her free one into the sculptor's left; so that they were a linked circle of three, with many reminiscences and forebodings flashing through their hearts. Kenyon knew intuitively that these once familiar friends were parting with him, now.

"Farewell!" they all three said, in the same breath.

No sooner was the word spoken, than they loosed their hands; and the uproar of the Carnival swept like a tempestuous sea over the spot, which they had included within their small circle of isolated feeling.

By this interview, the sculptor had learned nothing in reference to Hilda; but he understood that he was to adhere to the instructions already received, and await a solution of the mystery in some mode that he could not yet anticipate. Passing his hands over his eyes, and looking about him, (for the event just described had made the scene even more dream-like than before,) he now found himself approaching that broad piazza, bordering on the Corso, which has for its central object the sculptured column of Antoninus. It was not far from this vicinity, that Miriam had bid him wait. Struggling onward—as fast as the tide of merry-makers, setting strong against him, would permit—he was now beyond the Piazza Colonna, and began to count the houses. The fifth was a palace, with a long front upon the Corso, and of stately height, but somewhat grim with age.

Over its arched and pillared entrance, there was a balcony, richly hung with tapestry and damask, and tenanted, for the time, by a gentleman of venerable aspect, and a group of ladies. The white hair and whiskers of the former, and the winter-roses in his cheeks, had an English look; the ladies, too, showed a fair-haired, Saxon bloom, and seemed to taste the mirth of the Carnival with the freshness of spectators to whom the scene was new. All the party—the old gentleman with grave earnestness, as if he were defending a rampart, and his young companions with exuberance of frolic—showered confetti inexhaustibly upon the passers-by.

In the rear of the balcony, a broad-brimmed, ecclesiastical beaver was visible. An Abbate, (probably an acquaintance and cicerone of the English family,) was sitting there, and enjoying the scene, though partially withdrawn from view, as the decorum of his order dictated.

There seemed no better nor other course for Kenyon, than to keep watch at this appointed spot, waiting for whatever should happen next. Clasping his arm round a lamp-post, to prevent being carried away by the turbulent stream of way-farers, he scrutinized every face, with the idea that some one of them might meet his eyes with a glance of intelligence. He looked at each mask—harlequin, ape, bulbous-headed monster, or anything that was absurdest—not knowing but that the messenger might come, even in such fantastic guise. Or, perhaps, one of those quaint figures, in the stately ruff, the cloak, tunic, and trunk-hose, of three centuries ago, might bring him tidings of Hilda, out of that long-past age. At times, his disquietude took a hopeful aspect; and he fancied that Hilda might come by, her own sweet self, in some shy disguise which the instinct of his love would be sure to penetrate. Or, she might be borne past on a triumphal car, like the one just now approaching; its slow-moving wheels encircled and spoked with foliage, and drawn by horses that were harnessed and wreathed with flowers. Being, at best, so far beyond the bounds of reasonable conjecture, he might anticipate the wildest event, or find either his hopes or fears disappointed in what appeared most probable.

The old Englishman and his daughters, in the opposite balcony, must have seen something unutterably absurd in the sculptor's deportment, poring into this whirlpool of nonsense, so earnestly, in quest of what was to make his life dark or bright. Earnest people, who try to get a reality out of human existence, are necessarily absurd in the view of the revellers and masqueraders. At all events, after a good deal of mirth at the expense of his melancholy visage, the fair occupants of the balcony favoured Kenyon with a salvo of confetti, which came rattling about him like a hail-storm. Looking up, instinctively, he was surprised to see the Abbate, in the back-ground, lean forward and give a courteous sign of recognition.

It was the same old priest with whom he had seen Hilda, at the confessional; the same, with whom he had talked of her disappearance, on meeting him in the street.

Yet, whatever might be the reason, Kenyon did not now associate this ecclesiastical personage with the idea of Hilda. His eyes lighted on the old man, just for an instant, and then returned to the eddying throng of the Corso, on his minute scrutiny of which depended, for aught he knew, the sole chance of ever finding any trace of her. There was, about this moment, a bustle on the other side of the street, the cause of which Kenyon did not see, nor exert himself to discover. A small party of soldiers or gensd'armes appeared to be concerned in it; they were perhaps arresting some disorderly character, who, under the influence of an extra flask of wine, might have reeled across the mystic limitation of Carnival-proprieties.

The sculptor heard some people, near him, talking of the incident.

"That contadina, in a black mask, was a fine figure of a woman."

"She was not amiss," replied a female voice; "but her companion was far the handsomer figure of the two. Could they be really a peasant and a contadina, do you imagine?"

"No, no," said the other. "It is some frolic of the Carnival, carried a little too far."

This conversation might have excited Kenyon's interest; only that, just as the last words were spoken, he was hit by two missiles, both of a kind that were flying abundantly on that gay battle-field. One, we are ashamed to say, was a cauliflower, which, flung by a young man from a passing carriage, came with a prodigious thump against his shoulder; the other was a single rosebud, so fresh that it seemed that moment gathered. It flew from the opposite balcony, smote gently on his lips, and fell into his hand. He looked upward, and beheld the face of his lost Hilda!

She was dressed in a white domino, and looked pale, and bewildered, and yet full of tender joy. Moreover, there was a gleam of delicate mirthfulness in her eyes, which the sculptor had seen there only two or three times, in the course of their acquaintance, but thought it the most bewitching and fairy-like of all Hilda's expressions. That soft, mirthful smile caused her to melt, as it were, into the wild frolic of the Carnival, and become not so strange and alien to the scene, as her unexpected apparition must otherwise have made her.

Meanwhile, the venerable Englishman and his daughters were staring at poor Hilda in a way that proved them altogether astonished, as well as inexpressibly shocked, by her sudden intrusion into their private balcony. They looked —as, indeed, English people of respectability would, if an angel were to alight in their circle, without due introduction from somebody whom they knew, in the court above—they looked as if an unpardonable liberty had been taken, and a suitable apology must be made; after which, the intruder would be expected to withdraw.

The Abbate, however, drew the old gentleman aside, and whispered a few words that served to mollify him; he bestowed on Hilda a sufficiently benignant, though still a perplexed and questioning regard, and invited her, in dumb-show, to put herself at her ease.

But, whoever was in fault, our shy and gentle Hilda had dreamed of no intrusion. Whence she had come, or where she had been hidden, during this mysterious interval, we can but imperfectly surmise, and do not mean, at present, to make it a matter of formal explanation with the reader. It is better, perhaps, to fancy that she had been snatched away to a Land of Picture; that she had been straying with Claude in the golden light which he used to shed over his landscapes, but which he could never have beheld with his waking eyes, till he awoke in the better clime. We will imagine that, for the sake of the true simplicity with which she loved them, Hilda had been permitted, for a season, to converse with the great, departed Masters of the pencil, and behold the diviner works which they have painted in heavenly colours. Guido had shown her another portrait of Beatrice Cenci, done from the celestial life, in which that forlorn mystery of the earthly countenance was exchanged for a radiant joy. Perugino had allowed her a glimpse at his easel, on which she discerned what seemed a Woman's face, but so divine, by the very depth and softness of its Womanhood, that a gush of happy tears blinded the maiden's eyes, before she had time to look. Raphael had taken Hilda by the hand, (that fine, forcible hand which Kenyon sculptured,) and drawn aside the curtain of gold-fringed cloud that hung before his latest master-piece. On earth, Raphael painted the Transfiguration. What higher scene may he have since depicted, not from imagination, but as revealed to his actual sight!

Neither will we retrace the steps by which she returned to the actual world. For the present, be it enough to say that Hilda had been summoned forth from a secret place, and led, we know not through what mysterious passages, to a point where the tumult of life burst suddenly upon her ears. She heard the tramp of footsteps, the rattle of wheels, and the mingled hum of a multitude of voices, with strains of music and loud laughter breaking through. Emerging into a great, gloomy hall, a curtain was drawn aside; she found herself gently propelled into an open balcony, whence she looked out upon the festal street, with gay tapestries flaunting over all the palace-fronts, the windows thronged with merry faces, and a crowd of masquers rioting upon the pavement below.

Immediately, she seemed to become a portion of the scene. Her pale, large-eyed, fragile beauty, her wondering aspect, and bewildered grace, attracted the gaze of many; and there fell around her a shower of bouquets and bon-bons—freshest blossoms and sweetest sugar-plums, sweets to the sweet—such as the revellers of the Carnival reserve as tributes to especial loveliness. Hilda pressed her hand across her brow; she let her eyelids fall, and, lifting them again, looked through the grotesque and gorgeous show, the chaos of mad jollity, in quest of some object by which she might assure herself that the whole spectacle was not an illusion.

Beneath the balcony, she recognized a familiar and fondly remembered face. The spirit of the hour and the scene exercised its influence over her quick and sensitive nature; she caught up one of the rosebuds, that had been showered upon her, and aimed it at the sculptor. It hit the mark; he turned his sad eyes upward, and there was Hilda, in whose gentle presence, his own secret sorrow and the obtrusive uproar of the Carnival alike died away from his perception.

That night, the lamp beneath the Virgin's shrine burned as brightly as if it had never been extinguished; and though the one faithful dove had gone to her melancholy perch, she greeted Hilda rapturously, the next morning, and summoned her less constant companions, whithersoever they had flown, to renew their homage.

L

MIRIAM, HILDA, KENYON, DONATELLO

THE GENTLE READER, we trust, would not thank us for one of those minute elucidations, which are so tedious, and, after all, so unsatisfactory, in clearing up the romantic mysteries of a story. He is too wise to insist upon looking closely at the wrong side of the tapestry, after the right one has been sufficiently displayed to him, woven with the best of the artist's skill, and cunningly arranged with a view to the harmonious exhibition of its colours. If any brilliant or beautiful, or even tolerable, effect have been produced, this pattern of kindly Readers will accept it at its worth, without tearing the web apart, with the idle purpose of discovering how its threads have been knit together; for the sagacity, by which he is distinguished, will long ago have taught him that any narrative of human action and adventure —whether we call it history or romance—is certain to be a fragile handiwork, more easily rent than mended. The actual experience of even the most ordinary life is full of events that never explain themselves, either as regards their origin or their tendency.

It would be easy, from conversations which we have held with the sculptor, to suggest a clue to the mystery of Hilda's disappearance; although, as long as she remained in Italy, there was a remarkable reserve in her communications upon this subject, even to her most intimate friends. Either a pledge of secrecy had been exacted, or a prudential motive warned her not to reveal the stratagems of a religious body, or the secret acts of a despotic government, (whichever might be responsible, in the present instance,) while still within the scope of their jurisdiction. Possibly, she might not herself be fully aware what power had laid its grasp upon her person. What has chiefly perplexed us, however, among Hilda's adventures, is the mode of her release, in which some inscrutable Tyranny or other seemed to take part in a frolic of the Carnival. We can only account for it, by supposing that the fitful and fantastic imagination of a Woman (sportive, because she must otherwise be desperate) had arranged this incident, and made it the condition of a step which her conscience, or the conscience of another, required her to take.

A few days after Hilda's re-appearance, she and the sculptor were straying together through the streets of Rome. Being deep in talk, it so happened that they found themselves near the majestic, pillared portico and huge, black rotundity of the Pantheon. It stands almost at the central point of the labyrinthine intricacies of the modern city, and often presents itself before the bewildered stranger, when he is in search of other objects. Hilda, looking up, proposed that they should enter.

"I never pass it, without going in," she said, "to pay my homage at the tomb of Raphael."

"Nor I," said Kenyon, "without stopping to admire the noblest edifice which the barbarism of the early ages, and the more barbarous Pontiffs and Princes of later ones, have spared to us."

They went in, accordingly, and stood in the free space of that great circle, around which are ranged the arched recesses and stately altars, formerly dedicated to heathen gods, but

Christianized through twelve centuries gone by. The world has nothing else like the Pantheon. So grand it is, that the pasteboard statues, over the lofty cornice, do not disturb the effect, any more than the tin crowns and hearts, the dusty artificial flowers, and all manner of trumpery gew-gaws, hanging at the saintly shrines. The rust and dinginess that have dimmed the precious marble on the walls; the pavement, with its great squares and rounds of porphyry and granite, cracked crosswise and in a hundred directions, showing how roughly the troublesome ages have trampled here; the gray Dome above, with its opening to the sky, as if Heaven were looking down into the interiour of this place of worship, left unimpeded for prayers to ascend the more freely;—all these things make an impression of solemnity, which Saint Peter's itself fails to produce.

"I think," said the sculptor, "it is to the aperture in the Dome—that great Eye, gazing heavenward—that the Pantheon owes the peculiarity of its effect. It is so heathenish, as it were; —so unlike all the snugness of our modern civilization! Look, too, at the pavement directly beneath the open space! So much rain has fallen there, in the last two thousand years, that it is green with small, fine moss, such as grows over tombstones in a damp English churchyard."

"I like better," replied Hilda, "to look at the bright, blue sky, roofing the edifice where the builders left it open. It is very delightful, in a breezy day, to see the masses of white cloud float over the opening, and then the sunshine fall through it again, fitfully, as it does now. Would it be any wonder if we were to see angels hovering there, partly in and partly out, with genial, heavenly faces, not intercepting the light, but only transmuting it into beautiful colours? Look at that broad, golden beam—a sloping cataract of sunlight—which comes down from the aperture and rests upon the shrine, at the right hand of the entrance!"

"There is a dusky picture over that altar," observed the sculptor. "Let us go and see if this strong illumination brings out any merit in it."

Approaching the shrine, they found the picture little worth looking at, but could not forbear smiling, to see that a very plump and comfortable tabby-cat (whom we ourselves have often observed haunting the Pantheon) had established herself on the altar, in the genial sunbeam, and was fast asleep among the holy tapers. Their footsteps disturbing her, she awoke, raised herself, and sat blinking in the sun, yet with a certain dignity and self-possession, as if conscious of representing a Saint.

"I presume," remarked Kenyon, "that this is the first of the feline race that has ever set herself up as an object of worship, in the Pantheon or elsewhere, since the days of ancient Egypt. See; there is a peasant from the neighboring market, actually kneeling to her! She seems a gracious and benignant Saint enough."

"Do not make me laugh," said Hilda reproachfully, "but help me to drive the creature away. It distresses me to see that poor man, or any human being, directing his prayers so much amiss."

"Then, Hilda," answered the sculptor, more seriously, "the only place in the Pantheon for you and me to kneel, is on the pavement beneath the central aperture. If we pray at a Saint's shrine, we shall give utterance to earthly wishes; but if we pray, face to face with the Deity, we shall feel it impious to petition for aught that is narrow and selfish. Methinks, it is this that makes the Catholics so delight in the worship of Saints; they can bring up all their little worldly wants and whims, their individualities, and human weaknesses, not as things to be repented of, but to be humoured by the canonized humanity to which they pray. Indeed, it is very tempting!"

What Hilda might have answered, must be left to conjecture; for, as she turned from the shrine, her eyes were attracted to the figure of a female penitent, kneeling on the pavement, just beneath the great central Eye, in the very spot which Kenyon had designated as the only one whence prayers should ascend. The upturned face was invisible, behind a veil or mask, which formed a part of the garb.

"It cannot be!" whispered Hilda, with emotion. "No; it cannot be!"

"What disturbs you?" asked Kenyon. "Why do you tremble so?"

"If it were possible," she replied, "I should fancy that kneeling figure to be Miriam!"

"As you say, it is impossible," rejoined the sculptor. "We know too well what has befallen both her and Donatello."

"Yes; it is impossible!" repeated Hilda.

Her voice was still tremulous, however, and she seemed unable to withdraw her attention from the kneeling figure. Suddenly, and as if the idea of Miriam had opened the whole volume of Hilda's reminiscences, she put this question to the sculptor:—

"Was Donatello really a Faun?"

"If you had ever studied the pedigree of the far-descended heir of Monte Beni, as I did," answered Kenyon, with an irrepressible smile, "you would have retained few doubts on that point. Faun or not, he had a genial nature, which, had the rest of mankind been in accordance with it, would have made earth a Paradise to our poor friend. It seems the moral of his story, that human beings, of Donatello's character, compounded especially for happiness, have no longer any business on earth, or elsewhere. Life has grown so sadly serious, that such men must change their nature, or else perish, like the antediluvian creatures that required, as the condition of their existence, a more summer-like atmosphere than ours."

"I will not accept your moral!" replied the hopeful and happy-natured Hilda.

"Then, here is another; take your choice!" said the sculptor, remembering what Miriam had recently suggested, in reference to the same point. "He perpetrated a great crime; and his remorse, gnawing into his soul, has awakened it; developing a thousand high capabilities, moral and intellectual, which we never should have dreamed of asking for, within the scanty compass of the Donatello whom we knew."

"I know not whether this is so," said Hilda. "But what then?"

"Here comes my perplexity," continued Kenyon. "Sin has educated Donatello, and elevated him. Is Sin, then— which we deem such a dreadful blackness in the Universe— is it, like Sorrow, merely an element of human education, through which we struggle to a higher and purer state than we could otherwise have attained. Did Adam fall, that we might ultimately rise to a far loftier Paradise than his?"

"Oh, hush!" cried Hilda, shrinking from him with an expression of horrour which wounded the poor, speculative sculptor to the soul. "This is terrible; and I could weep for you, if you indeed believe it. Do not you perceive what a mockery your creed makes, not only of all religious sentiment, but of moral law, and how it annuls and obliterates whatever precepts of Heaven are written deepest within us? You have shocked me beyond words!"

"Forgive me, Hilda!" exclaimed the sculptor, startled by her agitation; "I never did believe it! But the mind wanders wild and wide; and, so lonely as I live and work, I have neither pole-star above, nor light of cottage-windows here below, to bring me home. Were you my guide, my counsellor, my inmost friend, with that white wisdom which clothes you as with a celestial garment, all would go well. Oh, Hilda, guide me home!"

"We are both lonely; both far from home!" said Hilda, her eyes filling with tears. "I am a poor, weak girl, and have no such wisdom as you fancy in me."

What further may have passed between these lovers, (while standing before the pillared shrine, and the marble Madonna that marks Raphael's tomb, whither they had now wandered,) we are unable to record. But when the kneeling figure, beneath the open Eye of the Pantheon, arose, she looked towards the pair, and extended her hands with a gesture of benediction. Then they knew that it was Miriam. They suffered her to glide out of the portal, however, without a greeting; for those extended hands, even while they blessed, seemed to repel, as if Miriam stood on the other side of a fathomless abyss, and warned them from its verge.

So, Kenyon won the gentle Hilda's shy affection, and her consent to be his bride. Another hand must henceforth trim the lamp before the Virgin's shrine; for Hilda was coming down from her old tower, to be herself enshrined and worshipped as a household Saint, in the light of her husband's fireside. And, now that life had so much human promise in it, they resolved to go back to their own land; because the years, after all, have a kind of emptiness, when we spend too many of them on a foreign shore. We defer the reality of life, in such cases, until a future moment, when we shall again breathe our native air; but, by-and-by, there are no future moments; or, if we do return, we find that the native air has lost its invigorating quality, and that life has shifted its reality to the spot where we have deemed ourselves only temporary residents. Thus, between two countries, we have none at all, or only that little space of either, in which we finally lay down our discontented bones. It is wise, therefore, to come back betimes—or never.

Before they quitted Rome, a bridal gift was laid on Hilda's table. It was a bracelet, evidently of great cost, being composed of seven ancient Etruscan gems, dug out of seven sepulchres, and each one of them the signet of some princely personage, who had lived an immemorial time ago. Hilda remembered this precious ornament. It had been Miriam's; and once, with the exuberance of fancy that distinguished her, she had amused herself with telling a mythical and magic legend for each gem, comprising the imaginary adventures and catastrophe of its former wearer. Thus, the Etruscan bracelet became the connecting bond of a series of seven wondrous tales, all of which, as they were dug out of seven sepulchres, were characterized by a sevenfold sepulchral gloom; such as Miriam's imagination, shadowed by her own misfortunes, was wont to fling over its most sportive flights.

And, now, happy as Hilda was, the bracelet brought the tears into her eyes, as being, in its entire circle, the symbol of as sad a mystery as any that Miriam had attached to the separate gems. For, what was Miriam's life to be? And where was Donatello? But Hilda had a hopeful soul, and saw sunlight on the mountain-tops.

POSTCRIPT

THERE comes to the Author, from many readers of the foregoing pages, a demand for further elucidations respecting the mysteries of the story.

He reluctantly avails himself of the opportunity afforded by a new edition, to explain such incidents and passages as may have been left too much in the dark; reluctantly, he repeats, because the necessity makes him sensible that he can have succeeded but imperfectly, at best, in throwing about this Romance the kind of atmosphere essential to the effect at which he aimed. He designed the story and the characters to bear, of course, a certain relation to human nature and human life, but still to be so artfully and airily removed from our mundane sphere, that some laws and proprieties of their own should be implicitly and insensibly acknowledged.

The idea of the modern Faun, for example, loses all the poetry and beauty which the Author fancied in it, and becomes nothing better than a grotesque absurdity, if we bring it into the actual light of day. He had hoped to mystify this anomalous creature between the Real and the Fantastic, in such a manner that the reader's sympathies might be excited to a certain pleasurable degree, without impelling him to ask how Cuvier would have classified poor Donatello, or to insist upon being told, in so many words, whether he had furry ears or no. As respects all who ask such questions, the book is, to that extent, a failure.

Nevertheless, the Author fortunately has it in his power to throw light upon several matters in which some of his readers appear to feel an interest. To confess the truth, he was himself troubled with a curiosity similar to that which he has just deprecated on the part of his readers, and once took occasion to cross-examine his friends, Hilda and the sculptor, and to pry into several dark recesses of the story, with which they had heretofore imperfectly acquainted him.

We three had climbed to the top of Saint Peter's, and were looking down upon the Rome which we were soon to leave, but which (having already sinned sufficiently in that way) it is not my purpose further to describe. It occurred to me that, being so remote in the upper air, my friends might safely utter, here, the secrets which it would be perilous even to whisper on lower earth.

"Hilda," I began, "can you tell me the contents of the mysterious pacquet which Miriam entrusted to your charge, and which was addressed to 'Signor Luca Barboni, at the Palazzo Cenci'?"

"I never had any further knowledge of it," replied Hilda, "nor felt it right to let myself be curious upon the subject."

"As to its precise contents," interposed Kenyon, "it is impossible to speak. But Miriam, isolated as she seemed, had family connections in Rome, one of whom, there is reason to believe, occupied a position in the Papal Government. This Signor Luca Barboni was either the assumed name of the personage in question, or the medium of communication between that individual and Miriam. Now, under such a government as that of Rome, it is obvious that Miriam's privacy and isolated life could only be maintained through the connivance and support of some influential person, connected with the administration of affairs. Free and self-controlled as she appeared, her every movement was watched and investigated far more thoroughly by the priestly rulers than by her dearest friends. Miriam, if I mistake not, had a purpose to withdraw herself from this irksome scrutiny, and to seek real obscurity in another land; and the pacquet, to be delivered long after her departure, contained a reference to this design, besides certain family documents, which were to be imparted to her relative as from one dead and gone."

"Yes; it is clear as a London fog," I remarked. "On this head no further elucidation can be desired. But when Hilda went quietly to deliver the pacquet, why did she so mysteriously vanish?"

"You must recollect," replied Kenyon, with a glance of friendly commiseration at my obtuseness, "that Miriam had utterly disappeared, leaving no trace by which her whereabout could be known. In the mean time, the municipal authorities had become aware of the murder of the Capuchin; and, from many preceding circumstances, such as his strange persecution of Miriam, they must have been led to see an obvious connection between herself and that tragical event. Furthermore, there is reason to believe that Miriam was suspected of implication with some plot or political intrigue, of which there may have been tokens in the pacquet. And when Hilda appeared as the bearer of this missive, it was really quite a matter of course, under a despotic government, that she should be detained."

"Ah! quite a matter of course, as you say," answered I. "How excessively stupid in me not to have seen it sooner! But there are other riddles. On the night of the extinction of the lamp, you met Donatello in a penitent's garb, and afterwards saw and spoke to Miriam, in a coach, with a gem glowing on her bosom. What was the business of these two guilty ones in Rome? And who was Miriam's companion?"

"Who?" repeated Kenyon. "Why, her official relative, to be sure; and as to their business, Donatello's still gnawing remorse had brought him hitherward, in spite of Miriam's entreaties, and kept him lingering in the neighborhood of Rome, with the ultimate purpose of delivering himself up to justice. Hilda's disappearance, which took place the day before, was known to them through a secret channel, and had brought them into the city, where Miriam, as I surmise, began to make arrangements, even then, for that sad frolic of the Carnival."

"And where was Hilda, all that dreary time between?" inquired I.

"Where were you, Hilda?" asked Kenyon, smiling.

Hilda threw her eyes on all sides, and seeing that there was not even a bird of the air to fly away with the secret, nor any human being nearer than the loiterers by the obelisk, in the piazza below, she told us about her mysterious abode.

"I was a prisoner in the Convent of the Sacré Cœur, in the Trinità de' Monti," said she; "but in such kindly custody of pious maidens, and watched over by such a dear old priest, that—had it not been for one or two disturbing recollections, and also because I am a daughter of the Puritans—I could willingly have dwelt there forever. My entanglement with Miriam's misfortunes, and the good Abbate's mistaken hope of a proselyte, seem to me a sufficient clue to the whole mystery."

"The atmosphere is getting delightfully lucid," observed I, "but there are one or two things that still puzzle me. Could you tell me—and it shall be kept a profound secret, I assure you—what were Miriam's real name and rank, and precisely the nature of the trouble that led to all these direful consequences?"

"Is it possible that you need an answer to these questions?" exclaimed Kenyon, with an aspect of vast surprise. "Have you not even surmised Miriam's name? Think awhile, and you will assuredly remember it. If not, I congratulate you most sincerely; for it indicates that your feelings have never been harrowed by one of the most dreadful and mysterious events that have occurred within the present century."

"Well," resumed I, after an interval of deep consideration, "I have but few things more to ask. Where, at this moment, is Donatello?"

"In prison," said Kenyon, sadly.

"And why, then, is Miriam at large?" I asked.

"Call it cruelty, if you like—not mercy!" answered Kenyon. "But, after all, her crime lay merely in a glance; she did no murder."

"Only one question more," said I, with intense earnestness. "Did Donatello's ears resemble those of the Faun of Praxiteles?"

"I know, but may not tell," replied Kenyon, smiling mysteriously. "On that point, at all events, there shall be not one word of explanation."

LEAMINGTON,
March 14th, 1860

THE END.

APPENDIXES

TEXTUAL NOTES

11.2 Nature] In MS Hawthorne personified "Nature" by capitalization more times than he failed to indicate personification (as "nature"). No system can be observed in his variable practice. But since his general intention to personify is clear, the Centenary text capitalizes whenever, as here, personification seems to be desired.

17.28 Faun in red marble, . . .] Since MS fol. 21 ends "Faun, who keeps up a", the chances for Jenkins' eyeskip creating this variant between MS and $E1^a$ are negligible. It would seem that Hawthorne worked over the passage in proof in order to make the immediate association of "that other Faun" with the marble statue without waiting for the phrase "who keeps up a motionless dance". He may also have been worried about the syntax, since "dance" and "marble" were so closely associated in MS.

25.16 appetite] For this and other of Sophia Hawthorne's alterations of MS, see the Textual Introduction, pp. lxv–lxx.

36.12 influencies] an -ies ending like this is occasionally written by Hawthorne, especially in the word "excellencies". The modernization of these acceptable forms by the $E1^a$ printer effectively prevented the O.E.D. from recording them although The Marble Faun (in its American edition) was a book used in the preparation.

41.15 canvases] In his earlier romances Hawthorne's spelling was regularly the old-fashioned "canvass", as in MS here and at 47.23. But elsewhere in this text MS uses the modern spelling to which it appears Hawthorne was tending. The two anomalies have, therefore, been normalized.

44.2 feeling] The E1ᵃ variant "feelings" seems to be a sophistication by Mintern, who similarly at 337.23 alters MS singular to plural. Although Hawthorne was accustomed to using the plural "feelings", he attempted to distinguish between a specific "feeling", or emotion (as in 105.21, 365.21), and "feelings" as a collective emotional response (384.3). See also the Textual Note to 105.9 for the same distinction applied to *affection-affections*.

45.13 subtly] E1ᵃ "subtilely" for MS "subtly" is the one occurrence in this text in which the print has the long and the MS the short form (some MS long forms are followed but others are shortened). Also, this variant appears in the work of Hobson who at 22.14 had altered MS "subtile" to "subtle". Thus a slight possibility exists that a Hawthorne proof-change may have been made here despite the fact that Hawthorne in his manuscripts uses the *subtile-subtle* doublet so interchangeably that the Centenary editions do not attempt to normalize his usage. But that this reading is an adverb, not the common adjective, may have some bearing, and it seems safest to retain the form that Hawthorne manifestly wrote in this case. The point is raised, however, for the benefit of linguists who may be interested in this text.

47.32 if even so many, in] Farley's insertion of "times" after "many" seems to be a sophistication reflecting his misunderstanding of the sense. In MS Hawthorne is remarking that in one's life one normally sees only two or three such beautiful women; not, as Farley would have it, that one sees beautiful women (or their portraits) only two or three times. Hawthorne's phrasing is abrupt here, however, and the sophistication a natural one to attempt.

49.13 their reality and truth is] Farley's change to "are" seems to be mere sophistication. Hawthorne occasionally employs just such a collective singular, as in the manuscript for "Leamington Spa," "swans, whose aspect and movement in the water is most beautiful and stately", or at Centenary 214.14 in *The House of the Seven Gables*, "Moonlight, and the sentiment in man's heart, responsive to it, is the greatest of renovators and reformers."

68.4 Signor] The editorial emendation to "Signor" of the few and erratic appearances of "Signore" simplifies by anglicizing a most complex matter of Italian usage that Hawthorne was not equipped to deal with. The alternative to this minor emendation would be to change most of his "Signor" forms to "Signore" in indirect address without a following name; but Hawthorne was not writing in Italian.

77.19 sun-flickered] E1ᵃ "sun-fleckered" is a sophistication. Besides the blessing of the *O.E.D.* on "flickered", see 73.33–34, "The flicker of the sunshine, the sparkle of . . . "

83.34–84.2 youth; for (so . . . life) they seemed] E1ᵃ reads here, "youth. So much had they flung aside the sombre habitudes of daily life, that they seemed . . . " The origin of the change seems to rest in a mistake that Sophia made in tinkering with the manuscript. That is, she may have been disturbed by the lack of a relative "that" before "they seemed", and hence she altered Hawthorne's "they" to "that" and neglected to restore the "they"; but in this case it would seem that she thought she was correcting, not revising, the manuscript, since the "they" of "they flung" begins the same line (which slants upward) and the eye is easily deceived into taking it that this "they" actually starts the line below. Hence we may conjecture that Sophia wrongly believed that the MS read "they | they" in a typical example of Hawthorne's dittography, and she altered what she took to be the first "they" to "that", thus creating the impossible phrasing "of daily life) that seemed born . . . " Whether Farley took it upon himself to attempt to straighten out this tangle, or whether he set the MS literally and Hawthorne made what he could in proof of the apparent misprint, cannot be determined. What is important is the recognition that in some manner the variant in E1ᵃ from MS is dependent upon an error that had been created in MS, and the change in syntax results from the mending of the impossible "for . . . that seemed" or sophisticated "for . . . that they seemed". Even if Hawthorne himself marked the change in proof, the final reading may not be accepted, in part because it would have been made in ignorance of the MS reading, and in part because the alteration was ill-considered. In the MS the explanation for their play like children or immortally youthful creatures is that they are endowed not with a deep joy (nature) but with (a shallower) eternal mirthfulness. This makes sense. On the other hand, when in the E1ᵃ version the parentheses are removed the explanation applies, instead, to what had been formerly the parenthetical matter; the result is incoherent, for whether their joy was deep or was mirthful has nothing to do with their flinging aside "the sombre habitudes of daily life". The sense of the MS clearly shows that the original inscription, before the Sophia meddling, is right and the print is wrong and must be ignored.

88.30 attentively] The omission of this word by Mintern may perhaps be put down to the fact that it is not altogether clearly inscribed in MS. It is difficult to believe, according to the sense, that E1ᵃ represents a Hawthorne proof-alteration.

105.9 affection] E1ᵃ "affections" represents Hobson's misreading of an upstroke following an imperfectly formed final "n"; the MS word, on examination, is clearly singular. The analogy is not to "affections" in 105.13 where more than one object is implied but to "affection" as used in 105.22,26. See also the Textual Note above to "feeling" at 44.2.

105.11 No, no no] Evidently MS omission of the comma between "no no" is an intentional effect; see the same omission at 130.23.

109.12 rejoined] Ordinarily a change like this from MS "rejoined" to E1ᵃ "replied" would be imputed to the author. But the word is not very legible and could readily be confused by such a careless compositor as Mintern.

113.5 staked] The syntax associates the MS preterite here with the preterite in the parallel following clause. The staking of his hopes was not in the past, or over with, as in the past perfect of "had invited". This latter seems by contamination to have caused Farley to commit a memorial error or conscious sophistication in altering "staked".

117.4 judgment] In his other romances, in the early 1850's, Hawthorne in his manuscripts had spelled "judgement". In *The Marble Faun* he has shifted in the interval to "judgment" except here and at 117.19 where his old habit creeps in.

119.12 observed] As at 109.12, mentioned in the Textual Note above, a change like this might ordinarily be taken as authorial. But the word is not very legible in MS, and it seems probable that, unable to read it, Farley from context chose the neutral word "said" and let it go at that.

126.28 full₍ₐ₎] The comma present in MS, and reproduced in E1ᵃ, was inscribed to separate "full" from another adjective preceding "Nubian". When this adjective was deleted, the comma was retained in error.

139.24 the divinest] For a discussion of this emendation adopted from E1ᵃ, see the Textual Introduction, pp. cxiv–cxv.

143.5 at the city] MS and E1ᵃ "at" may seem odd instead of conventional "of" in this phrase. In truth, the word is not at all well formed in MS, except that an "f" would need to be extremely truncated if it had been intended. The vowel is open at the top and could be anything. However, the reading is vindicated when one observes an identically inscribed "at" on fol. 200, line 13 (Centenary 177.11) where the context is not ambiguous.

143.34 glistening, and dimpling] E1ᵃ's omission of MS "whitening," after "glistening," is very troublesome and no decision about its authority can be at all certain. A possibility exists that Barnett was not sure of the word in MS and thus chose the easy course of omitting it. Although most letters are clearly inscribed, the "n" is not wholly legible and this, plus the unusualness of the word, may have thrown Barnett off. On the other hand, there is a possibility (see Textual Note for 139.24) that Hawthorne made a proof-correction in this sheet 16, and thus the present may also represent an authorial intervention in the same sheet. Whether the retention in E1^a of the comma after "glistening" is evidence for deletion in proof is difficult to say. Did the fountain glisten in the moonlight, or did it glisten anyway and only "dimple" in the moonlight? Even if the question could be decided, Hawthorne's frequent use of a rhetorical comma in this position would qualify the evidence. It is possible that Hawthorne felt that "whitening" and "dimpling" were too close, or that "whitening" was too strained a usage.

150.1 holding] The E1^a reading "keeping" is probably Barnett's version, from context, of a slightly unusual word not written very legibly in MS.

180.9 on purpose] For the authority of this MS reading over E1^a "or" see Textual Introduction, pp. xcvii and ci, and 429.9–11, "There is a Providence purposely for Hilda, as I remember to have told you, long ago."

198.4–5 unintentionally] Although the between-lines error in MS is clearly enough written "un-|tentionally", Hobson's misreading as "intentionally" was perhaps a natural one. However, the evidence of MS is decisive in restoring the true word, with its important values, to the text: the symbolism requires Donatello to be unaware, at least until the moment of contact with his breast (and perhaps not even then), that he has placed Miriam's hand on his heart.

204.22 them] That I^a "there" (MS, E1^a "them") could derive from a misreading corrected only very late in the proof may be indicated by the mending of MS "them" from "there" and the possibility that Farley mistook the reading as a consequence. For the conjectural bibliographical reconstruction of the events leading to this I^a error and its correction in I^c, see the Textual Introduction, p. xcvii.

234.27 beyond memory] Some slight support for the conjecture that the omission of "human" in E1^a from MS "human memory" was authorial may be found in the MS inscription whereby the "h" of "human" is written over a wiped-out "th", perhaps indicating some such phrase in the draft manuscript as "beyond the memory of man" or "of mankind". The alteration to the adjective "human" condensed the phrase, but the change in MS may suggest that in proof Hawthorne was still not satisfied and that he finally removed the redundant "human" since no other memory is, after all, possible.

275.6 circumgyratory] The manuscript spelling looks like "circumgyrotory", but Hawthorne's writing is such that "circumgyrotary" as in E1ᵃ is possible. This interesting word is given so few illustrations in the *O.E.D.* that it is a pity the compilers' use of the American edition, with its "circumgyratory" correction prevented them from reproducing the linguistically interesting original spelling.

281.13 development] In the earlier romances Hawthorne's typical spelling was "developement", but in *The Marble Faun* MS only here and at 380.26 and 411.25 does he use "developement" instead of "development", which is also the spelling in the MSS of *Our Old Home* (1863). Nevertheless, Hawthorne continued to write "develope" and "developes", forms that are reproduced in this text.

324.2 become] The syntax is involved here but that the change from MS "become" to E1ᵃ "became" was a typical Mintern sophistication may be indicated by the initial inscription in MS of the present-tense "catch" and then its deletion and the interlineation of "become aware of" as a substitute.

331.33 and understood] It is difficult to decide whether in the copying of his draft Hawthorne in MS slipped and omitted "been" before "understood" but then supplied it in proof, or whether Mintern—not liking or understanding the somewhat harsh construction with its effective compression—sophisticated the reading. A straw in the wind that "been" was never written may be the comma that follows "understood", although this is only the airiest of evidence. On the whole, it seems better to credit Hawthorne with a rhetorically effective series than with the E1ᵃ blander version that does not read nearly so well aloud. Cf. the effect of "had been told, and understood, and pitied".

386.6 ¶ "Miriam loved me . . .] Superficially this sentence in the MS seems to follow along as the conclusion of the preceding paragraph; but a close inspection reveals that an indention was indeed intended and that the confusion results from Hawthorne having saved space by infringing on the blank of the line above, which had ended in the left margin with the single word "off."

414.15 shrine, on] This is the reading of MS. For the evidence that the uncorrected proof-sheet of E1ᵃ read "shrine, or" and that the E1ᵃ reading "shrine, or on" was Hawthorne's correction of the error in proof but without consultation of copy, see the Textual Introduction, pp. xciv–xcv.

434.8 on] In Hawthorne's hand unless the dot can be seen there is often no way to distinguish "in" from "on". In the MS here the loop of the long "s" of "playfulness" in the line above almost intercepts the vowel and could, by its position, cover the dot of an "i". But since no such dot can be seen in the MS after the most careful examination, we must assume that the word is "on" and the E1ᵃ variant "in" is a mistake by Shand that was not detected in the proof.

EDITORIAL EMENDATIONS IN THE COPY-TEXT

NOTE: Except for such silent typographical alterations as are remarked in the appendix on general textual procedures as applying to all Centenary texts, supplemented by the statement at the end of the Textual Introduction, every editorial change made from the final inscription of the printer's-copy manuscript of *The Marble Faun* is listed here. Only the immediate source of the emendation is noticed; the Historical Collation may be consulted for the complete history, within the editions collated, of any substantive readings that qualify for inclusion in that listing. An alteration assigned to CENTENARY is made for the first time in the present edition if by "the first time" is understood "the first time in respect to the editions chosen for collation." Asterisked readings are discussed in the Textual Notes. The following texts are referred to: MS (the British Museum manuscript), E1 (1860 first English edition, two printings—second printing marked "SECOND EDITION."), E2 (1860 second English edition, marked "THIRD EDITION."), E3 (1861 English one-volume edition), I (1860 first American edition), II (1876 Little Classics Edition), III (1883 Riverside Edition), IV (1900 Autograph Edition). The wavy dash ⁓ represents the same word that appears before the bracket and is used in recording punctuation variants. A caret ∧ indicates the absence of a punctuation mark.

2.20	grave-stone] CENTENARY; gravestone MS,E1–E3,II–IV; ⁓-|⁓ I
4.17–19	Were . . . noble . . . Zenobia.] E1; *omit* MS
4.31	October 15th,] CENTENARY; ⁓ 15th. MS; *December* 15, E1–E3,I–IV

5.0   THE MARBLE FAUN: OR, THE RO-
MANCE OF MONTE BENI] CENTENARY;
THE ROMANCE OF MONTE BENI
E1–E3,I–III; THE MARBLE FAUN IV;
omit MS

7.10   master-piece] CENTENARY; masterpiece
MS,E1–E3,I–IV

7.17   half-illusive] CENTENARY; ~ₐ~ MS,E1–E3,
I–IV

8.15   wonderful,] E1; ~ₐ MS

9.6   inward,] E1; ~; (*semicolon doubtful*) MS

10.32   discoloured] E1; discolored MS

*11.2   Nature] CENTENARY; nature MS,E1–E3,I–IV

12.1   Miriam,] E1; ~ₐ MS

12.7   earnestness.–] CENTENARY; ~ₐ– MS; ~.ₐ
E1–E3,I–IV

12.8   granted.] E1; ~ₐ MS

12.21   "your] E1; ₐ~ MS

13.10   Nature] CENTENARY; nature MS,E1–E3,I–IV

13.17   long-past] I; ~ₐ~ MS,E1–E3

13.23   unless,"] E1; ~,' MS

13.23   sculptor] CENTENARY; *reading obscured by
blot* MS; ~, E1–E3,I–IV

13.28   life,] E1; ~ₐ MS

13.29   Nature] CENTENARY; nature MS,E1–E3,I–IV

14.7   "like]E1; ₐ~ MS

14.7   thunder-shower] E1; ~ₐ~ MS

15.8   Hilda?"] E1; ~?ₐ MS

15.25   sometimes.] E1; ~ₐ MS

16.26   incrusted] II; encrusted MS,E1–E3,I

17.12   discoloured] E1; discolored MS

*17.28   Faun in red marble, who . . . dance,] E1;
Faun, who . . . dance, in red marble, MS

18.10   exhilaration] E1; exhiliration MS

19.3   wrath."] E1; ~.ₐ MS

19.8   of] E1; *omit* MS

19.11   Saints] CENTENARY; saints MS,E1–E3,I–IV

21.15   subtile] E2; subte MS; subtle E1

23.4   hinted] E1; bore MS

23.16   studio.] E1; ~ₐ MS

*25.16	appetite] MS *(original)*; fancy *(Sophia MS alteration)*, E1
25.33	catacombs] E1; Catacombs MS
26.5	guide.] E1; ~∧ MS
29.8	inquiries] E1; inquries MS
29.12	tremour] CENTENARY; tremor MS,E1–E3,I–IV
29.21	back?] IV; ~. MS,E1–E3,I–III
30.2	endeavouring] E1; endeavoring MS
30.3	him.] E1; ~∧ MS
30.13;31.34	Spectre . . . Catacomb] E1; spectre . . . catacomb MS
31.27	torch-light] E1; torchlight MS
32.3	when] E1; whence MS
32.18	Anglo-Saxons] E1; ~∧~ MS
32.22	Hoffmann] I; Hoffman MS,E1–E3
32.25	acceptable] E1; acceptible MS
35.18	beggar,] E1; ~∧ MS
35.20	pilgrims] E1; Pilgrims MS
*36.12	influencies] *stet* MS; influences E1
37.20;38.16	courtyard] E1; court-yard MS
38.16	door-way] III; door way MS; doorway E1–E3; door-|way I–II
38.25	ambassadours] CENTENARY; ambassadors MS,E1–E3,I–IV
38.28	panelled] E1; pan-|neled MS
38.30	palace] E1; ~, MS
38.32	fireside] E1; fire side MS
39.9	white-wash] CENTENARY; whitewash MS,E1–E3,I–IV
*41.15	canvases] E1; canvasses MS
42.33	lay-figure] E1; ~∧~ MS
43.17	Jael] MS *(original)*; Jaël *(Sophia MS alteration)*, E1
43.32	Old Masters] CENTENARY; old masters MS,E1–E3,I–IV
*44.2	feeling] *stet* MS; feelings E1
44.22	Uffizi] CENTENARY; Uffizzi MS,E1–E3,I–IV
*45.13	subtly] *stet* MS; subtilely E1
45.27	half-worn] CENTENARY; ~∧~ MS,E1–E3,I–IV
46.30	Miriam.] E1; ~∧ MS

47.12	this.] E1; ~ʌ MS
47.14	like] E1; ~, MS
47.23	canvas] E1; canvass MS
*47.32	many, in] *stet* MS; many times, in E1
48.15	perchance] E1; per chance MS
48.27	Signorina] II; Signora MS,E1–E3,I
*49.13	is] *stet* MS; are E1
49.33	terrour] CENTENARY; terror MS,E1–E3,I–IV
51.8	sentinel] E1; centinel MS
51.12	whereon] E1; wheron MS
52.6	Virgin's] E1; virgin's MS
52.7	at noon] E1; at | at noon MS
52.12	Church] E1; church MS
52.19	pushing] E1; shoving MS
52.20	favourite] E1; favorite MS
52.21	tumultuously] E1; tumultously MS
53.18	thrusts] E1; thusts MS
53.26	of] E1; of | of MS
53.33	neighbors] I; neighbours MS,E1–E3
53.34	Saint] CENTENARY; saint MS,E1–E3,I–IV
54.16	exhilarates] E1; exhilirates MS
54.16	half-inclined] CENTENARY; ~ʌ~ MS,E1–E3,I–IV
55.11	distant,)] CENTENARY; ~ʌ) MS; ~ʌ– E1–E3,I–IV
55.24	centuries.ʌ] E1; ~.– MS
56.9	aërial] E1; aerial MS
56.19	sending] E1; projecting MS
57.11	indispensable] E1; indispensible MS
58.4	unconscious] E1; unconcious MS
58.12	-coloured] E1; -colored MS
58.33	Heaven] CENTENARY; heaven MS,E1–E3,I–IV
59.2	retouched] E1; re-touched MS
59.28	Old Masters] CENTENARY; old Masters MS; old masters E1–E3,I–IV
60.1	reproduce] E1; re-produce MS
60.18	spectator] E1; spector MS
61.1	in] E1; in in MS
62.3	of] E1; of | of MS
62.17	Anglo-Saxon] E1; ~ʌ~ MS

62.18	become] E1; be |come MS
63.1	shabbily dressed] E1; ~-~ MS
63.3	her] E1; *omit* MS
64.2	new-comer.] E1; ~-~ᴀ MS
67.9	Heaven's] E1; heaven's MS
67.26	Hilda.] E1; ~ᴀ MS
*68.4	Signor] Cᴇɴᴛᴇɴᴀʀʏ; Signore MS,E1–E3,I–IV
68.16	it.–] Cᴇɴᴛᴇɴᴀʀʏ; ~ᴀ– MS,E1–E3; ~,– I–III; ~·ᴀ IV
69.17	something] E1; some thing MS
70.6	Rome)] E1; ~,) MS
70.8	Michel] Cᴇɴᴛᴇɴᴀʀʏ; Michael MS,E1–E3,I–IV
70.16	life.] E1; ~ᴀ MS
71.2	be,] Cᴇɴᴛᴇɴᴀʀʏ; ~ᴀ MS,E1–E3,I–IV
71.8	inferiour] Cᴇɴᴛᴇɴᴀʀʏ; inferior MS,E1–E3,I–IV
71.16	Western] E1; western MS
71.17	-honoured] E1; -honored MS
73.1	wood-paths] E1; woodpaths MS
73.22	thrown] E1; thown MS
74.13	exhilarating] E1; exhilirating MS
75.2	Nature] Cᴇɴᴛᴇɴᴀʀʏ; nature MS,E1–E3,I–IV
*77.19	sun-flickered] *stet* MS; sun-fleckered E1
80.11	had] Cᴇɴᴛᴇɴᴀʀʏ; have MS,E1–E3,I–IV
82.34	ever-varying] E1; ~ᴀ~ MS
83.26	exhilaration] E1; exhiliration MS
84.2	they] MS *(original)*; that *(Sophia MS alteration)*, E1
84.4	glimpse] E1; glimpe MS
84.15	coloured] E1; colored MS
86.11–12	Fauns . . . Satyrs] Cᴇɴᴛᴇɴᴀʀʏ; fauns . . . satyrs MS,E1–E3,I–IV
86.20	Dance,] E1; ~; *(doubtful)* MS
86.21	glade,] Cᴇɴᴛᴇɴᴀʀʏ; ~ᴀ MS,E1–E3,I–IV
86.23	stone-seats] Cᴇɴᴛᴇɴᴀʀʏ; ~ᴀ~ MS,E1–E3,I–IV
86.25	stone-benches] Cᴇɴᴛᴇɴᴀʀʏ; ~ᴀ~ MS,E1–E3,I–IV
86.34	Church] E1; church MS
87.31	Michel] Cᴇɴᴛᴇɴᴀʀʏ; Michael MS,E1–E3,I–IV
87.34	goat-skin] E1; goatskin MS

*88.30	attentively] *stet* MS; *omit* E1
90.2	fantasy] E1; phantasy MS
90.25	"Hush] E1; ∧~ MS
90.29	terrour] CENTENARY; terror MS,E1–E3,I–IV
91.12	Heaven's] E1; heaven's MS
91.13	controul] CENTENARY; control MS,E1–E3,I–IV
94.4;95.13	Model] CENTENARY; model MS,E1–E3,I–IV
94.25	mortal.] E1; ~∧ MS
95.21	"Pray] E1; ∧~ MS
98.18	Papal] CENTENARY; papal MS,E1–E3,I–IV
99.4	exhilarating] E1; exhilirating MS
100.10	Garden] CENTENARY; garden MS,E1–E3,I–IV
100.25	burthened] CENTENARY; burdened MS,E1–E3,I–IV
100.33–34	well-worth] CENTENARY; ~∧~ MS,E1–E3,I–IV
101.4	echoless] E1; echoeless MS
101.18	frame-work] CENTENARY; framework MS,E1–E3,I–II,IV; ~-|~ III
102.2	Summer] E1; summer MS
102.13	ilex-trees] E1; ~∧~ MS
102.18	By-and-by] CENTENARY; ~∧~∧~ MS,E1–E3,I–IV
103.28	Apennines] E1; Appenines MS
104.11	Hilda,] E1; ~∧ *(interlined)* MS
*105.9	affection] *stet* MS; affections E1
*105.11	No, no no] *stet* MS; No, no, no E1
105.34	throughout.] E1; ~∧ MS
106.15	Michel] CENTENARY; Michael MS,E1–E3,I–IV
106.19–20	Empire, Republic . . . Kings] CENTENARY; empire, republic . . . kings MS,E1–E3,I–IV
106.22	Israelites,] CENTENARY; ~∧ MS,E1–E3,I–IV
106.27	Nile!"] E1; ~!' MS
106.32	Sant'] CENTENARY; St∧ MS; St. E1–E3,I–IV
106.33	Archangel] CENTENARY; archangel MS,E1–E3,I–IV
107.6	Saint] CENTENARY; St. MS,E1–E3,I–IV
107.11	Chief-Priest] CENTENARY; ~∧~ MS; chief priest E1–E3,I–IV
107.13	assistance] E1; asistance MS

108.22	Emperour's] CENTENARY; Emperor's MS; emperor's E1–E3,I–IV
108.24	errour] CENTENARY; error MS,E1–E3,I–IV
109.4	Anglo-Saxon] E1; ~∧~ MS
*109.12	rejoined] *stet* MS; replied E1
109.16	Papal] CENTENARY; papal MS,E1–E3,I–IV
109.24	di] CENTENARY; della MS,E1–E3,I–IV
110.2	Column] CENTENARY; column MS,E1–E3,I–IV
110.9	senators] E1; Senators MS
111.19	sculptor.] E1; ~∧ MS
111.23	Saint] CENTENARY; St∧ MS; St. E1–E3,I–IV
*113.5	staked] *stet* MS; had staked E1
114.6	di] CENTENARY; della MS,E1–E3,I–IV
114.20	plaistered] CENTENARY; plastered MS,E1–E3,I–IV
114.28	plaister] CENTENARY; plaster MS,E1–E3,I–IV
114.33;115.14	plaister-] CENTENARY; plaster- MS,E1–E3,I–IV
115.2	Carrara] E1; Carrera MS
115.25	sculptor's] E1; Sculptor's MS
115.33	stopt] MS (*original*); stopped (*Sophia MS alteration*) E1
116.8	Carrara] E1; Carrera MS
116.18	ante-chamber] CENTENARY; antechamber MS,E1–E3,I–IV
116.19	visitor.] E1; ~∧ MS
*117.4	judgment] E1; judgement MS
117.10	plaister] CENTENARY; plaster MS,E1–E3,I–IV
117.19	judgment] E1; judgement MS
118.2	Grey Friars] E1; MS *may possibly read* Grey-Friars
*119.12	observed] *stet* MS; said E1
121.9	reproduce] E1; re-produce MS
121.21	Nature] CENTENARY; nature MS,E1–E3,I–IV
124.4	half-smiling, half-seriously] CENTENARY; ~∧~,~∧~ MS,E1–E3,I–IV
124.20	Uffizi] CENTENARY; Uffizzi MS,E1–E3,I–IV
124.32	Carrara] E1; Carrera MS
125.25	"No] E1; ∧~ MS
*126.28	full∧] II; ~, MS,E1–E3,I
128.14	too—] E1; ~,— MS

130.18	honourable] E1; honorable MS
130.23	No, no no] *stet* MS; No, no, no E1
131.3	Anglo-Saxons] E1; ~ˌ~ MS
131.13	æsthetic] E1; aesthetic MS
134.2	above] E1; a-|above MS
134.26	pagan] CENTENARY; Pagan MS,E1–E3,I–IV
136.11	Carrara] E1; Carrera MS
136.28	æsthetics] E1; aesthetics MS
137.13	is] *stet* MS; are E1
137.32	discoloured] E1; discolored MS
138.8	palace] CENTENARY; Palace MS,E1–E3,I–IV
138.18	inferiour] CENTENARY; inferior MS,E1–E3,I–IV
139.14	Church] I; church MS, E1–E3
139.23	contemptuously] E1; contempt-|tuously MS
*139.24	the divinest] E1; *omit* the MS
140.6	Archangel's] E1; archangel's MS
140.24	half-playfully, half-seriously] CENTENARY; ~ˌ~,~ˌ~ MS,E1–E3,I–IV
141.7	Archangel] E1; archangel MS
142.7	courtyard] E1; court-yard MS
*143.5	at the city] *stet* MS,E1
143.6	Emperours, and Popes] CENTENARY; emperours, and popes MS; emperors, and popes E1–E3, I–IV
143.16	Borghese grounds] E1; Borghese-grounds MS
143.27	art.] E1; ~.— *(justifying dash)* MS
*143.34	glistening, and] E1; glistening, whitening, and MS
144.6	aqueducts] E1; acqueducts MS
145.17	chestnut] I; chesnut MS,E1–E3
146.4	Kenyon;] CENTENARY; ~, MS *(interlineation; deleted 'Graydon' was followed by a semicolon)*, E1–E3,I–IV
146.6	-States] CENTENARY; -states MS; ˌStates E1–E3,I–IV
146.12	lavatory] E1; lavoratory MS
146.17,27	Nelvil] CENTENARY; Neville MS,E1–E3,I–IV
146.20	water."] E1; ~ˌ" MS
147.9	of you] E1; if you MS
147.20	is] E1; *omit* MS

147.27   terrour] CENTENARY; terror MS,E1–E3,I–IV
148.2   holy-water] CENTENARY; ~ᴧ~
            MS,E1–E3,I–IV
148.19   rage.–] CENTENARY; ~ᴧ– MS; ~.ᴧ
            E1–E3,I–IV
149.33   Emperour's] CENTENARY; Emperor's
            MS,E1–E3,I–IV
*150.1   holding] *stet* MS; keeping E1
150.15   noonday] I; noon-day MS,E1–E3
150.17   half-rubbed] CENTENARY; ~ᴧ~
            MS,E1–E3,I–IV
151.12   handfull] CENTENARY; handful
            MS,E1–E3,I–IV
151.12   to] E1; to to MS
151.14   artists.–] E1; ~ᴧ– MS
151.14   "Besides] E1; '~ MS
151.19   Emperour] CENTENARY; Emperor
            MS,E1–E3,I–IV
151.20   Emperours] CENTENARY; emperors
            MS,E1–E3,I–IV
153.11   structure] E1; ~, (*doubtful*) MS
154.18   cross] E1; Cross MS
156.10   Emperour] CENTENARY; Emperor
            MS,E1–E3,I–IV
156.15   melancholy] E1; melan-| MS
156.19   horrour] CENTENARY; horror MS,E1–E3,I–IV
156.25   suppose,)] CENTENARY; ~ᴧ) MS; ~ᴧ–
            E1–E3,I–IV
156.30   amphitheatre."] E1; ~.ᴧ MS
157.12   horrour] CENTENARY; horror MS,E1–E3,I–IV
157.19   the] MS (*original*); their (*Sophia* MS
            alteration), E1
157.22   -controul] CENTENARY; -control
            MS,E1–E3,I–IV
158.32   him,] E1; ~ᴧ (*doubtful*) MS
159.23   flag-stones] CENTENARY; flagstones
            MS,E1–E3,I–IV
160.5   hundredfold] CENTENARY; ~ - ~
            MS,E1–E3,I–IV
161.19   friend.–] MS (*possibly justifying dash*);
            ~.ᴧ E1
163.4   cross] E1; Cross MS

163.26	Hail, Columbia!] E1; $\sim_\wedge\sim$, MS
166.1	heathen] E1; Heathen MS
166.1	Emperour] CENTENARY; Emperor MS,E1–E3,I–II; emperor III–IV
166.26	King] CENTENARY; king MS,E1–E3,I–IV
167.30	Dome] CENTENARY; dome MS,E1–E3,I–IV
167.30	Saint] CENTENARY; St. MS,E1–E3,I–IV
168.19	Nature's] E1; nature's MS
168.31	Senate-House] CENTENARY; $\sim_\wedge\sim$ MS,E1–E3,I–IV
169.6	favoured] E1; favored MS
169.8	at] E1; at | at MS
170.2	horrour] CENTENARY; horror MS,E1–E3,I–IV
170.4	farther] E1; *doubtful* 'farther' *or* 'further' MS
172.1	swang] *stet* MS; swung E1
172.10	horrour-] CENTENARY; horror- MS,E1–E3,I–IV
173.1,6;174.1	horrour] CENTENARY; horror MS,E1–E3,I–IV
174.14	terrour] CENTENARY; terror MS,E1–E3,I–IV
175.8	before.—] CENTENARY; $\sim_\wedge$— MS; $\sim\cdot_\wedge$ E1–E3,I–IV
176.21	forum.] E1; $\sim_\wedge$ MS
178.4	Barberini] E1; Barbeini MS
178.15	passion,] CENTENARY; $\sim_\wedge$ MS,E1–E3,I–IV
180.5	a-light] CENTENARY; alight MS,E1–E3,I–IV
*180.9	on] *stet* MS; or E1
180.22	Apennines] E1; Appennines MS
181.27	a-light] CENTENARY; alight MS,E1–E3,I–IV
182.12	cunningly wrought] E1; $\sim$-$\sim$ MS
185.26	sidelong] II; side-long MS,E1–E3,I
188.17	It] E1; It|it MS
188.27	horrour-] CENTENARY; horror- MS,E1–E3,I–IV
189.11	unsolved.] E1; $\sim_\wedge$ MS
189.30	physician)] E1; $\sim$,) *(doubtful)* MS
190.10	henceforth] E1; hence|forth MS
191.23	endeavouring] E1; endeavoring MS
192.19	sacristan's] E1; Sacristan's MS
192.34	friars] E1; Friars MS
193.18	frame-work] CENTENARY; framework MS,E1–E3,I–IV
194.13	disagreeable] E1; disgreeable MS

194.24   sacristan] E1; Sacristan MS
197.18   half fancied] E1; ~ - ~ MS
*198.4–5   unintentionally] II; un-|tentionally MS;
          intentionally E1–E3,I
198.8   Miriam] E1; ~, MS
199.15   have] E1; have | have MS
199.25   commiserating] E1; commisserating MS
200.34   Donatello.] E1; ~ₐ MS
202.8   Church]CENTENARY; church MS,E1–E3,I–IV
202.15   been compelled to] E1; been to MS
203.6   squatted] MS (original); huddled (Sophia MS
          alteration), E1
*204.22   them] stet MS,E1
206.4   no] E1; no | no MS
207.2   you!"] E1; ~!ₐ MS
207.14   wantonness] E1; wantoness MS
207.16   Hilda.] E1; ~ₐ MS
207.32   suffering] E1; sufferring MS
208.26–27   her . . . her . . . she] E1; me . . . me . . .
          I MS
209.33   courtyard] E1; court-yard MS
210.9   Hilda,] E1; ~ₐ MS
210.28   threshold.] E1; ~ₐ MS
213.16   terrours] CENTENARY; terrors MS,E1–E3,I–IV
214.3   visit,)] CENTENARY; ~ₐ) MS; ~), E1–E3,I–IV
214.12   works, which] E1; works, in that kind,
          which MS
214.15   Nature] CENTENARY; nature MS,E1–E3,I–IV
214.27   hill-side] E1 (hill-|side); hillside (doubtful) MS
215.7   stone-work] II; stonework MS,E1–E3,I
215.23   roundabout] CENTENARY; round about
          MS,E1–E3,I–IV
215.33   yellow-wash] CENTENARY; ~ₐ~
          MS,E1–E3,I–IV
216.28   countenance,)] CENTENARY; ~ₐ) MS,I; ~),
          E1–E3,II–IV
218.2   prison-chambers] CENTENARY; ~ₐ~
          MS,E1–E3,I–IV
218.5   dimly lighted] E1; ~ - ~ MS
218.8   "I] E1; '~ MS
218.23   courtyard] E1; court-yard MS

218.29	great-grandsire] E1; ~ᴧ~ MS
219.6	Count] II; count MS,E1–E3,I
219.22	staircase] E1; staicase MS
219.30	an] E1; and MS
220.6	door-ways] I; doorways MS,E3; door-|ways E1–E2
221.16	favourable] E1; favorable MS
222.19	summer-noon] CENTENARY; ~ᴧ~ MS,E1–E3,I–IV
223.12	liquour] CENTENARY; liquor MS,E1–E3,I–IV
224.13,28,32	Signor] CENTENARY; Signore MS, IV; signore E1–E3,I–III
225.4	it,)] I; ~ᴧ) MS,E1–E3
225.14	exhilaration] E1; exhiliration MS
227.26	sculptor's] E1; sculptor MS
229.8	minds,)] CENTENARY; ~ᴧ) MS; ~), E1–E3,I–IV
229.10	terrour] CENTENARY; terror MS,E1–E3,I–IV
229.21	Church] I; church MS,E1–E3
229.29	change,)] CENTENARY; ~ᴧ) MS; ~ᴧ– E1–E3; ~,– I–IV
229.34	bridal,] E1; ~ᴧ MS
231.17–18	and arrive nowhither] E1; and probably arrive no whither MS
232.4	say,)] CENTENARY; ~ᴧ) MS; ~,ᴧ E1–E3,I–IV
232.11	Republic] CENTENARY; republic MS,E1–E3,I–IV
232.20	descent ( ] CENTENARY; ~,(MS; ~ᴧ– E1–E3,I–IV
234.3	Nature] CENTENARY; nature MS,E1
234.9	eir own part g] E1; MS *mutilated*
*234.27	beyond memory] E1; beyond human memory MS
234.34	Nature] CENTENARY; nature MS,E1–E3,I–IV
235.3	that, once] E1; MS *mutilated*
235.30	vineyard.] E1; ~ᴧ MS
236.5	re-appear] CENTENARY; reappear MS,E1–E3,I,III–IV; ~-|~ II
236.19	Dark] CENTENARY; dark MS,E1–E3,I–IV
236.21;237.7	Kenyon] E1; Graydon MS
236.29	neighboring] I; neighbouring MS,E1–E3

237.29	valleys] E1; vallies MS
239.31	Nature] CENTENARY; nature MS,E1–E3,I–IV
241.11	handfull] CENTENARY; handful MS,E1–E3,I–IV
241.30	store,)] CENTENARY; ~ₐ) MS; ~ₐ– E1–E3, I; ~,– II–IV
243.9	maiden-hair] E1; ~ₐ~ MS
243.30	imagination.] E1; ~ₐ MS
244.1	he] E1; he | he MS
244.2	well.] E1; ~ₐ MS
244.5	Donatello.] E1; ~.– (justifying dash) MS
244.7	more sad] E1; more than sad MS
245.16	point.] E1; ~, MS
246.9	sculptor.] E1; ~ₐ MS
246.11	horrour-] CENTENARY; horror- MS,E1–E3,I–IV
246.30	Nature] CENTENARY; nature MS,E1–E3,I–IV
247.18	the] E1; the the MS
247.30	persuasibility] E1; persuadability MS
247.31;248.23	Kenyon's] E1; Graydon's MS
248.18	Nature] CENTENARY; nature MS,E1–E3,I–IV
249.12	Nature] CENTENARY; nature MS,E1–E3,I–IV
249.21	a] E1; a | a MS
249.23	friend's] E1; friends MS
249.32;250.11	Nature] CENTENARY; nature MS,E1–E3,I–IV
250.9	Donatello.] E1; ~ₐ MS
251.19	spirit.] E1; ~ₐ MS
251.23	"Ah] E1; ₐ~ MS
252.14	without.] E1; ~ₐ MS
252.19	too,)] CENTENARY; ~ₐ) MS; ~ₐ– E1–E3,I–IV
253.22	"Like] E1; ₐ~ MS
253.31	door-way] I; doorway MS,E1–E3
254.16	ghosts?"] E1; ~?ₐ MS
255.27	holy-water] CENTENARY; ~ₐ~ MS,E1–E3,I–IV
257.13	picture.] E1; ~.– (justifying dash) MS
257.22	gray convents] E1; gray-convents MS
258.18	His] E1; his MS
261.1	"That] E1; ₐ~ MS
262.28	battle-field] E1; battle field (doubtful) MS
263.4	endeavoured] E1; endeavoued MS

263.10 summer-afternoon] Centenary; ∼ˌ∼
 MS,E1–E3,I–IV

263.21 distinctly] E1; distincly MS

264.19 Count.] Centenary; ∼, MS; count; E1–E3;
 Count; I–IV

266.23 cry,(] Centenary; ∼ˌ(MS; ∼ˌ– E1–E3;
 ∼,– I–IV

267.10 it.] E1; ∼ˌ MS

267.32 Heaven] II; heaven MS,E1–E3,I

267.34 it.] E1; ∼ˌ MS

268.19 advantages] E1; ad-|tages MS

268.33 Donatello's] E1; Dontatello's MS

273.10 onward.] E1; ∼ˌ MS

274.8 past] *stet* MS

274.19 chanced to find] E1; happened upon MS

274.26 figures] E1; shows MS

274.31;275.2 liquour] Centenary; liquor MS,E1–E3,I–IV

275.2 sadder] E1; sorrier MS

*275.6 circumgyratory] I; circumgyrotory(?) MS;
 circumgyrotary E1–E2

275.17 Nature] Centenary; nature MS,E1

276.4 this.] E1; ∼ˌ MS

276.29 tapestry.] E1; ∼ˌ MS

277.12 martyrdom] E1; martydom MS

277.14 half-a-century] Centenary; ∼ˌ∼ˌ∼
 MS,E1–E3,I–IV

277.17 holy-water] Centenary; ∼ˌ∼
 MS,E1–E3,I–IV

278.25 verd] I; verde MS,E1–E3

279.2 Oriental] II; oriental MS,E1–E3,I

279.8 excellencies] *stet* MS; excellences E1

279.12 hundredth] E1; hundreth MS

280.26 horrour] Centenary; horror MS,E1–E3,I–IV

281.9 Donatello,] Centenary; ∼ˌ MS,E1–E3,I–IV

*281.13 development] E1; developement MS

281.17 not] E1; *just possibly* 'out' MS

281.23 moment, he] E1; moment? He MS

283.9 however)] Centenary; ∼,) MS;
 ∼ˌ– E1–E3,I–IV

283.20 Eye-Witness] Centenary; Eye Witness MS;
 eye witness E1–E3; eye-witness I–IV

284.27	valleys] E1; vallies MS
285.10	woman—] E1; ~, MS
286.24	she. "More] CENTENARY; ~ₐ"~ MS; ~; "more E1–E3,I–IV
288.19	sluggishness] E1; slugglishness MS
289.4	valleys] E1; vallies MS
290.16	great-grandmothers] E1; ~ₐ~ MS
290.21	Western] II; western MS,E1–E3,I
290.22	sun-burnt] CENTENARY; ~ₐ~ MS; sunburnt E1–E3,I–IV
291.16	flower,)] CENTENARY; ~ₐ) MS; ~), E1–E3,I–IV
291.17	loves.] E1; ~ₐ MS
292.7	victim] E1; victims MS
292.16	gateway] E1; gate-way MS
293.15	sentinels] E1; centinels MS
294.2	his] E1; his	his MS
295.30	endeavours] E1; endeavors MS
295.32	door-steps] CENTENARY; doorsteps MS,E1–E3,I–IV
296.27	penitential] E1; penintential MS
297.2	Blessed] II; blessed MS,E1–E3,I
298.16	Heaven] CENTENARY; heaven MS,E1–E3,I–IV
298.21	iniquities] E1; inquities MS
298.21	Papal] CENTENARY; papal MS,E1–E3,I–IV
298.23	Cross] CENTENARY; cross MS,E1–E3,I–IV
298.33	Cross . . . Cross] CENTENARY; cross . . . cross MS,E1–E3,I–IV
299.8	faintly heard] E1; ~-~ MS
300.6	hill-side] CENTENARY; hillside MS,E1–E3,II; ~-|~ I,III–IV
301.9	Republic] E1; republic MS
303.20	bear)] CENTENARY; ~,) MS; ~ₐ— E1–E3,I–IV
304.2	school] E1; School MS
304.25	horrour] CENTENARY; horror MS,E1–E3,I–IV
305.13	inseparable] E1; insep-|erable MS
305.31	Himself] CENTENARY; himself MS,E1–E3,I–IV
306.9	exteriour] CENTENARY; exterior MS,E1–E3,I–IV
307.28	well fed] E1; well-fed MS
307.28	The] E1; They MS

308.12   Donatello] E1; Dontello MS
309.9   Italy alone] E1; only Italy MS
310.16   depth,] E1; ~∧ MS
311.6   Cathedral] CENTENARY; cathedral
                MS,E1–E3,I–IV
311.12   hats] E1; ~, MS
311.18   Donkeys] E1; Donkies MS
313.8   piazza] E1; Piazza MS
313.14   Middle-Age] CENTENARY; middle-age MS;
                ~∧~ E1–E3,I–II; Middle Age III–IV
314.27   market-place] E1; ~∧~ MS
315.8   Pontiff's] CENTENARY; pontiff's
                MS,E1–E3,I–IV
315.11   Wilderness] E1; wilderness of Egypt MS
315.13   Blessed] II; blessed MS,E1–E3,I
315.18   neighboring] I; neighbouring MS,E1–E3
316.19   tremour] CENTENARY; tremor MS,E1–E3,I–IV
317.6   cathedral] E1; Cathedral MS
317.32   me,] E1; ~; MS (doubtful)
318.8   up] E1; upon MS
318.32   piazza] E1; Piazza MS
318.34   store.] E1; ~∧ MS
319.8   a] E1; a a MS
319.11   quick] E1; much MS
319.12   her?] E1; ~. MS
322.1   Donatello] E1; Dontello MS
322.29   earnestly.] E1; ~∧ MS
323.11   eye-witnesses] E1; eyewitnesses MS
323.21   Miriam.] E1; ~∧ MS
323.22   too.] E1; ~∧ MS
*324.2   become] stet MS; became E1
324.4   sculptor] E1; Sculptor MS
327.12   visitors] E1; visiters MS
327.19   aërial] I; aerial MS,E1–E2
329.27   echoless] E1; echoeless MS
*331.33   and understood] stet MS; and been understood
                E1
333.0   PICTURE-GALLERIES] I; ~∧~ MS,E1–E3
333.18   never more] E1; MS could just possibly read
                nevermore

334.11	reproduce] E1; re-produce MS
334.15	"Yes] E1; $_\wedge\sim$ MS
334.23	di] CENTENARY; da MS,E1–E3,I–IV
334.27	"But] E1; $_\wedge\sim$ MS
335.26	creating.] E1; $\sim_\wedge$ MS
336.13	Douw] E1; Duow MS
337.29	Heaven-] CENTENARY; heaven- MS,E1–E3,I–IV
337.30	Barberini] I; Baberini MS,E1–E2
337.31	trollop] E1; trollope MS
338.4	Paradise] CENTENARY; paradise MS,E1–E3,I–IV
338.16	have$_\wedge$)] E1; $\sim$,) MS
339.29	ground$_\wedge$] MS (original); $\sim$, (Sophia MS alteration), E1
339.31	loneliness.$_\wedge$] E1; $\sim$.— (possibly justifying dash) MS
340.9	heavens] E1; Heavens MS
343.5	battlements] E1; battements MS
344.9	Fathers] CENTENARY; fathers MS,E1–E3,I–IV
345.23	interiour] CENTENARY; interior MS,E1–E3,I–IV
346.5	Dome] CENTENARY; dome MS,E1–E3,I–IV
349.8	work] MS (original); $\sim$, (Sophia MS alteration), E1
349.24	actual] E1; omit MS
349.27	'How] CENTENARY; "$\sim$ MS,E1–E3,I–IV
350.31	heart$_\wedge$)] CENTENARY; $\sim$,) MS; $\sim_\wedge$– E1–E3,I–IV
351.28	Peter,] E1; $\sim_\wedge$ MS
352.18	Michael] E1; Michel MS
353.10	Will-o'-] E1; Will-of- MS
354.8	as] E1; as as MS
356.13	Confessional] CENTENARY; confessional MS,E1–E3,I–IV
358.11	Confessor] CENTENARY; confessor MS,E1–E3,I–IV
359.13	my] E1; omit MS
361.29	burthened] CENTENARY; burdened MS,E1–E3,I–IV
362.17	cross] E1; Cross MS
364.9	it.] E1; $\sim_\wedge$ MS

364.21   moment."] E1; $\sim_\wedge$" MS
365.21   overbrimming] CENTENARY; over-brimming MS,E1–E3,I–IV
366.26   Hierarchies] CENTENARY; Hierrarchies MS; hierarchies E1–E3,I–IV
366.27   purple,] E1; $\sim_\wedge$ MS
367.8–9   New England] E1; New-England MS
367.21   confessional] E1; Confessional MS
368.12   errour] CENTENARY; error MS,E1–E3,I–IV
369.35   Sant'] CENTENARY; St. MS,E1–E3,I–IV
370.10   as] I; *omit* MS,E1–E2
370.13   motion] E1; motions MS
370.17,23   Saint] CENTENARY; St. MS,E1–E3,I–IV
373.0   SNOW-DROPS] III; SNOWDROPS MS,E1–E3,I–II
376.6   hand,] E1; $\sim_\wedge$ MS (*see list of Alterations in MS*)
376.10   within-doors] E1; $\sim_\wedge\sim$ MS
376.19   door-ways] I; doorways MS,E1–E3
379.10   original."] E1; $\sim_\wedge$" MS
380.3   long-past] E1; $\sim_\wedge\sim$ MS
380.26   development] E1; developement MS
381.12   unsuccessful] E1; unsuccessul MS
383.1   —you] E1; —then you MS
385.23   for better] E1; for for better MS
385.24   ourselves] E1; our ouselves MS
*386.6   ¶"Miriam loved me . . .] *stet* MS,E1
387.15   terrours] CENTENARY; terrors MS,E1–E3,I–IV
387.26   had trodden] E1; trod MS
387.34   of] E1; of of MS
388.2   close,] E1; $\sim_\wedge$ MS
388.4   overpopulate] CENTENARY; over-populate MS,E1–E3,I–IV
388.15   incrusting] I; encrusting MS,E1–E3
389.11   baiòcco] CENTENARY; baioccho MS,E1–E3; baiocco I–IV
389.19   Anglo-Saxon] E1; $\sim_\wedge\sim$ MS
391.14   Belvedere] E1; Belvidere MS
391.31   Sculpture] CENTENARY; sculpture MS,E1–E3,I–IV
392.23   proceeds] E1; avails MS

393.11   conversation] E1; converstation MS
393.15   penitence.] E1; ~ʌ MS
393.22   and was] E1; and was was MS
397.8   out] E1; out out MS
398.5   thus!] E1; ~? MS
398.19   Virgin's] E1; Virgins MS
399.0   DESERTED] E1; deserted MS
399.2   daughter] E1; Daughter MS
399.6   aërial] I; aerial MS,E1–E2
399.7   a-light] CENTENARY; alight MS,E1–E3,I–IV
400.7   him.] E1; ~ʌ MS
403.13   were so far] MS (*original*); ~,~~, (*Sophia MS alteration*), E1
404.13   pacquet] CENTENARY; packet MS,E1–E3,I–IV
405.7   Blessed] II; blessed MS,E1–E3,I
405.9   Blessed] III; blessed MS,E1–E3,I–II
406.21   Signor] E1; Signore MS
407.26   surface.] E1; ~ʌ MS
410.3   heaped-up] E1; ~ʌ~ MS
410.15   Palace] CENTENARY; palace MS,E1–E3,I–IV
411.25   development] E1; developement MS
412.6   Vandal] E1; ~, MS
412.20   opportunity] E1; opportuni-| MS
412.26   handfull] CENTENARY; handful MS,E1–E3,I–IV
*414.15   shrine, on] *stet* MS; shrine, or on E1
415.13   must] *stet* MS; *omit* E1
416.1   Blessed] II; blessed MS,E1–E3,I
416.13   apprehended] E1; ~, MS
418.10   plaistered] CENTENARY; plastered MS,E1–E3,I–IV
418.19   interiour] CENTENARY; interior MS,E1–E3,I–IV
419.13   massiveness.] E1; ~ʌ MS
419.19   olive-trees] E1; ~ʌ~ MS
420.8   columbarium] II; columbaria MS,E1–E3,I
420.9   graveyard] E1; grave yard MS
420.28   handfull] CENTENARY; handful MS,E1–E3,I–IV
421.13–14   half fancied] E1; ~-~ MS
421.17   himself.] E1; ~ʌ MS

422.4   indescribable] E1; indescrible MS
422.10   half-an-hour] CENTENARY; ~ʌ~ʌ~
             MS,E1–E3,I–IV
422.13   exceedingly] E1; exceedinly MS
424.9   Nature] CENTENARY; nature MS,E1–E3,I–IV
424.23   Emperour] CENTENARY; Emperor MS; emperor
             E1–E3,I–IV
426.13   half-mirthful] CENTENARY; ~ʌ~
             MS,E1–E3,I–IV
426.20   Carnival-time] CENTENARY; carnival-time MS;
             ~ʌ~ E1–E3,I–IV
427.32   you,"] E1; ~ʌ" MS
429.17   Heaven] CENTENARY; heaven MS,E1–E3,I–IV
429.25   Will-o'-the-Wisp] E1; ~ʌ~ʌ~ʌ~ MS
430.7   recall] E1; recal MS
431.1   breeds] MS (original); races (Sophia MS
             alteration), E1
431.5   Some time] E1; Sometime MS
431.6   Miriam alluded] stet MS; Miriam had alluded
             E1
433.29   smiling.] E1; ~ʌ MS
434.7   re-appeared] CENTENARY; reappeared
             MS,E1–E3,I–IV
*434.8   on] stet MS; in E1
434.19   blessing] MS (original); ~, (Sophia MS
             alteration), E1
434.22   discipline?"] E1; ~?ʌ MS
435.5   feet!] CENTENARY; ~? MS; ~. E1–E3,I–IV
435.24   -journey] E1; -jouney MS
439.14   the powdered] E1; the the powdered MS
441.6   Carnival] III; carnival (doubtful)
             MS,E1–E3,I–II
442.9   Anglo-Saxon] E1; ~ʌ~ MS
442.30   gilding.] E1; ~, MS
443.2   cardinals] CENTENARY; Cardinals
             MS,E1–E3,I–IV
443.12   New Englander] E1; New-Englander MS
443.12   Englander,)] CENTENARY; ~ʌ) MS; ~ʌ–
             E1–E3, ~,– I–IV
446.6   dumb-show] E1; dumb-shew MS

450.5	best,] E1; ~$_\wedge$ MS
450.19	back-ground] CENTENARY; back ground MS; background E1–E3,I–IV
450.23	street.] E1; ~$_\wedge$ MS
451.2	Carnival-] CENTENARY; carnival- MS; carnival$_\wedge$ E1–E3,I–IV
452.11	dumb-show] II; ~$_\wedge$~ MS,E1–E3,I
452.22	imagine$_\wedge$] E1; MS *just possibly has a comma*
452.27	portrait] E1; portait MS
453.2	master-piece] CENTENARY; masterpiece MS,E1–E3,I,II,IV; ~-|~ III
453.9	know] E1; known MS
453.22	bon-bons] CENTENARY; bonbons MS,E1–E3,I–III; ~-|~ IV
453.23	sugar-plums] E1; sugarplums MS
456.5	government,] E1; *comma doubtful* MS
456.17	re-appearance] CENTENARY; reappearance MS,E1–E3,I–IV
456.34	dedicated] E1; dedi-|dicated MS
458.16	neighboring] I; neighbouring MS,E1–E3
459.28	Paradise] CENTENARY; paradise MS,E1–E3,I–IV
459.33	required] E1; reequired MS
460.30	agitation;] E1;~$_\wedge$ MS

NOTE: The Centenary Edition uses E1^b—the second English printing—where the Postscript first appeared, as copy-text, since no MS survives. The first American printing to include the Post-script, headed "Conclusion", was presumably I^d—i.e., the fourth printing.

463.1	Author] CENTENARY; author E1^b–E3,I^d–IV
463.6	dark;] I^d; ~;– E1^b–E3
463.16	Author] I^d; author E1^b–E3
463.19	Real . . . Fantastic] I^d; real . . . fantastic E1^b–E3
464.4	Author] I^d; author E1^b–E3
464.12	Saint] I^d; St. E1^b–E3
464.14–15	which (having . . . way)] I^d; ~,~ . . . ~, E1^b–E3

464.20	pacquet] CENTENARY; packet E1b–E3,Id–IV
464.21,29	Signor] CENTENARY; Signore E1b–E3,Id–IV
464.22	Cenci'?"] CENTENARY; ~?' " E1b–E3; ~?" Id–IV
464.28	believe] E2; belive E1b
465.6,12,24	pacquet] CENTENARY; packet E1b–E3,Id–IV
465.17	mean time] Id; meantime E1b–E3
465.34	Rome? And] CENTENARY; Rome? and E1b–E3; Rome, and Id–IV
466.4	neighborhood] Id; neighbourhood E1b–E3
466.19	Trinità] Id; Trinita E1b–E3
466.23	forever] Id; for ever E1b–E3
466.24	Abbate's] Id;E1b–E3

REJECTED FIRST-EDITION SUBSTANTIVE VARIANTS

NOTE: Although the readings below are listed in the Historical Collation, they are given separately here since the information is of critical importance. An asterisk indicates that a Textual Note discusses the reading. E1[a] is the first English printing.

3.19	like] MS; *omit* E1[a]
3.32	find in] MS; find it in E1[a]
4.31	October] MS; *December* E1[a]
8.30	claw] MS; claws E1[a]
9.24	nor] MS; or E1[a]
14.2,30	neither] MS; either E1[a]
15.31	should] MS; shall E1[a]
16.33	mischievously. "You] MS; mischievously, "you E1[a]
17.32	would] MS; could E1[a]
18.1	on] MS; in E1[a]
18.5	subtile] MS; subtle E1[a]
20.13	put up her] MS; put her E1[a]
20.13	shown] MS; showed E1[a]
21.10	those] MS; these E1[a]
21.14	further] MS; farther E1[a]
21.15	than] MS; then E1[a]
21.15	subtile] II; subtle MS,E1[a]
22.14	subtile] MS; subtle E1[a]
*25.16	appetite] MS *(original);* fancy *(Sophia MS alteration)* E1[a]
25.25	my] MS; *omit* E1[a]

26.34	around] MS; round E1ᵃ
28.18	uttermost] MS; utmost E1ᵃ
32.22	Hoffmann] I; Hoffman MS,E1ᵃ
*36.12	influencies] MS; influences E1ᵃ
37.12	elder] MS; older E1ᵃ
38.7	weed] MS; weeds E1ᵃ
39.23	from] MS; form E1ᵃ
42.8	Miriam] MS; Mariam E1ᵃ
43.10	man or woman] MS; men or women E1ᵃ
*44.2	feeling] MS; feelings E1ᵃ
44.4	mustachios] MS; moustaches E1ᵃ
44.7	at] MS; in E1ᵃ
*45.13	subtly] MS; subtilely E1ᵃ
*47.32	many, in] MS; many times, in E1ᵃ
48.27	Signorina] II; Signora MS,E1ᵃ
*49.13	is] MS; are E1ᵃ
52.30	beaksful] MS; beakfuls E1ᵃ
52.31	rustled] MS; rushed E1ᵃ
55.1	woman] MS; women E1ᵃ
55.17	angel's] MS; angels' E1ᵃ
57.21	now] MS; more E1ᵃ
58.2	her] MS; the E1ᵃ
59.25	processes] MS; process E1ᵃ
60.34	adducing] MS; admiring E1ᵃ
62.15	excellencies] MS; excellences E1ᵃ
64.19	eyelids] MS; eyes E1ᵃ
69.12	tower] MS; lower E1ᵃ
72.3	what] MS; which E1ᵃ
72.4	funereal] MS; funeral E1ᵃ
72.22	of a] MS; of the E1ᵃ
72.34	granite,] MS; ∼₍ₗ₎ E1ᵃ
77.12	could] MS; would E1ᵃ
*77.19	sun-flickered] MS; sun-fleckered E1ᵃ
80.11	had] CENTENARY; have MS, E1ᵃ
83.32	they] MS; *omit* E1ᵃ
*83.34–84.2	youth; for (so . . . life) they] MS (*original*); youth. So . . . life, that they (that *Sophia MS alteration; the following they is Hawthorne's addition*) E1ᵃ
85.5	moment] MS; movement E1ᵃ

86.19	Here] MS; There E1[a]
*88.30	attentively] MS; *omit* E1[a]
88.34	on] MS; to E1[a]
90.7	sylvan] MS; silver E1[a]
95.6	could] MS; would E1[a]
95.29	could] MS; would E1[a]
96.32	immitigable] MS; unmitigable E1[a]
97.19	could] MS; would E1[a]
100.24	long] MS; *omit* E1[a]
*105.9	affection] MS; affections E1[a]
106.9	prospect] MS; prospects E1[a]
106.16	eldest] MS; oldest E1[a]
106.34	building] MS; buildings E1[a]
108.9	in] MS; of E1[a]
108.23	could] MS; would E1[a]
*109.12	rejoined] MS; replied E1[a]
109.24	di] CENTENARY; della MS,E1[a]
110.10	these] MS; those E1[a]
110.32	the] MS; *omit* E1[a]
*113.5	staked] MS; had staked E1[a]
114.6	di] CENTENARY; della MS,E1[a]
*119.12	observed] MS; said E1[a]
122.5	probability] MS; possibility E1[a]
124.5	neither] MS; either E1[a]
127.17	never] MS; ever E1[a]
137.13	is] MS; are E1[a]
145.3	this] MS; their E1[a]
145.20	come] MS; came E1[a]
146.17,27	Nelvil] CENTENARY; Neville MS,E1[a]
149.18	farther] MS; further E1[a]
149.29	elder] MS; older E1[a]
*150.1	holding] MS; keeping E1[a]
153.22	inherit] MS; inhabit E1[a]
154.12	lie] MS; lay E1[a]
154.12	area] MS; arena E1[a]
154.15	song] MS; songs E1[a]
154.18	especial] MS; special E1[a]
157.15	her] MS; *omit* E1[a]
157.19	the] MS (*original*); their (*Sophia MS alteration*) E1[a]

157.34	with] MS; *omit* E1ª
160.9	nor] MS; or E1ª
163.27	exceedingly] MS; exceeding E1ª
166.1	this] MS; the E1ª
169.2	literally] MS; literary E1ª
169.14	has] MS; had E1ª
171.2	neither] MS; either E1ª
172.1	swang] MS; swung E1ª
180.7	downward] MS; downwards E1ª
*180.9	on] MS; or E1ª
188.23	musings] MS; musing E1ª
189.9	explanation] MS; exclamation E1ª
*198.4–5	unintentionally] II; un-|tentionally MS; intentionally E1ª
199.23	others'] MS; other's E1ª
203.6	squatted] MS (*original*); huddled (*Sophia MS alteration*) E1ª
207.8	sides] MS; side E1ª
212.19	dove's] MS; doves' E1ª
216.15	Tomaso] MS; Thomaso E1ª
219.23	ascended] MS; ascending E1ª
224.27	kindliness] MS; kindness E1ª
225.15	round] MS; around E1ª
233.28	sprung] MS; sprang E1ª
239.16	days] MS; day E1ª
240.2	surest] MS; soonest E1ª
241.13	or spectator] MS; or a spectator E1ª
241.22	established] MS; establishing E1ª
243.33	eldest] MS; oldest E1ª
245.6	glowing] MS; glancing E1ª
247.32	shrubbery] MS; shrubberies E1ª
250.32	further] MS; farther E1ª
254.12	Granducal] MS; Grand-ducal E1ª
254.20	came] MS; come E1ª
259.5	of mid-sky] MS; of the mid-sky E1ª
259.21	this] MS; the E1ª
262.19	a nobler] MS; *omit* a E1ª
266.29	further and further] MS; farther and farther E1ª
269.22	could] MS; would E1ª

271.13   this] MS; his E1ᵃ

*275.6   circumgyratory] I; circumgyrotory(?) MS; circumgyrotary E1ᵃ

276.11   could] MS; would E1ᵃ

277.16   into] MS; in E1ᵃ

278.12   himself] MS; *omit* E1ᵃ

279.8   excellencies] MS; excellences E1ᵃ

281.18   misery] MS; mystery E1ᵃ

287.4   but] MS; and E1ᵃ

290.3–4   indistinguishable] MS; undistinguishable E1ᵃ

292.14   and surrounding] MS; and its surrounding E1ᵃ

292.17   when] MS; where E1ᵃ

294.32   deep-hued] MS; deep, mild E1ᵃ

296.18   was] MS; were E1ᵃ

297.31   wreathe] MS; wreath E1ᵃ

298.27   pursues] MS; possesses E1ᵃ

306.17   And] MS; All E1ᵃ

306.33   grandams] MS; grandames E1ᵃ

307.28   need] MS; needs E1ᵃ

321.10   may] MS; nay E1ᵃ

*324.2   become] MS; became E1ᵃ

326.19   threading] MS; treading E1ᵃ

*331.33   and understood] MS; and been understood E1ᵃ

334.23   di] CENTENARY; da MS,E1ᵃ

335.5   these] MS; those E1ᵃ

336.15   reflections] MS; reflection E1ᵃ

336.20   works] MS; work E1ᵃ

337.23   feeling] MS; feelings E1ᵃ

346.18   infrequent] MS; unfrequent E1ᵃ

350.18   of] MS; at E1ᵃ

352.27   whether for] MS; whether from E1ᵃ

360.27   consequencies] MS; consequences E1ᵃ

370.10   as] I; *omit* MS, E1ᵃ

375.24   when] MS; where E1ᵃ

375.29   artists] MS; artist E1ᵃ

400.18   upward] MS; upwards E1ᵃ

402.18   thither] MS; hither E1ᵃ

404.31   within] MS; with E1ᵃ

410.13   roughnesses] MS; roughness E1ᵃ

*414.15   shrine, on] MS; shrine, or on E1ᵃ

415.13	must] MS; *omit* E1ᵃ
418.20	goat's] MS; goats' E1ᵃ
431.1	breeds] MS *(original)*; races *(Sophia MS alteration)* E1ᵃ
431.6	Miriam alluded] MS; Miriam had alluded E1ᵃ
432.12	penances] MS; penance E1ᵃ
433.20	immitigable] MS; unmitigable E1ᵃ
433.24	whatever] MS; whatsoever E1ᵃ
*434.8	on] MS; in E1ᵃ
438.34	secrets] MS; secret E1ᵃ
441.11;442.27	gensd'armes] MS; gendarmes E1ᵃ
444.3	the Contadina] MS; *omit* the E1ᵃ
446.24	horrour] MS; sorrow E1ᵃ
446.31	to let] MS; to him let E1ᵃ
450.32	gensd'armes] MS; gendarmes E1ᵃ
456.11	a] MS; the E1ᵃ
461.1	with] MS; *omit* E1ᵃ

WORD-DIVISION

1. *End-of-the-Line Hyphenation in the Centenary Edition*

NOTE: No hyphenation of a possible compound at the end of a line in the Centenary text is present in the manuscript except for the following readings, which are hyphenated within the line in the manuscript. Hyphenated compounds in which both elements are capitalized are not included.

4.15	bas-|reliefs	119.2	great-|grandchildren
38.27	marble-|panelled	125.12	clay-|model
41.19	half-|startled	126.16	pulse-|throbs
42.20	hide-and-|seek	130.18	true-|hearted
43.12	pencil-|drawings	138.8	half-|a-dozen
52.7	twenty-|four	142.16	cigar-|vender's
53.8	paving-|stones	145.16	fruit-|dealers
62.20	wild-|bearded	147.20	time-|stains
65.19	oil-|paintings	154.7	ground-|tier
72.26	water-|weeds	159.33	half-|worn
73.22	half-|development	164.13	hill-|side
100.24	nursery-|maids	182.13	clay-|cold
102.11	half-|development	192.32	longest-|buried
106.8	lattice-|work	193.29	earth-|damps
106.24	awe-|stricken	222.18	window-|blinds
117.23	sea-|weeds	229.34	death-|chamber
118.25	quick-|lime	230.5	By-|and-by

245.5	rain-|drops	334.34	first-|love
246.17	blood-|stain	336.6	picture-|galleries
253.29	entrance-|hall	336.28	quarter-|part
255.1	fountain-|side	345.31	many-|coloured
255.6	eye-|shots	349.26	dream-|edifice
255.32	eye-|caverns	376.27	frost-|bitten
266.31	cross-|wise	377.34	tiger-|like
268.6	fellow-|creatures	380.33	chance-|result
275.22	dark-|cheeked	389.18	brown-|haired
277.20	family-|banner	390.11	pre-|occupation
280.29	ill-|regulated	402.13	half-|hidden
289.24	mid-|day	407.5	kind-|hearted
290.25	broad-|brimmed	412.10	standing-|room
290.26	head-|apparel	414.3	starting-|point
292.34	house-|tops	414.19	dove-|cotes
293.4	wild-|flowers	431.33	ill-|omened
294.28	often-|tried	442.12	damask-|curtained
307.12	village-|maids	442.32	three-|cornered
311.33	market-|day	443.10	well-|directed
325.8	alley-|like	446.15	parti-|coloured
326.25	summer-|atmosphere		

2. End-of-the-Line Hyphenation in the Manuscript

NOTE: The following compounds, or possible compounds, are hyphenated at the end of the line in the manuscript copy-text. The form in which they have been transcribed in the Centenary Edition, as listed below, represents the practice of the manuscript as ascertained by other appearances or by parallels within the manuscript. Other Hawthorne manuscripts of the period have been consulted when evidence was not available in *The Marble Faun* manuscript.

7.12	dark-eyed	24.10	torch-light
10.7	leaf-shaped	24.24	daylight
15.19	twenty-five	38.7	maiden-hair
18.32	footsteps	39.3	door-ways
22.20	key-note	39.9	white-wash

41.34	lay-figure		152.19	hedge-bordered
42.18	now-a-days		155.34	moonshine
44.3	by-the-by		156.19	moonlight
51.6	linen-draper's		159.9	half-hidden
51.8	fruit-stand		160.10	footsteps
54.32	artist-life		162.30	commonwealth
60.30	daylight		163.19	moonlight
61.2	handmaid		172.10	horrour-stricken
71.17	ilex-trees		177.3	grandsire's
72.8	rose-coloured		181.33	bas-relief
74.15	overhanging		184.2	to-day
77.15	wood-path		184.32	smoke-blackened
77.19	sun-flickered		187.13	eyelids
80.23	wood-anemones		190.6	convent-church
81.15	vintage-time		201.19	noonday
86.30	feast-day		204.29	straightforward
88.30	merry-makers		212.2	new-born
89.13	tiptoes		213.2	country-house
90.8	merry-makers		215.18	last-mentioned
90.14	pleasure-ground		217.1	side-portal
91.17	playmate		217.27	now-a-days
92.18	footsteps		218.5	dimly lighted
99.2	dove-cote		218.7	midnight
100.19	flower-beds		218.29	grandsire
101.6	countrywoman		219.23	resting-places
101.22	re-crossed		223.1	Sunshine
103.28	moss-grown		225.4	vintage-time
106.19	far-off		226.25	Sunshine
124.18	half-a-dozen		226.27	banquet-hall
126.25	midway		228.15	bust-makers
128.6	wrong-doing		231.3	family-history
133.6	well-deserving		237.1	topmost
143.15	a-dancing		237.29	hill-sides
145.6	never-ceasing		245.6	rainbow
145.7	marble-brimmed		251.13	entrance-hall
145.8	semi-circle		257.12	frame-work
145.10	snow-points		258.3	bald-peaked
146.5	one-and-thirty		266.30	drum-beat
146.15	moonlight		266.31	convent-bells

271.8	pre-conceptions	375.2	Snow-drop
285.29	noontime	375.10	picture-galleries
285.30	outstretched	378.24	offspring
290.14	stern-looking	384.24	coexist
290.31	long-buried	389.12	ill-omen
291.18	earthlike	394.28	seaside
291.21	wayside	395.18	Sunshine
292.34	earthen-tiled	404.12	fruit-seller
293.1	grape-vines	406.4	to-day
294.30	wine-shop	406.13	writing-desk
295.33	grass-plots	410.12	bitter-sweetness
296.7	brick-work	413.1	pitfall
296.12	countrymen	419.1	uprises
297.28	flower-pots	423.5	earth-stained
297.30	flowering-shrubs	430.13	footsteps
301.15	mountain-side	431.20	saintlike
309.3	midnight	435.15	farewell
312.31	black-letter	435.27	to-day
313.14	Middle-Age	436.12	store-house
314.14	market-cries	438.33	gala-dress
318.17	Anglo-Saxons	439.30	battle-field
325.19	fireside	446.16	orang-outangs
326.4	half-lifeless	446.17	dog-headed
330.23	print-shops	449.7	winter-roses
333.1	dove-cote	450.32	gensd'armes
333.4	door-keepers	451.15	battle-field
342.12	elm-trees	458.8	sunbeam
342.24	week-days	461.22	fireside
353.10	Will-o'-the-Wisp	462.13	sevenfold
370.28	mud-puddle		

3. *Special Cases*

(a)

NOTE: In the following list the compound, or possible compound, is hyphenated at the end of the line in the manuscript and in the Centenary Edition.

23.31	sprite-|like (i.e. spritelike)
70.15	day-|dream (i.e. day-dream)
177.6	wrong-|doing (i.e. wrong-doing)
219.13	farming-|tool (i.e. farming-tool)
290.29	witch-|like (i.e. witch-like)
403.14	brown-|haired (i.e. brown-haired)

(b)

NOTE: In the following cases the hyphenated compound appears at the end of the line in the Centenary Edition, but the hyphen is an editorial emendation not present in the manuscript.

| 100.33 | well-\|worth (i.e. well-worth *for MS* well worth) |
| 101.18 | frame-\|work (i.e. frame-work *for MS* framework) |

HISTORICAL COLLATION

This Historical Collation records substantive variants between editions as well as all accidentals changes in the 1860 English and American editions. Typographical errors not forming accepted words are not listed for editions after E2 unless they involve revision of the plates. The basis of record is the reading to the left of the bracket, which is that of the Centenary text but not always that of the copy-text manuscript. Where "MS" is not specified as the source for a rejected reading, it is to be understood that the Centenary reading is the manuscript reading. Any unlisted edition is presumed to agree with Centenary.

The following editions were collated, and their substantive variants recorded: E1ª, 1860, first edition, first printing; E1ᵇ, first edition, second printing (i.e. "SECOND EDITION."); E2, second English edition (i.e. "THIRD EDITION."); E3, 1861, third English edition; Iᵃ⁻ᵉ, 1860, first American edition, with seven printings in 1860, five of which have been differentiated; II, 1876 Little Classics Edition; III, 1883 Riverside Edition; IV, 1900 Autograph Edition. The plates of I were used for the 1865 untitled collected edition, 1876 Illustrated Library, 1879 Fireside, 1880 Globe, 1884 Globe (Crowell), and 1886 New Fireside editions; the plates of II, for the 1891 Popular, 1894 Salem, and 1899 Concord editions; and the plates of III for the 1884 Wayside, 1884–85 Complete Works (London), 1891 Standard Library, 1902 New Wayside, and 1909 Fireside editions.

Since the plates for the first American edition were the only ones that could have been revised during Hawthorne's lifetime, the intermediate printings of I have been cross-collated to identify the variants within this edition. Machine collations of the plates of II and III record variants between the first and last printings of these plates, but the provenience of intermediate variants is not further specified in this listing. No attempt has been made to check the plates of IV after the first printing.

In this list the superior letter "a" indicates first printing, "z" the last. See the Textual Introduction for a discussion of the concealed printings of the 1860 American edition, and also for information about the three English editions in 1860–61.

3.19	like] *omit* E1–E3,I–IV
3.21	these volumes] this romance E3
3.32	find in] find it in E1–E3,I–IV
4.17–19	Were . . . noble . . . Zenobia.] *omit* MS; Were . . . admirable . . . Zenobia. I–IV
4.31	October] *December* E1–E3,I–IV
7.6	gaily] gayly Ie–IV
7.14	of marble] of the marble E3
7.25	faces,] ~∧ E1b
8.30	claw] claws E1–E3,I–IV
9.24	nor] or E1–E3,I–IV
13.32	morality] mortality E2–E3
13.34	burthen] burden E2–E3,II–IV
14.2,30	neither] either E1–E3,I–IV
15.31	should] shall E1–E3,I–IV
16.30	or] of II–IV
16.33	mischievously. "You] ~, "you E1–E3,I–IV
17.28	Faun in red marble, who . . . dance] Faun, who . . . dance, in red marble, MS
17.32	would] could E1–E3,I–IV
18.1	on] in E1–E3,I–IV
18.5	subtile] subtle E1–E3,IV
19.8	of] *omit* MS
20.13	put up her] put her E1–E3,I–IV
20.13	shown] showed E1–E3,I–IV
20.18	distinguish] distinguished E3
21.10	those] these E1–E2
21.14	further] farther E1–E3,I
21.15	than] then E1
21.15	subtile] subte MS; subtle E1,I
22.14	subtile] subtle E1–E3,I–IV
22.34	Oriental] oriental E2

23.4	hinted] bore MS
24.30	marble-work] ~ₐ~ E2
25.16	appetite] fancy E1–E3,I–IV
25.25	my] *omit* E1–E3,I–IV
26.34	around] round E1–E3,I–IV
28.18	uttermost] utmost E1–E3,I–IV
31.4	what fearful] what a fearful III–IV
31.15	Henceforth,] ~ₐ E2
31.23	farther] further II–IV
32.3	when] whence MS
32.22	Hoffmann] Hoffman MS,E1–E3
33.31–32	perplexing itself] perplexing in itself III–IV
36.12	exhausting] exhaustive III–IV
36.12	influencies] influences E1–E3,I–IV
36.13	an] *omit* II–IV
36.32	upon] up on E3
37.12	elder] older E1–E3,I–IV
38.7	weed] weeds E1–E3,I–IV
38.15	of] at II–IV
39.23	from] form E1
40.31	Nature] nature E1–E3,I[a-d]
42.8	Miriam] Mariam E1
43.10	man or woman] men or women E1–E3,I–IV
44.2	feeling] feelings E1–E3,I–IV
44.4	mustachios] moustaches E1–E3,I–IV
44.7	at] in E1–E3,I–IV
45.9	subject] subjects E3
45.13	subtly] subtilely E1–E3,I–IV
46.18	spiritualize] spiritualized E3
47.32	many, in] many times, in E1–E3,I–IV
48.27	Signorina] Signora MS,E1–E3,I
49.13	is] are E1–E3,I–IV
51.8	fruit-stand] ~ₐ~ E1,E3
52.7	at noon] at at noon MS
52.19	pushing] shoving MS
52.30	beaksful] beakfuls E1–E3,I–IV
52.31	rustled] rushed E1–E3,I–IV
53.26	of] of of MS
54.20	angel] ~, E1–E3,I–IV
55.1	woman] women E1–E3,I–IV

55.17	angel's] angels' E1–E3,I–IV
56.19	sending] projecting MS
57.21	now] more E1–E3,I–IV
57.34	of] by II–IV
58.2	her] the E1–E3,I–IV
58.33	face;—] ~$_\wedge$— E1–E3,I^{a-d}; ~,— I^e–IV
59.9	sensibility,] ~$_\wedge$ E1–E3,I^e–IV
59.23	artists] artist E3
59.25	processes] process E1–E3,I–IV
59.31	work] ~, E2,III–IV
60.18	spectator] spector MS
60.34	adducing] admiring E1–E3,I–IV
61.1	in] in in MS
61.9	literature!] ~? E3
62.3	of] of of MS
62.15	excellencies] excellences E1–E3,I–IV
63.2	her] omit MS
63.28	subtle] subtile II–IV
64.3	lucky] luckily III
64.19	eyelids] eyes E1–E3,I–IV
67.11	again,] ~! E1,E3,I–IV; ~; E2
67.16	subtle] subtile E2
67.26	asked] ask III
67.30	good] omit III–IV
67.34	malaria] malarial III–IV
68.27	good bye] ~-~ E2; good by I^e–II; good-by III–IV
69.12	tower] lower E1–E3,I–IV
70.22	remote,] ~$_\wedge$ E2
71.9	being] beings E3
72.3	what] which E1–E3,I–IV
72.4	funereal] funeral E1–E3,I–IV
72.22	of a] of the E1–E3,I–IV
72.34	granite,] ~$_\wedge$ E1–E3,I–IV
73.10	imitations,] ~ E1^b
75.6	after long] after a long III–IV
75.17	home,] ~$_\wedge$ E2
75.29	fairy] fairly E3
77.12	could] would E1–E3,I–IV

77.19	sun-flickered] sun-fleckered E1–E3,I–IV
78.14	hereabouts,] $\sim_\wedge$ E2
78.20	propose] proposed E3
79.4	ecstasy] ecstacy E1–E3,I–IV
80.11	had] have MS,E1–E3,I–IV
83.20	the] *omit* E3
83.32	up again, they twined] up again, twined E1–E3,I–II; up twined III–IV
83.34–84.2	youth; for (so . . . life) they] youth. So . . . life, that they E1–E3,I–IV
84.4	farther] further II–IV
85.5	moment] movement E1–E3,I–IV
85.7	motion] notion E3
86.19	Here] There E1–E3,I–IV
88.18	thrummed] thummed E2
88.30	attentively] *omit* E1–E3,I–IV
88.34	on] to E1–E3,I–IV
90.7	sylvan] silver E1–E3,I–III^c
91.9	Donatello,] $\sim_\wedge$ E2
95.6	could] would E1–E3,I–IV
95.19	those] these III–IV
95.29	could] would E1–E3,I–IV
96.32	immitigable] unmitigable E1–E3,I–IV
96.34	within short] within a short II^{1879}–IV
97.19	could] would E1–E3,I–IV
100.22	sunshine] suhshine E2
100.24	long] *omit* E1–E3,I–IV
101.17	aërial] aerial E2,II–IV
101.24	history–] $\sim$,– I^e–IV
101.27	ink–] $\sim$,– I^e–IV
102.23	grounds] ground II–IV
102.32	a] *omit* III–IV
104.3	Faun!] $\sim$: E2
105.9	affection] affections E1–E3,I–IV
106.9	prospect] prospects E1–E3,I–IV
106.16	eldest] oldest E1–E3,I–IV
106.34	building] buildings E1–E3,I–IV
108.9	in] of E1–E3,I–IV
108.23	could] would E1–E3,I–IV

109.12	rejoined] replied E1–E3,I–IV
109.24	di] della MS,E1–E3,I–IV
109.32	besides] beside II–IV
110.7	ruin] ruins II–IV
110.10	these] those E1–E3,I–IV
110.32	the] *omit* E1–E3,I–IV
111.22	millionaire] millionnaire E1b–E3,I–IV
113.5	staked] had staked E1–E3,I–IV
114.6	di] della MS,E1–E3,I–IV
117.14	experiments,] ~∧ E2
118.4	work;] ~: E2
118.21	argued] augured II–IV
119.4	farthest] furthest II–IV
119.12	observed] said E1–E3,I–IV
119.18	burthen] burden E2,I–IV
122.5	probability] possibility E1–E3,I–IV
123.1	statue!] ~? E3
124.5	neither] either E1–E3,I–IV
127.17	never] ever E1–E3,I–IV
134.2	above] a-|above MS
134.12	sculptor,] ~∧ E2, II–IV
135.15	mildly] mildy III[a-c]
137.13	is] are E1–E3,I–IV
137.22	and,] ~∧ E2
139.12	paper!] ~. E2
139.24	the divinest] *omit* the MS
143.5	at] of II–IV
143.34	glistening, and] glistening, whitening, and MS
144.26	ever] even II
145.3	this] their E1–E3,I–IV
145.20	come] came E1–E3,I–IV
145.28	nearly] early III–IV
146.12	lavatory] lavoratory MS
146.17,27	Nelvil] Neville MS,E1–E3,I–IV
147.9	of you] if you MS
147.20	is] *omit* MS
147.30	flinging it] fling-| it E2
147.32	vanish] Vanish E2
149.5	Miriam,] ~∧ E2

149.18	farther] further E1–E3,I–IV
149.29	elder] older E1–E3,I–IV
150.1	holding] keeping E1–E3,I–IV
150.32	conjuncture] conjecture II–IV
151.12	to] to to MS
152.14	slily] slyly Ie–IV
152.18	and] ~, E2,III–IV
152.27	Hadrian] Hadriau E2
153.22	inherit] inhabit E1–E3,I–IV
154.12	lie] lay E1–E3,I–IV
154.12	area] arena E1–E3,I–IV
154.15	song] songs E1–E3,I–IV
154.18	especial] special E1–E3,I–IV
155.9	praying,] ~∧ E1–E2†
156.15	melancholy] melan-| MS
157.15	her] omit E1–E2†, I
157.19	the] their E1–E3,I–IV
157.34	with] omit E1–E3,I–IV
158.1	yourself–] ~, E1–E2†,I–II; ~; E2††–E3,III–IV
158.5	if] omit E3
159.5	by,] ~∧ E2††–E3
160.9	nor] or E1–E3,I–IV
162.13	stept] stepped E2,I–IV
162.18	grieves] grives Ia-d
162.28	deeper;] ~: E2
163.3	battle-fields] battlefields E2,IV
163.27	exceedingly] exceeding E1–E3,I–IV
164.12	rose] arose II–IV
164.32	farther] further II–IV
165.6	dilapidated] delapidated E1
165.32	figure as it were] ~, ~~~, E2
166.1	this] the E1–E3,I–IV
168.18	a-down] adown E2,IV
169.2	literally] literary E1
169.8	at] at at MS
169.14	has] had E1–E3,I–IV
170.4	farther] further MS

† First state only.
†† Second state only.

170.8	were] are II–IV
170.34	deep,] ~_∧ E2
171.2	neither] either E1–E3,I–IV
172.1	swang] swung E1–E3,I–IV
172.22	heart,] ~_∧ E2
173.3	madly,] ~_∧ E2
174.20	union,] ~_∧ E1,E3
175.3	breadth] breath III–IV
175.6–7	that word] the word III–IV
180.7	downward] downwards E1–E3,I–IV
180.9	on] or E1–E3,I
180.10	if for] if on I^{c-e}
182.13	figure–] ~_∧ E1,E3,I–IV; ~, E2
185.6	vivacity;] ~: E2
185.26	nor a] *omit* a III–IV
188.23	musings] musing E1–E3,I–IV
188.32	connect,] ~_∧ E2
189.9	explanation] exclamation E1–E3,I–IV
190.1	away,] ~. E1
191.26	Judgment Seat] judgment-seat E1,E3,I–IV; judgment seat E2
192.24	chapels,] ~_∧ *(press variant)* E1^b
193.33	which perhaps] ~, ~, E2
198.4–5	unintentionally] un-|tentionally MS; intentionally E1–E3,I
198.19	ask,] ~_∧ E2,III–IV
199.15	have] have have MS
199.23	others'] other's E1,I–IV
200.9	charm] charms E2
200.26	May] may E2
202.6	up] *omit* III–IV
202.7	aëry] eyrie E1–E3,I; eyry II–IV
202.15	been compelled to] been to MS
203.6	squatted] MS; huddled E1–E3,I–IV
203.15	And,] ~_∧ E2
203.29	heretofore?] ~. E1,E3,I
204.22	them] there I^{a-b}
205.19	baby's] babe's IV
206.4	no] no no MS

206.28	convulsively] conclusively III–IV
207.8	sides] side E1–E3,I–IV
208.26,27	her . . . her] me . . . me MS
208.27	she] I MS
210.6	all] *omit* III–IV
212.19	dove's] doves' E1–E3,I–IV
214.12	works, which] works in that kind which MS
216.15	Tomaso] Thomaso E1
217.31	gazer?] ~! E2
218.19	nevertheless] ~, I^e–IV
219.8	gray] grey E2
219.23	ascended] ascending E1–E3,I–IV
219.30	an] and MS
220.4	as much] *omit* I–IV
222.13	plate-full] plate full E1,E3,I–IV; plateful E2
223.19	subtle] subtile II–IV
224.27	kindliness] kindness E1–E3,I–IV
225.15	round] around E1–E3,I–IV
225.28	figures,] ~$_\wedge$ E2
225.32	enlivening;] ~: E2
226.27	Yes;] ~: E1,E3; ~, E2
226.30	mirth,] ~$_\wedge$ E2
226.30	see;] ~: E1, E3
227.4	joyous,] ~$_\wedge$ E2,III–IV
227.10	banquet-hall] ~$_\wedge$~ E1,E3,IV
231.17	and arrive nowhither] and probably arrive no whither MS
232.3	farther] further II–IV
233.13	friend;] ~– E1–E3,I^{a-d}; ~,– I^e–IV
233.15	woods;–] ~– E1–E3,I^{a-d}; ~,– I^e–IV
233.21	subtle] subtile II–IV
233.28	sprung] sprang E1–E3,I–IV
234.27	beyond memory] beyond human memory MS
236.21;237.7	Kenyon] Graydon MS
238.14	and] or III–IV
239.4	era, ( ] ~– E1–E3,I^{a-d}; ~,– I^e–IV
239.5	abundant,)] ~– E1–E3,I^{a-d}; ~,– I^e–IV
239.16	days] day E1–E3,I–IV
240.2	surest] soonest E1–E3,I–IV

240.3	Tomaso] Tomasa II
241.4	often was] was often II–IV
241.13	or spectator] or a spectator E1–E3,I–IV
241.22	established] establishing E1–E3,I–IV
243.33	eldest] oldest E1–E3,I–IV
244.1	he] he he MS
244.7	more sad] more than sad MS
244.27	for,] ∼∧ E2
245.6	glowing] glancing E1–E3,I–IV
246.16	Never,] ∼∧ E1,E3,I–IV
247.7	added,] ∼∧ E2
247.18	the] the the MS
247.30	persuasibility] persuadability MS,I–IV
247.31;248.23	Kenyon's] Graydon's MS
247.32	shrubbery] shrubberies E1–E3,I–IV
248.34	could] would I
249.21	a] a a MS
249.23	friend's] friends MS
250.32	further] farther E1–E3,I
251.6	could] would I–IV
254.12	Granducal] Grand-ducal E1–E3,I–IV
254.20	came] come E1–E3,I–IV
255.8	of the] *omit* the I–IV
255.13	simplicity] sim |plicity E1^b
256.20	us;] ∼! E2
259.5	of mid-sky] of the mid-sky E1–E3,I–IV
259.21	this] the E1–E3,I–IV
262.8	subtile] subtle I–IV
262.19	a nobler] *omit* a E1–E3,I–IV
263.23	were] was E3
264.12	All,] ∼∧ E2
264.14	life-line] lifetime I–IV
265.17	art] heart I,II[a-1878],III–IV; hart II[1879-z]
266.29	further and further] farther and farther E1–E3,I–IV
267.1	adding,] ∼; E1
267.5	Would] Should II–IV
268.19	advantages] ad-|tages MS
269.8	sang] sung I–IV

269.22	could] would E1–E3,I–IV
270.16	kindly] kind I–IV
270.19	passing. If] passing. ¶ If E2
271.13	this] his E1–E3,I–II
272.24	reason,] ∼∧ E2
273.12	unutterable] unalterable III–IV
274.19	chanced to find] happened upon MS,I–IV
274.26	figures] shows MS,I–IV
275.2	sadder] sorrier MS,I–IV
275.6	circumgyratory] circumgyrotory MS;
	circumgyrotary E1–E2
276.11	could] would E1–E3,I–IV
276.11	redundant] abundant III–IV
276.15	site] sight I
277.16	into] in E1–E3,I–IV
278.12	himself] *omit* E1–E3,I–IV
279.8	excellencies] excellences E1–E3,I–IV
280.15	he–] ∼, E1,E3,I–IV; ∼; E2
281.18	misery] mystery E1–E3,I–II[a]
281.23	moment, he] moment? He MS,I–IV
282.14	man save one] ∼,∼∼, E2
285.9	heart-sustenance] ∼∧∼ E1–E3,II–IV; ∼,∼ I
286.24	taste] tastes E3
287.4	but] and E1–E3,I–IV
287.21	bound,] ∼∧ E1,E3,I–II
288.11	familiar;] ∼, E2
290.3–4	indistinguishable] undistinguishable
	E1–E3,I–IV
290.7	scenes] things E3
290.14	stern-looking] stain-looking I
290.20	sum] hum I–IV
292.7	victim] victims MS
292.14	and surrounding] and its surrounding
	E1–E3,I–IV
292.17	when] where E1–E3,I–IV
293.3	roughnesses] roughness III–IV
294.2	his] his his MS
294.12	caucus] canvass I–IV
294.22	intercourse,] ∼∧ I[b-d]

294.32	deep-hued] deep, mild E1–E3,I–IV
296.18	was] were E1–E3,I–IV
296.19	pincers] pinchers I
297.31	wreathe] wreath E1–E3,I
298.13	himself] herself E2
298.27	pursues] possesses E1–E3,I–IV
301.20	Etruscan] Etrucean I[a-b]
301.24	fall–] ~,– I[e]–IV
301.24	away–] ~,– I[e]–IV
302.11	habitations such] such habitations I–IV
302.18	country–] ~,– I[e]–IV
302.18	here–] ~,– I[e]–IV
306.3	exclaimed] said III–IV
306.3	strangely] strangelg I[d-z]
306.4	figure!] ~: I[d-z]
306.6	"it] ':it I[d-z]
306.7	himself.] ~∧ I[d-z]
306.17	And] All E1–E3,I–IV
306.19	Belief] belief E1–E3,I[a-c],II–IV; belife I[d-z]
306.33	grandams] grandames E1–E3,I–IV
307.3	boneless] ~, I[a-d]
307.11	dirty] dirtly I[a-b]
307.28	need] needs E1–E3,I–IV
307.28	The] They MS
309.6	loitered,] ~∧ E1[b]–E2
309.9	Italy alone] only Italy MS
309.9	was the] was all the III–IV
312.24	indestructibly] indestruc |tibly E1[b]
312.24	achieving,] omit III–IV
312.30	to] into I–IV
313.32	eyes] eye II–IV
315.11	Wilderness] wilderness of Egypt MS
315.18	of] in II–IV
318.8	up] upon MS
319.8	have] has II–IV
319.8	a] a a MS
319.11	quick] much MS
319.12	her?] ~. MS
321.10	may] nay E1–E3,I–IV
322.32	ever,] ~∧ I[d]–IV

324.2	become] became E1–E3,I–IV
326.19	threading] treading E1–E3,I–IV
331.33	and understood] and been understood E1–E3,I–IV
334.23	di] da MS,E1–E3,I–IV
335.5	now] *omit* IV
335.5	these] those E1–E3,I–IV
336.15	reflections] reflection E1–E3,I–IV
336.20	works] work E1–E3,I–IV
337.23	feeling] feelings E1–E3,I–IV
337.30	Barberini] Baberini MS,E1–E2
341.25	had] and III
344.3	sky] sun IV
346.9	which] when III–IV
346.18	infrequent] unfrequent E1–E3,I–IV
349.24	actual] *omit* MS
350.18	of] at E1–E3,I–IV
352.7	subtle] subtile I–IV
352.16	ray] rays III–IV
352.27	whether for] whether from E1–E3,I–IV
353.10	Will-o'-the-Wisp] Will-of-the-Wisp MS
354.8	as] as as MS
355.5	impression!] ~? E3
357.19	towards] toward III–IV
359.13	my] *omit* MS
360.8	burthen] burden E1–E3,I–II; burn III–IV
362.5	him] me III–IV
368.14	perversion] conversion II–IV
369.31	I] *omit* E2
370.10	as] *omit* MS,E1–E2
370.13	motion] motions MS
373.6	nearer to one] near one III–IV
374.19	inner] minor III–IV
374.22	none that] none but that E3
375.24	when] where E1–E3,I–IV
375.29	artists] artist E1–E3,I–IV
376.15	held] hold E3
376.26	togaed] togated III–IV
378.32	poems] poem II–IV
383.1	—you] —then you MS

385.23	for better] for for better MS
385.24	ourselves] our ouselves MS
387.16	ninety] ninty III[a-b]
387.26	had trodden] trod MS,I–IV
387.34	of] of of MS
390.16	medium.] ~, I[a-b]
391.10	art] heart I[a-b]
391.14	Belvedere] Belvidere MS,I
391.22	Errour . . . Evil] Error . . . Evil E1–E3,I[c]–IV; error . . . evil I[a-b]
392.23	proceeds] avails MS,I–IV
393.22	and was] and was was MS
394.12	are] is III
397.8	out] out out MS
398.19	Virgin's] Virgins MS
398.26	puts] put III–IV
400.3	become] be|come E1[b]–E2
400.18	upward] upwards E1–E3,I–IV
401.17	when] where I–IV
401.34	whatever] what E3
402.18	thither] hither E1–E3,I–II
404.27	at] as I
404.29	a narrow] the narrow E3
404.31	within] with E1–E3,I–IV
406.8	anxiety,] ~; I[a-b]
406.33	Heaven] heaven I[a-b]
408.8	efficacy] efficiency II[1879]–IV
410.13	roughnesses] roughness E1–E3,I–IV
410.33	before—] ~, I[a-b]; ~,— II–IV
412.17	dead] dread I[a-b]
413.18	vain;] ~∧ I[b]–IV
414.15–16	shrine, on the] shrine, or on the E1–E3; shrine, or the I–IV
415.13	must] omit E1–E3,I–IV
416.23	forever?] ~. I[a-d]
416.26	aid?] ~. I[a-d]
418.20	goat's] goats' E1–E3,I–IV
419.22	funereal] funeral E3
420.8	columbarium] columbaria MS,E1–E3,I–II[1878]
421.10	a] omit I[a-b]

423.8	elbows] elbow II–IV
423.11	further] farther I
423.19	de'] de I[a-b]
426.19	labyrinth!] ~. I–IV
429.0	CONTADINA] CONTADINO E1[a]
429.26	we] I I–IV
430.2	a] *omit* II[1879]–IV
430.14	about] across E3
430.32	wild] vile II[1879]–IV
431.1	breeds] races E1–E3,I–IV
431.6	Miriam alluded] Miriam had alluded E1–E3,I–IV
432.12	penances] penance E1–E3,I–IV
433.1	Cleopatra,] ~; E1,I–IV; ~– E2–E3
433.20	immitigable] unmitigable E1–E3,I–IV
433.24	whatever] whatsoever E1–E3,I–IV
434.8	on] in E1–E3,I–IV
434.29	farther] further II–IV
434.33	lost] last I
438.34	secrets] secret E1–E3,I–IV
439.14	the powdered] the the powdered MS
439.15	cart] car E3
441.11	gensd'armes] gendarmes E1–E3,I–IV
441.19	tips] tip III–IV
442.27	gensd'armes] gendarmes E1–E3,I–IV
443.16	could] would I–IV
443.18	bestrewn.] ~∧ I[a-b]
444.3	the Contadina] *omit* the E1–E3,I–IV
445.25	aggregated] aggregate I–IV
446.15	parti-] party- II–IV
446.24	horrour] sorrow E1–E3,I–IV
446.31	to let him blood] to him let him blood E1; to him to let him take blood I–IV; to him to let him blood E3
448.32	Piazza] Palazzo I–IV
449.4	damask] damasked E3
449.18	of] for III–IV
450.32	gensd'armes] gendarmes E1–E3,I–IV
452.19	straying] staying E3
453.9	know] known MS

454.1   upward] upwards E3
455.11–12   the web . . . its] its web . . . the I–IV
456.11   a] the E1–E3,I–IV
458.2   this] the E3
460.25   sentiment] sentiments I–IV
461.1   with] *omit* E1–E3,I–IV

The POSTSCRIPT *first appeared in* E1ᵇ.

463.0   POSTSCRIPT] CONCLUSION Iᵈ–IV
464.13   which] *omit* Iᵈ–IV
464.19   of the] of that Iᵈ–IV
464.28   believe] belive E1ᵇ
464.34   person,] ∼ₐ E3
465.16   whereabout] whereabouts Iᵈ–IV
465.19   strange] *omit* Iᵈ–IV
465.20   been led to see] seen Iᵈ–IV
465.23   implication] connection Iᵈ–IV
466.10   Carnival] carnival E3
466.31   trouble] troubles Iᵈ–IV
466.31   these] those Iᵈ–IV
466.33   these] those Iᵈ–IV
467.9   "In . . . sadly.] "The . . . Faun." Iᵈ–IV

ALTERATIONS IN THE MANUSCRIPT

NOTE: With the exceptions listed below, all alterations made in the manuscript during its inscription or review before submission (the two classes are not always distinguishable with certainty) are described here. The exceptions are as follows: (1) Letters or words that have been mended or traced-over for clarity without alteration of the original; (2) interlineations that repeat in a more clearly written form the identical original (unless inscribed by Sophia, in which case they are noted); and (3) deletions, mendings, or readings under alterations that could not be read. In this last connection, empty square brackets signify one or more illegible letters. Letters within square brackets are conjectural on some evidence although not wholly certain. In the descriptions of manuscript alterations, *above* means "interlined" and *over* means "in the same space." The presence of a caret is always noticed.

A dagger alongside the page-line reference indicates an inscription by Sophia Hawthorne; but the substitutions of *Kenyon* for *Graydon* after 7.12 are not so marked. Her alterations are detailed in the Textual Introduction.

1.4	each of] *interlined with a caret*
1.11	than a] *written over smudged* 'to [ ]'
1.11	critic] *written over wiped-out* 'fri'
2.5	Reader] 'a' *written over wiped-out* 'd'
2.17	outlasts] 'lasts' *written over* 'lives'
3.17	annals] *first* 'a' *written over* '[c]'
3.20	Ruin] 'R' *altered from* 'r'

4.24	imbedded] 'i' *altered from* 'e'
4.26	say] 'sa' *written over wiped-out* 'st'
5.4	was] *interlined above deleted* 'is'
5.18	one of the] *written over wiped-out* 'the wind'
6.15	half-] 'ha' *written over* '[wa]'
6.17	Etruscan] *at end of preceding line* 'E' *wiped out*
6.27	which] 'w' *written over wiped-out* 'th'
6.29	human] *written over wiped-out* 'existence'
6.29	different] *a following comma presumably wiped out*
†7.12	Kenyon] *interlined by Sophia above deleted* 'Graydon'. *An ink cross appears above following* 'dark-'
7.31–32	Donatello] 'Don' *written over* 'he'
7.34	of rustic creatures,] *interlined with a caret*
8.1	one!] *exclamation altered from comma*
8.6,15	Kenyon] *interlined by Sophia above deleted* 'Graydon'
8.17	however—] *dash written over comma*
8.21	attention] *interlined above deleted* 'eyes'
9.9	statue—] *dash written over wiped-out comma*
10.7	in little] 'in l' *written over wiped-out* 'each'
10.33	surface] 'sur' *written over wiped-out* 'of the'
†12.13	Apennines] *a second* 'p' *deleted by Sophia*
13.15,32	Kenyon] *interlined by Sophia above deleted* 'Graydon'
13.30	four] *written over wiped-out* 'foot'
15.13	Miriam] 'Mir-'| *written over wiped-out* 'Gra'
15.16	Kenyon] *interlined by Sophia above deleted* 'Graydon'
15.20	Donatello?] *query added before wiped-out comma*
16.8	assigning] 'in' *written over wiped-out* 'ig'
16.10	made] 'm' *altered from* 'a'
16.18	Kenyon] *interlined by Sophia above deleted* 'Graydon'
16.33	mischievously.] *period altered from comma*
17.23	realization] 'reali' *written over doubtful* 're-app'
18.3	round its verge] *interlined with a caret*
18.14	To] *written over wiped-out doubtful* 'It'
18.15	Kenyon] *interlined by Sophia above deleted* 'Graydon'

20.18	practice] *just possibly second 'c' is altered from 's'*
20.19	Nevertheless] *'I' written over wiped-out 's'*
21.9	brief contact] *interlined with a caret above deleted* 'casual intercourse'
21.29	high] *interlined with a caret*
21.34	chose] *'s' altered from 'o'*
22.4	Kenyon] *interlined by Sophia above deleted* 'Graydon'
22.17	and half-] *written over wiped-out* 'regard of'
23.7	a third] *interlined with a caret above deleted* 'another'
23.15	pencil] *mended so that it falsely resembles* 'penccil'
23.24	a great] *'a' interlined with a caret*
23.31	result] *interlined with a caret above deleted* 'effect'
23.33	Kenyon] *interlined by Sophia above deleted* 'Graydon'
24.24	through] 'thro' *written over wiped-out* 'thou'
†25.16	appetite] 'fancy' *interlined by Sophia above deleted original* 'appetite'
25.25	my] *written over wiped-out* ' "sh' *or* ' "she' *and omitted by the printer either because it was illegible or thought to have been deleted*
26.4	Kenyon] *interlined by Sophia above deleted* 'Graydon'
26.25	Kenyon.] *written by Sophia after deleted* 'Graydon'
26.26	a] *written over wiped-out* 'I'
28.1,13	Kenyon] *interlined by Sophia above deleted* 'Graydon'
†28.5	desperately] 'er' *written by Sophia over doubtful* 'ar'
28.13	bass] *followed by wiped-out semicolon*
28.20	on] *written over wiped-out* 'f'
29.6	fearful] 'fea' *written over wiped-out* 'girl'
29.26	Kenyon] *interlined by Sophia above deleted* 'Graydon'
30.1,28	Kenyon] *interlined by Sophia above deleted* 'Graydon'
30.25	Steps] 'S' *altered from 's'*
31.12	Kenyon's] *interlined by Sophia above deleted* 'Graydon's'

33.3	Christian] *preceded by deleted* 'any'
33.14	misery,] *comma altered from semicolon*
34.12	Art] 'A' *altered from* 'a'
34.25	ear)] *parenthesis written over dash*
34.31	attendant.] *followed by wiped-out* 'This s'
34.34	Miriam's] 'M' *written over wiped-out doubtful* 'H'
35.19	in] *a following* 'in' *deleted*
35.24	city,] *comma written over wiped-out semicolon*
36.3	singular] *a following comma partly wiped out*
36.15	Kenyon] *interlined by Sophia above deleted* 'Graydon'
37.1	built] *interlined with a caret above deleted* 'of'
37.9	invariably] 'in' *written over wiped-out* 'los'
37.10	lay aside] *interlined with a caret above deleted* 'lose'
38.2	stone] *written over wiped-out* 'basin'
38.16	door] *written over doubtful wiped-out* 'entrance'
39.14	means of] *interlined with a caret*
39.20	extremely] *interlined with a caret above deleted* 'very'
40.17	allowing] 'all' *written over wiped-out* 'and'
41.6	are] *interlined with a caret*
42.17	at the] 'at t' *written over wiped-out* 'in r'
43.16	rough] *interlined above deleted* 'first'
†43.17	Jael] *a dieresis added above the* 'e' *possibly by Sophia*
44.7	which] 'ch' *written over wiped-out* 'le'
45.27	an infant's] 'an' *altered from* 'a'; 'little' *after* 'a' *deleted*
46.2	dear] *written over wiped-out* 'rich'
46.8	thus] *interlined with a caret above deleted* 'so'
47.25	have] *interlined with a caret*
48.24	tell!] *exclamation altered from comma*
48.33–34	descriptively] *interlined with a caret*
49.9	illustrious;] *semicolon altered from comma*
49.12	been] *interlined with a caret*
49.31	friend!] *exclamation altered from comma*
50.8	this] *interlined above deleted* 'tomorrow'
51.6–7	a pipe and cigar-shop;] *interlined with a caret*
51.7	soldiers,] *the comma is faint*

52.1	Virgin] 'V' *altered from* 'v'
52.5	is a] *written over wiped-out* 'was'
52.7	at noon] 'at' *interlined above deleted* 'and'
52.7	twenty-four] *interlined with a caret above deleted* 'day'
52.10	belongs to] *written over wiped-out* 'i[ ] to it'
52.26	showed] *written over wiped-out* 'appeared'
52.28	small] *interlined with a caret above deleted* 'little'
53.1	The other] 'y' *wiped out after* 'The'; 'ot' *written over wiped-out* 'kno'
53.5	loftiness] 'i' *written over wiped-out* 'y' *and* 'ness' *added*
53.13	threw] *altered from* 'throw'
54.5	call] 'ca' *written over letters that just might be* 'acc'
54.28–30	street;— ... tended;—] *dashes squeezed in after semicolons*
54.34	narrower] 'er' *added*
55.1	scope] 'sc' *written over wiped-out doubtful* 'cho'
55.2	we] *a second* 'we' *beginning the next line deleted*
55.23	future] 'fu' *altered from* 'cen'
55.26	Italy] 'I' *altered from* 'R'
55.32	her] *interlined with a caret above deleted* 'herself'
55.33	in] 'i' *altered from* 'o'
56.2	, possessing] *interlined with a caret above deleted* 'with' *and preceding comma added*
56.4	own. They] *period altered from comma;* 'They' *interlined with a caret above deleted* 'and who'
56.5	became] *written over wiped-out* 'grew as'
56.8	called Hilda] 'called' *interlined above deleted* 'gave'; *following* 'Hilda' *is deleted* 'the name of'
56.9	aërial] *interlined with a caret*
56.11	such ethereal] 'such' *interlined above deleted* 'in many a'; 'ethereal' *starts as an interlineation and then runs down over wiped-out* 'treasure'
57.3	viewed it] 'it' *interlined with a caret*
57.4	hence] *interlined with a caret*

57.22	desirable] *followed by wiped-out comma*
57.30	pencils] *altered from* 'pincils'
58.32	Angel] 'A' *altered from* 'a'
58.33	Heaven] *second* 'e' *altered from* 'i'
59.6	Old] 'O' *altered from* 'o'
59.6	in bestowing] *written over wiped-out* 'as he bestowed'
59.12	result] *followed by wiped-out comma*
59.14	the] 't' *altered from* 's'
59.27	attempt] 'a' *written over wiped-out* 'g'
60.2	these men] 'ese m' *written over wiped-out* 'ey are'
60.8	her] 'h' *written over wiped-out* 'th'
60.15	has been] *interlined with a caret above deleted* 'can be'
60.34	adducing] *altered from* 'admiring'
61.1	in] *interlined with a caret after deleted* 'preferr' *which is preceded by blotted* 'in'
61.1	be] *interlined with a caret*
62.3	sweet labour] *interlined with a caret above deleted* 'performance'
63.4	picture] *follows deleted* 'old'
63.7	have] 'ha' *written over wiped-out* 'be'
63.10	light] *interlined with a caret*
64.3	to-day!] *exclamation altered from comma*
64.16	luxuriance] 'lu' *written over wiped-out doubtful* 'el'
64.21	the girl] 'the' *altered from* 'she'; 'girl' *interlined with a caret*
65.5	exquisite] *interlined with a caret above deleted* 'great'
65.26	ascend] *interlined with a caret above deleted* 'go to'
65.27	what] 'w' *written over wiped-out* 'it'
66.31	may have] 'may h' *written over wiped-out doubtful* 'was[ ]'
67.17	Well] *second* 'l' *written over wiped-out semicolon and followed by wiped-out comma*
67.26	yourself?] *query altered from period*
67.30	good] *interlined with a caret*
67.31	of] *interlined with a caret*
67.31	slight] 'sl' *altered from doubtful* 'ob'

68.4	Luca] *interlined with a caret*
68.11	to her] 'to' *added later in left margin*
68.11	would] *followed by deleted* 'would' *beginning next line*
68.12	better] *followed by deleted* 'freely to a friend'
68.17	woman] 'w' *written over wiped-out doubtful* 's'
68.30	the] *interlined with a caret*
69.22	Kenyon] *interlined by Sophia above deleted* 'Graydon'
69.22	passing] 'in' *written over wiped-out doubtful* 'th'
69.23	that] *followed by deleted* 'it had been meant for him'
70.13	priest] *plural* 's' *wiped out*
71.21	ago] *interlined above deleted* 'since'
71.25	in ponderous grace] *interlined with a caret above deleted* 'in attitudes of indolent repose'
72.19	and still bestowed,] *interlined with a caret*
72.22	Faun] *followed by wiped-out comma*
72.30–31	inscriptions. Statues] *period altered from semicolon;* 'S' *from* 's'
72.33	or] *followed by deleted* 'or' *beginning next line*
72.33	turf. Terminal] *period altered from semicolon;* 'T' *altered from* 't'
73.10	sportive] 'i' *altered from* 's'; 've' *written over wiped-out* 'and'
73.13	sober] *interlined with a caret above deleted* 'sad'
73.16	that] *interlined above deleted* 'which'
73.28	Eden in] 'E' *written over doubtful* 'p'
74.7	heavy] *interlined with a caret*
74.10	cloud] *follows deleted* 'heavy'
74.29	and blue] *interlined with a caret*
75.5	existence] *interlined with a caret above deleted* 'life'
75.6	blood] 'bl' *written over wiped-out* 'g'
75.17	had] *interlined with a caret*
75.22	living] 'li' *written over wiped-out* 'f[]'
75.23	beneath] 'n' *written over wiped-out* 'l'
76.6	alighted] *followed by deleted* 'close'
76.8	among] *interlined with a caret above deleted* 'through'
77.1	an] *altered from* 'on'

78.1	by other men,] *interlined with a caret*
78.29	to inquire] 'to in' *written over wiped-out* 'with'
78.33	the sylvan] *interlined with a caret above deleted* 'delightful'
79.16	come under] *interlined with a caret above deleted* 'reached'
81.17	evenings;] *semicolon altered from period*
81.27	again—] *dash written over comma*
82.21	be] *interlined with a caret*
83.6	that] *interlined with a caret*
83.8	cheerily] *interlined above deleted* 'merrily'
83.18	both] 'oth' *written over wiped-out* 'ound'
83.22	hours;] *semicolon altered from period*
84.1–2	(so . . . life)] *parentheses written over commas*
†84.2	they] *altered by Sophia in error to* 'that'
84.8	Happiness] 'H' *altered from* 'h'
84.11	triumph;] *semicolon altered from period*
85.14	apart] *interlined with a caret above deleted* 'aside'
86.16	companion] 'com-'| *interlined above deleted* 'Miriam'; 'panion' *begins next line*
86.21	(of] *parenthesis written over comma*
86.23	kindly] *interlined with a caret*
86.25	-benches] *followed by wiped-out comma*
86.31	in the] *written over wiped-out* 'bene'
86.32	windows] 'w' *written over* 's'
87.3	among] 'am' *written over wiped-out* 'the'
87.4	each] *interlined with a caret*
87.18	were] 'wer' *written over wiped-out* 'had'
87.29	German] *interlined with a caret*
87.31	Guardsmen] 'G' *altered from* 'g'
†87.33	contadine] 'e' *interlined possibly by Sophia above deleted* 'a' *which had been altered to* 'e'
88.4	knees;—] *semicolon written over dash, then followed by dash*
88.11	mingling] *follows deleted* 'and'
89.19	saw] *interlined for clarity with a caret above deleted* 'seemed to see' *in which* 'see' *has been altered to* 'saw'
89.21	the] *written over* 'her'
89.32	chanced] *written over wiped-out* 'was tha'

89.33	abruptly] 'abru' *written over wiped-out* 'sudde'
90.2	as] *interlined with a caret*
90.13	old] *interlined with a caret*
90.14	people's] 'eo' *written over wiped-out* '[ ]p'
90.17	creating] *interlined above deleted* 'and created'
90.19	me!] *exclamation altered from comma*
90.20	imperatively] 'im' *written over wiped-out doubtful* 'th'
90.20–21	look not] 'not' *interlined with a caret; an original* 'not' *before* 'look' *deleted*
91.17	let myself] 'let m' *written over* '[ ]d[ ]', *possibly* 'made'
91.19	more] 'm' *written over wiped-out* 'the'
92.11	of] *written over* 'in'
92.20	that of] *written over wiped-out* 'a gathering'
94.10	with] *written over wiped-out* 'which'
95.28	awful for] *separately interlined with carets above deleted* 'awul to'
96.8	her] *interlined with a caret*
96.21	trial] *interlined above deleted* 'mode'
97.5	own] *written over wiped-out* 'de'
97.20	washed clean] 'washed cle' *written over wiped-out* 'made clean!'
97.28	fair] *a following accidental mark in MS is not a comma*
97.31	imagine] *a following comma wiped out*
97.33	like] *followed by deleted* 'from the spectre which she had herself evoked out of the darkness that like'
99.6	Kenyon] *interlined by Sophia above deleted* 'Graydon'
100.5	borders] *written over wiped-out* 'avenues'
100.6	with] *interlined with a caret*
100.12	an] *interlined in margin with a caret*
100.18	peaceful] *interlined with a caret above deleted* 'easy'
100.23	instils] 'inst' *written over wiped-out* 'kills'
†100.30	thorough] *interlined for clarity by Sophia above deleted* 'thourough' *in which the first* 'u' *had been independently deleted*
100.31	Rome] 'Ro' *written over* 'the'

100.32	here . . . sunsets;] *interlined with a caret misplaced between* 'promenades' *and following semicolon*
100.33	here, whichever] 'which-'| *interlined above deleted* 'are', *and the comma added*
100.34	gazing at] 'gazing' *written over wiped-out* 'looking'; *and* 'at' *interlined with a caret*
101.11	oldest] *altered from* 'eldest'
101.20	page of] 'of' *interlined with a caret*
101.21	memorable] 'mem' *written over wiped-out* 'events'
†101.32	thicker] *interlined for clarity by Sophia above* 'thicker' *that has been mended from doubtful* 'richer'
102.1	earlier—even in February—] *dashes written over commas*
102.8	virgin] 'v' *written over wiped-out* 'V'
102.10	which] *interlined above deleted* 'that'
†102.13	ilex-] *written in MS as* 'i-|lex' *but Sophia for clarity deleted* 'i' *and wrote in* 'i' *in the next line before* 'lex'
102.14	Kenyon] *interlined by Sophia above deleted* 'Graydon'
102.25	Is] 'I' *altered from* 'i'
102.31	we] *written over erased* 'ha'
103.6	the] 'th' *written over wiped-out* 'H'
103.20	Kenyon's] 'Kenyon' *interlined by Sophia above deleted* 'Graydon'
104.1	reverentially] *interlined with a caret above deleted* 'respectfully'
104.2	Excellency] 'Exce' *written over wiped-out* 'Ellen'
104.7	Kenyon] *interlined by Sophia above deleted* 'Graydon'
104.11	replied Hilda] *interlined with a caret*
104.14	back] 'ba' *written over wiped-out* 'aw'
104.15	do] *written over wiped-out* 'did'
104.23	a] *written over wiped-out* 'g'
104.27	shaggy] *interlined with a caret*
105.7	then?"] *query written over double quotes, then quotes added*
105.9	Kenyon.] *added by Sophia after deleted* 'Graydon.'

105.10	She] 'S' *written over wiped-out dash*
106.2	knowledge] *interlined above deleted* 'thing'
106.6	slowly] *written over wiped-out very doubtful* 'calmly'
106.10	and] 'an' *written over wiped-out* 'them'
106.16	red] *follows deleted* 'obelisk'
106.21	indestructible] 'indestr' *written over wiped-out doubtful* 'enduring'
106.24	cloudy] 'clou' *written over wiped-out* 'fiery'
106.29	Gate] 'G' *altered from* 'g'
106.32	Emperour] *altered from* 'emperor'
107.2	long] 'lon' *written over wiped-out* 'befor'
107.4	precisely] 'p' *written over wiped-out* 'th'
107.12	debarred] 'de' *written over wiped-out* 'ba'
107.20,24	Kenyon] *interlined by Sophia above deleted* 'Graydon'
107.29	the] *written over wiped-out* 'Gra'
108.6	Kenyon's] *interlined by Sophia above deleted* 'Graydon's'
108.14	Kenyon] *interlined by Sophia above deleted* 'Graydon'
108.19	then] *interlined with a caret*
108.24	Kenyon] *interlined by Sophia following* 'Graydon' *which had been interlined with a caret by Hawthorne above deleted* 'he'
108.31	What] *follows wiped-out double quotes*
109.3	she] 'sh' *written over wiped-out* 'the'
109.4	Saxon] 'Sa' *written over wiped-out* 'sa'
109.12	Kenyon] *interlined by Sophia above deleted* 'Graydon'
109.13	we need] 'we' *interlined with a caret;* 'n' *written over wiped-out* 'wh'
109.15	utter] *written over wiped-out* 'speak'
109.33	taller] *followed by deleted* 'palace'
110.26	its recumbent form] 's' *added after* 't' *and* 'recumbent form' *interlined with a caret*
110.29	alleys] 'eys' *written over wiped-out* 'ies'
111.7	an] *written over wiped-out* 'un'
111.8	Rome?—the] *query written over semicolon and the dash over wiped-out* 'the'
111.9	Man's] 'M' *written over* 'm'
111.10	glory] 'g' *written over wiped-out* 'Gl'

111.20	stairs] *interlined above deleted* 'staircase'
111.20	ascend] *final* 's' *erased*
112.5,20	Kenyon] *interlined by Sophia above deleted* 'Graydon'
112.13	and] *interlined with a caret*
112.21	Model] 'M' *altered from* 'm'
113.4,8	Kenyon] *interlined by Sophia above deleted* 'Graydon'
113.8	difficulties] 'difficult' *written over wiped-out* 'many crises'
113.9	feminine] 'feminin' *written over wiped-out* 'sympathy'
114.5	Kenyon's] *written by Sophia before deleted* 'Graydon's'
114.12	artist] *interlined with a caret above deleted* 'sculptor'
114.19	or plank] *written over wiped-out* ', and plastered'
114.24	earliest] *interlined above deleted* 'first'
114.27	little] *interlined with a caret*
115.4	Kenyon's] *interlined by Sophia above deleted* 'Graydon's'
115.9	exquisite] 'is' *interlined with a caret*
†115.33	stopt] *Sophia wrote* 'ped' *over* 't'
116.2	its hard substance] 's' *added after* 'it' *and* 'hard substance' *interlined with a caret*
116.6	countenance] *interlined with a caret above deleted* 'face'
116.9	Kenyon's] *interlined by Sophia above deleted* 'Graydon's'
116.17	Kenyon] *written by Sophia before deleted* 'Graydon'
116.21	than] *interlined with a caret*
117.3,12	Kenyon] *interlined by Sophia above deleted* 'Graydon'
117.5	generally] *interlined with a caret*
118.13	Kenyon] *interlined by Sophia above deleted* 'Graydon'
119.2	renders] *interlined with a caret above deleted* 'makes'
119.10	infallibly] 'infa' *written over wiped-out* 'inall'
119.20,31	Kenyon] *interlined by Sophia above deleted* 'Graydon'

119.22	it] *interlined with a caret*
120.1	meant,] *comma written over wiped-out exclamation*
120.6	Kenyon] *interlined by Sophia above deleted* 'Graydon'
120.18	had] *written over wiped-out* 'if the'
120.22	Loulie's] 'ou' *has been strengthened;* 'ie' *written over erased* 'y'
120.31	Kenyon.] *written by Sophia following deleted* 'Graydon.'
121.1	had] *followed by deleted* 'not'
121.4	Kenyon,] *interlined by Sophia above deleted* 'Graydon' *and undeleted comma*
121.8	me—] *dash written over comma*
121.10	day!] *exclamation written over wiped-out comma*
121.15	its] 'it' *written over wiped-out* 'the'
121.21	which] *followed by deleted* 'you'
121.31	Kenyon] *interlined by Sophia above deleted* 'Graydon'
122.5	he] 'h' *written over wiped-out* 's'
122.7	himself] *interlined with a caret*
123.1	Kenyon] *interlined by Sophia above deleted* 'Graydon'
123.17–18	as modest . . . and] *interlined with a caret*
123.20	all] *interlined with a caret*
124.3,30	Kenyon] *interlined by Sophia above deleted* 'Graydon'
124.24	Kenyon,] *interlined by Sophia above deleted* 'Graydon' *and undeleted comma*
124.33	probably] *first* 'b' *written over erased* 'p'
124.34	quality] 'qu' *written over wiped-out* 'tex'
125.9	me] *interlined with a caret*
125.12,25	Kenyon] *interlined by Sophia above deleted* 'Graydon'
125.15	members of] *interlined with a caret*
125.26	special] 'spe-|cial' *in which the hyphen is written over a wiped-out* 'c'
†125.32	Egypt] *Sophia added the tail of the* 'y'
126.2	to] *interlined with a caret*
126.8	the Ptolemies] 'the' *interlined with a caret;* 't' *of* 'Ptolemies' *altered from* 'T', *and the* 'T' *written over wiped-out* 't'

126.14   Cleopatra] *interlined with a caret above deleted* 'she'

†126.28   Nubian] 'Nubia' *written over wiped-out illegible letters and the whole word interlined above deleted* 'negro' *which follows a heavily deleted word that just possibly may be* 'sensual', *the spiral deletions made by Sophia.*

126.30   Cleopatra's] *first* 'a' *written over wiped-out* 'I'

127.15   which] 'w' *written over wiped-out* 'th'

127.23;128.1   Kenyon] *interlined by Sophia above deleted* 'Graydon'

128.14   too] *interlined as* 'too,' *with a caret*

128.29   Kenyon's] 'Kenyon' *interlined by Sophia above deleted* 'Graydon's'

128.33   girl] *interlined with a caret above deleted* 'woman'

128.34   say] *interlined above deleted* 'tell'

129.3   it] *interlined with a caret*

129.12   Kenyon] *interlined by Sophia above deleted* 'Graydon'

129.18   half-] *written over wiped-out* 'alm'

129.22   (however] *parenthesis written over wiped-out dash*

129.31   sisterhood,] *comma altered from period*

130.11   Kenyon] *interlined by Sophia above deleted* 'Graydon' *which had been written over a wiped-out word, possibly* 'Miriam'

130.23   she] 's' *written over wiped-out* 'th'

130.24   Unless] *follows wiped-out single quote*

130.25   would] 'wo' *written over wiped-out* 'do I'

130.29   Shadow] 'S' *altered from* 's'

131.1   Kenyon's] *interlined by Sophia above deleted* 'Graydon's'

131.19   whose] 'wh' *written over wiped-out* 'all'

131.20   enlarging] 'larging' *written above deleted* 'riching'

132.5   In] 'I' *written over wiped-out* 'E'

132.25   special] *interlined with a caret above deleted* 'own'

132.27   professional] 'profe' *written over wiped-out* 'grudges'

133.12   titillation] *final* 's' *wiped out*

133.18	to her] *written over wiped-out* 'into in'
†134.34	buff] *written over* 'rose' *by Sophia; before writing* 'rose', *Hawthorne may have started* 'pink'
135.26	pre-conceptions] *hyphen added by writing* '-c' *over wiped-out* 'co'
136.7	No ideas] *follows deleted* 'How terrible should be the thought'
136.18	are] 'ar' *written over wiped-out* 'h[ ]'
137.3	talk] 'ta' *written over wiped-out doubtful* 'do'
138.18	inferiour] 'inf' *written over* 'ig'
138.29	at] *interlined with a caret*
139.31	you] 'y' *written over wiped-out* 't'
139.33	that] *interlined with a caret*
140.3	Demon] 'De' *written over wiped-out* 'fig'
140.4,21	Kenyon] *interlined by Sophia above deleted* 'Graydon'
140.12	Kenyon.] *written by Sophia after deleted* 'Graydon' *and undeleted period*
140.21	that] *written over wiped-out* 'they'
140.33	when] 'w' *altered from doubtful* 'd'
141.6	am] *written over wiped-out doubtful* 'seem'
141.8	visit] 'v' *written over wiped-out* 'go'
142.10	cold] 'co' *written over wiped-out* 'w'
143.1	falling] *just possibly altered from* 'fallen'
143.25	choosing] 'choo' *written over wiped-out* 'select'
143.27	Kenyon] *interlined by Sophia above deleted* 'Graydon'
143.31	either] *interlined with a caret*
144.3	came] *written over wiped-out* 'emer'
144.6	and sparkles forth,] *interlined with a caret*
†144.19	with] *followed by* 'many' *deleted by Sophia*
†144.19	and many bas-reliefs,] *interlined by Sophia with a caret drawn over a comma; the* 'a' *of* 'and' *is written over Sophia's pencil cross*
145.4	with] *written over wiped-out* 'and'
145.8	continually] 'con' *written over wiped-out* 'a sn'
145.10	multitude] *followed by deleted* 'as a multitude'
145.11	flights] 'fl' *written over wiped-out* 'of'
145.15–16	the piazza] 'the pia' *written over wiped-out* 'it is filled'
145.21	Here, also, are] *written over erased* 'Hither, also, come'

146.4   Kenyon,] *interlined by Sophia above deleted* 'Graydon' *and undeleted semicolon*

146.6   silver] *interlined above deleted* 'separate'

146.23   moonshine] *interlined with a caret above deleted* 'moonlight'

146.33   indeed,] *interlined with a caret*

147.1   shadows of] 'of' *written over wiped-out and erased* 'fro'

147.17   concluded] 'con-'| *interlined above deleted* 'gathered'; |'clu' *written over* 'that'

†147.27   real] *originally* 're-|al' *but Sophia wrote* 'al' *over the hyphen and deleted* 'al' *in the next line*

147.31   persecutor's] *first* 'r' *written over wiped-out* 's'

148.6   all the] *written over wiped-out* 'expecting'

148.12   looked] *second* 'o' *written over wiped-out* 'k'

148.19   mischief] 'ef' *written over wiped-out* 'f'

148.28   smoothed] 'sm' *written over wiped-out* 'so'

149.3   hot?] *query probably altered from wiped-out exclamation*

149.4   and] *written over some illegible wiped-out letters followed by a wiped-out comma*

149.8   your] 'y' *written over wiped-out* 'h'

149.9   (as] *parenthesis altered from comma*

149.10   delights!] *exclamation altered from period*

149.23   came] 'ca' *written over wiped-out* 'arr'

149.26   sexton;] *semicolon altered from period*

149.29   This] *written over wiped-out* 'So it'

150.6   immense] *interlined with a caret*

150.6   shafts] *interlined with a caret above deleted* 'pillars'

150.12   Kenyon] *interlined by Sophia above deleted* 'Graydon'

150.17   centuries] 'u-'| *over wiped-out* 'ur'

150.19   almost] 'al' *written over wiped-out* 'eq'

150.33   away'] *single quote written over wiped-out double quotes*

151.21   Kenyon] *interlined by Sophia above deleted* 'Graydon'

151.24   that] *written over wiped-out* 'this'

151.30   Kenyon's] *interlined by Sophia above deleted* 'Graydon's'

151.32	The party] 'The p' *written over wiped-out* 'They m'
152.4	violence] 'i' *altered from* 'o'
152.5	midway] 'mid' *written over* 'a'
†152.8	on one side;] *interlined by Sophia above deleted* 'between two of the splendid Corinthian columns;'— *and the* 'o' *of* 'on' *inscribed over her pencil cross*
152.8	remnants] *final* 's' *doubtfully an addition*
152.12	Kenyon] *interlined by Sophia above deleted* 'Graydon'
152.17	Alessandria] 'A' *altered from* 'a'
152.23	antique] *interlined with a caret above deleted* 'old'
152.24	yet] *interlined with a caret*
153.4	sentinel] 's' *altered from* 'c'
153.9	revelation] *a following comma deleted*
153.9	took] *a following comma deleted*
153.11	build] *a following comma deleted*
153.12	Coliseum,] *comma deleted and then reinserted*
†154.14	black] *written over* 'iron' *by Sophia; a pencil cross appears above*
†154.17	black] *interlined by Sophia above deleted* 'Iron' *and pencil cross*
†154.26,29	black] *interlined by Sophia above deleted* 'iron' *and pencil cross*
155.15	a heap] *written over wiped-out* 'some tufts of'
155.16	adventurously] *interlined with a caret above deleted* 'strangely'
155.20	paying] *interlined with a caret above deleted* 'doing'
155.29	fragrance] 'nce' *written over wiped-out* 'nt'
155.30	endowed] 'en-'| *written over wiped-out* 'seem'
156.3	Kenyon,] *interlined by Sophia above deleted* 'Graydon' *and undeleted comma*
156.6	see] *followed by deleted* 'lions and tigers tear'
156.6–7	torn . . . tigers] *interlined with a caret*
156.13	people] *followed by deleted* 'to'
156.14	Kenyon] *interlined by Sophia above deleted* 'Graydon'
156.21	authority] *interlined with a caret*

156.24   in which] 'in whi' *written over wiped-out* 'where'

†156.25   black] *interlined by Sophia above deleted* 'iron' *and pencil cross*

156.27   eyes—] *dash written over comma*

156.28   aspect—] *dash written over comma*

†156.34   one!] *original exclamation altered by Sophia to query*

157.3   Kenyon.] *interlined by Sophia above deleted* 'Graydon' *and undeleted period*

157.15   as] *written over wiped-out* 'if'

157.17   labouring] 'labour' *written over wiped-out* 'undergo'

†157.19   the] *Sophia added* 'ir' *to form* 'their'

157.26   Signorina! Signorina!] *in each* 'ina' *is written over* 'a'; *following second is wiped-out double quote*

157.34   almost] *interlined with a caret*

158.30   Ah,] *comma written over wiped-out exclamation*

158.32   him,] 'T' *of* 'They' *in line below obscures the comma*

159.4   Kenyon] *interlined by Sophia above deleted* 'Graydon'

159.7   that] *followed by deleted* 'it'

159.11   is] *written over wiped-out doubtful* 'af' *or possibly* 'ap'

159.13   ancient] 'an' *written over wiped-out* 'old'

159.16   perform] 'perf' *written over erased* 'effect'

160.10   was wont] *interlined with a caret above deleted* 'used'

160.11   ringing] *interlined with a caret*

161.0   EDGE] 'E' *mended from* 'e'

161.1   Kenyon] *interlined by Sophia above deleted* 'Graydon'

161.20   of blackness] 'of bla' *written over wiped-out* 'that lies'

162.6   in Curtius] *interlined with a caret*

162.16   gallant] 'g' *written over wiped-out* 'b'

162.18   thus,] *followed by wiped-out single quote*

162.27   wrong] 'w' *written over wiped-out* 'th'

163.12   bloodshed?] *query altered from period*

163.25	choral strain] *interlined with a caret above deleted* 'thunderous anthem'
164.16	Capitol] 'C' *altered from* 'c'
164.28	lie] 'ie' *written over wiped-out doubtful* 'ies'
165.5	the oldest pillar] *interlined with a caret above deleted* 'anything'
165.11	This] *written over wiped-out* 'Nat'
165.18	forthwith] 'i' *written over wiped-out* 't'
165.21	disadvantage] 'ta' *written over wiped-out* 'ge'
165.30	glistened] 'glis' *written over wiped-out* 'shone'
165.32	figure] *follows deleted* 'imperial'
166.9	benediction.] *followed by deleted* 'The sculptor'
166.11,22	Kenyon] *interlined by Sophia above deleted* 'Graydon'
167.9	cityward] 'c' *written over wiped-out* 'at'
167.21	other] *interlined with a caret*
167.24	a] *written over wiped-out* 'the'
168.7	of soil] *interlined with a caret*
168.28	Kenyon] *interlined by Sophia above deleted* 'Graydon'
169.3	precipice.] *period altered from comma*
169.8	at] *second* 'at' *of* 'at	at' *deleted*
169.9	had] *interlined with a caret*
169.13	Kenyon's] *interlined by Sophia above deleted* 'Graydon's'
169.16	back!] *exclamation inserted before deleted* 'with me!'
169.31	(of] *parenthesis altered from comma*
169.32	side;] *semicolon possibly over period*
170.1	tempting] 'em' *written over wiped-out* 'ep'
170.9	have] *written over wiped-out* 'were'
170.16	precipice] 'ec' *written over wiped-out* 'ep'
170.18	persons] 'perso' *written over wiped-out* 'people'
170.23	sidelong] *interlined with a caret*
171.11	no, not] *written over wiped-out doubtful* 'not even'
171.14	her] *written over wiped-out* 'the f'
171.15	late] 'la' *written over wiped-out* 'co'
171.17	melody] *interlined with a caret above deleted* 'music'
173.1	horrour] 'horror' *interlined to clarify* 'horror' *mended to* 'horrour'

174.21   if] *inserted in left margin*

175.3   ever] 'e' *written over wiped-out* 'cl'

175.13   short] *written over wiped-out* 'brief'

175.30   ever-] *first* 'e' *written over wiped-out* 'l'

176.7   foremost] 'fore' *written over wiped-out* 'first'

176.8   sense of] 'of' *interlined with a caret*

176.15–16   (as . . . shapes)] *parentheses altered from commas*

176.26   now?] *query altered from comma*

177.2   it—] *dash altered from comma*

177.13   no] *interlined with a caret*

177.30   snowy] *interlined with a caret above deleted* 'white'

177.31   cry] *interlined with a caret above deleted* 'prayer'

178.4   hour] 'ho' *written over wiped-out* 'tim'

178.7   careful] *interlined with a caret above deleted* 'cautious'

178.22   Kenyon] *interlined by Sophia above deleted* 'Graydon'

†179.3   artificial] 'cial' *added by Sophia below* 'artifi-'| *at end of folio*

179.7   hearing] *interlined with a caret above deleted* 'presence', *probably by Hawthorne but just possibly by Sophia*

179.21   us?] *query altered from comma and double quotes*

179.33   Kenyon] *interlined by Sophia above deleted* 'Graydon'

179.34   alarm.] *followed by wiped-out* ' "Not'

180.2   closely] *followed by wiped-out comma*

180.8   tower-] *written over wiped-out* 'house-top'

180.17   Kenyon] *written by Sophia before deleted* 'Graydon'

180.25   be] *interlined with a caret*

180.27   it was] 'it' *written over wiped-out* 'l'

181.3   Kenyon] *interlined by Sophia above deleted* 'Graydon'

181.4   indifferently] *written over wiped-out* 'indiferrently'

181.11   nobody] 'n' *written over wiped-out doubtful* 'b'

†181.15   so much] 'so' *interlined by Sophia above deleted* 'thus'; *above and below* 'much' *are pencil crosses*

181.26   closely] 'cl' *written over wiped-out* 've'

182.5   aspect] 'as' *written over wiped-out* 'of' *or possibly* 'od'

182.13   figure—] *dash written over wiped-out comma*

182.13–14   wax— . . . be—] *dashes written over commas*

183.12   that] 'tha' *altered from* 'the'; *final* 't' *written over wiped-out* 'tri'

183.14   the triumph] 't' *of* 'the' *written over wiped-out* 'T'

183.15   Kenyon] *interlined by Sophia above deleted* 'Graydon'

183.34   more] 'm' *written over wiped-out* 'c'

184.3   Kenyon.] *written by Sophia after deleted* 'Graydon' *and undeleted period*

184.7   sky-] *interlined with a caret*

184.9   on] *written over wiped-out doubtful* 'of'

184.11   No,] *comma written over wiped-out semicolon*

184.21   all] *written over wiped-out* 'th'

184.24   mouth.] *period written over erased exclamation*

184.26   Kenyon,] *interlined by Sophia above deleted* 'Graydon' *and undeleted comma*

184.27   the picture] 'th' *altered from* 'a'; 'e pic-' | *written over wiped-out* 'Saint'

185.14   and] *followed by deleted* 'probabl'

185.20   it] *interlined with a caret*

185.31   him] 'h' *written over wiped-out* 'up'

188.17   idea] *interlined with a caret*

188.20   baby, and] ', a' *written over wiped-out left parenthesis*

188.23   fanciful] 'i' *written over wiped-out* 'f'

188.27   and bewildered] 'and b' *written over wiped-out* 'glance'

189.2   Kenyon,] *interlined by Sophia above deleted* 'Graydon' *and undeleted comma*

189.19   Kenyon.] *interlined by Sophia above deleted* 'Graydon' *and undeleted period*

189.19   of] *written over wiped-out* 'by'

189.23   which] 'w' *written over wiped-out* 'th'

189.30	church?] *query altered from period*
189.31	Kenyon] *interlined by Sophia above deleted* 'Graydon'
189.34	unexpectedly] 'unex-'| *written over wiped-out* 'involun-'|
191.3	between] |'tween' *interlined above deleted* |'neath'
191.24	he] *followed by deleted* 'seemed to	to'
191.24	threw] 'e' *altered from* 'o'
†192.5	Signorina] 'ina' *written over* 'a' *by Sophia; a pencil cross appears below*
192.7	Kenyon] *interlined by Sophia above deleted* 'Graydon'
192.33	skeleton] *follows deleted* 'skeleton' *altered from* 'sketon'
193.12	entire] 'ire' *written over wiped-out* 'rie'
193.20,22	are] *interlined above deleted* 'were'
193.24	up] *interlined with a caret*
193.29	has] 's' *written over erased* 'd'
193.30	look] *final* 'ed' *deleted*
193.33	even] *written over erased* 'still'
194.2	But] 'B' *written over doubtful* 'T'
194.5	death;] *semicolon doubtfully mended from period*
194.5	holy earth] 'holy' *written over illegible wiped-out letters;* 'ea' *of* 'earth' *written over wiped-out* 'fr' *or* 'fe'
194.6	grown] *written over wiped-out* 'become a'
194.6	the] *interlined with a caret*
194.16	smell] *interlined above separately deleted* 'have smelt'
†194.22	Signorina,] 'ina,' *written over* 'a,' *by Sophia; a pencil cross appears below*
194.28	in] 'i' *altered from* 'o'
194.30	Is] 's' *altered from* 't'
194.32	in] *follows deleted* 'undisturbed'
†195.1	Signorina,] 'ina,' *written over* 'a,' *by Sophia; a pencil cross appears below*
196.5	Yes,"] *left quote altered semicolon to comma*
196.13	alleys] 'eys' *altered from* 'ies'
†197.17	to] *interlined with a caret by Sophia*

†197.18   cling!] *altered by Sophia from* 'cling to!'; *a pencil cross appears above*

197.30   uneasily] 'un' *written over wiped-out* 'wi'

198.30   to let fall] *follows deleted* 'for'; 'to' *written over wiped-out* 'a'; 'let fall' *written over wiped-out and erased* 'fling upon'

198.31   of] *interlined with a caret*

199.3   would] 'w' *altered from* 'm'

199.15   have] *written in error* 'have | have' *with second* 'ha' *written over wiped-out* 'fou'

199.29   your] *interlined with a caret above deleted doubtful* 'our'

199.33   should] *interlined with a caret above a highly doubtful deleted word that just possibly could be* 'shunned'

201.7   she] *interlined with a caret*

201.24   little] 'lit' *written over wiped-out* 'lef'

202.17   unhesitatingly] *first* 'i' *written over wiped-out* 'ti'

203.3   were] 'w' *written over what is propably a wiped-out uncrossed* 't'

†203.6   squatted] *Sophia deleted this word, without a pencil cross, and interlined* 'huddled'

203.12   expectation] 'expecta' *written over wiped-out* 'anticipa'

203.23   world—] *dash written over comma*

203.28   clasp] 'c' *written over wiped-out* 'to'

204.6   more] *interlined with a caret above much-mended deleted* 'more'

204.20   impalpable] *second* 'p' *written over wiped-out* 'ab'

204.22   them] *mended from* 'there'

204.32–205.1 permitted] 'per-'| *written over wiped-out* 'only'

205.20   was] 'w' *written over wiped-out doubtful* 'i'

205.23–24   It was . . . face.] *inserted later at end of line, and interlined below*

206.17   only] 'o' *written over wiped-out doubtful* 'h'

206.24   vanished] 'v' *written over wiped-out doubtful* 'b' *perhaps followed by* 'e'

207.9   bridged] *first* 'd' *written over wiped-out* 'ge'

207.10   Eternity] 'E' *altered from* 'e'

207.16   Miriam!] *exclamation altered from comma*

207.33	is] *inserted in left margin*
208.17	personally?] *query altered from exclamation*
208.20	Miriam!] *exclamation altered from comma*
209.3	with] *interlined with a caret*
209.8	earthly] *interlined with a caret*
209.10	needlessly] *interlined with a caret*
209.12	Miriam.] *period altered from comma*
209.14	what] *followed by deleted 'you'*
209.14	you] *interlined with a caret*
209.25	angels.] *following double quotes deleted*
209.25	perceive] *interlined with a caret*
210.16	it!] *followed by wiped-out double quotes*
210.20	look!—] *exclamation written over wiped-out dash and then a dash added*
210.29	young] *'y' written over erased doubtful 'm'*
211.13	As] *preceded by wiped-out double quotes*
211.32	Kenyon!] *interlined by Sophia above deleted 'Graydon' and undeleted exclamation*
211.33–34	because—I] *dash written over wiped-out comma*
212.10	the] *'t' written over wiped-out 'so'*
213.1	June] *interlined with a caret above deleted 'May'*
213.1	Kenyon] *interlined by Sophia above deleted 'Graydon'*
213.5	accompany] *'acc' written over wiped-out 'shift'*
213.10	The] *written over wiped-out 'For,'*
213.14	other] *written over wiped-out 'forei'*
213.22	City] *'y' written over wiped-out 't'*
214.9	in] *written over wiped-out 'wh'*
214.15	inadequately] *interlined with a caret*
214.20	for,] *interlined with a caret*
214.23	Kenyon] *written by Sophia before deleted 'Graydon'*
215.25	a] *interlined with a caret*
†215.33	yellow] *interlined by Sophia above deleted 'white-', the hyphen not being restored, in error; a pencil cross appears below*
216.1,21	Kenyon] *interlined by Sophia above deleted 'Graydon'*
216.3	above] *interlined above deleted 'over'*
216.8	from] *interlined above deleted 'between'*

216.8	an] *written over wiped-out* 'the'
216.11	hat;] *semicolon mended from period; a comma was possibly intended*
216.11	for] *written over wiped-out* 'This'
216.27	Kenyon] *written by Sophia before deleted* 'Graydon'
217.17,28;218.6,27	Kenyon] *interlined by Sophia above deleted* 'Graydon'
†219.18	Etruscan] 'E-' *at end of folio deleted by Sophia and* 'E' *added before* 'truscan' *starting next folio*
219.23	degrees] *followed by erased comma*
219.25	Kenyon] *interlined by Sophia above deleted* 'Graydon'
†219.33	enough] *Sophia deleted* 'e-'| *and added* 'e' *in next line before* 'nough'
220.7	Beni.] *followed by deleted* ' "Come," said the Count, "I see you already find the old house dismal'
221.8	hearts] 'ts' *altered from* 't'
221.10	so large] 'so lar' *written over wiped-out* 'such a'
221.20	Kenyon.] *written by Sophia after* 'Graydon' *and undeleted period*
222.6	that?" asked] *query, quotes, and* 'a' *of* 'asked' *written over wiped-out* 'ask'
222.12	plums,] *interlined with a caret*
222.33	some of] 'of' *interlined with a caret*
223.2	name."] *a line below is deleted* ' "Taste it; but first smell its fragrance'
223.8	Kenyon] *interlined by Sophia above deleted* 'Graydon'
223.12	invaluable] *written over wiped-out* 'precious'
223.25	the wine's] *interlined with a caret above deleted* 'its'
223.26	and] 'a' *written over wiped-out* 'd'
223.31	Kenyon's] *interlined by Sophia above deleted* 'Graydon's'
224.4	surely] *a doubtful following comma seems to have been erased*
224.15	were] *followed by deleted* 'to be'
224.16	At] *written over wiped-out* 'The'
224.18	Emperour] 'E' *mended from* 'e'

224.18	Pope] 'P' *mended from* 'p'
224.23	Kenyon] *interlined by Sophia above deleted* 'Graydon'
225.10	you] *written over wiped-out* 'the'
225.15	Kenyon] *interlined by Sophia above deleted* 'Graydon'
225.18	supporting] *interlined above deleted* 'and supported'
225.31	presented] *interlined with a caret*
226.14	funereal] 'n' *written over wiped-out* 'e'
226.19	Kenyon] *interlined by Sophia above deleted* 'Graydon'
227.3	how] *interlined with a caret*
227.6	answered] 'ans' *written over wiped-out* 'sai'
227.12	Kenyon] *interlined by Sophia above deleted* 'Graydon'
227.14	It] *written over wiped-out* 'Yo'
227.23	(as] *parenthesis written over comma*
228.20	it] *interlined with a caret*
228.22;229.6,13,19	Kenyon] *interlined by Sophia above deleted* 'Graydon'
229.8	minds,)] *parenthesis may be written over a comma*
†229.10	terrour,] *between folios Hawthorne had written* 'ter-| ror,' *which Sophia clarified by adding* 'ror,' *over the hyphen and deleting the syllable heading the next folio but leaving the comma*
229.14	resuming] *interlined with a caret; the caret had first been misplaced before* 'from' *but was erased*
229.23	tell] 'ell' *written over wiped-out* 'i[ ]'
229.32	Kenyon] *written by Sophia before deleted* 'Graydon'
230.6,15	have] *interlined with a caret*
230.17	Kenyon] *interlined by Hawthorne above deleted* 'Graydon'; *from this point the change in name is to be taken as in Hawthorne's hand unless specifically noted*
230.18	visitor] *interlined with a caret above deleted* 'guest'
230.18	roof.] *below, indented to begin a new paragraph, is wiped-out* 'F'

231.2	Kenyon] *interlined above deleted* 'Graydon'
232.1	Middle Ages] 'M' *and* 'A' *altered from* 'm' *and* 'a'
232.3	flower;] *semicolon altered from period*
232.13	strayed] *interlined with a caret*
232.15	gold, and] *the comma is an addition; the* 'd' *of* 'and' *written over wiped-out* 'g'; *just possibly the* 'an' *of* 'and' *written over the word* 'or'
232.21	upon] *interlined with a caret*
232.27	one] 'o' *written over wiped-out* 'a'
232.29	which] *interlined with a caret above deleted* 'that'
232.33	at] 'a' *written over wiped-out* 'i' *followed by partly formed* 't'
233.9	the] *followed by deleted* 'the'
233.13	inhabitants] *first* 'i' *written over wiped-out* 'h'
233.15	at that] *follows deleted* 'the lineage of Monte Beni had its rise'
233.18	be] 'b' *written over doubtful* 'a'
234.19	generations] 'gener' *written over wiped-out* 'ages, l'
234.22	supernumerary] 'ra' *written over wiped-out* '[ ]y'
234.27	beyond] *followed in MS by* 'human' *in which* 'hu' *is written over wiped-out* 'th'
234.32	descent] *interlined with a caret*
235.29	which] *written over wiped-out* 'that would'
236.8	race] *followed by wiped-out comma*
236.9	accumulating] *follows deleted* 'advancing age'
236.14–15	investigate] *interlined with a caret*
237.1	branches] *interlined with a caret above deleted* 'boughs'
237.2	tall] *interlined with a caret*
237.3	child] *written over erased* 'boy'
237.12	(and] *parenthesis written over comma*
237.14	Their] *written over wiped-out* 'His'
237.28	Kenyon] *interlined above deleted* 'Graydon'
238.1	added] 'a' *written over comma*
238.15	antique] 'ti' *written over* 'cie' *during inscription*
238.19	Kenyon] *interlined above deleted* 'Graydon'
238.21	Counts] 'C' *altered from* 'c'

239.2	gladden] 'den' *written over wiped-out* 'en the'
239.3	seeming] 'see' *written over wiped-out doubtful* 'ap'
239.5	before] *written over wiped-out* 'were'
239.10	as at] *written over wiped-out doubtful* 'such'
240.3,12,23	Kenyon] *interlined above deleted* 'Graydon'
240.5	still] *written over wiped-out* 'enjoy'
240.30	an] 'n' *written over wiped-out* 'd'
241.4	whom] *interlined with a caret*
241.4	Kenyon] *interlined above deleted* 'Graydon'
241.15	presence] *written over wiped-out* 'elastic'
242.6	Kenyon] *interlined above deleted* 'Graydon'
242.21	with a] *followed by deleted* 'with a'
243.1	Kenyon's] 'Kenyon' *interlined above deleted* 'Graydon's'
243.6	small] *written over wiped-out* 'water'
243.13	it] *interlined with a caret*
243.26;244.3,11	Kenyon] *interlined above deleted* 'Graydon'
244.8	formerly] *followed by deleted* 'that it ends in did'
244.23	changeable] *followed by erased comma*
245.8	pebbles?—] *query written over erased dash and then new dash added*
245.14	the] *written over wiped-out* 'a'
245.17	watery] *written over wiped-out* 'watry lady'
245.32	something] 'thing' *written over wiped-out* 'what'
246.4	the brook] 'the' *written over wiped-out* 'a'
246.15,27	Kenyon] *interlined above deleted* 'Graydon'
246.23	have] *interlined with a caret*
246.29	effects] *first* 'e' *written over wiped-out doubtful* 'f' *or* 'b'
247.30	persuasibility] MS *has* 'persuadability' *with* 'abi' *written over wiped-out doubtful* '[ ]eb'
248.2	Any] *written over wiped-out doubtful* 'Hear'
248.4	more] 'm' *written over wiped-out* 'd'
248.19	inarticulate] *first* 'i' *altered from* 'a'
248.34	Kenyon] *interlined above deleted* 'Graydon'
249.1	shadow,] *comma written over wiped-out* 'y'
249.13,20,27;250.1,10,20	Kenyon] *interlined above deleted* 'Graydon'
250.15	very] *written over wiped-out* 'absu'

251.5	Kenyon] *interlined above deleted* 'Graydon'
252.7,21	Kenyon] *interlined by Sophia above deleted* 'Graydon'
252.22	mansion] *interlined with a caret above deleted* 'house'
253.1	close . . . Vecchio,] *interlined with a caret*
253.14	some] 'som' *written over wiped-out* 'the [ ]'
253.17	we climb] *interlined with a caret above deleted* 'I see'
253.19	Count] 'C' *mended from* 'c'
253.25	resembles] 'r' *written over wiped-out* 's'
253.32	turret-] *interlined with a caret*
254.17	Kenyon] *interlined by Sophia above deleted* 'Graydon'
254.21	So] 'S' *written over erased* 'T'
254.25	by] *written over wiped-out* 'of'
254.28	showed] *interlined above deleted* 'gave'
255.1,6,30	Kenyon] *interlined by Sophia above deleted* 'Graydon'
255.24	boy,] *followed by deleted* 'reclining'
256.15;257.5,20	Kenyon] *interlined by Sophia above deleted* 'Graydon'
257.11	in] *written over wiped-out* 'it'
257.30	at] *written over wiped-out* 'th'
257.31	black] *followed by deleted* 'of'
258.7	Art] 'A' *mended from* 'a'
258.26;259.20	Kenyon] *interlined by Sophia above deleted* 'Graydon'
259.26	your] 'y' *written over wiped-out* 'us'
259.30	stooping] *interlined above deleted* 'bending'
260.21;262.1	Kenyon] *interlined by Sophia above deleted* 'Graydon'
262.9	those] *currently altered from* 'the'
262.21	human] 'hu' *written over wiped-out* 'life'
262.23	without] *interlined with a caret*
262.29	Calamity] 'C' *altered from* 'c'
262.31	Kenyon] *interlined by Sophia above deleted* 'Graydon'
263.9	ascended] *interlined with a caret above deleted* 'rose'
263.26	Kenyon] *interlined by Sophia above deleted* 'Graydon'

263.27	out] 'ou' *written over wiped-out* 'of'
263.30	positive] *first* 'i' *interlined with a caret*
264.3	by] *interlined with a caret*
264.9	Kenyon] *interlined by Sophia above deleted* 'Graydon'
264.31	vividly] *interlined with a caret above deleted* 'sky,' *and the comma preceding* 'vividly' *added*
265.5	finally] *interlined with a caret*
265.7	fancied] 'fa' *written over* 'im'
265.30	Kenyon] *interlined by Sophia above deleted* 'Graydon'
266.5	day] *interlined with a caret*
266.8	Kenyon] *interlined by Sophia above deleted* 'Graydon'
266.15	on] *altered from* 'in'
266.22	The two owls] *interlined with a caret, and the preceding period added*
267.7	monk?] *query altered from exclamation*
267.9	True,] *comma altered from semicolon*
267.28	Kenyon] *interlined by Sophia above deleted* 'Graydon'
269.8	that sang them.] *interlined with a caret*
269.19	voice] 'v' *written over wiped-out* 'r'
269.22	melody,] *interlined with a caret above deleted* 'song' *which is followed by an undeleted comma*
269.25	there was silence] *interlined with a caret above deleted* 'it was still'
269.27	receive] *second* 'e' *altered from* 'i'
269.29	it] *interlined with a caret*
270.1	Kenyon] *interlined by Sophia above deleted* 'Graydon'
270.10	which] 'wh' *written over wiped-out* 'that'
270.19	through] *altered from* 'though'
271.3	or clay] *interlined with a caret*
271.8	Kenyon] *interlined by Sophia above deleted* 'Graydon'
271.16	substance] *followed by wiped-out comma*
271.31	man] *written over erased doubtful* 'self'
272.13	Kenyon] *interlined by Sophia above deleted* 'Graydon'

272.23	uglier] *interlined with a caret above deleted* 'fiercer' *with the preceding* 'a' *altered to* 'an'
272.26	to] *interlined with a caret*
272.30	face] *follows deleted* 'living'
273.8	long; there] *semicolon altered from period; and* 't' *written over erased* 'T'
273.15	noisome] *interlined with a caret*
273.23;274.4,15.31	Kenyon] *interlined by Sophia above deleted* 'Graydon'
274.10	melting] *interlined with a caret above deleted* 'tempting'
274.12	that] 't' *written over wiped-out* 'A'
274.25	shaggy] *interlined with a caret above deleted* 'hairy'
274.26	Scripture] 'S' *written over wiped-out* 's'
274.28	effusion,] *interlined with a caret above deleted* 'juice'
274.31	sample] *interlined with a caret above deleted* 'specimen'
275.6	creaking] *interlined with a caret*
275.28	which] 'whi' *written over wiped-out* 'that'
277.22	roof.] *period written over wiped-out comma*
278.2	hapless] *interlined with a caret above deleted* 'very'
278.3	had] *follows deleted* 'there'
278.15	He] 'H' *written over wiped-out* 'K'
278.19	Kenyon had] *written over wiped-out* 'he had leis'
279.8	excellencies] 'ie' *written over* 'es'
279.30	Miriam!] *exclamation written over comma*
280.5	energy] *interlined with a caret above deleted* 'strength'
280.6	—or] *written over wiped-out* 'weari'
280.8	on] 'o' *written over wiped-out* 'i'
280.8	utterly.] *interlined with a caret drawn over original period*
280.23–24	for a woman] *written over wiped-out* 'to tell a man'
280.25	certainty] 'y' *written over wiped-out* 'I'
280.26	sight!] *exclamation added after wiped-out period*
281.1	merely;] *semicolon written over wiped-out comma*

281.19	shock] 'sh' *written over doubtful* 'sli'
281.20–21	all the circumstances] 'all the c' *written over wiped-out* 'the circumst'
281.25–26	experienced] 'ex' *written over wiped-out doubtful* 'h'
281.33	had] 'ad' *written over wiped-out* 'ave'
282.1	longs] 'lon' *written over wiped-out* 'des'
282.2	it.] *interlined with a caret*
282.3	strong] *interlined with a caret*
282.10	her] *interlined with a caret*
282.19	activity] *interlined with a caret above deleted* 'life'
282.23	former] 'for-'| *written over wiped-out* 'older'
282.29	good! To] *exclamation inserted before erased comma and* 'T' *written over erased* 't'
282.32	which] 'w' *written over wiped-out* 't'
282.33	me] 'm' *written over wiped-out doubtful* 'I'
283.18	Eye] 'E' *altered from* 'e'
283.22	far as] 'as' *written over wiped-out* 'I'
283.27	at] *interlined with a caret*
284.6–7	flinging . . . hands,] *interlined with a caret; the preceding comma added*
284.7	acknowledged,] *comma perhaps altered from period*
285.25	is a] 'a' *interlined with a caret*
286.1–2	tour, (. . . meet,)] *parentheses written over commas, and new commas added*
286.4	after] *interlined with a caret*
286.5	contemplated] *interlined with a caret above deleted* 'proposed'
286.31	however] *followed by deleted* 'the'
287.8	Womanhood] 'W' *written over erased* 'w'
287.13	not] *interlined with a caret above deleted* 'nothing of'
287.18	are] *followed by deleted* 'as'
287.22	keep] *interlined with a caret*
287.24	right!] *exclamation written over erased comma*
287.24	Miriam.] *period altered from comma*
288.10	visits] *followed by deleted* ', therefore,'
288.18	easily] *interlined above deleted* 'readily'
288.21	and] 'an' *written over erased doubtful* 'he'

289.13   vagrant] 'vagr' *written over wiped-out* 'purp'

289.19   fancy] *interlined with a caret above deleted* 'imagine'

289.20   in] *interlined with a caret*

289.20   Unexpected] 'U' *altered from* 'u'

289.22   The] *final* 'y' *erased*

289.34   existence] *interlined with a caret above deleted* 'life'

290.13   yarn] *interlined with a caret*

290.25   -crowned] 'c' *written over wiped-out doubtful* 'b'

290.30   black-] *written over wiped-out* 'hats of'

291.2   burthen] *interlined with a caret above deleted* 'bundle'

291.8   which] *interlined with a caret*

291.15   like] 'l' *written over wiped-out right parenthesis*

291.22   trunks] *written over wiped-out* 'trees'

291.28   an] *interlined with a caret*

292.25   ruined] *interlined above deleted* 'broken'

292.27   (that] *parenthesis written over comma*

292.32   needless] *interlined with a caret above deleted* 'massive'

293.8   rural peace] 'rural p' *written over wiped-out* 'rustic pea'

293.20   half-] *written over wiped-out* 'covere'

293.23   one] *interlined with a caret*

293.24   habitations] *followed by wiped-out comma*

294.2   is] *interlined with a caret above deleted* 'sits'

294.28   of] *interlined with a caret*

294.33   water] 'w' *written over wiped-out* 'th'

295.4   are] *followed by deleted* 'as'

295.5   devout,] *comma added; and following* 'as he' *mended from* 'as him' *deleted*

296.6–7   plaister] 'plai' *written over wiped-out* 'plas'

296.28   Cross] 'C' *altered from* 'c'

297.1   but] *followed by deleted* |'but'

297.5–6   as accorded] 'as ac-'| *interlined above deleted* 'according' *and text continued on next line with* 'corded'

297.12–13   or at . . . bridge;] *interlined with a caret misplaced before the semicolon after* 'farm-house'

297.32   should] *interlined with a caret above deleted* 'might'

298.6	blossoms] *follows deleted* 'flowers'
298.15	he] *interlined with a caret*
299.5	Kenyon] *interlined with a caret above deleted* 'his companion'
299.9	like] 'li' *written over wiped-out* 'a'
301.7	bridge] *interlined with a caret*
†303.9	desperate] *Sophia altered* 'ar' *to* 'er'
303.23	illusions—] *dash intended to delete comma*
†303.24	Pinturicchio] *Sophia altered* 'cio' *to* 'chio'
304.5	surely] *followed by independently deleted* 'the' *and then by deleted* 'mind of man has never imagined, nor his'
304.29	to] *written over wiped-out* 'th'
305.18	to] 't' *altered from* 's'
305.23	but the] *followed by deleted* 'dusty pictures of English cathedrals,'
306.2	divine] 'di' *written over wiped-out* 'Di'
306.12	nor] *interlined with a caret above deleted* 'or'
306.20	Faith] 'F' *altered from* 'f'
306.24	emerged from] *interlined with a caret above deleted* 'left'
307.20	that] *interlined with a caret*
307.31	in availing] 'in a' *written over wiped-out* 'of ava'
308.4	death] 'd' *altered from* 'a'
308.13	as] 'a' *written over wiped-out* 'h'
308.25	replied;] *semicolon altered from period*
309.17	admirable] *interlined with a caret*
309.19	it was] *interlined with a caret above deleted* 'they were'
310.1	look] *written over wiped-out* 'see'
310.2	not] *interlined with a caret*
310.6	of] *added later in left margin*
310.11	Saints] *final* 's' *added and a following comma wiped out*
310.12	to have lived] 'to have' *interlined with a caret*
310.14	holy] *interlined with a caret*
311.2	than] *written over wiped-out* 'though'
311.18	Donkeys] *MS* 'Donkies' *has* 'ies' *written over wiped-out* 'eys'
311.21	room] *interlined with a caret above deleted* 'space'

311.32	in Perugia] *interlined with a caret*
312.8	echo] *final 'e' wiped out*
312.18	Council-House] 'C' *and* 'H' *altered from* 'c' *and* 'h'
312.25	such] *preceded by deleted* 'such'
312.28	have] *interlined with a caret*
312.30	hardened] 'h' *written over wiped-out doubtful* 'c'
313.17	civilization] 'iz' *written over wiped-out* 'is'
313.18	get from] *interlined with a caret above deleted* 'find in'
313.25	made] 'mad' *written over wiped-out* 'approac'
313.33	forth] 'for' *written over wiped-out* 'ben'
314.1	(so] *parenthesis written over wiped-out comma*
314.1	wise, and] *written over wiped-out* 'serenely af'
314.2	regard)] *parenthesis inserted before wiped-out comma*
314.4	his] *interlined with a caret*
314.14	listening] 'lis' *written over wiped-out* 'and'
314.32	hopeful] *followed by deleted* 'light'
315.8	excellent] 'excel-'| *written over wiped-out* 'Excel-'
315.21	one and all] *interlined with a caret above deleted* 'them'
315.24	sculptor] 's' *written over wiped-out* 'S'
316.10	that] *interlined with a caret above deleted* 'which'
317.5	with . . . light] *interlined with a caret*
317.20	Kenyon] *written over wiped-out* 'asked'
317.25	inestimable] 'b' *written over wiped-out* 'g'
318.8	into] 'n' *written over wiped-out and erased* 't' *and* 'to' *added*
318.9	benignant] *interlined with a caret*
318.9	, as if she had] *written over wiped-out* 'to ask of him if she had'
318.10	vast] *interlined with a caret above deleted* 'great'
318.32	to] *written over wiped-out* 'th'
319.2	glance] 'g' *written over wiped-out* 'lo'
319.7	one] *interlined with a caret*
319.27	Ah;] *semicolon written over wiped-out exclamation*

320.4	that—] *dash deletes comma*
320.14	and] 'a' *altered from* 'A'
320.19	so rare a being] *interlined with a caret above deleted* 'such a creature'
320.31	the] 't' *written over wiped-out* 'o'
321.16	uttering] 'u' *written over wiped-out* 'th'
321.22	incurred] *interlined with a caret*
321.22	responsibility] *followed by wiped-out comma*
321.27	of] 'o' *written over wiped-out doubtful* 'h'
321.28	magnetic] 'm' *written over wiped-out* 's'
321.33	should] *interlined with a caret above deleted* 'to'
†322.7	it] *inserted in the left margin by Sophia*
322.22	life,] *interlined with a caret*
322.29	say?] *query altered from comma*
322.32	, dear] *written over wiped-out* 'Miriam'
†323.16	guest] *Sophia made a pencil cross above this word*
323.22	Farewell!] *exclamation altered from comma*
323.25	Pope] 'Po' *written over wiped-out* 'the'
323.33	eyes] 'ey' *written over wiped-out* 'al'
324.2–3	become aware of] *interlined with a caret above deleted* 'catch'
325.1	her] *written over erased* 'it'
325.4	all] *interlined with a caret*
325.5	features;—] *semicolon altered from comma and dash added*
325.5	her in utter] 'her in u' *written over wiped-out* 'it[ ]'
325.8	indescribably] 'a' *written over wiped-out* 'l'
325.10	our] *written over erased* 'your'
325.10	lungs;—] *semicolon altered from comma and dash added*
325.13	weary] *interlined with a caret*
325.14	climbing] *interlined with a caret*
325.15	stalls] *interlined with a caret*
325.16	middle] *first* 'd' *over two illegible wiped-out letters; second* 'd' *lacks an upright, but intention was to inscribe* 'middle'
326.9	our] *interlined with a caret above deleted* 'your'
326.9	our] *interlined with a caret above deleted* 'your'
326.15	were more] 'more' *interlined with a caret*

327.5	a reality] 'a' *interlined with a caret*
327.6	show] *preceded by deleted* 'bright'
327.13	cheek] 'c' *written over wiped-out* 'th'
327.25	Virgin's] 'V' *altered from* 'v'
328.5	however,] *interlined with a caret*
328.23	whom] 'w' *written over wiped-out doubtful* 't' *or* 'f'
329.2	discovery—] *dash deletes comma*
329.5	and] *followed by deleted* 'which'
329.9	one] 'o' *written over wiped-out* 'to'
330.14	Leonardo da Vinci's] *interlined with a caret above deleted* 'the'
330.17	to] *interlined with a caret*
331.6	has] *interlined with a caret*
331.11	spirting] 'ti' *written over wiped-out* 'iti'
331.14	she] *followed by deleted* 'don't	she'
331.17	The] 'T' *written over erased* 't'
331.23	world's] ' 's ' *written over comma*
332.5	knelt—] *dash deletes comma*
332.7	the] *written over wiped-out doubtful* 'me'
333.6	which] *interlined with a caret*
334.11	his miracles] 's' *of* 'his' *written over wiped-out* 'm'
334.22	just] *written over wiped-out and erased doubtful* 'beside'
334.29	The] 'e' *written over wiped-out* 'ey'
334.30	they] *interlined with a caret*
335.10	departed] *followed by deleted* 'from her' *with a caret after* 'from'; *another* 'her' *interlined but deleted*
336.7	Mephistophiles] *second* 'i' *may be altered from* 'e'
336.20	their works] *interlined with a caret above deleted* 'themselves'
337.10	day] *interlined with a caret*
338.1–12	But . . . said.] *inscribed on verso; in text is* '(Insert paragraph on the opposite page)' *following* 'Fornarina!'
338.3	see] *followed by wiped-out* 'a'
338.33	these] 'se' *written over erased* 'y'
338.33	painters] *interlined with a caret*

339.17   therefore] *preceded and followed by erased commas*

339.20   imagine.] *followed by a pencil query within an oval written in another hand*

339.25   inexpressibly] *'in' is written over wiped-out 'ex'; preceded by deleted ', indeed,'*

†339.29   ground] *a following comma may have been added by Sophia*

340.1   and reverent] *interlined with a caret*

340.15   Revelation] *'R' altered from 'r'*

341.11   ten] *interlined with a caret above deleted 'a'*

341.28   over] *interlined with a caret above deleted 'or'*

342.2   further] *interlined with a caret*

342.27   windy] *'win' written over wiped-out 'sea'*

342.28   heart] *'he' written over wiped-out 'gre'*

342.29   that were awakened] *interlined with a caret*

343.4   summer] *'su' written over wiped-out 'af'*

343.5   upon] *interlined above deleted 'over'*

344.3   sky;] *semicolon written over wiped-out dash*

344.7   hardly] *written over wiped-out 'scar'*

344.9   Knowing] *'Know-'| written over wiped-out 'H[   ]'*

344.10   it] *written over wiped-out 'she'*

344.14   the faith] *interlined with a caret above deleted 'it'*

344.16   Spiritual] *'S' altered from 's'*

344.16   be] *written over wiped-out and erased 'clothe'*

344.19   visions] *'v' written over wiped-out 'f'*

345.9   it] *interlined with a caret*

345.21   often] *'o' written over wiped-out 'f'*

347.10   plead] *followed by wiped-out comma*

347.16   youth] *'th' written over wiped-out 'ng'*

348.5–6   from . . . downward.] *interlined with a caret*

348.21   He] *written over wiped-out 'he'*

348.24   Saint] *'a' written over wiped-out 't'*

348.25   Dome] *'D' written over erased 'd'*

348.34   no] *'n' written over wiped-out 'def'*

349.2   Dome] *'D' written over erased 'd'*

349.3   as she . . . them,] *interlined with a caret*

349.6   actual] *interlined with a caret*

†349.8   -work] *a following comma added, possibly by*
          Sophia
349.22   with] *interlined with a caret*
349.23   but] 'b' *written over wiped-out* 'w'
350.10   Dome] 'D' *written over erased* 'd'
350.13   whatever] *interlined with a caret above inde-*
          pendently deleted 'all' *and* 'that'
351.7,23 Dome] 'D' *written over erased* 'd'
351.26   up the] *written over wiped-out* 'toward'
352.13   as Catholics] 'as' *interlined with a caret above*
          deleted 'and'
352.14   as] *written over wiped-out* 'if'
352.15   shrine] *with wiping-out, altered from* 'shine'
353.1   if it were] *preceded by deleted* 'if it | were'
353.4   looked] 'lo' *written over wiped-out* 'ga'
353.10   Will-o'-the-Wisp] *each* 'W' *altered from* 'w'; 'is'
          written over wiped-out 'hi'
354.12   Angels] 'An' *written over wiped-out* 'ang'
354.12   hover] *interlined above deleted* 'show
          themselves'
355.7   sacred] *written over wiped-out* 'holy'
355.14   dark] 'd' *written over wiped-out* 'b'
356.18   Saviour] 'S' *altered from* 's'
356.21   sake,] *comma written over wiped-out exclama-*
          tion
357.7   the] *interlined with a caret*
357.13–14 passionately] 'pass' *written over wiped-out* 'with'
357.23   acted] *written over wiped-out* 'attrac-'
357.31   revealed] *interlined with a caret above deleted*
          'told'
358.1   gone;] *semicolon written over wiped-out ex-*
          clamation
358.5   that] *followed by deleted* 'had'
358.19   countenance] *interlined with a caret above*
          deleted 'face'
359.14   best] 'be' *written over wiped-out* 'ef'
359.26   which] 'wh' *written over wiped-out* 'th'
359.28   in the] *written over wiped-out* 'as it'
359.30   I could] 'c' *written over wiped-out* 't' *of original*
          'It'
359.31   grew] *written over wiped-out* 'became'

359.35	know."] *quotes written over wiped-out exclamation and period inserted*
361.6	perpetrate] *followed by deleted* 'at' *mended from* 'it'
361.13	a smile] 'a' *interlined with a caret*
362.14	farther] 'ar' *written over erased* 'ur'
363.17	Kenyon] *squeezed in the right margin by Hawthorne, but later touched up for clarity by Sophia*
364.8	of religious] *written over wiped-out* 'that emerged from'
364.28	heart] 'h' *written over wiped-out* 'g'
†365.3	in] *interlined with a caret by Sophia*
365.30	had] *followed by deleted* 'had'
366.1	sculptor] *interlined with a caret*
366.10	Faith] 'F' *written over wiped-out* 'f'
366.17	only] *written over wiped-out very doubtful* 'less'
366.27	Dogmas] 'D' *written over erased* 'd'
367.5	finer] *interlined with a caret*
367.6–7	supposed] *interlined with a caret above deleted* 'imagined'
367.11	reliable] 'r' *written over wiped-out and erased doubtful* 'th' *or* 'tr'
367.24	deem] 'd' *written over wiped-out* 'th'
368.2	or have] 'have' *interlined with a caret*
368.35	temperature] *interlined with a caret above deleted* 'atmosphere'
369.10	dwell] 'd' *written over wiped-out doubtful* 'li'
369.16	(or] *parenthesis written over comma*
369.31	answered] 'ans' *written over wiped-out* 'rejoi'
370.11–12	exquisite] 'ex' *written over wiped-out* 'equ'
370.19	Archangel] 'A' *mended from* 'a'
370.23	she] *written over wiped-out* 'Hild'
370.27	look] *followed by deleted* 'down'
370.28	yellow] *interlined with a caret above deleted* 'eddying'
370.34	imbedded] 'i' *written over wiped-out* 'e'
371.6	Would] 'Wo' *altered from* 'Is'
371.10	all] *written over wiped-out* 'the'
371.18	of] *interlined with a caret*

371.18   seven poets] 'poets' *interlined with a caret above deleted* 'of them'

371.27   Portoghese,] *comma written over wiped-out doubtful* 'e' *or* 'a'

372.6   little] *interlined with a caret*

372.12   street!] *exclamation written over comma*

373.0   SNOWDROPS] 'd' *probably written over a hyphen*

373.11   they] 'y' *heavily altered over erased doubtful* 'se'

375.25   the Saviour] 'the Sa' *written over wiped-out* 'other [   ]'

375.27   one.] *followed by deleted* 'How, indeed, should she have found such!'

376.6–7   like . . . grasshoppers] *interlined with a caret misplaced before the comma following* 'hand'

376.10   Keeping] *written over erased very doubtful* 'Without f'

376.21   dwellings] *followed by erased comma*

376.21   the] *final* 'ir' *erased*

376.24   over] 'ov' *written over wiped-out doubtful* 'of'

376.34   when] *interlined with a caret*

377.20   one] 'o' *written over wiped-out* 'of'

379.28   and of] 'of' *interlined with a caret*

379.30   white] *interlined with a caret*

380.1   countenance,] *interlined with a caret above deleted* 'shape'

380.14   deal] *interlined with a caret*

380.25   him;] *semicolon altered from period following which double quote has been erased*

381.9   bust] *followed by erased comma*

381.15   it,] 'it' *interlined above comma*

381.22   adventures] 'adven' *written over erased* 'history'

382.5   is] *interlined with a caret above deleted* 'has'

382.10   (as] *parenthesis written over comma*

383.3   Hilda,] *just possibly comma intended to be wiped out*

383.11   wonder] 'w' *written over wiped-out* 'd'

383.15   indeed!] *exclamation altered from comma*

383.15   now] 'n' *written over wiped-out* 'I'

384.2   you—] *dash altered from comma*

384.9	Love!'] *single quote preceding exclamation is wiped out*
384.16	another;] *semicolon altered from comma*
384.16	foes—] *dash written over wiped-out left parenthesis*
384.18	is] *inserted in left margin*
384.21	at] *written over wiped-out* 'and'
385.23	other] *interlined with a caret*
†385.26	desperate] 'er' *touched up by Sophia, possibly over* 'ar'
386.18	adopt] 'ad' *written over wiped-out doubtful* 'su'
386.28	and] *preceded by deleted* 'and'|
387.3	How] *written over doubtful* 'And'
387.5	friend.] *period altered from exclamation*
387.23–24	New England] *written over erased* 'native village'
387.31	Innocence] 'I' *altered from* 'i'
389.18	portal,] 'port' *written over wiped-out* 'door,'
391.11	Sculpture] 'S' *altered from* 's'
392.7	uneasy] 'u' *written over wiped-out* 'e'
392.22	out of] *interlined with a caret above deleted* 'by'
393.30	other] *written over wiped-out* 'more'
394.23	purpose] *followed by wiped-out comma*
394.30	daisies] 'dais' *written over wiped-out* 'viole'
394.32	that Hilda] 'that Hil-'| *written over wiped-out* 'which H'
395.9	yesterday] 'y' *written over wiped-out doubtful* 'h'
395.22	resulting] *preceded by deleted* 'following'
396.2	face, and] *written over wiped-out* 'carriage'
396.16	were] 'ere' *written over erased* 'as'
396.23	had] 'ha' *written over wiped-out* 'wo'
396.28	had] *interlined with a caret above deleted* 'were'
396.32	and Hilda] 'and' *written over wiped-out* 'Hil'
397.3	him] *interlined with a caret*
397.10	go on] *written over wiped-out* 'walk'
397.31	were] 'ere' *written over erased* 'as'
398.11	must] *interlined with a caret*
398.18	elevation] *preceded by deleted* 'height'
398.21	inconsiderable] 'inc' *written over wiped-out* 'con'

399.6	her aërial] *written over wiped-out* 'the |up[\]'
399.7	There] 'T' *written over wiped-out* 'H'
399.9	that] *written over erased* 'which'
399.17	be] *interlined with a caret*
399.17	smoke-] *interlined with a caret*
400.1	tower;] *semicolon written over erased comma*
400.6	evidence] *interlined with a caret above deleted* 'testimony'
400.11	Signor!] *exclamation altered from comma*
400.26	del Torre] *interlined with a caret*
401.1	noon—] *dash written over wiped-out right parenthesis*
401.10	-panels—] *dash written over wiped-out comma or semicolon*
401.14	at] *altered from* 'on'
402.27	with] 'w' *written over wiped-out doubtful* 'h'
†403.13	were so far] *commas after* 'were' *and* 'far', *in blacker ink such as was used by Sophia, seem to have been added later*
403.14	brown-] *written over wiped-out* 'fair-haired'
403.16	distant] 'd' *written over wiped-out* 'fa'
404.29	of] *inserted with a caret in left margin*
405.23	herself] 'he' *written over wiped-out doubtful* 'Ke'
406.4	own] 'o' *written over erased* 'd'
406.5	they] *interlined with a caret*
406.14	been] 'b' *written over wiped-out* 's'
406.16	as other] 'as' *inserted with a caret in left margin*
407.5	appeared] 'appea' *written over wiped-out* 'seeme'
407.6	hearted] *interlined with a caret above deleted* 'heared'
407.8	individual] *interlined above deleted* 'indivual'
407.12	spoken] *interlined with a caret above deleted* 'uttered'
407.25	turning] *followed by deleted* 'her'
408.8	police] *interlined with a caret*
408.10	wear] *interlined above deleted* 'make'
408.12	too often] *interlined with a caret*
408.17	to him] 'to' *interlined with a caret*
408.22–23	Hope— . . . upward—] *dashes written over erased commas*

409.10	himself] *followed by deleted* 'all astray'
410.17	which] *interlined with a caret above deleted* 'that'
410.21–22	of progressive generations] *interlined with a caret*
410.25	hinting at] *interlined with a caret above deleted* 'telling of'
410.27	distance;] *semicolon altered from comma*
410.28	gleam of] *interlined with a caret above deleted* 'little'
411.30	a vicious] 'a vi-'| *written over wiped-out* 'their'
412.10	one place] *written over wiped-out* 'fallen sto'
412.13	tide] *interlined with a caret*
412.16	appeared] 'appear' *written over wiped-out* 'seemed'
412.23–24	dungeons] *written over wiped-out* 'chambers that'
412.25	but] 'b' *written over wiped-out* 'o' *or* 'a'
413.13	round, and] ', and' *written over wiped-out* 'and it'
413.19–20	(and . . . reason,)] *interlined with a caret misplaced before comma after* 'wise'
415.13	remember] 'remem-'| *interlined with a caret above deleted* 'rember'
415.21–22	for . . . mankind] *interlined with a caret*
415.29	will] *interlined with a caret above deleted* 'may'
416.1	at] 'a' *written over wiped-out* 't'
416.11	reflections] *followed by wiped-out comma*
416.11	his] *followed by deleted* 'conjectures and'
416.18	prowl about] *interlined with a caret above deleted* 'watch'
416.20	expectations] 'expec' *written over wiped-out* 'hopes'
416.32	safe] *written over wiped-out* 'free'
418.4	The] *written over wiped-out* 'Ken'
418.15–16	inhospitably] *interlined with a caret above deleted* 'ominously'
419.31	vast] 'v' *written over erased* 'f'
420.6	of everlasting] 'of' *altered from* 'as'; 'everlas' *written over erased* 'they were'
420.20	broad] 'br' *written over wiped-out* 'su'

420.25	become the] 'come' *altered from doubtful* 'en' *after* 'the' *was inscribed*
421.1	with a blue atmosphere between,] *interlined with a caret misplaced before comma after* 'away'
421.9	nigh] *mended from* 'near'
421.26	him] *interlined with a caret*
421.29	that] *written over erased* 'which'
422.2	a more] *written over wiped-out* 'another'
422.3,6	Summer] 'S' *mended from* 's'
422.6	and which] 'an' *written over wiped-out* 'wh'
423.3–4	(which . . . recently)] *parentheses mended from commas*
423.18	antique] *written over wiped-out* 'old artist'
423.19	as] *interlined with a caret above deleted* 'which'
424.4	cleared] *written over wiped-out and erased doubtful* 'brushed'
426.15	sculptor] *followed by erased comma*
426.16	Hilda] 'Hild' *written over wiped-out* 'they,'
428.22	answered Donatello] *interlined with a caret*
428.29	said Donatello] *written over wiped-out* 'answered Donatello'
429.25	Will-] 'W' *seems altered from* 'w'
430.1	yet] *interlined with a caret above deleted* 'and'
430.1	few] *interlined with a caret*
430.4	only] *written over wiped-out* 'a few'
430.16	upon] *interlined with a caret*
430.26	was] *interlined with a caret*
430.32	and] *followed by wiped-out comma*
†431.1	breeds] *Sophia deleted this original reading and interlined* 'races' *above it, a reading followed by* E1
431.21	saw] *above* 'saw' *was interlined with a caret* 'beheld'; *when* 'beheld' *was wiped out,* 'saw' *was affected*
431.28	obvious and] *interlined with a caret*
431.33	Then came] 'Then c' *written over wiped-out* 'But, then'
432.2	she] *followed by deleted* 'had'
432.8	that] *interlined with a caret above deleted* 'which'

432.8	followed] *interlined with a caret above deleted* 'attended'
432.9	dark] *written over wiped-out* 'wild'
432.13	sanctity] 'san' *written over wiped-out* 'piety'
433.26	none] *interlined with a caret*
433.31	may] *interlined with a caret*
434.11	sculptor's] *interlined with a caret*
†434.19	blessing] *a following comma added by Sophia*
435.23	she] 'sh' *written over wiped-out* 'Mi'
435.24	both] *interlined with a caret*
436.17	barren,] *followed by deleted* 'in productions of the'
437.12	but for] *written over wiped-out* 'if it we'
437.27	again] 'a-'| *written over wiped-out* 'g'
437.32	Kenyon] 'yon' *added with a caret in left margin*
†438.8	hand] *interlined with a caret by Sophia*
438.10	if] *interlined with a caret*
438.26	could] 'c' *written over wiped-out* 'h'
438.32	had] *interlined with a caret*
439.14	coachman] 'coa' *written over wiped-out* 'foot'
439.22	one another] *interlined with a caret*
439.29	threw] *interlined with a caret*
440.4	bouquets] 'u' *written over wiped-out* 'q'
440.7	regarded] *written over wiped-out doubtful* 'f[avoured wi]th'
440.13	her tender] *interlined with a caret above deleted* 'such a'
441.7	seemed] 'ed' *mended from* 's'
441.32	fiercer] *written over erased doubtful* 'wilder'
442.1	even] *followed by deleted* 'in'
442.3	we] *interlined with a caret above deleted* 'they'
442.5	popular] 'pop' *written over wiped-out doubtful* 'vul'
442.12	damask-] *hyphen written over wiped-out* 'ed'
442.14	were] *interlined with a caret*
442.17	which] *followed by wiped-out comma*
442.30	gilding. Like] 'L' *mended from* 'l' *and a preceding* 'and' *deleted; in error, the comma after* 'gilding' *was not altered*
442.30	they] *interlined with a caret*
442.30	coachmen] 'c' *written over wiped-out* 'f'

442.32	powdered] *interlined with a caret*
443.16	fact] 'fac' *written over erased doubtful* 'trut'
444.20	himself] 'self' *added in left margin with a caret*
445.16	legs)] *parenthesis mended from comma*
446.11	covering] *interlined above deleted* 'enveloping'
446.11	with] *interlined above deleted* 'in'
446.12	shelter] *interlined with a caret above deleted* 'cover'
446.17	that] *written over wiped-out* 'with'
447.27	us] *interlined with a caret*
449.6	former] *interlined with a caret above deleted* 'gentleman'
449.15	(probably] *parenthesis added later*
449.16	family,)] *parenthesis possibly intended to delete a comma*
449.25	mask—] *dash mended from comma*
449.26	anything] 'an' *written over erased doubtful* 'wh'
449.28	quaint] 'q' *written over wiped-out* 'f'
450.1	borne] *followed by deleted* 'on a'
450.24	not] *interlined with a caret*
450.27	his] *written over wiped-out* 'the'
450.31	Kenyon] 'K' *written over wiped-out* 'h'
451.1	flask] *written over wiped-out* 'draught'
451.3	The sculptor] 'The scul' *written over wiped-out* 'He heard'
451.16	from] *interlined with a caret above deleted* 'in'
451.24	her] *interlined with a caret*
452.7	withdraw.] *followed by deleted* 'The Abbate'
452.21	could] *interlined with a caret*
452.21	have] *interlined with a caret*
452.26	in] *interlined with a caret above deleted* 'with'
453.4	may] *interlined with a caret above deleted* 'can'
453.13	breaking] *interlined with a caret above deleted* 'bursting'
453.16	out] *interlined above deleted* 'down'
455.9	any] 'a' *written over wiped-out* 'b'
455.13	long] *written over wiped-out* 'have'
456.3	of] *inserted in left margin*
456.4	stratagems] 'ta' *interlined with a caret*
456.11	a frolic] 'a' *written above wiped-out* 'the'

456.14   desperate] *second 'e' altered from* 'a'

456.21   stands almost] 'stands a' *written over wiped-out* 'is almost'

457.13   unimpeded] *interlined with a caret above deleted* 'open'

457.21   has fallen] *interlined with a caret*

457.29   hovering] 'hove' *written over wiped-out* 'there'

459.23–24   the far-descended heir of] *interlined with a caret at top margin after the foliation number had been inscribed*

459.29   Donatello's] *interlined with a caret above deleted* 'his'

460.17   it] 'i' *written over wiped-out* 'l'

460.25   religious sentiment] 'religious' *mended from* 'religion'; *and* 'sentiment' *interlined with a caret*

460.33   bring] *written over wiped-out* 'guide'

461.22   human] *interlined with a caret*

461.30   we] 'w' *written over wiped-out* 'h'

462.13   characterized] 'characteri' *written over wiped-out* 'distinguished'

COMPOSITORIAL STINTS IN *TRANSFORMATION*, THE FIRST ENGLISH EDITION OF 1860

NOTE: This table gives the facts about the compositorial stints from the start of one signed paragraph to the next paragraph marked by a compositorial signature, or, in rare cases, from one signature to a bracket and signature within a paragraph. The items are, in order: (a) name, (b) within parentheses the number of folios in the take, (c) Centenary page-line references, (d) within square brackets the first and last words of the stint, (e) the manuscript folio references, (f) the volume-page-line references of the first edition, and (g) within parentheses the number of lines of type in the stint.

Hobson (2)	5.0–6.32	[Chapter . . . alike.] MS 7–9. I,1.0–4.9 (63)
Orr (3)	6.33–8.25	[It . . . words.] MS 9–11. I,4.10–7.22 (79)
Spech (1)[1]	8.26–9.9	[The . . . The] MS 11–12. I,8.1–8.22 (22)
Farley (4)[2]	9.9–14.2	[whole . . . neither!"] MS 12–17. I,8.22–16.12 (148)

[1] This compositor (if the notation actually is to a compositor) does not appear again. The final "h" of his name is not wholly certain, and might just possibly be a "k".

[2] To begin this stint a square bracket drawn over an original half-bracket and then Farley's name (written over some erased name) is placed within the paragraph apparently to mark a special takeover. Oddly, an ink square bracket comes within the first paragraph on fol. 13 before "capacity" (9.25) beginning line 21 of *Transformation*, and near the foot of the leaf a pencil bracket and Farley's name before "caudal" (10.12)

Shand (4)[3]	14.3–17.8	["What . . . warm."] MS 17–21. I,16.13–22.16 (136)
Jenkins (3)[4]	17.9–19.14	["Ah . . . Model!"] MS 21–23. I,22.17–26.22 (94)
Hobson (3)[5]	20.0–22.20	[Chapter . . . narrative.] MS 24–27. I,27.0–31.13 (94)
Farley (4)[6]	22.21–25.24	[Such . . . region.] MS 27–31. I,31.14–37.13 (132)
Orr (4)[7]	25.25–29.10	["What . . . looked] MS 31–34. I,37.14–43.6 (104)
Jenkins (4)[8]	29.10–33.11	[pale . . . conviction.] MS 34–39. I,43.7–51.3 (173)
Farley (5)[9]	33.12–36.32	[Thenceforth . . . remained.] MS 39–43. I,51.4–58.6 (157)
Hobson (4)[10]	37.0–40.20	[Chapter . . . amiss.] MS 44–47. I,59.0–65.13 (138)

beginning line 3 of I, 11. A half-bracket and Hobson's name are deleted before "Chapter II" on fol. 15 (12.0).

[3] Farley's name was written in the first-paragraph indention of this take (14.3) but then deleted and Shand's substituted after the preceding paragraph.

[4] Originally Orr was assigned this, but his name in the paragraph indention is deleted and Jenkins' substituted after the preceding paragraph.

[5] Hobson's name was first deleted but then added below in the same hand.

[6] Orr's name was written in the first-paragraph indention but then deleted and Farley's substituted after the preceding paragraph.

[7] Hobson's name was written in the first-paragraph indention but then deleted and Orr's substituted after the preceding paragraph.

[8] Jenkins' take of four leaves originally started with fol. 35 when Farley's name in the first-paragraph indention (30.4) was deleted and Jenkins' added at the end of the preceding paragraph. It would seem, though, that Jenkins had time to work back onto fol. 34, the last of Orr's take, since a bracket and his name before "pale" (29.10) come in the middle of the first paragraph starting a line of type (*Transformation* I, 43.7). That Orr's take was originally planned as three leaves may be suggested by the presence of an unsigned bracket in the first-paragraph indention on fol. 34 (29.3).

[9] Jenkins' name was deleted in the first-paragraph indention and Farley's substituted after the preceding paragraph. This alteration was presumably connected with the alteration on fol. 35 whereby Jenkins was substituted for Farley. Farley's take here was four leaves, but the text was the equivalent of five folios since the Chapter IV ending numbered 43 was written on the verso of fol. 42.

[10] Orr's name originally headed this take but was deleted and Hobson's substituted. In the indention of the first paragraph on fol. 46 (39.1) Shand's name and a half-bracket are deleted.

Mintern (4)[11]	40.21–44.10	["Dear . . . -pot.] MS 48–52. I,65.14–72.20 (161)
Hobson (4)[12]	44.11–47.3	[Over . . . appreciate."] MS 52–55. I,72.21–78.7 (119)
Farley (4)[13]	47.4–50.9	[The . . . pleasure."] MS 56–59. I,78.8–84.12 (136)
Jenkins (4)[14]	51.0–55.8	[Chapter . . . cities.] MS 60–64. I,85.0–92.15 (162)
Shand (4)[15]	55.9–58.15	[Hilda . . . works.] MS 64–68. I,92.16–98.20 (137)
Mintern (4)[16]	58.16–61.9	[Her . . . literature!] MS 68–71. I,98.21–104.7 (119)
Hobson (4)[17]	62.0–65.29	[Chapter . . . it."] MS 72–75. I,105.0–112.2 (149)
Farley (4)	65.30–68.34	["Nor . . . sunset."] MS 76–79. I,112.3–118.3 (133)
Mintern (4)	69.1–72.24	["Farewell . . . this.] MS 80–84. I,118.4–124.17 (129)
Shand (4)	72.25–76.3	[In . . . tree.] MS 84–88. I,124.18–131.6 (143)
Jenkins (4)	76.4–79.23	[He . . . reason."] MS 88–92. I,131.7–136.20 (116)
Hobson (4)	79.24–83.10	[Certainly . . . summers.] MS 92–96. I,136.21–143.20 (154)

[11] Hobson's name was deleted in the first-paragraph indention and Mintern's substituted above the opening words. On fol. 50 Farley's name and a half-bracket are deleted in the first-paragraph indention (42.16).

[12] Hobson's name and a half-bracket in the first-paragraph indention were deleted but then his name restored written vertically.

[13] Orr's name was deleted in the first-paragraph indention and Farley's substituted above the first words.

[14] Jenkins' name was first deleted but then restored in a different hand.

[15] Hobson's name in the space after the preceding paragraph was deleted and Shand's written vertically in ink (in one of the hands used in the making-up annotations elsewhere) before the half-bracket beginning the paragraph.

[16] A half-bracket is drawn before the first-paragraph indention. In the space after the preceding paragraph appear, in order from left to right: "Farley" (deleted), "Mintern" (undeleted), "Hobson" (deleted). Below the first line of the paragraph and underneath Farley's deleted name is another deleted inscription of "Farley". A half-bracket appears before the first-paragraph indention on fol. 70 (60.7).

[17] Jenkins' name was deleted before "Chapter" and Hobson's substituted.

Farley (4)	83.11–87.2	["How . . . pastime.] MS 96–100. I,143.21–150.15 (156)
Mintern (6)[18]	87.3–91.28	[As . . . now!"] MS 100–105. I,150.16–159.12 (195)
Shand (4)	92.0–95.20	[Chapter . . . submit!"] MS 106–110. I,160.0–166.12 (137)
Farley (4)	95.21–98.25	["Pray . . . vain.] MS 110–113. I,166.13–172.15 (135)
Jenkins (4)	99.0–102.24	[Chapter . . . gateway.] MS 114–118. I,173.0–179.18 (143)
Hobson (4)	102.25–105.34	["Look . . . throughout."] MS 118–121. I,179.19–186.7 (143)
Mintern (4)	106.1–109.19	["I . . . ourselves."] MS 122–126. I,186.8–193.3 (150)
Shand (4)	109.20–112.25	["The . . . vanished.] MS 126–129. I,193.4–199.6 (135)
Farley (8)[19]	113.0–119.33	[Chapter . . . sit?"] MS 130–138. I,200.0–213.2 (281)
Mintern (4)	120.1–124.8	["Poh . . . -petticoat?"] MS 138–142. I,213.3–219.20 (135)
Shand (4)	124.9–127.15	["That . . . centuries.] MS 142–145. I,219.21–226.2 (136)
Mintern (4)	127.16–130.30	["What . . . street.] MS 146–149. I,226.3–232.13 (143)
Farley (4)	131.0–135.7	[Chapter . . . life.] MS 150–154. I,233.0–240.20 (167)
Jenkins (4)	135.8–137.34	[This . . . genius.] MS 154–158. I,240.21–246.8 (120)

[18] A half-bracket appears in the first-paragraph indention on fol. 104 in the fifth leaf of this take (90.19).

[19] A half-bracket and Mintern's name are deleted in the first-paragraph indention on fol. 134, the fifth leaf of this take (116.28).

Barnett (16)[20]	138.1–152.30	[According . . . Coliseum.] MS 158–174. I,246.9–273.6 (584)
Mintern (4)	153.0–156.18	[Chapter . . . again!"] MS 174–178. II,1.0–7.13 (133)
Farley (5)	156.19–160.25	["You . . . Forum.] MS 178–182. II,7.14–15.16 (179)
Jenkins (5)	161.0–165.25	[Chapter . . . venerable.] MS 183–188. II,16.0–24.13 (182)
Mintern (4)	165.26–169.11	[The . . . behind.] MS 188–192. II,24.14–31.8 (149)
Shand (2)	169.12–171.5	["I . . . was] MS 192–194. II,31.9–34.19 (77)
Hobson (6)[21]	171.5–177.11	[the . . . other.] MS 194–200. II,34.20–46.16 (238)
Mintern (4)	177.12–180.27	["But . . . too!"] MS 200–203. II,46.17–53.2 (131)
Farley (6)[22]	180.28–186.6	[The . . . Father.] MS 204–209. II,53.3–63.15 (233)
Barnett (6)	187.0–193.3	[Chapter . . . lodger.] MS 210–216. II,64.0–75.9 (244)
Mintern (3)	193.4–195.11	[The . . . soul.] MS 216–218. II,75.10–79.17 (96)

[20] This take begins on fol. 158 with a half-bracket before the first-paragraph indention (138.1) and Barnett's name appears after the preceding paragraph. In the first-paragraph indention on fol. 159 Barnett's name is deleted (138.29). On the fifth leaf of the take "Barnett" and a half-bracket are inscribed before "Chapter" (142.0). (On fol. 164 the make-up annotation for gathering 17 lists Barnett's name.) This long take ends the first volume.

[21] A bracket and Hobson's name intervene on fol. 194 (171.5 before "the very") in the middle of a paragraph, but a half-bracket is inscribed above the first-paragraph indention on fol. 196 (173.7) (with Hobson's name written above the first words), a place that would have given Shand a four-leaf, not a two-leaf, take. It seems probable, therefore, that Hobson went back to assist Shand after completing his original four-leaf take.

[22] A half-bracket made out of a full bracket appears in the first-paragraph indention on fol. 208 (184.26), the fifth leaf of the take.

Hobson (5)[23]	196.0–200.31	[Chapter . . . respond.] MS 219–224. II,80.0–88.19 (188)
Farley (4)	200.32–205.11	["That . . . timorously.] MS 224–228. II,88.20–96.19 (160)
Barnett (3)	205.12–208.3	["Am . . . humankind!"] MS 228–231. II,96.20–102.4 (116)
Farley (5)	208.4–212.22	["It . . . own!] MS 231–235. II,102.5–111.4 (198)
Barnett (2)	213.0–215.11	[Chapter . . . now.] MS 236–238. II,112.0–116.5 (86)
Farley (3)	215.12–217.19	[Up . . . here] MS 238–240. II,116.6–120.14 (97)
Barnett (12)[24]	217.19–229.15	[abouts . . . quietude.] MS 240–253. II,120.15–142.2 (465)
Shand (19)[25]	229.16–246.26	["You . . . see!"] MS 253–272. II,142.3–175.21 (704)
Hobson (4)	246.27–250.8	[Kenyon . . . -friends."] MS 272–276. II,175.22–182.12 (145)
Barnett (2)	250.9–251.24	["They . . . head.] MS 276–277. II,182.13–185.9 (63)
Shand (3)	252.0–254.31	[Chapter . . . abroad.] MS 278–281. II,186.0–191.4 (108)
Hobson (3)	254.32–257.27	["They . . . beautiful.] MS 281–284. II,191.5–196.17 (123)
Farley (3)	257.28–259.33	[What . . . battlements."] MS 284–286. II,196.18–200.21 (92)

[23] On fol. 220, the second leaf, Hobson's name appears written above the first-paragraph indention (197.10), indicating that Mintern's preceding original take had been assigned as four leaves, not three.

[24] Barnett's bracket and name are written on fol. 240 near the foot of the third leaf of Farley's take in the middle of a paragraph (217.19). His name also appears in the making-up annotation on fol. 245 for gathering 27. Otherwise no compositorial marking, whether of bracket or of name, is found until the start of Shand's take on fol. 253.

[25] No bracket or other compositorial marking appears in the nineteen leaves of this longest take.

Barnett (1)	260.0–261.14	[Chapter . . . more!"] MS 287–288. II,201.0–203.11 (48)
Hobson (1)	261.15–262.13	["How . . . afterwards.] MS 288–289. II,203.12–205.7 (40)
Farley (3)	262.14–264.21	[From . . . sought."] MS 289–291. II,205.8–209.19 (100)
Shand (4)[26]	264.22–268.10	[As . . . Heaven.] MS 292–296. II,209.20–217.3 (160)
Farley (2)	268.11–269.26	[The . . . ear?"] MS 296–297. II,217.4–220.3 (66)
Mintern (3)[27]	269.27–272.23	["I . . . one!"] MS 298–301. II,220.4–225.11 (99)
Hobson (2)	272.24–274.17	["For . . . wine.] MS 301–303. II,225.12–228.21 (76)
Barnett (1)	274.18–275.14	[Unexpectedly . . . vinegar.] MS 303–304. II,228.22–230.16 (39)
Shand (2)	275.15–276.30	[Yet . . . summons.] MS 304–305. II,230.17–233.14 (64)
Farley (2)	277.0–279.7	[Chapter . . . them.] MS 306–308. II,234.0–237.22 (81)
Mintern (3)	279.8–281.27	[It . . . love."] MS 308–311. II,238.1–242.19 (107)
Hobson (3)	281.28–284.24	["But . . . world."] MS 311–314. II,242.20–248.11 (124)
Shand (3)	284.25–287.3	["What . . . suppose.] MS 314–317. II,248.12–252.22 (99)
Barnett (1/2)[28]	287.4–287.11	["I . . . her!"] MS 317. II,253.1–11 (11)

[26] Barnett's name and bracket are deleted in the first-paragraph indention (266.20) on fol. 294, the third leaf of Shand's take.

[27] A half-bracket is written in the first-paragraph indention (271.28) on fol. 300, the third leaf of Mintern's take. However, his take continues since lower on the same folio the making-up annotation for gathering 33 gives his name.

[28] Barnett's one-paragraph stint began with the first-paragraph indention on fol. 317; a bracket appears in the second-paragraph indention below, with Mintern's name at the end of the preceding paragraph.

Mintern (1/2)	287.12–30	["I . . . yourself!"] MS 317. II,253.12–254.11 (22)
Farley (2)	288.0–289.23	[Chapter . . . journey] MS 318–319. II,255.0–257.18 (55)
Hobson (1)[29]	289.23–290.32	[ings . . . husbands.] MS 319–320. II,257.19–260.7 (53)
Barnett (1)[30]	290.33–291.32	[Another . . . growth] MS 320–322. II,260.8–262.5 (42)
Mintern (2)[31]	291.32–294.8	[imprisoned . . . nothing.] MS 322–324. II,262.6–266.15 (98)
Farley (3)[32]	294.9–296.15	[From . . . eye.] MS 324–327. II,266.16–271.3 (98)
Shand (2)	296.16–298.8	[As . . . flower.] MS 327–329. II,271.4–274.15 (74)
Hobson (2)	298.9–299.20	[The . . . woman!"] MS 329–330. II,274.16–277.5 (56)
Barnett (1)	300.0–301.3	[Chapter . . . was] MS 331–332. II,278.0–279.17 (32)

[29] Farley's take marked on fol. 318 is confirmed near the head of fol. 319 when his name appears in the making-up annotation for gathering 35. Hobson's setting starts below on fol. 319, in the second line of the first paragraph opening (289.23 breaking "journeyings"), but his name has been substituted in another hand for Mintern's, which is deleted. On fol. 320 a half-bracket is inscribed in the first-paragraph indention (290.8).

[30] Barnett's bracket and name appear in the indention of the second paragraph on fol. 320, the last line on the manuscript page. A half-bracket, as remarked above, had been drawn in the first-paragraph indention but without a signature.

[31] A half-bracket appears before the first-paragraph indention on fol. 322 (292.9) and Mintern's name is inscribed in the space after the preceding paragraph. However, in the fourth manuscript line of this folio a bracket is drawn before "imprisoned" (291.32), which in *Transformation* becomes II,262.5–6 "im-|prisoned". The odds favor the hypothesis that this is a significant bracket and that Mintern worked back to it from the start of his normal stint at 292.9, but by an error did not sign his name at the bracket. His typesetting, hence, has been taken to include the material after this internal bracket on fol. 322. If, instead, Barnett set down to 292.8, then Barnett would have set 54 lines, not 42, and Mintern 86 lines, not 98. For something of a parallel, see footnote 33 below, but especially footnote 35.

[32] A half-bracket is drawn in the first-paragraph indention (295.19) on fol. 326, the third leaf of Farley's take.

Hobson (2)[33]	301.3–302.19	[capable . . . would] MS 332–333. II,279.18–282.12 (61)
Farley (0)[34]	302.19–302.31	[be . . . ruin.] MS 333–334. II,282.13–283.5 (15)
Barnett (1)	302.32–303.26	[Yet . . . wash!] MS 334–335. II,283.6–284.18 (35)
Mintern (2)	303.27–305.13	[Kenyon . . . soul!"] MS 335–337. II,284.19–287.21 (69)
Farley (2)	305.14–307.2	["I . . . displayed] MS 337–338. II,287.22–291.7 (74)
Shand (2)[35]	307.2–308.26	[their . . . Perugia."] MS 339–340. II,291.8–294.13 (72)
Farley (3)	309.0–311.33	[Chapter . . . month.] MS 341–344. III,1.0–6.14 (112)
Shand (3)[36]	312.1–315.2	[Through . . . influence.] MS 344–347. III,6.15–12.11 (129)
Mintern (6)	315.3–320.23	["Yes . . . evil!"] MS 347–353. III,12.12–22.15 (213)
Farley (3)	320.24–323.19	["Miriam . . . crime!] MS 353–356. III,22.16–28.4 (121)
Mintern (2)	323.20–326.16	["Farewell . . . born!] MS 356–358. III,28.5–32.11 (76)

[33] A half-bracket is drawn in the first-paragraph indention on fol. 332 (301.10) but without signature. However, above, in the second manuscript line on the page, a bracket is drawn before "capable" (301.3), with Hobson's name above led to it, beginning a line of type and marking the adjusted start of Hobson's stint.

[34] Toward the end of the first new paragraph on fol. 333 in the lower quarter of the page, a pencil bracket is drawn before "be impossible" (302.19), which was then traced over with ink and Farley's name added in ink. This compositor must have been brought in to complete Hobson's setting, in a hurry, and could not have been originally assigned a take at this point.

[35] A half-bracket and Shand's name are deleted at the first-paragraph indention on fol. 339 (307.20) and in a different hand are substituted before "their wooden" (307.2), which are the first words on the folio.

[36] On fol. 346, the third leaf of Shand's take, a half-bracket appears in the first-paragraph indention (313.28).

Barnett (2)	326.17–327.24	[It . . . did.] MS 358–360. III,32.12–34.19 (52)
Hobson (2)	327.25–329.13	[With . . . again!] MS 360–362. III,34.20–37.21 (68)
Shand (2)	329.14–330.32	[Hilda's . . . -stain!'] MS 362–364. III,37.22–40.20 (65)
Mintern (2)	330.33–332.10	["Your . . . Mother!] MS 364–365. III,40.21–43.15 (61)
Hobson (2)	333.0–335.2	[Chapter . . . another!"] MS 366–368. III,44.0–47.11 (71)
Farley (2)	335.3–336.25	[Hilda . . . them!] MS 368–370. III,47.12–50.17 (72)
Mintern (2)[37]	336.26–338.19	[Then . . . them.] MS 370–372. III,50.18–54.7 (78)
Barnett (1)	338.20–339.22	[Hilda's . . . pillar.] MS 372–373. III,54.8–56.11 (48)
Shand (3)	339.23–342.2	[In . . . one.] MS 373–376. III,56.12–61.3 (102)
Farley (2)	342.3–343.14	[Such . . . Beni.] MS 376–377. III,61.4–63.16 (57)
Hobson (2)	344.0–345.34	[Chapter . . . chapel.] MS 378–380. III,64.0–67.9 (68)
Farley (2)	346.1–348.2	[Restless . . . shrine.] MS 380–382. III,67.10–71.12 (91)
Barnett (2)	348.3–349.9	[She . . . magnified.] MS 382–384. III,71.13–73.19 (51)

[37] On fol. 371, the second leaf of Mintern's take, in the fifth line from the foot (the second line of the first-paragraph indention) appears one bracket drawn over another before the words "in the above" (338.14) and the deleted name of Hobson. Just possibly this marking has something to do with the inserted paragraph (338.1–12) written on the verso of fol. 370 and marked for insertion in the line above the paragraph indention. Oddly, however, the bracket marks the first word of page 54 in volume III of *Transformation*.

Hobson (4)[38]	349.10–352.21	[This . . . little.] MS 384–388. III,73.20–80.3 (138)
Farley (3)	352.22–356.2	[In . . . church.] MS 388–391. III,80.4–85.13 (102)
Barnett (1)	356.3–356.23	[Approaching . . . you!"] MS 391. III, 85.14–86.16 (25)
Shand (4)[39]	356.24–360.8	[She . . . more!"] MS 392–396. III,86.17–93.14 (152)
Hobson (2)	360.9–361.25	["But . . . consequence?"] MS 396–397. III,93.15–96.14 (66)
Farley (2)	361.26–363.19	["Hush . . . happy!] MS 398–400. III,96.15–100.9 (66)
Hobson (4)	363.20–367.15	[In . . . yourself!"] MS 400–404. III,100.10–107.9 (154)
Shand (2)	367.16–368.33	["I . . . irreverence.] MS 404–406. III,107.10–110.9 (66)
Farley (3)	368.34–371.12	["The . . . Truth!"] MS 406–409. III,110.10–115.6 (107)
Hobson (3)	371.13–374.4	["Positively . . . rose.] MS 409–412. III,115.7–120.17 (99)
Farley (3)	374.5–376.22	[With . . . tomb.] MS 412–415. III,120.18–125.16 (109)
Hobson (3)	376.23–379.6	[They . . . embrace."] MS 415–418. III,125.17–130.11 (105)
Farley (3)	379.7–381.22	["And . . . adventures.] MS 418–420. III,130.12–135.6 (105)
Hobson (3)	382.0–384.26	[Chapter . . . any!"] MS 421–424. III,136.0–140.22 (103)

[38] A half-bracket appears in the first-paragraph indention on fol. 386 (351.3), the third leaf of Hobson's take.

[39] A half-bracket appears in the first-paragraph indention on fol. 394 (358.13), the third leaf of Shand's take.

Farley (6)[40]	384.27–389.22	["That . . . bound.] MS 424–429. III,141.1–150.12 (210)
Jenkins (4)	390.0–393.19	[Chapter . . . him?"] MS 430–434. III,151.0–157.10 (135)
Hobson (3)	393.20–396.11	[He . . . ominous.] MS 434–437. III,157.11–162.13 (113)
Farley (3)	396.12–398.30	["All . . . burn.] MS 437–440. III,162.14–167.15 (112)
Jenkins (3)	399.0–402.29	[Chapter . . . it.] MS 440–444. III,168.0–175.2 (149)
Hobson (2)	402.30–404.18	[In . . . for.] MS 444–446. III,175.3–178.7 (71)
Farley (4)	404.19–407.27	[The . . . her."] MS 446–449. III,178.8–184.15 (140)
Hobson (4)	407.28–412.6	[It . . . by.] MS 450–454. III,184.16–192.17 (157)
Jenkins (4)	412.7–415.5	[And . . . him.] MS 454–458. III,192.18–198.14 (129)
Farley (4)	415.6–419.13	[It . . . massiveness.] MS 458–462. III,198.15–205.6 (132)
Jenkins (4)	419.14–422.33	[Even . . . earth.] MS 462–466. III,205.7–212.6 (154)
Hobson (4)	423.1–427.15	[But . . . be!"] MS 466–470. III,212.7–219.9 (142)
Farley (4)[41]	427.16–431.12	["Most . . . herself.] MS 470–474. III,219.10–226.19 (164)
Shand (4)	431.13–435.2	["But . . . can?"] MS 474–478. III,226.20–234.3 (160)
Jenkins (4)	435.3–439.7	["It . . . mortals.] MS 478–482. III,234.4–241.20 (158)

[40] A half-bracket appears in the first-paragraph indention on fol. 427 (387.12), the third leaf of Farley's take.

[41] On fol. 473, the fourth leaf of Farley's take, the making-up annotation for gathering 52 lists Hobson's name in error. No sign of a bracket to mark the start of a new take appears in fols. 470–474 except for Farley on fol. 470; moreover, this four-leaf Farley take comes in a sequence of takes of four leaves. The identification of the take as Hobson's by the maker-up must be wrong: one may notice that Hobson had had the take just before this one of Farley's.

Hobson (8)	439.8–446.13	[All . . . away.] MS 482–490. III,241.21–255.3 (271)
Farley (4)	446.14–449.13	[Hereupon . . . -by.] MS 490–494. III,255.4–260.22 (129)
Jenkins (4)	449.14–453.5	[In . . . sight!] MS 494–498. III,261.1–268.5 (159)
Shand (4)	453.6–457.15	[Neither . . . produce.] MS 498–502. III, 268.6–275.8 (137)
Hobson (2)	457.16–458.33	["I . . . tempting!"] MS 502–504. III,275.9–278.9 (67)
Jenkins (2)	459.1–460.11	[What . . . knew."] MS 504–505. III,278.10–280.18 (53)
Farley (3)[42]	460.12–462.21	["I . . . -tops.] MS 505–508. III,280.19–285.8 (100)

[42] A half-bracket appears in the indention of the fourth paragraph on fol. 505, with Farley's name written at the end of the preceding paragraph. Since there are only seven manuscript lines remaining on this page, the folio is estimated as part of Jenkins', not of Farley's, take. The anomaly must have something to do with the fact that Farley's take is the last of the third volume's text. A half-bracket appears in the first-paragraph indention on fol. 507 (461.17). Farley's three-page take includes the end of the volume written on the verso of fol. 507, this being numbered 508.

THE CENTENARY TEXTS:
EDITORIAL PRINCIPLES

T HE CENTENARY EDITION of Hawthorne provides
for the first time established texts of the romances, tales,
and associated shorter works. The general procedures
governing this establishment are outlined here, whereas the
specific problems for each text are treated in the separate
Textual Introductions.

The text itself is a critical unmodernized reconstruction.
It is critical in that it is not necessarily an exact reprint of any
individual document: the print or manuscript chosen as copy-
text (i.e., as the basis for this edition) may be emended by
reference to other authorities or by editorial decision. The
Centenary text, in short, has been established by the application of bibliographical and analytical criticism to the evidence
of the various early documentary forms in which the text has
appeared.[1] It is unmodernized in that every effort has been
made to present the text in as close a form to Hawthorne's
own inscription as the surviving documents for each work
permit of such reconstruction, subject to normal editorial
procedure.

[1] Various terms used here are discussed at length in Fredson Bowers,
"Established Texts and Definitive Editions," *Philological Quarterly*, XLI
(1962), 1–17.

The first step in the establishment of a critical text is the determination of the exact forms of the texts in the early documents and of the facts about their relationship to one another. When manuscripts are extant, the establishment of the texts of these documents involves the checking of the written form of all words and the determination of the texture of their spelling, capitalization, word-division, and punctuation, i.e., the "accidentals" of a text as distinguished from its "substantives," or the forms of the words as distinguished from the words themselves. Any manuscript alteration of the initial inscription is noticed, and whenever possible the author's rejected forms are reconstructed from the available evidence and recorded.

Since the first editions printed from Hawthorne's preserved manuscripts have a supplementary authority, the duty is placed on an editor to identify and analyze any variation in the readings of the printed texts that have primary or supplementary authority. To this end a number of copies of the first—and of any other edition possessing authority—have been mechanically compared for variation on the Hinman Collating Machine. Previously unknown differences that developed in the text during the course of printing have been discovered by this process, as well as such major variation within editions as the duplicate typesetting of the last gathering of the first and of the preliminary gathering of the second edition of *The Scarlet Letter*. Although it is too much to hope that every minor variant in an impression has been discovered by the extensive multiple collation, one can state with some confidence that the majority have probably been noticed; unknown major variation, at least, is not likely to exist in unseen copies of the editions examined by this method. Hence, the readings of the text in the authoritative documents, even in relatively minor respects of form, have been substantially established from the evidence of the machine comparison by superimposition of a number of exemplars, letter for letter and word for word.

The forms of other editions chosen for examination have also been established by multiple collation of copies on the Hinman Machine. Technically, an edition comprises a particular typesetting, without regard for the number of different printings made at various times from this typesetting or its plates.[2] Since most Hawthorne book editions after the first (and often the first, too) were printed from stereotype plates, the history of the usual edition is the history of the textual variation in its set of plates throughout the various printings. Plates were occasionally altered between impressions, at times to correct errors in the edition-typesetting, at times to incorporate editorial normalizations and fancied improvements, and at times to repair plate damage caused by handling accidents and normal wear on the press. Therefore, in order to establish the exact forms of the editions (in respect to the history of their plates), the first impression from the plates of any edition-typesetting has been compared on the Hinman Machine against the last ascertained impression (in the Boston line of publication), and those variants affecting substantives have been recorded as between the early and late states of the plates. However, only when changes in plates were made before 1865 (Hawthorne died in 1864) have the individual variants been tracked down through the intermediate impressions in order to establish the dates of their first appearances. Finally, no attempt has been made to record variation in the plates in respect to non-verbal alteration. In punctuation readings, for instance, actual alterations are often impossible to distinguish from anomalies caused by plate wear and damage; moreover, for the purposes of the present edition non-verbal

[2] In the Centenary Edition the use of the bibliographical terms "edition," "impression" (or "printing"), "issue," and "state" follows that recommended in Fredson Bowers, *Principles of Bibliographical Description* (Princeton, 1949), pp. 379–426.

variants in unauthoritative prints have no textual significance, interesting as they might prove to a historian of printing practice.

Following the establishment of the variant documentary forms of all editions chosen as significant in the history of Hawthorne's text, these different edition-typesettings have been individually hand-collated against the first edition; and all substantive, or word, variants recorded, as well as such occasional variants among the accidentals as might bear on the question of the authority of any of the documents by which the texts were transmitted. From this evidence, printed in the Historical Collation appended to each edited work, the line of textual transmission can be traced from document to document and the general authority of each edition can thus be determined. This evidence, also, determines in large part the specific authority of any document, since bibliographical and critical analysis of the textual variants has demonstrated which are mere reprint editions—that is, editions in which the cumulative transmitted error was never corrected systematically but, instead, largely by chance. Evidence of this nature indicates that no comparison of the printer's copy had been made against any authoritative document, and thus that the various alterations observed (when not mechanical corrections) were in their turn corruptions and could not represent, in some manner, an editorial return to a purer version of the text.

On internal evidence like this, combined sometimes with external evidence, one can determine, usually with precision, the printed texts that have Hawthorne's immediate authority as against the number that are simply derived reprints without authority. In this connection, authority is defined as resident in any document printed directly from a Hawthorne manuscript or from some other document, such as another edition, that had been corrected or revised by Hawthorne or by some other person utilizing a Hawthorne manuscript. Such authoritative texts are called substantive, as contrasted with derived. Only substantive texts have been used as documentary sources of revisory emendation, although occasional correction may be drawn, for convenience, from derived editions.

After the derived reprints have been isolated, the next step in the editorial process is the selection of the copy-text from among the established substantive texts. In practice, the selection may differ from literary work to literary work according to the distinctive conditions, but the theory is firm: whenever practicable the copy-text selected is that form of the text, no matter how it may subsequently have been revised, that is nearest to the primary authority of Hawthorne's manuscript.

Obviously, when the manuscript is no longer in existence, the copy-text must be the first printed edition that was set directly from such a manuscript, since only this edition can preserve in any authoritative form such characteristics of the manuscript as have escaped the normalization of printing-house style imposed on the copy. If Hawthorne never intervened to revise or correct this text in any subsequent edition, the first edition remains the sole authority. However, if Hawthorne introduced corrections and revisions to a later edition the claims of more than the single, or copy-text, authority must be considered.

The editorial procedure in such cases follows the principles laid down by Sir Walter Greg.[3] That is, a double authority is recognized. The copy-text remains the supreme authority for the accidentals, since it alone was set directly from Hawthorne's manuscript. On the other hand, the substantive variants in other texts not thought to be printer's errors must be

[3] "The Rationale of Copy-Text," *Studies in Bibliography*, III (1950–51), 19–36. See also Fredson Bowers, "Current Theories of Copy-Text," *Modern Philology*, LXVIII (1950), 12–20.

taken to represent Hawthorne's revisions, and to these must be added such alterations in the accidentals as appear to derive from the author, although this last is a much more difficult matter to determine. Hence the resulting critical Centenary text will incorporate in the first-edition copy-text such variants from later demonstrably authoritative editions as pass the editorial tests for authorial alterations. In effect this procedure attempts to reproduce the lost marked-up printer's copy that Hawthorne furnished for the revised text, and in this reconstruction to filter out the unauthorized printing-house variants that creep into any reprint and are thus found in the printed form even of a revised edition. Despite the fact that he "accepted" them (provided he read the proof for a revised edition), Hawthorne did not authorize these printing-house variants; hence they can have no place in the pure text that the Centenary Edition endeavors to establish.

Correspondingly, when Hawthorne's manuscript of a work has been preserved, this manuscript becomes the copy-text. In each case this manuscript has been collated against the first printed edition and all details of substantive variance have been recorded. However, the printing-house style imposed on the authoritative manuscript has been rejected except for necessary corrections,[4] and only those variants from the manuscript in substantives or in accidentals that appear to have been inserted by Hawthorne in the proof have been accepted and incorporated in the critical text. Thereafter, the determination of the history of the text and of the authority of all variants in editions after the first follows the regular procedures outlined above.

[4] When in such a text as *The House of the Seven Gables* the printer of the first edition made on an average about fifteen alterations per page in conformity with house style, the cumulative effect on Hawthorne's own modes of expression as seen in the manuscript is very serious indeed. Only the manuscript contains the full record of the subtleties of Hawthorne's parenthetical expression and emphasis.

Hawthorne's shorter works that might have been published in periodical and gift-book form several times before collection present a special problem. In general, the Greg theory of copy-text holds, and an attempt has been made to separate the authority of the substantives from that of the accidentals in the different versions of the text and thus to establish the most authoritative form of each in a critical text that may fairly be said to synthesize the most authoritative versions. Only when one can determine that a later edition was set from an independent manuscript (not from marked-up copy of an earlier print) or was so thoroughly revised from printed sheets as to make distinction impossible between Hawthorne's and the printer's alterations, has the copy-text been shifted from the earliest printing from manuscript to a later substantive edition.

To repeat, the purpose of the Centenary Edition is to establish the text in as close a form, in all details, to Hawthorne's final intentions as the preserved documents of each separate work permit. This aim compels the editors to treat each work as a unit, with its own separate textual problems. That is, no attempt is made between texts to secure a uniformity of style that is not authorized from those documents for the texts in question that establish their most authoritative preserved forms. It follows that the texture of accidentals in a work like *The House of the Seven Gables,* established from authorial manuscript, will differ from that in a work like *The Scarlet Letter,* established from the first printed edition.

In the latter, the printing-house style imposed on the text removes it in various respects from conformity with Hawthorne's known practices in spelling, punctuation, capitalization, and word-division as seen in his manuscripts of about the same date. One might be able to alter some of these forms in *The Scarlet Letter* to bring the critical text, in theory, into a closer relationship with what one may reasonably suppose to have been certain of the details of the lost manuscript. But interesting as such an experiment might be, the result could never be wholly consistent and could not lead to any demonstrably established form of the text. Hence, each work in the Centenary Edition rests as a separate unit on the evidence of its own preserved documents, and represents a faithfulness to Hawthorne's full intentions in varying degrees of exactitude according to the authority of this evidence.

Editorial treatment of the text, then, is primarily concerned with synthesizing the evidence of all manuscripts and authoritative printed editions in order to arrive at Hawthorne's detailed final intentions as nearly as may be determined from the documents. In this situation any alteration believed to be Hawthorne's must be adopted, regardless of critical estimate of its literary worth, although, of course, an editor's literary judgment is one of the various criteria that operate to establish any alteration as a Hawthorne variant instead of the printer's. On the other hand, not all Hawthorne revisions are literary in their nature. When Hawthorne softened his original satire, or excised sections for personal reasons as with the passage on saloons in *The Blithedale Romance,* crossed out in the manuscript and therefore not present in the first edition, presumably in deference to his wife's prejudices, the original manuscript version has been retained in the established text as more faithfully representing Hawthorne's true intentions than the results of censorship even though self-imposed.

Revision of the copy-text, therefore, can be admitted only from the evidence of authoritative documents. On the other hand, correction may be drawn from any source, whether a substantive or reprint edition, or from independent editorial judgment. Indeed, no correction from an unauthoritative document can have any more validity than editorial correction; hence reprint editions are noted as sources for emendation only as a convenience and not because there is any secondary value in the fact that the chosen emendation first originated in them.

Editorial correction is of five kinds. First, since Hawthorne appears to have been a rapid and far from accurate proof-reader,[5] he did not catch in proof all of the printer's errors that manifestly need setting right; hence some substantive emendation has proved necessary.

Second, inconsistencies may be present in the manuscripts in respect to spelling, capitalization, and division of words that were regularized in the prints. Such regularization of a manuscript has generally been accepted when the printer's version appears to coincide with Hawthorne's usual practice; however, if the print regularizes anomalies in opposition to Hawthorne's more habitual practice, or else fails to normalize an irregularity, independent emendation has been admitted.

Third, if Hawthorne's own usual practice cannot be determined (as in his frequent undifferentiated use of "subtle" and "subtile" and sometimes of "farther" and "further"), the variant forms are retained in the established text unless normalization seems justified on the authority of the dictionary that Hawthorne used—*A New Critical Pronouncing Dictionary of the English Language . . . By an American Gentleman* (Burlington, N. J.: Allinson, 1813).[6]

Fourth, whereas all characteristic spellings are followed in our unmodernized text when they are acceptable variants of more common forms and are regular in the literary text in question, misspellings, like Hawthorne's habitual manuscript "cieling", are always corrected.

[5] For some information on this and other matters affecting the text, see Fredson Bowers, "Hawthorne's Text," in *Hawthorne Centenary Essays*, ed. Roy Harvey Pearce (Columbus, O., 1964), pp. 401–25.

[6] This Hawthorne family dictionary was identified and described in Carroll A. Wilson, *Thirteen Author Collections of the Nineteenth Century and Five Centuries of Familiar Quotations*, ed. Jean C. S. Wilson and David A. Randall (New York, 1950), I, 154.

Fifth, word-division is regularized according to the practice in the most authoritative documents for each text. If the matter is in doubt within a given text, the form has been adopted that agrees with parallels within the text or that is most characteristic of manuscripts closest in date to the print. When in the original documents a possible compound is hyphenated at the break between two lines, the editorial decision whether to establish the word in the Centenary Edition as a hyphenated compound or as a single word conforms to the same principle.

No attempt has been made in the Centenary Edition to reproduce the typographical details of the original documents such as the lineation, the number of lines of indentation for display capitals and the number of capitalized text-letters following them, or the capitals or lower case in running-titles and chapter headings. For instance, the customary periods after running-titles, and chapter numbers and headings, have been omitted, and old-fashioned wide spacing like "I 'll" or "that 's" (not always uniform in Hawthorne's manuscripts) has been ignored. Although the text has been scrupulously treated, its appurtenances have been modernized.

In every other respect, however, the Centenary Edition reproduces the features of the copy-text or else notes an alteration. No variation of any kind from the copy-text (other than those enumerated above) has gone unreported; hence, the interested reader at any point can reconstruct the copy-text from the Centenary print in tandem with its records of emendation. These records are contained in an appendix to each literary work, where specialists may consult the details at leisure. The basis for the record is the page and line number in the Centenary text; *viz.*, 42.15 means page 42, line 15.

The usual textual appendix contains the following sections:

Textual Notes: Whenever an emendation of the copy-text, or a refusal to emend, seems to require special notice, a brief comment upon the reading is provided.

Editorial Emendations: All alterations to the copy-text made in the present edition are recorded, together with the immediate source of the approved reading, always the first appearance of the emendation in the editions consulted in the preparation of the particular text. Since the purpose of this emendations list is to present at a view only the departures from the copy-text, and the origin for each reading of the correction or revision, the history of the copy-text reading up to the point of emendation is provided, but not its subsequent history. For substantives, this last can be found in the Historical Collation.

The basic note provides, first, the precise form of the emended reading in the Centenary text. Following the square bracket appears the identification of the earliest source of the emendation in the editions collated. A semicolon succeeds this notation, and following this appears the rejected copy-text reading with the sigla of editions that provide its history up to the point of emendation. In these notations certain arbitrary symbols appear. When the variant to be noted is one of punctuation, a wavy dash ∼ takes the place of the repeated word associated with the pointing. An inferior caret ∧ calls attention to the absence of punctuation either in the copy-text or in the early edition from which the alteration was drawn. Three dots indicate one or more omitted words in a series. The sigla for denoting the editions recorded are explained in the Textual Introduction for each work. In general, editions listed by their dates are those set from type, whereas roman numbers are used to identify the stereotype plates first put into use from a new typesetting in the listed edition. If a second edition were printed in the same year from a different setting of type, the two would be differentiated as in 1850^1 and 1850^2. All editions are American unless otherwise noted. English editions are identified as E. The notation (r) indicates reset type, and (s) standing type. Unless specifically excepted, the reading listed as originating in a plated edition comes from the original state of the plates and is constant in all recorded impressions made from these plates. An emendation assigned to CENTENARY is made for the first time in the present edition if by "the first time" is understood "the first time in respect to the listed editions chosen for collation."

The following examples are from *The Scarlet Letter*:

133.33   broad,] E,III; $\sim_\wedge$ $1850^{1\text{-}2\,(r)}$

Here the copy-text first edition in 1850 (1850^1) places no punctuation after "broad", and the lack of punctuation is followed in the second edition of 1850, this reading occurring in one of the reset pages. The necessary comma, adopted in the Centenary text, was first inserted in the third American edition, printed from plates in 1850; and it is also found in the first English edition of 1851. Since this English edition was set from a copy of 1850^2 independently, its sigla are placed for convenience before that of III in order not to interrupt the sequence of American plated editions beginning with III.

*262.25   sombre-hued] CENTENARY; sombre-hued $1850^{1\text{-}2\,(s)}$, E, L; sober-hued III–VII

In the above the Centenary original emendation of "sombre-" substitutes for the copy-text (1850^1) misprint "sobre-" followed in the standing type of the second edition (1850^2), by the first English edition, and by the Levin 1960 Riverside paperback, but sophisticated to "sober-" in the third edition (III) and repeated in this form by all subsequent texts collated, including the 1900 Autograph Edition (VII). The asterisk preceding the reference indicates that a Textual Note discusses this reading. Discussion of a reading that has not been emended is indicated in the emendations list as in the following, with the editions noted in which the unemended reading appears:

*221.29   such personage] *stet* 1850[1]–III

Word-Division: Hyphenation of a possible compound at the end of a line in the Centenary Edition poses a problem for the reader as to the exact form in the copy-text. Moreover, end-of-the-line hyphenation in the copy-text itself requires editorial decision whether the reading should be reproduced in the Centenary text as one word or as a hyphenated compound. This double problem is faced in the appendix section on Word-Division, which is designed to record all the essential facts about the forms of possible compounds both in the Centenary and in the copy-text.

No hyphen at the end of a line in the Centenary text is present in the copy-text unless listed in this section of the apparatus, as in the form:

6.21   grizzly-|bearded

This notation indicates that "grizzly-", ending the line in the Centenary Edition, page 6, line 21, is printed as part of a hyphenated compound within the line in the copy-text.

Since many hyphens ending lines in the copy-text may actually break an original hyphenated compound, not just the syllables of a single word, the second part of this appendix section lists all occurrences of established hyphenated compounding and of possible compounding broken at the end of a line in the copy-text itself, except when the hyphen joins capitalized units and there can be no ambiguity. Here the reading is that of the Centenary Edition; whether the compound is hyphenated or unhyphenated in the listing is in accord with the determined practice of the copy-text or (failing this evidence) of the manuscripts closest in date. It is to be understood that each reading was broken in the copy-text at the point of the hyphen, or where one would normally have occurred if the compound had been hyphenated.

3.18	lifemates
7.21	slop-sellers

Here the copy-text readings were, respectively, "life-|mates" and "slop-|sellers".

The third section lists those rarer examples when, by chance, the same compound reading is broken at the hyphenation in both the copy-text and the Centenary Edition. Within parentheses, the established correct form is thereupon provided for the information of the reader.

These precautions being observed, anyone may transcribe a passage from the Centenary Edition with no ambiguity about word-division in the copy-text.

Historical Collation: A list is provided of all substantive variants from the Centenary text in the editions chosen for collation. Variant readings in the accidentals are ignored because of their copiousness and their basic lack of significance save when they affect the sense in a substantive manner and thus qualify for listing, or for some special reason in connection with the tracing of the family tree of textual derivation. Moreover, the various accidental forms in different editions of a recorded substantive reading are ignored.

The first reading, to the left of the bracket, is that of the Centenary Edition, which will not necessarily be that of the copy-text if emendation has taken place. To the right of the bracket is placed the variant and the sigla for the specific collated editions in which it appears. The reading is that of the Centenary text in any such edition not listed.

21.29 all of his] all his IV–VII

This example from *The Scarlet Letter* signifies that the first three American editions, the first English edition, and the Levin text read with the Centenary Edition "all of his" but that the variant "all his" appears first in the Little Classics Edition of 1875 (IV) and continues through the intervening collated editions, the Red-Line of 1878 (V), the Riverside of 1883 (VI), and the Autograph of 1900 (VII) and all their collated platings.

In this Historical Collation an attempt is made to distinguish the states of the plates of the various editions in respect to substantive readings. Thus in *The Scarlet Letter,* for example,

50.30 They] Thed III^a

records the fact that the first impression made from the plates of the third edition, in 1850, misprinted "They" as "Thed" at page 50, line 30, of the present edition; but that the error was corrected in the 1851 second impression of these plates.[7] For each work the special sigla identifying the plates and their printings are explained in a headnote preceding the Historical Collation. The entry

26.12 make] made III^{e-g}; have made IV–VII

indicates that as part of a repair of the third-edition plates for the Illustrated Library Edition of 1871 (e), "make" was inadvertently altered to "made", a reading that was reproduced in the 1876 Illustrated Library Edition state of the

---

[7] If the error had appeared in all the impressions of the third-edition plates, the notation would read simply: They] Thed III.

plates (f) and the *c.* 1880 Globe Edition state (g) including the last impression of this state to be collated, the undated (*c.* 1886) New Fireside Edition. This error was sophisticated to "have made" when type was set for the Little Classics Edition of 1875, a reading that persisted through the Autograph typesetting (VII) but not in the Levin text (L).

An attempt is made in this Historical Collation to be complete and accurate in respect to this substantive plate variation in the several editions and their numerous impressions. Additional plate variants, discovered after a Centenary volume has gone to press, will be recorded in the Descriptive Bibliography of Hawthorne that will be appended to the Centenary Edition.

Variants in the First Edition: Any differences in the typesetting or plates that appear during the course of printing the first edition, or any other substantive edition, are recorded and identified in respect to the collated copies.

Special Lists: Whenever the textual situation warrants the addition of further information than that supplied in the standard sections of the textual appendix, special lists record the necessary data.

For example, in *The Scarlet Letter* the variants in the standing type of the second edition seem to have been ordered by the publisher and not by the author; thus, they have not been regularly incorporated as part of the establishment of the Centenary text. In addition, the variants in the reset pages of the second edition must represent a mixture of printer's divergences from copy and the publisher's markings for alteration similar to those made in standing type. Since a difficult and not wholly demonstrable decision about authority has had to be a matter of editorial judgment, the whole list is provided so that the reader may be in possession of all the evidence in the event that he wishes to make an independent study of the problem.

Also, when the manuscript of a Hawthorne text has been preserved, an appendix list details the facts of revision or alteration in the inscription of this manuscript insofar as recovery can be made from a close examination of the documents.

On the other hand, a full record of the differences between the manuscript and the first edition printed from it would usually run to quite extraordinary length: about five thousand items, for instance, for *The House of the Seven Gables*. As a consequence, the editors' early hope that every variant between the manuscript copy-texts and the initial prints could be recorded has had to be abandoned, regretfully, in respect to the accidentals. However, all substantive variation will be found recorded in the Historical Collation for such works, with the Editorial Emendations list indicating those readings in which the manuscript copy-text has been altered by reference to a variant in the prints.

In order to secure a common ground for collation of the different Hawthorne works, the following procedures have been adopted.

Multiple copies (usually eight or more) of the first appearances in print and of any later substantive editions[8] have been mechanically collated on the Hinman Machines at the

[8] Only substantive editions printed from type metal (and hence subject to change during impression) have been collated from multiple copies on the Hinman Machine, for the chances are infinitesimal that the plates of an edition would be altered during the course of an impression of a sheet. Nevertheless, since accidents will happen, the editors have taken certain precautions against such an occurrence, however remote the possibility. When hand collation of the copy-text edition is made against later editions for the record of the Historical Collation, different copies of the primary edition are used as the basis for the comparison of every subsequent edition. In this manner, plate variation if present in the copy-text should be reflected in variant readings of a kind that are automatically checked.

Ohio State University and the University of Virginia where extensive collections of Hawthorne have been gathered in the Ohio State University Center for Textual Studies and in the University of Virginia's Alderman Library, including the Clifton Waller Barrett Collection.

The establishment of the text has then proceeded by the determination of the family tree and of the authority or non-authority of editions after the first. These facts are recorded in the Historical Collation appended to each work. The following collected editions have always been collated against the copy-text: Little Classics (1875), Riverside (1883), and Autograph (1900). These are the only collected editions in the Boston line of publishers to Houghton Mifflin Company that represent different typesettings.[9]

For each of these editions the latest identified impression made from the edition-plates has been collated on the Hinman Machine against the first impression in order to secure the maximum information about the changes made in the history of the plates. But only the blue-bound form of the Autograph Edition has been collated (not the form with the signed illustrations), and no further account of its plates has been provided beyond this one impression.

Within the limits of the information about impressions available at the time of editing each text, an attempt has been made to identify the exact printing in which each plate-variant originated up to 1865. Thereafter, only the last known impression has been collated against the first, the differences being recorded without specifying the impression in which they originated. *The Scarlet Letter* has been given fuller

[9] The succession of the publishers is as follows: Allen and Ticknor (1832–34); William D. Ticknor, (1834–43); William D. Ticknor and Company (1843–49); Ticknor, Reed, and Fields (1849–54); Ticknor and Fields (1854–68); Fields, Osgood and Company (1868–71); James R. Osgood and Company (1871–78); Houghton, Osgood and Company (1878–80); Houghton, Mifflin and Company (1880–1908); Houghton Mifflin Company (1908——).

treatment than other texts, in that plate variation has been identified in specific impressions later than 1865.

As well as the collected editions issued by Hawthorne's Boston publishers and their successors to the present Houghton Mifflin Company, all separate editions representing different typesettings put out by these publishers before 1900, and a few later, have also been collated and their variants noted. For each work the first English edition has also been collated, in part to establish its derivation, and in part to determine whether authoritative alterations were made in the American sheets sent to England to serve as copy. When a work was first published in England, something of the English history of the text has been investigated by collation of later editions; the usual history of the American line of the text has, of course, also been established.

This extensive collation has been carried forward well beyond 1864, the year of Hawthorne's death, in order to insure against the possibility (however faint) that fresh authority has entered a text if it was compared with an authoritative manuscript by some conscientious editor; and partly to provide for its own sake the history of the text, in detail, in the standard editions up to the present.

The textual record is a sad one of pyramiding corruption, sometimes trivial but often serious. Yet occasionally a purpose may be served in this section by demonstrating in detail that the editions commonly used by scholars and critics for analysis and quotation are unreliable. More important, the Historical Collation provides for the reader the total substantive evidence for textual transmission available to the textual editor, who has been chiefly responsible for the establishment of the text. All the cards are on the table, face up.

To insure maximum accuracy, all hand collation of the different typesettings of later editions against the copy-text was duplicated by individual workers at the Ohio State University and the University of Virginia, the results conflated, differences checked, and every variant wherever noted was rechecked through the whole list of editions. This process should have produced exactness of fact unless the collators of an edition at both universities simultaneouly passed over a variant unique to that edition, in which case no system of double checking could catch the error. All proofs have been read at least five times and by three or more editors.

F. B.

THE MARBLE FAUN

Volume IV in the Centenary Edition of the Works of Nathaniel Hawthorne.

Published by the Ohio State University Press, Columbus.

The text of the novel is set in eleven-point Fairfield, with Caslon initial capitals. Chapter headings are set in fourteen-point Caledonia capitals.

Composition, presswork, and binding by the Heer Printing Company, Columbus, Ohio.

Paper for the Centenary Edition is Permalife Text, manufactured by the Standard Paper Manufacturing Company of Richmond, Virginia.

Binding cloth for the Edition is Colonial Linen, manufactured by the Columbia Mills, Inc., Syracuse, New York.

Preliminary pages designed by Turck and Reinfeld, Inc., New York City.